# The Nineteenth-Century Novel

The Open University

Routledge
Taylor & Francis Group

*REALISMS*

*edited by* DELIA DA SOUSA CORREA

# The Nineteenth-Century Novel

This series comprises:

*The Nineteenth-Century Novel: Realisms*, edited by Delia da Sousa Correa
*The Nineteenth-Century Novel: Identities*, edited by Dennis Walder
*The Nineteenth-Century Novel: A Critical Reader*, edited by Stephen Regan

Published by Routledge
11 New Fetter Lane
London EC4P 4EE

Written and produced by The Open University
Walton Hall
Milton Keynes MK7 6AA

Simultaneously published in the USA and Canada by Routledge
29 West 35th Street
New York, NY 10001

First published 2000; reprinted 2001, 2004

Edited, designed and typeset by The Open University

Printed in the United Kingdom by Scotprint

A catalogue record for this book is available from the British Library

A catalog record for this book is available from the Library of Congress

ISBN 0 415 23826 9

This text forms part of an Open University course: AA316 *The Nineteenth-Century Novel*. Details of this and other Open University courses can be obtained from the Course Reservations Centre, PO Box 724, The Open University, Milton Keynes MK7 6ZS, United Kingdom: tel. +44 (0)1908 653231.

For availability of this or other course components, contact Open University Worldwide Ltd, The Berrill Building, Walton Hall, Milton Keynes MK7 6AA, United Kingdom: tel. +44 (0)1908 858585, fax +44 (0)1908 858787, e-mail ouwenq@open.ac.uk

Alternatively, much useful course information can be obtained from The Open University's website: http://www.open.ac.uk

1.4

B/aa316_b1_e1i4_0415238269

# Contents

# General introduction

*by Dennis Walder*

This book is the first of a series of two volumes and a critical reader, designed to encourage enjoyment and understanding of the nineteenth-century novel. The majority of the works discussed here are from England, but we have also included novels from France and the USA as an integral part of the project. The characteristic concerns and achievements of nineteenth-century novels are, we believe, displayed best by reading both deeply and widely – which means close study of a select group of individual texts, but also drawing those texts from more than one of the countries in which the novel flourished. The first volume, *Realisms*, explores novels by Jane Austen, Charlotte Brontë, Charles Dickens, George Eliot, Thomas Hardy and Émile Zola; the second, *Identities*, explores novels by Gustave Flaubert, Wilkie Collins, Henry James, Bram Stoker, Kate Chopin and Joseph Conrad.

The focus throughout is on writing in society: not only in the sense that every literary work inevitably draws from, as it also influences, its social environment; but also in the sense that novels in the nineteenth century saw themselves as particularly engaged with the events, circumstances, beliefs and attitudes of their time. Of all the literary genres, the novel is probably the best adapted to the representation and exploration of social change. This was especially evident immediately before and during the nineteenth century, when society was undergoing the massive and lasting change inaugurated by the 'twin revolutions' of the industrial revolution in England and the French Revolution. Our accounts of the novels discussed in this volume draw attention to their engagement with social attitudes as these have come to be discussed today, including the political discourses of class, gender and race.

The novel as a genre is of course defined by formal as well as by historical elements, and we concentrate also on the characteristic themes and issues articulated by the genre's typical features – character, plot, image, setting, point of view and, indeed, all aspects of narrative function. We look at the novels in broadly chronological order according to publication, as a way of conveying a strong sense of their changing engagement with the times; but this linear narrative is interrupted in these volumes from time to time by thematic grouping, in order to clarify what strikes us as most worthy of discussion in relation to the specific novels chosen at any one point – the representation of rural life, for example, or of crime, or of the heroine, or the *fin de siècle*.

Novels would not exist but for their writers. However, the *survival* of novels depends on their writers less than their critics, and on their critics less than their readers – although there is a closer connection between the critical reception of novels and their composition and consumption than most readers are willing to credit. Hence, in the following chapters on the novels, our approach involves a strong awareness of the interrelatedness of writing, reading and criticism: by demonstrating how the novelists themselves became increasingly self-conscious of what they were doing (notably Flaubert, Zola and James); by looking at some of the reviews and publishing statistics of the time; and by taking account of more recent developments in the study of the novel. The critical reader that accompanies these two volumes consequently contains a range of nineteenth-century primary material – essays by George Eliot, Henry James and Robert Louis Stevenson, for example – as well as examples of more recent critical approaches.

Among the latter, most readers will be aware of the impact of feminism on the writing and reception of recent fiction, and we aim to show how this has affected our understanding of nineteenth-century novels. Equally political, in the broadest sense, have been recent readings of nineteenth-century novels as participating in the discourses of empire, readings made possible by the rise of what has been called 'post-colonial' criticism. Indeed, we take it as part of our brief to alert you to many of the ways in which discourses outside the strictly 'literary' (such as the discourses of science) have been increasingly used to illuminate the reading and understanding of nineteenth-century novels.

We aim to show how various forms of narrative theory can help us to enjoy the 'made-ness' of fiction; it can also help us to analyse its technical effects. As critics such as Roland Barthes (1915–80) have shown, the novel is only one of many kinds of narrative, which can be looked at and compared with others, to the delight as well as to the occasional bemusement of readers. It is important to acknowledge the diversity and reach of narrative, as a cultural arena in which the nineteenth-century novels we look at have participated. The fluidity and openness of the genre should ensure that we do not rush towards a fixed idea of what it is about. We should, for example, be wary of unquestioningly taking the nineteenth-century novel as an exemplification of the 'rise' of a certain kind of 'realist' writing. It is our aim to suggest that there is more than one version of the development of the nineteenth-century novel, most obviously in the emergence of fantasy and romance as features which provide an alternative and sometimes subversive idea of the form. These competing strands are to be found in some of the more popular novels by Dickens (see *Realisms*), Collins or Stoker (see *Identities*). Awareness of previously less-respected subgenres has also contributed to the way we read the nineteenth-century novel in general.

Chapters 1 and 8 in *Realisms* and chapters 8 and 15 in *Identities* are designed to be read as part of the general context; the rest are designed to be read in conjunction with individual novels. At the beginning of each of these chapters, you will find that we have recommended a particular edition of each novel; thereafter page references are given to this edition. (For those who are not reading in this edition, a general chapter reference is given.) You will notice that the text is punctuated with questions in bold-face; these are signals for you to pause in your reading, either to consider general questions or to focus on a certain passage which is about to be discussed in detail. We strongly recommend that you engage in these mental exercises as and when the text suggests. The authors follow each question or set of questions in bold with a detailed discussion of those questions, often referring closely to the text, which it would be helpful to have open before you at the relevant passage. Such discussion then broadens out to consider other relevant topics or material. You will also discover that the text will refer you to essays collected and excerpted in the critical reader, which you are invited to read and consider so that you can then engage with the discussion of the material that follows. The critical reader also provides materials, both contemporary and modern, which are not dealt with at length in the text; they will provide you with a wider library of some of the most important relevant materials within which to contextualize your novel-reading.

These volumes were conceived and prepared by the following team: Sue Asbee, Marilyn Brooks, Hazel Coleman (editor), Delia da Sousa Correa, Nicolette David, Julie Dickens (course manager), Simon Eliot, Alan Finch (editor), Jane Lea (picture researcher), Sebastian Mitchell, Valerie Pedlar, Lynda Prescott, Stephen Regan, Nora Tomlinson, Dennis Walder (chair) and Nicola Watson (deputy chair). Our thanks go to Rosemary Ashton (University College London), who advised on the early stages of this project, and to Jacques Berthoud (University of York) for his guidance throughout.

# PART 1

# Introduction to part 1

*by Delia da Sousa Correa*

The first part of this volume looks particularly at relationships between literary realism and romance in three novels from the first half of the nineteenth century. The first novel we deal with is Jane Austen's *Northanger Abbey* (1818), written well before forms of literary realism and romance had achieved the dominance they increasingly enjoyed in mid-nineteenth-century fiction. We aim to show how *Northanger Abbey* can be read as pioneering a more realist type of fiction in its parody of Gothic forms, whilst retaining a highly complex and ambivalent relationship with the Gothic. The Gothic is also investigated as one of several non-realist modes of crucial importance to Charlotte Brontë's *Jane Eyre* (1847), the second novel considered in this volume. Brontë's innovative blending of realist and non-realist literary genres is explored alongside the relationship of her novel with non-fictional texts, including natural history and psychology. The first part of this volume concludes with an account of Charles Dickens's *Dombey and Son* (1846–8), which draws attention to the plethora of forms in Dickens's work. Dickens is shown to accommodate both realist and symbolic modes in his complex treatment of contemporary social, economic and industrial activity, including Britain's expanding imperial role.

Dickens's literary career coincided with a transformation in publishing – a transformation in which he played an influential role. The way in which nineteenth-century novels were published is another important dimension to understanding them – many of the melodramatic crises in their plots were created specifically for the end of a serial number, for example. Magazine editors acted as censors over the novels appearing within their pages. We need to be aware of this context, as we need to be aware of the historical, critical-theoretical, and formal or generic contexts in which we read novels. It is not authors alone who make books. Authors need publishers and booksellers, and their writings are accordingly embedded in the material conditions and constraints of publication and book production. A knowledge of the ways books were consumed by their readers at the time illuminates not only many of the narrative structures and stances adopted by the novel, but also its attitude to the whole enterprise of reading and writing. Bibliographical studies has accordingly developed as an important discipline within literary and historical scholarship. The first chapter, 'Books and their readers – part 1', is designed to provide an additional frame to the detailed readings of individual novels that occupy subsequent chapters. Our interest in what these novels mean to us now at the beginning of the twenty-first century can only be enhanced by an awareness of how these texts were produced and read in the nineteenth.

# CHAPTER 1

# Books and their readers – part 1

*by Simon Eliot*

## By way of an introduction: money, death, literacy and light

> The past is a foreign country: they do things differently there.
>
> (L.P. Hartley, *The Go-Between* (1953), prologue)

The novels that we study in this book were not written for us at all. They were written for readers most of whom have been dead for more than a hundred years. These readers, and those who wrote for them, knew a very different life from the one we lead. Of course, ultimately, we must read the novels with our own eyes and in the light of our own experience. Nevertheless, we shall miss a lot if we do not try to understand something of the economic, social and cultural context in which readers and writers lived their lives in the nineteenth century. Many references – many passing allusions which would have had a meaning to a reader in 1850, and would thus have affected his or her view of a novel – will be lost on us unless we make a positive effort to come to grips with the feel of life at the time of a novel's first publication.

I stress 'publication', because it is not just a novel's text that might have had a somewhat different meaning for its contemporaries. The books that contained the texts that we arc now studying were different in the nineteenth century. They looked different, they felt different, they were acquired differently and their cost was significantly different. In other words, the material form a novel took in, say, 1850 would have had an economic and social significance to a reader that is lost to us who read the text in the form of a cheapish, modern paperback.

In the chapters entitled 'Books and their readers' we shall be looking at the ways in which knowledge of some of the material and cultural details of our period can enrich our understanding of its novels and their readers.

### *Money*

**Northanger Abbey**

[B]y what means their income was to be formed, whether landed property were to be resigned, or funded money made over, was a matter in which her disinterested spirit took no concern.

(Austen, [1818] 2003, 1.15; p.90; all subsequent page references are to this edition)

*Figure 1.1   'The Rivals, Which Shall It Be?' This cartoon illustrates well the battle for disposable income and time: are you to be a respectably dressed person spending your time (and saving your money) in a free library? Or are you to be a poorly dressed individual in a battered hat giving your time to drinking, smoking and gambling (note 'bagatelle' and 'billiards') with the workhouse threatening in the background. Originally published as the frontispiece to Thomas Greenwood,* Free Public Libraries *(1886). Reproduced from Thomas Kelly,* A History of Public Libraries in Great Britain 1845–1975, *London: The Library Association, 1977, frontispiece. By permission of Mrs Joan E. Kelly*

Of a very considerable fortune, his son was, by marriage settlements, eventually secure; his present income was an income of independence and comfort. (2.16; p.185)

[I]n no sense of the word were they necessitous or poor ... Catherine would have three thousand pounds. (2.16; p.186)

### Jane Eyre
'It would, indeed, be a relief', I thought, 'if I had ever so small an independency.'
> (Brontë, [1847] 2000, 2.9; p.268; all subsequent page references are to this edition)

'Your fortune is vested in the English funds.' (3.7; p.382)

### Dombey and Son
Mr Dombey ... was one of those close-shaved, close-cut, moneyed gentlemen who are glossy and crisp like new bank-notes.
> (Dickens, [1846–8] 2001, 2; p.19; all subsequent page references are to this edition)

'Money, Paul, can do anything.' He took hold of the little hand, and beat it softly against one of his own, as he said so. (7; p.99)

'The fact is,' said Mr. Brogley, 'there's a little payment on a bond debt – three hundred and seventy odd, overdue: and I'm in possession.' (9; p.123)

At most times, and in most of its forms, the novel has been characterized by a preoccupation with two subjects: love and money. Let us begin with one of those two universals: money.

What about incomes, prices and expenditure in the nineteenth century? Of course, it is very difficult to generalize: incomes and prices varied considerably between 1800 and 1900 though not, perhaps, as much as you might have expected. Inflation, which was a hallmark of most of the twentieth century, was not so obvious in the nineteenth. For instance, a recent calculation (Twigger, 1997, pp.10–12) suggests that, if you take prices as they were in 1974 and call that 100, then prices in 1799 would have been 9.7. In other words, in 1799 things roughly cost one-tenth of what they were to cost in 1974. To put it another way, if you think of the pound in 1974 being equal to 100 pence, then a pound in 1799 would have been worth 1,034 pence. The first fifteen years of the nineteenth century covered the Napoleonic wars, and wars always tend to create inflation. Thus by the year of Waterloo, 1815, the price index was up from 9.7 to 12.4 and the value of the pound had fallen from 1,034 pence to 809 pence in 1974 values.

This trend did not continue. As the Napoleonic wars passed into history, the economy settled down, prices dropped again and the value of the pound rose. By 1836, when Dickens published his first novel, *Pickwick Papers*, the price index was down to 9.6 and the pound was worth 1,040 pence – more than it had been worth at the end of the eighteenth century.

The Crimean War (1854–6) saw a new bout of inflation with prices going up and the value of the pound going down, but it was only a blip. Amazingly, between the late 1860s and the late 1890s there was a long period of deflation in which prices generally fell and the value of money went up. Thus by 1899 the price index was at 8.5 and the value of the pound at 1,172 pence, higher than it had been in 1799!

Incomes show a similar stability. Unlike the mid- to late twentieth century where incomes went up to try to match inflation, incomes didn't increase dramatically during the nineteenth century. They did increase, particularly in the later part of the century, but only slowly and patchily. However, as the value of the pound was increasing between 1865 and 1895, if you earned £200 per annum in 1865 and you still earned the same amount in 1895, those 1895 pounds would buy you more, and therefore you would be, marginally at least, richer.

If you have no experience of pre-decimal British coinage the following might help. The old pound was made up of 240 pennies (denoted as 'd'), so a decimal penny is worth about two and a half times more than an old penny, i.e. 1p = 2.4d. A penny could be divided into two halves ('halfpennies', written as '½d') and into four quarters ('farthings', written as '¼d'). Twelve old pennies (12d) made one shilling (1s), which was the exact equivalent of 5p. Twenty shillings (20s) made up one pound. One pound and one shilling (21s) made up a guinea. Sums of money were written up in the following order: pounds, shillings and pence, so, for instance, £2.51 would be £2 10s 2½d.

It is very difficult to generalize about incomes, then as now. They varied over time, they varied from region to region within the country, and they varied enormously both between and within social classes. In the 1860s, for instance, working-class incomes could vary from agricultural labourers earning between twelve and seventeen shillings (60–85 pence) a week to highly skilled craftsmen earning 28s–35s a week (£1.40–£1.75).

Middle-class incomes were equally variable. In the 1860s, income tax tended to be applied only to what were regarded as middle-class incomes. Income tax applied to all incomes above £160 per annum, roughly 60s (£3) a week. If £150–£160 per annum was the minimum, middle-class incomes could sometimes be much higher: for instance, successful lawyers and doctors could earn £800–£1,000 per annum or more.

For a moment let's think of the minimum middle-class income of £150–£160. This could be derived from employment, of course, but if you were a woman that would be difficult to achieve in a respectable occupation. If you were a man, and had pretensions to being a gentleman, then it would be socially preferable to gain this sum from interest payments rather than work. Throughout the nineteenth century one of the safest ways of generating interest was to invest a capital sum in 'Consols' or British Government stock. Interest rates varied a bit but they usually hovered around 3 per cent per annum. **With this in mind, look at the quotations above from *Northanger Abbey* and *Jane Eyre*.** Catherine Morland's £3,000 invested in Consols would produce an annual income of about £90. This would not be enough to provide an independent income, but would usefully augment a husband's property. This sort of income assumed that a woman would marry. Now think for a moment about Jane Eyre's legacy. She, of course, insists on splitting the £20,000 into four portions of £5,000 each. The money is in the 'English funds' (presumably government stock paying about 3 per cent). **What, to contemporaries, would be significant about the income derived from £5,000 invested at 3 per cent?**

It would usually generate about £150 per annum in interest, just enough income to sustain a frugal middle-class existence. This delivers Jane Eyre's longed-for 'small independency', which would give her a middle-class life without needing to marry. As Jane earned £30 per annum as a governess at Thornfield (1.10; p.88) and the same sum as a schoolmistress at Morton (3.4; p.355), this modest capital sum would have increased her annual income fivefold.

However, simply knowing a person's total income is not enough. We need to know about their 'disposable income'. Disposable income is that part of your income you have left over when you have bought all the necessities of life for you and your family: housing, food and drink, clothing, heating, lighting, and so on. Of course, the concept of 'necessity' changes over time and between classes; in 1860, for instance, even for a lower-middle-class family, one necessity would be a servant. But then servants came cheap or, at least, unskilled female ones did. A general maid in 1860 would cost £10–£16 a year plus board and lodging.

It is worth reminding ourselves how common servants were in eighteenth- and nineteenth-century novels. They were common in novels because they were common in real life. In 1861, when the total population of England, Scotland and

Wales was just over 23 million, there were over 1.5 million people in domestic service. By 1871 there were more servants than agricultural labourers.

Below the servant-employing class disposable incomes were small. A working-class family in 1860 earning 20s 6d would, it has been calculated, have about 1s 3d per week as disposable income. A family earning 27s 6d would have a disposable income of about 3s.

The higher up the social scale you went, the higher the proportion of your income could be regarded as disposable. Middle-class incomes varied over a wider range, as did expenditure, but one commentator has suggested that necessities may have accounted for about 84 per cent of total income of an average middle-class family, leaving about 16 per cent as disposable income (Burnett, 1969). If we think of a modest middle-class income of about £5 per week, that would leave about 16s per week disposable income.

Let's take an example. In *Jane Eyre*, St John Rivers gives Jane a copy of Sir Walter Scott's poem *Marmion* that was first published in 1808. On first publication this cost £1 11s 6d (£1.58), but let's assume that he gave her the cheaper edition without illustrations which was listed at 12s in 1811. Whatever St John's income, and it cannot have been great, a copy of *Marmion* must have represented a goodly part of his disposable income for that week, if not for many weeks. As far as Jane was concerned, even the cheaper version represented 2 per cent of her total annual income. It is difficult to think of a modern equivalent, but if we think of a very low modern annual wage of £5,000 a year, 2 per cent of this would be £100. **Given the figures, what would a reader in 1848 make of St John's gift?**

It's a significant expenditure and thus would not have been undertaken lightly. As St John is a man of rigid self-denial, we should not be surprised at this sacrifice. However, for a contemporary reader it would be further evidence as to the nature and importance, for St John, of his relationship with Jane.

A note of caution: it is the nature of disposable income that it is disposable on anything available. Books and newspapers were but one temptation offered to an individual with a few coins to spend. There were many others that might offer stronger attractions: drinking and smoking, theatres, circuses, concerts, high days and holidays. When Dickens's characters have some time off, how many settle down with a good book – or, indeed, any sort of book?

## *Death*

### *Northanger Abbey*
[T]he seizure which ended in her death *was* sudden. The malady itself, one from which she had often suffered, a bilious fever – its cause therefore constitutional. (2.9; p.145)

### *Jane Eyre*
[D]isease had thus become an inhabitant of Lowood, and death its frequent visitor. (1.9; p.77)

The next day Bessie was sent for home to the deathbed of her little sister. (2.6; p.220)

### *Dombey and Son*

The old, old fashion – Death! (16; p.241)

The power that forced itself upon its iron way – its own – defiant of all paths and roads, piercing through the heart of every obstacle, and dragging living creatures of all classes, ages, and degrees behind it, was a type of the triumphant monster, Death. (20; p.297–8)

Somebody's always dying. (32; p.490)

The population of the British Isles had been growing since the mid-eighteenth century, sometimes because of a drop in death rates, sometimes because of an increase in birth rates. In 1801 the population of England, Scotland and Wales was 10.5 million. By 1851 it was 20.8 million and by 1901 it had reached 37 million. Despite this, death came more frequently and earlier in the nineteenth century than now, and in particular it struck most often at children. Infant mortality rates are commonly the last to show improvement during a process of economic and social development, and so it was in Great Britain. It was only at the very end of our period that rates of death among children began to decline significantly and consistently. In 1850, 16.2 per cent of children died before their first birthday. In 1900 it was still 15.4 per cent. Only in 1912 did this rate drop below 10 per cent for the first time (by contrast infant mortality in the UK in 1998 was about 0.59 per cent). For most of our period parents expected that not all their children would survive their early years. It is often thought a symptom of Victorian mawkishness that its novels should frequently involve the death of children. But it could be argued that this frequency was little more than an honest reflection of social reality. Many parents would not have escaped the anguish of seeing at least one of their children die. Similarly, with obstetrical care at a very primitive stage, with the germ theory of infection only to be established at the end of the century, and with contraception not widely available, the death of mothers in childbirth was not an uncommon experience. Divorce was, of course, difficult to obtain (until 1857 it required an Act of Parliament) but, with high death rates among women of childbearing age, many Victorian marriages did not have a very long life expectancy. In this context the death of Paul Dombey's mother, and his own subsequent death, are little more than commonplaces – as are most of the deaths of children in Dickens's novels. The only unusual feature was that children died later in his novels than they did in real life. Most deaths in childhood occurred in the first five years of life. Dickens himself, who fathered ten children, was lucky to have only one die in infancy, but then he was middle-class and affluent. **In this context, what can we say about the Toodle children as they are first presented in *Dombey and Son* in chapter 2?**

The remarkable thing is that they are all alive; a feature of which Toodle himself is acutely aware:

'You have a son I believe?' said Mr Dombey.

  'Four on 'em Sir. Four hims and a her. All alive!'

  'Why, it's as much as you can afford to keep them!' said Mr. Dombey.

  'I couldn't hardly afford but one thing in the world less, Sir.'

  'What is that?'

  'To lose 'em Sir.' (2; p.19)

The death of infants was likely to touch most families, but it was more likely in low-income families where overcrowding, ignorance, poor nutrition and inadequate sanitation took a particularly heavy toll. This is clearly what Mr Dombey implies, but Toodle neatly turns this by using the other sense of 'afford', that of emotional cost (a form of reckoning of which Dombey is almost wholly ignorant).

Nonplussed by Toodle's answer, Dombey abruptly changes the subject. The new topic he chooses is significant. It is the subject of literacy.

## *Literacy*

'Can you read?' asked Mr. Dombey.
   'Why, not partick'ler Sir.'
   'Write?'
   'With chalk, Sir?'
   'With anything.'
   'I could make shift to chalk a little bit, I think, if I was put to it,' said Toodle after some reflection. (2; p.19)

**Do you notice anything odd about this approach to literacy, compared with a modern one?**

Two things struck me. The first was that both Dombey and Toodle separated reading and writing, while we tend to think of them as going together. The second was that Toodle thought of writing as being linked to a particular medium: in this case, chalk. He could write a little bit in chalk, if nothing else.

Historians have always argued about literacy rates in the past, and will no doubt continue to do so. The main problem is evidence. The act of reading, unless it's a highly unusual one (such as the public readings of excerpts from his novels that Dickens gave in the 1850s and 1860s), does not leave any historical evidence behind. Writing, of course, does, but until Hardwick's Marriage Act of 1754 required all marriages to be recorded in a parish register by the signature of bride, groom and two witnesses (see Figure 1.2), there was no large-scale, consistent source of information on the ability to write. After 1754 historians can see the numbers of those who could sign their names in comparison with those who just made their mark. This is a crude technique, but it's the best we've got for the late eighteenth and early nineteenth centuries.

The biggest problem with registers is that they equate reading and writing. But Toodle knew better. Until the late nineteenth century reading and writing were two distinct skills and were treated as such. Reading was taught first, and then writing. If you came from a low-income family, it might be able to afford to send you to school to learn to read, but could probably not afford to keep you there for another year or two to learn to write. By that time you would be old enough to work to supplement the family's income.

In most cases, until the last part of our period, reading and writing were not taught as good things in themselves, as things intimately associated with self-development, the pursuit of happiness or some other romantic aspiration. Reading and writing were skills that were taught for a purpose. Reading was

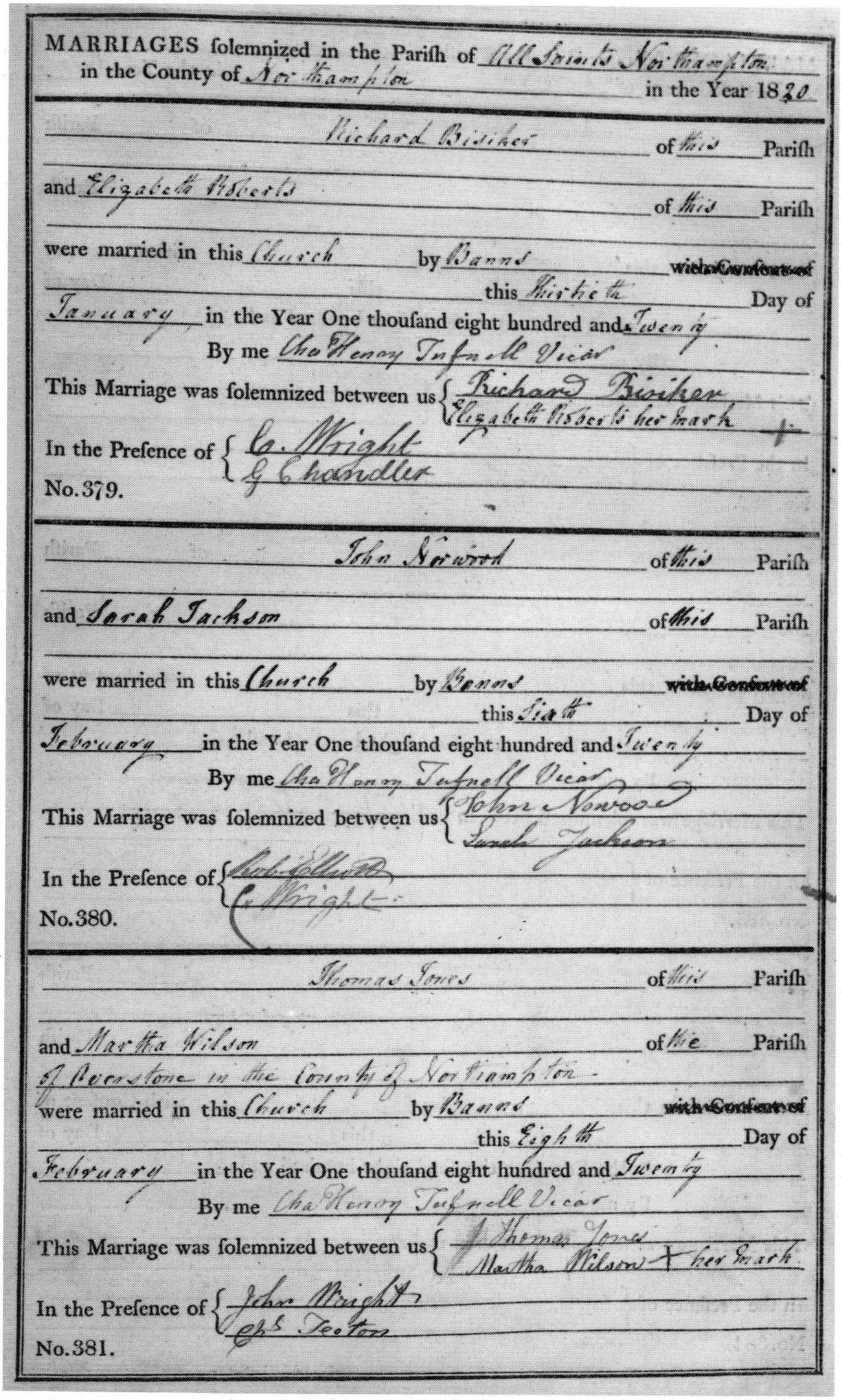

MARRIAGES solemnized in the Parish of *All Saints Northampton*
in the County of *Northampton*                          in the Year 18*20*

*Richard Bisiker*                                    of *this*  Parish

and *Elizabeth Roberts*                               of *this*  Parish

were married in this *Church*      by *Banns*      ~~with Consent of~~

_____ this *Thirtieth* _____ Day of

*January* ____ in the Year One thousand eight hundred and *Twenty*

By me *Cha. Henry Tufnell Vicar*

This Marriage was solemnized between us { *Richard Bisiker*
{ *Elizabeth Roberts* to her *mark* +

In the Presence of { *C. Wright*
{ *G Chandler*

No. 379.

*John Norwood*                                      of *this*  Parish

and *Sarah Jackson*                                of *this*  Parish

were married in this *Church*      by *Banns*      ~~with Consent of~~

_____ this *Sixth* _____ Day of

*February* ____ in the Year One thousand eight hundred and *Twenty*

By me *Cha. Henry Tufnell Vicar*

This Marriage was solemnized between us { *John Norwood*
{ *Sarah Jackson*

In the Presence of { *Rob. Colliott*
{ *C. Wright*

No. 380.

*Thomas Jones*                                      of *this*  Parish

and *Martha Wilson*                                of *the*  Parish

*of Overstone in the County of Northampton*

were married in this *Church*      by *Banns*      ~~with Consent of~~

_____ this *Eighth* _____ Day of

*February* ____ in the Year One thousand eight hundred and *Twenty*

By me *Cha. Henry Tufnell Vicar*

This Marriage was solemnized between us { *Thomas Jones*
{ *Martha Wilson* + her *mark*

In the Presence of { *John Wright*
{ *Jos. Texton*

No. 381.

*Figure 1.2   Page of an early marriage-register with signatures and marks.
This shows Hardwick's Marriage Act in action: all three grooms and all the
witnesses could write their names, but two out of the three brides made a
mark rather than wrote their signature. Northamptonshire Records Office*

usually taught to equip you for a job or, in Protestant countries, to save your soul. Remember that most Protestant sects put a great stress on each individual achieving his or her own salvation through an understanding of God's word. God's word was in the Bible, so it was necessary to read it. Writing and numeracy, however, were skills more associated with higher-level jobs: the filling of ledgers, the recording of bills, the writing of letters of credit, and so on. Many Sunday schools, which in the late eighteenth and early nineteenth centuries were the means by which many children from low-income families learned to read, would be concerned exclusively with reading as a means of spiritual exercise.

To put it briefly, it is likely that more people could read than write, so any literacy study based on the signing of marriage-registers is likely to underestimate reading rates.

Toodle can read a bit, and write a bit; and this raises a very important problem that is with us still today: semi-literacy. There were probably many readers in the nineteenth century who could pick out a few words, or read a simple sentence, albeit painfully slowly. An extreme version of this is to be found in Dickens's *Great Expectations* (1860–1), where Joe Gargery is explaining his love of reading to a very young Pip:

'Tho' I'm oncommon fond of reading, too.'

'Are you, Joe?'

'On-common. Give me,' said Joe, 'a good book, or a good newspaper, and sit me down afore a good fire, and I ask no better. Lord!' he continued, after rubbing his knees a little, 'when you do come to a J and a O, and says you, "Here, at last, is a J-O, Joe," how interesting reading is!'

I derived from this, that Joe's education, like Steam, was yet in its infancy.

(Dickens, [1860–1] 1994, 1.7; p.45)

Pip, who is himself just learning to read, resolves to educate Joe. You will recall that Toodle comments 'One of my little boys is a-going to learn me, when he's old enough, and been to school himself' (2; p.19). It is quite likely that the inversion of the roles of parents and children (a recurrent theme in Dickens's work) was relatively common during the nineteenth century as literacy education became much more available to younger generations than it had been to their elders. It was certainly the case that much literacy education in lower-income families would have been done at home, by husbands, wives – and children.

Toodle could write a bit with chalk. This may reflect the medium in which he was taught (chalk on a board or a slate). Chalk allows you, forces you, to write large, and mistakes are easily erased. Fully literate people would be expected to write with a pen, and that was another skill entirely.

In the early nineteenth century, writing was costly in both money and effort. Paper was much more expensive than it is today. Commonly people would re-use odd scraps of paper wherever the original writing left enough space; of Catherine Morland, Jane Austen observes that she did this 'whenever she could obtain the outside of a letter from her mother, or seize upon any other odd piece of paper' (2003, 1.1; p.6). Writing was certainly more difficult: there were no fountain pens, ballpoints or rollerballs. You had the choice of a quill or a steel pen, both of which you had to replenish by dipping the tip into an inkwell. The steel pen became much more common after 1828 when it could be made by machine.

Even so, it would have taken many years to become universal, so many people in the earlier nineteenth century would have written with a quill pen. This would have to have been cut and shaped by penknife before use, and re-trimmed as and when necessary. Loading either sort of pen with ink was a skilled business: too little and you would be scratching the paper and then have to return to the inkwell almost immediately; too much and there was a considerable danger of blotting. If you made a mistake, it was difficult to erase it. A pen nib hitting an irregularity in the paper would often splutter, sending ink droplets in all directions. No wonder Toodle wouldn't go further than chalk!

Literacy was not evenly spread in the nineteenth century. It was inevitably less common in low-income families. In Europe, literacy rates tended to be higher in Protestant than in Catholic countries. On the whole, more people were literate in towns than in the countryside. Until around 1900 men were more likely to be literate than women.

Despite all the problems, by 1841 in England and Wales (until around 1900 literacy rates were always somewhat higher in Scotland) about 67 per cent of men and 51 per cent of women were able to sign a marriage-register. By 1871 these figures were 81 per cent and 73 per cent respectively. By 1900, 97 per cent of both men and women signed the register. It was 1913 before over 99 per cent of both sexes could sign. We achieved a fully literate population just in time for everyone to be able to read the posted lists of the dead and missing in the First World War.

We ought to go back to 1850 for one important detail. In that year almost all marriages involving a middle-class groom were fully literate, that is, all four participants (bride, groom, both witnesses) could sign the register. But in marriages where the groom was an unskilled labourer only one marriage in thirteen had four literate signatories. However, in three-quarters of these unskilled labourer marriages, at least one participant could write. In other words, by 1850 at the latest, literacy and illiteracy were inextricably mixed socially. Most illiterates had at least one literate person in their immediate circle of family or friends. This is important because to experience text you do not have to read text. Remember, there is a very ancient tradition going at least as far back as Homer (and almost certainly much further) which suggest that, in the past, the majority of people heard literature rather than read it. (Shakespeare's contemporaries would commonly speak of going to 'hear' rather than to 'see' a play.) In the nineteenth century, newspapers were read out aloud in pubs, Dickens's novels were commonly read out aloud to the assembled members of a family at home, and sometimes people were hired to read to workers in manual factories to keep them entertained (see Figure 1.3).

You didn't need to be literate to enjoy literature. However, the reader you might be listening to would need adequate light to read by.

*Figure 1.3    There were many ways of gaining access to literature other than by private reading. Here, cigar-makers are being read to by a reader hired for the purpose,* The Practical Magazine, *New York, 1873*

# Light

### Northanger Abbey
The dimness of the light her candle emitted made her turn to it with alarm ... she hastily snuffed it. Alas! it was snuffed and extinguished in one. (2.6; p.124)

### Jane Eyre
Seen by the dim light of the dips [candles made by repeated dipping of a wick into molten animal fat], their number to me appeared countless, though not in reality exceeding eighty. (1.5; pp.43–4)

'Only, master had been reading in his bed last night; he fell asleep with his candle lit, and the curtains got on fire.' (2.1; p.154)

### Dombey and Son
[G]as itself couldn't light her up after dark, and her presence was a quencher to any number of candles. (8; p.105)

It was quite late at night before candles were brought; for at present they made Mrs Skewton's head ache. (30; p.455)

Its dirty wick burnt dimly at first, being choked in its own grease. (34; p.513)

If, before the invention and widespread use of electric light, you had wanted to read in anything but daylight you would have been faced with a number of difficulties. Actually, even during the day, if you were indoors, you might have had a problem. Between 1696 and 1851 you would have been taxed on the number of windows in your house. The Window Tax was at its highest at the beginning of our period: houses with six windows or fewer paid between 6s 6d and 8s. Seven windows cost £1, nine windows cost £2 2s 0d. The temptation to build houses with very few windows must have been irresistible because, just before abolition, only one-seventh of the housing stock in the country was subject to the Window Tax. **What effect do you think that would have had on domestic reading?**

Put bluntly, it meant that many houses simply could not let in enough daylight, even if outside the sun were blazing. Apart from low light levels, there would also be a significant lack of ventilation. Older buildings, being built substantially of wood, were great fire risks and fewer windows also meant fewer escape points.

What was available to a reader in terms of artificial light? Before 1784 you had the choice of simple oil lamps, wax candles, tallow candles, rush lights and firelight. Oil lamps had not changed much since the Roman legions had left Britain: basically they were a container of, usually, animal oil (commonly made from fish or sheep fat) with a wick. Tallow candles were made usually of clarified, solidified mutton fat. Rush lights were long pieces of rush dipped in hot tallow fat and then dried. All three produced a low light output; as all were animal-based, they were greasy and smelt. All three, but particularly the tallow candle, produced a lot of smoke which, along with the grease, could seriously damage paintwork, plaster and upholstery. Rush lights, which were burnt in a holder almost horizontally, left a line of greasy spots as they burned back. Wax candles burnt with a stronger and more consistent flame, but were much more expensive. They also had another drawback: they were inedible. All lights based on animal fats were, by definition, edible, and so if *in extremis* it became a toss-up between food and light, food usually won. Trinity House lighthousekeepers, it was discovered, were supplementing their wretched rations by eating some of the tallow candles provided for them.

All sources of light that relied on a naked flame had another drawback that became evident whenever a large quantity of light was required: for instance, at a social function such as a ball. A large number of candles in a room produced as much heat as light, and consumed a considerable amount of oxygen. Young women fainting at such balls may have been less to do with romantic conventions of femininity and more to do with high temperatures, high levels of carbon dioxide and low levels of oxygen. If there were fewer windows than there should have been, that would simply have added to the dangers.

Candles, particularly cheap tallow candles, demanded a considerable amount of maintenance. Until the 1820s (when candle technology started to improve markedly) both wax and tallow candles needed frequent 'snuffing'. Many of us commonly misunderstand the term 'snuffing'. It did not mean to put a candle flame out; it meant to trim the candle's wick. If you did not do this, the wick would grow longer as the wax melted, would curve over towards the small wall

*Figure 1.4   This painting illustrates the problem of artificial lighting before gas: most light sources were low in luminescence, flickering and highly localized. At best they created small pools of light in a desert of darkness. Gerard Dou,* The Night School, *oil on panel, 52.7 × 40 cm. Rijksmuseum, Amsterdam*

of solid material holding in the melted wax or tallow. The curving wick would then melt the wall, causing the molten material to flow down the candle and be lost. This was called 'guttering' and made the candle burn less efficiently and for a shorter time. Tallow candles left unattended might only use 5 per cent of their material and burn out within half an hour. In 1838 it was calculated that, if a tallow candle gave off 100 per cent of light when it was first lit, within 19 minutes it was only giving off 23 per cent of its light, unless you had snuffed it in the meantime. However, snuffing a candle, even a wax candle, was a skilled operation, and if you didn't do it properly you could extinguish the flame, as Catherine Morland did when she was reading the laundry-list she found in Northanger Abbey.

As a candle burnt down, or as a feeble rush light burnt along, the light source changed its position so, if you were reading by its light, you would have to keep adjusting the position of the book or newspaper. Most candles and oil lamps threw a lot of their light upwards and sideways rather than downwards, so exact, and sometimes uncomfortable, positioning of the book was necessary. Any naked flame moves, particularly in a draft, so the light would be inconstant. Being usually located nearer to the floor than the ceiling (on a table, for example), candles and lamps tended to throw large, moving and distracting shadows.

**Think for a moment of the plot of *Jane Eyre*. What other problems were associated with domestic lighting that was dependent on a naked flame?**

We are reminded by Bertha Mason in *Jane Eyre* that naked flames could be a fire hazard, particularly in rooms (such as bedrooms) with large quantities of hangings. Bertha Mason caused a fire on purpose, of course, but accidental fires were much more common. Let's take 1848, by which time both *Jane Eyre* and *Dombey and Son* had been published. Of the 767 fires recorded in London whose causes were known, 237 of them had been caused by candles, many of which ignited bedclothes, hangings or curtains.

Things had begun to improve in the 1780s with the invention of the oil Argand lamp which had a tubular cotton wick and a glass chimney that improved combustion and light output and made things somewhat safer. Unfortunately such lamps were very expensive, used up a lot of oil, and needed a great deal of maintenance.

The real changes came with gas lighting. This was used as early as 1805 to illuminate factories, and by 1823 London had 40,000 gas lamps lighting its main thoroughfares. Gradually gas, though still expensive, was introduced into affluent homes. By the 1850s new burners were ensuring a brighter and more consistent light output, and by the 1870s a gas chandelier that could be moved up and down at will was available. This allowed the ordinary domestic room to be lit by a high, even light source that tended to kill shadows.

By the 1860s new oil lamps – using paraffin derived from petroleum oil wells in Pennsylvania – were being introduced. Paraffin was relatively cheap, clean, and almost odourless.

Domestically usable electric light had been devised by Swan in England and Edison in the USA in the late 1870s. Electrical power stations were set up by Edison and others in the USA in the 1880s, but this process took somewhat longer in the British Isles. However, by the 1880s some public buildings were being lit by electric light. In 1881 W.S. Gilbert had to redesign the set and costumes of *Patience* when the production moved into the new Savoy Theatre with its 1,200 Swan electric lights. One of George Gissing's characters in *New*

*Figure 1.5   One of the many dangers of close reading with a naked flame. 'The Short-Sighted Man', after a print by Hogarth. Reproduced from William T. O'Dea,* The Social History of Lighting, *London: Routledge & Kegan Paul, 1958, p.22*

*Grub Street* (published in 1891 but set in the 1880s) complained of the headaches she got from working in the new electric light in the British Museum.

However, practice always dawdles behind innovation, and many domestic interiors, particularly in lower-income families, provided serious obstacles to reading in terms of inadequate light throughout most of our period.

To read a novel in such circumstances represented a great cost to the individual in terms of time, risk and effort. Economically and domestically, reading – until the widespread use of the electric light in the early twentieth century – had a cost, and therefore a significance, which it has now almost completely lost.

Despite all the obstacles and all the costs, people read a lot during our period. They read more as our period unfolded and they read more diverse sorts of texts. What were these texts, how much did they cost, and how did readers get hold of them?

*Figure 1.6 The system may be crude, but the light generated by gas brackets set relatively high on the wall provided a level of steady illumination unknown before. Gustave Doré,* Scripture Reader in a Night Refuge, *1872. Reproduced from William T. O'Dea,* The Social History of Lighting, *London: Routledge & Kegan Paul, 1958, p.56*

# Books and newspapers in the nineteenth century

### *Northanger Abbey*

Let us leave it to the Reviewers ... over every novel to talk in threadbare strains of the trash with which the press now groans. (1.5; p.23)

Miss Morland has been talking of ... a new publication which is shortly to come out, in three duodecimo volumes, two hundred and seventy-six pages in each, with a frontispiece to the first, of two tombstones and a lantern. (1.14; p.82)

Could [such atrocities] be perpetrated without being known ... in a country such as this, where roads and newspapers lay everything open? (2.9; pp.145)

### *Jane Eyre*

With these words Mr. Brocklehurst put into my hand a thin pamphlet sewn in a cover. (1.4; p.35)

I found Burns, absorbed, silent, abstracted from all round her by the companionship of a book, which she read by the dim glare of the embers. (1.6; p.55)

Most of the books were locked up behind glass doors; but there was one bookcase left open containing everything that could be needed in the way of elementary works, and several volumes of light literature, poetry, biography, travels, a few romances, &c. (1.11; p.103)

He saw nature – he saw books through me. (3.12; p.451)

### *Dombey and Son*

The books precisely matched as to size, and drawn up in line, like soldiers, looked in their cold, hard, slippery uniforms, as if they had but one idea among them, and that was a freezer. The bookcase, glazed and locked, repudiated all familiarities. (5; p.56)

The Major ... could make out ... the Copenhagen and Bird Waltzes in a Music Book of Miss Tox's own copying. (7; p.93)

The books were not easy to procure; and the answer at several shops was, either that they were just out of them, or that they never kept them, or that they had had a great many last month, or that they expected a great many next week. But Susan was not easily baffled in such an enterprise; and having entrapped a white-haired youth, in a black calico apron, from a library where she was known, to accompany her in her quest, she lead him such a life in going up and down, that he exerted himself to the utmost ... and finally enabled her to return home in triumph. (12; p.177)

That young man was generally required to read out of some book to the Captain, for one hour, every evening. (39; p.575)

Sometime in the 1820s James Nesbitt of Berwick opened a pleasantly bound book of blank pages and began to write. On most occasions he did not compose original pieces but instead copied out texts that he had enjoyed or that had particularly stuck him. In many ways Nesbitt was acting in a very traditional manner. He was compiling a 'commonplace book' – a collection of excerpts, sayings, nostrums, recipes (often for medicines), jokes, riddles and the occasional pasted-in picture. Some books might have contained music (Miss Tox's book was exclusively of music and Jane Austen compiled a similar book). Such books had been a standard feature of literate people's lives for centuries. The inclination to anthologize is an ancient one which can be found in *The Greek Anthology* (1st century BCE – 13th century CE), a collection of some 6,000 short elegiac poems by more than 300 writers; and in the gathering together of bits and pieces that made up books called 'florilegia' (or books of little flowers) of the later medieval period. In the later part of the nineteenth century and in the twentieth this tradition was carried on through the album and the scrapbook.

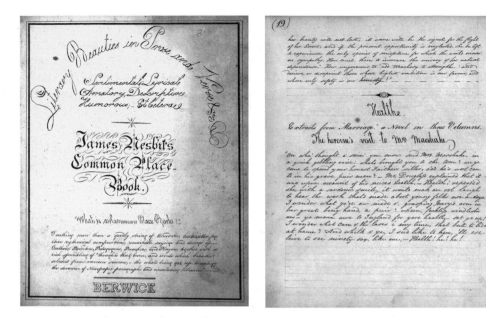

*Figure 1.7 The interchange between manuscript and print: the title-page of Nesbitt's commonplace book is handwritten but imitates the elegant title-pages of the printed gift books of the period. From the Book History Archive, London Regional Centre. By permission of William St Clair*

*Figure 1.8 Here Nesbitt is copying out a comic scene from a minor novel, Susan Ferrier's* Marriage. A Novel in Three Volumes. *From the Book History Archive, London Regional Centre. By permission of William St Clair*

Thus that James Nesbitt was compiling a commonplace book in the 1820s and 1830s should not surprise us. What he included in it might, however, make us pause. It was not just poems and witty sayings that were written down in his careful hand; he also laboriously transcribed whole chunks of prose. **Given the time and expense, why did Nesbitt bother?**

One possible answer, and one that may have some truth to it, is that it was a good way to learn passages, particularly of poetry. Many periods before our own valued the 'art of memory' and the ability to create a well-stocked mind. There is also the sense that in writing something out you 'make it your own' in a much more emphatic way than by simply reading it. However, the overwhelming reason for commonplace books was preservation. That is, a significant number of the books and newspapers that were copied from were not owned by the copyist and would have had to be returned. Copying text was the only way of keeping text.

Now to some extent we share the same culture: we, too, borrow books from libraries or from friends and sometimes, as students, we will make hand-written notes. But they will be notes, not exactly copied passages. If we wanted long passages we would get them photocopied. We usually regard this as work, not as a leisure activity.

Parts of books were copied because books were expensive. Novels not only talked about money, they cost money, often a great deal of money. If you wanted to read them you had buy them or borrow them, and frequently borrowing was not free. Although the legislation to set up free public libraries had been passed in 1850, there were relatively few of them until the 1880s. Until the late nineteenth century, most libraries that you could borrow a novel from were commercial organizations that required you to pay an annual subscription. The commonest subscription rate was one guinea (£1 1s 0d or £1.05). In 1850 that was a lot of money: as we have seen, many of the working class, particularly agricultural labourers, earned around that, or less, per week.

# *The cost of books*

Until 1814 all books and newspapers, indeed every printed item, had been produced on a handpress. That is, a simple, human-powered machine built of wood until around 1800 and, after that, of iron. In either case it required two people to operate it (one to ink the type, one to fit the sheet of paper and press the paper onto the inked type) and could only print one sheet of paper, on one side, at a time. Nowadays we tend to think that producing more of something at one go reduces the price per unit; that is the basis of all mass production. But if your power is human, you cannot speed it up; in order to produce more you have either to ask human beings to work longer (and you may have to pay overtime to do this), or you have to hire more people. In either case your wage costs go up. Thus more, in pre-industrial printing, did not necessarily mean cheaper. This was particularly the case with newspapers. The nineteenth century was the period in which newspapers grew up and became the predominant form of printed matter. There were certainly many newsworthy events that cried out for widely sold newspapers. However, as the owner of, say, *The Times*, you would have had a problem. Imagine that you have just received the news of the battle of Trafalgar (1805) – a famous victory but one that also saw the death of Nelson. What a double story! You naturally want to print a lot of copies fast. How do you go about doing this? A pair of printers working one machine, even one of the new metal handpresses, could only produce a maximum of 250 sheets printed on one side every hour. You obviously needed more than one machine. Indeed, you probably needed dozens of machines with two printers each to produce a sufficient number of copies quickly enough. You didn't save because each printer had to be paid. Worse, each printing machine needed its own type from which to print. Thus for each machine you had to have a compositor to set up, by hand, all the type you needed. More expense and expense that is multiplied each time you add another handpress. Worse is to come. In 1805 almost all paper was handmade. Handmade paper (mostly made of linen rags) was durable but expensive. Indeed paper for both books and newspapers was, until the later nineteenth century, often the single most expensive item in the whole printing process. Certainly many of the rags that Good Mrs Brown was accumulating in *Dombey and Son* would have been destined for the paper-makers.

*Figure 1.9    The Stanhope press, made of iron and introduced around 1800. In the background a compositor is selecting type from the upper and lower case with his right hand and holding a composing stick in his left. Paper was slightly dampened before printing so that it would offer a softer surface for inked type. After printing it was, as you can see here, hung up to dry. There would usually be two people working a handpress. Reproduced from James Morgan,* Printing Presses, *Berkeley: University of California Press, 1973, p.28*

There was one other factor that added to the cost of newspapers in the early nineteenth century: tax. In 1819 the Seditious Publication Act was passed: this imposed a 4d per copy tax on any periodical containing news or comment on the news which was published more frequently than every twenty-eight days and cost less than 6d. Its title suggests its purpose: in the wake of the French Revolution and the Peterloo massacre this was an attempt to prevent the working classes getting hold of newspapers that might stir them into revolutionary fervour. This was one of the notorious 'taxes on knowledge' which were progressively repealed as the century advanced (the newspaper tax was reduced to 1d in 1836 and finally abolished in 1855). Another of these taxes was on paper, which was at the rate of 3d per pound (lb) weight (this was only finally abolished in 1861). A tax on newspaper advertisements of 3s 6d (18p) each was a further restriction, for it reduced the indirect income of newspapers.

The upshot of all this was that newspapers, for the first half of the century at least, were expensive. That Dombey is frequently seen reading what is obviously his own newspaper is but one indication of his affluence. Many of the commonplace books from the early nineteenth century have material copied from newspapers as well as books. **Why didn't the owner simply cut out and stick the newspaper passage in the commonplace book and have done**

**with it? After all, newspapers weren't like books, they had a strictly limited life.**

Newspapers had a longer life in the early nineteenth century than they do today. Partly this was because of their expense, and partly because of the way they were made. We are all used to buying a paperback and over a few years seeing its paper turn yellow-brown and become fragile. Much modern paper is made out of wood pulp that has a high acid content. The acid attacks the paper, discolouring and weakening it. But most paper before the mid-nineteenth century was made out of rags, not wood pulp. It was much more chemically stable and physically robust. This was fortunate because, with newspapers often costing as much as sixpence (a considerable sum in 1800), only the well-off could afford to buy a newspaper exclusively for their own use.

Many copies of, say, *The Times* would be circulated through many hands. Our 1805 copy reporting the battle of Trafalgar might well, for instance, not be sold outright by the newspaper seller but loaned to the reader for 1d an hour. Over the day of publication such a copy might be read by seven or eight borrowers. The firm of W.H. Smith began in the late eighteenth century as a small 'newswalk' which would have both sold and loaned out newspapers. At the end of that first day our copy might well then have been sent into the country – once the newspaper stamp had been paid on a given paper, that paper could be sent through the mails for free. It might be sent to a small market town (to the sort of community Jane Austen commonly wrote about) and then circulated over the next couple of weeks around a newspaper club composed of the middle-class families of the area. After that it might have been given to the local tailor or some other literate artisan who might well read parts of it out loud to his less literate friends and family. A single copy of a newspaper might thus last for weeks and go through dozens of hands. The news may have been old by the time it got to the tailor but, given the robust rag paper, it would still not be in tatters. Thus, if you saw a newspaper from which you wished to copy something, it may not have been yours to cut up. As with books, newspapers might just have been passing through your life. If you wanted to hold on to a bit of text you would have had to copy it out.

Renting books and newspapers sounds peculiar to us, but it is worth remembering that for most people for most of the nineteenth century, renting was the norm. Until the expansion of building societies, even many middle-class families, unless they were very well off, did not own their own homes. Renting houses or parts of houses was a common practice. Even a distinguished and pretty affluent writer such as Dickens only bought one house, Gadshill Place near his boyhood home in Kent, and then only twelve years before his death. Without building society mortgages, and without hire purchase, many middle-class families were never able to afford high-cost goods. In lower-class families even kitchen equipment such as ovens was rented (commonly from the local baker) when a particularly large meal was required. Hired houses, hired transport (horses), hired help (servants); if many of the books and newspapers they read were also transitory, then we should not be surprised. As the nineteenth century progressed it became more and more likely that at least the more affluent members of the middle classes would own their own homes, and even working-class people, by the end of the century, were able to make relatively major purchases (for instance, pianos, sewing machines or bicycles). However, it was to be the middle of the twentieth century before the working-class rental culture was substantially overturned.

Book prices were generally quite high in the first half of the nineteenth century. As an example let's take novels. In the eighteenth century, novels could come in one volume, but more commonly they were published in multiple volumes: Henry Fielding's *Tom Jones* (1749) in six volumes, Laurence Sterne's *Tristram Shandy* (1760–7) in nine volumes, Fanny Burney's *Cecilia* (1782) in five volumes. By the early nineteenth century things were becoming a bit more uniform, and the standard number of volumes for a first edition of a novel had settled down to three or four. Each volume normally cost about 5s or 6s, so a three-volume novel would normally retail at between 15s and 18s. The author who changed all that was someone we have already met as author of *Marmion* – Sir Walter Scott. Scott's long sequence of novels began with *Waverley* in 1814. This was published in three volumes but the set cost 21s. Despite this high price the novel went through eight editions in seven years (a total of 11,500 copies – a huge number for such a costly book). Scott clearly had a captive market, and his publishers exploited it. *Ivanhoe*, published in 1820, cost 30s and *Kenilworth*, published in 1821, sold for 31s 6d, or a guinea and a half (see Figure 1.10). There the price for a new novel in three volumes stuck. Between 1821 and 1894, despite inflation and deflation, criticism and attack, the price for a three-decker remained at 31s 6d. This was more than most working-class men earned in a week, and was almost twice the weekly disposable income of someone at the bottom end of the middle classes. The publishing history of the novel for most of the nineteenth century is the history of how publishers, librarians and readers adapted to, or got around, this price.

The most obvious way was the circulating library, thus named because the books 'circulated' around the readers. There had been many such libraries during the eighteenth century but they came into their own in our period. Essentially a circulating library was a commercial organization charging a monthly or annual subscription for the right to borrow books. There were many subscription rates but the most famous was one guinea (21s or £1.05) a year, which was charged by Mudie's Circulating Library, the largest in the British Isles. For this you could borrow just one volume at a time. To such a library the three-decker novel, as it was called, was a godsend. As a library you could lend the three volumes of a single novel to three separate subscribers. Such libraries bought novels in considerable numbers from publishers so they often got substantial discounts (sometimes up to 50 per cent or more). A three-decker novel might cost the library only 15s or 20s so, if it circulated the volumes for about a year, it would make a profit on each. As readers could not afford to buy, they had no alternative to borrowing. As publishers could ask a high price for their new novels (even 15s was a high price in relation to the actual production costs of such a novel), selling a few hundred sets to the circulating libraries meant that they made money even if they sold no other copies. This arrangement was often denounced at the time as a conspiracy against the reading public, as indeed it was, but nothing much changed until the end of our

*Figure 1.10   Sir Walter Scott's* Kenilworth *(1821), the three-decker novel that established 31s 6d as the standard price. Note the generous margins and the heavy leading (that is, the wide gap between the printed lines). Note also that this binding is not the original one. Photo: Mike Levers*

period. So convenient to the publishers was it, that when Mudie's was threatened with bankruptcy in the 1860s, many of the major London novel-publishers banded together to save it by becoming shareholders in the company.

Novels were frequently forced into sets of three or more to make sure that they would be acceptable to the circulating libraries. You will have noticed that *Northanger Abbey* was published in 1818 with Jane Austen's last complete novel, *Persuasion*, in order to provide a multi-volume set that the circulating libraries would buy in substantial numbers. *Jane Eyre* first came out in 1847 as a three-decker novel. Charlotte Brontë's sister Emily had to publish her novel *Wuthering Heights* (1847) with Anne Brontë's *Agnes Grey* in order to bulk the work out to three volumes and thus make it marketable to the circulating libraries.

The three-decker novel was a socially respectable form; it was accessible only to those with a middle-class income or above. Working-class literature was of a totally different sort. Traditionally, from the sixteenth century onwards, the cheapest literature tended to be chapbooks and broadsheets. Neither was usually sold in a bookshop but instead was hawked about the streets, fairs and markets by itinerant sellers. 'Chapbook' means a 'book to be sold at a market' (from the Old English 'ceap' meaning 'market'). Such books were usually little more than pamphlets with sixteen or thirty-two pages recounting the deeds of traditional and legendary heroes (such as Robin Hood). They usually sold for 1d or 2d (see Figure 1.11). A broadsheet or broadside was a single, long sheet of paper, printed on one side only and giving an account of some exciting or horrendous event (a murder, an execution or a monstrous birth). They were often 'multi-genre' publications with a prose account, a poem on the subject (sometimes a song) and a woodcut illustration. They commonly sold for ½d or 1d (see Figure 1.12).

*Figure 1.11 Traditional cheap popular reading: the chapbook.* The History of Valentine and Orson. *British Library 1578/4470* © *The British Library*

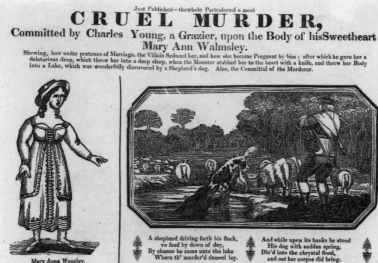

*Figure 1.12 Early nineteenth-century popular literature: the broadside. Note the mix of prose, poetry, woodcut illustrations (often used again and again) and typographic decoration: the broadsides were the multimedia of their day. J. Catnach was one of the major producers of this literature in the early nineteenth century. 'Cruel Murder'. John Johnson Collection; Murders and Executions Broadsides Folder 5, Bodleian Library, University of Oxford*

In the 1830s and 1840s a new working-class form emerged: a lengthy prose fiction serialized weekly parts costing 1d or 2d. These were frequently concerned with adventures or with Gothic-like narratives. Many had the quality of soap operas in the sense that there was no close to the narrative, it just went on until the public lost interest. Some penny weekly novels in the 1850s and 1860s were serialized over four or more years.

Dickens was one of a number of authors who tried to break through the rigid system of the three-decker novel. He took the idea of novels in parts from the working-class form – essentially a form of hire purchase for literature – and went up-market with it. Instead of weekly parts at 1d he offered monthly parts at 1s. There were a strictly limited number of parts: twenty, which were serialized over nineteen months (the final part was a double issue at 2s). Thus at the end of nineteen months you had an entire novel for £1 rather than 31s 6d. It was still expensive, but the investment was spread. One shilling was a middle-class price; however, even if the 3d a week that it represented was three times what most working-class fiction cost, it was still more within reach of those on lower incomes. In terms of sales, Dickens's novels certainly went much farther down the social scale than those of most other serious novelists. Even so, Dickens's sales figures cannot begin to compare with the sales of genuine working-class texts. *Dombey and Son* sold on average about 32,000 copies of each monthly issue. Dickens's most successful novel in terms of immediate sales, *The Old Curiosity Shop* (1840–1), was selling about 100,000 a month by the end of its run. But, in contrast, as early as 1828 a broadside, 'Confession and execution of William Corder', sold an estimated 1,166,000 copies.

Being a single sheet printed crudely on one side and over a number of months, the 'Corder' broadside did not present any technical problems. But producing 100,000 copies of monthly parts of *The Old Curiosity Shop* on time and quickly was a very different matter. How was this possible by 1840?

# *The printing revolution of 1800–1840*

The printing industry had undergone a revolution between 1800 and 1840. There were many aspects to this, but the most important were the application of steam power to paper-making machines and to printing machines, and the development of stereotyping.

Until the first decade of the nineteenth century, all paper was made by hand, and the maximum size of a sheet of paper was determined by the largest size of wooden-framed wire tray that a man could dip into a vat of 'stuff' (a pulp of linen fibres and water with the consistency of porridge). In the first decade of the nineteenth century the first powered paper-making machine (called a 'Fourdrinier' after the stationers who had funded its development) was introduced. Instead of making separate sheets of paper, the Fourdrinier machine made paper in a continuous strip or 'web'. Over the next few decades paper production went up dramatically and the price of paper began slowly to fall as the machines took over.

*Figure 1.13    The* Illustrated London News *being printed on a steam press, 1843. At this time newspapers were still printed on single sheets of paper (not on a continuous roll or 'web'). Note the drive belt in the foreground: this transferred power from the steam engine (not shown here but presumably below) to the machine*

The application of steam power to printing was brought about by pressure from newspaper publishers: they needed to produce papers more quickly and more cheaply. In November 1814 *The Times* was, for the first time, printed on steam-driven machines that were capable of producing between 1,100 and 1,800 sheets per hour as opposed to the 250 on a handpress. Machines were then produced that could print on both sides of the paper in the same process (called 'perfecting') and by 1827 newspaper presses could produce 4,000 perfected sheets an hour. As book printing didn't require the sort of volume or speed newspapers needed, it lagged behind somewhat, although by the 1830s book machines capable of producing 800 perfected sheets an hour were in use.

In order to print you need to set type. Typesetting ('composition' as it was called) was a manual job. The compositor stood in front of two large, subdivided trays, each subdivision holding a particular letter, punctuation mark or spacer to create gaps between words or lines. The upper case held capital letters, the lower case contained what we, in everyday speech, still call 'lower case' letters. Each letter had to be picked up and placed in the right order, which – as far as the compositor was concerned – was upside down and mirror-fashion if it was eventually to print the right way round. Books were not printed page by page, of course. Printing normally consisted of printing a number of pages (commonly eight) simultaneously on one large piece of paper, printing another eight on the back of the sheet, and then folding the sheet and cutting its edges so that the pages were in the correct order. One sheet folded and cut was called a 'gathering' or 'quire', and most books were made up of a number of gatherings put together.

Each piece of type was separate from every other piece, so that the type for, say, eight pages, had to be locked firmly into a wooden or iron frame called a 'chase'. It is this chase, with its locked-in type, that then went to the printing machine. Once the printing had been done and the type cleaned, every single piece of type had to be put back by hand into the correct subdivision of the upper or lower case (this was called 'distributing' the type). **Just think for a moment of the sort of things that might go wrong during such a process.**

There are many, but what about: the compositor's finger missing the correct subdivision of the case and choosing the wrong piece of type; reversing a letter so it prints the wrong way around; dropping the chase so all its individual bits of type scatter all over the printing shop; imagine having individually to clean and then return the type to its correct subdivision. Then, above all, imagine doing this as a rush job in the winter months by light from a tallow candle or fitful oil lamp.

Type was expensive, so unless you were a very large-scale or affluent printer you would not have enough type to print the whole novel at once. You had to print the first few gatherings and then distribute the type before you then set up the next few gatherings. Once the job was finished the type would be used for another job. **Imagine what would have to happen if the novel was a success, and another print run was called for.**

The whole process would have to begin again, so the costs of the second edition would not be much less than the first. Also, almost certainly, the second printing would not be the same as the first; it might possibly be even worse than the first for, rather than using the author's manuscript again, the type would be set from the first edition. The first edition's mistakes might well be copied into the second and then, almost inevitably, other errors would be introduced on top of these.

Stereotype, although invented in the eighteenth century, was not widely used until the nineteenth century but, when it was, it revolutionized print production. The stereotype process works as follows: a page of type is set up by the compositor as usual but then a plaster cast is taken of that page of type. The type is then distributed and further pages are set up and casts taken of those. When you want to print, you simply pour molten type metal into each cast, allow it to cool, and you then have a solid plate of metal from which you can print. After printing you can either store the stereotype plates much more easily than heavy movable, vulnerable type, or melt the plates and keep the plaster moulds. If another printing is called for you use the plates or recast them in the moulds. This was a technique introduced to print long works in constant demand (such as Bibles) but gradually the technique spread so that by the mid-nineteenth century any work that might need reprinting was 'plated', just in case.

In these three technologies – the Fourdrinier, steam-powered printing and stereotype – we see the beginning of an industrial revolution in print production that was to gather momentum throughout our period and result, by its end, in a total transformation of the ways in which newspapers and book were made – and read.

# The communications revolution

## *Trains*

Part of this transformation was dependent on a technology that was not directly related to print production. When the firm of W.H. Smith began it was successful because the first W.H. Smith mastered the intricacies of the mail coach timetable from London to the provinces, and was thus able to ensure that his newspapers were as widely distributed as possible. However, even the fastest horse-drawn coaches, working at competition speed in the 1830s, took seven and a half hours to get from London to Birmingham and eighteen hours to get from London to Manchester. In *Northanger Abbey* it was John Thorpe's proud boast that his horse could manage 10 miles per hour (1.7; p.29).

It was the railways that transformed everything. Between 1824 and 1848 some 4,646 miles of railway were built. By 1852 there were only three sizeable towns in England (Hereford, Yeovil, Weymouth) not served by a railway line. Average speeds were modest at first (about 37 miles per hour in 1845) but they were still more than three times what the fastest mail coach could achieve. The railways also ran in all weathers and did not require stops at various stages as horse-drawn vehicles did. In 1820 it would have taken about thirty hours to travel from London to Hull; by 1845 it was taking just eight hours. Newspapers could now reach every major centre of population in hours rather than days. Perishable food could be transported in bulk quickly and safely to the growing towns crying out for it. And people could be transported everywhere. Large cities with larger suburbs and commuter belts beyond, cities as we know them, were the creation of the railways.

Significantly, the building of railways reached a peak in 1847, during which year more than a quarter of a million men were employed on building 6,455 miles of railway. In 1847 expenditure on railways represented 12 per cent of total national income. This was, of course, the year during which the largest part of *Dombey and Son* was being written and published. **Consider the following three quotations from Chapter 15 of *Dombey and Son*. What can we learn from them?**

There were railway patterns in its drapers' shops, and railway journals in the windows of its newsmen. (15; p.233)

There was even railway time observed in clocks, as if the sun itself had given in. (ibid.)

*Figure 1.14    George Scharf,* The Birmingham Railroad being extended from Chalk Farm to Euston (May 1836). © *British Museum*

> Wonderful Members of Parliament, who, little more than twenty years before, had made themselves merry with the wild railroad theories of engineers, and given them the liveliest rubs in cross examination, went down into the north with their watches in their hands, and sent on messages before by the electric telegraph, to say that they were coming. (p.234)

As the railway has transformed Staggs's Gardens, so it was transforming Britain. William Makepeace Thackeray (1811–63), Dickens's great contemporary, once observed that the railways had divided the past from the present. Everything before the railway was archaic, everything since was the modern world. But surely it's more specific than that here?

It has affected culture: there are even newspapers devoted to it. But it has also created 'railway time'. Difficult as it may be to imagine, prior to the coming of the railways time was not uniform throughout the British Isles. Local towns often ran on local time. Indeed, how could you have co-ordinated clocks when the fastest means of communication was either a man on a horse or a series of signal fires on beacon hills?

## *Time and the telegraph*

With the coming of the railways came railway timetables, and they would only work if everyone operated on the same time. Note that the MPs travelling down to the North carry their own watches against which they check time. For people such as Dombey time became personal: it structured their individual lives and they carried it around with them in the form of pocket watches. Has it struck you how many references there are in *Dombey and Son* to watches?

There was no sound in answer but the loud ticking of Mr Dombey's watch and Doctor Parker Peps's watch, which seemed in the silence to be running a race ... The race in the ensuing pause was fierce and furious. The watches seemed to jostle, and to trip each other up. (1; pp.9–10)

[H]e even knew the difference in the sound of their watches. (16; p.237)

Today we are used to carrying precise time about with us in the form of electronic watches, but the nineteenth century was the first to see a significant proportion of the middle class carrying watches. The industrial revolution

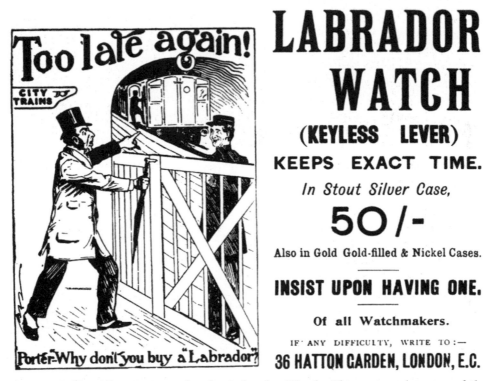

*Figure 1.15   Advertisement for the Labrador Watch. The temporal power of the railways standardized time and then required individuals to run to it*

affected watches just as it did most other goods: between 1800 and 1875 the production of watches increased tenfold. Mechanical time, from clocking-on in factories through to MPs checking railway time, started to regulate human conduct with an exactitude that had never been possible before:

'[W]e go on in our clock-work routine, from day to day.' (33; p.505)

But how were clocks and watches in various parts of the country to be co-ordinated? We have talked much about the communication revolution represented by the changes in newspaper and book production, but there were other such technical revolutions happening at the same time. **Look again at the quotation about MPs travelling. What might have been used to co-ordinate all those clocks and watches, wherever they were in the country?**

The electric telegraph. This was developed in Britain and the USA in the 1830s and early 1840s and first installed by railway companies in this country (one of the first was a line between Euston and Camden Town ('Camberling Town') in the late 1830s). It is not insignificant that it was at the end of 1847, as *Dombey and Son* was being serialized, that time was, for the first time, co-ordinated throughout the country by telegraph.

The telegraph was, until the development of the telephone system in the 1870s and 1880s, the only means of near-instantaneous communication. However, it depended on trained operators using Morse code and its costs were relatively high. It was invaluable for newspapers (how many of these technical changes were accelerated by the demands of newspapers?), for government, for businessmen and stock exchanges; it was useful to the private individual in an emergency – but it was not usually a common means of personal communication. For that the written letter was still the obvious choice.

## *The postal system*

The letter and the novel have been intimately connected since the rise of the novel in the eighteenth century. Indeed, many of the early novels, such as Samuel Richardson's *Pamela; or Virtue Rewarded* (1740), were epistolary in form, that is, they were constructed as a series of letters to and from the main characters. Even when the form is not epistolary, letters often play a significant role in novels. **Think of one important event in each of the three novels covered in part 1 of this book that involves a letter**.

In *Northanger Abbey* there is James Morland's letter to Isabella Thorpe carrying the news of his parents' approval of his marriage; there is James Morland's letter to Catherine with the news of Isabella's duplicity and, of course, Isabella's own letter to Catherine which fully reveals Isabella's true nature. In *Jane Eyre* there is Mrs Reed's letter to Brocklehurst which sets Jane up for the punitive early years at Lowood; there is the letter to 'J.E.' offering her the job at Thornfield; there is Jane's letter to her uncle that alerts Mason to the intended bigamous marriage; there is the letter from the solicitor with news of Jane Eyre's inheritance and there is the final letter from St John that ends the novel. In *Dombey and Son* there is the letter that fatefully Walter Gay picks up which starts in train his journey to the West Indies and there is Solomon Gill's letter to Captain Cuttle. Most notable is the way in which the images of letters and correspondence cluster around Carker, the man of business.

Before 1840, and Rowland Hill's reforms, sending a letter was a difficult and expensive business. Letters were charged on the basis of distance sent: from 1812 onwards, for instance, charges ranged from 4d for fifteen miles to 1s for 300 miles plus a further 1d for each additional 100 miles. Letters were usually paid for on delivery so, if you were sending a letter to someone with little disposable income, there was no guarantee that they could pay for it at the other end. Rowland Hill's reforms were simple and radical: there would be a standard charge regardless of distance and this charge would only vary according to weight; the charge was to be one penny and it was to be prepaid by the sender in the form of an adhesive stamp.

The penny post was in its way as revolutionary as the railways and, indeed, these two systems reinforced each other. With the introduction of pre-paid postcards at ½d in 1870, the creation of the General Postal Union (1875) to improve the international postal system, and the arrival of the picture postcard at the end of the century, our period witnessed both the birth and the maturity of a modern postal system. This growth was very rapid: the annual number of letters received per capita in 1839 was four; in the first year of the penny post the figure doubled to eight; by 1871 it was thirty-two and, by 1900, sixty. In February 1850 more than 500,000 valentines were sent by post, and by 1877 4.5 million Christmas cards were being delivered.

As with the railways and the telegraph, the period covered by the publication of *Jane Eyre* and *Dombey and Son* was also significant for books, newspapers and the new postal system: in 1848 special, cheaper postal rates for printed matter were introduced. The final monthly parts of *Dombey and Son* may well have been sent more cheaply through the post than its earlier parts had been.

As printed books and letters moved in ever-increasing quantities – and as people (consulting their watches) travelled ever faster – along the railway line, so also did uniform time flow down the iron rails. All this was accompanied and paralleled by electrical information buzzing in Morse code through the telegraph wires that followed the railway tracks. We are not the first to undergo an information revolution.

# Literature and commodities; or, advertising and the novel

There was one more information revolution that we have not yet considered, and yet which used the railways, the postal system and print to achieve its ends. As the industrial revolution created both the goods and the population capable of buying them, so a mode of communication came to maturity that was able to convey the promise and excitement of buying things: advertising. The nineteenth century was the first great century of universal advertising, of commodities being made, packaged and sold on a scale and with an intensity that had never been seen before. Dickens's novels are full of allusions to advertisements but, more strikingly, Dickens's novels were furiously promoted by advertising and were also, literally, surrounded by advertisements.

The first part of *Dombey and Son* was issued on Thursday 1 October 1846. However, prior to that there had been a massive advertising campaign. In August and September, to build up interest, 240,000 handbills had been issued; in September and early October 10,000 posters had been printed that were then flyposted everywhere. In the first few months of the novel's publication the publishers, Bradbury and Evans, had spent substantial sums on newspaper and magazine advertisements. Dickens's popularity, though genuine, was not left to develop naturally: it was stimulated and hyped as much as the promotion system of the mid-nineteenth century would allow.

Each part of every novel that Dickens published in monthly parts came in pamphlet form with a coloured and engraved paper cover and thirty-two pages of letterpress (that is, print). But that was not all. Surrounding the letterpress were a certain number of pages devoted to advertising. The 'Dombey Advertiser', as these additional leaves were called, ran to sixteen pages in the first part of the novel. So what sorts of commercial goods surrounded *Dombey and Son*?

On the back (or verso) of the front covers of issues 1 and 2 was, very appropriately, the advertisement of an optician and telescope-maker, Thomas Harris & Son. As with Sol Gills, this instrument-maker seems to have been having trouble keeping his customers for 'Crystal Spectacles', 'Achromatic Telescopes' and 'Deer-Stalking Telescopes', for he warns:

> CAUTION – To prevent mistakes, the public are requested to notice the name THOMAS HARRIS & SON, and the number [52], is laid in MOSAIC PAVEMENT on the footway contiguous to their shop. Attention to this *Caution* is necessary to prevent mistakes, in consequence of the *unprincipled* conduct of a person in the immediate neighbourhood.

Not surprisingly many of the pages were taken up with advertisements from publishers of books and magazines. Of the first sixteen pages in issue 1, eleven were occupied by publishers and their wares. From then on, however, the Advertiser opens up to the cacophony of early Victorian commercialism. There were advertisements for waterproof overcoats, umbrellas and general tailors (most notably for E. Moses & Son of the Minories and Aldgate; these tended to include a parody of a well-known traditional or contemporary poem; in their amended form these poems celebrated the glories of Moses's tailoring). Food and drink featured strongly, with patented Carrara water, Worcestershire sauce, tea, coffee and Cognac. Aids to personal appearance were much touted, with Rowland's Macassar oil (for hair), Kalydor (skin cream) and Odonto (tooth powder); Comprimo braces; Gowland's lotion (another skin preparation) – and the 'Invisible Peruke' (a wig). Patent medicines and medical aids were commonly promoted in literary publications, and the 'Dombey Advertiser' was no exception, for it includes advertisements for the 'Elastic Chest Expander' and 'Bailey's Trusses'.

Most touchingly appropriate of all, and an advertisement that appeared in every serialized part of *Dombey and Son*, is a half-page announcement, accompanied by an engraving of its imposing building, of the extensive stock of the 'London General Mourning Warehouse'. This was a department store devoted to equipping the grief-stricken for the long and elaborate Victorian process of mourning the dead. No doubt Mr Dombey or his servants visited such an emporium as occasions in the novel required.

This first issue of the 'Dombey Advertiser' brought in £124 7s 9d in income to Dickens and his publishers, Chapman & Hall. By the end of the nineteen months of serialization, gross advertising income alone stood at £2,027 1s 0d. As early as April 1847, the overall profits from *Dombey and Son* were substantial enough for Dickens to invest the sum of £600 in Consols.

And what happened to James Nesbitt of Berwick, the compiler of 'James Nesbitt's Commonplace Book ... Literary Beauties in Prose and Verse &c Sentimental, Lyrical, Amatory, Descriptive, Humorous Etceterae'? He too was affected by the changes we have been describing in this section. In 1842 he moved to Manchester – to work as an engineer.

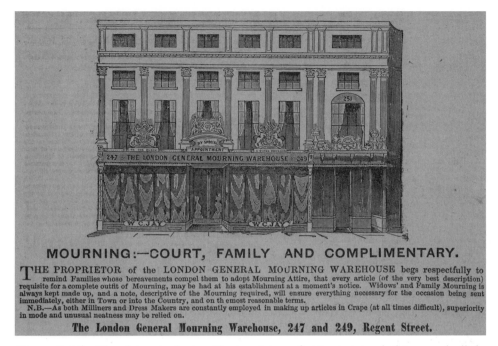

*Figure 1.16   The dying industry: the provision of appropriate clothing and all the accessories for formal mourning resulted in a considerable retail trade. Photo: Mary Evans Picture Library*

# Works cited

Austen, Jane. [1818] 2003. *Northanger Abbey*, ed. by James Kinsley and John Davie, with an introduction and notes by Claudia L. Johnson, Oxford World's Classics, Oxford: Oxford University Press.

Brontë, Charlotte. [1847] 2000. *Jane Eyre*, ed. by Margaret Smith, with an introduction and revised notes by Sally Shuttleworth, Oxford World's Classics, Oxford: Oxford University Press.

Burnett, John. 1969. *A History of the Cost of Living*, Harmondsworth: Penguin.

Dickens, Charles. [1846–8] 2001. *Dombey and Son*, ed. by Alan Horsman, with an introduction and notes by Dennis Walder, Oxford World's Classics, Oxford: Oxford University Press.

Dickens, Charles. [1860–1] 1994. *Great Expectations*, ed. by Margaret Cardwell, with an introduction by Kate Flint, Oxford World's Classics, Oxford: Oxford University Press.

Twigger, Robert. 1997. *The Value of the Pound 1750–1996*, London: House of Commons Library.

Suggestions for further reading can be found at the end of chapter 8.

# CHAPTER 2

# *Northanger Abbey*: a novel's entry into the world

*by Nicola Watson*

## Introduction

*Northanger Abbey* was the first novel that Austen wrote (at the age of about twenty-four) and had accepted for publication. Drafted in 1798 or 1799, revised in 1803 and possibly again, very lightly, in 1816, it was none the less not published until after Austen's death in 1817 (1818 appears on the title-page), a delay that remains unexplained. It is very much the product of the last decades of the eighteenth century and the first decades of the new. These decades saw the political experiment of the French Revolution and witnessed its aftermath, the Napoleonic Empire. They were a time of political and intellectual ferment in which writers, artists, philosophers, politicians and the ordinary working man were engaged in an urgent rethinking of 'things as they are' and 'things as they should be' (to borrow two much-used phrases from polemicists including William Godwin, Mary Wollstonecraft and their associates). Rooted in this period, then, *Northanger Abbey* has a special status here because it self-consciously foregrounds in comic mode an (implicitly political) struggle over how to represent 'things as they are', or 'reality', an argument which we also take to govern, overtly or covertly, the entire history of the nineteenth-century novel.

*Northanger Abbey* has generally been taken to mark the full flowering and completion of Austen's juvenilia, that is to say, the sketches and so on that she wrote before completing a major work. Generalizations are always risky, but it is possible to say that the juvenilia develop the art of burlesque and parody. Burlesque is when you take a 'high' or serious art form but fill it with 'low' or comic content. Henry Fielding, for example, took the plot and language of heroic tragedy but peopled it with figures from popular culture in his *The Tragedy of Tragedies, or The Life of Tom Thumb the Great* (1730). One of its effects is therefore 'bathos' – laughter at the comically anticlimactic incongruity between form and matter. Parody is related, though not necessarily so good-tempered, and may deploy burlesque along with other techniques, but usually shadows a parent text or style, producing a kind of literary satire by following its conventions and structure faithfully but in a ludicrously truncated or exaggerated manner. In the juvenilia, Austen's targets include a number of inherited novelistic conventions, together with many of the values they articulate, but it is not until *Northanger Abbey* that she harnesses this satiric impulse to make a free-standing moral, political and social fable. By making use of so many other texts and genres – the novel (sentimental and Gothic) and related genres, such as sermons directed at young women, conduct-book literature, history, and guidebooks – this novel sets up large questions that would preoccupy Austen for the rest of her career about what might be at stake in the 'proper' perception of social reality.

What this comes down to in practice is a novel preoccupied with genre and with acts of reading, reading represented by *Northanger Abbey* as 'at once a trivial pursuit, a form of social bonding, the quest for pleasure and satisfaction, and a trainee's preparation in reading the world'. Reading is not just of books, of course, but ultimately of people, dress, behaviour, language and the games played out in conversation – the world, in short (Butler, 1995, pp.xx–xxi). Austen's elaborate exploration of signs and how they can be understood and misunderstood demands that you read with a sophisticated alertness to intertextual games of allusion and genre. As we plunge into the first chapter and meet our heroine, you need to activate all that sophistication because this isn't a heroine with whom you will be allowed to identify in any simple fashion.

# A heroine

**Reread volume 1, chapter 1, and, as you read, ask yourself what attributes and circumstances threaten to disqualify Catherine Morland as a 'heroine'. From that, what do you infer about how you qualify as a 'heroine'? What do you need to be, and what do you need to do?**

As you open this book you know, as the first readers of this volume knew, that you are about to read a novel – and a novel, at this time, generally (if not always) had a heroine. The opening of *Northanger Abbey* is designed to play off and to laugh at contemporary and stereotypically feminine, even silly expectations of what such a heroine would have been like, and what sort of things would happen to her. Indeed, the chapter, like others after it, as we shall see, is full of sly references to various celebrated and important novels of the day by Frances Burney, Ann Radcliffe and Maria Edgeworth. To put it another way, Austen opens with burlesque, although that term, carrying connotations of the bombastic or rowdy, doesn't quite do justice to Austen's subtler, more ladylike effects. (One of Austen's most innovative techniques here is to allow the narratorial voice to slip in and out of characters' consciousnesses – a technique called 'free indirect discourse'. The first tiny example of this mode is the tone of fifteen-year-old innocent indignation that the narrative voice momentarily assumes in the exclamation 'as any body might expect' on page 5. You should be able to identify more examples as you read on.) She punctures the high-flown glamorous improbabilities of heroism by showing how a good-tempered but thoroughly commonplace girl falls hopelessly short of its standards. 'Reality' shows up 'fiction' to comic effect.

So what or who is this 'heroine' at whom we are so neatly being made to laugh? Well, for one thing, you might have noticed that a real heroine is somehow 'born to be an heroine', devoted from 'infancy' to this vocation. But by nature Catherine is neither beautiful, accomplished nor clever, nor is she the conventional paragon of the sentimental novel, brimming over with super-refined and virtuous feeling. That is the point of that reference to 'the more heroic enjoyments of infancy' (Austen, [1818] 2003,1.1; p.5; all subsequent page references are to this edition) in which other heroines of the period are in fact displayed for our edification, and it's also why her inability to write sonnets is remarked upon – the heroines of Ann Radcliffe and Charlotte Smith are particularly liable to break out into extemporary effusions. Worse, she hasn't been born into any of a range of suitable plots, such as that of conflict with her parents. Catherine's father is respectable and thoroughly middle-class rather than poor, neglected, remarkably handsome or wickedly tyrannical; her mother is comfortably alive, disconcertingly fertile, possessed of good nature, good health and good sense. Nor has she been provided with a suitable local hero of mysterious or noble origin with whom to fall in love. Labouring under the disadvantages of being a respectable, good-hearted, good-natured, kind, scatterbrained and thoroughly ignorant tomboy in her youth, she is obliged instead to be 'in training for a heroine' as she hits adolescence. Her appearance improves, she becomes 'almost pretty', she amasses a scrappy, hackneyed stock of second-hand literary sentiment – 'those quotations which are so serviceable and so soothing in the vicissitudes of their eventful lives' (1.1; p.7) ('vicissitudes' is a standard over-inflated sentimental term), and as Austen points out slyly, a much more useful if unglamorous ability to endure social fatigue even if she can't dazzle company or a lover with her accomplishments either artistic or musical.

# Bath and the perils of 'the world'

At the end of the chapter, Austen says laughingly that 'when a young lady is to be a heroine ... something must and will happen to throw a hero in her way' (1.1; p.8) and promptly sets about doing exactly that by sending her off to Bath. In doing so, Austen enters Catherine into a particular plot, perhaps most successfully and charmingly realized by Frances Burney's first novel *Evelina: A Young Lady's Entrance into the World* (1771) but also the mainspring of Burney's later mature novels, *Cecilia* (1782) and *Camilla* (1796), both much admired by Austen. For the first volume of *Northanger Abbey*, Austen will move Catherine through a range of social anxieties and difficulties characteristic of the novels of Burney and her imitators. To take just one instance, like Evelina, Catherine will suffer the pains of dance-etiquette because she is 'engaged' to dance with one man when she would rather dance with another. Refusing to dance with one man, and then accepting another man's invitation, Evelina commits a serious social solecism. But while Evelina comes close to irretrievable social disaster, Catherine, courtesy of Austen's lighter touch, survives these 'female difficulties' unscathed. In chapter 3 we'll be coming back to the question of why Austen might think it pertinent to poke fun at the novel of manners and sentiment, but meanwhile, let's follow our heroine to Bath. You'll find that from here on, *Northanger Abbey* is constructed principally as a set of conversations in charged settings, so we're going to be looking first at individual conversations and then contrasting them.

**Reread volume 1, chapter 2. What, in practice, are 'all the difficulties and dangers of a six weeks' residence in Bath' (p.8) as Austen puts it, tongue-in-cheek?**

Why does Catherine go to Bath? Bath was booming in the second half of the eighteenth century as a 'watering-place' – that is to say, somewhere people went to drink or bathe in the waters for the relief of various ailments. But alongside its function as a spa-resort, Bath was also part of the 'season' and the fashionable congregated there every year. It boasted public Assembly Rooms, balls, masquerades, fireworks, concerts, shops and a circulating library – for those who lived in the country, visiting back and forth in a confined ambit of a few families in the immediate neighbourhood, it was a thoroughly cosmopolitan public space. By 1800 when Austen herself went to live there with her father and sister, Bath had become less aristocratic than Brighton, and a later Austen heroine, Anne Elliott of *Persuasion*, is described as particularly disliking the pretensions of the place. Nevertheless, Bath stands, in *Northanger Abbey* and *Persuasion*, as in innumerable novels and satirical poems right across the last half of the eighteenth century, for 'the world'. In this context, 'the world' means separation from the family circle and local society and entry into the marriage-market. Bath was a place where a young man or woman could meet eligible strangers through the good offices of the master of ceremonies of the Upper and Lower Assembly Rooms (if you go to Bath you can still visit them), and in fact, that is exactly how Catherine Morland first meets our hero, Henry Tilney.

Bath also offered the promiscuous and semi-anonymous excitement of the crowd – a fluid, treacherous social nexus possessed by fashion and display, floating free from the solid, verifiable worth of property. As Catherine reflects later, it is composed of a quicksand of proprieties and customs:

> She knew not how such an offence as her's might be classed by the laws of worldly politeness, to what a degree of unforgivingness it might with propriety lead, nor to what rigours of rudeness in return it might justly make her amenable. (1.7; p.66)

In this place of leisure, pleasure and affectation, it is possible to deceive and be deceived, intentionally or otherwise, about a potential marriage-partner.

Bearing all this in mind, you'll have already seen that we're to be disappointed of all sorts of conventional thrills. In exchange, we're offered exquisite comedy. The traditionally risky passage into 'the world' is burlesqued: Catherine's mother isn't full of high maternal solicitude of the sort that was frequently purveyed in conduct-book literature aimed at mothers and daughters, but only of pragmatic advice on health and money-matters; the journey into the unknown is disturbed only by Mrs Allen thinking that she might have left her clogs behind (she hasn't). Austen is punningly down-to-earth even in the matter of footwear. Nor is our heroine going to write letters home full of candid reflections upon her experiences in the manner of Evelina and countless other heroines whose letters form the substance of their novels. Hence Henry Tilney will remark with mock-surprise on Catherine's failure either to write such letters, or to keep a proper journal recording her fluctuating feelings in minute detail (1.3; pp.15–16). Later

*Figure 2.1   Bath Assembly Rooms: general view of the Ballroom. National Trust Photographic Library/Andreas von Einsiedel*

on there will be other jokes at the improbable conventions of such novels, for example, Austen's jibe at 'conversations, which had passed twenty years before ... minutely repeated' (1.4; p.21) or her casual dismissal of the cumbersomeness of epistolary realism: 'I leave it to my reader's sagacity to determine how much of all this it was possible for Henry to communicate at this time to Catherine, how much of it he could have learnt from his father, in what points his own conjectures might assist him, and what portion must yet remain to be told in a letter from James. I have united for their ease what they must divide for mine' (2.15; p.183). You should be able to identify many more such moments.

If the discourse of the novel is to be anti-sentimental, so, apparently, is the plot. No exciting abductions in high-life Burney-style, no wicked surrogate mother to 'reduce poor Catherine to all the wretchedness of which a last volume is capable ... whether by intercepting her letters, ruining her character, or turning her out of doors' (1.2; p.10). Rather, 'the difficulties and dangers' of Bath are deliberately cut down to size to conform to 'the common feelings of common life' (1.2; p.9) – and they resolve themselves at the first ball into discomfort, boredom, disappointment, embarrassment and the awkward negotiation of conversational platitudes.

The work that Austen does in these first two chapters, then, is to lay out the general project of *Northanger Abbey*. Austen sets up a heroine and a situation which cut sentimental conventions down to size, while (and this is important), faithfully shadowing them. For as we go on reading, we find that Catherine experiences many of Evelina's feelings and adventures, but in a thoroughly mundane mode. Her social embarrassments and misadventures happen in the same sort of places but have less startling consequences – even her abduction by an unwanted suitor only takes the shape of a forced and incompetent tourist excursion. Austen subjects contemporary conventions of romance or fantasy to the mere discomfort of realities.

# Friends and lovers

Once in Bath, Catherine meets two families, the Tilneys and the Thorpes. The most important members of these families – Eleanor and Henry Tilney and Isabella and John Thorpe – are symmetrically counterpoised as brother–sister pairings with the pairing of Catherine and her brother James Morland, and the novel from here on orchestrates a sort of country-dance whereby they constantly shift partners, making of each other different sets of 'brothers' and 'sisters' – as Isabella will say later, 'there are more ways than one of our being sisters' (2.3; p.105). In this next section, we're going to be thinking about the effects Austen gets by juxtaposing these characters. You will find that she is interested especially in registering discrepancies between what is said and what is really so, discrepancies that result first in little misunderstandings and then in major ones.

## *The Thorpes*

**Now read volume 1, chapter 6. How would you describe Isabella Thorpe's characteristic way of talking? Why is this conversation funny, and at whose expense? In what ways do you think Isabella might be taken to typify Bath society?**

One of the things you might have noticed about Isabella is her tendency to sloppy, slangy, and self-serving hyperbole – 'I have been waiting for you at least this age!', 'I have an hundred things to say to you', she would have been 'thrown ... into agonies' if there had been a shower to prevent their meeting (1.6; pp.24–5). This inaccurate and unspecific language of feeling is thrown into sharp relief by the sudden change of gear as she starts talking about something that really interests her, in this instance a hat she's seen 'just now' described suddenly in minute detail: 'in a shop window in Milsom-street ... very like yours, only with coquelicot ribbons instead of green: I quite longed for it' (1.6; p.25). Coquelicot, being the latest shade of red, would have quite outdone Catherine's hat – so much for friendship. Watch too how her language inclines to poverty-stricken repetition of conventional intensifiers – look at the way the words 'sweet' and 'sweetest' recur around the discussion of Miss Andrews, or the way Isabella uses the adjective 'amazing'.

This language of extravagant feeling marks Isabella, Austen's anti-heroine, as deriving from a stock sentimental convention – the bosom friend and confidante of the heroine. But whereas in the sentimental novel proper, this extravagance of language and feeling is numbingly sincere, in Isabella's mouth it becomes self-serving posturing. Handsome, worldly, and with one eye always to her own advantage, she speaks in a curious mélange of threadbare novelistic sentiments which imperfectly cover up hard-headed and hard-hearted common sense about her marriage prospects. Whether or not she is, as she says, a passionate reader of trashy novels (if she is, why does she need Miss Andrews's library-list?), she is a parody of the sentimental heroine, and her relationship with Catherine satirizes sentimental representations of female friendship. This conversation with Catherine, which Austen ironically describes as 'a specimen of their very warm attachment, and of the delicacy, discretion, originality of thought, and literary taste which marked the reasonableness of that attachment' (1.6; p.24), is funny principally because Isabella is always trying to make Catherine take up the other half of a conventionally sentimental conversation, an effort constantly frustrated by Catherine's endearingly inadequate performance. Catherine is so bad at this sentimental game because she is unversed in the genre – her artless feeling, being real rather than assumed, speaks a different language. As she later puts it, 'I cannot speak well enough to be unintelligible' (2.1; p.96).

In general, one of the most untrustworthy and vulgar things about Isabella is her bustling and unscrupulous desire to script Catherine into implausible fantasies: 'I must tell you, that just after we parted yesterday, I saw a young man looking at you so earnestly – I am sure he is in love with you' (1.6; p.26). (You might like to take a moment to see if you can analyse the conversation in volume 1, chapter 10, in this way, too.) This assertion is followed almost immediately by the adoption of a sentimental pose, again on Catherine's behalf, though Isabella, who has already been hinting at an attachment to James Morland, would also like to present herself in this way:

> Nay, I cannot blame you – (speaking more seriously) – your feelings are easily understood. Where the heart is really attached, I know very well how little one can be pleased with the attention of any body else. Everything is so insipid, so uninteresting, that does not relate to the beloved object! I can perfectly comprehend your feelings. (1.6; p.26)

All of this is of a piece with Isabella's preference for the cheap thrills of the Gothic novel, mouth-wateringly 'horrid', over the moral weightiness and 'horrid' prosiness of Samuel Richardson's *Sir Charles Grandison* (1755), one of Austen's favourite novels. Catherine's innocence at once makes her vulnerable to corruption by Isabella and impervious to it; she honestly doesn't understand Isabella's language of flirtation – the come-hither delivered as a 'scold' or a slight, or her sentimental innuendo – and betrays her youth and innocence by preferring to speculate on Laurentina's skeleton in Radcliffe's *The Mysteries of Udolpho* than on any number of possible lovers in real life.

We've spent so much time on this trifling conversation because it sets up Isabella's linguistic, social and marital strategies in miniature. (You might also find it rewarding to glance at volume 1, chapter 15, and think about it in this way.) On the whole, Isabella says exactly the opposite of what she means, because what she means, as she is all too aware, is inadequately 'feminine' in its naked ambition. What the scheming, speculating, managing Isabella is principally interested in, understandably enough, is organizing herself, and perhaps her brother, into an establishment rather above what they might reasonably hope for. In order to do this, she will ruthlessly manoeuvre Catherine and her brother, only abandoning them when better prey comes her way (or so she thinks) in the shape of Captain Frederick Tilney. At one level this will amount simply to involving her in conversations that Catherine doesn't really understand; at another, it will extend to involving her in a highly improper chase after two unknown young men, and to promoting her 'involvement' with Thorpe in unsuitable outings and in the face of Catherine's stated liking for Tilney.

These qualities make Isabella especially at home in Austen's Bath. Her ambition is to be mobile, or unfixed – her walking around the town, her familiarity with the Pump Room, the Assembly Rooms, the circulating library, the shops, and all the best vantage points to see and be seen, her conscious up-to-dateness in matters of cheap finery and cheap novels, in short, her at-homeness in this promiscuous and manoeuvring place all speak a ruthless determination to marry up, something, incidentally, that all heroines do, including Catherine Morland. But more of the problem of why it's all right for Catherine to marry up but not Isabella later – for the moment we have an appointment with John Thorpe.

Volume 1, chapter 7, opens with an instance of Austen's structural irony – worth pausing on briefly since it is easy to miss the ways in which this novel is elegantly structured on doubles and substitutes. The two young men Isabella had insisted on pursuing are lost and replaced at a stroke with their doubles, James Morland, the lover of Isabella, and John Thorpe, the soon-to-be would-be lover of Catherine.

**Reread volume 1, chapter 7. Is there any family resemblance between Isabella's way of talking and her brother's?**

I don't suppose it has taken you as long as it seems to take Catherine to work out that John Thorpe is a lumpen, ignorant, boastful, conceited bore, of limited intelligence and even more limited charm, manners or feeling. The conversation between him and James Morland repeats in a different, heavily masculinized mode some of the shape of Isabella's conversation with Catherine. While on the whole the Morlands reveal themselves as well-meaning and literal-minded with a strong fund of common sense rather overborne by their inability quite to recognize or identify their companions' failings, the Thorpes share a sort of hyperbolical and selfish conversational violence. Thorpe's hyper-masculinity translates as careless, even impudent, manners, slovenly clothes and a bullying style of interlocution that takes no account of anybody else's interests. In his preoccupation with horses, carriages, mileage and routes, he is a worthy precursor of the car-bore. And, ominously, he talks about money, good bargains and the like, revealing himself to be at once by temperament a greedy cheat and in practice everyone's dupe. Like his sister, the literary taste of this 'discerning and unprejudiced reader', as Austen sardonically calls him, marks him out as suspect. He parrots masculine conventionalities such as 'I never read novels', then turns out to prefer two novels regarded at the time as improper, Henry Fielding's *Tom Jones* and Matthew Lewis's *The Monk*, to Burney's *Camilla*. As you have already seen in the case of Isabella, a character's reading and what they make of it are, in this novel so concerned with literariness, made to function as

*Ref. Analysing Text for TMAOI.*

cultural indicators of a character's moral standing. As the novel wears on, Thorpe turns out in addition to be a rude and unfeeling son and brother, given to swearing, braggadocio, drink, hunting and horseflesh, a much coarsened escapee rake from the Richardson–Burney tradition.

The next few very funny chapters will develop Isabella as a selfish, manipulative coquette, and Thorpe as a burlesque villain, unscrupulous and utterly wearisome rather than a desperate danger. As we've already remarked, the stock seduction and abduction dwindles to an aborted tourist excursion to Blaize Castle behind a surprisingly slow horse. The blundering and brutal Thorpe's faked message from Catherine to Eleanor Tilney breaking her engagement to walk with them is a reduction of countless scenes in previous novels where the villain forges a letter which involves the heroine in delicious miseries. But however banal their vices seem, both brother and sister deliberately plunge Catherine into social embarrassment and real distress in the service of their own social-climbing marital plans:

> To be disgraced in the eye of the world, to wear the appearance of infamy while her heart is all purity, her actions all innocence, and the misconduct of another the true source of her debasement, is one of those circumstances which peculiarly belong to the heroine's life. (1.8; p.36)

Austen is of course laughing here at Catherine's ten minutes' discomfiture over the non-appearance of her partner at the ball, setting up a disproportion between the heroinical discourse and the actual occasion which manages to be at once comic and touching. But, if we set aside the inflated language, this is more or less what will happen to Catherine as the Thorpes' constant manoeuvrings and fictioneerings first block, then facilitate, and finally all but destroy her new acquaintance with another brother–sister pair, the Tilneys.

## *The Tilneys*

**Refresh your memory of volume 1, chapter 3 (the first appearance of Henry Tilney in the Pump Room and his introduction to Catherine), and then look carefully at volume 1, chapters 10 and 14, in particular the conversations between the Tilneys and Catherine. Contrast the Tilneys with the Thorpes, paying special attention to the similarities/ differences in their styles of language and subjects of conversation.**

Catherine's hesitant but growing conviction that perhaps neither Thorpe was 'altogether completely agreeable' (1.9; p.47) contrasts with her growing intimacy with the Tilneys. The Tilneys offer themselves as alternatives to the Thorpes. Eleanor is older and more sophisticated; like Isabella she is pleasing, fashionable, sensible, intelligent, refined, and, like Isabella, finds the artless Catherine completely transparent, though, unlike Isabella, she doesn't therefore try to manipulate her. Where Isabella is supposedly an ally, but always puts her own interests first, as at the ball where she abandons Catherine to sit by herself while she goes and dances with Frederick Tilney, Eleanor will be a true ally, defending Catherine first against her brother's playful conversational attacks on Beechen Cliff, and ultimately against her father General Tilney by lending

Catherine money to see her home safely. By the end of the novel, Eleanor will have replaced Isabella as true sentimental friend, confidante, sister, companion and correspondent. Something of this outcome is already signalled by the contrast between Eleanor's language and Isabella's.

**Now read the representation of Isabella's conversation and body language in the passage beginning 'When they arrived at Mrs. Allen's door ...' (p.47) and running to '... she bade her friend adieu and went on' in volume 1, chapter 9 (ibid). Compare and contrast it with the passage beginning 'Miss Tilney met her with great civility ...' (p.51) and ending '... the smallest consciousness of having explained them' in volume 1, chapter 10 (ibid).**

Isabella's noisy, self-centred, and affected performance contrasts sharply with Eleanor's deployment of the conventionalities of small talk. She opens with polite platitudes which, unusually, have 'the merit of ... being spoken with simplicity and truth, and without personal conceit'. Her replies to Catherine are characterized by tact, delicacy and a reserved truthfulness – and where it would be unsuitable to say anything, she is politely receptive: 'Miss Tilney could only bow.' Structured in complete sentences and balanced clauses, free from colloquialisms, affectations and exaggerations, and innocent of the jolting between registers and perspectives that characterizes Isabella's artificiality, her language is that of restrained sincerity tempered with unobtrusive feeling, with a polish of wit, discretion and delicacy that her future sister-in-law – 'open, candid, artless, guileless, with affections strong but simple, forming no pretensions, and knowing no disguise' (2.10; p.152) – has yet to attain. Indeed, Eleanor's language bears the closest similarity of any character's to the narrator's own style – always a strong vote of confidence in an Austen novel.

It is a good deal more difficult to decide what to make of the adequately tall, not quite handsome, pleasing, lively, intelligent and arch Henry Tilney. As a hero, he derives from the long-standing tradition of the lover-mentor, most influentially embodied earlier in the century by Samuel Richardson's creation Sir Charles Grandison, but also making regular appearances in Frances Burney's novels. If you have read *Mansfield Park* or *Emma* you will recognize that Edmund and Mr Knightley are also versions of this figure. Critical opinion is much divided on quite what view we are supposed to take of Tilney. For Butler, he is 'a mysterious, almost allegorical figure, who stands for androgynous ideas, youthful play, the comic spirit, romance' (1995, p.xlii), a 'big brother' who courts Catherine in scenes of instruction along the lines of popular educators of the day: Thomas Day, the Barbaulds and Maria Edgeworth. On the other hand, Claudia L. Johnson (1988), and others, read him as not at all unlike John Thorpe and General Tilney, if a little more polished, pointing to a similar tendency alternately to silence Catherine and to put words into her mouth. In this reading, Tilney's imagined interpolation in Catherine's journal about her meeting him (1.3; p.15), is similar to John Thorpe's message to Eleanor that he pretends comes from Catherine, and to General Tilney's self-serving habit of imputing words to her that she hasn't said:

> Which would she prefer? He was equally at her service. – Which did his
> daughter think would most accord with her fair friend's wishes? – But he

thought he could discern. – Yes, he certainly read in Miss Morland's eyes a judicious desire of making use of the present smiling weather. – But when did she judge amiss? ... He yielded implicitly. (2.7; p.129)

Where you place yourself in this debate largely depends on what you think about Catherine's 'education' and Tilney's place in it. Butler (1995) and Terry Castle (1990) on the whole feel that Henry Tilney differs from the Thorpes and General Tilney because he is, for a mentor-hero, unusually playful with Catherine, meeting her on her own terms, posing her questions, to be sure, but leaving her to answer them herself. Johnson (1988) feels, on the other hand, that Tilney is patronizing and bullying, regularly reducing Catherine to silence. One of the reasons that these opposed readings are possible is that the scenes of instructive conversation between Henry and Catherine are so delicately balanced that it is not at all easy to tell who is being made fun of at any one time.

One of the most peculiar things about Tilney is his disconcertingly protean ability to talk like a woman. In the glittering first pages of our acquaintance he can shift from a facile parody of the affected small talk and smirk of a Bath miss, to teasing Catherine about the thoroughly femininocentric literary conventions associated with her visit to the watering-place, to nattering about muslins and the sorrows of shopping with the silly, inconsequential but essentially harmless Mrs Allen, until even the surprised and attracted Catherine fears 'that he indulged himself a little too much with the foibles of others' (1.3; p.17). It is a strange performance, of a piece with the flighty flirtatiousness of his remarks on the similarities between a country-dance and marriage (1.10; pp.54–5), and it's hard to know what view we are supposed to take of it. Are we to be critical, with Catherine, of his strange presumptuousness, or are we to be attracted, with Catherine, to his game-playing? Volume 1, chapter 14, the outing with Catherine and Eleanor to Beechen Cliff, flagged up as an important moment by Austen's comical remark that 'my heroine was most unnaturally able to fulfil her engagement, though it was made by the hero himself', offers us an extended chance to see him speaking both masculine and feminine languages, so let's take a careful look at the conversation.

**Reread volume 1, chapter 14, and make a list of the subjects of conversation. If you think of the conversation as a sort of game, who wins each point?**

'I never look at it [Beechen Cliff],' said Catherine, as they walked along the side of the river, 'without thinking of the south of France.'

'You have been abroad then?' said Henry, a little surprized.

'Oh! no, I only mean what I have read about. It always puts me in mind of the country that Emily and her father travelled through, in the "Mysteries of Udolpho".' (1.14; p.77)

Catherine's opening gambit surprises Henry with its suggestion of an unsuspected sophistication. Is this a silly Isabella-ish second-hand affectation, or just sheer naivety? In fact, as Catherine almost instantly makes clear, she has given a misleading impression solely because she hasn't quite got her language of literary criticism disentangled from the sort of language used to talk about 'reality' – and Austen is also, incidentally, making a joke at the expense of Radcliffe herself, who, famous for her portrayals of 'sublime' scenery, had actually never been abroad and borrowed her scenery from books of engravings. But it's not just that Catherine's language is sufficiently undiscriminating to promote misunderstanding – her sense of generic fitness is too, for the environs of Bath are emphatically not the same thing as the wildnesses of the south of France, teeming as they conventionally are with banditti. As this tiny exchange moves into a conversation about *The Mysteries of Udolpho*, it sets the structure and terms of reference for the big confrontation between hero and heroine to come in volume 2.

As we move on, you'll notice that this conversation looks quite a lot like a version of Catherine and Isabella's first substantial conversation about novels, that we've already read. In fact, this exchange starts to set Henry up as a rival 'female friend'. Henry does read novels, and Mrs Radcliffe's novels too, and he reads them for a self-consciously feminine pleasure – 'my hair standing on end the whole time' – and with a self-consciously feminine voracity, cheating his sister out of the book. Of this episode he says to Catherine, claiming a strategically giggly sisterhood, 'I am proud when I reflect on it, and I think it must establish me in your good opinion.' But it is important to notice that Tilney portrays himself as adopting a conventional, appropriate and limited readerly stance for the enjoyment of the genres of the Radcliffean Gothic and sentimental 'Julias and Louisas'. His reading is what we call 'mediated' by an understanding of literary conventions – that's where his knowing and arch tone derives from, so different to Catherine's artless enthusiasm. This, too, is the point of Henry's pedantry over Catherine's use of the word 'nice', though whether you are supposed to approve of Henry (as most critics do) or whether with me you feel more in sympathy with Eleanor who rebukes him for being 'more nice than wise', I leave you to decide!

The conversation now ranges to history, regarded by all conduct books of the period as an altogether more suitable sort of reading for young women than novels, which were supposed to encourage romantic flightiness and dissatisfaction with reality. If Eleanor's liking for history marks her out as a more suitable friend than Isabella, it also stands for a more fluidly gendered reading habit (the mirror-image of her brother) – for as Catherine comments, her father, brothers and the sensible Mr Allen also read it. Their conversation about history is also serving another function here, pointing up the complexly interdependent relation between fact and fiction (this is the point of Catherine's remarks on 'invention') gendered respectively masculine and feminine. There is a seeping sense that there is something to Catherine's strictures on history, however naively expressed – 'the men all so good for nothing and hardly any women at all'.

The rest of the chapter is concerned with the conflict between the languages of aesthetics and everyday languages of common sense. The confused Catherine, introduced to a new aesthetic language – that of the picturesque – learns 'that a clear blue sky was no longer a proof of a fine day'. She applies common-sense criteria to an aesthetic that would much prefer a hurrying swirl of cloud – in a picture, that is. But who is the laugh here really at? At Catherine? Or at the language of aesthetics that the Tilneys are so well versed in? The importance of knowing the conventions you're operating in is repeated in the famous misunderstanding that next follows between Catherine, who is talking about the publication of the new Gothic novel in London, and Eleanor, who imagines her to be speaking of riots. Henry has in fact been speaking of politics, so Eleanor's mistake is perfectly understandable. But what is interesting is the way that Henry is enabled to resolve the misunderstanding because of his insistently masculine facility at moving between 'languages':

> 'Come, shall I make you understand each other, or leave you to puzzle out an explanation as you can? No – I will be noble. I will prove myself a man, no less by the generosity of my soul than the clearness of my head. I have no patience with such of my sex as disdain to let themselves sometimes down to the comprehension of yours.' (1.14; p.82)

Such a reading of the conversation puts Tilney rather thoroughly in the right. And usually it is read as though this were a major scene of instruction in which Catherine's reading skills are put to the test, while Henry demonstrates his superior reading skills, and educates her in other available (masculine) discourses – not just the novel, history and education, but aesthetics, politics and economics. But do you think the narrative voice entirely approves of Tilney? Isn't Austen sometimes laughing at him?

**Take another look at the passage in volume 1, chapter 14, beginning 'Where people wish to attach ...' (p.81) and ending '... an easy step to silence' (ibid). Who is being laughed at here? And for what?**

This passage indicts Catherine for being ignorant, credulous and so attracted to Henry that she is willing to suspend the wisdom of the past, common sense and her own judgement, as when she 'voluntarily rejected the whole city of Bath, as unworthy to make part of a landscape'. But surely it also blames Henry for being the other half of the equation – the vanity that can be flattered by affectionate ignorance – and surely Austen must be laughing when she briefly takes on Henry's consciousness to say 'delighted with her progress, and fearful of wearying her with too much wisdom at once', and then offers a slither down what must have been, from Catherine's point of view, an increasingly boring and incomprehensible conversation: 'forests, the inclosure of them, waste lands, crown lands and government'. Moreover, what are we to make of Eleanor's strictures on her brother's rather strikingly illiberal opinions on the intelligence of women? Are we indeed to understand that he is just teasing? If he is teasing, what function does teasing have in this novel? One way of making sense of this instability is to refuse to regard Henry Tilney as entirely identified with the narratorial voice. To be sure, he comes close in his elegant playfulness, and occasionally anarchic wit, but it is possible to read this scene as a scene of false instruction where on the whole the lover-mentor doesn't teach the heroine anything. The scene asks whether learning is growth or loss of self, whether teaching is generosity or manipulation, instruction or torment. As Susan Morgan has said of this episode, it shows that 'the ignorant have their truths that the clever need to learn' (1980, p.72). When Catherine trusts her own observation it strikes a real chord ('the men all so good for nothing and hardly any women at all'), when she parrots Henry's discourse, she is made absurd, as in the matter of the panorama of Bath.

You will have to decide yourself where to place the emphasis; my own view is that part of the point of this scene is the way that our sympathies are flexed and surprised – it is perhaps not only Catherine who is being instructed. This scene serves as a reminder that novel-reading of the period, especially in the Austen household, was often a social event and that this conversation would have been meant both to represent and to instigate similar conversations in the readership.

As you continue to read the novel, you will find many other scenes of instruction played out between Catherine and Henry. The sequence will culminate in the celebrated rebuke outside the door of Mrs Tilney's bedroom; thereafter, Henry abandons this role. However, when you're thinking about the dynamics of the relationship between the two, take a look at some less famous moments, for example, the short and flirtatious conversation about 'learning to love a hyacinth' at the beginning of volume 2, chapter 7, and the very important conversation about Frederick and Isabella's flirtation in volume 2, chapter 4, a scene of true instruction in which Tilney instructs Catherine by refusing to instruct her:

> 'Nay, if it is to be guess-work, let us all guess for ourselves. To be guided by second-hand conjecture is pitiful. The premises are before you.' (2.4; p.110)

We will be coming back later to the question of what moral and social point there is to Catherine's 'education' in linguistic discriminations. For now, we should take note that the dangers of Bath, and later of the Abbey, turn out to be generated by linguistic inaccuracy – a failure, deliberate or involuntary, to say what is meant. Two instances conclude volume 1; engaged to James Morland, Isabella manages to mislead both herself and anyone else who is not listening carefully by talking heroinically about hard cash:

> 'For my own part,' said Isabella, 'my wishes are so moderate, that the smallest income in nature would be enough for me. Where people are really attached, poverty itself is wealth: grandeur I detest: I would not settle in London for the universe. A cottage in some retired village would be exstasy. There are some charming little villas about Richmond.' (1.15; p.88)

Secondly, in a brilliantly comic and technically accomplished scene, Thorpe all but proposes without realizing that Catherine has no idea of what he is saying, 'leaving him to the undivided consciousness of his own happy address, and her explicit encouragement' (1.15; p.92).

# The Abbey and the terrors of the domestic

With Catherine's departure for a visit to the Tilneys at Northanger Abbey, the novel activates another set of generic expectations, those associated with the Radcliffean Gothic, a genre which is essentially domestic, speaking of horrors committed against women in the home. Chapter 3 will be discussing the Gothic more extensively, but here you need to know that Mrs Radcliffe effectively restaged the sentimental heroine in sixteenth-century France and Italy's castles and convents, translating and heightening the dangers and difficulties of the entry into the 'world' into the exploration of a fantasy architecture which speaks of incest, rape and murder past and to come. The heroine's bravery in overcoming her fear, whether this is represented as rational or irrational (critics disagree!), eventually qualifies her to marry the hero and to exit into a regenerate and safely feminized companionate domesticity. From now on, *Northanger Abbey* will faithfully shadow this structure, at the same time as explicitly educating Catherine out of Gothic fantasy. We will be asking again what is at stake in this process of educating Catherine in reading strategies, a process again presided over by Henry Tilney.

## *Imaginary terrors*

**Reread volume 2, chapter 5. What does Catherine expect Northanger Abbey to be like? What can you deduce about the 'Gothic' from her expectations and from her seduction by Henry Tilney's teasing rundown of delights in store?**

As we already know from Catherine's desire to see Blaize Castle, she has strong romance expectations of castles. Talking of the proposed excursion with Thorpe, she betrays that she expects the castle to be 'old' and 'like one reads of' with 'towers and long galleries' (1.11; p.60). She anticipates a certain emotional state: an enjoyable melancholy over past grandeur and present decay, enlivened by adventurousness and a delicious frisson of fright:

> the happiness of a progress through a long suite of melancholy rooms, exhibiting the remains of magnificent furniture, though now for many years deserted – the happiness of being stopped in their way along narrow, winding vaults, by a low, grated door; or even of having their lamp, their only lamp, extinguished by a sudden gust of wind, and of being left in total darkness.
> (1.11; pp.62–3)

These preoccupations betray her frame of reference as romance rather than the sort of tourism that Thorpe hints at when he describes it as 'the finest place in England – worth going fifty miles at any time to see' (1.11; p.60). Thorpe's castle is by implication a well-maintained, well-furnished seat of the local aristocracy. Catherine carries these expectations over to Northanger Abbey itself. Endearingly, she doesn't ask, as it were, the 'right' questions about the Abbey: the balanced and well-read Eleanor gives her a good guidebook line on the Abbey (its history, its acquisition, its architecture and its situation), the predatory Isabella, with her wonderfully vulgar grip on the essentials (class and money), is well aware that it is 'one of the finest old places in England', a coded way of talking about what sort of money a girl might marry in the shape of a Tilney; General Tilney, as Butler remarks, will give her a sort of auctioneer's tour. But Catherine's desires run another way; she longs to experience a real, live 'Gothic' building. Symptomatically, she never gets to Blaize Castle, her first temptation, and this will be true too of the pleasures that Henry promises her from the Abbey. They will turn out to be unavailable, not to say improper. She indulges in Disneyworld hopes of a building redolent of a (not very obviously attractive but thoroughly Radcliffean) past: 'long, damp passages', 'narrow cells and ruined chapel' enlivened with 'some traditional legends, some awful memorials of an injured and ill-fated nun'. These features, familiar to us from horror films and computer games, were already conventional for Austen's readership from popular fiction. Henry, with his facility in the rules of genre, recognizes and is able to enter into Catherine's expectations. Shamelessly plagiarizing Ann Radcliffe's bestsellers, *A Sicilian Romance* (1790), *The Romance of the Forest* (1791) and Catherine's current favourite, *The Mysteries of Udolpho* (1794), Henry teasingly conjures up the anxieties and incomprehensibilities of a strange house and household, a heroine possessed with fatal curiosity, a manuscript detailing the past mysterious ill-treatment of an imprisoned woman, for a rapt if intermittently sceptical Catherine. Within a very few minutes, however, all these expectations are disappointed by the fashionable, wealthy, technological modernity of the place: modern, lightweight furniture, a Rumford grate, English china, and modern glass in the windows.

What sort of pleasure or desire is embodied in Catherine's fantasizing? Principally, surely, the pleasure of improper speculation and investigation, a freedom of a female imagination, with the proviso, of course, that the danger of such speculations is always literalized, as it is in *The Mysteries of Udolpho* or in the story of Bluebeard, in the corpse of some other too adventurous woman. At best, then, this sort of female desire is morally ambiguous. Conjuring up a little novel of her own, borrowed pretty much wholesale from Henry's collaboration with Radcliffe, Catherine sets about filling out domestic cosiness with domestic violence.

**Reread volume 2, chapters 6, 7, 8 and 9, concentrating on the episodes of the mysterious chest, the japanned cabinet, and the visit to Eleanor Tilney's mother's bedroom. What do these episodes have in common?**

The first thing these episodes share is their shape. Catherine's imagination and curiosity are aroused by some chance correlation between Henry's fiction and the circumstances within which she finds herself; she becomes prey to febrile excitement, rather against her better judgement; and she makes a discovery, which, far from being the hoped-for dagger, instrument of torture, or first-person confessional manuscript, then turns out to be boringly modern, determinedly domestic and pointedly free of the sort of narrative excitement (murder, inquisition or a tale of sorrows) that Catherine is hoping for – 'a white cotton counterpane, properly folded' in the chest, a 'washing-bill' and 'a farrier's bill' left 'by the negligence of a servant' in the cabinet, and finally, in Mrs Tilney's bedroom, 'a large, well-proportioned apartment, an handsome dimity bed, arranged as unoccupied with an housemaid's care, a bright Bath stove, mahogany wardrobes and neatly-painted chairs'. Revelation is succeeded by mortification, in two instances compounded by discovery by one or other of the surprised Tilneys. In the culminating sequence, even the mother's death is made tiresomely banal – she dies of 'a bilious fever'. The upshot is the humiliation of Catherine in her own eyes, and an end to her 'visions of romance'. She draws the moral at length:

> It had been all a voluntary, self-created delusion, each trifling circumstance
> receiving importance from an imagination resolved on alarm, and everything
> forced to bend to one purpose by a mind which, before she entered the Abbey,

had been craving to be frightened. She saw that the infatuation had been created, the mischief settled long before her quitting Bath, and it seemed as if the whole might be traced to the influence of that sort of reading which she had there indulged. (2.10; p.146)

Perhaps you may have picked up one other element that each of these episodes has in common. Each self-indulgent flight of Catherine's imagination involves her in a real social impropriety productive of actual if unspectacular evil. Her flirtation with the old chest makes her late for dinner, and Eleanor is consequently scolded by her father. Her hurrying away from the discomfiture of the laundry-list means that she is embarrassed by the General's innuendo on finding her alone with Henry in the breakfast-room. Her Jane Eyreish adventures alone into the deserted wing end in shame at her folly and absurdity and a horrid consciousness of the sheer rudeness, the 'liberty' (2.10; p.146), into which she has strayed. As this might suggest, and as critics have often remarked, the exploded Gothic is faithfully shadowed by a cut-down version, the everyday terrors and tyrannies of the domestic. Some critics have even wondered whether Catherine's assessment of life at the Abbey was quite so far out, after all.

## *Domestic economies*

**Read volume 2, chapter 7, from 'Catherine was saved the embarrassment of attempting an answer ...' (p.127) to the end of the chapter, and volume 2, chapter 11, from 'A day or two passed away ...' (p.154) to the end of the chapter. How would you describe the relation between the Tilney siblings and their father? What forms does General Tilney's less than perfect amiability take? What sort of household is Northanger Abbey, and what values does it stand for? How is the Abbey contrasted with Woodston?**

If John Thorpe is the burlesque rake-villain of the first part of the novel, General Tilney is the quasi-Gothic villain of the second, and it is appropriate that the two are linked. We will learn later on that both General Tilney's attentions and the climax of the novel, the sudden expulsion of our heroine, are owing to two conversations with Thorpe, the first in which Thorpe's greedy conceit leads him into exaggerating Catherine's wealth under the persuasion that she has encouraged his attentions, the second in which his angry vanity leads him into equal and opposite inaccuracies. This late revelation of a like-mindedness makes explicit what we should already have picked up as readers even before Catherine decides firmly that, even if her future father-in-law is not the wife-murderer she fantasized,

> she need not fear to acknowledge some actual specks in the character of [General Tilney], who, though cleared from the grossly injurious suspicions which she must ever blush to have entertained, she did believe, upon serious consideration, to be not perfectly amiable. (2.10; p.147)

(Note how Catherine's youthful hesitation has been refined into a new-found moderation signalled by the delaying subordinate clauses and the final statement in the negative.)

It is our discovery, in retrospect, of what Thorpe has told General Tilney of Catherine's fortune, that makes sense of the General's volte-face from obliging his daughter to tell our heroine that she is 'not at home', to scolding the servant William for not opening the door quickly enough to her when she practically takes the Tilney household by storm in her anxiety to vindicate herself. On the whole, this logic will operate for the rest of the novel – when Catherine is thought to have money, she gets inside the Tilney house, when she is thought not to, she finds herself outside it. If the General falls a little short of the glamour and sexiness of Radcliffe's villain Montoni (though he's sexy enough to put Catherine to the blush on occasion), he is just as interested in the heroine's money.

Though the Tilney household is, unlike Udolpho, banditti-free, it is ruled by the same sort of tyranny, albeit in a commonplace register. The General's style of elaborate compliment, bullying politeness, pompous modesty and arch circumlocution blight rather than facilitate happy social intercourse. Listen to him here inviting Catherine to Northanger Abbey:

> If you can be induced to honour us with a visit, you will make us happy beyond expression. 'Tis true, we can offer you nothing like the gaieties of this lively place; we can tempt you neither by amusement nor splendour, for our mode of living, as you see, is plain and unpretending; yet no endeavours shall be wanting on our side to make Northanger Abbey not wholly disagreeable. (2.2; p.101)

Once we arrive at the Abbey, it turns out that the Tilney lifestyle is anything but plain and unpretending. As the General shows off the amenities and improvements of the estate to the imagined heiress, and Catherine politely digests her disappointment at not finding a romantic interior, we discover that the General's household is fitted out as the last word in modern consumerist luxury, from the brand-new porcelain tea set to the 'village of hot-houses' (including a fashionable pinery for growing pineapples), and the state-of-the-art kitchens and sculleries. The immoderate vanity and sheer greed this suggests (who ate the hundred pineapples in a household of two?) is reiterated in the little episode of the dinner at Woodston, which takes Henry three days to prepare, and even then is found wanting in the matter of cold meats on the sideboard.

The General's greed and conceit are not, apparently, redeemed by any other domestic virtues. Far from being fond of him, his wife seems to have been unhappy and his children are frightened of him. Indeed, at the last moment, Eleanor, self-confessedly only the 'nominal mistress' of the household, turns out to have been a closet Gothic heroine after all, shut up and prevented from marrying the man of her choice who has an insufficient fortune. The last instance of the General's tyranny forms the climax of the second volume. The whirlwind return of the General, the midnight conversation with Eleanor and Catherine's sleepless night fill Gothic conventions with substance: 'Her anxiety had foundation in fact, her fears in probability' (2.13; p.167). The expulsion of Catherine at an unreasonably early hour without any of the common civilities, to travel on a Sunday (especially insulting to a clergyman's daughter) for eleven hours in a post-chaise unaccompanied by a servant and unprovided with cash, is a real distress rather than a merely romantic evil.

The aggressive modernity of the Abbey is thus revealed to be more Gothic than the Gothic – the domestic is more violent and unpredictable than the formulae of the novel of terror would suggest. Catherine eventually finds a home at Woodston, which is carefully contrasted with the Abbey, and represented as a better version of her childhood home, the parsonage at Fullerton; as Austen puts it, following Catherine's thought processes by way of the technique of 'free indirect discourse':

> the Abbey in itself was no more to her now than any other house ... What a revolution in her ideas! she, who had so longed to be in an abbey! Now, there was nothing so charming to her imagination as the unpretending comfort of a well-connected Parsonage, something like Fullerton, but better: Fullerton had its faults, but Woodston probably none. (2.11; p.156)

I expect you will have noticed how in this instance this technique of representing Catherine's thoughts delicately distances the reader in a stance of affectionate intimacy and amusement at what is Catherine's resurgent habit of speculation. The naive quality of the 'probably', however, robs the speculation of any suggestion of conscious cupidity; though Catherine here constructs herself as now so grown-up ('what a revolution in her ideas!') she remains sweetly innocent of her own desires, entirely transparent though they are to us.

Where the Abbey testifies to selfish modern consumerism, the 'new-built' Woodston has by contrast a social conscience, as befits a parsonage. As Butler (in Austen [1818] 1995, Notes to Text, n.89) has pointed out, Austen's word 'well-connected' refers to the way the house is integrated within a working community and has not subordinated the interests of that community to the aesthetics of 'improvement'. Catherine proves her entitlement to this establishment by her approval of the view of the cottage from the drawing-room, that otherwise the improving General had planned to sweep away in pursuit of the sort of landscaping currently favoured by the fashionable designer Humphrey Repton. This preoccupation with houses and landscapes as political, social and moral indicators will run throughout the nineteenth-century novel.

# 'I leave it to the reader to determine ...'

**Read through the final chapters once more, concentrating on volume 2, chapters 13–16. What do you take to be the point of Catherine's 'education'?**

If this is a novel about educating a heroine, what exactly does she learn? Clearly, one way of reading Catherine's mortifications in the Abbey is that she exchanges adolescent fantasy for the solid benefits of matrimony. Accepting a thoroughly English, provincial, well-connected modernity identified with Henry Tilney, she conforms to his adjuration to

> 'Remember the country and the age in which we live. Remember that we are English, that we are Christians. Consult your own understanding, your own sense of the probable, your own observation of what is passing around you –

> Does our education prepare us for such atrocities? Do our laws connive at them?
> Could they be perpetrated without being known, in a country like this, where
> social and literary intercourse is on such a footing; where every man is
> surrounded by a neighbourhood of voluntary spies, and where roads and
> newspapers lay everything open?' (2.9; p.145)

Henry's language relies heavily on a lexicon of rational and empirical understanding – 'consider', 'judge', 'consult' – and on invoking institutionalized discourses, that of the law, religion, education, the constitution, the economy, common sense which go to make up the national character. As Johnson (1988) points out, this lexicon practically suffers a fit trying to reschedule Catherine's vagaries: 'If I understand you rightly', says Henry, 'you had formed a surmise of such horror as I have hardly words to—' (2.9; p.145). Catherine is to realign herself with Henry's 'our' and 'we'; renouncing the heroine's language, her plots and her imaginative vagaries, she finally becomes marriageable to Henry and the substantial rewards which that implies in money, status and establishment. What inflection you put on this depends rather on what you think about the real violence Catherine (not to say, Mrs Tilney and Eleanor) endures from the General despite the safeguards Henry invokes of 'a country like this'. Johnson (1988), for example, along with others, has taken the view that Austen's dénouement shows Catherine to have been right all along – the domestic is inhabited by patriarchal violence and oppression of women – and that therefore to laugh at Catherine for an overactive imagination is to align yourself with these forces of oppression in silencing women's perceptions and protests. Others, like Castle (1990), less inclined to read against the comedic grain of Austen's text, argue that Catherine is not finally obliged to renounce her own judgement, but to come into the full use of it, and that this includes discarding the platitudes of the sentimental and Gothic, entering instead a partnership with Henry, a union that only then can outgrow the erotics of instruction. Like Austen, I leave it to you to decide, observing only that it might be worth being a fraction sceptical about the function of the Gothic interlude. What strikes me is the way that this flight into heroinical speculation allows Catherine a sort of alibi; while her gaze has been firmly fixed on this sort of juvenile indulgence, she has unconsciously been enabled to prosecute her relationship with Henry Tilney. Her childishness – innocently improper, if there can be such a thing – substitutes for the sort of marital manoeuvring that is punished in an Isabella. Indeed, as the subject of matrimony comes ever nearer, Catherine characteristically flees it into childhood activities – at Woodston, for example, finally noticing the wedding-list impending, she escapes first outside and back briefly into tomboy mode ('Mamma says, I am never within' (2.7; p.127)), and then to play with a litter of puppies. Notwithstanding all this, if we are to take seriously the matter of 'perfect felicity' then we at least have to agree that this is a story of how Catherine grows up and learns to exercise her own judgement. Once we recognize this, the two parts of the novel fall into their proper relation: structurally, the episodes in Northanger Abbey recapitulate in a different register the scenes of instruction, misconception and enlightenment that happen at Bath.

The indecorously swift last chapter of *Northanger Abbey* is famous; as Austen mischievously says to her readers, they 'will see in the tell-tale compression of the pages before them, that we are all hastening together to perfect felicity' (2.16; p.185. With material that in any other contemporary novel would have filled up a third volume – a correspondence between hero and heroine, an intransigent father, a previously unsuspected suitor to Eleanor produced like a rabbit out of a hat, and two weddings, here reduced to 'the bells rang and everyone smiled' (2.16; p.186) – Austen refuses to provide any of the romantic pleasures of the happy ending: no proposal, no anxious letters, no wedding finery. Instead, Austen's narrative voice takes up the foreground to an unprecedented extent (take a look at her remarks on Eleanor's marriage, for example (2.16; pp.185– 6)), culminating in the unintelligible moral with which we are blandly abandoned:

> I leave it to be settled by whomsoever it may concern, whether the tendency of this work be altogether to recommend parental tyranny, or reward filial disobedience. (2.16; p.187)

The novel suddenly jumps out of focus – does it 'recommend parental tyranny' in claiming that the General's opposition brought about the happiness of Henry and Catherine, or does it suggest instead that 'filial disobedience' in the shape of Henry's defiance of his father is what is being rewarded by the happy ending? Generations of readers have felt cheated and annoyed by this puppet-show ending with its unctuously parodic, imploding 'moral', its irony that twists and turns undecidably, flowing back on itself. What is Austen up to?

The short answer, I suppose, is that this chapter represents the final exit from novelistic conventions, so thoroughly have they by now been turned inside out and upside down. As readers we have been (supposedly) educated out of the same sort of postures and pleasures that Isabella tries on and Catherine craves – romance, sentimental or Gothic, is here once more ruthlessly cut down to size. We shouldn't need the 'fix' of a happy ending beyond that alluringly solid parsonage. In return for agreeing not to read in a naive, childlike and feminine mode, we are offered a number of compensations for this enforced distancing from the pleasures of identification: the pleasures of comic condescension identified with Austen's narrative voice, pleasures which include picking up the generic jokes but are not confined to them. That's the short answer. But in the next chapter, in dealing with *Northanger Abbey* in cultural and political context, we'll be going on to explore what the contemporary political implications might have been of educating the heroine and the reader in this way.

# Works cited

Austen, Jane. [1818] 1995. *Northanger Abbey*, ed. by Marilyn Butler, Harmondsworth: Penguin.

Austen, Jane. [1818] 2003. *Northanger Abbey*, ed. by James Kinsley and John Davie, with an introduction and notes by Claudia L. Johnson, Oxford World's Classics, Oxford: Oxford University Press.

Butler, Marilyn. 1995. 'Introduction' to Jane Austen, *Northanger Abbey*, Harmondsworth: Penguin. (Extract in Regan, 2001.)

Castle, Terry. 1990. 'Introduction' to Jane Austen, *Northanger Abbey*, ed. by John Davie, Oxford World's Classics, Oxford: Oxford University Press.

Johnson, Claudia L. 1988. *Jane Austen: Women, Politics and the Novel*, Chicago and London: University of Chicago Press.

Morgan, Susan. 1980. *In the Meantime: Character and Perception in Jane Austen's Fiction*, Chicago: University of Chicago Press.

Regan, Stephen. Ed. 2001. *The Nineteenth-Century Novel: A Critical Reader*, London: Routledge.

Suggestions for further reading can be found at the end of chapter 3.

CHAPTER 3

# *Northanger Abbey*: contexts

*by Marilyn Brooks, with Nicola Watson*

*Northanger Abbey* is the most openly literary of Austen's novels, casting Catherine's development as a young woman in terms of her maturation as a critical reader of texts, people and situations, and choosing literary spoof as its vehicle. Light-hearted *Northanger Abbey* may be, yet in its concern with Catherine's 'education' it self-consciously enters into the lively political debates of the period. In this chapter we'll be exploring the contexts of *Northanger Abbey*, considering comparable polemics on the dangers of reading, speculating on why Austen and others might have been interested in debunking both the sentimental novel and in particular its cousin the Gothic novel, and concluding with an overview of some critical debates surrounding Austen's own position.

## Reading and its dangers

Let us start with Austen's famous defence of the genre she was working in – the novel:

> I will not adopt that ungenerous and impolitic custom so common with novel writers, of degrading by their contemptuous censure the very performances, to the number of which they are themselves adding – joining with their greatest enemies in bestowing the harshest epithets on such works, and scarcely ever permitting them to be read by their own heroine, who, if she accidentally take up a novel, is sure to turn over its insipid pages with disgust. Alas! If the heroine of one novel be not patronized by the heroine of another, from whom can she expect protection and regard? I cannot approve of it. Let us leave it to the Reviewers to abuse such effusions of fancy at their leisure, and over every new novel to talk in threadbare strains of the trash with which the press now groans. Let us not desert one another; we are an injured body. Although our productions have afforded more extensive and unaffected pleasure than those of any other literary corporation in the world, no species of composition has been so much decried. From pride, ignorance, or fashion, our foes are almost as many as our readers. And while the abilities of the nine-hundredth abridger of the History of England, or of the man who collects and publishes in a volume some dozen lines of Milton, Pope, and Prior, with a paper from the Spectator, and a chapter from Sterne, are eulogized by a thousand pens, – there seems almost a general wish of decrying the capacity and undervaluing the labour of

the novelist, and of slighting the performances which only have genius, wit, and taste to recommend them. 'I am no novel reader – I seldom look into novels – Do not imagine that *I* often read novels – It is really very well for a novel.' – Such is the common cant. – 'And what are you reading, Miss —?' 'Oh! It is only a novel!' replies the young lady; while she lays down her book with affected indifference, or momentary shame. – 'It is only Cecilia, or Camilla, or Belinda;' or, in short, only some work in which the greatest powers of the mind are displayed, in which the most thorough knowledge of human nature, the happiest delineation of its varieties, the liveliest effusions of wit and humour are conveyed to the world in the best chosen language.

> (Austen, [1818] 2003, 1.5; pp.23–4; all subsequent page references are to this edition)

This passage is famous because it is one of the few occasions in Austen's novels where the authentic voice of the novelist seems to come through; famous for being a rare instance when Austen aligns herself as a woman author with her distinguished colleagues Frances Burney (author of *Cecilia* and *Camilla*) and Maria Edgeworth (author of *Belinda*); famous, too, for marking a historical moment when a defence of the novel as not only a respectable genre but a genre demanding high genius first becomes possible. Here, Austen attacks the cultural assumption that the popularization of history or the selection of sentimental literary extracts for young ladies were both more suitable and more elevated reading matter than the novel. Yet this manifesto comes in the context of a novel in which novel-reading, both on the part of the characters and by implication on the part of the reader, comes under serious critical scrutiny. True, the unattractive John Thorpe epitomizes the 'pride, ignorance, [and] fashion' that Austen remarks upon; true, too, that our hero Henry Tilney is an inveterate novel-reader; true, finally, that what and how characters read serves as a gauge of intelligence and humanity throughout, yet Catherine finds herself apologizing to Tilney for liking novels because 'they are not clever enough for you – gentlemen read better books' (1.14; p.77), and this sentiment is only partially discredited. This critical scrutiny of the practice of novel-reading is, as we have seen, built into the fabric of the novel as burlesque. We have already noted how Austen's skilful use of parody shows the young Catherine Morland as an inversion of the conventional heroines found in the popular sentimental and Gothic novels of the time (Terry Castle calls this an 'ironic dislocation' of the text whereby the original is 'recalled' to memory only to be 'displaced' (1990, p.xi)). Such parody depends upon the reader recognizing the hidden presence of other texts or subgenres and making connections and comparisons. Austen had a number of novelistic models in mind as she composed *Northanger Abbey*, most of them very popular with contemporary readers. Some of these novels simply make their appearance by name: *Camilla*, *Belinda*, and Isabella's library-list of Gothic shockers – Radcliffe's *The Italian*, plus *The Castle of Wolfenbach*, *Clermont*, *Mysterious Warnings*, *Necromancer of the Black Forest*, *Midnight Bell*, *Orphan of the Rhine* and *Horrid Mysteries*. Others provide a more fundamental structural logic. Whilst the most obvious literary presence is that of Ann Radcliffe's *The Mysteries of Udolpho* (1794), other novels are also 'present' in, and inform, *Northanger Abbey*. Marilyn Butler has made the case for the importance of *Camilla* as a model (1995, pp.xxi–xxii). Below, we'll be arguing for the importance of Charlotte Smith's *Emmeline, the Orphan of the Castle* (1788), mentioned by Austen in two of the juvenile skits written for the amusement of her family which predate her career as a published author, namely 'The History of England' (1791) and 'Catherine, or, the Bower' (1792). But, despite Austen's spirited defence of the genre and wide-ranging evocation of contemporary texts, the main project of *Northanger Abbey* is to chart the ways in which Catherine is deluded by her reading of novels and to extricate her from these delusions. As such, it is very much a novel of its time.

Jane Austen was not the first (and nor would she be the last) to be concerned about the influence of reading on women's lives. Numerous books and sermons were directed at the female reader, designed to chasten and channel her imagination. Among the authors of such tracts, the conservative Dr Fordyce was influential enough to become a target for Mary Wollstonecraft in her feminist polemic *A Vindication of the Rights of Woman* (1792). The issue was important right across the political spectrum, as demonstrated by both the radical Mary Wollstonecraft's and the liberal Maria Edgeworth's entry into the debate. **Read the following extracts from Dr Fordyce's *Sermons to Young Women* (1765), Mary Wollstonecraft's *A Vindication of the Rights of Woman* (1792) and Maria Edgeworth's *Practical Education* (1798). What do they identify as the perils of reading?**

> There seem to me to be very few, in the style of Novel, that you can read with safety, and yet fewer that you can read with advantage. – What shall we say of certain books, which we are assured (for we have not read them) are in their nature so shameful, in their tendency so pestiferous, and contain such rank treason against the royalty of Virtue, such horrible violation of all decorum, that she who can bear to peruse them must in her soul be a prostitute, let her reputation in life be what it will. But can it be true ... that any young woman, pretending to decency, should endure for a moment to look on this infernal brood of futility and lewdness? ... the general run of Novels [is] utterly unfit for you ... They paint scenes of pleasure and passion altogether improper for you to behold, even with the mind's eye.
>
> (Fordyce, 1765, sermon 4, pp.148–50)

> Novels, music, poetry, and gallantry, all tend to make women the creatures of sensation and their character is thus formed in the mould of folly during the time they are acquiring accomplishments, the only improvement they are excited, by their status in society, to acquire. This overstretched sensibility naturally relaxes the other powers of the mind, and prevents intellect from attaining that sovereignty which it ought to attain to render a rational creature useful to others, and content with its own station; for the exercise of the understanding, as life advances, is the method pointed out by nature to calm the passions.
>
> (Wollstonecraft, [1792] 1975, p.152)

> Sentimental stories, and books of mere entertainment ... should be sparingly used, especially in the education of girls. This species of reading cultivates what is called the heart prematurely, lowers the tone of mind, and induces indifference for those common pleasures and occupations which, however

trivial in themselves constitute by far the greatest portion of our daily happiness ... To those who acquire this taste every object becomes disgusting which is not an attitude for poetic painting; a species of moral picturesque is sought for in every scene of life, and this is not always compatible with sound sense, or with simple reality.

(Edgeworth, 1798, pp.332–3)

Fordyce holds the view that 'the general run of novels' are 'pestiferous' and 'shameful' despite his airy masculine assertion that 'we have not read them'. They are 'rank treason against the royalty of Virtue' because they encourage the imagination to dwell upon 'scenes of pleasure and passion'. The language suggests that sympathetic imagination, to which women were supposed particularly susceptible on account of their more sensitive bodies, would in time, if focused on fictitious depictions of passion and pleasure, lead to the real thing – 'violation', 'prostitution', and ultimately (without benefit of contraception) to an 'infernal brood'. (We're not suggesting that he actually says this, but the choice of vocabulary produces this effect, revealing what we might call the 'unconscious' of the text; so, for example, the alliterative phrase 'loose and luscious' adds to the idea of prostitution and 'horrible violation'.) He contends that a young woman's moral worth can be gauged by her reading matter more accurately than by her 'reputation'. The inflated language has, too, a political edge – the phrase 'rank treason against the royalty of Virtue' might perhaps recall to you the dialogue at Beechen Cliff (1.14; pp.77–83) where novel-reading gets muddled up with sedition and riot. Most striking, and by no means unusual in such discussions of the perils of women's reading, is the edge of hysteria and hyperbole, betraying that something fundamental to social stability is felt to be at stake. Wollstonecraft argues that novel-reading makes women 'creatures of sensation', prey to an 'overstretched sensibility' that is unrestrained by reason and so doomed to be both unhappy and useless. Edgeworth similarly thinks that popular novels should be read with care, but for slightly different reasons. Making roughly the same point about the unsuitable cultivation of 'the heart', she fears that such reading raises unrealistic expectations in the young woman and that this leads to inevitable dissatisfaction. She insists that life consists of 'common pleasures' rather than the stuff of novels which, she thinks, is incompatible with 'simple reality', presumably the humdrum of dutiful marriage and motherhood.

As you'll have noticed, Austen's tone is far nearer Edgeworth's than Fordyce's, more interested in subjecting picturesque 'attitudes' to 'common reality' than in painting the tragic and well-deserved consequences of unbridled sentimental indulgence, as others such as Jane West would do. Jane West's *Tale of the Times* (1799), for example, described the way in which an overly sentimental education betrayed a young woman into adultery, misery and a repentant death-bed, deriving much of this conventional trajectory from an unsympathetic reading of Jean-Jacques Rousseau's great proto-Revolutionary novel *La Nouvelle Héloïse* (1761). Austen instead chose to borrow from a special tradition of rather gentler satire, a tradition which stresses the dangers involved in the inability to distinguish between life and art, reality and romance, and the misconceptions which arise from the uncritical absorption of a particular type of literature.

'Quixotic' satire had been made popular through Charlotte Lennox's *The Female Quixote: or, The Adventures of Arabella* (1752), which used as its model Cervantes's *Don Quixote* (1605), whose hero mistook reality for situations he had read in romance literature, most famously when he mistakes a windmill for a giant and prepares to fight it. In her female version, Lennox derives all of her heroine's predicaments from the ideas she has gleaned from the romantic novels she has injudiciously devoured:

> Her ideas, from the manner of her life, and the objects around her, had taken a romantic turn; and supposing romances were real pictures of life, from them she drew all her notions and expectations. By them she was taught to believe that love was the ruling principle of the world; that every other passion was subordinate to this; and that it caused all the happiness and miseries of life ... Her mind being wholly filled with the most extravagant expectations, she was alarmed by every trifling incident; and kept in a continual anxiety by a vicissitude of hopes, fears, wishes, and disappointments.
>
> (Lennox, [1752] 1986, p.7)

Arabella is eventually educated out of her folly in part through the kind offices of her lover, who, like Henry Tilney, takes up her literary language as a courtship strategy. The genre was to take on a new lease of life in the politically charged years of the 1790s and after, when 'romantic' ideas might well extend to 'revolutionary' ones. A spate of foolish heroines led astray by their sentimental or political reading would follow, amongst them E.S. Barrett's Cherubina, heroine of *The Heroine* (1813), eager and silly reader of sentimental/Gothic novels and revolutionary polemics, who revolts against her father, denying his paternity, and sets the fashionable world by the ears by occupying a mildly Gothic castle and defending it against the local militia. But even she is eventually rescued from the lunatic asylum and reformed, as usual, by a thoroughly sensible lover. Let's look more closely at the 'sentimental' novel, and why it should have been the subject of satire across the political spectrum.

# The sentimental novel and its politics

You will probably have already worked out a good deal about the sentimental novel from Austen's parodic inversions of its generic expectations. It boasts a heroine (more rarely a hero) whose main characteristic is an abundance of refined and virtuous feeling. The action consists in her misfortunes and vicissitudes, in one way or another brought about as a consequence of social convention. It may culminate in a tear-jerking death-scene, or in a happy marriage. Its characteristic narrative conventions are the letter or the journal, which purport to represent feeling straight from the heart. Its (sometimes suffocatingly extravagant) discourse is all feeling rather than action. It is often said to derive from Samuel Richardson's great novel *Clarissa: The History of a Young Lady* (1747–8), and is developed in Frances Burney's novels, and in important examples such as Henry Mackenzie's *The Man of Feeling* (1773). The 'cult of sensibility' associated with sentimental fiction – evaluating people according to their capacity for intense benevolent feeling, and regarding the whole of human society as held together by primarily affective, emotional bonds – probably reached its zenith as a fashion in the 1780s, when Austen was in her childhood and adolescence.

Clearly *Northanger Abbey* engages with sentimental fiction principally in the shape of first Catherine's and then Isabella's shortcomings as sentimental heroines. Luckily for her, Catherine doesn't quite measure up to generic specifications. One predecessor, the heroine of Charlotte Smith's *Emmeline, the Orphan of the Castle* (1788), is by contrast the prototype of the sentimental and accomplished heroine, displaying 'uncommon understanding' and 'unwearied application'. She also had 'a kind of intuitive knowledge' and a 'generous sympathy' with nature, with physical beauty to match: 'her figure was elegant and graceful ... there was a sweetness in her countenance' (Smith, [1788] 1971, pp.2, 5). Compared to this paragon who had 'of every useful and ornamental feminine employment ... long since made herself mistress without any instruction' (ibid., p.6), Catherine falls woefully short. But her comic failure to 'learn or understand any thing before she was taught' (1.1; p.5) and her confessed inability to love so much as a rose are blessings in disguise; she is already disqualified from inhabiting the fictional universe of *Emmeline*, which divided reviewers and public alike over its dubious tendency to make a woman's adultery sympathetic and even acceptable. By contrast, the sentimental poseur Isabella Thorpe is regularly shown up as deploying an empty and extravagant language which imperfectly masks her self-seeking ambition. To get a more precise sense of the ways in which Isabella parodies the sentimental, let us take a look at a representative passage from Frances Sheridan's sentimental bestseller *Memoirs of Miss Sidney Bidulph* (1761).

**Read the following passage in which the heroine is writing to her sister. What sort of effects is Sheridan aiming at? Can you identify any that Austen sends up in *Northanger Abbey*? Compare this passage with Isabella's letter to Catherine in volume 2, chapter 12 (pp.159–60).**

1708.

*June* 28. And shall I really be so blessed, my ever beloved Cecilia, as to see you at the time you mention? Oh, my dear, after an absence of five long years, how my heart bounds with joy at your approach! The two months that are to intervene before we meet will appear very tedious to me. But it is always so with happiness that is within our view. Before I expected you, though I regretted your absence, yet did I patiently acquiesce under it, and could entertain my thought with other objects; but I am now, I cannot tell you how anxious and impatient to see you. And yet, my Cecilia, we shall have nothing new to say to each other, knowing as we both do every circumstance of each other's life since we parted. Mine has been a strange one; but my lot has now fallen on a fair ground, where, I hope, it will please heaven to continue me whilst I am to remain in this world ... Let me but live to embrace my Cecilia, and then, providence, thy will be done!

*June* 29. Gracious God! for what am I yet reserved? My trembling hand can scarce hold my pen, but I will try to tell you the event which yesterday produced.

(Sheridan, [1761] 1995, pp.419–20)

The first thing you might have noticed is that this novel is written in a quasi-documentary form – a first-person letter-cum-daily journal addressed to a female friend (in this case, the heroine's sister). The advantages of this form include the immediacy of the representation of feeling as trembling 'effusion', and the ability to mimic the heroine's exciting 'vicissitudes' of fortune by her change of mood between one diary entry and another. The heroine can also be displayed as full of proper pious principles derived from the conduct-book advice of the day – principles which will not save her from one jot of the four hundred pages plus of social torture that she undergoes. In chapter 2 we've already looked at the way in which Henry pretends astonishment that Catherine is not planning to write a journal of this sort; in fact, this heroine is a second sister not to Catherine but to Isabella, whose imperfectly sentimental letter to Catherine arrives in the second volume. It lurches between ready-made effusion and what she is genuinely thinking, signalled by colloquialism:

> Thank God! we leave this vile place tomorrow. Since you went away, I have had
> no pleasure in it – the dust is beyond everything; and every body one cares for
> is gone. I believe if I could see you I should not mind the rest, for you are dearer
> to me than anyone can conceive. I am quite uneasy about your dear brother,
> not having heard from him since he went to Oxford and am fearful of some
> misunderstanding. Your kind offices will set all right: he is the only man I ever
> did or could love, and I trust you will convince him of it. The spring fashions are
> partly down; and the hats the most frightful you can imagine. (2.12; p.159)

She casts herself mendaciously as a sentimental heroine bewildered by the mysterious behaviour of the men around her, but this sentimental letter, far from merely describing feeling in an artless and beleaguered girl, has the transparently self-serving objective of turning Catherine into a go-between. The true sentimental discourse will take place between Eleanor and Catherine; as Butler has remarked, the delicately drawn scene between them in Catherine's bedroom has an air of having escaped from 'some elegant tale of pathos and sentiment' (1995, p.xliii) and it is the precursor to their correspondence, to which, however, we are never made privy.

One of the main effects of the sentimental mode was to pit the individual against the social formation and to ratify the self's individualistic response at the expense of social convention. By the 1790s, in the context of the widespread fear of revolutionary fervour spreading to Britain from France which had escalated after the execution of King Louis XVI in 1792, such sentimental individualism was taking on a distinctly radical tone. It might seem that the French Revolution had little to do with British novel-readers, but rather than being seen as simply a revolt against a particular obsolete and absolute monarch it was quickly perceived as potentially against all government. The Revolution had many supporters in Britain (known as 'Jacobins'), supporters who proclaimed libertarian and democratic principles; among them were the writers Charlotte Smith, Mary Wollstonecraft, Mary Hays, Robert Bage and William Godwin, and the playwrights Thomas Holcroft and Elizabeth Inchbald, all of whom were active in the 1790s when Austen was working on *Northanger Abbey*. When William Godwin published his anarchic philosophical treatise *An Enquiry Concerning Political Justice and its Influence on Modern Morals and Happiness* in 1793, his call for the complete abolition of government and reliance on 'private judgement' influenced the thinking of a generation, including that of such romantics as Coleridge, Wordsworth and Shelley. In 1794 he popularized his anti-establishment ideas through his novel *Caleb Williams*; its contents were considered to be so subversive that he was forced to suppress its inflammatory preface which alluded to 'the modes of domestic and unrecorded despotism, by which man becomes the destroyer of man' (Godwin, [1794] 1977, preface). Some women, such as Mary Wollstonecraft and her admirer and fellow feminist Mary Hays, extended the analysis of despotism to the issue of women's oppression. Of especial interest to us here is their attack on the ideology of sentimentalism, which they saw as a way of perpetuating imaginary and debilitating gender differences. They argued for improved female education and consequent opportunities to procure economic and emotional independence from the chancy goodwill of men – fathers, brothers or husbands. Their experimental novels, however, in trying to protest against the individual sufferings of women, found themselves obliged to adopt both the form and the language of the sentimental novel, as in Charlotte Smith's *Desmond* (1792), Hays's notorious semi-autobiographical novel *The Memoirs of Emma Courtney* (1795) and Wollstonecraft's unfinished novel *The Wrongs of Woman* (1798), and this strengthened the association between the sentimental and the radical still further.

While these writers were generally supported in liberal pamphlets and journals, they were lampooned by the conservative press of the 1790s, and the discussion of the proper form and concerns of fiction became an important medium for the discussion of political and social issues more generally. Certainly commentators of all shades of opinion were conscious that the novel had taken on a new seriousness and depth of social concern. In 1808, for example, the *Monthly Review* commented on the general politicization of literature, and especially of the novel over the previous ten years:

> Romances and novels were formerly written to make old women sleep, and to keep young women awake. They interfered not with the serious affairs of the world, but dwelt in a region of their own, and revelled there free and unconfined ... Now, however, they are frequently made the vehicles of the most marked and serious instruction ... they discuss and settle the most doubtful points in politics; – and instead of being toys to amuse, they have occasionally become extremely useful as mines to blow up, or as battering rams to throw down, whatever is deemed hurtful to society.

> (*Monthly Review*, 1808, vol.107, p.378)

Reaction against the more 'seditious' exponents of this newly politicized fiction, the radical novelists associated with Godwin and Wollstonecraft, appears in a deluge of so-called 'anti-Jacobin' writings – abusive, ridiculing satires and burlesques. Some were directed at particular individuals, such as Charles Lloyd's *Edmund Oliver* (1798) and Elizabeth Hamilton's *Memoirs of Modern Philosophers* (1800), both of which took Mary Hays as their target. In Hamilton's satire, Hays is represented as a posturing sentimentalist, but her inflated language of refined feeling is undercut by her ugly and absurd limp and squint. Others condemned the 'new philosophy' of individualism in general terms and in 1798 a popular journal entitled the *Anti-Jacobin Review and Magazine* was established as a platform for doing just that. Less direct attacks were made implicitly through the exoneration and bolstering up of the Establishment and through the articulation of conservative values, an articulation arguably only necessary when such values are already under threat. This is the political and literary context out of which *Northanger Abbey* (drafted and redrafted over the 1790s) emerged. We'll be returning to consider the political implications of Austen's deployment of sentimental conventions at more length later, but before we do that, let's glance at the other genre that Austen activates, sentimental fiction's cousin, the controversial and bestselling Gothic novel.

*Figure 3.1 'The crumbling ruins of a mighty castle', by Samuel Read, from the* Illustrated London News. *A conventionally 'Gothic' depiction of a castle, emphasizing its awesome sublimity. Catherine's ideas of Blaize Castle and, later, Northanger Abbey are drawn from depictions of this sort. Photo: Mary Evans Picture Library*

# The Gothic novel and its politics

The Gothic novel is first cousin to Richardsonian sentimental fiction. The plots are very similar: the entry of a heroine into the wider world and her efforts to achieve a suitable and happy marriage which are regularly frustrated by social conventions and the machinations of the predatory – male and female. The principal difference lies in the heightened and fantastical setting – country and town houses are turned into castles or monasteries, cruel fathers change into murdering noblemen, social restrictions metamorphose into supernatural phenomena. Heightened, too, are the stakes – women in these novels die not from declines but are murdered, and heroines do not merely suffer social anxiety or humiliation but outright imprisonment and the threat (at least) of rape and/or forced marriage, usually at the hands of some man determined to appropriate their property. While the Gothic novel is often divided up by critics into 'male' and 'female' Gothic – the former preoccupied with the consciousnesses of transgressive men, the latter with those of victimized women – it is almost uniformly interested in depicting violences perpetrated against women (especially women who, like their avatar Clarissa, have been bequeathed money in their own right). *Northanger Abbey*, modelled upon (and against) the novels of Mrs Radcliffe, is of course most interested in 'female' Gothic, seen through the eyes of the powerless heroine, but Austen is conscious too of the 'male' variant – one of the most revealing things we are told about the predatory John Thorpe is that he is an eager reader of Matthew Lewis's shocking novel *The Monk* (1796), the semi-pornographic account, visibly written when Lewis was only eighteen, of the crimes of the hypocritical Brother Ambrosio, which include incarceration, incest and rape.

The whole genre of the Gothic novel is usually thought to have been inaugurated with the publication of Horace Walpole's *The Castle of Otranto: A Gothic Story* in 1764. This, like most of its successors, was set in the medieval past of southern Europe in a man-made landscape of dungeons, monasteries and castles and within a natural setting of perilous mountain ranges. The critic David Punter suggests that a particular set of characteristics are present in all Gothic literature: 'an emphasis on portraying the terrifying, a common insistence on archaic settings, a prominent use of the supernatural, the presence of highly stereotyped characters and the attempt to deploy and perfect techniques of literary suspense' (1980, p.1). Figure 3.2, *Carceri d'invenzione* (prisons) by Giovanni Battista Piranesi, may stand here as shorthand for the characteristic Gothic situation, a nightmarish imprisonment of the individual in a labyrinthine structure.

It has been argued that Gothic sensibility arose as a reaction against the Enlightenment's emphasis on reason and the ordered symmetry of neoclassicism. Simultaneously, a waning in religious belief and an acknowledgement of the poverty of Enlightenment scepticism may have made exploration of the inexplicable attractive. The fad for Gothic fiction was facilitated too, as Emma Clery has pointed out in *The Rise of Supernatural Fiction 1792–1800*, by the contemporary rise of consumerism, the expansion of

*Figure 3.2   Giovanni Battista Piranesi,* Carceri d'invenzione *(prisons), plate VII. British Architectural Library, RIBA, London*

the reading public and new methods for distributing and marketing books, especially the circulating library (1995, see introduction, passim).

In the popular imagination, Gothic was heavily associated with women, both as consumers and producers. It may have been that the form was especially attractive to middle-class women, readers and writers, because it mirrored in a fantastic register their social reality, confined to the home, legally subservient to

*This attempt to describe the effects of the Sublime & Wonderful is dedicated to M.G. Lewis Esq.r M.P*

TALES of WONDER!

*Figure 3.3 James Gillray,* Tales of Wonder!, *1802. Photo: Mary Evans Picture Library*

father or husband, or, when out in the 'world', vulnerable to male predators. Alternatively it has been argued that it offered a fantasy space outside the confines of such domesticity, providing a chaotic space where heroines could travel over craggy mountain-tops, or along dimly lit corridors in foreign parts, where they demonstrated bravery and initiative, and made their own decisions. The Gillray caricature (Figure 3.3) of fat middle-aged women, initiating a younger woman into the indulgence of absurd and sensual thrills (compare the emotionally cross-dressed Henry Tilney's ironically sensual epicureanism in reading, his 'hair standing on end the whole time'), certainly suggests that this sort of reading was felt to provide a fantasy experience, regularly repeatable thanks to the formulaic qualities of the Radcliffean novel which were elaborated by her many inferior imitators and recognized by many readers beside Henry Tilney.

In 'Terrorist novel writing', published in a review of 1798, for example, the following blueprint was offered to 'female readers ... desirous of catching the season of terrors':

*Take* – An old castle, half of it ruinous.
A long gallery, with a great many doors, some secret ones.
Three murdered bodies, quite fresh.
As many skeletons, in chests and presses.
An old woman hanging by the neck; with her throat cut.
Assassins and desperadoes, '*quant. suff.*'

Noise, whispers, and groans, threescore at least.
Mix them together, in the form of three volumes, to be taken at any of the
watering places before going to bed.

(quoted in Clery, 1995, p.147)

Devastatingly accurate in its ingredients, this joke recipe for a Gothic novel
invents it as a sort of medicine or cosmetic for the female reader, to be mixed up
and taken in lodgings at a fashionable watering-place (such as Bath) during the
'season'. It identifies it as formulaic and therefore repeatable, as fashionable and
therefore ephemeral, and as fare for the addicted, aspirational and consumerist
reader. It also identifies it as something that has invaded domestic routine, a
private indulgence to be swigged secretly at bedtime. Other reviews of the time
make it clear that there was a loose but tenacious cultural chain of associations
working to bind novel-reading to eating, female sexual promiscuity, the failure
of class distinctions, fashion, and the manufacture of commodities – a chain that
suggests some of the anxieties that underlie any discussion of women's reading
in the period.

Clery argues that Radcliffe's *Mysteries of Udolpho* and its many imitators
appear at the moment that 'the idea seems to emerge ... that romance, by its very
inclusion of the marvellous or the apparently marvellous, can reveal the
unpleasant truth about real life in a way impossible in the referential narratives
of realist novelists' (1995, p.129). *Udolpho* 'displayed in the form of romance the
real contradictions and dangers which every gentlewoman of the period
potentially faced', dramatizing the fears of the middle classes whose social
standing was most unstable and who were consequently, as a group, 'most
attentive to the taboos surrounding femininity' (ibid., p.128). But by the 1790s,
this feminocentric Gothic fiction was accruing another, less gender-specific if
equally unstable, political significance. Punter construes it as a 'gesture of
defiance' in the face of the established conventions of eighteenth-century social
life and literature: 'every coping-stone that crashes from a castle battlement into
the undergrowth beneath is a small victory for liberty, a snap of the fingers in the
face of autocratic power' (1980, p.15). Because it subverts what is knowable and
controllable, according to this view, it is therefore dangerous to the status quo.
Others, notably Ronald Paulson, have pointed to the generalized way in which
the Gothic seems to evoke the *ancien régime* – 'the castle, prison, tyrant, and
sensitive young girl ... had all been familiarized and sophisticated by the events
in France' (1983, p.221), and, it might be added, by the portrayal of Marie
Antoinette as just such a Gothic heroine by texts such as Edmund Burke's
*Reflections on the Revolution in France* (1790); Paulson goes on to claim that the
Gothic articulates middle-class anxieties about the power of the aristocracy
(1983, pp.57–73). Formally speaking, the Gothic novel seemed potentially
politically subversive in challenging the idea that domestic realism is more
suited to represent social reality than, say, the supernaturally charged romance
laden with the 'un-realism' of 'extravagance, disorder, frenzy, and the irrational'
expressed as incest, murder, parricide (Punter, 1980, p.5; Karl, 1975, p.237).
Indeed, the mode was consciously deployed on occasion to elaborate a radical
political agenda. We have already mentioned William Godwin's politico-Gothic

thriller *Caleb Williams*; Mary Wollstonecraft also adopted the Gothic in her novel *The Wrongs of Woman*. But here plain reality outdoes Gothic conventions:

> Abodes of horror have frequently been described, and castles, filled with spectres and chimeras, conjured up by the magic spell of genius to harrow the soul, and absorb the wondering mind. But, formed of such stuff as dreams are made of, what were they to the mansion of despair, in one corner of which Maria sat, endeavouring to recall her scattered thoughts!
>
> (Wollstonecraft, [1798] 1980, p.75)

Imprisoned wrongfully by her ruthless husband in a madhouse, Maria endures truly 'Gothic' terrors and restraints, but these are the realities, not the fantasies of her life, and represent the universal 'wrongs of woman'.

Armed with this sense of the possible political valences of the Gothic, let us look more closely at *The Mysteries of Udolpho* (1794), the novel Austen uses as the model that Catherine projects onto the state of affairs at the Abbey. Radcliffe's novel was published to great acclaim and in her introduction to the World's Classics edition of *Northanger Abbey* Terry Castle points out that 'to debunk such a work – however insouciantly – was to debunk one of the cherished icons of late-eighteenth-century popular taste' (1990, p.xi). The setting is Gascony and the Italian Apennines during the sixteenth century, where the beautiful orphan Emily St Aubert is made ward to a tyrannical aunt who unexpectedly and unwisely marries the sinister Montoni. Emily's tender attachment to Valancourt, who is not rich enough for the greedy aunt, is disapproved of and, as punishment, Emily is secluded in Montoni's castle, Udolpho. Here Emily experiences a series of apparently supernatural occurrences and finds herself in the power of Montoni following the unnatural death of her aunt. Emily manages to escape, is finally reunited with her lover, Valancourt, and the evil Montoni is captured and brought to justice. Despite the apparent supernatural nature of the occurrences experienced at the castle – mysterious music, ghostly apparitions, strange dancing lights, a concealing black veil and so on – Radcliffe takes pains to produce rational explanations for all of them in her last pages. With its emphasis on reason overcoming terror, *The Mysteries of Udolpho* might best be termed 'Enlightenment Gothic'. In Austen's variation upon the form, Catherine plays Emily, and General Tilney plays Montoni both in Catherine's imagination – 'It was the air and attitude of a Montoni!' (2.8; p.137) – and 'for real'. His character is clearly modelled on Radcliffe's superior and sexy villain; his efforts to annexe the heroine's fortune are as whole-hearted if less picturesque.

The following is 'the black veil scene' from Ann Radcliffe's *The Mysteries of Udolpho* to which Catherine and Isabella Thorpe refer in their conversation in volume 1, chapter 6:

> [Emily] determined to explore the adjoining chambers of the castle. Her imagination was pleased with the view of ancient grandeur, and an emotion of melancholy awe awakened all its powers, as she walked through rooms obscure and desolate, where no footsteps had passed probably for many years, and remembered the strange history of the former possessor of the edifice. This brought to her recollection the veiled picture which had attracted her curiosity on the preceding night, and she resolved to examine it. As she passed through

the chambers that led to this, she found herself somewhat agitated; its connection with the late lady of the castle, and the conversation of Annette, together with the circumstance of the veil, throwing over the object that excited a faint degree of terror. But a terror of the nature, as it occupies and expands the mind, and elevates it to high expectation, is purely sublime, and leads us, by a kind of fascination, to seek even the object from which we appear to shrink.

Emily passed on with faltering steps; and having paused a moment at the door before she attempted to open it, she then hastily entered the chamber, and went towards the picture, which appeared to be enclosed in a frame of uncommon size, that hung in a dark part of the room. She paused again, and then with a timid hand lifted the veil; but instantly let it fall – perceiving that what it had concealed was no picture; and before she could leave the chamber she dropped senseless on the floor.

(Radcliffe, [1794] 1962, 1.19; p.252)

Catherine would have to read on to the end of the second volume to discover what was concealed behind the black veil; what appeared to be 'a human figure, of ghastly paleness, stretched at its length, and dressed in the habiliments of the grave', the face appearing 'partly decayed and disfigured by worms', turns out in fact to have been only a waxen image or *memento mori* of a decaying body (2.55; p.334). Emily has another encounter with a concealing veil in the second volume:

When her spirits had overcome the first shock of her situation, she held up the lamp to examine if the chamber afforded a possibility of an escape ... Here again she looked round for a seat to sustain her, and perceived only a dark curtain, which, descending from the ceiling to the floor, was drawn along the whole side of the chamber. Ill as she was, the appearance of this curtain struck her, and she paused to gaze upon it in wonder and apprehension.

It seemed to conceal a recess of the chamber; she wished, yet dreaded, to lift it, and to discover what it veiled; twice she was withheld by a recollection of the terrible spectacle her daring hand had formerly unveiled in an apartment of the castle, till, suddenly conjecturing that it concealed the body of her murdered aunt, she seized it in a fit of desperation, and drew it aside. Beyond appeared a corpse stretched on a kind of low couch, which was crimsoned with human blood, as was the floor beneath. The features, deformed by death, were ghastly and horrible, and more than one livid wound appeared in the face. Emily, bending over the body, gazed, for a moment, with an eager, frenzied eye; but, in the next, the lamp dropped from her hand, and she fell senseless at the foot of the couch (2.26; pp.17–18).

**Now compare and contrast the similar situation in volume 2, chapter 5, of *Northanger Abbey* when Catherine arrives at the Abbey with Henry's Gothic description of its horrors still ringing in her ears. Read from 'Oh! Mr Tilney, how frightful! – This is just like a book! ...' (p.115) to '... a white cotton counter-pane, properly folded, reposing at one end of the chest in undisputed possession!' in chapter 6 (p.120).**

Comparing these passages, what might strike us first is that Emily's curiosity, her desire to reveal the hidden and her fainting horror on her discovery are all

*Figure 3.4* The Ghost Story, *engraved by R. Graves after the painting by R.W. Buss. Another, altogether gentler, satire on young women's indulgence in the pleasurable terrors of the Gothic novel late at night in the boudoir. Photo: Mary Evans Picture Library*

doubled by Catherine. The sequence of emotion is the same: apprehension, anticipation, disappointment, renewed anticipation and so on, and this passage syntactically mimics Catherine's fear and excitement. But here, of course, Austen's doubling of the Gothic set piece is immediately undermined by the discovery, not of the feared and desired skull, will or corpse, but of the homely counterpane. Where Radcliffe withholds the discovery for maximum shudders ('I know it must be a skeleton. I am sure it is Laurentina's skeleton', as Catherine exclaims lusciously (1.6; p.25)), Austen blandly reveals all to plain, all too plain, view. This is not the sublime, but the domestic. Yet for all that *Northanger Abbey* may debunk *The Mysteries of Udolpho*, the two novels retain some intriguing similarities. The two heroines are united in their imaginative curiosity, their transgressive need to know. During his pastiche novelization of Catherine's imminent arrival and first night at Northanger Abbey Henry stresses that Catherine would be 'unable of course to repress [her] curiosity in so favourable a moment for indulging it, [she] will instantly arise, and throwing [her] dressing-gown around [her], proceed to examine this mystery' (2.5; pp.115–16). Henry is not only basing his scenario on Gothic heroines but also on ancient stories – Eve, Pandora, Bluebeard's wife – of female curiosity which discovers what should remain hidden. Emily is punished for her curiosity by seeing the unseeable and Catherine also is punished for thinking the unthinkable, by, as she thinks, losing Henry's esteem: 'Her folly, which now seemed even criminal, was all exposed to him, and he must despise her for ever' (2.10; p.146). Making no discoveries, Catherine is herself exposed or 'discovered'.

As we have already noted in chapter 2, Catherine is doomed to a whole set of further disappointments, although at the very moment of abandoning her 'craving to be frightened' she finds herself reluctantly starring in a modern version of the Gothic novel, complete with a tyrannical fortune-seeking surrogate father in the shape of General Tilney, a dead mother and immured sister in the shape of Mrs Tilney and Eleanor, and a lost-and-found lover, Henry Tilney, a less sentimental Valancourt. This dénouement is what divides critics, some inclining to argue that *Northanger Abbey* is interested in showing the Gothic of 'real life' (the terrors of the domestic), and some arguing that Austen demonstrates that real life is on the whole more benevolent and civilized than Gothic fantasy admits. Whether you regard Austen as 'conservative' or 'radical' therefore depends rather on what you think Catherine's education implies.

# Jane Austen: 'conservative' or 'radical'?

Prior to the 1970s, Austen was regarded as a ladylike, quintessentially English, middle-class conservative, with little awareness of or interest in the larger political picture of her times. Concerned with educating her heroines to take their places within traditional family structures, through marriages which are designed to uphold, rather than challenge, the status quo, Austen's plots seemed eager to support the Establishment (whether represented by church, government or family), and to avoid at all costs any disturbance of it. The novels' structure too – comic resolutions of marriage after order has been restored, truth triumphing over falsehood, right choices being made – have been seen as temperamentally conservative yet politically disengaged. However, since the 1970s, this view has been challenged.

Marilyn Butler's influential work argued that while Austen might not have explored topics such as the Napoleonic wars and the impact of industrial change in her novels, 'at a subtler and profounder level she was engaged in the controversies of her class and generation' (1981, p.98) – specifically considering the extent of paternalistic responsibilities, the fusion of aristocratic and middle-class interests, the nature of moral education, and the question of individual rights and duties within the family and society at large. Elsewhere, in her seminal study *Jane Austen and the War of Ideas*, Butler has argued that Austen bears 'the lineaments of the committed conservative' ([1975] 1987, p.165), largely by examining the values her novels seem to uphold within the social and literary context of the 1790s and 1800s.

**Now read Marilyn Butler, 'The juvenilia and *Northanger Abbey*' (1987, pp.172–81; extract in Regan, 2001), and her introduction to *Northanger Abbey* (1995, pp.xiv–xlv; extract in Regan, 2001). On what grounds does Butler interpret *Northanger Abbey* as 'conservative'?**

*Northanger Abbey* is very much a novel of its time, and not merely because of its interest in debunking contemporary sentimental and Gothic fiction. It is riddled with topical references: the picturesque and the 'improvement' of the estate – a term that covered garden landscaping and the practice of enclosure – are both canvassed; Henry Tilney's reference to a mob attempting to seize the Tower may have been partly suggested by the Spa Fields riot of 2 December 1816; the interests of General Tilney may reflect the national concerns of the second half of 1816 (Butler, 1981, p.106). On the whole, like other Austen novels, *Northanger Abbey* can be read as being very much about the anxieties of the gentry, 'threatened from within and from without', partly because the role of the aristocracy was being redefined and partly because of fears that French Revolutionary fervour might spread to England (ibid., p.99). More specifically, or so argues Butler, it can be read as a self-consciously 'anti-Jacobin' novel of the nineties. The young heroes and heroines in radical novels (generically called 'Jacobin' novels) were usually shown to be suffering from 'the dangerous vice of individualism' and a dependence on their 'individual' judgement, making them vulnerable to 'false' judgement, for instance of unworthy suitors such as the two-timing Willoughby who captivates Marianne in *Sense and Sensibility*, the duplicitous Wickham who initially attracts Elizabeth Bennet in *Pride and Prejudice*, or the devious Frank Churchill who at first intrigues the eponymous heroine of *Emma*. Catherine's intermittently 'romantic' perspective and willingness to fantasize (counterpointed in material matters by the selfishness of the scheming Isabella and John Thorpe as they ruthlessly try to secure rich marriage-partners) form critical threats to the stability of society, and affiliate her to these other potentially errant heroines. But while other anti-Jacobin novelists have a strong tendency to kill off these individualists, Austen, with characteristic moderation, simply educates them through humiliation. Hence Catherine must learn to align her wayward imagination with the perspective of the community, apparently articulated by Henry Tilney, before she can marry and become established. *Northanger Abbey*, then, suggests that overemphasis on subjective responses may result in an inability to discriminate true from false, which in Catherine's case leads to folly, and in Isabella's to a species of folly altogether closer to vice.

Butler describes Catherine's awakening as 'the typical moment of *éclaircissement* [revelation] towards which all the Austen actions tend, the moment when a key character abandons her error and humbly submits to objective reality' (1987, p.176). According to Butler, Catherine had been inhabiting a 'ready-made inner world' acquired by reading other people's books rather than by engaging with reality, but she ultimately resolves that 'henceforth she will apply more caution, more scepticism, more concern for the objective evidence' (ibid., p.177). Like Catherine, the reader too is induced to reject the flippancy and selfishness of the Thorpes and to value instead the sincerity and accuracy of the Tilneys. Butler goes on to point out that 'formally it requires [the reader] to use his [*sic*] judgement and not his feeling'; the text values third-person narration over first-person effusion and games of allusion over sympathetic identification. As judgement is based on reason and feeling is guaranteed by subjective response, Butler concludes that 'ideologically' *Northanger Abbey* is 'a very clear statement of the anti-jacobin position', with the threatening 'revolutionary character' being depicted in Isabella Thorpe who pursues 'the modern creed of self', as do her brother and the General, all of whom are confounded over the course of the novel.

This is a persuasive argument, but not the only one available to us, as some diametrically opposed readings have shown. Other commentators have argued that it is possible for Austen's novels to encourage radical readings. **Now read Isobel Armstrong, ' "Conservative" Jane Austen? – some views' (1988, pp.95–104; extract in Regan, 2001). What arguments does Armstrong put forward, and do you find them convincing?**

Whereas Butler practises historical contextualization to understand the text in its period, Armstrong is interested in reading the text against itself. If for Butler *Northanger Abbey* is self-consciously an anti-Jacobin polemic, for Armstrong it has a sort of unconscious, something of which it is not itself fully aware or in control, something which can be articulated at this particular historical moment by us in a way that it perhaps couldn't be by Austen's contemporaries. Armstrong claims that in Austen's novels radical readings can be made to emerge because 'moments of cultural stress or lack of cohesion' open up conservative readings of Austen's works to 'inspection' and 'disclose elements in the texts which have been ignored or have remained unnoticed'. Thus she thinks that 'perhaps one could say that they hardly existed until they were named'. She further argues that 'areas of unease, unsolved problems and contradictions' in Austen's writing permit contradictory readings. In other words, she is interested in the novels' processes rather than their overt solutions, in the ways that the novels might be said to be *exploring* rather than *finding*, *asking* questions rather than *answering* them.

**Try transferring some of Armstrong's insights to a reading of *Northanger Abbey*. Where might *Northanger Abbey* appear to be ambiguous or unstable? Are there any moments at which the text seems sympathetic towards the ostensible targets of its satire?**

If Butler's historicization demands the reconstruction of the early nineteenth-century reader's range of reference, Armstrong calls for a consciously modern reader positioned within an (unspecified) twentieth-century moment of 'cultural stress'. Her reader is born from post-structuralist analyses of the way texts are internally conflicted and unstable. We have already seen in chapter 2 how Austen's use of parody and intertextuality promotes a stereoscopic readerly sensibility, relying for its effects on a reader positioned at once as typical naive consumer of fiction and as astute, self-conscious literary critic. This produces an ever-hovering instability – in the first chapter, for instance, is 'the heroine' being used to ridicule Catherine, or is Catherine being used to ridicule 'the heroine'? Or does it cut both ways? Austen's famous 'irony' is akin to this effect. For example, she parrots the style of conduct-book conventionalities but jams them with indigestible paradox – 'where people wish to attach, they should always be ignorant. To come with a well-informed mind, is to come with an inability of administering to the vanity of others, which a sensible person would wish to avoid' (1.14, p.81). To unpack this successfully, you need to concentrate on the impossible and potentially subversive, even feminist, opposition between the 'well-informed' and the 'sensible' person. (You might try extending this to other examples of Austen's irony exercised on conduct-book admonitions, for instance on the vanity of dress in volume 1, chapter 10, from 'What gown and what head-dress ...' (p.52) to '... impropriety will be most endearing to the latter' (ibid.). If you have worked out how to reconcile these sort of moments with the main thrust of Austen's plot-line, then you are some way towards adopting Armstrong's reading strategy. She argues that, instead of 'tidying up' 'areas of unease, unsolved problems and contradictions' into closure in 'fixed positions', it is more fruitful to explore 'a text in dialogue with itself', and to discover critique in process. This formulation might perhaps recall our discussion of the Beechen Cliff conversation (chapter 2 above) and its problematic representation of Henry's influence over Catherine, or return us to the sardonic 'moral' offered at the close of the novel and its uneasy fit with all that has preceded it. If *Northanger Abbey* is indeed an anti-Jacobin tale, why does it appear so much like its radical counterparts in at least half-endorsing Henry's 'filial disobedience'? And why represent 'parental tyranny' at all? And more difficult than either of those questions, what about the peculiarly disengaged, even flippant, tone of these last words? Is Austen pointing playfully at the fact that while fiction may conventionally deprecate such evils it depends upon them for the generation of plot and the satisfactions of resolution? But above all, scanning for textual ambivalence tends to revive the strange way in which *Northanger Abbey* slips in and out of being 'Gothic'.

**Now read Claudia L. Johnson, *Jane Austen: Women, Politics and the Novel* (1988, pp.32–41, 47–8; extract in Regan, 2001). How does Johnson argue for Austen's radicalization of the Gothic?**

Recent feminist commentators have argued that the issues which concerned Austen were very close to those which designated the eighteenth-century feminist Mary Wollstonecraft a radical: Austen too is explicitly concerned with women's position in society, the inadequacy of female education, women's lack of independence, their vulnerability under patriarchy and so on. Like Johnson, such critics read Catherine as having been 'right' rather than 'wrong' all along; Austen, in this view, is not just making Catherine see that reality is not romance, she is implicitly showing her that real life can also be 'Gothic' – full of anxieties, disappointments, fears, cruelties and plottings. Austen cleverly debunks the Gothic novel and its careless readers only to reinvest it with bigger fears based on reality and experience rather than on the clichés of popular fiction. Underlying Henry's assured confidence in 'the country and the age in which we live' lies an unpalatable truth that Catherine is about to discover, as she unwittingly features in General Tilney's Gothic plot of marrying an heiress (a fiction in his mind) to his son. The unequal power relationship between Catherine and the General demonstrates how, despite what Henry claims, the women in 'this England' are as dependent, unprotected and vulnerable as the Eleanor Tilney who confesses to Catherine 'that I am but a nominal mistress of [this house], that my real power is nothing' (2.13; p.166). Catherine's musings about Mrs Tilney's fate at the hands of her husband, too, are less wild than Henry would wish: Catherine concludes that in suspecting General Tilney of either murdering or shutting up his wife, 'she had scarcely sinned against his character, or magnified his cruelty' (2.15; p.183). The news Eleanor brings of Catherine's imminent expulsion so closely follows her new-found ability to distinguish between fantasy and reality that feminist commentators such as Sandra M. Gilbert and Susan Gubar (1979) suggest that Catherine has been right to confound the two, perceiving the potential for the 'atrocities' which Henry had insisted were impossible 'in a country like this' (2.9; p.145). Austen makes Catherine's journey into 'real' Gothic even more explicit through the use of patterning. Hence Catherine, hearing Eleanor at the door, transposes the situation into and then out of remembered Gothic thrills:

> At that moment Catherine thought she heard her [Eleanor's] step in the gallery, and listened for its continuance; but all was silent. Scarcely, however, had she convicted her fancy of error, when the noise of something moving close to her door made her start; it seemed as if some one was touching the very doorway – and in another moment a slight motion of the lock proved that some hand must be on it. She trembled a little at the idea of any one's approaching so cautiously; but resolving not to be again overcome by trivial appearances of alarm, or misled by a raised imagination, she stepped quietly forward, and opened the door. (2.13; p.164)

Again, Catherine is housed in the same bedroom when she leaves the Abbey as when she arrived 'groping her way to bed' where 'she jumped hastily in, and sought some suspension of agony by creeping far underneath the clothes' (2.6; p.124. Seven chapters later, after she hears of her dismissal she undergoes a similar experience, this time tormented by real rather than imaginary anxieties:

> That room, in which her disturbed imagination had tormented her on her first arrival, was again the scene of agitated spirits and unquiet slumbers. Yet how different now the source of her inquietude from what it had been then – how mournfully superior in reality and substance! Her anxiety had foundation in fact, her fears in probability; and with a mind so occupied in the contemplation of actual and natural evil, the solitude of her situation, the darkness of her chamber, the antiquity of the building were felt and considered without the smallest emotion; and though the wind was high, and often produced strange and sudden noises throughout the house, she heard it all as she lay awake, hour after hour, without curiosity or terror. (2.13; p.167)

The Austen of feminist criticism, then, is concerned with women's lack of credibility and worth unless they are financially marketable. And it is not simply because the Gothic is silly fantasy, but because the clichés of the Gothic romance are inadequate to portray the real horrors of a woman's life that Austen ridicules them, portraying the real danger as embedded at the heart of Henry Tilney's England, in patriarchy and perhaps marriage itself. It seems significant that Catherine is introduced to Gothic romances precisely at the time she is introduced to 'the world' and the marriage-market at Bath, as if the terrors of both are interchangeable; as Ellen Moers argues, the female perils attendant on entering 'the world'

> seem to issue from the same grim realities of eighteenth-century girlhood that inspired the Gothic novels Catherine was reading: the same unjust accusations and uncaused severities; the same feminine malice and masculine cruelty; the restraints on her freedom, all the way to actual imprisonment; the mysterious, unexplained social rituals; the terrible need always to appear, as well as always to be, virtuous; and, over all, the terrible slippage from the respectable to the unrespectable class of womanhood.
>
> (Moers, 1978, p.136)

Perhaps, as Catherine's exploration of hidden secrets in the Abbey bedroom reveals a laundry-list of male attire, it is growing up into marital domesticity that Catherine justly fears? Or, as Johnson puts it, perhaps 'the convention of the happy ending conceals our all-too-legitimate cause for alarm'.

As we have seen, elements of Gothic inform *Northanger Abbey* and perform several functions in it. Austen adopts it primarily to burlesque it but, at the same time, both burlesque and Gothic perform serious tasks. Burlesque encourages a disposition to criticize what is being burlesqued through the technique of what Castle terms 'recall-and-displace' (1990, p.xi). The presence of humour, especially through the use of satire and burlesque, helps distance the reader from Catherine's plight and encourages that reader to expect a comic resolution. Gothic romance, the narrative suggests, distorts reality and may result in moral blindness because of the reader's non-discriminating indulgence in its extravagance and falsehood, its 'un-realism'. Consequently, Catherine has to learn to distinguish between fiction and reality and, more importantly, to *choose* to inhabit the latter. Reality, together with the formal structures of a narration based on conversation, seems to be associated with Henry Tilney's view of a safe and secure English nation which counters Catherine's imaginings with tangible realities: social structure, law, religion, education, the constitution, economy, common sense, which are summed up in the ideal of national character – 'we are English'. Nevertheless, Catherine's fictioneering is capable of threatening, intermittently, this 'England', and the flickering presence of the Gothic helps to realize real dilemmas and anxieties threatening women in late eighteenth- and early nineteenth-century England. Over the next hundred years, as we shall see in the following chapters, writers as diverse as Charlotte Brontë and Bram Stoker were to pit Gothic conventions against realism so as to explore the blurred boundaries between socially sanctioned 'reality' and individual perception.

# Works cited

Armstrong, Isobel. 1988. 'Conservative Jane Austen? – some views', in *Jane Austen, 'Mansfield Park'*, Penguin Critical Studies, London: Penguin. (Extract in Regan, 2001.)

Austen, Jane. [1818] 2003. *Northanger Abbey*, ed. by James Kinsley and John Davie, with an introduction and notes by Claudia L. Johnson, Oxford World's Classics, Oxford: Oxford University Press.

Butler, Marilyn. 1981. *Romantics, Rebels and Reactionaries: English Literature and its Background 1760–1830*, Oxford: Oxford University Press.

Butler, Marilyn. [1975] 1987. 'The juvenilia and *Northanger Abbey*', in *Jane Austen and the War of Ideas*, new edn, Oxford: Oxford University Press. (Extract in Regan, 2001.)

Butler, Marilyn. 1995. 'Introduction' and 'Notes' to Jane Austen, *Northanger Abbey*, Harmondsworth: Penguin. (Extract in Regan, 2001.)

Castle, Terry. 1990. 'Introduction' to Jane Austen, *Northanger Abbey*, ed. by John Davie, Oxford World's Classics, Oxford: Oxford University Press.

Clery, E.J. 1995. *The Rise of Supernatural Fiction, 1762–1800*, Cambridge: Cambridge University Press.

Fordyce, James. 1765. *Sermons to Young Women*, London.

Gilbert, Sandra M. and Gubar, Susan. 1979. *The Madwoman in the Attic: The Woman Writer and the Nineteenth-Century Literary Imagination*, London: Routledge.

Godwin, William. [1794] 1977. *Caleb Williams*, Oxford: Oxford University Press.

Johnson, Claudia L. 1988. *Jane Austen: Women, Politics and the Novel*, Chicago: University of Chicago Press. (Extract in Regan, 2001.)

Karl, Frederick. R. 1975. *A Reader's Guide to the Development of the English Novel in the Eighteenth Century*, London: Thames & Hudson.

Lennox, Charlotte. [1752] 1986. *The Female Quixote*, with an introduction by Sandra Shulman, London: Pandora.

Moers, Ellen. 1978. *Literary Women*, London: The Women's Press.

Paulson, Ronald. 1983. *Representations of Revolution (1789–1820)*, New Haven: Yale University Press.

Punter, David. 1980. *The Literature of Terror: A History of Gothic Fictions from 1765 to the Present Day*, London: Longman.

Radcliffe, Ann. [1794] 1962. *The Mysteries of Udolpho*, London: Dent.

Regan, Stephen. Ed. 2001. *The Nineteenth-Century Novel: A Critical Reader*, London: Routledge.

Sheridan, Frances. [1761] 1995. *Memoirs of Miss Sidney Bidulph*, ed. by Patricia Koster and Jean Coates Cleary, Oxford World's Classics, Oxford and New York: Oxford University Press.

Smith, Charlotte. [1788] 1971. *Emmeline, the Orphan of the Castle*, ed. by Anne Henry Ehrenpreis, London: Oxford University Press.

Wollstonecraft, Mary. [1792] 1975. *A Vindication of the Rights of Woman*, ed. by Miriam Brody Kramnick, Harmondsworth: Penguin.

Wollstonecraft, Mary. [1798] 1980. *Mary and The Wrongs of Woman*, ed. by James Kinsley and Gary Kelly, The World's Classics, Oxford: Oxford University Press.

# Further reading

Butler, Marilyn. 1981. *Romantics, Rebels and Reactionaries: English Literature and its Background 1760–1830*, Oxford: Oxford University Press. Sets Austen within an influential survey of the period as a whole.

Butler, Marilyn. [1975] 1987. *Jane Austen and the War of Ideas*, new edn, Oxford University Press. Study of Austen's novels in historical context that argues broadly for Austen's conservatism and sets the agenda for much Austen criticism to the present.

Butler, Marilyn. 1995. 'Introduction' and 'Notes' to Jane Austen, *Northanger Abbey*, Harmondsworth: Penguin. Updates her thinking on *Northanger Abbey*, providing much new context.

Clery, E.J. 1995. *The Rise of Supernatural Fiction, 1762–1800*, Cambridge: Cambridge University Press. A study of the phenomenon of Gothic fiction which is especially interested in its place in the literary marketplace.

Copeland, Edward and McMaster, Juliet. Eds. 1997. *The Cambridge Companion to Jane Austen*, Cambridge: Cambridge University Press. General conspectus of current critical concerns, and a lively essay on irony and romance in *Northanger Abbey* by Rachel Brownstein.

Gilbert, Sandra M. and Gubar, Susan. 1979. *The Madwoman in the Attic: The Woman Writer and the Nineteenth-Century Literary Imagination*, London: Routledge. Ground-breaking American feminist reading of subversive subtexts in Austen.

Hill, Mary K. 1989. *Bath and the Eighteenth Century Novel*, Bath: Bath University Press.

Johnson, Claudia L. 1988. *Jane Austen: Women, Politics and the Novel*, Chicago: University of Chicago Press. A reading of Austen in political context that argues for a strongly liberal, if not radical stance on women's issues.

Kelly, Gary. 1981. *Fiction of the Romantic Period*, London: Longman. Conspectus of fiction of the period, including Austen.

Moers, Ellen. 1978. *Literary Women*, London: The Women's Press. Early but still fresh feminist readings.

Mooneyham, Laura G. 1988. *Romance, Language, and Education in Jane Austen's Novels*, Basingstoke: Macmillan.

Paulson, Ronald. 1983. *Representations of Revolution (1789–1820)*, New Haven: Yale University Press. Important study of response to the French Revolution in the literature of the period, with stimulating if not altogether convincing psychoanalytical slant.

Punter, David. 1980. *The Literature of Terror: A History of Gothic Fictions from 1765 to the Present Day*, London: Longman. Politico-psychoanalytical readings of Gothic.

Sedgwick, Eve Kosofsky. 1986. *The Coherence of Gothic Conventions*, London: Methuen.

# CHAPTER 4
# *Jane Eyre* and genre

*by Delia da Sousa Correa*

## Introduction

'There was no possibility of taking a walk that day.' The opening of *Jane Eyre* takes us directly to the heroine's thoughts on a bleak November afternoon. A 'cold winter wind', 'sombre' clouds and 'penetrating' rain are observed by Jane from her window seat (Brontë, [1847] 2000, 1.1; p.7; all subsequent page references are to this edition). From the outset we are aware of the intense relationship in Brontë's novel between the description of external conditions and the portrayal of individual thoughts and feelings. This technique helps establish Jane's consciousness at the centre of the narrative where it remains throughout the novel. Sequestered between the window curtains and 'the drear November day' outside, Jane is poised between two scenes jointly eloquent of her circumstances. Beyond the curtains, the Reed children cluster around their mother at the fireside, enjoying a family intimacy from which Jane is excluded. Outside the window lies 'a scene of wet lawn and storm-beat shrub, with ceaseless rain sweeping away wildly before a long and lamentable blast' (1.1; p.8). In her cold hiding-place Jane reads Thomas Bewick's *A History of British Birds* by the dim light of the fading day. The desolation of the scene is enhanced by her contemplation of the 'solitary rocks and promontories' and bleak shores of the northern wastes depicted there (1.1; p.8).

The first-time reader of *Jane Eyre* is thus immediately made conscious of Jane as an outsider, literally banished from the warmth of the hearth, scarcely protected by the windowpane from the hostile wilderness beyond. Brontë's very syntax contributes to the intensity of her writing: 'dreadful to me was the coming home in the raw twilight ... Me, she had dispensed from joining the group' (1.1; p.7). The unusual word order in these sentences is a hallmark of Brontë's style. Such inversions, which are more frequently associated with poetry, contribute significantly to the vigour and tension of the novel's language. 'I was glad of it: I never liked long walks ... dreadful to me ...' (1.1; p.7); this series of short clauses is also characteristic of Brontë's writing. The insistent repetition of 'I' and 'me' ensures that the sensations of the first-person heroine are kept constantly before us.

In rereading the opening chapter, we notice not only how forcefully every detail of external description conveys Jane's situation and feelings, but how it also prefigures her quests and ordeals for the rest of the novel, offering in microcosm events, themes and images which will recur in the text. We are to be intensely aware of Jane's physical experience of the absence of warmth and light, and Jane's story is to be dominated by the search for a home and 'family' to replace those which rejected her at its outset. Helen Burns, Miss Temple, Rochester as she first knows him, all offer temporary substitutes, with the Rivers family, and finally Rochester, ultimately providing lasting blood and legal relationships. Meanwhile, Jane's pilgrimage is to take her as a wanderer over just such wastes as she currently surveys beyond the window and in Bewick. As Jane lies recuperating from her collapse in the red-room, the theme implicit in the desolate landscapes of the novel's opening is augmented as Bessie sings a ballad about the lonely wandering of the 'poor orphan child' through a 'wild', 'moonless' and 'dreary' landscape (1.3; p.22). Jane then undertakes her journey to Lowood, across 'remote and mysterious regions' (1.5; p.41). These again recall the strange landscapes illustrated in Bewick and look forward to the wilderness through which she eventually travels on her flight from Thornfield. The opening scene at the window, fire within, snow without, is to be repeated: at Lowood (1.6; p.54) and at Thornfield (1.13; pp.118–19; 3.1; p.313), becoming a recurrent motif. This trope is closely associated with the 'general blending of snow and fire' which pervades the language of the novel (1.11; p.104). You will continually find these repeated patterns when rereading *Jane Eyre*.

# Pictured thoughts

Jane sits hidden by 'Folds of scarlet drapery', the first of countless occasions in the novel when she seeks the protection of a literal or metaphorical 'veil' to screen her from other people (1.1; p.8). In a structurally parallel scene at Thornfield, for example, she finds a similar curtain to shield herself from Rochester's guests (2.2; p.166). For the reader, however, the window, and the account of Jane's reading, offer a privileged view into her powerfully introspective imagination. From Bewick, Jane imbibes a synthesis of words and landscape. Passages of poetry and prose enter her inner world alongside visual representations of shipwrecks, graveyards, fiends and snowy wastes. The significance of these allusions to Bewick is enhanced when we discover how popular his work was at the time. Charlotte Brontë could be confident of her audience's appreciation of the importance of these references. Bewick's woodcuts were especially admired: his illustrations of birds in their natural habitats and, above all, the tiny vignettes, or 'tail pieces', with which he decorated the ends of individual sections. In these, Bewick allowed his imagination free rein, depicting scenes unconnected with the ornithological text: atmospheric seascapes, isolated Gothic buildings and alienated figures in moonlit landscapes. The scenes described by Jane Eyre derive from vignettes in *A History of British Birds*. Brontë incorporates into her chapter a verse of Thompson's poem *The Seasons,* which Bewick has also used, and she quotes Bewick's own romantic prose account of the 'death-white realms' of northern lands (1.1; p.8). 'The words in these introductory pages connected themselves with the succeeding vignettes', Jane remarks. 'Each picture told a story; mysterious often to my undeveloped understanding and imperfect feelings, yet ever profoundly interesting' (1.1; p.9). **Look at the reproductions of some of**

**Bewick's vignettes in Figure 4.1, then reread Brontë's quotations from his written text and Jane's description of the vignettes. What elements in Bewick's text seem relevant to Jane's story?**

We can assume that the atmosphere of desolation and even horror are relevant to Jane's current and future experience. Details are important too: here is the moon, for instance, so constant a symbolic presence in the novel. The 'desolate coast', 'solitary churchyard' and 'object[s] of terror' establish a harrowing intensity. Later we will have Jane's own strange romantic paintings, which recall the tone and some of the details of Bewick's drawings, to provide a similar 'visual' context for the novel, and insight into her psyche. Brontë's account of Bewick epitomizes the way in which she incorporates details of external landscape into the powerful psychological portrayal of her heroine. This was a quality she found in Bewick's writing itself. In 1832, Brontë had composed a poem in praise of Bewick, recounting the 'fresh delight' always to be found in 'the enchanted page / Where pictured thoughts ... breathe and speak and burn' (quoted in Stevens, 1968, p.25).

'She calls in nature to describe a state of mind which could not otherwise be expressed': in '*Jane Eyre* and *Wuthering Heights*', Virginia Woolf noted Brontë's capacity to make landscape acutely expressive of emotion and meaning. Woolf saw Charlotte and Emily Brontë as displaying unique poetic power in the way that:

> They seized those aspects of the earth which were most akin to what they themselves felt or imputed to their characters, and so their storms, their moors, their lovely spaces of summer weather are not ornaments applied to decorate a dull page or display the writer's powers of observation – they carry on the emotion and light up the meaning of the book. ([1923] 1979, p.130)

**Can you identify other passages in the novel to which Woolf's comment would apply?**

My suggestions include volume 1, chapter 4, and volume 2, chapter 11, which I discuss below. You will find many further examples in the novel.

Perhaps your list is not restricted to descriptions of nature alone. Woolf's observations on Brontë's internalizations of nature could be expanded to characterize Brontë's representation of external environments in general. This aspect of her narrative technique was astutely observed by the critic George Henry Lewes in his 1847 review of the novel in *Fraser's Magazine*, where he praised Brontë's 'strange power of subjective representation':

> We do not simply mean the power over the passions – the psychological intuition of the artist, but the power also of connecting external appearances with internal effects – of representing the psychological interpretation of material phenomena.

(in Allott, 1974, p.86)

The psychological significance of outer circumstances becomes most intensely evident in these early chapters when Jane is confined to the red-room. Jane's enraged rebellion against the tyranny of her cousin John Reed and her subsequent confinement introduces central themes and issues, and foreshadows subsequent events in the plot. Her rebellion is expressed in the images of fire

(a)

(d)

(b)

(e)

(c)

(f)

(g)

*Figure 4.1  Vignettes from Bewick's* A History of British Birds, *Newcastle:*
*F. Graham, 1971; facsimile of 1826 edn; (a) and (b) from vol.1,* Land Birds,
*pp.99, 183, (c)–(g) from vol.2,* Water Birds, *pp.109, 196, 245, 421 and 256*

which are to recur and ultimately to be dramatized in the conflagration at
Thornfield. Jane's terror at the possible manifestation of her uncle's ghost is to be
realized in the appearance of Bertha in her room on the night preceding her
planned marriage to Rochester. Her experience of self-alienation as she looks at
her unrecognizable image in the red-room mirror is also recalled in the later
scene, when Jane sees Bertha's reflection as she looks into the mirror to try on
the wedding-veil. The insanity which will re-emerge with Bertha at Thornfield is
presaged in Jane's rage and terror at her confinement in the red-room, which
brings about her mental collapse. Afterwards, she seems on the threshold of
madness, seeing before her only 'a terrible red glare, crossed with thick black
bars' (1.3; p.18).

As Woolf expressed it in her comment quoted earlier, Brontë's 'landscapes'
'carry on the emotion and light up the meaning of the book'. Brontë effectively
makes an explicit declaration of this poetic method in the account of the
progress of Jane's emotions after her confrontation with her aunt in chapter 4:

> A ridge of lighted heath, alive, glancing, devouring, would have been a meet
> emblem of my mind when I accused and menaced Mrs. Reed: the same ridge,
> black and blasted after the flames are dead, would have represented as meetly
> my subsequent condition. (1.4; pp.37–8)

The novel gains much of its psychological power from the spatial expression of
Jane's inner life: both rooms and 'regions' are recurrent images of her mind.
Brontë's readers become accustomed to this technique and the blending of
literal and metaphorical landscapes. We are ultimately unsurprised when Jane
declares that, after her discovery of Rochester's marriage to Bertha, the view
from her window at Thornfield has changed overnight from summer to winter:

> Jane Eyre, who had been an ardent, expectant woman – almost a bride – was a
> cold, solitary girl again: her life was pale; her prospects were desolate. A
> Christmas frost had come at midsummer; a white December storm had whirled
> over June; ice glazed the ripe apples, drifts crushed the blowing roses; on hay-
> field and corn-field lay a frozen shroud: lanes which last night blushed full of
> flowers, to-day were pathless with untrodden snow; and the woods, which
> twelve hours since waved leafy and fragrant as groves between the tropics, now
> spread waste, wild, and white as pine-forests in wintry Norway. (2.11; p.295)

We are recalled to Bewick, and the solitary haunts 'of the coast of Norway' (1.1;
p.8).

The passages of *Jane Eyre* discussed here offer examples of the repeated and
opposing patterns of imagery fundamental to its structure. The figurative unity
of the novel has frequently been noted. As an example of just one figure central
to *Jane Eyre*, David Lodge (1966), in a now classic essay, 'Fire and Eyre', traces
the prevalence of both literal and metaphorical references to fire, and the
frequency with which these modulate into one another. As we have already
seen, Jane is deprived of the warmth of a literal fire at the novel's opening and
fire becomes a metaphor for her fury in her confrontation with Mrs Reed. At
Thornfield Jane longingly imagines a life of 'incident, life, fire, feeling' for herself
(1.12; p.109). St John Rivers later invokes the purgatorial fire and brimstone of
the biblical Book of Revelation (3.9; p.416). The purging conflagration at
Thornfield is both literal and symbolic – as is the prophetic lightning which

strikes the chestnut tree. Allusions to fire thus link very different aspects of the text: hearth, home and comfort on the one hand, imaginative power, passion, rebellion, fury and purgation on the other (this list is not exhaustive). Frequently too, as in the novel's opening chapter, or in the image of Jane as first 'ardent' and then 'cold', images of fire appear in conjunction with opposing images of snow and ice. You will notice these patterns as a constant feature of Brontë's language in the novel, and one which repays close attention.

Such figurative clustering helps provide coherence and intensity of atmosphere within a text of extraordinary thematic and generic fluidity. The question of genre will underpin discussion of the novel throughout the rest of this chapter, for we address issues of genre every time we wonder what kind of novel we are reading and what might happen next. Elements from numerous different modes of literature combine in *Jane Eyre*. All of them influence our expectations as readers, and our interpretations of the novel.

# Realism and romance

The opening scenes of the novel, as discussed here, would seem to offer a mixture of realism and fantasy. The novel can be described as 'realist', in that we are presented with largely credible circumstances and events. However, this does not preclude the presence of non-realist elements also. In this volume, we are particularly concerned with relationships between realism and romance. **In what senses is *Jane Eyre* a 'romance'?**

In a specific sense, *Jane Eyre* is a romance because it is a love story. More generally, the novel might be described as a romance in that, as in the passages we have just been reading, it pursues the desires and fantasies of the protagonist, and of the reader. Linked with this is the celebration of the individual imagination associated historically with romanticism. 'Realist' novels frequently contain a good deal of romance, in all the senses outlined here. Indeed, *Jane Eyre* influenced the way in which many subsequent realist novels combined romantic elements into their narratives. The intersection of realism and romance in *Jane Eyre* was noticed by some of the early literary critics to write about the novel. Its introspective qualities, including Brontë's treatment of landscape discussed earlier, associated it with the subjectivity of Wordsworth, Byron and other romantic poets widely read at the time. Brontë therefore embodies in the novel qualities previously identified predominantly with poetic forms. Frederic Harrison, writing in 1895, praises her 'skill in the use of what Ruskin has called the "pathetic fallacy," the eye which beholds nature coloured by the light of the inner soul. In this quality she really reaches the level of fine poetry' (in McNees, 1996, vol.1, p.6). Harrison saw the novel as combining the essential features of romantic poetry and the realist novel: 'It stands just in the middle of the century, when men were still under the spell of Byron, Shelley, Coleridge and Wordsworth, and yet it is not wholly alien to the methods of our latest realists' (in ibid., p.260). In 1899, George Saintsbury also described Brontë as the first writer to find ways of bringing together the romance elements of writers such as Walter

Scott and the more realist depiction of precise character, dialogue and middle-class manners of a novelist such as Jane Austen. He sees her as having achieved

> the maintenance of the rule of exact and ... realistic observation of ordinary personality, of middle-class rank, of fairly usual incident, but the addition to these or the saturation of them with a new romance, a romance derived partly from the study of nature and partly from the working out of the passionate thoughts and feelings of the individual.
>
> (in ibid., p.287)

'What Emily and Charlotte Brontë did', Saintsbury concluded, 'was to effect the union of realism and of dream in the English novel' (ibid., p.289). However, the less realist elements of the novel's plot also received considerable criticism. Lewes saw the mad wife as a weak point (in McNees, 1996, vol.3, p.13). His view was endorsed by many critics during the succeeding century, who were often disturbed by the increasingly fantastic coincidences of the novel's plot. More recently, criticism of *Jane Eyre* has perceived productive tensions between aspects of realism and romance, and has increasingly paid most attention to the text's non-realist elements.

# Generic inheritance

Whilst reading the opening scenes of *Jane Eyre*, we begin to form an idea of some of the most significant literary modes to be employed in the novel. In the same way that Brontë integrates external landscapes into the psychological portrayal of her heroine, she incorporates a wealth of different literary elements into her text. Brontë's narrative declares from the outset the importance of its relationship with other literary texts Jane is reading: the novel quotes at length from Bewick, as we have already noted (1.1; p.8). The account of Bewick is rapidly followed by explicit references to three contrasting works of fiction: Richardson's *Pamela* (1740–1), Swift's satirical *Gulliver's Travels* (1726) and Wesley's *Earl of Moreland* (1781), a tale of innocence in a corrupting world. Another allusion is to didactic literature for children of the kind that Brocklehurst presents to Jane. The cautionary tale of 'the awfully sudden death of Martha G——, a naughty child addicted to falsehood and deceit' is typical of religious tracts such as those produced by Carus Wilson, the historical proprietor of the Clergy Daughters' School, Cowan Bridge, on which Brontë based her account of Lowood (1.4; p.35; see Allott, 1974, pp.74, 75). Not just morality literature, but the Bible itself is invoked here as part of the intertextual context for *Jane Eyre*: Jane's cheeky but logical recipe for the avoidance of hell-fire – 'I must keep in good health, and not die' – demonstrates her resistance to oppressive dogmas and institutions. It also importantly establishes her right to interpret biblical models for herself, rather than in deference to an authority such as Brocklehurst (1.4; p.32). She even asserts her right to determine which parts of the Bible she will respect: 'Psalms are not interesting' (1.4; p.33). In addition to these specific allusions, other, equally important intertextual relationships are implicit, rather than explicitly stated. They indicate not merely patterns of influence, but the degree to which Brontë was writing within a context which contemporary writers – and readers – shared.

To say that *Jane Eyre* is a novel especially rich in intertextual reference is not remotely to suggest that Brontë's writing is merely derivative. Rather, we can recognize that no writer – or reader – is innocent of previous literary experience, and find that the effect of this is a valuable focus of critical interest. We all bring our previous reading to bear on what we have before us. In Brontë's case this involved some surprising combinations, which were to contribute to the startling originality of her novel. To describe *Jane Eyre* as intertextual, then, is to draw attention not to a high incidence of passive reference to other works of literature, but to Brontë's active deployment of allusions to an extraordinary range of different genres and texts through which her work achieves its own unique character. We begin with Bewick, both a literary and a visual source of reference which Brontë works into her own text. A major emphasis in what follows will be on discovering how awareness of the intertextual prodigality of *Jane Eyre* can affect our reading of the novel.

As present-day readers, we need to explore, as far as we are able, how the novel relates to the contexts available to readers at the time of its publication. We can, of course, never achieve a perfect reconstruction of the literary, not to mention the social and ideological, contexts within which Brontë's original readers encountered the novel. Moreover, we need to see as valid what the novel means to us as readers now. None the less, an attempt to appreciate some of the expectations the novel would have aroused in its nineteenth-century readership can only enrich our own reading. Investigation of a wide range of historical contexts offers less a key to the text's meaning than a way of acknowledging the multiplicity of writing in *Jane Eyre*. We are assisted in this by the way in which the novel has attracted a wealth of new critical approaches. Since the 1970s, it has been of central interest to Anglo-American feminist critics, and in chapter 5 I shall be looking at some specific examples of feminist criticism. Formalist approaches have paid increasing attention to the novel's realist and non-realist elements and are reflected in the emphasis of my own discussion on issues of genre. My approach is also influenced by the increasing number of historicist studies of the novel's engagement in issues of its time.

# Fictional autobiography

Lewes defines the genre of *Jane Eyre* as autobiographical: 'It *is* an autobiography, – not, perhaps, in the naked facts and circumstances, but in the actual suffering and experience' (in Allott, 1974, p.84). The novel's emotional intensity, and retrospective, first-person narration, certainly suggest an autobiographical narrative. The fierce introspection in *Jane Eyre*, as much as correspondences with Brontë's own life, has led some readers, from the time of the novel's first publication, to see the work as literally its author's autobiography, despite its fictional status. The extent to which readers identify with Jane's experiences also has the effect of making them feel as if they are reading their *own* autobiography: 'It reads like a page out of one's own life', comments Lewes on the novel's vivid opening scene (in ibid., p.86). Intense identification with the heroine is thus one of the enduring responses provoked by this text. *Jane Eyre* is a novel in which there can seem to be little connection between our individual passionate response as readers and critical attempts to analyse the text. However, the fact that it apparently speaks so directly to us is arguably all the more reason to explore how the novel's historical relationships with the literature and issues of its time can inform our interpretation. Rather than reading *Jane Eyre* only to affirm our own experiences, we may also become aware of important respects in which we differ from the novel's original readers. In this way, we can hope to arrive at a better understanding of its distinctive power.

'It *is* an autobiography': in addition to the potent sympathetic identification provoked by Brontë's writing, reception of the novel as autobiographical was influenced by the way in which it echoed previous literary traditions of autobiography. Lewes's comment, in fact, refers directly to the novel's title-page. At her publisher's instigation, the first edition of *Jane Eyre* included the subtitle '*An Autobiography*', together with the claim: 'edited by Currer Bell'. For its first readers, the novel was thereby instantly placed within the familiar convention of fictional 'editions' of autobiographical narrative. This convention had been employed for such widely different narratives as Richardson's moral novel of society, *Pamela*, and Mary Shelley's 'Gothic' novel, *Frankenstein* (1818) – it does not therefore in itself signal any certainty as to the novel's precise genre. Although the setting of *Jane Eyre* is domestic, and invites us to suppose that we are embarking upon a realist novel, the snowy wastes depicted in Bewick may indeed suggest some affinity with *Frankenstein*. What kind of novel do we have before us? This is a question that remains pertinent throughout our reading of it.

As we read on, we gather increasing clues as to what kind of fictional autobiography is to be presented in *Jane Eyre* and about the other modes of writing on which it will draw. Fundamental to the preoccupation, throughout the novel, with the development of an individual consciousness is the long-standing tradition in English prose of what has come to be known as 'spiritual autobiography'. The introspective tradition, which made an important contribution to the development of the novel in the eighteenth and nineteenth centuries, includes such didactic and religious works as John Bunyan's *The Pilgrim's Progress* (1678–84), and his autobiographical work *Grace Abounding to the Chief of Sinners* (1666). Brontë's use of significant names for the places Jane journeys between – Gateshead, Lowood, Thornfield, Marsh End – is one specific way in which her text echoes Bunyan's allegorical style. More generally, a preoccupation shared by spiritual autobiography and the majority of nineteenth-century novels is self-interpretation. The conventions of spiritual autobiography generate certain narrative and moral expectations in the reader, above all the likelihood that the protagonist will grow in moral stature, developing a growing trust in God's providence and thankfulness for delivery from temptation. You can probably identify ways in which this mode is relevant to parts of Brontë's novel. However, it is by no means the sole mode of autobiography on which *Jane Eyre* draws, and not the one that is given primacy at the novel's opening.

*Jane Eyre* begins with a scene of rebellion. An alternative mode of autobiography is also at work within the text. Jane's rebellious outbursts against the tyrannies of John Reed and his mother may be identified with a tradition of radical autobiography inherited from writers such as the philosopher and novelist William Godwin (1756–1836). Godwin was the husband of the feminist Mary Wollstonecraft (author of *A Vindication of the Rights of Woman* (1792)), and father to Mary Shelley. His novels, which included such works as *Caleb Williams* (1794) – still the most frequently read of his novels today – were associated with revolutionary romanticism and were appreciated for their intense depictions of individual psychology. One of *Jane Eyre's* early reviewers, the editor of the radical *Examiner,* asserted that 'as an analysis of a single mind' the novel should be read alongside 'the autobiographies of Godwin' (in Allott, 1974, p.77). Godwin's narratives sympathized with the rebellious individual protesting against social and personal injustice. The opening chapters of *Jane Eyre* do the same.

Jane's first encounter with Brocklehurst seems to dramatize an opposition between his morality literature and the radical mode of biography already established in the text. The two different modes of autobiography, spiritual and romantic, obviously have the potential to set up confusing dramatic and ideological expectations in the reader. As we trace how Brontë blends together different modes, we become aware of ways in which such combinations complicate interpretation of the novel. Is *Jane Eyre* to be a story of spiritual development or of romantic rebellion?

In addition, the narrative voice of *Jane Eyre* vastly complicates attempts to fix an interpretation of the novel. Unlike the third-person narrative in *Northanger Abbey,* Jane Eyre herself speaks directly to us. But, despite the first-person narration, there are at least two Janes speaking. An older, wiser Jane tells her story with authority to comment, much as a third-person narrator might, on the 'undeveloped understanding' of her younger self (1.1; p.9). The voice of this younger Jane speaks out directly against the tyranny of John Reed and engages our sympathy. The two narrators can suggest contrasting views of Jane's situation. As the novel progresses, moreover, it frequently becomes difficult to distinguish which Jane is speaking. A third Jane emerges: the mature young woman and governess, in whose narrative we hear constant echoes of her angry younger self. If you look back at the passage I quoted towards the end of the section entitled 'Pictured thoughts', you can, in fact, find *two* Janes described by a *third,* narrative voice. Jane Eyre the 'ardent, expectant woman' is the 'cold, solitary girl again'. This reversal of identities dramatizes the difficulty we have in distinguishing which Jane is addressing us. In later sections ('The governess and the "Woman Question"' and 'The uncanny'), I quote Jane's description of Blanche Ingram and her monologue on 'presentiments'. Is it Jane the governess speaking in these passages, or is it Jane as Mrs Rochester? It could be either or both. In these examples, it may make little difference to how we read the passages, although the uncertainty is somewhat troubling in itself. You will identify other points in the novel where this uncertainty complicates interpretation. 'Millions are condemned to a stiller doom than mine' exclaims the narrator as she describes Jane pacing the battlements at Thornfield (1.12; p.109).

Is this present-tense declaration to be read as indirect speech – the older narrator reporting the thoughts of her younger self – or is Jane reflecting directly on her situation *as* Mrs Rochester? This could radically influence how we read the end of the novel. Moreover, this multiple Jane is not the only narrator in the novel. Both Rochester and St John have their moments of narrative too. The narrative voice(s) contribute another level of intricacy to this multi-genred text.

Autobiography, then, has no single voice in *Jane Eyre*. Even in all its variety, it represents but one dimension of the generic diversity within the novel. We have mentioned the novel's links with romantic poetry. As Jane's career develops, the romantic *Bildungsroman*, or novel of education, also suggests itself as an appropriate prose-fiction model. Affinities with a further variety of genres become apparent as the novel unfolds.

# Social comment

When Jane departs for Lowood, the reader may be reminded of a 'foundling novel' such as Dickens's *Oliver Twist* (1837). Like Oliver, Jane is poor and little, orphaned and homeless, and is required to make a testing moral journey through life. The subtitle of Dickens's novel, *The Parish Boy's Progress*, is an indicator of the common significance of the moral and social allegory inherited from Bunyan's *The Pilgrim's Progress*. Analogies with further Dickens novels come to mind. The death of Helen Burns also reminds us of the numerous child death-scenes in Dickens's work. *Nicholas Nickleby* (1840) and *Dombey and Son* (1846–8) deal, as does *Jane Eyre*, with repressive schools and the abuse of children. Indeed, a number of mid-nineteenth-century readers, including Lewes, identified the Lowood section of the novel with Dickens's Dotheboys Hall in *Nicholas Nickleby* (see Beaty, 1996, p.33). *Dombey and Son* was published just too late for Brontë actually to have responded to it in *Jane Eyre*. However, you will no doubt discover affinities between the two novels, when you come to study Dickens in chapters 6 and 7: evidence of how such parallels can be as much a question of a common literary inheritance and shared social preoccupations as of direct influence.

At the time of its publication, *Jane Eyre* was a novel as much admired for its realist detail as for its psychological power. Lewes extols Brontë's combination of psychological insight and realistic experience: 'reality is not confined to the characters and incidents, but is also striking in the descriptions of the various aspects of Nature, and of the houses, rooms, and furniture' (in Allott, 1974, p.86). Many of his contemporaries were conscious of *Jane Eyre* as a novel that combined elements of romantic individualism with social comment. For the novel's detractors, this made it a socially dangerous text. The fact that *Jane Eyre* is a novel with a passionate individual at its centre has tended to deflect readers from the extent to which it also deals with social issues. However, we can appreciate, from even the brief series of parallels with Dickens outlined above, that it is a novel which shares many other concerns with more overtly socially engaged novels of its time. The 1840s was a decade which saw the rise of what became known as the 'condition of England' novel, after Carlyle's coinage of this phrase. Novels such as Benjamin Disraeli's *Sybil* (1845), Elizabeth Gaskell's *Mary*

*Barton* (1848) or Charles Kingsley's *Yeast* (1848) directly addressed the conditions and causes of poverty in Britain, as did much of Dickens's work. They were influenced also by anxiety about revolutionary tensions in Europe. In her 1954 study *Novels of the Eighteen-Forties*, Kathleen Tillotson discussed *Jane Eyre* as a novel not just of its century but of its decade, emphasizing its connection with these social comment novels (in McNees, 1996, vol.3, pp.79–80). Marxist critics, above all Terry Eagleton, have examined the novel in relation to issues of class. His *Myths of Power: A Marxist Study of the Brontës* ([1975] 1988) analyses Jane's complex position as both inside and exiled from her class, with conflicting aspirations both to challenge and to conform to a secure social order. Feminist critics have discussed it as a novel that has radical things to say on issues of gender, and we shall be discussing ways in which *Jane Eyre* engaged with the debate on the 'Woman Question' that was current at the time.

Certain of *Jane Eyre*'s original reviewers found the work socially subversive, indicative even of revolutionary tendencies. After all, Jane assumes equality of both intellect and class with her employer. As a child, she perceives John Reed as a tyrant and her own situation as that of a 'revolted slave' (1.1; p.11; 1.2; p.14). Later, her famous speech on the 'stagnation' and 'restraint' suffered by women in mid-nineteenth-century society asserts an analogy with the 'silent revolt' of oppressed workers (1.12; p.109). 'Every page burns with moral Jacobinism', commented the reviewer for the *Christian Remembrancer*. '"Unjust, unjust," is the burden of every reflection upon the things and powers that be' (in Allott, 1974, p.90). '*Jane Eyre* is pre-eminently an anti-Christian composition', concluded Elizabeth Rigby, writing for the *Quarterly Review* in 1848:

> There is throughout it a murmuring against the comforts of the rich and against the privations of the poor, which as far as each individual is concerned, is a murmuring against God's appointment ... We do not hesitate to say that the tone of the mind and thought which has overthrown authority and violated every code human and divine abroad, and fostered Chartism and rebellion at home, is the same which has also written *Jane Eyre*.

(in Allott, 1974, pp.109–10)

Autobiography, romantic poetry, *Bildungsroman*, radical social comment: these are just some of the contexts we have already identified as important for reading *Jane Eyre*. We are constantly challenged to think about what sort of novel we are reading, adapting our ideas and expectations to accommodate the possibilities suggested by each new aspect of the text. The interaction of different generic modes during the first volume of the novel already suggests multiple potential developments for Jane's story. Will she be a martyr, a moral pilgrim, a rebel, or ... something else? By the end of Jane's time at Lowood, a further set of possibilities announces itself with the introduction of another genre of central importance to *Jane Eyre*.

# The governess novel

The governess was an extremely popular subject for fiction. Numerous novels earlier than *Jane Eyre* feature characters who are governesses, amongst them Jane Austen's *Emma* (1816) and Dickens's *Martin Chuzzlewit* (1843–4).

However, novels where the governess was the heroine are represented by such now-forgotten works as Mrs Sherwood's *The Governess* (1835), or Rachael McCrindell's *The English Governess* (1844). This was a genre highly available and familiar to Brontë's readers. Governess novels tended to follow one of two basic patterns: 'romantic' or 'providential'. Both modes of governess novel provided a realist, domestic, form of fiction, written by women authors for a predominantly female readership. In novels of the romantic type, the governess's true qualities are recognized by a gentleman, perhaps her employer, and the novel ends in their marriage. Governess novels of the providential type share some of the major traits of the spiritual autobiography tradition. Such novels thus represent a female form of autobiography in which the heroine grows in moral stature to pursue a life of service in increasing gratitude for God's providence and for protection from sin. This may entail the reform of an originally passionate temperament which has led her to near-disaster. Sometimes the providential and romantic forms of the governess novel combine, with the pious heroine finding romantic fulfilment in marriage to a clergyman of high moral stature. Anne Brontë's *Agnes Grey* (1847) follows such a pattern. Narrated by its morally inviolable, home-seeking heroine, this work was in numerous ways an important influence on *Jane Eyre*. **Can you identify ways in which the outcomes of both the romantic and the providential forms of governess novel are invoked as possibilities in *Jane Eyre*?**

Jane's courtship with Rochester sets up expectations of a romantic resolution. However, Jane is no typical romantic heroine. 'We never lose sight of her plainness; no effort is made to throw romance about her', wrote Lewes; 'you admire ... love her for the strong will, honest mind, loving heart, and peculiar but fascinating person' (in Allott, 1974, p.85). An outcome of the providential kind seems highly possible during the Morton section of the novel, where Jane offers thanks for her deliverance from the temptation of an illicit union with Rochester (2.5; p.360). She also finds vocational satisfaction in teaching the daughters of the local farmers and considers another possible future vocation as a missionary, albeit that this is offered on terms – marriage to St John – which she ultimately cannot accept.

Of course, *Jane Eyre* is not exclusively a governess novel. Jane is certainly not portrayed as a typical governess any more than she is portrayed as a typical romantic heroine. The novel's emphasis is on her unique qualities of character, rather than on her vocation as a teacher. We feel that she has been set apart from governesses in general well before Blanche Ingram launches her attack on that 'anathematized race' (2.2; p.177). Nevertheless, the governess novel was so widely familiar that Brontë's novel was indeed identified by some of its original readers as a version of the genre. The *Christian Remembrancer* reviewer was sure that the 'intensity of feeling' with which the novel portrayed 'a despised and slighted governess' indicated that its author had been a member of 'this ... class' (in Allott, 1974, p.89). The degree of public familiarity with governess fiction is indicated by the way in which Elizabeth Rigby reviewed both *Jane Eyre* and William Makepeace Thackeray's *Vanity Fair* (1847–8) in terms of the governess genre. She then completed the same article with a notice of the Report for 1847 of the Governesses' Benevolent Institution.

The 'heroine' of Thackeray's novel, Becky Sharp, sometime governess, attempts to make her fortune by marrying into her employer's family. Rigby saw Jane as a priggish Becky Sharp, less attractive because given to hypocritical moralizing about her quest for wealth and status (in Allott, 1974, pp.107–8). Rigby also saw Jane as 'merely another Pamela', the virtuous servant who, in Richardson's novel, persists in resisting the improper advances of her employer until he offers to marry her (in ibid., p.106). One of the novels specifically mentioned at the beginning of Brontë's work, *Pamela* is a text which significantly influenced the governess genre (1.1; p.9).

**At this point it would be useful to reread volume 2, chapter 2, noticing ways in which, in this chapter at least, it might be possible to read *Jane Eyre* as a governess novel.**

Jane's experience here is specifically that of a governess. The humiliating scene in which Blanche and her mother criticize governesses in Jane's hearing is typical of countless similar scenes in governess novels. (Jane Austen's *Emma* also alludes to this convention when describing the patronizing rudeness with which Jane Fairfax, a former governess, is regarded.) At this point, the novel dramatizes a contest between different novelistic genres: Blanche and the other fashionable guests whose arrival is described in this chapter, can be seen as representative of the genteel 'silver fork' novels of high society, such as those written by Countess Blessington (1789–1849), author of *Lionel Deerhurst; or, Fashionable Life Under the Regency*. Emphasizing Blanche Ingram's patently unjust criticism of governesses, Brontë apparently champions serious domestic fiction against the 'novel of fashionable life' with which characters like Blanche, or Jane's cousin Georgiana Reed, 'beguile' their time and identify themselves (2.6; p.234; 2.3; p.189; 2.6; p.237). The governess novel is thus maintained as a relevant model alongside which to read *Jane Eyre*. It forms one example of how the variety of genres referred to in Brontë's text enables her novel to engage with a corresponding multiplicity of contemporary issues and debates. We have already noticed how concern about the treatment and education of children is conveyed through allusions to the genres of the foundling and social comment novels. Our further exploration of the generic make-up of *Jane Eyre* during the course of chapters 4 and 5 will also highlight the novel's engagement with such discourses as religion, psychology and race. Meanwhile, references to the governess novel, and to several of the other genres we will go on to discuss, give *Jane Eyre* a manifest connection with the 'Woman Question' debate.

'It has no learning, no research, it discusses no subject of public interest', wrote Brontë of her novel in a letter to her publisher. 'A mere domestic novel will, I fear, seem trivial to men of large views and solid attainments' (in Helsinger *et al.*, 1983, vol.3, p.66). Whilst this expresses some anxiety that her novel would be regarded as 'merely' domestic, it is important to realize that realist domestic fiction in the 1840s was not as common as it was to become a decade later. Many of *Jane Eyre*'s first reviewers *praised* it because it *was* a 'domestic' novel and thus offered a refreshing change from the sentimental romances currently published in vast quantities by publishers such as the Minerva Press. 'It is one of the most powerful domestic romances which have been published for many years', proclaimed a review in the *Atlas*, meaning this as a compliment upon the novel's originality (in Allott, 1974, p.67). 'It is no mere novel, for there is nothing but nature and truth about it, and its interest is entirely domestic', agreed the review in the *Era* (in ibid., p.78). 'One of the most notable domestic novels', proclaimed the *People's Journal* (in ibid., p.80). In *Blackwood's Magazine*, John Eagles saw the novel as symptomatic of the end to an age of 'sickly sentimentality' (in ibid., p.95). As for any lack of 'learning', Thackeray (with Lewes, one of the few commentators to guess that *Jane Eyre*'s author might be a woman) noted that 'if a woman she knows her languages better than most ladies do, or has had a "classical education"' (in ibid., p.70). As for 'subject[s] of public interest', the plight of the governess and the general state of women's education certainly qualified as such.

## The governess and the 'Woman Question'

The governess was a topic as popular in fact as it was in fiction. Significant in terms of the novel's social context, of course, is the fact that Jane earns some measure of independence as a governess. The question of her financial security is undeniably a crucial one, and as such it reflects the vulnerable material circumstances of innumerable actual governesses. Public debate registered increasing concern over the situation of unemployed governesses and the exploitation of those in service. The Governesses' Mutual Assurance Society (1829) and the Governesses' Benevolent Institution (1841) were founded in response to the hardships suffered by governesses, especially those who became unemployed. Such organizations publicized the plight of the governess, provoking considerable alarm. After all, the problem concerned the middle classes intimately, as this class both provided women for employment as governesses and, increasingly, employed them. Economic crises resulted in numerous middle-class fathers suffering severe loss of income as a result of which they were unable to support unmarried daughters. Jane's cousins Mary and Diana Rivers become governesses after their father loses money and they have to provide for themselves (3.3; p.343). Of the same class as her employers, yet neither servant nor equal, the governess occupied a difficult position. The Rivers sisters 'each held a situation in families, by whose wealthy and haughty members they were regarded only as humble dependants, and who neither knew nor sought one of their innate excellences, and appreciated only their acquired accomplishments as they appreciated the skill of their cook, or the taste of their waiting woman' (3.4; p.352). When Rochester entertains Blanche Ingram and his other guests at Thornfield, Jane listens to the music and sounds of merriment from below, just as she had done when banished to the nursery by her Aunt Reed. Now, as then, she has 'not the least wish to go into company, for in company I was very rarely noticed' (1.4; p.28). In close proximity, yet an outsider to the family she served, the governess's role offered scant fulfilment for a seeker after hearth and home like Jane Eyre. In addition, with professions for women severely restricted, unemployment could bring terrible poverty.

One response to this worrying situation took the form of campaigns to enhance the status of governesses by improving their education and professional qualifications. Christian Socialists, Methodists and other religious and philanthropic affiliations were involved in attempts to achieve this. In the year of *Jane Eyre*'s publication, a series of lectures for women led to the founding in London of Queen's College in 1848, followed by the founding of Bedford College in 1849. There was a Ladies' Branch of the 'College of Preceptors' which was founded in 1846 for the improvement of the teaching profession. The College established its own periodical, the *Educational Times*, in 1847, publishing articles which defended the necessity for women to improve their educational attainments and to sit examinations by which they could be judged as properly qualified. The journal was intended primarily for '*professional educators*', but was also described as of interest to '*parental educators*' ([Mrs Bakewell] 'Editor', 1850, p.18). This recommendation was made by Mrs Bakewell, who was both editor of the Methodist *British Mothers' Magazine* and a leading member of the College of Preceptors – a combination of roles that aptly illustrates how closely contemporary debate over women's education was linked with the formation of domestic ideology. Debate about the education of governesses thus formed a specific part of the 'Woman Question' debate about what woman, in general, should be educated *for*. **Can you identify a broad critique of female education in *Jane Eyre* as well as particular concern over the status of the governess?**

The novel does offer general comment about the effects of a conventional female education. Blanche Ingram, for example, provides a striking model of the conventionally 'accomplished' woman. We appreciate that Jane herself has gained an education at Lowood, superior, despite its faults, to that of the frivolously accomplished lady. Blanche's talents are displayed in a way that immediately marks her out as detestable:

> Miss Ingram, who had now seated herself with proud grace at the piano, spreading out her snowy robes in queenly amplitude, commenced a brilliant prelude; talking meantime. She appeared to be on her high horse to-night; both her words and her air seemed intended to excite not only the admiration, but the amazement of her auditors. (2.2; p.179)

Later, her musical accomplishment provides the opportunity for a public flirtation with Rochester as Blanche accompanies his fine singing voice. Such accounts are commonplace in nineteenth-century fiction. Similar scenes are to be found in Anne Brontë's novels, and in the novels of Elizabeth Gaskell, especially her *Wives and Daughters* (1866). Perhaps you are reminded of aspects of Jane Austen's satirical portrayal of the results of female training in *Northanger Abbey*? You will certainly encounter a further critique of women's education in George Eliot's *Middlemarch* (1872) and in other of the novels discussed in this series.

Like these novels, *Jane Eyre* made a contribution – a dangerously radical one in the view of some of Brontë's contemporaries – to a fiercely contested ideological debate over woman's role and nature. In this respect, we can uncover an important intertextual relationship between *Jane Eyre* and the contemporary genre of the advice manual (a genre significant also for Eliot's work and for that of other female novelists of the time). Innumerable advice books and journals were published during the period, commenting on the educational attainments relevant for women's social and, above all, domestic roles. Many of their authors came from an evangelical or non-conforming religious background. Amongst these, the most popular and prolific was Sarah Ellis, born a Quaker, later an evangelical Anglican. Her works include titles such as *The Wives of England: Their Relative Duties, Domestic Influence, and Social Obligations* (1843) and a considerable quantity of domestic moral fiction besides.

Generalizations about Victorian gender ideology often imply that definitions of woman's nature and proper role were commonly understood and accepted. It is crucial for us to recognize that the domestic ideology of the time was not fixed, but was constantly questioned and redefined. The number of advice books in existence testifies to the extent to which the role of the woman was seen to require debate. These advice books varied considerably in their views on the extent of education necessary for women. None the less, it is fair to say that in general, advice material, and other contexts within which the Woman Question was debated, reveal an abhorrence of the 'vanity' and 'self-display' encouraged by too great an emphasis on conventional accomplishments. Brontë's portrayal of Blanche Ingram thus has affinities with views common to much advice literature as well as with those of more radical critics of female education such as Mary Wollstonecraft, who had maintained that, for women educated only in seductive accomplishments, marriage was a form of legalized prostitution. Like Rochester's former mistress, Céline Varens, Blanche exerts her siren charms to lure him. This parallel might lead us to consider whether her potential status as Rochester's wife would differ from Céline's only in its legality.

Jane herself plays the piano only 'a *little*' as Rochester sardonically affirms (1.13; p.124). Instead she paints, also a traditional accomplishment, but represented by Brontë as a valuable mode of self-expression, free from the commodifying self-display of musical performance. Jane's limitations as a pianist can be seen to count in her favour. She avoids any possibility of the artificial display and artful flirtation indulged in by Blanche, who for all her pride, is essentially educated for nothing more than the marriage-market, her sexual allure her only mode of exerting a temporary power. The piano, together with numerous trivial occupations, is also emblematic of the intolerable restrictions of enforced passivity which are placed upon women by their confinement within the domestic sphere. This is clear from Jane's statement about women's need for an active life in which she rails against the opinion that they 'ought to confine themselves to making puddings and knitting stockings, to playing on the piano and embroidering bags' (1.12; p.109). Jane's 'failure' to fulfil the musical duties conventionally expected of a dependent governess operates as an asset in her struggle for greater independence. During their engagement, Rochester has to accompany his own singing after Jane bungles his accompaniment (2.9; p.271). Albeit that Jane and Rochester's social positions are extremely unequal at this stage, Jane's lack of pianistic skill frees her from one aspect of the subservient role which would otherwise befall her (either as governess, mistress or wife).

The governess is in an especially anomalous position. Her duties are largely those of a mother, yet she performs them for hire. This dichotomy generated a considerable amount of anxiety. **Please read Mary Poovey, 'The**

**anathematized race: the governess and *Jane Eyre*' (1989, pp.126–48; extract in Regan, 2001). What are the most important insights we gain from Poovey's investigation of *Jane Eyre*'s engagement with contemporary domestic ideology?**

Notice that Poovey discusses not just contemporary concern over the plight of the governess, but ways in which governesses were seen as potentially threatening to family stability. She highlights the analogies implicit between the governess and the other woman from whom a wifely function could be procured for cash: the prostitute. The governess, as Poovey outlines, was frequently allied with the fallen woman in contemporary literature. Her position as a single female within middle- and upper-class households and the poverty she often faced presented a real risk of this fate. 'You are not what you ought to be' the Rivers's servant Hannah tells Jane (3.2; p.335). Jane is anxious to avoid the fate of Céline Varens (2.9; p.270; 3.1; p.311). Opera singer and kept woman (the two frequently synonymous at the time), Céline pursued one of the few professions open to women. Jane Eyre the governess pursues another. Perhaps Brontë's emphasis on Jane's lack of beguiling accomplishments bespeaks anxiety to dissociate her from this connection with the fallen woman, as much as from the objectified members of her own class. Anne Brontë's *The Tenant of Wildfell Hall* (1848) dramatizes just such a connection in the character of the 'governess' Miss Meyers, mistress to the heroine's husband, whose sole attainment is that, like Blanche, she can play the piano and sing.

Brontë is careful not to give Jane a conventional education and aspirations. Other teachers and governesses in the novel – Miss Temple, Diana and Mary Rivers – together with Helen Burns, provide the positive examples on which Jane partly models herself. Whilst the contrasts drawn between Jane and Blanche Ingram endorse many of the strictures common to domestic-advice literature, this is not to suggest that the novel's interests are identical to it. Sarah Ellis, the advice author mentioned earlier, was more struck, in the 1850s, with *Jane Eyre*'s 'glaring violations of good taste'. Fiction itself tended to be regarded as suspect by such authors unless composed specifically so as to 'elevate' or 'improve' the reader. Although she acknowledged the novel's emotive power, Ellis concluded that it represented a form of literature 'as unhealthy as it is absorbing' (in Glen, 1997, p.2). Moreover, the novel's positive representation of professional teachers and its protest against domestic constraints is a challenge to the emphasis in most advice material on woman's 'naturally' domestic role. This is an issue on which Brontë also expressed herself strongly outside her fictional writing: 'give [women's] existence some object – their time some occupation', she implored in a letter to her publisher, echoing Jane's assertion of women's need for 'a field for their efforts' (in McNees, 1996, vol.1, p.417; *Jane Eyre*, 1.12; p.109). Advice authors frequently advocated improvements in female education on the basis that, as mothers, women played a crucial role in the education of the next generation. In the case of Adèle, Jane's position as governess makes her a professional substitute mother-figure whose role as an educator is also a crucial reforming one – since Adèle, as she first appears, presents a miniature of the female vanity and self-display caricatured in Blanche Ingram. We may not see that Adèle receives much of an education at Jane's hands, and it would obviously be going too far to suggest we read *Jane Eyre* as a novel of vocation, which primarily extols the role of governess. Nevertheless, the novel implicitly comments on the state of contemporary female education and makes a radical claim for women's right to professional rather than merely domestic labour. Moreover, one implication of Jane's frustration with her lot at Thornfield, and subsequent offer to serve as St John's 'curate', is that opportunities for female professionalism should extend well beyond the relatively domestic role of the governess (3.9; p.413). This might also be read as a vindication of the professional woman author and of her authority to speak beyond the domestic sphere. 'Domestic' fiction is anything but non-political. It may reveal connections between supposedly separate private and public spheres and challenge male dominance of remunerative forms of labour – including authorship. Terry Eagleton, in an introduction to the second edition of *Myths of Power*, links the novel's formal plurality with resistance to patriarchy. He suggests that the 'discrepancy of *genres*' in Brontë's work might be seen as 'a radical challenge to orthodox realism ... to those seamless, organic, homogenous literary forms which have been the traditional prerogative of men' (1988, p.xvi). We might have difficulty identifying any novel which, on close examination, would represent the 'seamless, organic, homogenous' form of which Eagleton speaks. The extreme and conspicuous multiplicity of genres in *Jane Eyre* may none the less suggest a significant link between gender and genre.

# The Gothic

For the first volume of *Jane Eyre*, and for the first chapters set at Thornfield, the realist domestic modes of the foundling and governess novels dominate the foreground of the text. However, if readers are beginning to formulate any comfortable set of expectations in accordance with this, they are promptly to be startled out of their composure, as is Jane herself, by Bertha's 'preternatural' laughter (1.11; p.107). This signals the decisive introduction of the Gothic, a further crucial generic strand which thoroughly confuses any assumptions about the novel which may have survived the mixture of genres we have already encountered. Fantastical, romantic, uncanny: the Gothic joins domestic-realist governess fiction to become one of the most pervasive modes operating within the novel.

By now, we recognize that *Jane Eyre* combines elements of a variety of autobiographical forms, the social comment novel, the governess novel, the Gothic and other literary modes. **So what kind of novel *is Jane Eyre*? Does any one recognizable genre predominate in your view of the text?**

As different modes of writing are introduced we have constantly to revise and reform our assumptions about what kind of novel *Jane Eyre* is. This process of exploration on the part of the reader is a major part of the text's fascination. It is not so easy to predict how Jane's story will develop – or end. Even when we discover how the plot ends, the conglomeration of generic forms continues to make interpretation problematic, no matter how many times we read the novel.

The twentieth-century critic who has most influentially theorized the operation of different generic forms within fiction is Mikhail Bakhtin (1895–1975). Bakhtin devised the concept of 'dialogic form' to describe novels where a medley of competing 'voices' interrupt but do not silence one another. The Bakhtinian term for this blending of genres is 'hybridization'. A Bakhtinian account of *Jane Eyre* is provided in Jerome Beaty's *Misreading Jane Eyre* (1996) and my own generic 'map' of the novel is indebted to this. *Jane Eyre* is both connected to the other novels of its time and unique in the particular combination of genres through which it offers its readers a new kind of novel. In Bakhtinian terms, the mixture of genres within *Jane Eyre* makes it a 'hybrid' novel of enormous originality. In fact, as we have already established, *Jane Eyre* is a novel that has specifically advertised its hybrid status from the start. We began by noticing its incorporation of Bewick's also extremely hybrid text: his work mixes romantic poetry and prose with natural history and visual iconography. We then noted allusions to a number of specific book-titles which illustrate an even wider range of generic type. Brontë does not merely list these but actually demonstrates how elements of such disparate genres might be brought together. In Bessie's fascinating tales the older Jane recognizes a blending of 'fairy tales and older ballads' and scenes 'from the pages of *Pamela*, and Henry, Earl of Moreland' (1.1; p.9). Brontë's own text maintains an equivalent degree of generic freedom.

Different genres may dominate at different times, suggesting discrete interpretative models in accordance with the ideologies – religious, moral, romantic and so forth – which are most associated with them. But in the hybrid novel, no genre ever dominates exclusively. Generic modes which have been suggested, and which then recede, never fall entirely silent, but continue to echo within the text as disturbingly as does Bertha's uncanny laughter.

Once Bertha's 'demoniac' laugh has been heard for the first time, we become more conscious of the extent to which the Gothic has always been a significant presence in the novel. **What aspects of *Jane Eyre* would you define as Gothic? Your study of the Gothic in *Northanger Abbey* may help you here. You might begin by looking through chapters 1–3 of *Jane Eyre*.**

On a second reading it is especially clear how powerfully the Gothic pervades the novel's opening chapters. The scene is set by the eerie and frightening illustrations in Bewick depicting graves, fiends and moonlight. Jane's assertiveness distinguishes her from the typical passive Gothic heroine, but her confinement and mental collapse in the red-room none the less echo the plight of countless incarcerated Gothic heroines. The madwoman, and especially the incarcerated wife, were stock motifs of Gothic fictions such as Ann Radcliffe's *A Sicilian Romance* ([1790] 1998), a brief and enjoyable example of the form (still in print), which you may wish to read. Radcliffe is, of course, the novelist whose works haunt the imagination of the heroine of *Northanger Abbey*. You may have noticed that *Jane Eyre* shares many details of plot with Austen's novel: the journey to the forbidding mansion, the theme of the incarcerated wife, and many other details which you will be able to recall for yourself. These parallels between the Gothic elements in the two novels are coincidental – in the sense that Brontë had not read any Austen when she wrote *Jane Eyre* – but they serve to emphasize the familiarity of the elements most typical of the Gothic genre. Resemblances between Radcliffe, Austen and Brontë in this case are underpinned by their shared reference to another familiar genre, the fairytale. The Bluebeard story, to which they are all indebted, is central to much Gothic literature, particularly to those works which Ellen Moers (1976) defined as belonging to a tradition of 'female Gothic'. Moers reads the incarceration of a female character as emblematic of the position of women within Victorian domesticity and marriage, and this view of the Gothic is central to Sandra M. Gilbert and Susan Gubar's (1979) influential reading of *Jane Eyre* in *The Madwoman in the Attic*. We will be considering their approach in chapter 5, alongside a number of alternative readings.

Brontë's powerful internalizing technique allowed her to exploit Gothic conventions to enhance the portrayal of her heroine's inner life. Robert B. Heilman's essay on Brontë's 'new' Gothic is a classic of Brontë criticism, and discusses ways in which she mobilizes Gothic conventions to enhance the psychological power of her work. **Read Robert B. Heilman, 'Charlotte Brontë's "new" Gothic' ([1958] 1970, pp.98–101, 108–9; extract in Regan, 2001). What are the most important points Heilman makes? Do you agree with him?**

Heilman argues that Brontë transforms the conventions of the Gothic mode, investing it with real expressive power as part of the symbolic structure of her book. He sees her as using the Gothic to further her profound explorations of psychology and to facilitate her vivid and unconventional representations of passionate emotion. He distinguishes Brontë's Gothic from what he terms 'old Gothic', or 'straight Gothic', both because it is integral to the psychological interpretation in which her novel engages, and because she repeatedly modifies 'straight Gothic' by juxtaposing it with realist and even humorous detail. Heilman's verdict on Brontë's achievement of psychological realism echoes Lewes's judgement that 'Reality – deep, significant reality – is the great characteristic of the book' (in Allott, 1974, p.84). However, unlike Lewes, and many of the novel's subsequent critics, who saw the mad wife as one of the novel's weaknesses, Heilman concludes that the Gothic aspects of *Jane Eyre* 'increase wonderfully the sense of reality in the novel' (1970, p.109).

Since Heilman's essay was written, critical views on what he styles 'primitive Gothic' have changed. Readers of Ann Radcliffe, for example, would be less likely now to regard her as merely the practitioner of 'the relatively crude mechanisms of fear' (Heilman, 1970, p.98). Rather than the disparagement Heilman records, Brontë's use of the Gothic has correspondingly become the focus of intense interest, especially amongst feminist critics. Heilman is not writing from a feminist viewpoint. He also writes on the assumption that realism is the superior fictional mode and defends Brontë's use of the Gothic as ultimately enhancing the reality of her text. Recent criticism has been less concerned to defend the novel as realist. However, accounts of the Gothic in *Jane Eyre* owe much to Heilman's insights. His essay marks an important point in Brontë criticism, after which the workings of the Gothic in her text, its relation to the realist elements of the novel and its psychological importance, have received serious attention. 'Not only is Thornfield more realistically drawn than, say, Otranto or Udolpho', agree Gilbert and Gubar, 'it is more metaphorically radiant than most gothic mansions: it is the house of Jane's life' (1979, p.347).

Numerous critics have identified the third storey of Thornfield as emblematic of Jane's consciousness, and the madwoman Bertha as having an important, potentially parallel relationship to her. Does the third storey of Thornfield embody Jane Eyre's own repressed anger and rebellion, or does it contain a terrible madness which she must avoid? This question will be explored in some detail in chapter 5, which will investigate readings of the novel by several critics who see Bertha as having a significance that expands well beyond the Gothic genre. First, however, I should like to look more closely at how Gothic and realist elements interact in the novel. **Look again at volume 1, chapter 11. Which details are realist – or, more specifically, domestic – and which are Gothic? Does your view of which is which change, or become confused, on rereading?**

Jane reflects that the 'narrow, low, and dim' third-storey corridor is 'like a corridor in some Bluebeard's castle'. Immediately, as if in response to this thought, Bertha's 'preternatural' laugh is heard for the first time (1.11; p.107). Now we are firmly in the realm of the Gothic. Thinking back, we recognize how consistently Gothic and realist elements have been combined. We remember the apprehension Jane felt at not being met at the inn on her arrival, and on her strange dark journey to Thornfield Hall. The warmth of Jane's reception has since allayed her fears, Mrs Fairfax, her 'modern' bedroom – these things offer reassurance. The governess-novel mode is reaffirmed by Jane's favourable comparison between this welcome and the usual treatment of governesses (1.11; p.96). Perhaps this is to be a governess tale of the providential kind? Jane offers a prayer of thanks, the first explicit reference to religion since she expressed her doubts on that subject at the death of Helen Burns. Life seems secure, boring even, despite the necessity to pass up dark stairways and along galleries hung with portraits, with doors opening into a multitude of disused rooms (1.11; pp.97–8). Thornfield is church-like and 'A very chill and vault-like air pervaded the stairs and gallery' (1.11; p.97). Jane looks in on Mrs Fairfax as she dusts the unoccupied downstairs rooms. Notwithstanding the mundanity of Mrs Fairfax's comfortable domestic occupation, the room is damp, 'the air feels chilly', and the drawing-room 'feels like a vault' (1.11; p.104). They make a tour of the third storey, discussing it as a fitting haunt for a ghost (1.11; p.106). The furnishings are antiquated, macabre relics of antiquity: the fingers which undertook 'half-effaced embroideries' now 'coffin-dust' (1.11; p.105). We think back to the red-room: the former inhabitant of the old-fashioned mahogany bed also well on the way to being coffin-dust.

Later, we recognize that the red-room has also prefigured the gory chamber of horrors in which Jane (locked in once more) tends Mason, with Bertha snarling on the other side of the door, shadows gathering 'under the hangings of the vast old bed' and over the other bizarre furnishings of the room as she wipes away the 'trickling gore' from Mason's wound (2.5; p.210). Then there is the terrifying 'apparition' of Bertha herself in Jane's bedroom at Thornfield, and the final revelation of Bertha raging in her attic 'cell'. You will find a wealth of further

Gothic detail to add to what Jane describes as 'the web of horror' when rereading these chapters (2.5; p.210).

This image reminds us that the Gothic is frequently seen as analogous to the 'literature of horror'. I should like to amplify this account of the Gothic by investigating how it relates to the operation of the uncanny more generally within the novel. The uncanny is not, of course, an effect exclusive to Gothic literature, but is an element within numerous genres. However, with the Gothic so overwhelmingly present in *Jane Eyre*, uncanny effects frequently operate so as to augment its psychological power.

# The uncanny

'Here then I was in the third story, fastened into one of its mystic cells; night around me; a pale and bloody spectacle under my eyes and hands' (2.5; p.209). After hearing Bertha's 'goblin ha! ha!' we too began to ask 'what crime was this, that lived incarnate in this sequestered mansion' (2.5; pp.208, 210)? This is something we certainly might describe as 'uncanny'. We all have our own ideas about what is experienced as uncanny. **Can you define what you think of as 'uncanny' in general? What are some uncanny features of *Jane Eyre*?**

Here is a suggestion by two critics, Andrew Bennett and Nicholas Royle, of some of the essential features of the uncanny:

> The uncanny has to do with a sense of strangeness, mystery or eeriness. More particularly it concerns a sense of unfamiliarity which appears at the very heart of the familiar, or else a sense of familiarity which appears at the very heart of the unfamiliar. The uncanny is not just a matter of the weird or spooky, but has to do more specifically with a disturbance of the familiar. (1995, p.33)

The German romantic writer Schelling defined the uncanny in terms pertinent to the role of Bertha within *Jane Eyre* as that which 'ought to have remained ... secret and hidden but has come to light' (quoted in Freud, [1919] 1985, p.34). The third storey of Thornfield could certainly be described as the *locus suspectus* (literally 'suspect place') which Freud was to cite as the Latin equivalent of the uncanny in his account of E.T.A. Hoffmann, another German romantic and master of the uncanny (Freud, 1985, p.341). The German term for the uncanny is also literally appropriate: there is something *unheimlich* (literally 'un-homely') within the walls of Thornfield. Thornfield seems to Jane a 'home of the past' and 'a shrine of memory' (1.11; pp.105–6). We subsequently discover how literally it houses Rochester's past. Uncanny and Gothic elements of the novel also include strange affinities and portents of the future in the form of dreams or the natural phenomena of storm and moonlight.

Brontë gives this aspect of the uncanny explicit house-room in the chapter which begins:

> Presentiments are strange things! And so are sympathies; and so are signs: and the three combined make one mystery to which humanity has not yet found the key. I never laughed at presentiments in my life; because I have had strange ones of my own. Sympathies I believe exist: (for instance, between far-distant, long-absent, wholly estranged relatives; asserting, notwithstanding their

alienation, the unity of the source to which each traces his origin) whose workings baffle mortal comprehension. And signs, for aught we know, may be but the sympathies of Nature with man. (2.6; p.220)

**Could this effectively amount to an exposition of Brontë's own narrative method, embodying, as discussed at the beginning of this chapter, the 'sympathies of Nature with man'?**

Certainly it would appear to constitute a defence of specific details of Brontë's plot: proleptic weather-signs, splitting trees, visionary moonlight, moments of strange coincidence, or of uncanny sympathy – above all, Rochester's disembodied voice. This undeniably uncanny instance is prefigured in previous descriptions in the narrative of these 'sympathies of Nature', including the heightened perception of sound travelling over distance which preludes Jane's first meeting with Rochester. Here she describes a transcendent moment as she looks towards Hay, 'which, half lost in trees ... was yet a mile distant':

> but in the absolute hush I could hear plainly its thin murmurs of life. My ear too felt the flow of currents; in what dales and depths I could not tell but there were many hills beyond Hay, and doubtless many becks threading their passes. That evening calm betrayed alike the tinkle of the nearest streams, the sough of the most remote. (1.12; p.111)

This portrayal of the natural world, animated by currents in the air, could be described as uncanny in that inanimate nature is given attributes of life. Brontë here implicitly evokes the romantic image of the aeolian harp (a structure of horizontal strings, suitable for placing on a window ledge, which would emit sympathetic vibrations of sound when the wind passed through it). Romantic poets such as Coleridge frequently used the aeolian harp to emblematize a view of all organic nature inspired by one 'intellectual breeze' ('The Eolian Harp' (1795), line 47). It is an emblem of sympathy inherently invoked in the images of inspiriting wind that guide Jane's path from the Lowood portion of the novel onwards, becoming portentous blasts of storm after her engagement to Rochester (2.8; p.256). Is his disembodied voice perhaps an aeolian harp effect on a magnified scale? Brontë's insistence that it is the 'work of nature ... no miracle – but her best' would seem to propose such an explanation, yet we feel no certainty about how to read the event, which therefore remains an uncanny one (3.9; p.420).

Brontë's habitual depiction of internalized natural landscapes makes this 'work of nature' open to comprehension as either an acoustic or a psychological effect – or even as a psychic phenomenon. 'Telepathy' was a term not coined until the 1880s, but it is one that we might now employ to define the kind of 'sympathy' which the narrator and the narrative invoke. The intense affinities between Jane and Rochester, and between Jane and her external surroundings, might also be described as telepathic. When Rochester and Jane are sitting in the Thornfield garden, he suggests that they are joined by a cord running between their two hearts, a metaphor for the 'communion' between them which can simultaneously be read in biblical, physical and psychic terms (2.7; p.252). The garden is 'Eden-like' and Rochester's image of 'a string somewhere under my left ribs' echoes the passage in the Book of Genesis (2:21–2) where God fashions Eve out of Adam's rib (2.8; pp.248, 252). A physical 'string' joins Jane and

Rochester at the ribs, and 'cord' is a word often applied to the structures of the human body that are cord-like, such as the spinal, umbilical or vocal cords. At the same time, it suggests the sympathetic harmonies of a musical chord, as an emblem of their affinity (the *Oxford English Dictionary* explains that 'cord' and 'chord' are interchangeable spellings). A similar compound of associations with this image is widely to be found in Victorian writing. Metaphors derived from the sympathetically vibrating c[h]ords of musical instruments were often used to describe nervous and emotional response in scientific as well as in imaginative literature. G.H. Lewes was a scientist as well as a man of letters and wrote a number of accounts of the physical acoustics of sympathetic vibration and the physiology of nervous response. In his 1847 review of *Jane Eyre* his description of the emotional effect of the novel echoes Brontë's imagery: 'There is a chord in the human breast which vibrates sympathetically whenever it be touched' (in Allott, 1974, p.84). Like Lewes's imagery here, Rochester's cord operates as an embedded reference to the aeolian harp. The uncanny makes us uncertain. Rochester's 'cord' and his disembodied voice hover equivocally about the borders of the psychological, physical, perhaps even mystical and supernatural significance. If they are the work of nature, they are none the less uncanny.

Allied with the romantic and the uncanny, the Gothic, then, is in many respects in tension with the realistic domestic mode of the governess novel. We might define the mixing of genres in *Jane Eyre* as the ultimately uncanny aspect of the text, constantly disrupting our sense of what is familiar, or indeed unfamiliar. **What are the most significant contradictions – and connections – which you perceive between the Gothic and the realist elements in the novel?**

The dialogue in the novel between the Gothic and the governess modes is a conspicuous example of countless negotiations between forms of realism and romance. We could argue that, despite obvious contrasts, the two genres arc fundamentally linked in *Jane Eyre* through their respective central figures: the governess and the madwoman. The governess, we know, could represent a disturbing figure in Victorian society, 'Gothic' not just by virtue of her own incarceration. (The narrator in Henry James's *The Turn of the Screw* (1898) is the most famous literary example of an ambiguous governess figure.) We have mentioned affinities between the governess and the fallen woman, through which the governess may embody fears of the sexual depravity latent within respectable womankind. The governess was also frequently associated with that other 'outsider' to society in Victorian literature, the madwoman. There were fears that the repressive conditions of her employment and her spinsterhood might unsettle the governess's reason. So too, paradoxically, might the results of her vulnerability to sexual temptation. Female sexual appetite was widely associated with insanity in popular medical literature of the period. Bertha, according to Rochester, is 'unchaste' (3.1; p.306). One of the many contradictions arising from Victorian gender discourse is that, for women, both emotional repression and lack of restraint could lead to madness. The question of how to interpret Jane Eyre's relationship with the madwoman is one we shall explore in more detail in chapter 5.

Several critics have identified an increasing dominance of fantasy over realism in *Jane Eyre* from the point at which the Gothic becomes conspicuously present on Thornfield's third storey. The novel appears less realist as images that previously inhabited Jane's imagination – wilderness, fire, terrifying apparitions, the possession of home and family – become manifested at the level of plot. However, whilst concrete realization of events figuratively foreshadowed in the novel's opening chapters certainly proliferates, connections with realist modes of narrative are also maintained. **To explore this mixture of realism and romance further, reread volume 1, chapter 12, taking particular note of transitions between contrasting modes of writing.**

# Rochester and romance

Before we have had time to take much stock of the Gothic/domestic hybrid novel in which we have become enmeshed after Jane's visits to the third storey of Thornfield, Rochester arrives on the scene. His first appearance is Gothic. Jane's recollection of the 'Gytrash' myth provokes the resurfacing of Bessie's tales about ghosts and superstitions. However, the 'spell' which her terror casts over her is quickly 'broken' by Rochester's fall (1.12; p.112). The ensuing crash also signals a rapid transition from one set of generic expectations to another. The Gothic fades into the background glimmer, and, with Rochester fulminating on the ground, we too come back to earth, readers for a time at least, of a realist novel once more. Yet the Gothic lingers on as Jane recounts the psychological aftermath of this episode: she fancies she might see the rider and dog once again, though now she hears 'only the faintest waft of wind, roaming fitful among the trees round Thornfield' (1.12; p.116).

Gothic and realist modes of fiction cohabit at Thornfield. The arrival of Rochester also opens up possibilities for the further development of a realist governess plot. But of what kind? We anticipate a romance, but romance, to quote Beaty, is a 'trans-generic' mode (1996, p.6). Perhaps, as in *Pamela*, the virtuous servant will marry her reformed master. However, the catastrophe of Richardson's *Clarissa* seems equally possible: Rochester may be a seducing rake. Lovelace, Clarissa's aspiring seducer, wishes to load her with clothes and jewels, which, like Jane, Clarissa resists. This echo swells the note of danger already faintly audible amid the exuberance of the exchanges between Jane and Rochester. The potential for a seduction plot is further enhanced by the association of Rochester's name with the infamously libertine seventeenth-century writer, the Earl of Rochester.

The ambiguity of Rochester's character makes numerous outcomes possible. His combination of rude and oddly appealing behaviour suggests the characteristics both of a romantic Byronic hero and of a Gothic villain – owner of 'Bluebeard's castle'. Blanche Ingram imagines herself as the consort to Rochester's Corsair (2.2; p.179), invoking Byron's popular poem *The Corsair* (1814). Blanche constructs Rochester as a passionate, brooding and secretive Byronic hero. Because she is discredited in the novel, Rochester's identification as a Byronic man seems undermined – yet is it entirely? Jane herself describes his 'full falcon-eye flashing' (2.9; p.273). **The following passage from Byron's poem will allow you to think about how Brontë's portrayal of Rochester's physical appearance, demeanour and, above all, rankling secret disappointment, correspond with those of Byron's hero, 'That man of loneliness and mystery' in whose 'form seems little to admire / Though his dark eye-brow shades a glance of fire':**

> No giant frame sets forth his common height;
> ...
> Sun-burnt his cheek, his forehead high and pale
> The sable curls in wild profusion veil;
> And oft perforce his rising lip reveals
> The haughtier thought it curbs, but scarce conceals
> Though smooth his voice, and calm his general mien,
> Still seems there something he would not have seen:
> His features' deepening lines and varying hue
> At times attracted, yet perplexed the view,
> As if within that murkiness of mind
> Worked feelings fearful, and yet undefined.
>
> (Byron, 1981, canto 1, lines 173–212)

'Up the blood rushed to his face; forth flashed the fire from his eyes; erect he sprang ...' (3.1; p.319). Note the poetic inversion of syntax in this series of clauses. Rochester's last attempt to prevent Jane leaving Thornfield gives us the Byronic hero in action.

Rochester's character is connected with a bewildering multiplicity of fictional and psychological types and is too complex to read with confidence, as Jane herself is to discover. The erotic wrangling that constitutes the courtship between Jane and Rochester increases our sense that there are different possible outcomes to their romance. **Reread volume 2, chapter 9, and consider how Rochester's character is portrayed there. Is Rochester Jane's soul mate or an exulting Eastern potentate looking to augment his harem?**

Rochester's shower of gifts threatens to reduce Jane, at best, to the ornamental commodity into which Blanche and Adèle have been groomed, or, worse still, make her the equivalent of one of his kept mistresses. At this stage we cannot be clear whether marriage to him represents romantic escape, domestic security or a form of the slavery with which Jane identified her situation in the Reed household. The disruption of the courtship plot at this stage suggests answers to some of these questions but simultaneously raises others.

# Biblical typology

Revelation of the secret of Bluebeard's castle finally shatters Jane's romance. The Gothic also seems to have run its course. Jane is to become no passive incarcerated heroine. Her escape from Thornfield is a question of survival as well as of moral scruple. Thinking of Céline Varens and her other predecessors in Rochester's affections, she is clear that her fate, should she stay with Rochester, would eventually mirror that of 'these poor girls' (3.1; p.312). With the romance and Gothic modes subdued, Jane's wandering in the wilderness is also a time of generic uncertainty until her arrival at Marsh End seems to re-establish a providential version of the domestic governess novel – at the same time as it fulfils Jane's long quest for hearth and home.

This section of the novel is particularly rich in biblical parallels. Jane sees her dead hopes of romance by analogy with the suddenly slain first-born of Egypt in the Old Testament Book of Exodus (2.11; p.295). This pattern of interpretation according to biblical models follows a practice known as 'biblical typology'. Together with Jane's thankfulness for delivery from the temptation to become Rochester's mistress it seems to reaffirm the importance of providential modes of autobiography. Just as Jane uses biblical types to interpret herself, St John interprets her resistance to his will according to the 'twenty-first chapter of Revelations', threatening her with 'the lake which burneth with fire and brimstone' in return for her fearfulness and unbelief (3.9; pp.416–17). However, Jane crucially does not acknowledge St John's superior authority as 'man and priest' to impose biblical interpretations upon her. In this respect, Jane's rebellion against St John seems especially insurrectionary; 'You are killing me' (3.9; p.412) echoes her frenzied protest against her physical constraint in the red-room: 'I shall be killed' (1.2; p.18). It also recalls her early resistance to Brocklehurst's attempts to impose his interpretations of Scripture upon her. Moreover, Jane's response to Rochester's summons, 'I am coming!', echoes the words of the chapter of Revelation following that which St John quotes (3.9; p.420). Biblical typology is as radically modified as are the other modes on which Brontë draws for her bafflingly original novel.

Rochester and Jane enjoyed a brief sojourn in Eden before the portentous breaking of the storm which split the chestnut tree (2.8; p.257). The implication must be that Jane was beguiled by a false paradise from which a fall will be imminent. Ironically, however, unlike Eve, Jane seemed innocent of conscious transgression. It was Rochester who longed to taste forbidden fruit, and so, in gender terms, at least, the significance of the biblical model was reversed. Now, Jane's obedience to the summons by Rochester's voice both appropriates the providential tradition and subverts it. For this moment of romantic 'sympathy' is simultaneously biblical and Bunyanesque – as are the numerous guiding breezes and portentous storms throughout the novel. The incident when Jane hears Rochester's voice closely echoes a moment in *Grace Abounding* when Bunyan feels 'the noise of the wind upon me' and hears 'a Voice speaking' (quoted in Peterson, 1986, p.10). In Bunyan's text, God addresses the sinner from a cloud and saves him from temptation. Jane previously castigated herself for idolizing Rochester (2.9; p.274). Now, however, it is Rochester's summons she obeys, not God's, inverting and secularizing inherited models.

We have certainly not lost the rebellious Jane of the novel's opening. At this point *Jane Eyre* would seem to be a novel which rejects providence in celebration of its heroine's independence and her claims to passionate fulfilment. As she does not yet know that Bertha is dead, Jane's decision to return to Rochester has potentially radical moral implications. At the same time, the novel remains 'providential' in that the way *is* cleared for Jane's legitimate union with a humbled and newly pious Rochester (3.11; p.446). His summons, moreover, would seem to literalize Jane's 'vocation' as one of domestic wifehood. Can we interpret the novel as an endorsement of romantic rebellion, or of something far more conservative? This question underpins the account in the following chapter of critical debates concerning *Jane Eyre*.

# Works cited

Allott, Miriam. Ed. 1974. *The Brontës: The Critical Heritage*, London: Routledge.

[Mrs Bakewell] 'Editor'. 1850. 'What is the "Royal College of Preceptors"?' *British Mother's Magazine,* vol.6, no.18, pp.17–18.

Beaty, Jerome. 1996. *Misreading Jane Eyre: A Postformalist Paradigm*, Columbus: Ohio State University Press.

Bennett, Andrew and Royle, Nicholas. 1995. *An Introduction to Literature, Criticism and Theory*, Hemel Hempstead: Harvester Wheatsheaf.

Brontë, Charlotte. [1847] 2000. *Jane Eyre*, ed. by Margaret Smith, with an introduction and revised notes by Sally Shuttleworth, Oxford World's Classics, Oxford: Oxford University Press.

Byron, George Gordon. [1814] 1981. *The Corsair: A Tale*, in *The Complete Poetical Works,* vol.3, ed. by J. J. McGann, Oxford: Clarendon Press.

Eagleton, Terry. [1975] 1988. *Myths of Power: A Marxist Study of the Brontës*, 2nd edn, Basingstoke: Macmillan.

Freud, Sigmund. [1919] 1985. 'The "uncanny" ', in *Art and Literature: Jensen's Gradiva, Leonardo da Vinci and Other Works*, The Pelican Freud Library, vol.14, ed. by Albert Dickenson, Harmondsworth: Penguin.

Gilbert, Sandra M. and Gubar, Susan. 1979. *The Madwoman in the Attic: The Woman Writer and the Nineteenth-Century Literary Imagination*, London: Routledge.

Glen, Heather. Ed. 1997. *Jane Eyre*, New Casebooks, Basingstoke: Macmillan.

Heilman, Robert B. [1958] 1970. 'Charlotte Brontë's "new" Gothic', in *The Brontës: A Collection of Critical Essays*, ed. by Ian Gregor, Englewood Cliffs, NJ: Prentice-Hall. (Extract in Regan, 2001.)

Helsinger, Elizabeth K., Sheets, Robert Lauterbach and Veeder, William. Eds. 1983. *The Woman Question: Society and Literature in Britain and America 1837–1883*, 3 vols, Manchester: Manchester University Press.

Lodge, David. 1966. 'Fire and Eyre: Charlotte Brontë's war of earthly elements', in *The Language of Fiction*, London: Routledge.

McNees, Eleanor. Ed. 1996. *The Brontë Sisters: Critical Assessments*, 4 vols, Mountfield: Helm Information.

Moers, Ellen. 1976. *Literary Women: The Great Writers*, New York: Doubleday.

Peterson, Linda H. 1986. *Victorian Autobiography: The Tradition of Self-Interpretation*, New Haven: Yale University Press.

Poovey, Mary. 1989. 'The anathematized race: the governess and *Jane Eyre*', in *Uneven Developments: The Ideological Work of Gender in Mid-Victorian England*, London: Virago. (Extract in Regan, 2001.)

Radcliffe, Ann. [1790] 1998. *A Sicilian Romance*, ed. by Alison Millbank, Oxford: Oxford University Press.

Regan, Stephen. Ed. 2001. *The Nineteenth-Century Novel: A Critical Reader*, London: Routledge.

Stevens, Joan. 1968. '"A sermon in every vignette": Bewick and Brontë', *Turnbull Library Record*, vol.1, no.3, pp.12–28.

Woolf, Virginia. [1923] 1979. '*Jane Eyre* and *Wuthering Heights*', in *Virginia Woolf: Women and Writing*, ed. by Michèle Barrett, London: The Women's Press.

Suggestions for further reading can be found at the end of chapter 5.

# CHAPTER 5
# *Jane Eyre*: inside and out

*by Delia da Sousa Correa*

## Passion and restraint

*Jane Eyre* begins with an act of protest. This powerful opening to Jane's story stays with us and is both reaffirmed and questioned as we read on. The rebellious, passionate Jane is extremely attractive to modern readers and celebrated by critics such as Sandra M. Gilbert and Susan Gubar, whose 1979 study of nineteenth-century women writers, *The Madwoman in the Attic*, has become a classic of Anglo-American feminist criticism. Like Ellen Moers's (1976) *Literary Women* and Elaine Showalter's (1977) *A Literature of their Own*, their book is concerned to establish a specifically female literary tradition. They seek to 'provide models for understanding the dynamics of female literary response to male literary assertion and coercion' (Gilbert and Gubar, 1979, p.xii). Their readings of women writers concentrate on patterns of confinement and escape, which they see as mirroring the conditions of women under domesticity and the woman author's need to escape the patriarchal literary tradition. The key method women writers use to achieve this escape is by 'simultaneously conforming to and subverting patriarchal literary standards' (ibid., p.73).

A complete inversion of Bunyan's *The Pilgrim's Progress* is how Gilbert and Gubar read *Jane Eyre*: Brontë, they argue, borrowed the 'mythic quest-plot' but discarded 'the devout substance' to produce an '"irreligious" redefinition, almost a parody, of John Bunyan's vision' (ibid., pp.336, 370). Gilbert and Gubar see women's writing as fuelled by anger against the oppressions of patriarchy. In their chapter on *Jane Eyre*, they focus on Matthew Arnold's comment that Charlotte Brontë's mind 'contains nothing but hunger, rebellion, and rage' and define *Jane Eyre* as a text which champions repressed female rage (quoted in ibid., p.337).

Gilbert and Gubar's reading of *Jane Eyre* hinges upon the interpretation of Bertha as 'Jane's truest and darkest double ... the angry aspect of the orphan child, the ferocious secret self Jane has been trying to repress ever since her days at Gateshead' (ibid., p.360). Bertha they perceive as enacting Jane's 'disguised hostility' towards Rochester's mastery: attacking Rochester and Mason, tearing the wedding-veil, and finally burning down Thornfield 'as if she were an agent of Jane's desire as well as her own' (ibid.). Moreover, Gilbert and Gubar maintain, 'Bertha not only acts *for* Jane, she also acts *like* Jane.' 'The imprisoned Bertha, running "backwards and forwards" on all fours in the attic', recalls both 'Jane the governess' pacing 'backwards and forwards' along the third-storey corridor, and the 'bad animal' Jane imprisoned and screaming in the red-room (Brontë, [1847] 2000, 1.12; p.109; 1.1; p.9; 1.2; p.17; all subsequent page references are to this edition) (Gilbert and Gubar, 1979, p.361). **What are your**

**initial thoughts on these parallels? What problems, if any, do you perceive in Gilbert and Gubar's approach?**

Whilst their approach provides certain powerful insights into Brontë's text, it can be accused of ignoring the complexities of how issues of passionate expression and self-restraint are portrayed in *Jane Eyre*. After her outburst against Mrs Reed, Jane at first feels a sense of exulting triumph. But this is swiftly followed by 'the pang of remorse and the chill of reaction' at having given her 'furious feelings uncontrolled play' (1.4; p.37). Gilbert and Gubar cite the passage from this scene in which Jane's anger is compared with a ridge of lighted heath as epitomizing the burning anger she represents (1979, p.343). However, they do not complete the quotation: 'the same ridge, black and blasted after the flames are dead, would have represented as meetly my subsequent condition' (1.4; pp.37–8). Jane's initial sense of liberation is succeeded by a perception of 'the dreariness of my hated and hating position' (1.4; p.38). The bleak landscape, in which she then walks, augments this account, the 'congealed relics of autumn' trapped in dreary and negative stasis, with heaps of leaves stiffened together in unmelting ice under an 'opaque sky', and a barren view into 'an empty field where no sheep were feeding, where the short grass was nipped and blanched' (ibid.).

Jane's passionate outburst is thus represented in highly equivocal terms. She is described as wishing to exercise a 'better faculty than that of fierce speaking' and to 'find nourishment for some less fiendish feeling than that of sombre indignation' (ibid.). The critical importance of a balance between passionate expression and control is established very early in the novel: 'half an hour's silence and reflection', she recalls, revealed 'the madness of my conduct' (ibid.). The association of uncontrolled rage with insanity, implicit in the incident of the red-room, is here overt. Gilbert and Gubar describe Jane's incipient madness in the red-room as offering her a mode of 'escape' from confinement (1979, p.341). However, is the 'terrible red glare, crossed with thick black bars' which she sees before her suggestive of escape or rather of imprisonment, such as Bertha suffers (1.3; p.18)? We might wonder whether images of fire are celebratory only, or more ambivalent: suggestive also of self-consuming rage. We might also consider to what extent Jane's subsequent education and training in self-control suggest that she has developed different modes of behaviour since the incident of the red-room. The animal attributes and insanity associated with her there are later transferred to Bertha. Does this suggest parallels and/or a distinction between Jane and Bertha? **To what extent do you accept, reject or want to modify Gilbert and Gubar's reading of the madwoman as a celebration of female rage?**

Gilbert and Gubar's work generates undifferentiated readings of *all* nineteenth-century women's writing as embodying repressed anger against patriarchy. In a review of *The Madwoman in the Attic*, Mary Jacobus suggested that its thesis denies women the 'freedom of being read as more than exceptionally articulate victims of a patriarchally engendered plot'. The authors' preoccupation with 'plot' in the narrative sense, also becomes a

> form of tight lacing which immobilizes the play of meaning in the texts whose hidden plots they uncover. What they find there, again and again, is not just

'plot' but 'author', the madwoman in the attic of their title ... this is a plot
doomed to repetition; their book ... reenacts endlessly the revisionary struggle,
unlocking the secrets of the female text again and again with the same key.

(quoted in Moi, 1988, pp.64, 68)

Feminist critics have certainly taken a variety of views on the relationship
between Jane and Bertha. Elaine Showalter (1977), in *A Literature of their Own*,
saw Helen Burns and Bertha Mason as representing two aspects of Jane's
femininity – self-sacrificing and self-destructively angry – both of which she
must reject. In 'Jane Eyre: the temptations of a motherless woman' (in McNees,
1996, vol.3, pp.226–39), Adrienne Rich has also read Bertha as predominantly a
warning to Jane. Whatever the parallels established between Jane and Bertha,
they are perhaps too complex to allow a reading of Bertha as unambiguously
Jane's double. *Jane Eyre* is neither unequivocal nor univocal. Gilbert and
Gubar's assertion that the enraged double represents the 'true', albeit
duplicitously represented, meaning of women's texts, effectively reduces the
novel to a submerged single-voiced narrative rather than allowing the dialogic
complexity of competing voices which we have been tracing. A question
addressed throughout these chapters is whether we can attain a single 'true'
reading of *Jane Eyre*, or whether we have to recognize a multiplicity of writing
(and thus of meaning) in the novel.

# Nineteenth-century psychology

Gilbert and Gubar provide a powerful psychoanalytical reading of *Jane Eyre* as a
novel that continues to occupy a place of special significance for women readers
today. However, if we try to read the novel as a text of its time, we discover that
considering it alongside theories of psychology contemporary with its
publication, rather than in the light of later Freudian analysis, produces some
very different insights.

   At the time Brontë wrote *Jane Eyre*, the dominant psychological theory was
provided by the science known as 'phrenology', in which Brontë herself took an
intense interest. Phrenology was popularized in England by George Combe. In
*Elements of Phrenology* (1824) and subsequent works, Combe described the
mind in terms of physiologically located faculties which he termed 'organs' of
'veneration', 'beneficence' and so forth (see Figure 5.1). *Jane Eyre* is permeated
with references to phrenology. After her attack on her Aunt Reed, Jane is shown
wishing to exercise a 'better *faculty* [my emphasis] than that of fierce speaking'
(1.4; p.38). An early explicit reference occurs when Jane describes how her
'organ of veneration' is aroused by Miss Temple (1.5; p.47). References to
physiologically located faculties are an aspect of the 'spatial' description of
Jane's psyche, which we noted in chapter 4, in relation to Brontë's depictions of
inner 'landscape'.

   In her book *Charlotte Brontë and Victorian Psychology*, Sally Shuttleworth
(1996) has investigated the significance of phrenological theories for Brontë's
work. Shuttleworth points out that the phrenological doctrine of the
development of individual faculties was especially empowering for women.

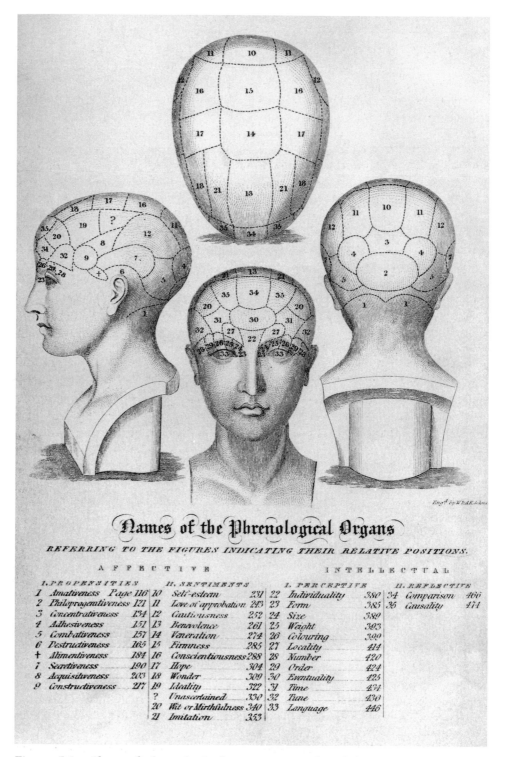

REFERRING TO THE FIGURES INDICATING THEIR RELATIVE POSITIONS.

AFFECTIVE — INTELLECTUAL

| I. PROPENSITIES | II. SENTIMENTS | I. PERCEPTIVE | II. REFLECTIVE |
|---|---|---|---|
| 1 Amativeness Page 116 | 10 Self-esteem 231 | 22 Individuality 380 | 34 Comparison 466 |
| 2 Philoprogenitiveness 121 | 11 Love of approbation 243 | 23 Form 385 | 35 Causality 474 |
| 3 Concentrativeness 134 | 12 Cautiousness 252 | 24 Size 389 | |
| 4 Adhesiveness 151 | 13 Benevolence 261 | 25 Weight 393 | |
| 5 Combativeness 157 | 14 Veneration 274 | 26 Colouring 399 | |
| 6 Destructiveness 165 | 15 Firmness 285 | 27 Locality 414 | |
| + Alimentiveness 184 | 16 Conscientiousness 288 | 28 Number 420 | |
| 7 Secretiveness 190 | 17 Hope 304 | 29 Order 424 | |
| 8 Acquisitiveness 203 | 18 Wonder 309 | 30 Eventuality 425 | |
| 9 Constructiveness 217 | 19 Ideality 322 | 31 Time 434 | |
| | ? Unascertained 350 | 32 Tune 430 | |
| | 20 Wit or Mirthfulness 340 | 33 Language 446 | |
| | 21 Imitation 353 | | |

*Figure 5.1 Chart of phrenological organs. Reproduced from George Combe,* A System of Phrenology, *3rd edn, Edinburgh: John Anderson, 1830, frontispiece. British Library 784.F.14*

Jane's proclamation that women need equal 'exercise for their faculties' (1.12; p.109) can be seen as a very historically specific reason why the novel appeared socially radical to critics such as Elizabeth Rigby (Allott, 1974, pp.90, 109–10). However, whilst Brontë's writing may be full of the 'hunger, rebellion and rage' that Matthew Arnold identified, Shuttleworth's work shows how crucially it is also concerned with self-control.

Combe saw the development of the individual's faculties as vital for both men and women. He defended expression of the passions as part of this process. However, it was essential that the development of the faculties be accompanied by the exercise of self-discipline. After Jane has conceived her wish to exercise a 'better faculty' she is portrayed as eager to acquire the benefits of a disciplined education (1.9; pp.74–5). Despite the sadness of Helen Burns's death, the end of the novel's first volume takes on a more energetic pace as the spring season parallels Jane's mental flowering. Later, her pupils at Morton seem 'hopelessly dull' at first, with 'faculties quite torpid', but become 'sharp-witted' and disciplined under the influence of Jane's training (3.6; pp.365, 366). Brontë especially admired Thackeray as a writer who kept his 'ardour under control' (Wise and Symington, 1993, vol.2, p.21). In *Jane Eyre*, Miss Temple's controlled demeanour, which 'precluded deviation into the ardent, the excited, the eager', may be an advantage (1.8; p.73) rather than merely a sign of extreme repression, as it is viewed by Gilbert and Gubar (1979, p.345).

A productive degree of discipline is contrasted in the novel with the effects of excessive constraint, as when Jane laments her 'stagnation' at Thornfield, where she feels obliged 'to slip ... over my faculties the viewless fetters of an uniform and too still existence' (1.12; pp.109, 116). Later she fears that to become St John's wife would 'stifle half my faculties' (3.8; p.398). St John himself is portrayed in phrenological terms. He complains that his faculties were 'paralyzed' (3.4; p.356) until he resolved to be a missionary, when, 'From that moment my state of mind changed: the fetters dissolved and dropped from every faculty' (3.5; p.362). The disciplining of his competing inclination to marry Rosamond Oliver ultimately liberates his more important energies. Whilst Jane describes St John as out of place at the domestic fireside (3.8; p.393), she recognizes the feverish ambitions which, as his sister describes, burn beneath his cold exterior (3.4; pp.356–7). After St John's narrative in which he describes the discovery of his vocation as a missionary, Jane realizes that 'he could not bound all that he had in his nature – the rover, the aspirant, the poet, the priest – in the limits of a single passion' (3.6; p.368). She agrees that 'He is right to choose a missionary's career' (3.8; p.393).

Brontë frequently uses phrenological vocabulary in her delineations of character. Note how often characters' foreheads, the site of several phrenological 'organs', are described. Miss Temple, whose name prompts both architectural and physiological associations, has an appropriately large 'front' (1.5; p.47), Mrs Reed a low 'brow' (1.4; p.35) and Jane herself a 'clear front' (1.8; p.69). Later, Jane expresses her dislike of Mason's physiognomy: 'unsettled and inanimate', 'no firmness' in the nose and mouth, 'no thought on the low, even forehead; no command in that blank, brown eye' (2.3; p.190). At Marsh End, the Rivers siblings read Jane's features as she lies ill. Diana finds them agreeable. St

John pronounces that she has 'rather an unusual physiognomy: certainly, not indicative of vulgarity or degradation'. However, he is also able to 'trace lines of force in her face which make me sceptical of her tractability' (3.3; p.339). In exchange for this scrutiny, she reads St John: 'Quiescent as he now sat, there was something about his nostril, his mouth, his brow, which, to my perceptions, indicated elements within either restless, or hard, or eager' (3.3; p.345).

Phrenology is often dismissed as a 'pseudoscience'. However, when referring to the time at which Brontë was writing, it is manifestly unfair to call phrenology this. For a start, the definition of what was, or was not, valid science was scarcely fixed at the period, nor for most of the remainder of the nineteenth century. There was no clear agreement amongst scientists on the status of phrenology (or on phenomena such as mesmerism, or spiritualism, which also aroused interest). It is important to remind ourselves how much more fluid the category 'scientific' was at the time. Phrenology became less significant as evolutionary theory gained the ascendancy. George Eliot's *Middlemarch*, as you will discover, is especially engaged with the impact of evolutionary thought. However, Brontë was writing in the years before evolutionary (or 'development') theory had shaped the study of psychology, when phrenology was still the dominant mode of psychological explanation. **Reread volume 1, chapters 13 and 14, and volume 2, chapter 4. What role does phrenology, as I have described it, seem to play in the assessments Jane and Rochester make of each other's character?**

The important conversational encounter between Jane and Rochester in volume 1, chapter 14, includes a phrenological dialogue, beginning 'does my forehead not please you?' (1.14; p.131). Jane's phrenological assessment of Rochester identifies him as lacking in the organ of 'benevolence', though well endowed with 'conscience' (ibid.). (According to Combe, the organ of benevolence was located high on the brow, whilst conscience occupied twin 'bumps' towards the back of the crown.) Brontë emphasizes distinctions between phrenology and other methods of interpreting character from external appearances, including physiognomy (by which facial features alone are seen as a guide to personality). Physiognomy, unsupported by phrenological evidence, is discredited when Lady Ingram sees 'all the faults of her class' in Jane's 'physiognomy' (2.2; p.177). Blanche, after her chastening interview with the 'gypsy' fortune-teller, lumps phrenology together with a thoroughly disreputable means of reading character: 'Really your organs of wonder and credulity are easily excited ... I have seen a gipsy-vagabond; she has practised in hackneyed fashion the science of palmistry, and told me what such people usually tell' (2.3; p.194). This incident may suggest some irony in Brontë's allusions to phrenology. Immediately afterwards, however, this gypsy is to be heard distinguishing phrenology from the palmistry ridiculed by Blanche. The gypsy drops Jane's hand to scrutinize her face and forehead instead: 'what is in a palm? Destiny is not written there.' 'I believe you,' Jane assents. '[I]t is in the face,' the gypsy continues: 'on the forehead, about the eyes, in the eyes themselves, in the lines of the mouth.' 'Ah!', exclaims Jane, 'Now you are coming to reality' (2.4; p.197).

These chapters show Jane and Rochester 'reading' one another. In a review of 1847, the critic H.F. Chorley described their mutual scrutiny in terms which neatly convey its disquieting intensity and the sense that Brontë has created a spatialized landscape of the mind. Chorley admired 'the fearless, original way in which the strong man and the young governess travel over each other's minds till, in a puzzled and uncomfortable manner enough, they come to a mutual understanding' (in Allott, 1974, p.72). From the beginning, Jane interprets Rochester's appearance phrenologically: a 'square forehead ... decisive nose, full nostrils denoting, I thought, choler ... grim mouth, chin and jaw' (1.13; p.119). Rochester gains some initial insight into Jane's personality from his scrutiny of her paintings. Now, Rochester's reading of Jane's eye, mouth and especially her brow, emphasizes a contest between strong passion and rational control:

> that brow professes to say, – 'I can live alone, if self-respect and circumstances require me so to do. I need not sell my soul to buy bliss ...' The forehead declares, 'Reason sits firm and holds the reins, and she will not let the feelings burst away and hurry her to wild chasms. The passions may rage furiously, like true heathens, as they are; and the desires may imagine all sorts of vain things: but judgement shall still have the last word in every argument, and the casting vote in every decision. Strong wind, earthquake-shock, and fire may pass by: but I shall follow the guiding of that still small voice which interprets the dictates of conscience.' (2.4; p.201)

Following his gypsy impersonation, Jane accuses Rochester of 'talking nonsense' to 'draw me out – or in ... It is scarcely fair, sir' (2.4; p.202). Nowadays we live with a general view that repression is unhealthy. However, Brontë indicates that interpretation of others, and protection from their scrutiny, are as vital to the preservation of autonomy as is the balance between self-expression and self-control. At the end of her conversation with Rochester in volume 1, chapter 14, Jane is 'sensible that the character of my interlocutor was beyond my penetration: at least, beyond its present reach; and feeling the uncertainty, the vague sense of insecurity, which accompanies a conviction of ignorance' (1.14; p.138). Rochester in fact eludes Jane's interpretation up until the moment when Bertha is revealed.

Jane and Rochester are keen not merely to assert self-control, but also to veil themselves from the intrusive scrutiny of others. This combination, notwithstanding their declarations of affinity, explains some of the singular terms of their courtship. Jane's preoccupation with retaining control over her own and Rochester's passionate impulses increases the erotic charge of this section of the novel. However, her efforts to interpret and control Rochester, whilst evading his efforts to control her, amount to more than flirtation. This is a real power struggle in which control and pleasure go hand in hand. Mrs Fairfax's unsettling warning that 'Gentlemen in [Rochester's] station are not accustomed to marry their governesses' results in Jane feeling a temporary loss of her 'sense of power over him' at his next piece of 'peremptory' conduct (2.9; pp.265, 266). She then impels herself to exert and protect this power for the remainder of their courtship. Her 'weapon of defence' is the 'needle of repartee' by which she keeps Rochester's advances, and her own desires, at bay (2.9; p.273).

Later, St John also indulges in intrusive 'reading' of Jane: St John 'seemed leisurely to read my face, as if its features and lines were characters on a page' (3.4; p.354). He used his eyes 'rather as instruments to search other people's thoughts, than as agents to reveal his own: the which combination of keenness and reserve was considerably more calculated to embarrass than to encourage' (3.3; p.346). St John gains a power over Jane that 'took away my liberty of mind' (3.8; p.397). However, as in her contest with Rochester, Jane relishes a final moment of triumph: 'It was *my* turn to assume ascendancy. *My* powers were in play, and in force' (3.9; p.420). The moment echoes that at Thornfield when, despite the almost overwhelming temptation to become Rochester's mistress, Jane shows some zest for her final contest with him: 'I was not afraid ... I felt an inward power; a sense of influence, which supported me. The crisis was perilous; but not without its charm' (3.1; p.302).

At these moments Jane makes triumphant assertions of autonomy. However, Shuttleworth points out that whilst the phrenological doctrine of the disciplined development of individual faculties may have been empowering for women, *Jane Eyre* also reflects the anxiety produced by other contemporary ideas of women as naturally lacking in self-control. Contemporary medicine was preoccupied by a view of women as subject to the fluctuating forces of their reproductive systems: literally 'hysterical' (of the womb). Finding means of control over these disruptive forces was all the more urgent in the light of anxiety that self-control was not possible for women. Bertha might be seen as an embodiment of this anxiety; her violent outbursts even seem to occur at monthly intervals, reflecting contemporary views of the violence and 'insane cunning' of women 'under the influence of their reproductive organs' (Shuttleworth, 1996, p.166). Gilbert and Gubar (1979) view *Jane Eyre* as a rejection of nineteenth-century gender ideology which can readily be assimilated to more modern feminist aspirations. However, Shuttleworth's investigation of the psychological context of the novel suggests it does not transcend but inscribes contradictions within Victorian thought on psychology and gender, which simultaneously emphasized a culture of self-control and the impossibility of attaining it (1996, p.164).

Shuttleworth (1996) notes that Jane's fierce assertions of self-determination alternate with fear that she may herself be subject to forces beyond her control. Moreover, phrenology itself paradoxically had the potential to strengthen such fears. Phrenology's view of the mind as consisting of separate faculties vying for fulfilment resulted in a model of the individual as made up of perpetually warring physical forces. These energies could be productively directed. Alternatively, individual 'propensities' could rage out of control, spilling over into madness and excess. Rochester confesses his own dissipated past (3.1; p.311). Bertha's incendiary interventions seem emblematic of Rochester's own uncontrolled sexuality as well as significant in relation to Jane. Bertha herself, Rochester records, was subject to 'giant propensities' (3.1; p.306). Her lack of control distinguishes Bertha from Jane, but also represents the risk that loss of self-control could potentially reduce Jane to the insane, animal status which threatened her in the red-room.

'Something spoke out of me over which I had no control', comments Jane on her outburst against her Aunt Reed (1.4; p.27). Her surrender to impassioned fury fragments her sense of identity. 'I was a trifle beside myself; or rather *out* of myself', she states of her enraged state as she resists being locked in the red-room, before becoming terrified at 'the strange little figure' of her own reflection in the red-room mirror (1.2; pp.12, 14). Bertha seems to operate as *both* warning and nascent parallel. The mad have no restraint, and no protective powers of concealment. In this respect, Bertha's tearing of the wedding-veil intimates the madness that may become Jane's in marriage to Rochester.

The terms of Jane and Rochester's courtship indicate that 'to surrender to passion is to surrender the very basis of selfhood', suggests Shuttleworth. She points out that 'The "real madwoman" of Thornfield breaks out on each occasion when Jane allows herself to be almost submerged within Rochester':

> On the night when she follows him 'in thought through the new regions he disclosed', and slips free from her usual 'painful restraint' his bed is set on fire ... Her sense of union with Rochester in his gypsy guise is similarly followed by the attack on Mason, and the final eruption occurs before the wedding when Jane has been absorbed, imaginatively in Rochester's world, thinking 'of the life that lay before me – *Your* life, sir'.

(Shuttleworth, 1996, p.174)

Bertha's madness disrupts Jane's 'realist narrative of self-improvement' (Shuttleworth, 1996, p.170). If the self is made up of competing energies, then such disruption always threatens. This leads Shuttleworth to suggest that the developmental model of the *Bildungsroman* genre is inappropriate as a description of *Jane Eyre*. Except for the exercise (and appearance) of self-control, Jane is the same character as she was in the red-room: a 'heterogeneous thing', as she describes herself (1.2; p.15). Rather than linear development, Jane undergoes cycles of conflict: alternations of passionate outburst and self-control. Shuttleworth offers a way of understanding how it is that we never seem to lose a sense of Jane as a rebellious character. **How does her account accord with your reading of Jane's narrative?**

The alternation of rebellion and control is perhaps a pattern embodied in the novel's constant alternations of images of fire and ice. It would seem also that the multiplicity of the narrative voice, which I discussed in chapter 4, is augmented by the psychological fragmentation figured in the text. It becomes difficult confidently to read Jane as pursuing a continuous line of development from the point when she flew like a 'mad cat' at John Reed (1.2; p.12). **Do Brontë's portrayals of self-control and passionate rebellion also have political implications?**

I commented in chapter 4 on the way in which Brontë appropriates the language of social revolt to describe Jane's initial passionate outburst of emotion, and how she compares Jane's restlessness at the stagnation of her faculties at Thornfield to the 'silent revolt' of oppressed workers (1.12; p.109). Brontë's engagement with contemporary psychology is examined by Shuttleworth within a wide framework of social explanation. She emphasizes the parallels the novel draws between social and mental conditions. Jane's political protest from the Thornfield battlements, Shuttleworth suggests, is 'not merely an isolated allusion, but rather raises to the level of explicit statement the implied parallels which run through the text' (1996, p.152). According to such a reading, the novel emerges both as the drama of an individual psyche and as a politically engaged text. Shuttleworth notes the common ground shared by nineteenth-century theories of political economy and psychology, each concerned with the controlled use of energy. Social revolt and lack of mental control thus become equivalent dangers: 'The dividing line between the forceful, useful channelling of energy, the full utilization of all resources, and the overspill into revolution or insanity was a thin one' (ibid., p.150). Judgements over justifiable levels of rebellious expression and restraint hover about a similarly narrow divide. A letter from Brontë to her publisher offers a microcosm of the ambivalent social and psychological attitudes evident in the novel. Brontë expands on the necessity for governesses to exercise 'self-control' and 'the art of self-possession', before doubling back on herself to assert that their rebellion against insupportable circumstances is justified:

> when patience has done its utmost and industry its best, whether in the case of women or operatives, and when both are baffled, and pain and want triumph, the sufferer is free, is entitled, at last to send up to Heaven any piercing cry for relief, if by that cry he can hope to obtain succour.
>
> (quoted in Shuttleworth, 1996, p.162)

Shuttleworth finds that *Jane Eyre* is a text which 'explores the intersection of models of the psyche and of the social order' (1996, p.153). This suggests that Brontë is as original in the conjunctions she brings about between different contemporary discourses as she is in amalgamations of literary genres. Rather than encouraging us to decide that *Jane Eyre* endorses *either* romantic rebellion *or* self-control, Shuttleworth's reading invites us to perceive an ambivalent alternation between the politics of control and rebellion on both the psychological and the social levels of the text. Shuttleworth finds this pattern embedded in the very features of Brontë's language that I discussed at the beginning of chapter 4: 'Syntactically, Jane's prose gives the impression of surges of energy which are yet restrained within legitimate social bounds' (ibid., p.152). Specifically, she suggests that Brontë's inverted sentence structures replicate Jane's attempts to cross social boundaries whilst remaining within accepted social frameworks (ibid.).

Brontë's attitude towards insanity, and the social insurrection it mirrors, emerges from Shuttleworth's reading as searching, albeit equivocal. As Jane crawls on the ground after fleeing Thornfield, the parallel between her and Bertha, running about her room on all fours, underscores the narrow divide between controlled sanity and madness. Shuttleworth sees Brontë as questioning categories by which individuals like Bertha (and potentially Jane) are defined as 'insane', 'animal' or in some other way not human (ibid., p.166). Jane herself importantly does not share Rochester's disgust at Bertha: 'Sir ... you are inexorable for that unfortunate lady: you speak of her with hate – with vindictive antipathy. It is cruel – she cannot help being mad' (3.1; p.301).

# Class and race

Exploring connections with nineteenth-century psychology expands our sense of the novel's engagement with other modes of discourse. As phrenology was the dominant psychological theory of the 1840s, looking at how the novel makes use of it helps us, as do the other intertextual relations we have explored, to see *Jane Eyre* as a text of its time. Shuttleworth's 'phrenological' reading of *Jane Eyre* is an example of a critical approach that allows us to perceive parallels and contrasts between Bertha and Jane by exploring what Heather Glen describes as the 'historical otherness' of the text (1997, p.25). In Shuttleworth's reading, Bertha emerges as the 'inverse image' of Jane's self-control, her madness the result of an 'eruption of uncontrollable energies', illustrative of the fine line dividing fruitful development of the individual's energies from the excesses of madness (1996, p.164). Whilst this establishes Bertha as psychologically less 'other' than 'opposite', a number of critics have suggested ways in which she is socially and racially distinguished from the novel's heroine.

In '*Jane Eyre* class-ified', Jina Politi ([1975] 1997) emphasized the issues of inequality implicit within the novel. Jane Eyre does not speak for other women in the text: either for those of other classes, such as Grace Poole, or for those who are 'foreign', such as Bertha Mason. This contradicts the conclusion reached by Gilbert and Gubar, who see the novel as drawing parallels, not only between Jane and Bertha, but also between the situation of middle-class governesses such as Jane and working-class servants such as Grace. Assessments of Grace Poole's status in the novel, and thus of its representation of class, vary widely. Shuttleworth sees divisions of class as running deeper than the separations between Jane and Bertha: Jane is less disgusted by the 'unfortunate lady' Bertha than by the thought that Rochester may have had a sexual relationship with the lower-class Grace (2.1; p.156; Shuttleworth, 1996, p.168). Politi and others have concluded that despite Jane's identification with the oppressed workforce in her famous 'silent revolt' speech, the novel is unconcerned about the fate of women like Grace Poole. Politi views *Jane Eyre*'s ideology of individual fulfilment as operating on behalf of narrow class and national interests. She highlights the novel's anti-French sentiments as epitomizing its hostility towards those of a different class and race. Subsequent critics have taken investigation of 'foreignness' in the novel further, to assert that implicit allusions to 'non-white' races define Bertha as 'other' from Jane Eyre, and that the novel may be seen to serve the interests of imperialist power.

Bertha is figuratively associated with colonized black races, and described in terms potentially both racial and racist: her face is 'savage' and 'blackened', her lips 'swelled and dark' (2.10; pp.283, 284). It has generally been assumed that, as a West Indian Creole, Bertha is not racially black. However, Susan L. Meyer has pointed out that the novel's racial overtones are complicated by the ambiguous application of the term 'Creole', which 'was used in the nineteenth-century to refer to both blacks and whites born in the West Indies' (1990, p.253). Gayatri Spivak ([1985] 1996) criticizes *Jane Eyre* as a novel that has been made a 'cult text' of Western feminism but that is written in the interests of a minority of women at the cost of the oppression of others. She reads Jean Rhys's *Wide*

*Sargasso Sea* (1966) as a partial critique of *Jane Eyre*'s unquestioning enmeshment in imperialist power. In *Jane Eyre*, Bertha must become the 'fictive Other' destroyed 'so that Jane Eyre can become the feminist individualist heroine of British fiction'. Spivak traces Jane Eyre's progression from a state of marginalized orphanhood at the novel's opening, via a sequence of unrealized unofficial 'families', to full and legal membership of a 'community of families' at the novel's end. This process she sees as epitomizing 'the active ideology of imperialism' as 'the woman from the colonies is ... sacrificed as the insane animal for her sister's consolidation' (Spivak, 1996, p.136). **Please read Gayatri Chakravorty Spivak, 'Three women's texts and a critique of imperialism' (1996, pp.132–41; extract in Regan, 2001 as 'Jane Eyre: a critique of imperialism'). Can *Jane Eyre* be read as a novel in which the European woman's assertive individualism is complicitous in imperialist rule?**

Spivak's answer to this question is an unambiguous 'yes'. She sees the novel as affirming the self-determination of its heroine at the cost of dehumanizing her non-European counterpart, so formulating her as irredeemably 'other'. However, Meyer (1990) usefully clarifies and augments details of Spivak's account whilst taking issue with her argument. Meyer finds in *Jane Eyre* 'not Spivak's "unquestioned ideology" of imperialism, but an ideology of imperialism which is questioned – and then reaffirmed – in interesting and illuminating ways' (1990, pp.251–2). **Now read Susan L. Meyer, 'Colonialism and the figurative strategy of *Jane Eyre*' (1990, pp.247–68; extract in Regan, 2001), and consider how far Brontë's analogies between different forms of oppression invite sympathy for black races. Does sympathy preclude racism?**

At the novel's opening Jane sees herself as a 'revolted slave' rebelling against the 'tyrannies' of John Reed (1.2; p.14). The identification between the oppressed Western woman – whether wife or governess – and the state of slavery is reaffirmed when Rochester calls Jane's work 'governessing slavery', just after she has asserted her refusal to become one of the enslaved inmates of his harem (2.9; pp.269–70). Meyer sees *Jane Eyre* as initially generating a degree of sympathy with the victims of colonization. However, whilst questioning imperialist oppression, this sympathy does not preclude racism – as the terms in which Bertha is described illustrate. As the novel progresses, sympathy is displaced by anxiety over ways in which Western culture – and the novel itself – becomes tainted by the practices and language of imperialism. **Are colonized peoples relegated permanently to 'otherness' by the novel's anxiety about English identity being contaminated by an involvement in imperialism?**

Meyer reads the novel as transferring to Bertha 'anxieties' previously attached to Jane herself and so 'preparing the way for [Bertha's] final annihilation' (1990, p.252). In this process, Meyer argues, the figurative language through which Bertha is represented means that she 'has *become* black, as she is constructed by the narrative', epitomizing the way in which an increasing anxiety about imperialism emerges throughout the novel. The incarceration of Bertha is the 'crime' which cannot be eradicated from Thornfield. The West Indies are, of course, the source of Rochester's wealth, and eventually Jane's also. The effects of the stained wealth acquired via colonial rule Meyer finds dramatized in the characters of Blanche Ingram and Rochester. Both 'dark and imperious', the incongruously named Blanche (French for 'white') embodies the disjunction between the ideal of white European femininity and the undesirable qualities imperialism brings out in Europeans 'besmirched by the contagious darkness and oppressiveness of British colonialism' (ibid., p.260). Shuttleworth suggests that Rochester's comments on Blanche Ingram specifically suggest male fear of the sexuality which was also to be found amongst respectable English women (1996, p.169). In Meyer's view, Rochester's darkness highlights his involvement in both gender and racial oppression. **Do you agree with Meyer's reading of the language of race in *Jane Eyre*? (You may wish to reread the extract, to remind yourself of her argument.) Does Brontë's use of metaphors of slavery and blackness to denote class and gender oppression in Britain dilute or displace the power of these figures to censure imperialism itself?**

We should be aware that connections between the oppression of women and slavery were frequently made at the time, and did not inevitably imply an immediate concern with slavery itself. Wollstonecraft and other feminists frequently drew analogies between marriage and slavery. In a more conservative context, the governess in Jane Austen's *Emma* (1816) quips that work as a governess involves the sale 'not quite of human flesh – but of human intellect', suggesting that the misery of the victims of the 'slave-trade' and the 'governess trade' may be equally great (chapter 35). Austen's prime concern seems to lie with the suffering of English women at home, rather than with the colonized slaves who provide a metaphor for their plight. In Meyer's view, the language of protest against imperialist oppression in *Jane Eyre*, including Jane's passionate identification with the state of slavery at the start of the novel, does have some connection with the real conditions of colonial power. However, rather than developing into a critique of imperialism, it ultimately becomes merely metaphorical in force: expressive of a narrow concern for the 'slavery' of English women of the lower middle class. She reads the novel's numerous portrayals of domestic house-cleaning as a 'symbolic alternative to an involvement in oppression' – but only for the favoured few (Meyer, 1990, p.264). Meyer perceives the novel as haunted by anxiety about the effects of imperialism, rather than celebrating the consolidation of its heroine's individuality. However, she sees the figurative strategy of Brontë's novel as having a 'conservative twist' by which it makes the power of oppression essentially 'other', non-British' and 'non-white', the result of besmirching contact with 'dark races' (ibid., p.262). The extent to which Jane herself is a victim of the same oppression as Bertha, or complicitous in it, remains unsettled and unsettling.

It is possible to read *Jane Eyre* as a narrowly feminist text which fails to address related issues of racial and class oppression. However, rather than taking an accusatory stance against Brontë as author, post-colonial critics such as Gayatri Spivak identify nineteenth-century society and ideology as failing to allow the energies which fuel the heroine's drive for self-realization to be extended to other races and classes. They share some ground in this respect with critics of *Jane Eyre* who are especially interested in the novel's interaction with nineteenth-century psychological, social and political thought. However, we need to recognize significant differences between critics such as Spivak, who assert *Jane Eyre*'s unquestioning enmeshment in imperialist power, and those such as Meyer and Shuttleworth, who find some measure of this critique within Brontë's novel itself, identifying a lingering anxiety about imperialist rule within the text.

The issue of imperialist control has both political and psychological significance. Shuttleworth cites the French cultural theorist Michel Foucault's observation that the Victorians were originally preoccupied with control not of other classes (or, we could add, races) but of their own minds (1996, p.11). This does not make *Jane Eyre* merely the story of an individual mind. Rather, 'the social is shifted, metonymically, into the psychological' (ibid., p.178). Meyer sees the language of race and slavery reduced to metaphorical significance for much of the novel. Shuttleworth's view of a metonymic, or associative, relationship emphasizes that the portrayal of Jane Eyre's psyche is an integral part of the novel's engagement with a complex, often contradictory debate which connected political economy, social theory and psychology.

Shuttleworth clearly sees the connections between Jane and Bertha as too ambiguous to construct Bertha as entirely 'other'. She questions whether *Jane Eyre* is the triumphant narrative of self-fulfilment which critics such as Spivak find it to be. In Spivak's view, Jane Eyre achieves individuality at the cost of dehumanizing Bertha. Does Spivak accept too readily the assumption of such critics as Gilbert and Gubar that *Jane Eyre* portrays a successful 'progress toward selfhood' (1979, p.364)? As we saw, Shuttleworth draws attention to Jane's anxiety about her lack of a unified centre of self, which runs alongside her passionate declarations of self-determination. Bertha thus becomes less 'self-consolidating Other' for Jane, as Spivak describes her (quoted in Shuttleworth, 1996, p.164), than 'a destabilizing agent undermining her attempts to construct a fiction of integrated selfhood'; thus Shuttleworth highlights the fragile basis of Jane's 'imperialist claims to self-domination' (1996, p.164). Selfhood in this analysis becomes 'not ... the unshakeable bedrock of the imperialist project, but rather the interiorized site of social conflict' (ibid., p.176). She finds that the novel's 'overarching narrative of self-improvement through self-control' is cut across by 'depictions of internal struggle cast in terms of racial and class conflict'. She sees the novel as an 'analysis of the ways in which ideological pressures of class, gender and economics are played out in the domain of subjectivity' (ibid., p.148). In chapter 4, I quoted Lewes's appreciation of Brontë's 'strange power of subjective representation', her ability to represent 'the psychological interpretation of material phenomena'. Could we now add to this her ability to represent the psychological interpretation of social and cultural relationships? It is possible to see the novel's political ambivalence dramatized in the psychological conflicts of its heroine. These conflicts reflect contradictions within contemporary discourse which make the novel especially difficult to interpret.

# Conclusion

Many of the issues which have been raised in preceding discussions, both in this chapter and in chapter 4, will influence how you read the novel's closing pages. **How do you read Jane's situation at the end of the novel: as the fulfilment of romantic individualism, of domestic romance, or as something more disturbing?**

Jane becomes the eyes and even the 'words' of the blinded Rochester, reading both books and the natural world on his behalf (3.12; p.450). This might indicate that she is taking control of the completion of her own narrative in defiance of all attempts, by St John, Brocklehurst and Rochester, to tell it for her. On the other hand, a romantic conclusion, in which the heroine is allowed no vocational scope, may undermine attempts to see the novel as a female *Bildungsroman*. Jane's assertions of domestic contentment sit uneasily alongside the passionate energies which have engaged us throughout the rest of the narrative. She sends Adèle to school for improvement, just as Mrs Reed previously sent Jane to Lowood. Brocklehurst's morality literature, we realize, has maintained a greater presence within the novel than its rebellious opening chapters might lead us to expect. We feel unsure whether Jane is now the representative of social conformity, or – though no passive Emma Bovary – is herself a victim of patriarchy. Rochester's Bluebeard past might well make us suspicious of the domestic idyll at the novel's close.

*Jane Eyre* draws on biblical models and the heroic Protestant 'epic' of *The Pilgrim's Progress*. Jane seems a radical questing heroine. 'George Eliot's heroines ask where social duty can lie, Charlotte Brontë's ask only how individual desires and ambitions can be achieved' (Shuttleworth, 1996, p.182). Even so, there are perhaps parallels, at the end of the novel, between Jane's situation and that of the very different heroine of *Middlemarch*. A comment made by Harriet Martineau that *Jane Eyre* concentrated too much on love was one of the most hurtful criticisms Brontë received (in Allott, 1974, pp.171, 172). Perhaps Brontë's narrative, like Eliot's, struggles to establish modes other than romance, only to find that there is no more a sphere for her heroine's self-realization than there is for the epic endeavours of Eliot's latter-day St Theresa?

The ending of *Jane Eyre* has frequently been read as a return to Eden. Jane now inhabits Ferndean, a name which contains both assonant and anagrammatical suggestions of 'Eden'. Yet, this is a dubious utopia, where the air is too 'insalubrious' for Rochester to have considered it fit for Bertha's confinement (3.11; p.430). Jane's last words before the novel's conclusion are to describe how, holding Rochester's hand as 'his prop and guide', they 'entered the wood, and wended homeward' (3.11; p.448). She echoes the haunting last lines of John Milton's *Paradise Lost*, where Adam and Eve go 'hand in hand with wandring steps and slow' after their expulsion from Paradise ([1667] 1935, book 12, lines 648–9).

'Reader, I married him' – this famous note of romantic resolution is not the end of *Jane Eyre* but merely the beginning of the last chapter, which ends with the death of St John. **What is the significance of this shift in focus away from Jane's story?**

Perhaps St John is killed off in revenge for his attempt to exert authority over Jane. Perhaps Jane is envious, even, of his more active sphere. Alternatively she may be calmly looking out from her personal Eden, able now to take a generous view of St John's vocation. Whichever interpretation you favour, the 'restless faculties' which made St John out of place at the domestic fireside certainly seem to have returned to haunt the hearth beside which Jane has finally found her place (3.8; p.392). The last words of the novel are not even Jane directly speaking to us, but her recounting of St John's final letter. **What is the effect of this transfer from Jane's to St John's voice at the end?**

St John's words echo the passages of the Book of Revelation following those which he had earlier preached at Jane, when threatening her with 'fire and brimstone' in punishment for her unbelief (3.9; p.417). Jane now compares him to Bunyan's warrior Greatheart, who guides Christian's wife in *The Pilgrim's Progress*. We might wonder whether Jane's story, despite her efforts to tell it herself, has been displaced by the authority of a male literary tradition which ultimately has no place for her. Previously Jane has described St John as 'of the material from which nature hews her heroes – Christian and Pagan – her lawgivers, her statesmen, her conquerors: a steadfast bulwark for great interests to rest upon' (3.8; p.393). Possibly she now endorses his mission and has even become complicitous in those 'great interests' he serves. Jane's West Indian legacy, after all, has facilitated both her own domestic security and St John's mission.

The ending, then, lends itself to equivocal, radical *and* conservative readings. Perhaps the crucial fact about the ending is that it closes in neither the words of Jane nor of St John, but of God. Jane and St John potentially represent two complementary Christian vocations: heroic martyrdom and domestic life. 'Household joys', she tells St John, are 'The best things the world has' (3.8; p.390). She accepts that the 'Himalayan ridge' will suit him better than the domestic hearth: is Jane's search for a home identified as *her* true religious vocation? Jane prays, she tells us, in her own way, 'a different way to St John's, but effective in its own fashion' (3.9; p.420). Rochester has also begun to pray and to acknowledge God's providential power (3.11; p.448). Perhaps the novel's conclusion, like that of *Paradise Lost*, represents a reconciliation between God and man. In this case, the echo of Milton could affirm a conformist providential reading.

This reading makes some sense of the last words of the novel, though it scarcely seems to cater for the restless faculties and rebellious energies of the Jane we think we know. A more radical reading emerges when we consider that Jane's absence as speaker could signal not exclusion but a radical evasion of a Christian ending, while affirming her claim for self-determination. St John's words are not his own, but those of the Bible, including those of St John (the Divine), writer of the Book of Revelation. We might then either regard St John Rivers as unable to speak for himself any more than he can speak for Jane, or as having placed himself in a powerful line of authority. In that case, so has Brontë. The ending of *Jane Eyre* completes the novel's continuing appropriation of the Book of Revelation with which Jane counters St John at the end of the Marsh End section (3.9; pp.420, 417). This is perhaps Jane's final riposte to both

Brocklehurst and St John. Brontë conceivably achieves a radical rejection of biblical authority and, simultaneously, an assumption of that authority by adopting what are practically the last words of the Bible as the ending of her own book.

No interpretation outlined here takes adequate account of questions raised by the novel and its ending. Perhaps no single reading can. The end of the novel is complex and troubling, and suggests a corresponding variety of critical interpretations. However, is the novel's final chapter the last word in any more than a temporal sense? Let me conclude by suggesting that a sense of whether the ending is either conservative or radical need not dominate our interpretation of the text. Even if we read it as a statement of conformity, other, more radical, voices are not cancelled out. The providential may seem to occupy a privileged position at the novel's close, but other generic and discursive strands echo in our memories. Until the very end, after all, we scarcely hear anything of a conformist Jane. The novel passes over the ten years of her marriage as it did over the eight years at Lowood during which she reputedly displayed a reformed character. The rebellious Jane dominates our *experience* of reading. On reflection we also recognize ways in which the novel qualifies its support for individual and social rebellion and even makes statements of religious and social conformity. All these are valid dimensions of reading a text which gives expression to such a wealth of discursive voices. These voices haunt our memories of *Jane Eyre* as well as the process of reading. This is a novel which, as Lewes described it: 'fastens itself upon your attention, and will not leave you. The book closed, the enchantment continues' (in Allott, 1974, p.84). The generic and historicist approaches emphasized here open up an increasing range of questions we can ask of the text rather than encourage us to formulate conclusive readings of *Jane Eyre*. For me, their attraction is that they allow for historically focused analysis of the novel whilst enhancing its continuing power to enchant and baffle us.

# Works cited

Allott, Miriam. Ed. 1974. *The Brontës: The Critical Heritage*, London: Routledge.

Brontë, Charlotte. [1847] 2000. *Jane Eyre*, ed. by Margaret Smith, with an introduction and revised notes by Sally Shuttleworth, Oxford World's Classics, Oxford: Oxford University Press.

Combe, George. 1824. *Elements of Phrenology*, Edinburgh: John Anderson.

Gilbert, Sandra M. and Gubar, Susan. 1979. *The Madwoman in the Attic: The Woman Writer and the Nineteenth-Century Literary Imagination*, London: Routledge.

Glen, Heather. Ed. 1997. *Jane Eyre*, New Casebooks, Basingstoke: Macmillan.

McNees, Eleanor. Ed. 1996. *The Brontë Sisters: Critical Assessments*, 4 vols, Mountfield: Helm Information.

Meyer, Susan L. 1990. 'Colonialism and the figurative strategy of *Jane Eyre*', *Victorian Studies*, vol.33, no.2, pp.247–68. (Extract in Regan, 2001.)

Milton, John. [1667] 1935. *Paradise Lost*, in *Milton's Poetical Works*, ed. by H.C. Beeching, London: Oxford University Press.

Moers, Ellen. 1976. *Literary Women: The Great Writers*, New York: Doubleday.

Moi, Toril. 1988. *Sexual/Textual Politics: Feminist Literary Theory*, London: Routledge.

Politi, Jina. [1975] 1997. '*Jane Eyre* class-ified', in *Jane Eyre*, ed. by Heather Glen, New Casebooks, Basingstoke: Macmillan.

Regan, Stephen. Ed. 2001. *The Nineteenth-Century Novel: A Critical Reader*, London: Routledge.

Showalter, Elaine. 1977. *A Literature of their Own: British Women Novelists from Brontë to Lessing*, Princeton, NJ: Princeton University Press.

Shuttleworth, Sally. 1996. *Charlotte Brontë and Victorian Psychology*, Cambridge: Cambridge University Press.

Shuttleworth, Sally and Bourne Taylor, Jenny. Eds. 1998. *Embodied Selves: An Anthology of Psychological Texts 1830–1890*, Oxford: Clarendon Press.

Spivak, G.C. [1985] 1996. 'Three women's texts and a critique of imperialism', in *A Practical Reader in Contemporary Literary Theory*, ed. by Peter Brooker and Peter Widdowson, Hemel Hempstead: Prentice-Hall. (Extract in Regan, 2001.)

Wise, T.J. and Symington, J.A. 1993. *The Brontës: Their Lives, Friendships and Correspondence*, 4 vols, Oxford: Blackwell.

# Further reading

Boumelha, Penny. 1990. *Charlotte Brontë*, London: Harvester Wheatsheaf. Boumelha's illuminating chapter on *Jane Eyre* is reprinted in Glen (1997).

Chase, Karen. 1984. *Eros and Psyche: The Representations of Personality in Charlotte Brontë, Charles Dickens, George Eliot*, New York: Methuen. An extract is reprinted in Glen (1997).

Delamotte, Eugenia. 1990. *Perils of the Night: A Feminist Study of Nineteenth-Century Gothic*, London: Edward Arnold. Chapters on *Jane Eyre* and *Villette* discuss Brontë as the most significant exponent of nineteenth-century female Gothic.

Gérin, Winifred. 1969. *Charlotte Brontë: The Evolution of Genius*, London: Oxford University Press. The standard biography.

Glen, Heather. Ed. 1997. *Jane Eyre*, New Casebooks, Basingstoke: Macmillan. An extremely useful (and affordable) collection of essays by Doreen Roberts, Karen Chase, Elaine Showalter, Jina Politi, Susan L. Meyer, Penny Boumelha, Margaret Homans, Mary Poovey, Elisabeth Bronfen, Peter Allan Dale and Carolyn Williams, with a valuable introductory essay by Heather Glen. Includes an annotated list of further reading.

Gordon, Lyndall. 1994. *Charlotte Brontë: A Passionate Life*, London: Chatto & Windus. A more recent biographical study.

Gregor, Ian. Ed. 1970. *The Brontës: A Collection of Critical Essays*, Englewood Cliffs, NJ: Prentice-Hall.

McNees, Eleanor. Ed. 1996. *The Brontë Sisters: Critical Assessments*, 4 vols, Mountfield: Helm Information.

Maynard, John. 1984. *Charlotte Brontë and Sexuality*, Cambridge: Cambridge University Press. Discusses Brontë as the most sophisticated writer on mid-nineteenth-century sexual issues before Thomas Hardy.

Moglen, Helene. 1976. *Charlotte Brontë: The Self Conceived*, New York: Norton. Examines connections between Brontë's psychological and literary development.

Rich, Adrienne. 1979. 'Jane Eyre: the temptations of a motherless woman', in *On Lies, Secrets, and Silence: Selected Prose 1966–1978*, New York: Norton; reprinted in McNees (1996). Reads *Jane Eyre* as offering alternatives both to conventional piety and to the social and cultural condition of women.

Showalter, Elaine. 1978. *A Literature of their Own: British Women Novelists from Brontë to Lessing*, London: Virago. A pioneering feminist study. Showalter's essay on *Jane Eyre* is reprinted in Glen (1997).

Shuttleworth, Sally. 2000. 'Introduction' to Charlotte Brontë, *Jane Eyre*, ed. by Margaret Smith, Oxford World's Classics, Oxford: Oxford University Press. This edition was completed too late to be discussed in the chapters on *Jane Eyre*, but the excellent introduction by Sally Shuttleworth is highly recommended reading.

Shuttleworth, Sally and Bourne Taylor, Jenny. Eds. 1998. *Embodied Selves: An Anthology of Psychological Texts 1830–1890*, Oxford: Clarendon Press.

Stoneman, Patsy. 1996. *Brontë Transformations: The Cultural Dissemination of 'Jane Eyre' and 'Wuthering Heights'*, London: Prentice-Hall. Traces the fascinating after-life of *Jane Eyre* not only in literature but also in such forms as stage, film and television adaptations of the novel.

# CHAPTER 6

# *Dombey and Son*: families and commerce

*by Sebastian Mitchell*

## Introduction

In a letter to his publisher John Forster dated 11 October 1846, Charles Dickens gives an unrestrained response to the news of the sales of the first instalment of *Dombey and Son*, which contained the first four chapters. 'The Dombey success is brilliant! I had put before me thirty thousand as the limit of the most extreme success, saying that if we should reach that, I should be more than satisfied, and more than happy; you will judge how happy I am!' (Dickens, 1977, p.631). Dickens's euphoria can be explained by a literary success after what had been a relatively frustrating period. He regarded his previous novel, *The Life and Adventures of Martin Chuzzlewit* (1843–4), as one of his best, but it sold about twenty thousand copies per month, fewer than any of his other works (Patten, 1978, p.133). His exuberant response to the news of the success of *Dombey and Son* no doubt contains an element of relief at the recovery of his reputation as the most popular and celebrated writer of prose fiction of his day, but it also perhaps acknowledges that this novel would be a turning point in his literary career. Dickens had planned the novel in more detail than his previous works. Much of the plot had been determined before he began writing. It is also the first of his major works which is set in the present rather than in the recent past, and comments critically on the prevailing social condition of England. As such, the novel can be seen as a bridging work between the more exuberant, farcical works of Dickens's early career, such as *Pickwick Papers* (1836–7), and the more sombre, socially concerned works of his late career, such as *Little Dorrit* (1855–7) and *Great Expectations* (1860–1).

The decade of the 1840s in which *Dombey and Son* is set was a period of considerable social and economic turbulence in England. The beginning of the decade saw one of the worst slumps of the century. Food shortages and unemployment contributed to intermittent unrest in rural England until 1848. The second half of the decade also saw, however, a tremendous increase in trade and the improved performance of the financial markets as bust turned to boom. In 1846, the year in which *Dombey and Son* began to be published, Robert Peel's Conservative administration repealed the Corn Laws (the legislation designed to protect the price of domestic grain from foreign imports), and the revocation of these acts was interpreted as a decisive victory of free-trade economics over traditional landed interests. The same year saw a boom in railway-building and the corresponding surge in investments in rail stock. Overall, the population of Britain grew about 11 per cent in this period. The demographic distribution of the population shifted decisively. By the end of the decade for the first time in Britain the majority of the population lived in cities and towns. This large-scale movement inevitably meant that large numbers of people experienced a sense of acute social dislocation as they moved from traditional rural communities to impersonal cities. The overall rate of employment was greater at the end of the decade than at the beginning, but the period also produced greater disparities of wealth and poverty. As the financial circumstances of the middle classes improved dramatically in the middle of the decade, the poor still suffered from economic depression and shortages which stemmed from earlier years (Hobsbawm, 1969, pp.79–96; McCord, 1991, pp.210–43).

As I hope will become clear, *Dombey and Son* is a novel which seeks to engage with the social transformations of its age. It deals extensively with the increasing industrialization and urbanization of early Victorian society and the effects of these changes on the way personal identity and familial relationships were shaped. The novel can consequently be seen to describe the process by which a recognizably modern society comes into being. By this I mean that it portrays both the destructiveness and dynamism of a society at the very moment of it becoming predominantly urban in its social and political organization, with a market economy, an industrial basis and an extensive internal and external transport network for the rapid movement of goods, services and people. Yet it would be doing *Dombey and Son* a disservice to see the narrative as only descriptive of its age, for what is impressive about the novel is its attempt both to produce a kind of social totality, an anatomy of social being, and to express this totality through a rich variety of narrative forms. I would suggest that it is this attempt to produce an inclusive social vision which makes *Dombey and Son* distinct from the novels we have encountered so far.

It is possible, for example, to consider *Northanger Abbey* and *Jane Eyre* in terms of the tension between their realist and non-realist elements. As you will be aware by now, realism is a problematic term that can be used in a variety of different ways, and it might be helpful if I provide a definition of what I regard as the standard realist components in the prose fiction of this period. There are four main points: firstly, the text attempts to produce a psychologically persuasive portrait of the central character, and account for his or her actions in terms of a prior state of mind; secondly, it attempts to locate this character within a coherent and credible representation of an external world; thirdly, the writing itself aims to be transparent, that is, the realist text attempts to persuade readers to forget that they are reading a novel and has some unmediated access to the lives of the characters it depicts; and finally, the realist text is predominantly concerned with middle-class social and moral concerns.

*Northanger Abbey* deals with the social circumstances and emotional upheavals of young marriageable women of the middling and better sort as they parade through the pump rooms and spas of Regency Bath. *Jane Eyre* recounts the trials and tribulations of a governess, which, as we have seen, is a problematic occupation for middle-class women in the early Victorian period.

Both works also contain Gothic and romantic components, and these elements can be interpreted as either contradicting or complementing the realist strands of the works. It is difficult, however, to conceive of *Dombey and Son* in terms of this dialectic of realist and Gothic elements, simply because the novel is composed of such a broad range of literary types. Realist description in Dickens's work has to contend with a 'veritable log jam of competing fictional modes' (Eagleton, 1976, p.154): theatrical melodrama, sentimental tale, eighteenth-century burlesque, poetic and symbolic narratives, urban folklore and, as eloquently demonstrated in Dennis Walder's account of the novel, fairytale (Walder, 2001, pp.xvi–xvii).

It is as though the novel attempts to incorporate within its bulky aesthetic as diverse a range of writing as it can possibly manage. This inclusivity in terms of different kinds of writing in the work is matched by the attempt to produce a comprehensive depiction of the various social types which composed early Victorian society. The relatively restricted focus on one or two households in Austen and Brontë is here replaced by an attempt to produce an account of as many households as possible, as the novel at one point describes its own social function as 'a good spirit who would take the house-tops off' (Dickens, [1846–8] 2001, 47; p.685; unless otherwise stated, all subsequent page references are to this edition). The novel's social vision consequently ranges from the lowest to almost the highest, from the desperately impoverished circumstances of Mrs Brown and her daughter, through the respectable working-class Toodle family, on to the somewhat less reputable but considerably more rumbustious MacStingers, on and up to the benevolent nautical company of Captain Cuttle, Solomon Gills and Walter Gay, the lower-middle-class brother and sister John and Harriet Carker, and finally up to the higher reaches of the gentry represented by Dombey and his social circle of Major Bagstock and Mrs Skewton.

If *Dombey and Son* is to be regarded as a dynamic literary work that attempts to express an inclusive social reality through a wide range of literary styles and registers, then it can perhaps be fruitfully regarded from a theoretical perspective offered by the Russian literary theorist M.M. Bakhtin. In a key essay, 'Epic and the novel', Bakhtin famously describes the inherent dynamism of the novel. He writes of the 'organically receptive' quality of this genre, and stresses its newness compared with such traditional forms of expression as the poetic and the dramatic. The novel for Bakhtin is *the* significant literary milieu. If you study prose fiction it is akin to 'studying languages which are not only alive, but still young'. In contrast, the study of the older literary forms demands a different set of forensic skills. The exercise of analysing poetry and plays, he claims, is more like 'studying dead languages, such as Latin or Greek' (Bakhtin, 1981, p.3). Moreover, the novel for Bakhtin is a form whose animation is displayed through its alertness to different styles and genres of writing. The novelistic is constantly seeking to incorporate other forms of writing within itself; it exemplifies 'an indeterminacy, a certain semantic open-endedness, a living contact with unfinished, still evolving contemporary reality (the open-ended present)' (ibid., p.7). In Bakhtin's writing, the novel often appears as though it were some vibrant, but rather cumbersome creature involved in a heroic struggle with itself in order to express the totality of the social reality (that is the experience of all social groups) within a given epoch.

In what follows, I intend to consider *Dombey and Son* in terms of this apparently paradoxical dynamic. Inevitably within such a comprehensive work, there are competing demands upon the text. Let me give you a brief example of what I mean. The social reality of the novel is conveyed through the actions and speech of such characters as Miss Tox, Mrs Pipchin, Captain Cuttle and Major Bagstock, yet the names of these characters by themselves are not straightforwardly realistic. They are not the sort of names we would usually encounter beyond the text-world of the novel itself, names such as Smith, Jones, or even Mitchell. Indeed, one might suggest that such names as Tox, Bagstock and Cuttle highlight the literary nature of the work by proclaiming the central properties of these particular figures. So 'Miss Tox' perhaps indicates there is something 'toxic' about her character, poisoned by the frustrations of her spinsterhood. 'Cuttle' has a maritime flavour, suggesting cuttlefish (and possibly even a cutlass), 'Pipchin' suggests a sharp blow, a pip-on-the-chin, and 'Bagstock' suggests, among other things, a 'windbag'. These proper names are self-reflective; that is, they prevent the reader from treating the text as though it were transparent. In fact, the names draw attention to the artifice of the characters they describe and encourage the reader to think of them in terms of their possible verbal associations. They belong to a symbolic mode of literary expression rather than to a straightforward realist realm of description. Yet these characters and their names also vividly express the social concerns of the early Victorian period, and by doing so contribute to the social reality of the novel. Mrs Pipchin, for example, is a striking example of the personal damage wrought by unwise financial speculation on a volatile stock market. The loss of the family's wealth for Mrs Pipchin is, figuratively speaking, 'a blow on the chin' from which she never recovers.

I should also perhaps mention one more stimulating, but unsettling aspect of Dickens's narrative. It can seem particularly difficult to arrive at a definitive critical judgement on *Dombey and Son*. This is partly because the range of styles which are deployed means that the work contains inherently contradictory modes of expression, and partly because there is a tension between the novel's socially descriptive and its socially critical components. As we discuss the novel you should see how sections of the narrative offer a complex range of perspectives on the same episode. Dickens is an acutely observant and trenchant critic of the individual, the institution of the family and urban society in the early Victorian period, but the discussion of contemporary society he offers is at once more suggestive and less clear cut than some other prominent novelists of this period. Unlike George Eliot and Elizabeth Gaskell, he does not often in his fiction complement social diagnostics with explicit social remedies.

This inclusivity of narrative allows considerable scope for interpretation of the social perspective of Dickens's fiction, precisely because the novel incorporates a range of critical perspectives and judgements, and resolutely refuses to advance one interpretation of the events it depicts over the others. One consequence of this range of narrative positions is that it invites conflicting interpretations of Dickens's social criticism. Two of the twentieth-century's major literary figures, George Bernard Shaw and George Orwell, held opposing views as to the social objectives of Dickens's fiction. In an introduction to *Great Expectations*, Shaw described Dickens as an unwitting revolutionary whose fiction in spite of his own professed views demands the sweeping away of the current social order. Orwell, however, did not detect any desire for such comprehensive social change in Dickens's work. Instead he reads the novels as being merely a corrective to the excesses and incidental cruelties of a liberal progressive Victorian society of which their narratives broadly approve. The overriding purpose of Dickens's fiction is consequently to effect in its middle-class Victorian audience 'a change of heart', which Orwell condemns as '*the* alibi of people who do not wish to endanger the status quo' (quoted in Brown, 1982, pp.28–9).

In order that we may explore how *Dombey and Son* utilizes its diverse literary materials to produce both a compelling representation of a social reality, and an exploration of the socially transformative power of such a representation, this chapter will consider the novel's depictions of the individual and the family and their relationship to commerce and class. In chapter 7, we will consider further the thematic significance of the supporting characters, explore the industrial and imperial concerns of the novel, and finish, appropriately enough, with a discussion of the conclusion. I'd like now, however, to begin right at the beginning of the novel, or rather just before its beginning, with the full title of the novel as displayed on the distinctive green wrapper of the first instalment, and the connection this title makes between business transactions and emotional attachments.

# Paul Dombey: money, trade and egotism

The full title of the book given on the green wrapper is *Dealings with the Firm of Dombey and Son, Wholesale, Retail, and for Exportation* (it is reprinted as the frontispiece of the Oxford World's Classics edition). Dickens himself was inordinately proud of this title, probably because it effectively draws together a number of the work's major themes. **Take a moment to consider how this title might serve as a pointer to the novel's preoccupations.**

The opening word, 'Dealings', is the first item which the potential purchaser of the instalment would see, and the invitation is consequently twofold – to have dealings with the novel in the sense of the financial transaction of purchasing the issue and to have dealings with the novel in terms of entering into an emotional relationship with its characters. The word at once conflates personal feeling and hard economics, and the relationship between these two spheres is one of the book's major themes. Dombey and Son is, of course, both the name of a commercial firm and a family unit (father and son). At the beginning of the work the firm of Dombey and Son is a traditional and successful London merchant company, whose wealth has been built on the buying, selling and transportation of various goods around Britain's maritime empire.

**Now reread the first chapter. There are three questions I would like you to consider as you read: firstly, how does Paul Dombey appear to us**

**at the beginning of the novel? Secondly, what is his attitude towards his business and family? And thirdly, what narrative techniques are used to portray him?**

The story begins with a familial image as the middle-aged Paul Dombey sits 'in the corner of the darkened room in the great arm-chair by the bedside, and Son lay tucked up warm in the little basket bedstead' (1; p.1). Note the use of capital letters for the description of the infant Paul Dombey. It allows us to make that central connection between Dombey and Son as a commercial enterprise and Dombey and his newly arrived son as part of a family. The capitalization of 'Son' at once suggests the overwhelming importance attached to the birth of this boy by his father. It is perhaps the first intimation of Dombey's cold vanity and rigid egotism, facets of his character which are quickly developed in the opening pages. When Dombey plays with his son, he does so with the appurtenances of his substantial wealth; he jingles and jingles that 'heavy gold watch-chain that depended from below his trim blue coat, whereof the buttons sparkled phosphorescently in the feeble rays of the distant fire' (ibid.).

The extent of Dombey's egocentric view of the world becomes apparent when he indulges himself in the fantasy that the world's natural features have been formed for the sole purpose of his firm's trading interests. 'The earth was made for Dombey and Son to trade in', the narrator states on his behalf, 'and the sun and moon were made to give them light. Rivers and seas were formed to float their ships' (1; p.2). Dombey also reinterprets common abbreviations in terms of his own immediate concerns, changing AD, anno Domini (in the year of the lord), into 'anno Dombei – and Son' (ibid.). There are, of course, faintly blasphemous overtones to this pronouncement, given that Dombey's child is referred to in its capitalized form as his 'Son'. The father and son relationship with which theirs is being implicitly compared is God and Christ. Dombey's egotism seems to lead towards a parody of the divine relationship depicted, for example, in *The Apostles' Creed*: 'I believe in God the Father Almighty, Maker of heaven and earth: And in Jesus Christ his only Son our Lord' (*Morning Prayer*, Book of Common Prayer 121:19; see also Walder, 1981, p.127).

Dombey's egotistical perspective on his trading interests and family is given full expression right at the start of the narrative, but it is also immediately exposed as being a false view. You may have noticed that the opening chapter is richly figurative in its expression. The opening description of the infant Paul, for example, has him lying in a basket bedstead. The idea of the basket is then used associatively. The image of the baby in the basket triggers the verbal association of a muffin in a basket, and the comparison is pursued further, as the narrative voice suggests that 'it was essential to toast him brown while he was very new' (1; p.1). Now, the effectiveness of this particular image depends on the reader being able to comprehend that the image of the muffin and the basket is distinct from the infant in his cot. The image demands that we see the associative possibilities between baby and muffin, but do not read the image literally: Dombey is not going to toast his newborn son. This kind of figurative language is a particularly distinctive and innovative feature of Dickens's prose. It is stimulating precisely because it encourages a multiplicity of verbal and imagistic connections. Dombey, in opposition to this expansive linguistic mode, either interprets matters in a literal way, or uses figurative language reductively to dismantle his relationships into their fundamental components. He is delighted, for example, that the birth of Paul transforms the name of the firm of Dombey and Son into the physical reality that once more the household is constituted by a father and son: 'The house will once again, Mrs Dombey', he declares, 'be not only in name but in fact Dombey and Son; Dom-bey and Son!' (ibid.).

Unlike his son, Dombey's daughter, Florence, is of little consequence to him. The narrator reveals through the mode of free indirect discourse the extent of Dombey's disdain (that is, the narrator expresses Dombey's views): 'But what was a girl to Dombey and Son! In the capital of the House's name and dignity, such a child was merely a piece of base coin that couldn't be invested – a bad Boy – nothing more' (1; p.3). There is clearly a pun on the use of capital here; the term is used to describe the social standing of the firm as well as its financial assets. Florence has no purpose in Dombey's world-view precisely because her sex disbars her from working for the firm, and from adding to its social credit. Her uselessness is expressed in a corrupted form of financial exchange; she is stripped of all her human qualities in Dombey's reductive figurative expression and dismissed as 'merely a piece of base coin that couldn't be invested'.

Dombey's egotism has essentially three elements to it: firstly, he is unable to disentangle his personal relationships from his business affairs and the social status which the standing of his business allows him to enjoy; secondly, he is not capable of making any meaningful emotional attachment to any of the other characters he encounters in the novel; and thirdly, as a result of these, he is a solitary figure, imprisoned by his entirely subjective and rigid consciousness. Dombey, to use a Marxian term, reifies all his relationships – that is, instead of viewing other people in terms of their affective capacities, he views them entirely in objective terms, making a judgement on their commercial and social use to him. Dombey assesses his family ties solely for their usefulness in the continuation of the family business. The point is skilfully and swiftly enforced when the narrative switches perspective from father to daughter, from Dombey's view to Florence's. She is, quite understandably, unable to see her father as an identifiable person in the sense of being someone who is capable of giving or receiving affection; and she consequently views him as a set of discrete signs which collectively represent his dispassionate authority: 'The child glanced keenly at the blue coat and the stiff white cravat, which, with a pair of creaking boots and a very loud ticking watch, embodied her idea of a father; but her eyes returned to her mother's face immediately, and she neither moved or answered' (1; p.3). Florence significantly cannot *see* her father's face; he is no more than an imposing collection of inanimate objects: collar, boots and watch; she consequently turns to her mother and focuses explicitly upon her face as a source of affection, security and identity.

The first chapter also reveals the cold and passionless state of Dombey's marriage to his first wife. Paul Dombey's difficulty is once more that he cannot see beyond his own conceptions of rank and status. He unreasonably suggests that his wife *should* be happy solely because of the social status which their marriage has bestowed upon her. The importance of this notion of social duty is underlined later in the chapter when Dombey's sister, Mrs Chick, recalls that

Fanny has given birth to a boy (rather than another useless girl); she remarks that 'after this, I forgive Fanny everything!' (1; p.8). The narrator observes ironically that the concession to her sister-in-law is made in a Christian spirit. Mrs Chick, like her brother, sees Fanny's principal function within the family as the preservation of the male line through the production of a son and heir. Having discharged her principal social duty according to the expectations of Dombey and his sister, she expires at the end of the first chapter, in the loving embrace of her distraught daughter, and under the distant gaze of her dispassionate husband.

Dombey is, of course, constantly concerned about social class. Hippolyte Taine, the leading French critic of English literature in the middle and later part of the nineteenth century, argued provocatively and influentially that Paul Dombey may well be a successful Victorian merchant, and therefore by rights should belong to the upper echelons of the middle class, but for much of the novel he behaves as though he were an aristocrat. Taine declares that you see in Dombey 'a character which could only be produced in a country whose commerce embraces the globe, where merchants are potentates, where a company of merchants has speculated upon continents, maintained wars, destroyed kingdoms, founded an empire of a hundred million men' (1871, vol.2, p.362). Taine's view of the merchant as imperial potentate seems to take Dombey rather too much at his own estimation instead of following the sustained critique the novel mounts against his vanity, pride and coldness. Nevertheless, Dombey does seem to possess some distinctive aristocratic traits. He handles his merchant business as though it were a landed estate which needs to be preserved intact and passed on through the male line. The offices of the firm are situated at the heart of the economic area, within 'the liberties of the City of London, and within hearing of Bow Bells' (4; p.36); and they have a faintly old-fashioned air to them; the firm's dealings are to be conducted in an ordered and traditional way. Dombey runs the company, but remains remarkably detached from its day-to-day affairs. Not unlike the way in which a landed aristocrat might leave the running of his estate to his agent, he surrenders much of the daily responsibility of the company to his manager, James Carker. It is precisely his lack of awareness of both the duplicitous conduct of his own most trusted agent and the rapidly changing nature of the British economy in the middle of the nineteenth century which ultimately contributes to Dombey's financial ruin at the end of the novel. Moreover, he demonstrates an aristocratic pride in his social position. He willingly accepts the flatteries of Major Bagstock and Mrs Skewton precisely because they readily remind him of their own aristocratic connections, and in doing so reassure Dombey's own sense of social worth.

Dombey's aristocratic will surfaces particularly clearly in the second chapter, as he makes the arrangements for the infant Paul's care after the death of his mother. He engages the impoverished Polly as his son's nurse, and in what at first seems to be a purely capricious act insists that she will be known henceforth in his house as Richards. Nina Auerbach has suggested that the name of 'Richards' is significant because of its masculine connotations. Dombey always feels compelled to exert his patriarchal authority over any threatening feminine intrusion into his world. He consequently renders down the prodigiously fecund 'Polly Toodle' to the much more abruptly masculine and controllable 'Richards' (Auerbach, 1976, pp 95–105). The renaming of Polly also seems to betray a deep sense of social anxiety on the part of Dombey. You may recall that Polly comes from a reputable working-class family and is married to an illiterate engine-stoker. Unlike any of the better-heeled couples in the novel, they have an abundance of children. Their fertility, of course, is one of the cumulative jokes in the text, as the Toodles reappear each time encumbered with yet more infants. Dombey's reaction when he first sees the Toodle children in his drawing-room, however, is informative. He observes that they look healthy, but baulks at the prospect of them having any kind of association with his son; he cannot tolerate their presence. He exclaims, 'think of their some day claiming a sort of relationship to Paul! Take them away Louisa' (2; p.17). It is as though such contact with the lower orders would involve a form of social pollution for Dombey, as though Polly's proletarian milk would provide some fatal contamination of his blood-line. He consequently insists that Polly, as Paul's nurse, should be thoroughly removed from her own family and that her name should be changed.

The novel, however, constantly challenges this notion that sympathetic feelings, or even social identification, can be constrained by the demands which Dombey makes of Polly. His authority and his effectiveness in this regard are explicitly confronted in what at first seems to be an inconsequential and somewhat arbitrary episode later in the narrative (in chapter 20). Shortly after his own son Paul has died, Dombey and Major Bagstock decide to travel to Birmingham from London by train. While they wait on the platform Dombey characteristically paces and broods. He does not see a stoker who periodically nods at him while tending a steam engine. The narrative voice emphasizes Dombey's *hauteur* at this point, suggesting that he 'habitually looked over the vulgar herd, not at them' (20; p.294). The stoker, however, is not to be denied; he approaches Dombey and reintroduces himself as Polly's husband, Toodle. The exchange seems fairly innocuous, polite even, but Dombey reacts to Toodle's presence with tight-lipped fury, wishing that 'he had rubbed the stoker underneath the wheels [of his carriage]' (20; p.295). The source of Dombey's seemingly disproportionate rage soon becomes apparent, as the narrator notes that the cap in Toodle's hand had caught Dombey's eye. The cap has a small symbol of mourning tucked into its brim. When Dombey and the Major are subsequently ensconced in their compartment on the train, the narrator reveals that Dombey was convinced from Toodle's 'manner and his answers, that he wore it for *his* son' (20; p.297). In other words, Toodle effectively ignores Dombey's initial order to have nothing to do with his son. Toodle mourns little Paul as though he had been one of his own ragged offspring. By doing so he outrages Dombey's social sensibilities. Toodle's symbol of mourning is for Dombey evidence of exactly the kind of social contamination he most wanted to avoid, and his recognition of this mixing of class and sentiment reduces him to mute fury.

As I have already suggested, one of the consequences of Dombey's vaulting pride is his inability to enter into any kind of fulfilling relationship with the other characters he encounters, and this includes his own son. Dombey's melancholy state of isolation becomes apparent just after Polly has taken up her duties as Paul's nurse (in chapter 3). He watches the renamed Richards walking up and down with his child; a sheet of glass separates them from him. **How is Dombey portrayed in the following passage, and how does this depiction relate to what happens to him at the end of the novel?**

> These three rooms opened upon one another. In the morning, when
> Mr Dombey was at his breakfast in one or other of the two first mentioned of
> them, as well as in the afternoon when he came home to dinner, a bell was rung
> for Richards to repair to this glass chamber, and there walk to and fro with her
> young charge. From the glimpses she caught of Mr Dombey at these times,
> sitting in the dark distance, looking out towards the infant from among the dark
> heavy furniture – the house had been inhabited for years by his father, and in
> many of its appointments was old-fashioned and grim – she began to entertain
> ideas of him in his solitary state, as if he were a lone prisoner in a cell, or a
> strange apparition that was not to be accosted or understood. (3; pp.24–5)

As you see, the scene begins with Dombey watching Richards, the very act of such dispassionate viewing seems to encapsulate Dombey's own sense of control over the affairs of the household. He surveys and monitors the development of his son and the conduct of his nurse. The glass chamber is itself an intriguing component in this scene. The glass perhaps indicates Dombey's emotional separation from everybody else; it forms an invisible wall between him and those he watches. Andrew Miller has written on the metaphoric possibilities of glass in nineteenth-century fiction. He points out that the manufacture of large expanses of glass only became possible towards the middle of the century, and one particularly common use for such glass sheets was the display of goods in shop windows (Miller, 1995, p.7). The grandest display of commercial wares in this period was the Great Exhibition of the Industries of 1851. The Great Exhibition was effectively a demonstration of British commercial prowess, with 15,000 exhibitors showing goods ranging from mighty production machinery, such as steam hammers and hydraulic presses, to rather more decorative items, such as candlesticks and asparagus tongs. The exhibition was housed in the purpose-built Crystal Palace, a vast and impressive construction of nearly one million square feet of glass and 3,300 iron girders which covered 18 acres of Hyde Park (Flint, 1986, p.24; May, 1995, pp.166–73). The idea of an expanse of glass can, therefore, be seen to become closely associated with the display of commercial wares. And it is therefore tempting to interpret Dombey's gaze through the glass at the nurse walking to and fro with her young charge as another instance of the commodification of his personal relationships. He sees the affection of the nurse for the child as an economic investment; it is a matter of financial and social expediency for him, so that the son will one day be able to take the place of the father, and carry on the success of the family firm.

Dombey may seek to exert his personal and financial control over his family by watching his son and his nurse from behind the glass screen, but the narrative once again suggests that this confidence in his position and his authority is misplaced. As we subsequently learn, little Paul dies young and the firm of

Dombey and Son collapses. It seems that this scene anticipates this sequence of events by suddenly inverting the direction of the gaze. Instead of Paul and Richards who are gazed upon, it is Dombey himself who is watched by both Richards and the reader as though through the sheet of glass. The narrative voice transforms the sense of display through glass from the perspective of Dombey to the sense of enclosure by the glass from the perspective of Richards. She reflects that Dombey sits as 'if he were a lone prisoner in a cell'. The house then assumes a double function in the narrative: it entraps Dombey and also serves as an extension of him. Richards perceptively observes that, in some sense, Dombey appears to be indivisible from the house he inhabits. The inversion of the gaze seems to suggest that if you treat others as so many goods and services then you eventually become an object yourself – with all vitality extinguished. Richards makes an interesting observation on this process in the above passage, when she suggests that Dombey appears as a ghostly figure. She sees him as 'a strange apparition', haunting a room which seems itself to be grimly reminiscent of a bygone era. The implication is not that Dombey himself is in any literal sense dead, but rather that the social form of hereditary capitalism which he represents is on the point of extinction. Dombey, of course, does not die in the novel, but the male lineage of which he is so proud in both the affairs of the business and the family is certainly curtailed by the death of one of the novel's principal characters, and indeed by one of the most notable of nineteenth-century fictional deaths, that of his son Paul.

# The life and death of little Paul

In writing about the death of a child who was one of the major characters in his novels, Dickens effectively reproduced the publishing coup he had enjoyed in 1841 with the description of the death of little Nell in *The Old Curiosity Shop*. The sentimental portrayal of the deaths of children had a considerable emotional impact on a public who often had to endure such bereavements in their own lives either as parents or siblings (Jalland, 1996, pp.119–42). Dickens himself famously endorsed the acute sense of personal loss which many of his readers felt on reading this scene. In the preface to the 1858 edition of the novel he writes of how he had roamed 'with a heavy heart' through the streets of Paris for a whole winter night after he had finished the chapter in which, as he puts it euphemistically, 'my little friend and I parted company' (see Dickens, 2001, appendix A, p.927).

Paul's death, however, had been planned meticulously. Dickens wrote in his private correspondence just before starting the fifth instalment that he was about to 'slaughter' the child (Dickens, 1977, p.676). One wonders if there isn't just a hint of glee in this prospective dispatching of innocence. Forster gives an indication of the public response to the demise of little Paul, claiming (perhaps with some exaggeration) that the episode flung 'the nation into mourning' (quoted in Collins, 1971, p.212). The Scottish jurist and critic Lord Jeffrey was reduced to a helpless state, writing to Dickens that 'I have so cried and sobbed over [the episode] last night, and again this morning; and felt my heart purified by those tears, and blessed and loved you for making me shed them' (quoted in ibid., p.217). The sheer technical bravura and innovation of the scene also caught the eye. The novelist William Thackeray, who was publishing *Vanity Fair* serially in direct competition with *Dombey and Son*, allegedly burst into the offices of *Punch* magazine, hurled the fifth number of Dickens's novel onto the editor's desk, and exclaimed in exasperation 'there's no writing against such power as this – one has no chance! ... It is stupendous' (quoted in ibid., p.219).

Some contemporary voices, however, were rather more sceptical. The satirical magazine *The Man in Moon*, for example, wittily held a mock inquest into Paul's death. The article has Dickens himself giving evidence and suggesting that the disease from which the character suffered was probably 'an attack of acute "don't-know-what-to-do-with-him-phobia". Had it not supervened, he would probably have succumbed at last to a chronic affection, technically called "being-in-the-way-ism"' (quoted in Ackroyd, 1991, p.549). The historian Henry Hallam wrote in a similarly sceptical vein: 'Everybody is pretending that the death of Paul Dombey is the most beautiful thing ever written ... I am so hardened as to be unable to look on it in any light but pure business' (quoted in Churchill, 1975, p.183). In other words, the accusations are that Dickens dispensed with little Paul because he obstructed the development of the plot, and the fashionable pathos of his demise was little more than a commercial gambit to boost still further the sales of the novel's monthly instalments. In commercial terms he was, of course, successful; this instalment pushed monthly sales up to 33,000 copies (Patten, 1978, p.188).

As wryly amusing and instructive as such sceptical observations are, they are ultimately rather too jaundiced in their conclusions for two reasons. It can be argued that the life and death of Paul is, firstly, integral to the unfolding of the social, economic and familial concerns of the novel, and, secondly, that it eloquently demonstrates the dynamic within Dickens's aesthetic between narrative innovation and conservative social vision. In his short life little Paul combines innocence with an almost uncanny world-weariness. As a very young child he has the look of an old man as he sits silently beside his brooding father. The narrative suggests that Paul is out of place in the hectic commercialism of mid-nineteenth-century London by repeatedly stressing his 'old-fashionedness' (a term which in the middle of the nineteenth century suggests something uncanny in addition to its literal meaning).

Little Paul is a curious child, unable fully to partake of the age into which he has been born. As such, he can be understood to play a significant part in the socially descriptive apparatus of the novel. He is inordinately useful because he provides a perspective from which conventional notions of early Victorian conduct and belief can be examined. Common events or received opinions are refracted through Paul's rather idiosyncratic view of the world, and the reader, in turn, is encouraged to reflect upon his or her own position on such matters (the technical term for this process in a literary context is defamiliarization). The clearest example of little Paul assuming this role is his discussion with his father on the topic of money. Dickens uses Paul's innocence (in chapter 8) to ask a number of searching questions about the nature of wealth. Paul asks his father 'what's money?' Dombey is bemused by this question; he wants to respond by deploying the full array of financial jargon at his disposal to describe the system of economic exchange, such as 'circulating-medium, currency, depreciation of currency, paper, bullion, rates of exchange, value of precious metals in the market, and so forth' (8; p.99). He recognizes, however, that this is an inappropriate vocabulary for a child (or indeed for anybody whose life has not already been organized by this economic order). Dombey asserts that money has the power to do anything, but little Paul's naive questioning exposes the limitations of this doctrine of financial omnipotence. Money is at best morally neutral and mostly impotent in its emotional influence; it is not able to revive Paul's mother or restore him to good health. Paul's questioning effectively exposes a certain arbitrariness in an order of economic exchange which Dombey accepts as a natural state of affairs and highlights the ease with which Dombey, and others like him, can confuse an economic conception of value with emotional and familial interest.

**Now reread the scene of Paul's death (chapter 16 'What the waves were always saying'). Use the following questions to guide your reading. How does Paul view the world? What is Paul's relationship with his father? How would you describe the style of writing in this scene?**

Paul, I think, is portrayed in this scene mainly as a passive observer. He listens to and envisages the hustle and bustle of the city life which takes place around him. As the narrator makes clear, 'he pictured to himself – pictured! he saw – the high church towers rising up into the morning sky, the town reviving, waking, starting into life once more' (16; p.237). In this death-bed scene Paul's perspective exposes a certain arbitrariness, or at least a lack of clear purpose, in much of the frantic social and commercial activity he imagines taking place beyond the confines of his bedroom. We can see with the benefit of hindsight that little Paul's world-weary demeanour, his old-fashionedness and the significant events of his life have steadily prepared us for the moment of his demise. You may recall that the narrator observed when the infant Paul was carried into the church for his christening, that he 'might have asked with Hamlet "into my Grave?" so chill and earthy was the place' (5; p.61). When Paul was a pupil at Blimber's academy he was wheeled down to the seaside, as though borne in the coffin in a funeral cortège. With a 'notable attendant to pull him along, and Florence always walking by his side, and the despondent Wickham bringing up the rear, [Paul] went down to the margin of the ocean every day; and there he would sit or lie in his carriage for hours together' (8; p.116). The more cynical of contemporary accounts may have seen Paul's demise as a piece of narrative expediency, but his death also perhaps suggests that the types of personal qualities he exemplifies cannot be readily accommodated within a modern commercial and industrial society.

There is in Paul's death-bed scene a striking but also perplexing moment in which he does not recognize his own father sitting at the bottom of his bed. Paul sees his father as though he were an inanimate object rather than a person, using the demonstrative pronoun 'that' to describe him: 'What *is* that? ... There! at the bottom of the bed'. Paul does subsequently recognize Dombey, but the face is transformed; it is 'so altered to [Paul's] thinking, thrilled while he gazed, as if it were in pain; and before he could reach out both his hands to take it between them, and draw it towards him, the figure turned away quickly from the little bed, and went out at the door' (14; p.238). **Why is Paul unable to recognize his father at this point?**

We might explain it away as a delusion brought about by Paul's chronic condition. But the scene is clearly reminiscent of Florence's perception of her father in the opening chapter as a sequence of discrete signs of parental authority (that imposing assemblage of watch, collar, blue waistcoat and boots) rather than a warmly responsive and readily identifiable human being. Paul seems to repeat this objectification of his father, and by doing so reminds us again of the emotional separation between Dombey and his children. Paul's inability to *see* his father underlines our sense of Dombey as a man who is systematically transforming himself into the kind of commodified object in which he trades.

Looked at from a slightly different angle, Paul's failure to recognize his father and Dombey's subsequent turning away perhaps also mark the beginning of Dombey's own collapse, as the approaching death of his son ends his hopes for the dynastic succession of the firm. In this sense the death of Paul ties neatly into the novel's frequent descriptions of Dombey as a shade or ghostlike apparition, as he sees himself effectively fading away, enacting, as it were, the extinction of his own family line. It is no accident, of course, that near the end of the novel, when Dombey has undergone a complete mental collapse, having lost his business, his house and his second wife, he recalls this turning away from his dying son. The description of Dombey at this late point of the narrative brilliantly fuses the extinction of his hopes, his hauntings, with the merest possibility of his salvation:

> In the miserable night [Dombey] thought of it; in the dreary day, the wretched dawn, the ghostly, memory-haunted twilight. He did remember it. In agony, in sorrow, in remorse, in despair! 'Papa! Papa! Speak to me, dear Papa!' He heard the words again, and saw the face. He saw it fall upon the trembling hands, and heard the one prolonged low cry go upward. (59; p.882)

Thackeray's declaration that the writing in the fifth instalment of *Dombey and Son* was 'stupendous' is an acknowledgement of the emotional power of these scenes but also, one suspects, a recognition of its technical innovations in the use of poetic and symbolic modes of narrative. The imagery of the water is sustained throughout 'What the waves were always saying'. Paul is introduced at the beginning of the chapter reflecting upon the River Thames as it flows through London. (The river, of course, is the basis for the commercial success of the merchant firm of Dombey and Son.) Subsequently the idea of the flowing river is transformed into the flowing tears shed at the prospect of Paul's imminent demise, and finally appears as an extended metaphor for death itself as 'the swift river' sweeps 'old fashioned' little Paul away, just as his own mother at the end of the first chapter was swept 'out upon the dark and unknown sea that rolls round all the world' (1; p.10).

Such symbolism is striking and intriguing because it connects those areas of the novel which seem to be mutually exclusive, the economic and the emotional. I will discuss the symbolic elements of Dickens's narrative in more detail in the next chapter, but I want now to extend this discussion of little Paul

*Figure 6.1    Late nineteenth-century study of St Paul's cathedral and the Thames. The photograph interestingly replicates* Dombey and Son*'s poetic and mercantile vision of the river. Reproduced from* The Victorian City: Images and Realities, *ed. by H.J. Dyos and Michael Wolff, London: Routledge & Kegan Paul, 1973, vol.2, figure 136. Photo: George Davison, Kodak Museum*

to consider the novel's representation of families in the wider terms of the domestic ideologies of the early Victorian period. And we might start with Paul's relationship with his sister, Florence.

## Brothers and sisters

Just before he dies, Paul reflects on his mother, and on the nature of her relationship with both his sister and his father: 'One night he had been thinking of his mother, and her picture in the drawing-room down-stairs, and had thought she must have loved sweet Florence better than his father did, to have held her in her arms when she was dying – for even he, her brother, who had such dear love for her, could have no greater wish than that' (16; pp.238–9). **Do you notice anything odd or ambiguous in the way things are expressed in this passage?**

The constant use of 'she' and 'her' makes it unclear as to whether Paul's greatest wish would have been to hold his mother in his arms when she was dying, or whether it would be to hold Florence in his arms, just like his mother, when he dies. The lack of clarity can, perhaps, be just dismissed as an oversight. Paul will, of course, perish while enfolded in the loving embrace of his sister (16; p.241). Nevertheless, the confusion between the respective roles of brother, sister and mother is also perhaps indicative of an instability in the depiction of familial relationships in the work as a whole.

The closeness of the relationship between the two Dombey children is subsequently used in one of the novel's more conventionally realistic strands. Dickens has often been accused of being that much more interested in the theatrical organization and external displays of his characters than in strictly auditing the minutiae of their intellectual processes. The close relationship of Paul and Florence, however, does explain persuasively the subsequent hardening of Dombey's attitude towards his daughter after his son's death. Dickens himself recognized the necessity for the depiction of an intense emotional relationship between Paul and Florence to account for Dombey's subsequent conduct. In an outline of the novel he sent to Forster in July 1846, he proposed from the moment of Paul's death to change 'Dombey's feeling of indifference and uneasiness towards his daughter into a positive hatred. For he will always remember how the boy had his arm around her neck when he was dying, and whispered to her, and would take things only from her hand' (Tillotson, 1977, p.590).

Yet there is still something perhaps slightly unsettling in the emotional intensity and insularity of this account of sibling affection. The closeness and significance of this relationship in the novel has been explored in an article by Catherine Waters. **Read through Catherine Waters, 'Ambiguous intimacy: brother and sister relationships in *Dombey and Son*' (1988, pp.9–26; extract in Regan, 2001). What is the main argument of this piece?**

Waters begins by stating that the novel demonstrates a range of brother and sister relationships, and that Dickens provides a complex vision of sibling affection which embraces an idealization of the relationship as well as suggesting a certain sexual ambiguity within it. In the case of Paul and Florence, as Waters points out, their love appears both ardent and, on occasion, quite desperate. Florence cries wildly to her nurse on one occasion 'oh pray, pray, let me lie by my brother tonight, for I believe he's fond of me!' (5; p.53). Paul subsequently reciprocates these feelings. When he is installed at Blimber's academy, he stares longingly each night out of his bedroom window just to catch a glimpse of his beloved sister. He shuns other children, preferring instead Florence's exclusive company. Sitting with Florence on the beach in Brighton, he confides, 'We don't want any others, do we? Kiss me, Floy' (8; p.116). Later still, he imagines a time when Florence and he can retire to the country in a state of domestic bliss. This will be an idyllic period when Paul can 'have a beautiful garden, fields, and woods, and live there with [Florence] all [his] life' (14; p.202). Their relationship consequently seems to stray perilously close to an intensity and intimacy that we might expect of lovers. Read in this way, Paul and Florence's final embrace on his death-bed perhaps takes on a certain erotic ambience, with a poetic confluence of love and death, as 'sister and brother wound their arms around each other, and the golden light came streaming in, and fell upon them, locked together' (16; p.240).

Waters entertains the possibility that such sentimental description is just a way of conveniently masking some dark, transgressive desires in the novel. She cites Mark Spilka's conclusion that 'Paul Dombey's affection for his sister is bathetic and incestuous', and Russell M. Goldfarb's opinion that 'in the foreground of *Dombey and Son* there is a complicated incestuous relationship' (quoted in Waters, 1988, pp.16–17). There are other episodes which seem to support an account of the general instability of the roles of brother, sister, husband and wife in *Dombey and Son*. One further example is Florence's relationship with her eventual husband, Walter Gay. **Florence encounters Walter after his rescue from shipwreck in the West Indies in the following passage. How does she view him?**

> She had no thought of him but as a brother, a brother rescued from the grave; a shipwrecked brother saved and at her side; and rushed into his arms. In all the world, he seemed to be her hope, her comfort, refuge, natural protector. 'Take care of Walter, I was fond of Walter!' The dear remembrance of the plaintive voice that said so, rushed upon her soul, like music in the night. 'Oh welcome home, dear Walter! Welcome to this stricken breast!' She felt the words, although she could not utter them, and held him in her pure embrace. (49; p.730)

It seems clear, then, that she sees her future husband as her brother, and in this regard Walter Gay serves as an emotional substitute for the deceased little Paul. Florence tellingly reacts to meeting Walter by recalling Paul. Walter's presence has the almost tangible effect of allowing her to 'feel' her dead brother's words. The confusion of familial roles is not confined to Florence, her brother and her future husband. The mixing of husband, brother and lover also occurs in one of the novel's subplots, in the relationship of the disgraced John Carker with his sister Harriet (the younger siblings of the principal villain of the piece, James Carker). John and Harriet live in a small house on the outskirts of North London. Waters draws at this point on the development of middle-class domestic ideology in the early Victorian period to explain Harriet's role in the novel.

In its most basic form, the ideology posits two spheres of influence, where men have to labour in a harsh public world, and women, as their wives, have responsibility for (and are effectively confined to) a private domestic sphere in which they provide a thoroughly well-organized, comfortable and morally secure environment for their families (Houghton, 1957; Poovey, 1989). The most famous and popular literary expression of this doctrine of female domestic responsibility is Coventry Patmore's sequence of poems *The Angel in the House* (1854–61). Patmore describes the happy, virtuous state of the wife compared with the worldly woes of her spouse:

> Her happy virtues taking hands
> Each smiling in another's face.
> So, dancing round the tree of life,
> They make an Eden of her breast,
> While his disjointed and at strife,
> Proud-thoughted and do not bring him rest.
>
> (quoted in Poovey, 1989, p.8)

Similarly conventional views on feminine selflessness and domestic duty are also expressed in a triptych of paintings by George Elder Hicks entitled *Women's Mission,* which was exhibited at the Royal Academy in 1863. The second of these, *Companion of Manhood* (see Figure 6.2), depicts a submissive but supportive wife as she comforts her grieving husband in the well-maintained parlour of their middle-class home. The figure of Harriet Carker in *Dombey and Son* seems initially at least to be just another embodiment of such domestic saintliness, as she too serves as the comforter of male woes with her virtues, making 'an Eden of her breast'. She cares tirelessly for the disgraced John Carker in reduced circumstances. The peculiarity of her state of affairs, however, is that

*Figure 6.2  George Elder Hicks, study for* Women's Mission: Companion of Manhood, *1863.* Tate Gallery, London 2000

John is not her husband, but her brother. Towards the end of the narrative the relationships in their household become even more confused. Harriet, in keeping with the notion of a suitable reward for virtuous conduct, gets to marry, the elderly, benevolent Mr Morfin, who has previously acted as their anonymous guardian. The brother John is as a result displaced from his position as quasi-husband to his sister, only to stay in the same house with Morfin and Harriet. The family ends up 'in a parodic *ménage à trois*' with the brother now 'filling the place conventionally occupied by the lover' (Waters, 1988, p.15).

Waters provides us with a spectrum of responses to the depiction of brother and sister relationships in the work: idealization on the one hand and 'ambiguous intimacy' on the other. She concludes by suggesting that 'the significance of this vision [of sibling affection] for nineteenth-century fiction lies in Dickens's identification and exploration of the way in which the sexual feeling underlying intense fraternal relationships emerges from the Victorian ideals of femininity and domesticity' (Waters, 1988, pp.25–6). **What do you make of this reading? Are you persuaded by its identification of a sexual undercurrent to the depictions of a sibling affection?**

For my part, I find this reading of the novel perceptive, and I do accept the argument of the presence of sexual feeling in these familial relationships, but the conclusion of Waters's article strikes me as being too neat, as though the novel can ultimately reconcile a harmonious vision of domesticity with the sexual tensions which such domesticity contains. I am inclined to see *Dombey and Son*'s depiction of hearth and home as remaining rather more fraught, and in order to illustrate this I'd like to look briefly at the triangular relationship of Florence, her stepmother Edith, and Dombey himself.

## Husband, stepmother and daughter

When Florence is first introduced to Edith, she reacts with a heady mixture of emotions, 'surprise, interest, admiration, and an indefinable sort of fear', and then responds by falling, 'weeping on the lady's bosom' (28; p.428). The intimate nature of this particular relationship is quickly established. In response to Florence's tearful collapse Edith clasps her 'close about her waist', and kisses 'her on the cheek' (ibid.). There follows a description of furtive glances, stolen kisses, passionate embraces and tender caresses. On the night before her marriage to Paul Dombey, Edith gazes on the sleeping Florence, and finds herself 'drawn nearer, nearer, nearer yet; at last, drawn so near, that stooping down, she pressed her lips upon the gentle hand that lay outside the bed, and put it softly to her neck' (30; p.461). Edith subsequently passes the night before her marriage sleeping on the same bed as her stepdaughter.

Edith's emotional reaction to Florence looks as though it is intended to contrast with her emotionally stultifying relationship with Dombey. The position of this scene is also significant. It comes immediately before Edith's marriage to Florence's father, and by doing so it emphasizes the difference between a relationship based on mutual affection, as is the case with Edith and Florence, and one undertaken purely for social and financial expediency, as is the case with Edith and Dombey. Some modern critics have identified a homoerotic undertow in the relationship between Florence and her stepmother (see, for example, Armstrong, 1996). It also should be said, however, that any such suggestion of homoeroticism is problematic. As Richard Altick has observed, modern readers may pick up on the novel's implications of lesbianism, but there is no clear evidence to suggest that the Victorians, at least on a conscious level, interpreted Edith and Florence's relationship in this way (1980, p.94). **So, how might we interpret this relationship?**

Both Edith and Florence are not realistic characters, or to put this point slightly differently, the characters appear to be drawn from traditions of writing which would not usually be associated with realism. Edith is described constantly in terms of her pride, her coolness and 'heaving bosom'; she looks as though she is the tragic queen of popular Victorian theatrical melodrama. Indeed she partakes in the most demonstrably theatrical scenes of the novel in her defiant exchanges with both Dombey and James Carker. Florence looks as though she has been drawn directly from a tradition of eighteenth-century sentimental writing. She is, in some respects, the most traditional of sentimental heroines; she is evidently kind, innocent, open-hearted, and, crucially in this particular genre, she is prone at the merest emotional disturbance to quiver and dissolve into a river of tears. Both characters consequently can be understood as conventional cultural types. And indeed one might argue that it is precisely their conventionality which allows them to represent such emotions and desires, which if presented directly would be unacceptable to mainstream Victorian opinion. Their very familiarity, their identification as stock characters, perhaps allows them at one and the same time both to mask and to transmit those forms of physical and emotional attractiveness which a censorious Victorian middle-class consciousness would find impossible to entertain.

Whatever one thinks about this apparent identification of both homoerotic and incestuous strands within *Dombey and Son*, one of the striking features of the triangular relationship of Florence, Edith and Dombey is the extent that it deviates from the ideological norm of the middle-class English family in the middle of the nineteenth century. In a more sophisticated version of the doctrine of the angel in the house, the most prominent art critic of the age, John Ruskin, evades the difficulty of seeing the separate spheres of men and women as a means of essentially preserving male authority and identity by acknowledging as much and recasting the relationship in chivalrous terms:

> The man, in his rough work in open world, must encounter all peril and trial; – to him, therefore, must be the failure, the offence, the inevitable error: often he must be wounded, or subdued; often misled; and *always* hardened. But he guards the woman from all this within his house, as ruled by her ... This is the true nature of home – it is the place of Peace.

(quoted in Gilmour, 1993, p.190)

The Victorian gentleman, in this view, is the successor of the medieval knight, following a strict moral code of honour, loyalty and valour. He is hardened by his battles in the public world of commerce and stands protective of his hearth. Judged by these standards it is difficult to imagine a more dysfunctional household than the Dombeys. Dombey thoroughly confuses the separate spheres of embattled commercial world and domestic retreat by entering into his marriage on economic grounds. The relationship between Dombey and Edith is without passion, and operates on the basis of a financial and social contract. Edith readily recognizes the market forces in their relationship and her status as something to be procured. As she tells her mother before the wedding: 'You know [Dombey] has bought me ... He has considered of his bargain; he has shown it to his friend ... he thinks that it will suit him, and may be had sufficiently cheap; and he will buy to-morrow' (27; p.417). Moreover, Dombey's hatred of Florence culminates in the most transgressive of actions, in an absolute denial of knightly virtue, when he physically strikes his daughter after Edith's elopement with Carker.

*Dombey and Son* gives us, then, examples of relationships which are more complex and unseemly than the more rigid ideological accounts of the family would allow. It suggests that the driving economic imperative of English society is likely to be destructive of any coherent and secure notion of family life, however this may be constituted. For the novel effectively poses its audience a question: how can one have a happy and secure family life if the economic basis of family life is constantly threatened by the very economic ideologies which finance it? Indeed, *Dombey and Son* displays the vagaries and destructiveness of free-market economics irrespective of one's position on the social ladder. The problem for those characters at the lowest end of the social scale, such as Good Mrs Brown and her daughter, is their wretched poverty; they lack the means either for emotional stability or for any kind of personal improvement. The problem for characters higher up the ladder, such as Mrs Pipchin and ultimately Dombey himself, is that one's apparent economic security can be swept away without warning, either through poor financial investment or through the cyclical booms and busts of the Victorian economy. If Dombey's actions are damnable in the moral schema of the novel, then they are at least explicable in terms of the social and economic pressures of the society in which he lives.

I'd like to finish this chapter by making one further observation on the representation of the family. We have seen the ways in which the family in all its perplexing complexity is portrayed in this work, and we might note that much of this portrayal is conducted in forms of writing which are not conventionally realist, such as the sentimental descriptions of Florence, the poetic symbolic descriptions of Paul, and the melodramatic descriptions of his second wife, Edith. Yet this range of styles appears to be marshalled for broadly realist ends. It can be argued that the overall effect of the novel is to produce a rich and highly varied form of expression which both masks and reveals the distorting and destructive effects of the cultural pressures of Victorian society. In other words, stylistic diversity in this area of narrative would appear to serve the realist purposes of producing both a description and a critique of the ideals of middle-class family life in this period. We can perhaps see rather more clearly how such forms of writing are used for the purposes of social description and social critique if we look at some of the secondary characters in this work, and in particular the idiosyncratic forms of their speech. So, we will begin the next chapter with some fisticuffs between the Game Chicken and the Larkey Boy.

# Works cited

Ackroyd, Peter. 1991. *Dickens*, London: Minerva.

Altick, Richard D. 1980. 'Varieties of reader response: the case of *Dombey and Son*', *Yearbook of English Studies*, 10, pp.70–94.

Armstrong, Mary. 1996. '*Dombey and Son*: female homoerotic desire, and the sentimental heroine', *Studies in the Novel*, 28, pp.281–302.

Auerbach, Nina. 1976. 'Dickens and Dombey: a daughter after all', *Dickens Studies Annual*, 5, pp.95–105.

Bakhtin, M.M. 1981. *The Dialogic Imagination*, ed. by Michael Holquist, trans. by Caryl Emerson and Michael Holquist, Austin: University of Texas Press.

Brown, James M. 1982. *Dickens: Novelist in the Market-Place*, Chippenham: Anthony Rowe.

Churchill, R.A. 1975. *A Bibliography of Dickensian Criticism 1836–1975*, Garland Reference Library of the Humanities, vol.12, Basingstoke: Macmillan.

Collins, Philip. Ed. 1971. *Dickens: The Critical Heritage*, London: Routledge & Kegan Paul.

Dickens, Charles. 1977. *The Letters of Charles Dickens*, vol.4: *1844–1846*, ed. by Kathleen Tillotson, Oxford: Oxford University Press.

Dickens, Charles. [1846–8] 2001. *Dombey and Son*, ed. by Alan Horsman, with an introduction and notes by Dennis Walder, Oxford World's Classics, Oxford: Oxford University Press.

Eagleton, Terry. 1976. *Criticism and Ideology: A Study in Marxist Theory*, London: Verso.

Flint, Kate. 1986. *Dickens*, Harvester New Readings, Brighton: Harvester.

Gilmour, Robin. 1993. *The Victorian Period: The Intellectual and Cultural Context of English Literature, 1830–1890*, Longman Literature in English, London: Longman.

Hobsbawm, E.J. 1969. *Industry and Empire: From 1750 to the Present Day*, The Penguin Economic History of Britain, vol.3, Harmondsworth: Penguin.

Houghton, Walter E. 1957. *The Victorian Frame of Mind, 1830–1870*, New Haven and London: Yale University Press.

Jalland, Pat. 1996. *Death in the Victorian Family*, Oxford: Oxford University Press.

McCord, Norman. 1991. *British History 1815–1906*, The Short Oxford History of the Modern World, Oxford: Oxford University Press.

May, Trevor. 1995. *An Economic and Social History of Britain 1760–1790*, 2nd edn, Harlow: Longman.

Miller, Andrew H. 1995. *Novels Behind Glass: Commodity Culture and Victorian Narrative*, Cambridge: Cambridge University Press.

Patten, Robert L. 1978. *Charles Dickens and his Publishers*, Oxford: Clarendon Press.

Poovey, Mary. 1989. *Uneven Developments: The Ideological Work of Gender in Mid-Victorian England*, London: Virago.

Regan, Stephen. Ed. 2001. *The Nineteenth-Century Novel: A Critical Reader*, London: Routledge.

Taine, Hippolyte. 1871. *History of English Literature*, trans. by H. Van Laun, 2 vols, Edinburgh.

Walder, Dennis. 1981. *Dickens and Religion*, London: Allen & Unwin.

Walder, Dennis. 2001. 'Introduction' to Charles Dickens, *Dombey and Son*, ed. by Alan Horsman, Oxford World's Classics, Oxford University Press.

Waters, Catherine. 1988. 'Ambiguous intimacies: brother and sister relationships in *Dombey and Son*', *The Dickensian*, 44, pp.9–26. (Extract in Regan, 2001.)

Suggestions for further reading can be found at the end of chapter 7.

# *Dombey and Son:* industrialization and empire

*by Sebastian Mitchell*

In the previous chapter we concentrated upon the depiction of the family in *Dombey and Son*. In this chapter I want to consider the novel's handling of wider social themes, such as the increasingly commercial and industrial nature of early Victorian society, and the economic and social importance of British imperial dominion. Implicit within this discussion is the question of the extent to which the novel criticizes the social processes it describes. Does it ultimately condone or condemn the substantial rebuilding of London, and the development of the railway? Similarly, does the novel approve or disapprove of British colonial policy? As I hope will become clear, the novel certainly articulates forthright views on all of these issues, but it does not necessarily provide us with any straightforward answers. We will finish with a consideration of the historical significance of the range of views which the novel expresses, but I want to start with an account of the secondary characters in *Dombey and Son*, and the ways in which these can be seen to focus a number of the novel's main social issues.

## Supporting characters in an industrial economy

In a highly influential account of Dickens's fiction, Raymond Williams, the leading Marxist literary critic of the 1960s, reflects upon the apparent eccentricity of many of Dickens's characterizations. Williams defends Dickens against the charge that his secondary characters are no more than caricatures. He suggests that he created these figures as an effective literary response to the volatile industrial age in which he lived. Dickens, he insists, 'was creating, openly and deliberately, a world in which people had been deprived of any customary identity, and yet in which, paradoxically, the deprivation was a kind of liberation, in which the most fantastic and idiosyncratic kinds of growth could come about' (Williams, 1970a, p.53; see also Williams, 1970b). Williams sees that identity for many individuals in this period becomes problematic, precisely because the dynamic nature of mid-nineteenth-century society did not provide a set of clear social roles for people to follow. Rather, the absence of clear social determinants for personal identity allows for the development of the most idiosyncratic of individuals. In *Dombey and Son*, we might regard the Game Chicken, the pugilist companion of scatter-brained Toots, as just such an idiosyncratic figure.

## *The Game Chicken*

**Read through the following report of the Chicken's defeat in the ring. The scene takes place in Toots's house just after Dombey has dismissed Susan Nipper from his household for confronting him over his treatment of Florence. What do you think is the intended effect of such writing? And what kind of language is being used here?**

> This Gentleman awakened in Miss Nipper some considerable astonishment; for, having been defeated by the Larkey Boy, his visage was in a state of great dilapidation, as to be hardly presentable in society with comfort to the beholders. The Chicken himself attributed this punishment to his having had the misfortune to get into the Chancery early in the proceedings, when he was severely fibbed by the Larkey one, and heavily grassed. But it appeared from the published records of that great contest that the Larkey Boy had had it all his own way from the beginning, and that the Chicken had been tapped, and bunged, and had received pepper, and had been made groggy, and had come up piping, and had endured a complication of familiar strange inconveniences, until he had been gone into and finished.
>
> (Dickens, [1846–8] 2001, 44; pp.658–9; unless otherwise stated, all subsequent page references are to this edition)

The scene is clearly intended to provide light relief after Susan's dramatic departure from Dombey's house. The comic intention of this episode is indicated by its circumlocutions (that is, the phrases are unnecessarily long to convey their meaning) and by the slightly arcane description of the Chicken's bruised face: 'his visage was in a state of great dilapidation, as to be hardly presentable in society with comfort to the beholders'. The Chicken's defeat in the ring is related entirely in an obscure (but no doubt accurate) boxing slang, which includes an array of colourful expressions such as 'severely fibbed', 'heavily grassed' and 'tapped, and bunged', and uses curious syntactical contortions such as 'endured a complication of familiar strange inconveniences'. One would not expect the majority of Dickens's Victorian audience to be able to follow the exact meaning of this description of the fight with any more ease than we can, although we all get the gist of the Game Chicken's unfortunate defeat.

The idiosyncratic Chicken himself is entirely constructed beyond familiar social constraints, and from the argot of prizefighting. The description of him, however, defies our immediate expectations of a boxer. Despite his profession of violence, the Chicken can be viewed as a pathetic figure. The reader is invited both to enjoy the description of the contest, and to pity the defeated fighter. Williams argues that the dynamic society offers both the removal of traditional social co-ordinates, and the possibility of the growth of strange, new types of individuals. The evidence of the Chicken, however, would seem to suggest that such new types are themselves not quite stable; they are prone to dissolution, or in the Chicken's case to being knocked over in the ring at any given moment.

**Have you noticed anything curious about the narrative perspective in this extract?**

The passage starts from the perspective of the Chicken, but then shifts to the position of the 'published records of that great contest'. That is to say, the second part of the passage is related from the standpoint of a newspaper report of the contest. It is as though the language with which the Chicken defines himself is at this moment wrested away from him and turned upon him so that he now becomes an object within the spectacle of the fight. He is to be 'gone into and finished' in both the fight itself and the language of prizefighting.

# Mrs Pipchin

The most obvious effect of the Chicken's boxing bout is the damage to his face caused by the blows of Larkey Boy. The cuts and bruises no doubt heal given time, but no such healing ever takes place from the metaphorical blows which little Paul's elderly nurse, Mrs Pipchin, has taken on the chin. You may recall that Mrs Pipchin is employed to care for Paul when he is moved to Brighton. She has a striking verbal mannerism, obsessively referring to Peruvian mines. Dickens's intention is to entertain us with the oddity of the association between an elderly infirm nurse from the south of England and some mining enterprise in remote South America. Such repetitious speech also has a practical purpose in a narrative which contains over 230 characters, and was originally related over nineteen months. Clearly, the use of highly distinctive phrases and improbable associations renders this character sufficiently memorable to be recalled with ease after a long absence.

The memorable speech, however, also has thematic implications. Mrs Pipchin's refrain of Peruvian mines is a reference to her husband's ill-advised investment in mining stock and the subsequent loss of the family's money when the share price collapsed. The shock of failure kills him, leaving his family in such straitened circumstances that his widow has to go out to work. The Peruvian mine becomes for her a mantra of personal disaster. She is both determined by the moment of the loss of independent means and social status, and entirely formulated by this trauma. She is a symbol of the self having been entirely consumed by the vagaries of the financial markets. Like the other secondary characters in this work, her utterances reiterate the central themes of the work and act as signs to provoke specific responses from the novel's contemporary audience. Mrs Pipchin's obsession with mines is certainly humorous, but her monomania – her compulsion to revisit this catastrophe – mirrors Dombey's own obsessiveness over the status of the family firm and anticipates his financial and mental collapse at the end of the novel. Pipchin's Peruvian obsession also expresses the deep-seated anxieties of early Victorian middle classes about the loss of capital, wellbeing and social esteem through the unpredictable movements of financial markets.

# Major Bagstock

One of the most prominent of the novel's supporting figures is the old colonial trooper, Major Bagstock. The following extract comes from his first meeting with Dombey in Brighton, when Dombey is out walking with Paul and Mrs Pipchin.

**How would you describe Bagstock's speech here? What sort of character is he?**

'An old campaigner, Sir,' said the Major, 'a smoke-dried, sun-burnt, used-up invalided old dog of a Major, Sir, was not afraid of being condemned for his whim by a man like Mr Dombey. I have the honour of addressing Mr Dombey, I believe?'

'I am the present unworthy representative of that name, Major,' returned Mr Dombey.

'By G—, Sir!' said the Major, 'it's a great name. It's a name, Sir,' said the Major firmly, as if he defied Mr Dombey to contradict him, and would feel it his painful duty to bully him if he did, 'that is known and honoured in the British possessions abroad. It is a name, Sir, that a man is proud to recognise. There is nothing adulatory in Joseph Bagstock, Sir. His Royal Highness the Duke of York observed on more than one occasion, "there is no adulation in Joey. He is a plain old soldier is Joe. He is tough to a fault is Joseph:" but it's a great name, Sir. By the Lord, it's a great name!' said the Major, solemnly. (10; p.135)

Bagstock's speech is highly distinctive, with its frequent interjections of 'Sir', its staccato delivery and those extended apparently self-deprecatory metaphors such as the particularly vivid: 'a smoke-dried, sun-burnt, used-up invalided old dog of a Major'. His rich speech conjures up an image of the bilious old soldier, but it also implies precisely the opposite of what it says. Bagstock presents himself as plain, bluff and modest, but his speech constantly betrays his egotism. He is intensely proud of his regal encounters, casually introducing the Duke of York to endorse his claims to plainness. And despite the opening compliment to Dombey, most of this speech, as with all his other speeches, is about himself. Just as Pipchin endlessly returns to the Peruvian mines, Bagstock constantly returns to Bagstock, referring to himself in the third person through a repertoire of synonyms such as JB, Joey B, Joe and Joseph. Bagstock may be an entertaining pastiche of retired Victorian soldiery, but he is also another instance of monomania in the novel, another distorting mirror-image of Dombey himself. On the surface of things his speech is about communicating with Dombey, but of course his communication is compromised, partly because his speech returns *ad nauseam* to his own pre-eminent qualities of slyness, toughness and plainness, and partly because his encounters with other characters are viewed in terms of their use value, rather than for the development of companionship or affection for its own sake. In this scene Bagstock cultivates Dombey for the purposes of conducting his petty vendetta against Miss Tox.

## *Captain Cuttle*

In direct contrast to the egotistical and manipulative Bagstock stands the old tar, Captain Cuttle. Cuttle forms part of an alternative community centred on the small nautical-instrument-makers with 'the wooden Midshipman', which is situated close to Dombey's offices in the city. The community consists of Cuttle himself, the maritime shopkeeper Solomon Gills, and his nephew Walter Gay. Like the Chicken, Pipchin and Bagstock, Cuttle has his own distinctive speech.

In his case it is a rich nautical dialect. His tar-laden speech is an expression of his character, an extraordinarily enticing blend of bluff exterior and instinctual benevolence. When he hears of Gills's financial difficulties he immediately collects everything he owns of value to put at his friend's disposal, including all his savings (thirteen pounds and half a crown), 'two withered atomies of teaspoons', 'knock-knee'd sugar-tongs' and his 'immense double-cased silver watch' (9; p.127). As Walter is about to depart for the West Indies on the ironically named merchant ship, *Son and Heir*, Cuttle attempts to press the self-same watch, sugar tongs and teaspoons into the young man's grasp (he refuses them, of course). When Walter does eventually leave, he spies the Captain and his uncle from the deck of his ship. They, in turn, catch sight of Walter, and at that moment, the narrator reveals, 'Captain Cuttle dropped the property into the bottom of the boat with perfect unconcern, being evidently oblivious of its existence, and pulling off the glazed hat hailed him lustily. The glazed hat made quite a show in the sun with its glistening, and the Captain continued to wave it until he could be seen no longer' (19; pp.287–8).

With his wide suit of blue, his hook, bushy eyebrows, stick and pitted nose, Ned Cuttle is a broadly drawn comic figure. Indeed, Dickens switched a chapter in which he is particularly prominent so that it would come immediately after the death of little Paul to provide some comic relief for his distraught readership. But Cuttle has a more serious purpose in the novel: he offers a vision of a society which does not fundamentally operate on the basis of the economic exchange value of goods and services. Cuttle inverts the economic order of much of the rest of the narrative, by suggesting that economic considerations, the ownership of property, should not determine the kinds of social relations one enters into, and that such financial matters should invariably be subordinated to matters of loyalty and friendship. The *only* value to him of his own meagre wealth is the benefit it can bestow upon his friends. When Walter departs on the *Son and Heir*, Cuttle symbolically discards all his earthly goods, dropping them 'with perfect unconcern' into the bottom of the rowing boat, in order that he might wave even more lustily at his departing friend. Cuttle's disregard of the dominant social and economic orders of the novel is further illustrated by the conclusion of this particular episode. The narrator describes how Cuttle glistens as he waves his glazed hat in the sun; it is as though the old sea-dog has been miraculously transformed into some glistening precious metal. His value, however, is not to be measured in financial terms, but in the wide compass of his benevolence and his unshakeable loyalty to his friends.

## A benevolent community

The notion that Cuttle and his cohorts operate as an alternative to the various self-serving and economically self-interested modes of behaviour exemplified in various ways by such characters as Dombey, Carker, Bagstock, Mrs Skewton and Edith, is supported by the physical space these figures mostly inhabit: Solomon Gills's maritime shop. As a number of critics have observed, what is particularly striking about this commercial establishment is that none of the goods are ever actually sold. The navigational bric-à-brac of weather glasses, keys, lodestones, telescopes, globes and parallel rulers remains pretty well undisturbed, except by the odd guest, such as Mr Brogley, who contents himself by browsing absent-mindedly among the instruments (9; p.132). The shop in which nothing is sold consequently looks as though it is a metaphor for an alternative form of life to the predominant capitalist mode of early Victorian society. Goods which should be just so many impersonal objects to be bought and sold to keep the business ticking over become an integral part of the shop itself, almost imbued with a personal vitality, as they contribute to the identity of this place and its community. Nevertheless, as beguilingly attractive as this uncommercial and mutually beneficial society may be, it is also, significantly, an idealized representation of the economic and social conditions of England in the 1840s.

It is not, I think, a matter of the characters and their circumstances being unrealistic in any absolute sense, but rather the novel itself stresses the fictional nature of these figures. The narrative of Gills's nephew clearly reworks the urban folklore of Dick Whittington, as Gay progresses from impoverished youth to wealthy merchant, but the mythical quality of the particular narrative is highlighted in the text when Gay is explicitly compared to Whittington. Cuttle himself seems to be drawn from an eighteenth-century tradition of comic prose writing, and his precursors are almost certainly the bluff nautical figures which populate the picaresque novels of Tobias Smollett (1721–71). Like Dickens's Cuttle, Smollett's sailors, such as Tom Bowling in *The Adventures of Roderick Random* (1748) and Hawser Trunnion and Lieutenant Hatchway in *The Adventures of Peregrine Pickle* (1751, rev. edn 1758), speak in a rich nautical dialect; they are coarsely benevolent, fiercely loyal, honest and unquestionably patriotic.

I suggested earlier that the sentimental strand of the novel, of which Florence forms a part, is used to provide contemporary social criticism. The dysfunctional aspects of middle-class Victorian life, or at least the inconsistencies within the Victorian ideology of the contented middle-class household, could be explored through these ostensibly sentimental and melodramatic modes of writing. The broad eighteenth-century characterizations of such characters as Cuttle and Gills, however, appear to function in a slightly different fashion. The use of these materials and character types, in this instance, looks as though it is intended to highlight the anachronistic qualities of this particular community. Cuttle and his cohorts express the virtues of another age (kindness, loyalty and generosity) which are set against the mercantile values of Dombey and his associates.

Dickens originally intended that Walter Gay, the favourite son of this benevolent nautical community, should be corrupted by his movement into the modern commercial world. He suggested to Forster when the novel was being planned that the boy should be shown 'gradually and naturally trailing away, from that love of adventure and boyish light-heartedness, into negligence, idleness, dissipation, dishonesty, and ruin' (Dickens, 1977, p.593). He changed his mind, of course, possibly due to the positive public response to the character, but in a sense the point about the idealized nature of this sentimental society did not need to be underscored by Walter's ruin. The narrative clearly demonstrates this community's anachronistic, idealized qualities. It shows us the extent to which the wooden Midshipman operates outside the present moment, outside the timescales and formal conceptions of economic authority which determined industrial and commercial life by the middle of the nineteenth century.

We may recall that one of the objects which Cuttle symbolically discards as he waves off young Walter in the *Son and Heir* is his watch, 'dropped with perfect unconcern' into the bottom of the boat. Watches have already been imbued with symbolic importance in the narrative; Paul Dombey entertains his newly born son with his watch chain, and the watch is one of the objects which encodes his dispassionate authority for Florence in the opening chapter. Cuttle has already been unsuccessful in pressing that great silver watch into Walter's hand. He assures Gay that the watch works – or rather works after a fashion. For as he goes on to explain, the chronometer will indeed keep perfect time, just so long as the hands are moved back about half an hour every morning, and 'about another quarter towards the arternoon' (19; p.287). For most purposes, then, Cuttle's watch is pretty useless, unable to measure with any accuracy or reliability the remorseless tick, tick, tick of the modern age, but it is an entirely appropriate timepiece for a community of friends which exists outside the exigencies of the present and still dances to the beat of a sentimental heart.

**What do you make of Gills's nautical community? What do you think is its principal function in the novel?**

I am inclined to read the wooden Midshipman as a matter of wistful regret, a kind of nostalgic reminiscence of social forms which seem to be rendered impossible by the commercial industrial nature of the modern world. The wooden Midshipman offers us an alternative social vision to the modern age but it ultimately does so by rendering that vision as unrealistic as Cuttle's own tar-stained speech. *Dombey and Son* may offer a backward glance in its description of this nautical society, but it also, in other respects, fully embraces the dynamic industrial spirit of its age. It seems to rush headlong into modernity, so much so that it has been argued that at its most vital Dickens's prose echoes the repetitive percussive rhythms of the industrial age. John Ruskin first enunciated this view of the progressive Dickens, suggesting that he should not be seen as a traditionalist, but as an impassioned advocate of industrial transformation. 'Dickens', he declared, 'was a pure modernist – a leader of the steam-whistle party *par excellence*' (quoted in Collins, 1971, p.443). Ruskin's view is too reductive, and does not do justice to the political and social complexities of Dickens's middle and late fiction. Nevertheless, it does correctly identify the industrial dynamic of much of his writing, and it is to *Dombey and Son's* engagement with the industrial and imperial aspects of English society in the 1840s that we now turn.

# Commercial and industrial London

In 1862, the journalist and novelist Henry Mayhew arranged to fly above London in a balloon in order to get a clearer impression of the shape, size and organization of the city. But when he was airborne, he found himself dumbfounded by what he saw. The city was massive, totally disorienting in its scale; there was not a hint of countryside beyond it, and try as he might he just

*Figure 7.1   A bird's-eye view over early Victorian London and the Greenwich railway. This lithograph by G.F. Bragg gives us an impression of the view of the 'monster city' that Henry Mayhew enjoyed from a balloon. Reproduced from* The Victorian City: Images and Realities, *ed. by H.J. Dyos and Michael Wolff, London: Routledge & Kegan Paul, vol.2, Figure 245. National Railway Museum/Science & Society Picture Library*

could not 'tell where the monster city began or ended' (Mayhew, quoted in Porter, 1994, p.186). London was indeed *the* monster city of the nineteenth century, the largest in the world, and for most of this period substantially bigger than any other conurbation in Britain. Its population expanded from just under a million inhabitants in 1800 to some 2.5 million in 1851; over 300,000 people settled in the metropolis during the 1840s, the decade of *Dombey and Son* (Dyos and Wolff, 1973, vol.2, p.414).

London was able to grow so rapidly because of its commercial success. By the middle of the century the city was at the heart of a global commercial empire, and it profited hugely from its monopolies on trade with colonial territories such as India, the Caribbean and the Pacific (Dombey himself is, of course, heavily involved in such colonial trading). The capital's commercial growth created a high-wage economy with huge numbers of middle-class jobs in such areas as banking, shipping and insurance. The affluence of the middle classes in turn produced demand for construction, railway transportation, the distributive trades, tailoring and dressmaking, food and drink, and retailing (Porter, 1994, pp.186–7). With such growth in the population London had to expand rapidly. Unlike other European cities which because of limited space tended to increase in height, London remained an essentially low-rise city spreading over the surrounding countryside.

Contemporaries wondered about the social and psychological effects of this enormous influx of people. In *The Condition of the Working Class in England*, Marx's collaborator and financial backer Friedrich Engels could not conceal his disgust at the impersonal nature of the busy London streets:

And still they crowd by one another as though they had nothing in common, nothing to do with one another, and their only agreement is the tacit one, that each keep to his own side of the pavement, so as not to delay the opposing stream of the crowd, while it occurs to no man to honour another with so much as a glance. The brutal indifference, the unfeeling isolation of each in his private interest, becomes the more repellent and offensive, the more these individuals are crowded together, within a limited space.

(Engels, [1844] 1987, p.69)

In *Dombey and Son*, Harriet Carker observes the steady flow of people arriving in the city. She watches them from her house, which is on the edge of the metropolis, in a space between country and city, 'only blighted country, and not town'. The narrator observes the encroaching industrial presence around Harriet's house as the few tall chimneys belch smoke all day and night (33; p.500). The novel subsequently describes how people arriving in the city are consumed, 'swallowed up in one phase or other of its immensity' (33; p.508). The anonymity and destructiveness of the modern city would seem also to be highlighted in the novel's account of Staggs's Gardens, the row of houses where the Toodle family live. The Gardens are part of Camden Town in North London (where Dickens himself lived for little over a year as a boy). Camden was substantially redeveloped in the 1830s and the 1840s, initially for the canal, and subsequently for the extensive rail network terminating at Euston.

*Figure 7.2  Late Victorian photograph of the heavy traffic on and below London Bridge. The picture seems to illustrate Engels's argument on the nature of the crowded London streets. Reproduced from* The Victorian City: Images and Realities, *ed. by H.J. Dyos and Michael Wolff, London: Routledge & Kegan Paul, vol.2, figure 135. Greater London Council*

**Now read two passages which describe the Gardens. The first runs from the beginning of chapter 6 (p.67) to '... with instructions to hail the failure with derisive cheers from the chimney pots' (p.69); the second runs from 'Oh, Mr Walter, Staggs's Gardens, if you please!' (p.232) to the end of chapter 15 (p.236). As you read the extracts, concentrate on the kind of language used to describe the changes taking place in this area. Are we to conclude from these descriptions that the material and social effects of industrial progress are to be regretted or welcomed?**

In the opening passage, we can see that the central distinction is made between the railway workings and the small community of the Gardens. Dickens employs a richly figurative language to evoke the anarchic and frightening vision of industrial works. The paragraph begins by specifically comparing this man-made upheaval of the landscape to the natural upheaval of an earthquake. The notion of natural disaster is repeated at the end of the passage with another reference to a geological episode, but the image has now become more volcanic than seismic: 'Boiling water hissed and heaved within dilapidated walls; whence, also, the glare and roar of flames came issuing forth; and mounds of ashes blocked up rights of way, and wholly changed the law and custom of the neighbourhood' (6; p.68).

You may also have noticed that the passage stresses the chaotic formless nature of this industrial prospect. Factory chimneys are transformed into 'Babel towers', where the biblical confusion of languages expresses the architectural confusion of the stacks of an industrial landscape. The sense of visual chaos is further emphasized by the lack of form of the objects in view, and indeed they cannot even be seen as objects as such. They can only be evoked in the most abstract of terms: 'There were a hundred thousand shapes and substances of incompleteness, wildly mingled out of their place, upside down, burrowing in the earth, aspiring in the air, mouldering in the water, and unintelligible as any dream' (ibid.). Some critics have argued persuasively enough that this imagery derives from the painting of industrial processes by J.M.W. Turner (see Figure 7.4) and, before him, Joseph Wright of Derby. I, however, prefer to see Dickens's elemental view of railway construction (composed as it is of earth, fire and water) as being reminiscent of a medieval vision of hell. It seems that the most traditional images of damnation are used to describe the most modern forms of industrial progress. Moreover, the use of such traditional Christian iconography has a moral implication. The industrial revolution essentially involves entering into a Faustian pact in which greater industrial and economic productivity is achieved at the price of the extinction of the warmth and vitality of human society, and the transformation of the modern city into the very place of damnation.

There are also religious connotations (though now expressed with a degree of ironic detachment) in the subsequent description of the Gardens. The narrative voice begins by stating that the Gardens occupies a small area, and is composed of readily identifiable features and objects as opposed to the vast formlessness of the railway works which it adjoins: 'It was a little row of houses, with little squalid patches of ground before them, fenced off with old doors, barrel staves, scraps of tarpaulin, and dead brushes; with bottomless tin kettles and exhausted iron fenders, thrust into the gaps' (6; p.69). The description of the Gardens certainly does not conform to any conventional notion of paradise with which one could readily contrast the preceding vision of a manufactured hell. It is a view of an older, pre-industrial London, and despite the area's evident dilapidation, it does conform to a human scale of things; it is a place where the eye can still survey, identify and organize an array of discrete objects, such as doors, tarpaulins and fenders. Staggs's Gardens possesses form whereas form is precisely what is absent in the elemental landscape of railway construction. The Gardens also has a clear sense of community, a sense of its common values and opinions. One could never describe Staggs's Gardens as a heaven on earth, but the narrative voice suggests, albeit ironically, that it has heavenly qualities for its inhabitants. The Gardens has become their hallowed ground. It was for its occupants '*a sacred grove* not to be withered by railroads' (ibid.; my emphasis). The community, however, in a dim echo of the failings of the book's central character, suffers from hubris. It scoffs at the idea of the railway ever being completed, or, if completed, then of being of any practical use or threat; the master chimney-sweeper at the end of the extract voices the Gardens' confidence by boasting that 'if [the railway] ever did open, two of his boys should ascend the flues of his dwelling, with instructions to hail the failure with derisive jeers from the chimney pots' (ibid.).

As we learn in the second passage, such confidence is misplaced. If even a London coachman, a forerunner of the London taxi-driver, cannot find Staggs's Gardens (his exasperation displayed in upper case, 'WHERE IS IT?'), then it seems likely that it is no longer there. And indeed Susan and Walter subsequently discover this to be the case. It is as though the area has been swept away overnight. The small, intertwined streets of the area have been replaced by the monolithic structures of the modern urban landscape, those 'granite columns of gigantic girth [which] opened a vista to the Railway world beyond' (15; p.233) (see also Figure 7.3 for a visual impression of the scale of contemporary railway construction). The environment is not in proportion to its inhabitants. There is no sympathy for a human scale in such buildings. Other new constructions threaten to overwhelm the senses with their abundance: there are now 'tiers of warehouses, crammed with rich goods and costly merchandise' (ibid.). The small and readily intimate community of Staggs's Gardens has been replaced by exactly the kind of impersonal metropolitan bustle which so offended Engels, with 'streets [which] now swarmed with passengers and vehicles of every kind' (ibid.). The passage finishes with the 'monster train', speeding from the heart of the city. The train looks to be a potent symbol of Victorian industrial and technological progress, a demon forged in the inferno of railway construction. But it also seems to represent the dynamism and destructiveness of the city itself, the monster train as the agent of the journalist Henry Mayhew's 'monster city', spreading ever more rapidly over the surrounding countryside.

Yet the passages taken together seem ultimately much more ambivalent about the development of the modern city. The monstrous train may well be an agent of death and destruction, leaving 'carcasses of houses' in its wake, but the narrative voice is ultimately bedazzled rather than horrified by the sheer scale and grandeur of the structures which finally emerge. The narrative now thrills at

*Figure 7.3   Hawkshaw's bridge and station at Cannon Street, with London Bridge in the background. From the* Illustrated Times *(1865). Note how this engraving, like Dickens's description of new railway buildings, emphasizes the grandeur of these constructions.*

the sight of the completed railway, at the absolute mastery of Victorian engineering, the slide-rule precision in the harnessing of those destructive elemental forces displayed in the first passage. Trains now roll into the station, 'gliding like *tame dragons* into the allotted corners grooved out to the inch for their reception' (15; p.234; my emphasis). Moreover, it is not necessarily the case that everything the industrial age swept away was worth preserving. Staggs's Gardens may have been a sacred grove for its inhabitants, but the narrator now implies that this was not sufficient grounds for its conservation. Who would, after all, wish to preserve those 'old rotten summer houses', and 'the miserable waste ground, where the refuse-matter had been heaped of yore'? At the end of the second extract, Susan and Walter finally manage to find Polly Toodle. The Toodle family, they discover, has not been cast into the outer darkness of the industrial revolution. They now inhabit a pleasant enough house, provided by the corporate paternalism of the railway company, and a sense of community remains in this area. The narrator reveals that Susan and Walter 'only had to ask for Toodle, Engine Fireman, and any one would show them which was his house' (ibid.).

This description of the disappearance of Staggs's Gardens consequently suggests a complex vision of urban and industrial development which contradicts Ruskin's straightforward assessment of Dickens as a member of the steam-whistle party. The novel suggests on the one hand that such change is clearly destructive, creating an urban environment unsuited by its very scale and dynamism to human habitation, but on the other hand the sight of such structures and the crowds and vehicles which flow through the newly built streets is inspiring, far more so than the derelict buildings, shoddy gardens and wastelands that this cityscape has replaced. We might also reflect that the spokesperson for this community at the end of the first extract is the master chimney-sweeper, a man who makes his dubious living by sending small boys up chimney flues. It may, of course, be just an incidental detail, but given that one of the central concerns of the novel is Dombey's negligent if not actually abusive relationship with his daughter, Florence, this reference to the employment of children is intriguing. As Raymond Williams points out, progress is always an ambivalent business. The enormous and, in some respects, socially destructive changes of such rapid revolution have to be weighed against the social benefits such traumatic change also produces. The revolution in industrial production and transportation in the 1840s also saw 'the influential social criticism of Carlyle and Engels, the great articulation of consciousness of Chartism and the struggle for the Ten Hours Bill' (Williams, 1970b, p.12). Such material and social benefits of the demonic railway are acknowledged in the Toodle family's new housing. Indeed, Toodle himself suggests later in the narrative – in a metaphor which derives again from a Christian iconography of light and darkness, of damnation and salvation – that the railway lifted him into the light from employment underground. And what of the ragged boys who were going to be sent up the chimneys of Staggs's Gardens by the master chimney-sweeper to celebrate the failure of the railway? The narrator reveals that the master is now one of 'the vanquished' of the Gardens, but his business is thriving; he has a lucrative contract to clean railway chimneys, and so industrial progress in this instance decreases to a smallest degree the sum of human misery. The monstrous railway is not cleaned by the monstrous labour of children, but by the labour of unfeeling, unthinking machinery (15; p.233).

# Two symbolic realms

Most critics of *Dombey and Son* agree that there are two main symbolic areas in the novel – trains and waves – but there the consensus ends. Critics have argued variously that the symbolic realms should be regarded as being contradictory, as being distinct but interconnected, or as being entirely resolvable into one unified whole – in other words, not distinct and not contradictory at all. The status of the symbolism in the narrative itself is also problematic. For the question arises as to the purpose of this particular mode of representation. It does not easily conform to a conventional realist mode of narrative representation. Indeed Dickens's use of symbolic narrative can be regarded as one of the most innovative aspects of his writing, as it seems to anticipate those forms of modernist narrative which explicitly oppose conventional realist forms of expression. There is also the question of the degree to which a literary symbol partakes of the object it represents. It is usual for the symbol to be separate from the object it denotes. A red rose can stand for England, but the flower remains conceptually distinct from the country it represents. Yet, as we have already seen, literary symbols in the novel complicate this distinction. The railway, for example, is the most prominent 'symbol' of industrial progress in the novel, but it is also the principal 'agent' of industrial and commercial development in the early Victorian period. It might be helpful if I gave some indication of my own position on the symbolism in the novel before I discuss some of the alternatives. I would argue that the narrative uses a range of symbolic modes, and that these can be usefully grouped into the categories of trains and waves, but that neither set of symbols is entirely consistent within this grouping; symbols tend to merge, to blend together at times, but even so, they still resist being resolved into a single unified vision.

The critic J. Hillis Miller has described *Dombey and Son* in terms of its tension between the materialism represented by the railway and a spiritual domain represented by water. The ocean is in his view 'a symbol of that realm beyond the earth where the seemingly inescapable separation between people will be transcended and the reciprocity of love will be possible' (Miller, 1958, p.149). In other words, the sea and the lapping waves operate as a kind of secularized vision of Heaven which is counterpoised to the sufferings and separations endured in this life. The waves offer a literary salvation, an aesthetic substitution for the comforts of religion, by symbolically carrying off both little Paul and his mother to a better place. Nina Auerbach (1976), in an influential account, follows this division of the novel into two spheres, but does not view this as a divide between the temporal and the transcendental. She sees the novel as being concerned with contemporary social and ideological tensions, and proposes a split along gender lines. The story, for her, is about the conflict between the symbolic spheres of the feminine fluid world exemplified by Florence, and the hard-bitten masculine capitalist, industrial world exemplified by Dombey. She finds no resolution of these two opposing domains in the novel. As early Victorian society was incapable of resolving such tensions between the ideological requirements of domesticity and the material requirements of commercial, industrial productivity, so the novel effectively dramatizes but cannot adequately resolve its ideological schism of the masculine and feminine. Auerbach concludes that 'the real and absolute barrier is sexual, and it separates not merely individuals, but the landscape of the novel itself' (1976, p.102).

## *Trains*

I find that the symbolism in *Dombey and Son* is rather more fluid, and less easily demarcated than either of these critics proposes. As we saw in the last section, the railway is an ambivalent symbol to represent the industrial world, as it is both the destructive industrial agent, and the means by which the dilapidated Staggs's Gardens can be cleared away. The train is a prominent symbol of modern destructiveness in nineteenth-century narrative fiction. In Leo Tolstoy's *Anna Karenina* (1874–6), for example, Anna famously perishes under the wheels of a train, but her whole sorry tale depends upon her ability to travel between Moscow and St Petersburg on the modern railway. In a memorable scene in Thomas Hardy's *Tess of the d'Urbervilles* (1891), Tess is momentarily brilliantly illuminated and transfixed by the light of the express train taking milk from rural

Wessex to London. The train seems in this moment both to capture Tess as a photographic image, and to express the transformative power of modernity, which will sweep away the rural society in which her tragedy is enacted.

In *Dombey and Son*, the train symbolizes death. In the description of Dombey's journey to Birmingham with Major Bagstock after the death of Paul, the train becomes the context for Dombey's own maudlin reflection on his son's demise: 'The power that forced itself upon its iron way – its own – defiant of all paths and roads, piercing through the heart of every obstacle, and dragging living creatures of all classes, ages, and degrees behind it, was a type of triumphant monster, Death' (20; pp.297–8). The train is used in this section to express specifically Dombey's own depressive state of mind and generally the social and personal destructiveness of the modern industrial age. The novel, however, remains more ambivalent about this gloomy theme. For this passage also conveys the novelty, the exhilaration and the sheer breathless excitement of travelling on a train through the landscape of England at high speed. The train thunders on, 'breasting the wind and light, the shower and sunshine, away, and

*Figure 7.4   J.M.W. Turner,* Rain, Steam and Speed – the Great Western Railway, *before 1844, oil on canvas, 90.8 × 121.9 cm. A number of critics have speculated that Turner's painting influenced Dickens's vision of the railway in* Dombey and Son. *The painting, like Dickens's depiction of the railway, seems to defy the formal constraints of realist representation. The landscape of swirling clouds, water and viaducts may express the dynamic possibilities of the train as social progress. Yet there is also, perhaps, an apocalyptic quality to those great arcs of deliberately roughened, scratched and pitted paint which swirl about the train in the middle of the canvas. Turner Bequest, 1856. National Gallery, London. Reproduced by courtesy of The Trustees, The National Gallery, London*

still away, it rolls and roars, fierce and rapid, smooth and certain; and great works and massive bridges crossing up above, fall like a beam of shadow an inch broad, upon the eye, and then are lost' (p.298).

The narrative appears to be half in love with the train, exhilarated by its speed and the conceptions of industrial progress it represents, and half detesting it for the social destructiveness and divisiveness it brings in its wake. The vocabulary in which the train itself is evoked is not primarily mechanical or temporal. Indeed in the description of Dombey's journey to Birmingham, the train seems almost to assume the qualities of a supernatural being, some form of terrifying industrial demon. Dickens describes the train pulling out of a station as follows: 'away, with a shriek and a roar, and a rattle, plunging down into the earth again, and working on in such a storm of energy and perseverance, that amidst the darkness and whirlwind the motion seems reversed, and to tend furiously backward, until a ray of light upon the wet wall shows its surface flying past like a fierce stream' (ibid). The symbolism of the train is further extended towards the end of the novel, and the train is instrumental in the death of James Carker, the principal villain of the piece.

Carker himself is a particularly interesting figure, because of the density of figurative language used to portray him, and the way in which much of this language is associated with the inanimate qualities of this character. As you will have noticed, he is most often referred to as a particularly shiny and sharp set of teeth. Some critics think this device is overused. John Carey, for example, has wittily suggested that *Dombey and Son* is the only novel in the English language which has a set of dentures as its principal villain (1973, p.126). In fact, the depiction of Carker relies on a sequence of metaphors and similes which are designed to stress his obsequious, devious and predatory nature. He is also compared at various points in the novel to a cat, a reptile and a scabrous monster lurking in the depths of the sea. Yet the image of the teeth does remain the most insistent representation of this figure. The technical term for this particular trope is synecdoche. That is, where a part of an object or individual is allowed to stand for the whole. A common example is the phrase 'all hands on deck', where 'hands' refers to the crew. In the case of Carker his teeth are allowed to stand for the whole of him. But these teeth have a death-like, inanimate quality to them, just as though they were either artificially manufactured (as in a set of dentures) or were the exposed teeth in a dead man's skull. Moreover, their movement, that constant masticating, has a certain precipitous mechanical quality about it.

The mechanized description of Carker appears consistent not only with the ruthless coldness he exhibits towards every other character in the novel, but also with the economic and social views he advances; he conceives of the world as an entirely impersonal place in which other people are treated as more or less effective instruments for furthering one's own aims. He, of course, meets a terrible fate towards the end of the novel. Dombey has by this stage become Carker's pursuer. Carker catches sight of him at a railway station and the surprise of seeing his former employer causes him to stumble backward off the platform and onto the line. Carker is subsequently hit by an oncoming train. The engine 'struck him limb from limb, and licked his stream of life up with fiery heat, and cast his mutilated fragments in the air' (55; p.823). The novel's symbolic connection between the railway and death is consequently made concrete; the two become connected by cause and effect, as it is the literal impact of the train that kills Carker. His demise is also satisfactory in terms of the symmetry of the inversions within the novel's figurative language. If Carker is characterized primarily by the automatic motions of his glinting teeth, through a constant reduction of the human, then by the same token his nemesis, the train, is endowed with dynamic, supernatural qualities. As the train appears in the journey with Dombey and Bagstock as some terrifying industrial demon, so it reappears in the description of Carker's death, still shrieking, whistling and thundering, but it has now become the moral agent of the narrative; the means by which Carker is to be punished for his actions. The train rattles and howls towards him as though it was an avenging angel sent to smite the unrepentant sinner.

## *Waves*

The train is of considerable symbolic importance in the narrative, but the difficulty with the symbol is the range of forces it represents: industrialization, technical progress, destructiveness, social improvement and biblical forms of vengeance, a kind of industrial *lex taleonis* (the scriptural law of proportionate vengeance, as in an eye for an eye, a tooth for a tooth). The train seems to connect the realm of the material with the transcendental, and by the same token the waves seems to connect the transcendental with the material. We may recall, for example, that in 'What the waves were always saying', the chapter begins with Paul envisaging the hustle and bustle of the city with the River Thames flowing through its centre, and concludes with the waves carrying Paul beyond this life. Mary McBride (1994) has pushed this argument further, suggesting that the waves in *Dombey and Son* should be regarded principally as an economic metaphor. She explains that the business cycle in the nineteenth century is frequently viewed as having wave-like movement, quoting the neo-Keynesian economist J.K. Galbraith: 'prices and production rose gradually, then more rapidly, reaching an apex and then subsided. One measured the length of the cycle from crest to crest, or trough to trough' (quoted in McBride, 1994, p.20). The waves in this interpretation of the novel consequently stand for both the cyclical movements within the British economy in the middle of the nineteenth century and the personal economic cycles of the characters. She points out that 'Paul Dombey rides a ten-year wave (1835–45) from the crest of prosperity to the trough of bankruptcy, and, as the novel ends, young Walter Gay begins his own economic cycle as a merchant' (McBride, 1994, p.21).

Railways and waves both operate as symbols of death and economics in the book, and the two are brought together in distinctly ironic fashion in the description of Staggs's Gardens. The Gardens has, of course, been swept away by the tide of railway-building, but the name of this particular street is also significant: 'stag' is Victorian slang for a speculator in railway stocks. An implication of having Staggs's Gardens swept away by this programme of railway-building is that the speculator's investment in railway shares is likely to be swept away with similar speed. Yet the importance of these symbolic aspects of the narrative and the attempt to see them as providing a unified and unifying perspective of English Victorian society will also inform the next part of this discussion, on the colonial aspects of *Dombey and Son*. In at least one critic's interpretation of the novel, the imperial domain offers a resolution of the novel's two opposing symbolic spheres.

# Empire

The theme of empire is present right at the beginning of *Dombey and Son*. Do you recall that the story begins with the middle-aged Dombey leaning over his newly arrived child, and playing with the infant with his watch chain? The narrator describes Dombey's smart (and expensive) jacket, 'whereof the buttons sparkled phosphorescently in the feeble rays of the distant fire' (1; p.1). The image of sparkling buttons can be read literally as the polished concave surfaces reflect the fire in the parlour. It can, however, also be read symbolically, the glistening buttons being an expression of Dombey's successful trading in the distant exotic climes of empire. As we saw earlier, Dombey's transformation of anno Domini into 'anno Dombei – and Son', along with his belief that the natural world had been entirely shaped for the benefit of his commercial transactions, is indicative of his narcissism. Dombey naturalizes this order of things, and views the world as having been devised exclusively for his economic interest, but this position is perhaps not that far from a more widely held view in England in the middle of the nineteenth century on the inherent legitimacy of British hegemony in the global economy.

The nineteenth century did see the consolidation of a global British Empire which included Africa, the Caribbean, India, the Middle East and Asia. Colonial territories were needed to maintain British dominance in the world economy. As Eric Hobsbawm has observed, Britain in this period 'increasingly became the agency of economic interchange between the advanced and the backward, the industrial and the primary producing, the colonial and quasi-colonial regions of the world' (1969, p.14). To summarize British economic aspirations in this period Hobsbawm subsequently uses a metaphor that comes close to Dombey's belief that the seas and land were created for him to trade in. He suggests that the 'ideal' result for the British balance of payments would have been to make every other economy dependent upon Britain's, and to have effectively turned the entire world into 'a kind of planetary system circulating round the sun of Britain' (ibid., p.136). *Dombey and Son* seems both to express a desire for just such a global economic dominance, and to indicate the hubris of such a scheme by placing it at the centre of Dombey's egotistical vision.

The notion of empire, then, is introduced in the novel in predominantly symbolic terms, as imperial trade is refracted through Dombey's narcissistic consciousness. We subsequently glimpse some of the material benefits of imperial trade. As we know, *Dombey and Son* is set mainly in the rapidly expanding London of the 1840s, and much of the city's expansion is fuelled by its economic position at the heart of a global empire. There is row upon row of warehouses filled with the goods of empire on the ground formerly occupied by Staggs's Gardens. Dombey's own offices are close to East India House. The narrator envisages (in chapter 4) the House filled with exotic goods; it teems 'with suggestions of precious stuffs and stones, tigers, elephants, howdahs, hookahs, umbrellas, palm trees, palanquins, and gorgeous princes of a brown complexion sitting on carpets with their slippers very much turned up at their toes' (4; p.36).

This imagery of oriental splendour clearly adds to the narrative richness of the novel, but there is also something troubling about these exotic associations and their proximity to the headquarters of Dombey's overseas trading activities. The East India Company had been established in the seventeenth century as the chartered trading company with the Indian sub-continent. It lost its trading monopoly in 1813, but continued as the main commercial organization in India, as well as effectively providing the civil administration of territories under British rule. The British presence in India expanded substantially between 1813 and 1823 (McCord, 1991, pp.57–8). The company had been associated in its earlier days with corruption, and representatives of the firm had used their positions to line their own pockets. The rich exotic goods which adorn the East India building may be seen as testament to the commercial acumen of the company, the rightful rewards of successful business transactions, but on the other hand, 'the tigers, elephants, howdahs, [and] hookahs' could be seen as just so much colonial booty, a great haul of oriental artefacts illegitimately expropriated from the territories the company was supposed to manage and govern impartially.

The clearest example in the novel of illegitimate colonial conduct, however, is Major Bagstock's treatment of his native servant. Bagstock is an old colonial trooper, who, as Miss Tox points out (in the manuscript of the novel), 'did all sorts of things in the Peninsula, with every description of fire-arm; and in the East and West Indies' (Dickens, [1846–8] 1974, pp.129). He is initially impressed by Dombey's extensive colonial dealings, flattering him that the name of Dombey 'is known and honoured in the British possessions abroad' (10; p.135). It is possible to view Bagstock as a cruder version of Dombey, in which Dombey's abusiveness and monomania are pushed to extremes. Indeed, some critics argue that the primary function of such characters as Bagstock is to provide an example of someone with whom Dombey can be favourably compared. Bagstock's treatment of his nameless, mute servant is clearly monstrous. The following description of the Major's conduct while he dresses for dinner with Dombey is representative:

> Nor was the Major less exasperated as he dressed for dinner, during which operation the dark servant underwent the pelting of a shower of miscellaneous objects, varying in size from a boot to a hairbrush, and including everything that came within his master's reach. For the Major plumed himself on having the Native in a perfect state of drill, and visited the least departure from strict discipline with this kind of fatigue duty. Add to this, that he maintained the Native about his person as a counter-irritant against the gout, and all other vexations, mental as well as bodily; and the Native would appear to have earned his pay – which was not large. (26; pp.395–6)

I think we can see in this passage a significant representation of a colonial cast of mind. The Major constantly abuses his servant; he pays him miserably; he subjects him to a constant low level of physical and verbal abuse, and he prides himself on his absolute dominion. 'For the Major plumed himself on having the Native in a perfect state of drill, and visited the least departure from strict discipline with this kind of fatigue duty.' The extract, however, also intriguingly reveals the Major's reliance on his native servant. Such dependence has been seen as axiomatic of the relationship between the colonizer and the colonized. The passage perceptively exposes the Major's total psychological and physical dependency on his servant, as Bagstock maintains him 'about his person as a counter-irritant against the gout, and all other vexations, mental as well as bodily'. In one sense the servant acts as a displacement for the Major's personal difficulties, a mute and compliant figure onto which his own vexation and anxieties can be projected, but in another sense the Major's identity as bilious colonial master is entirely dependent on the constant presence of his servant. To see yourself as absolutely dominant you need somebody to dominate. One suspects that if the servant disappeared so would the Major: with no one to subject, his sense of self as the colonial master would be critically undermined.

As far as I am aware, the first critics of the novel did not discuss the colonial aspects of Bagstock's behaviour; understandably, perhaps, they focused on the comic aspects of his portrayal. It was the novelist, poet and critic G.K. Chesterton, writing in 1907, who first drew attention to the seriousness of the colonial critique contained within Bagstock's bombast and slapstick. Bagstock was for him 'simply the perfect prophesy of that decadent jingoism which corrupted England' (Chesterton, 1965, p.186). Yet Chesterton's undoubtedly perceptive interpretation of this figure does itself invite further questions as to the extent of the criticism of colonialism in the novel. Does the novel mount a fundamental critique of the project of colonial expansionism or does it only satirize its excesses? I want to return to this question at the end of this section, but there is one more significant area of the novel in which imperial motifs are readily apparent, and that, perhaps surprisingly, is in the sentimental bosom of the wooden Midshipman.

The wooden Midshipman occupies the same dock as Dombey's business and the East India Company. Indeed, the description of the exotic contents of East India House is at the beginning of the chapter in which Gills, Cuttle and Gay are introduced. Their first scene is a celebration of Walter's employment as a clerk with the firm of Dombey and Son. Cuttle and Gills celebrate Walter's success by breaking open the last bottle of 'the wonderful Madeira', and the bottle itself becomes the subject of an imperial maritime romance, as its crossings and re-crossings of Britain's various trading routes are lovingly recounted. 'To be sure', as Solomon reminisces, think what 'this wine has passed through. Think what a straining and creaking of timbers and masts: what a whistling and howling of the gale through ropes and rigging' (4; p.43). Gills and Cuttle's joint narrative includes a fair number of shipwrecks, the lusty singing of some patriotic songs (mostly by brave British sailors on their way to watery graves) and the consumption of a considerable amount of the aforementioned Madeira.

Walter, as we know, will himself subsequently be shipwrecked in the Caribbean when Dombey's *Son and Heir* sinks on its way to Barbados. By being shipwrecked in this fashion, Walter is placed in a clear line of mythical maritime representations of Britain as a colonial power. The literary nautical antecedents are clearly Shakespeare's *The Tempest* (1611), and Daniel Defoe's *Robinson Crusoe* (1719). Shipwrecks were also of considerable symbolic significance to the Victorians. Nineteenth-century newspapers were full of detailed accounts of wrecks. Similarly it was an extremely popular topic for poetry in this period, and such poems were used in educational primers, as exemplars of a heroic national spirit. Walter's own imperial romance repeats the odyssey of the bottle of Madeira – shipwreck in the colonies, improbable survival, and a warm return to the wooden Midshipman. Yet the question arises as to the relationship between this romantic vision of a trading empire exemplified by Walter and the hard-edged economic materialism of Dombey's global trading network. The sinking of the *Son and Heir* for Walter is an episode on his journey to romantic fulfilment; for Dombey it is the start of the downward economic spiral to bankruptcy and suicidal depression. It is this tension between romantic and commercial visions of British colonial trade which is the central concern of an article by Suvendrini Perera. **Now read through Suvendrini Perera, 'Wholesale, retail and for exportation: empire and the family business in *Dombey and Son*' (1990, pp.603–20; extract in Regan, 2001). The article is quite difficult, so don't worry if you can't follow it all. At this stage see if you can identify the central argument.**

It is helpful if you can identify the intellectual co-ordinates of academic discussion of this kind. Academic articles invariably begin by placing themselves within a tradition of critical writing on their chosen subject. You can also be fairly sure that the next step will be to argue against such received interpretations of the text, or at least point out that there are certain crucial components which earlier readings fail to consider. In this instance Perera establishes the context of this account of *Dombey and Son* by referring to Nina Auerbach's account of the novel, which we encountered in the last section. She argues, you may recall, that the novel should be split along gender lines. The story, for Auerbach, is about the conflict between two symbolic spheres, the feminine fluid world exemplified by Flora and the hard-bitten masculine capitalist, industrial world exemplified by Dombey. She considers that the two opposing spheres are not resolved within the novel as whole. For her part, Perera agrees with this division of the text, but suggests that when the romantic and industrial aspects are viewed from a colonial perspective then they become mutually reinforcing rather than antagonistic. So, she claims that 'instead of an opposition structure of masculine/feminine and railroad/ocean, *Dombey and Son* can be seen as a complex interchange between the key categories of capital and adventure, or "romance," each is enmeshed in the overarching ideology of Empire' (Perera, 1990, p.609). The case can be seen particularly clearly in the apparent contrast of the world of Gills's wooden Midshipman with the world of Dombey's business. In this view of the novel, the two worlds converge in Walter's voyage to Barbados. Instead of the little shop providing a sentimental alternative to modern self-interested economic modes, it now provides a romantic legitimization for the colonialism upon which Dombey's trading depends. The central relationship between Paul and Florence similarly becomes a narrative of colonial displacement in which trading and social tensions are enacted in the metropolitan family rather in the developing world. The reconciliation of Dombey and his daughter becomes, for Perera, just a final soothing reassurance for the novel's British readership about the natural rightness of British colonial dominion. **How convincing do you find this post-colonial reading of the novel?**

I certainly find Perera's treatment of the novel perceptive and highly stimulating, but I am not sure that I am entirely persuaded by her argument. I have three reservations: firstly, I suspect that the article overplays the significance of the colonial components at the expense of the other elements of the narrative; secondly, I suspect it does not fully acknowledge the extent of the criticism of British colonization within the work; and thirdly, I am sceptical that a text which is so evidently heterogeneous can be resolved into a single coherent ideological position by shifting the focus of the analysis to a colonial perspective, however worthwhile such a shift of focus may be. Such imperial elements are of considerable importance, and as we have seen they are present in a number of strands of the narrative, but that is not to say they are the most significant aspects of the narrative, or that all other elements of the work can or should be readily subordinated to them. The colonial reading suffers by comparison with Dickens's later works *Bleak House* (1852–3) and *Great Expectations* (1860–1), in which there are more thorough and explicit discussions of British imperial aspirations in this period. I am also inclined to see the critique of British imperial influence in this narrative as more prominent and anxious than Perera perhaps allows.

Dickens was not consistent in his explicit pronouncements on British colonial policy and conduct. In 1848, the same year as the final publication of *Dombey and Son*, he satirized British imperial aspirations in Africa in a review in the *Examiner* of an account of the Niger expedition, but he also subsequently responded to the news of the Indian Mutiny by exclaiming of the mutineers 'exterminate the brutes' (see Gribble, 1999, pp.92–3). *Dombey and Son*, however, does not appear to endorse colonialism. Major Bagstock embodies a monstrous jingoism. The Major magnifies the faults of Dombey; his abuse of his native servant looks as though it is an extreme version of Dombey's treatment of Florence, and he similarly transforms Dombey's colonial narcissism (in his belief that the land and seas were created for him to trade) into outright xenophobia. Dombey may be favoured by any comparison with Bagstock, but he cannot entirely escape the implications of Bagstock's satire. Bagstock provides both insight into and criticism of the iniquity of the colonial relationship, and that criticism should be extended to Dombey himself. And in this respect we can make a case that Bagstock is not just a satire on the excesses of colonialism, but a direct challenge to the institutional basis of colonialism itself.

Yet the colonial critique supplied by Bagstock is still complicated by its form. The scenes between the Major and his servant often look like music-hall routines. The conventional stage business of choreographed kicks, slaps and prods renders these scenes entertaining, but in doing so it perhaps also blunts the colonial critique, turning the colonial relationship into a burlesque in which Bagstock's behaviour becomes more risible than damnable. Part of Perera's argument focuses on the end of the novel. She, like many other critics, is struck by the conventionality of the conclusion, or the way in which the last few chapters attempt to resolve the divergent strands of the narrative. Perera sees the resolution of the relationship of Dombey and his daughter as a legitimating myth for British colonial expansionism. Even if we do not agree with every aspect of this reading of *Dombey and Son*, it does raise the issue of the significance of the ending, and whether the conclusion should be regarded as an effective and appropriate resolution of the narrative.

# A conventional conclusion?

In a postscript to his biography of Dickens, Peter Ackroyd attempts to distil the essence of Dickens's life and work. Ackroyd stresses the early Victorian or pre-Victorian character of much of Dickens's writing. He was a product of Regency rather than Victorian London, and he was indelibly stamped with the social characteristics and expectations of the generation which emerged in the 1820s and 1830s. Dickens, for Ackroyd, was a pre-Victorian as much in 'his capacity for excitement and exhilaration, in his radicalism ... in his earnest desire for social reform', as in his 'theatricality, even his vulgarity' (1991, p.1141). He was a man who stood apart from the pragmatism and practicality which characterized the later Victorians. This view of the most prominent and popular of Victorian novelists as being at odds with the dominant current of his age is certainly consistent with some of the strands of *Dombey and Son*.

In the use of such types of writing as character comedy, sentimental tale and melodrama, Dickens can be seen to be drawing upon narrative forms of the late eighteenth and early nineteenth centuries to make social judgement and criticisms of the standards of the present, whether these be the unstable commercial nature of modern Britain, the disturbing and distorting emotional relations which characterize the middle-class Victorian family, the wretched conditions in which the poorest members of society are forced to live, the pernicious effects of a utilitarian educational system, the destructiveness of increasing industrialization, or the jingoism of British colonialism. In strict generic terms, it is difficult to make a case for Dickens as a realist writer. Those elements which we have associated with conventional realist writing – the insistent objectification, the recording of intellectual minutiae, and the precise plotting of the correspondence between subjective emotional and intellectual responses and subsequent actions – are certainly present in Dickens's fiction, but they never become entirely dominant. It is rather as though such forms of realist expression are visited fleetingly, as the prose moves swiftly from the styles of writing which derive from the Regency period to the kind of symbolic, lyrical form of expression characteristic of modernist writing in the late nineteenth and early twentieth centuries.

Yet in another sense Dickens appears to be an exemplary realist, as long as one defines the central objective of realist fiction as the production of a compelling depiction of the social diversity and ethical complexities of contemporary society. For no other writer of the period attempts to produce such a socially inclusive vision of early Victorian England. Moreover, it seems to be difficult to place Dickens and his writings in any age other than his own. Dickens himself seemed to work at an industrial rate of literary productivity, producing in his career fifteen novels, twenty stories, assorted journalism, non-fiction including *A Child's History of England*, as well as volumes of letters, diaries and speeches. It is a colossal output, the contemplation of which, as the journalist Robert McCrum has dryly observed, 'is enough to make the average reader want to go and have a quiet lie down' (1999, p.11). In this regard Dickens appears to be absolutely of his time, fashioning himself as a metaphor for the productive progressive spirit of the mid-nineteenth century, and exemplifying the Victorian belief in the rectitude of hard work. In *Dombey and Son*, we can see that the social upheavals of English society of the 1840s are recorded and expressed though the most innovative of literary forms. The novel uses symbolism (such as the trains and the waves) and figurative language to express the alienation of a society in the midst of such rapid economic and technological transformation. This writing is mostly descriptive and critical of its age, but there is also, at times, an almost visceral thrill at the prospect of change, as though the writing is pitched against itself, both critical of and enthralled by the dynamic flux of the society it seeks to depict.

*Dombey and Son* ultimately appears, then, to be a novel of sublime contradictions, a non-realist novel which appears to have realist social objectives, a novel which uses traditional narrative types both to describe and to criticize the contemporary state of society, a novel which presents a dynamic inclusive social vision, but concludes in an apparently conventional fashion with middle-class domestic and economic harmony restored. At the end of the book Florence and Walter are married and have produced two healthy and well-adjusted children. The little boy is called Paul and the daughter, though not named, is regarded by Dombey as a young Florence. The family replicates itself, but it is now free of the social and emotional problems of its earlier form. Florence also gets her wish to serve as a dutiful daughter and care for her father in his declining years. The novel closes with the repentant Dombey doting on his granddaughter (in the way he should have doted on his daughter). The transformation of Dombey is made even clearer at the end of the manuscript of the novel. He can now hear the sound of the sea: the waves 'speak to him of Florence, and his altered heart; of Florence and their ceaseless murmuring to her of the love, the eternal and illimitable, extending still, beyond the sea, beyond the sky, to the invisible country far away' (Dickens, [1846–8] 1970, p.976). Domestic harmony emerges from the dysfunctional family, and Dombey crosses decisively from the world of money and trade to the world of family and domestic affection.

Thackeray, among others, complained of the loss of quality in the later chapters of the novel. The difficulties are perhaps predominantly technical; the necessity of tying up various loose ends of the narrative produces a sense of restraint and artifice in the concluding section. The closing portrait of Dombey, for example, as the benevolent grandfather is so remarkably different from the rigid egotist of the rest of the novel that it is difficult to recognize him as the same character. Dombey does not commit suicide, but the appearance of this grey-haired family man suggests that he might well have done – so radically different is his appearance in the closing chapters.

We could perhaps simply discount the ending as a set of formal devices to polish off the work. Alternatively, we could see the final depiction of the contented middle-class family as being disappointing in thematic terms. The ending can be regarded as a dissipation of the more radical possibilities of the novel. It is as though the conclusion attempts to confound the dynamic inclusive possibilities of the narrative that we discussed in the introduction to the previous chapter. The Bakhtinian vision of the novel – that attempt to produce a plurality of narratives, to capture the full range of social forms – is abandoned for a closing affirmation of the conventional ideology of comfortable, caring middle-class domesticity.

Perhaps, in historical terms, such ambivalence is entirely appropriate, given the time and place of the novel's composition. The book was finished in 1848. This was a year of enormous importance in European history: while Britain contended with industrial revolution, the capitals of Europe were rocked by a sequence of social and political revolutions in Paris, Berlin, Vienna, Venice, Rome, Milan, Naples, Prague and Budapest. The events of 1848 form a key point in one of the most prominent sociohistorical theories of realism produced in the twentieth century, that put forward by the Hungarian literary critic and philosopher Georg Lukács (1885–1971) in *The Historical Novel* ([1937] 1962). In this work Lukács identifies 1848 as a key year in the development of bourgeois realism. Before this date he conceives of realism as being in its self-confident, heroic phase, embracing the idea of social progress. The possibility of the perfectibility of humankind and the imminent if not the immediate alleviation of social suffering are characteristics of a fundamentally optimistic and progressive bourgeois ideology which finds its concrete expression in realist prose fiction. After 1848, so Lukács argues, the threat of social revolution stifles the optimistic, progressive strands of bourgeois thought. Social dynamism is replaced by stasis in which the current social hierarchy becomes entirely fixed as an immutable natural hierarchy. In effect, 1848 marks for Lukács the movement from the dynamism of realism to the socially determinate forms of naturalism in which characters are depicted as being born, living and dying in social conditions which they have no capacity to change. (You will encounter such a grimly pessimistic vision of society in Émile Zola's *Germinal*.)

There are a number of problems with this historical, ideological understanding of realism: not least, that some socially critical and optimistic novels were produced after 1848 and, similarly, a good number of socially determinist novels appeared before this date. Indeed, the socially determinist agenda of such naturalist fiction is open to reinterpretation. Some critics uncover elements of social and formal flexibility in the most rigidly naturalistic novels. Yet even given the historical contentiousness of Lukács's theory, it is perhaps still worth considering *Dombey and Son* in the light of it. The novel was completed in the seminal year of 1848, and it can perhaps be interpreted as being right on the edge of a divide between radical and conservative impulses, simultaneously promoting a better, more inclusive and tolerant vision of society, and preserving a static hierarchical world in its view of middle-class respectability. This is not to suggest that we should finally follow either Orwell's judgement of Dickens's work as a justification of the social dominance of the middle class in nineteenth-century England, or Shaw's interpretation of Dickens's fiction as an instigation to revolution. And neither should we see *Dombey and Son* as a novel which just passively sits on the fence between these two very different interpretations. It is rather that the novel possesses a dynamic scope which allows it to embrace both these views: the central achievement of *Dombey and Son*, then, is that it vividly and compellingly displays in the same moment both the radical and conservative forces which shaped its own age.

# Works cited

Ackroyd, Peter. 1991. *Dickens*, London: Minerva.

Auerbach, Nina. 1976. 'Dickens and Dombey: a daughter after all', *Dickens Studies Annual*, 5, pp.95–105.

Carey, John. 1973. *The Violent Effigy: A Study of Dickens's Imagination*, London: Faber.

Chesterton, G.K. 1965. *Charles Dickens*, New York: Schoken.

Collins, Philip. Ed. 1971. *Dickens: The Critical Heritage*, London: Routledge & Kegan Paul.

Dickens, Charles. [1846–8] 1970. *Dombey and Son*, ed. by Peter Fairclough, with an introduction by Raymond Williams, Harmondsworth: Penguin.

Dickens, Charles. [1846–8] 1974. *Dombey and Son*, ed. by Alan Horsman, The Clarendon Dickens, Oxford: Clarendon Press.

Dickens, Charles. 1977. *The Letters of Charles Dickens*, vol.4: *1844–1846*, Oxford: Oxford University Press.

Dickens, Charles. [1846–8] 2001. *Dombey and Son*, ed. by Alan Horsman, with an introduction and notes by Dennis Walder, Oxford World's Classics, Oxford: Oxford University Press.

Dyos, H.J. and Wolff, Michael. Eds. 1978. *The Victorian City*, 2 vols, paperback edn, London: Routledge & Kegan Paul.

Engels, Friedrich. [1844] 1987. *The Condition of Working Class England*, ed. by Victor Kiernan, Harmondsworth: Penguin.

Flint, Kate. 1986. *Dickens*, Harvester New Readings, Brighton: Harvester.

Gribble, Jennifer. 1999. 'Borrioboola-Gha: Dickens, John Jarndyce and the Heart of Darkness', in *Dickens, Europe and the New Worlds*, ed. by Anny Sadrin, Basingstoke: Macmillan.

Griffiths, Eric. 1989. *The Printed Voice of Victorian Fiction*, Oxford: Clarendon Press.

Hobsbawm, E.J. 1969. *Industry and Empire: From 1750 to the Present Day*, The Penguin Economic History of Britain, vol.3, Harmondsworth: Penguin.

Lukács, Georg. [1937] 1962. *The Historical Novel*, trans. by Hannah and Stanley Mitchell, London: Merlin.

McBride, Mary. 1994. 'Contemporary economic metaphors in *Dombey and Son*', *The Dickensian*, 90, pp.19–24.

McCord, Norman. 1991. *British History 1815–1906*, The Short Oxford History of the Modern World, Oxford: Oxford University Press.

McCrum, Robert. 1999. 'The world of books', *Observer*, 14 March, Review section, p.11.

Miller, J. Hillis. 1958. *Charles Dickens: The World of his Novels*, Bloomington: Indiana University Press.

Palmer, William J. 1997. *Dickens and New Historicism*, Basingstoke: Macmillan.

Porter, Roy. 1994. *London: A Social History*, London: Hamish Hamilton.

Perera, Suvendrini. 1990. 'Wholesale, retail, and for exportation: empire and the family business in *Dombey and Son*', *Victorian Studies: A Journal of the Humanities, Arts and Sciences*, 33, pp.603–20. (Extract in Regan, 2001.)

Regan, Stephen. Ed. 2001. *The Nineteenth-Century Novel: A Critical Reader*, London: Routledge.

Williams, Raymond. 1970a. *The English Novel from Dickens to Lawrence*, London: Chatto & Windus.

Williams, Raymond. 1970b. 'Introduction' to Charles Dickens, *Dombey and Son*, ed. by Peter Fairclough, Harmondsworth: Penguin. (Extract in Regan, 2001.)

# Further reading

Ackroyd, Peter. 1991. *Dickens*, London: Minerva. The best modern biography of Dickens.

Connor, Stephen. Ed. 1996. *Charles Dickens*, Longman Critical Readers, Harlow: Longman. Worthwhile introduction to a variety of theoretical approaches to Dickens's novels.

Nead, Linda. 1988. *Myths of Sexuality: Representations of Women in Victorian Britain*, Oxford: Blackwell. Interesting and accessible account of the representation of women in visual culture in this period.

Shelston, Alan. Ed. 1985. *Charles Dickens: 'Dombey and Son' and 'Little Dorrit': A Casebook*, Basingstoke: Macmillan. A useful selection of critical writings on *Dombey and Son* from its publication through to 1976.

Tambling, Jeremy. 1995. *Dickens, Violence and the Modern State: Dreams of the Scaffold*, London: Macmillan. Interesting discussion of ideology and power in Dickens's work.

Waters, Catherine. 1997. *Dickens and the Politics of the Family*, Cambridge: Cambridge University Press. Modern full-length study of the representation of the family in Dickens's major fiction.

# PART 2

# Introduction to part 2

*by Stephen Regan*

*Middlemarch* (1872), *Far from the Madding Crowd* (1874), *Germinal* (1884–5) – what critical insights might we derive from looking at these three novels in close succession? What might we learn about the art of fiction in the later decades of the nineteenth century?

To begin with, we ought to consider the range and diversity of these three novels, both as statements about the world and as formal experiments with language. We are likely to find ourselves challenging any easy or simple account of the development of the novel. After reading these novels in close relation to each other, we might wish to avoid the suggestion of a smooth chronological history of literary forms and be tempted, instead, to applaud the sheer heterogeneity and multifariousness of nineteenth-century fiction. We would be giving our consent to 'novels' rather than to some individuated, idealized 'novel'.

One of the most powerful critical orthodoxies in twentieth-century literary study was the idea of 'the rise of the novel'. Compelling as it seems, the idea must be approached with a degree of scepticism. We need to be fully alert to what it implies, both in terms of the ascent towards a perfect form and in terms of the singular 'novel' that might represent the pinnacle of achievement. Ian Watt's highly influential account of the origins and development of English fiction, *The Rise of the Novel* (1957), provided an impressive and valuable study of the social and political conditions in which philosophical and literary realism came to the fore, but just as persuasively it seemed to privilege one kind of novel over another. Central to Watt's thesis was an undisguised preference for a subtle, psychological realism – the realism of Samuel Richardson, Jane Austen and Henry James – and a conviction that here was the destiny of realist fiction, slowly but steadily unfolding in a mode of writing that took the exploration of consciousness as its central task.

Such was the impact of *The Rise of the Novel*, that for several decades it retained its force and appeal as the most authoritative account of the origins and subsequent development of realist fiction. In terms of establishing a highly selective canon of novels worthy of critical scrutiny, however, the most powerful and influential study was undoubtedly *The Great Tradition*, in which F.R. Leavis confidently proclaimed that 'the great novelists are Jane Austen, George Eliot, Henry James and Joseph Conrad' ([1948] 1962, p.1). The criteria on which this judgement was based were formal perfection and moral seriousness. According to Leavis's standards, Charles Dickens, the Brontës and Thomas Hardy were all found wanting and summarily dismissed from the great tradition. Leaving aside the narrowness of his selection, what Leavis also produced (with little concern for the national origins of Henry James and Joseph Conrad) was an insistently English tradition. Even Raymond Williams, who did more than any other critic to counter Leavis's lofty assessments, was inclined to adopt the same kind of national emphasis, as indicated in the title of *The English Novel from Dickens to*

*Lawrence* (1970). To turn from George Eliot, not just to Thomas Hardy, but to Émile Zola as well, is one way of testing and disrupting habitual notions of tradition.

It was only in the 1970s that a serious challenge began to be mounted and a new generation of critics turned their attention to other plausible explanations of realism or pointed searchingly to various omissions in *The Rise of the Novel* and *The Great Tradition*. It was in the 1970s, too, that the very notion of 'realism' came under sustained attack and the 'classic realist text', as it came to be called, was condemned as naively expressive by critics such as Colin MacCabe, intent on promoting a more 'interrogative' and 'self-reflexive' mode of writing. Much of the impulse behind this concern with the 'classic realist text' came from Colin MacCabe's *James Joyce and the Revolution of the Word* (1979), a book adrift on the big waves of modern linguistic theory and semiotics washing in somewhat belatedly from the shores of France. Putting the arguments crudely, what MacCabe was intent on showing was the difference between James Joyce's highly playful, highly self-conscious preoccupation with the problematics of rendering experience in language, and the calm and skilful illusionist technique, typified by Eliot's *Middlemarch*, that purports to offer a stable and coherent representation of the world.

The critique of classic realism was taken up and widely popularized by Catherine Belsey's *Critical Practice*, first published in 1980 and reprinted numerous times since. Earlier critics had taken for granted the idea that realism was 'a mode that depends heavily on our commonsense expectation that there are direct connections between word and thing' (Levine, 1981, p.9), but it was precisely this 'commonsense expectation' that was now being exposed as deficient. Belsey made a sharp distinction between those literary forms that tend to efface or conceal their own textuality (their own linguistic artifice) and those that explicitly draw attention to their own vulnerable and questionable status as representations of the world. Realism, she argued, tends to offer itself as a transparent medium that gives us immediate access to experience: 'The reader is invited to perceive and judge the "truth" of the text, the coherent, non-contradictory interpretation of the world' (Belsey, [1980] 1994, p.69).

The intense debate over the meaning and function of realism in the 1970s and 1980s was valuable in revising and reconsidering the basic empirical assumption that novels simply 'reflect' the world. Criticism began to turn, in fruitful ways, towards a new consideration of the rhetorical devices and narrative techniques through which novels seek to persuade us of their grasp of truth and reality. Even so, these debates did not always recognize that even in the nineteenth-century the very notion of realism was a matter of profound uncertainty and disagreement; nor did they always register just how complex and complicated so-called classic realism can be. There was a tendency, evident in Belsey's book, to regard realism as 'a predominantly conservative form' because of its ultimately reassuring effect on readers and its habit of confirming 'the patterns of the world we seem to know' (Belsey, 1994, p.51).

*Middlemarch* was a key text in this debate, largely because of its reputation as the very epitome, the very highpoint, of nineteenth-century realist fiction. In a crucial intervention in the heated argument about the classic realist text, David

Lodge (following the earlier example of J. Hillis Miller) argued that beneath the serene surface of Eliot's fictional world there existed 'a gnawing epistemological doubt' – a fundamental uncertainty about whether we can ever be sure of what we know – and that her seemingly 'smooth, unproblematic narrative style' was riven with 'paradox and contradiction' (1981, p.219). Lodge in no way implied that these observations should be read as a negative response to her fiction; rather, the discontinuities and disruptions in the narrative were in keeping with the massive ambition of a novel like *Middlemarch*. He concluded that, far from being naive in her view of how language might operate, Eliot was 'well aware of the indeterminacy that lurks in all efforts at human communication' (ibid., p.236). Similarly, Miller had argued a few years earlier that Eliot's apparent aim in 'presenting a total picture of provincial society in England at the period before the first Reform Bill of 1832' was continually undermined by shifting and conflicting metaphors or ways of looking at the world. In flagrant opposition to those critics who had praised the unity and symmetry of *Middlemarch*, Miller drew attention (approvingly) to the 'incoherent, heterogeneous, "unreadable", or nonsynthesisable quality of the text' ([1975] 1987, pp.9, 24).

An important consequence of the prolonged debate about the nature and function of realism was a renewed attention to the actual diversity of fictional types and an emphasis on comparative rather than narrowly English models. Much of the impetus came from genre criticism, which questioned the assumption that realism was a single, homogeneous narrative method and suggested instead that it might be forged from a multiplicity of styles and voices. To take the novels of Hardy as an example, critics began to give much greater emphasis than before to the curious mingling of generic forms, from popular ballads and romantic melodrama to classical tragedy and scientific discourse. *Far from the Madding Crowd* can now be seen and appreciated more fully as a novel in which many different literary modes are brought into play. Realism had habitually been seen as the opposite of romance, but closer inspection revealed in the novels of Hardy, Dickens, the Brontës and others a surprising persistence of interest in Gothic and sensational devices that had previously been considered the preserve of earlier, romantic authors.

To turn from *Middlemarch* to *Far from the Madding Crowd* and then to *Germinal* is to become aware, even within the scope afforded by just three novels, of the remarkable range of fictional techniques and experiments being conducted in the 1870s and 1880s. One of the unfortunate consequences of a long, relentless harping on the classic realist text was that realism became narrowly identified with a strict mimesis or imitation of people, places and things. The power of *Middlemarch* lay in its capacity for verisimilitude, for a persuasively meticulous documentation of actuality. What a careful reading or rereading of the novel ought to reveal, however, is that *Middlemarch* acquires its force and conviction not through a comprehensive cataloguing of objects and events, but through a highly figurative and imaginative rendering of dreams and desires, aspirations and ambitions, often at the extreme edge of consciousness. *Middlemarch* has a quality of intuition, intrigue and surprise that seems at odds with what we usually understand by 'documentation'.

To take just one example, from Dorothea's troubled honeymoon in Rome: the arrival of Will Ladislaw brings about a transformation in Dorothea's thoughts and feelings, especially with regard to her marriage. As Will converses with Dorothea he seems to 'shake out' rays of light, but her scholarly husband Casaubon stands 'rayless' in comparison (Eliot, [1872] 1998, 2.21; p.196). The confrontation is deeply ironic: Will appears to Dorothea as a young Apollo, a figure of redemption lifted out of classical mythology, while Casaubon, the hapless compiler of the Key to all Mythologies, looks on in uncomprehending blankness at the metamorphosis in his wife's attentions and affections. But the episode does more than this: it shows us that we can't begin to do justice to the flexibility and complexity of 'realism' until we appreciate its capacity for apprehending events and experiences well beyond the level of immediate description or denotation. *Middlemarch* lifts us here into some strange mythopoeic mode of awareness; for a moment it enters the realm of the magical.

Hardy's fiction, too, is powerfully alert to those aspects of emotional and psychological experience that can't be rendered by what he terms mere 'copyism'. In his essay 'The science of fiction', he dwells upon 'the impossibility of reproducing in its entirety the phantasmagoria of experience with infinite and atomic truth' (Hardy, [1891] 1997, p.262). The essay was part of a debate about realism conducted in the 1880s and 1890s by writers and critics such as Henry James and Walter Besant. It shows that Hardy was clearly conversant with that debate, but it also reveals the considerable complexity and sophistication of his own views about fiction and artistic representation. As Peter Widdowson has repeatedly argued, Hardy's critical reputation has borne the weight of considerable condescension over the years, and only now is the image of Hardy the rustic clodhopper giving way to a more accurate assessment of his achievements as a novelist. Widdowson's excellent work on Hardy, especially on those novels (like *The Hand of Ethelberta*, 1876) that resist the usual stereotyping of the rough-edged, rural author, has helped to dispel the kind of easy qualitative distinction between James and Hardy that Leavis was prepared to make.

'The science of fiction' is also of interest for what it reveals about Hardy's response to Zola and prevailing ideas of a meticulously detailed, purportedly 'scientific' realism or 'naturalism' in fiction. Hardy is sceptical about Zola's writings on the experimental novel, but accepts that Zola's essay is itself carefully qualified in its views on the matter, conceding that 'the novel should keep as close to reality *as it can*'. Hardy comments wryly that this is 'a remark which may be interpreted with infinite latitude' (1997, p.261). Hardy, like some later critics, believes that the author of *Germinal* abandons in practice what he maintains in theory, but we should perhaps record that Zola was not so stubbornly 'scientific' as to eliminate all traces of what Hardy calls 'natural magic' (ibid., p.262). One of the most memorable statements about the narrative technique in *Germinal* is Zola's own conviction that it constituted 'a leap to the stars on the springboard of the exactly observed' (quoted in Lethbridge, 1993, p.xi).

Along with a new interest in the complexities of realism and in questions of representation, there has been in recent literary criticism a renewed interest in the history of ideas: a new historicist interest in the fascinating interplay of literary works and other cultural artefacts, including scientific, sociological, political and religious texts. Within the sphere of 'discourse', nineteenth-century fiction can be seen to have an active role in shaping or constituting ideas rather than passively receiving and transmitting them. The work of Gillian Beer on Darwinian ideas in nineteenth-century fiction and of Sally Shuttleworth on scientific models of enquiry are exemplary instances of this kind of literary history (see Beer, 1983, and Shuttleworth, 1984). It is only when we begin to situate our three chosen novels in relation to the history of ideas that we can begin to appreciate the profound impact of agnosticism, a word that had hardly been used before the 1870s. We can then begin to hear 'the melancholy, long withdrawing roar' of what Matthew Arnold in 'Dover Beach' (1867) so memorably called 'the sea of faith' (Arnold, 1930, p.402).

Michael Wheeler has made the vital point that Eliot's fiction 'investigates the problem of moral choice in a world without God' (Dorothea is a latter-day St Theresa of Avila, as the prelude to the novel suggests), but the same observation applies equally well to the writings of Hardy (Wheeler, [1985] 1994, p.8). In *Far from the Madding Crowd*, Hardy's main protagonists, Bathsheba Everdene and Gabriel Oak, attend church services, but their sentiments are distinctly lukewarm. Towards the end of the novel (chapter 56), Bathsheba overhears the choir learning a new hymn, which turns out to be 'Lead, kindly Light' (based on a poem by John Henry Newman). The children, we are told, sing 'without thought or comprehension'. The words of the hymn have a special poignancy for Bathsheba in view of the tragic circumstances that have previously befallen her: 'Lead, kindly Light, amid the encircling gloom, / Lead Thou me on'. In a telling remark, the narrator suggests that Bathsheba began to cry 'for she hardly knew what', and she wishes she could be like the children, 'unconcerned at the meaning of their words' (Hardy, [1874] 2002, 56; p.377). The episode is crucially important in Hardy's work in marking a transition from conventional religious belief to secular humanism, from a sense of providential design to one of painful bewilderment, alleviated only by mutual help and loving kindness.

Recent criticism has tended to emphasize the diversity of fictional types and the range of thematic preoccupations in nineteenth-century fiction, so much so that in the early twenty-first century, we are more likely to talk about 'novels' than 'the novel', and more likely to think of realist fiction as a composite form than as a smooth and seamless artefact. To borrow a pertinent phrase from David Musselwhite (musing on *Great Expectations*), novels are 'the welding together of so many partings', a brittle forging of materials that often seem inclined to fracture and disperse (1988, p.2). The generic instability of nineteenth-century fiction is not a purely formal matter, but a powerful indication of the clash of languages and voices, attitudes and ideas, at a time when so much in the social and political realm was still uncertain, still unknown. In meeting and contending with the social and economic forces that regulate behaviour, works like *Middlemarch*, *Far from the Madding Crowd* and *Germinal* push against generic constraints and expose the limitations of conventional expression. In the three novels discussed here, experiments with narrative technique are not simply attempts to 'tell it as it is', but efforts to imagine how it might otherwise be.

The three novels discussed in part 2 of this book belong to the closing decades of the nineteenth century, and yet in many ways they are as preoccupied with 'the exploration of community' as the novels of the 1840s that Raymond Williams fastened upon in *The English Novel from Dickens to Lawrence*. Williams saw the social and political crises of that particular decade extending across the century, as 'the substance and meaning of community' became increasingly difficult to know and understand. *Middlemarch*, *Far from the Madding Crowd* and *Germinal*, all in different ways confront dilemmas and difficulties that have to do with community: 'What community is, what it has been, what it might be ... how men and women, directly engaged, see within them or beyond them, for but more often against them, the shape of a society' (Williams, 1970, p.11). Society, as Williams attests, is a process that enters lives 'to shape or to deform'; a process that seems 'personally known but then again suddenly distant, complex, incomprehensible, overwhelming' (ibid., p.12).

New social forces, new social experiences, are powerfully evident in the three novels we have chosen to study here. They make their way into people's lives as surely and as steadily as the railway cuts across the landscape, but they are known, as well, in less obvious ways: in the complicated patterns of work and marriage, of wealth and property, of religious belief and scientific discovery. In these novels we see a critical process of change and readjustment in relations between men and women, and in relations within and between social classes. New forms of identity and selfhood and vocation are painfully worked out, as we see with Dorothea Brooke and Will Ladislaw, and again with Bathsheba Everdene and Gabriel Oak. In *Middlemarch* and *Far from the Madding Crowd*, the processes of change are gradual, though marked by moments of sudden drama and crisis. Inequalities of wealth and opportunity and power are steadily observed. In *Germinal*, however, the social process is laid bare with astonishing energy and momentum. As Robert Lethbridge comments, 'Few novels, of any period or in any language, so forcefully dramatize the cruel exploitation of men, women, and children in the interests of unseen shareholders; and perhaps none shows with such clarity the emergence of a new historical force in the shape of the working-class struggle for dignity and justice' (1993, p.xx).

It is worth highlighting two related concerns – love and labour – running very palpably through all three novels. It is through love and work that men and women seek fulfilment and come to know their roles within a particular community, whether it be Eliot's provincial Middlemarch, Hardy's rural Wessex or Zola's industrial northern France. So often, though, it is also in love and work that men and women find frustration and disappointment, and sometimes nineteenth-century novels seem obsessively preoccupied with showing the destructive impact of one aspiration upon the other rather than depicting their harmonious resolution. What all three novels show unflinchingly, as well, is the extent to which that frustration and denial of fulfilment is perpetuated by stubborn ideologies of class and gender, and how these ideological constraints must be fought and overthrown.

Frequently in nineteenth-century fiction, love and work find some provisional meeting place in the ideal of 'vocation', but just as frequently they appear intractably at odds. The impulse of desire, which should be productive and transformative, is thwarted or diminished. Whatever disappointments and disturbances are confronted in *Middlemarch*, in *Far from the Madding Crowd* and in *Germinal*, all three novels look beyond the confines of an oppressive and divisive society to other forms of existence, other ways of being. It is here, finally, that we might turn in looking for some common pursuit within these three novels of the 1870s and 1880s. Failure and resignation cast long shadows over all three novels, but do not prevent them reaching out, miraculously it seems, to grasp new hopes and possibilities. These complicated feelings of intransigence and anticipation find a sudden clarification in the marvellous metaphorical sweep at the end of *Germinal*, as Étienne takes the road to Vandame: 'Beneath the blazing rays of the sun, in that morning of new growth, the countryside rang with song, as its belly swelled with a black and avenging army of men, germinating slowly in its furrows, growing upwards in readiness for harvest to come, until one day soon their ripening would burst open the earth itself' (Zola, [1884–5] 1993, 7.6; p.524).

George Eliot, Thomas Hardy and Émile Zola in different ways encounter the processes of division and alienation, but their novels project us beyond the pain and waste of their own time towards an existence that even now we can only imagine. In the words of the German critic Ernst Bloch, these novels are works of 'anticipatory illumination', the harbingers of a better future (Bloch, 1996, p.xvii).

# Works cited

Arnold, Matthew. 1930. *The Poems of Matthew Arnold 1840–1867*, Oxford: Oxford University Press.

Beer, Gillian. 1983. *Darwin's Plots: Evolutionary Narrative in Darwin, George Eliot and Nineteenth-Century Fiction*, London: Routledge & Kegan Paul.

Belsey, Catherine. [1980] 1994. *Critical Practice*, London: Routledge.

Bloch, Ernst. 1996. *The Utopian Function of Art and Literature*, trans. by Jack Zipes and Frank Mecklenburg, Cambridge, MA: MIT Press.

Eliot, George. [1872] 1998. *Middlemarch*, ed. by David Carroll, with an introduction by Felicia Bonaparte, 3rd impression, Oxford World's Classics, Oxford: Oxford University Press.

Hardy, Thomas. [1891] 1997. 'The science of fiction', in *Thomas Hardy: Selected Poetry and Non-Fictional Prose*, ed. by Peter Widdowson, Basingstoke: Macmillan.

Hardy, Thomas. [1874] 2002. *Far from the Madding Crowd*, ed. by Suzanne B. Falck-Yi, with an introduction by Linda M. Shires, Oxford World's Classics, Oxford: Oxford University Press.

Leavis, F.R. [1948] 1962. *The Great Tradition: George Eliot, Henry James, Joseph Conrad*, Harmondsworth: Penguin.

Lethbridge, Robert. 1993. 'Introduction' to Émile Zola, *Germinal*, trans. by Peter Collier, Oxford World's Classics, Oxford; Oxford University Press.

Levine, George. 1981. *The Realistic Imagination: English Fiction from Frankenstein to Lady Chatterley*, Chicago and London: University of Chicago Press.

Lodge, David. 1981. '*Middlemarch* and the idea of the classic realist text', in *The Nineteenth-Century Novel: Critical Essays and Documents*, ed. by Arnold Kettle, 2nd edn, London: Heinemann.

MacCabe, Colin. 1979. *James Joyce and the Revolution of the Word*, London: Macmillan.

Miller, J. Hillis. [1975] 1987. 'Optic and semiotic in *Middlemarch*', in *George Eliot's 'Middlemarch'*, ed. by Harold Bloom, Philadelphia: Chelsea House.

Musselwhite, David. 1988. *Partings Welded Together: Politics and Desire in the Nineteenth-Century English Novel*, London: Routledge.

Shuttleworth, Sally. 1984. *George Eliot and Nineteenth-Century Science*, Cambridge: Cambridge University Press.

Watt, Ian. 1957. *The Rise of the Novel*, Harmondsworth: Penguin.

Wheeler, Michael. [1985] 1994. *English Fiction of the Victorian Period*, Harlow: Longman.

Williams, Raymond. 1970. *The English Novel from Dickens to Lawrence*, London: Chatto & Windus.

Zola, Émile. [1884–5] 1993. *Germinal*, trans. by Peter Collier, with an introduction by Robert Lethbridge, Oxford World's Classics, Oxford: Oxford University Press.

# CHAPTER 8
# Books and their readers – part 2

*by Simon Eliot*

## Authors, copyright and money: or, how do you turn literature into cash?

Most authors were notoriously bad about money. This was partly because most of them had very little of it so they never got enough practice, and partly because there had been, in Western culture at least, a long-held belief that writing and authorship were on a higher plain – and were thus sullied if they got involved with filthy lucre.

Before the eighteenth century there were four main ways of surviving as an author. One, you were independently wealthy, so you wrote for pleasure, and possibly fame, and would have been insulted had anyone offered you money. Two, you had a day job and wrote in your spare time (lawyers, civil servants and clerics were particularly inclined to this). Three, you had a patron who gave you cash presents or sinecures. Four, you worked for someone who could use your writing for commercial or other purposes (for instance, Shakespeare wrote his plays for a theatre company; Daniel Defoe wrote for various political masters).

None of these sources of income depended on authors realizing the value of their literary property by controlling its copyright. This was fortunate because, before the eighteenth century, there was very little idea of authors having what we would call 'copyright' over their work. The history of copyright is a difficult and sometimes obscure one. Suffice it to say here that copyright only became a serious issue when many copies could be produced quickly, that is, after printing by movable type had been developed by Johann Gutenberg in Mainz in Germany in the 1450s.

In England from 1504 onwards, various printers (not authors) were given the right, through Letters Patent granted by the Crown, to print certain types of text (such as royal proclamations, statutes, Bibles, school books and law books) or specific books (such as particular dictionaries or a specific translation of a classical author). Letters Patent were official documents, usually from the sovereign, in the form of an open letter that granted a named individual the exclusive right to make use of an invention or a text for a specified amount of time. Such a document made it clear that the printer who held it was exclusively privileged and could stop other printers from producing copies of the work. But such privileges applied only to a specific and limited number of works; most books had no protection at all.

*Figure 8.1 The Stationers' Company Hall as it was in the early nineteenth century. Between 1557 and the early nineteenth century the Company was the most important means of controlling and recording book production in the country. By permission of The Stationers' Company*

From 1557 onwards, with the creation of the Stationers' Company (a City Livery Company, or trade guild) by Mary I, a new sort of protection emerged; one that, potentially at least, could apply to all new books.

In 1559 Elizabeth I, Mary's successor, decreed that no book could be published unless censors, appointed by the Crown, licensed it. This system was never perfectly enforced, but the Stationers' Company did gradually develop a system of recording licences to print by listing them in what were called 'Entry Books'. An entry in such a book gradually came to mean not only the right to print the book so registered, but also the right to prosecute another printer who produced unauthorized copies of that book.

Through such slow and uncertain processes – much more concerned with political control and censorship than the granting of literary property rights – did 'copyright' emerge in England. This copyright, however, was almost always vested in the printer or, later, the 'bookseller' (a combination of publisher and seller of books), who dominated the trade in the sixteenth and seventeenth centuries. The author rarely, if ever, got a look in.

What was striking, at least to modern eyes, was that, in theory at least, this 'copyright' was perpetual. That is, literary property was treated as though it were any other sort of property: once you had it, you owned it for ever unless you gave it away, sold it or bequeathed it. This is the common-law view of literary property.

During the English Civil War control over what could be printed broke down. However, soon after the Restoration came a Printing Act (1662) that in essence

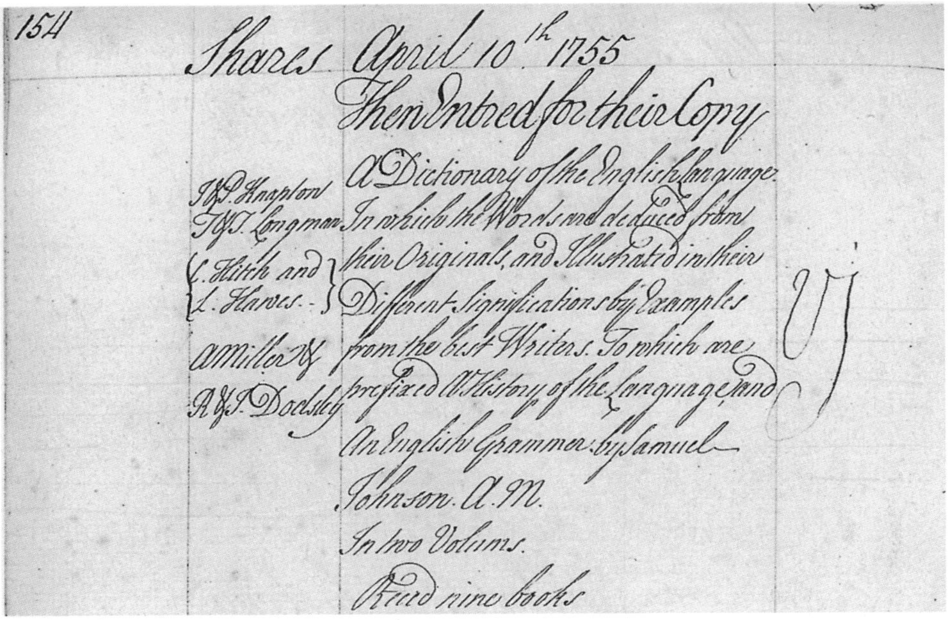

154 Shares April 10th 1755
Then Entred for their Copy
J&P. Knapton | A Dictionary of the English Language
T&T. Longman | In which the Words are deduced from
C. Hitch and L. Hawes | their Originals, and Illustrated in their Different Significations by Examples
A Millar & | from the best Writers. To which are
R&J. Dodsley | prefixed A History of the Language and
An English Grammar. by Samuel
Johnson. A.M.
In two Volums.
Recd nine books

*Figure 8.2 Stationers' Hall Entry Book recording the entry of Samuel Johnson's* Dictionary. *The second column, 'Shares', indicates the names of the booksellers (publishers) who had joined together to finance the project. The 'nine books' on the last line would have been the nine copies of the two-volume work, the number required for legal deposit at that time. Reproduced from Robin Myers,* The Stationers' Company Archive 1554–1984, *Winchester: St Paul's Bibliographies, 1990, p.[xlviii].*

attempted to re-establish the State's control over what could and could not be published. This Act was renewed by Parliament a number of times until 1695, when it lapsed altogether without anything being put in its place. Political control, and its rather accidental by-product of registerable literary property, had gone hand-in-hand. With the lapsing of the Printing Act, the status of copyright was also brought into question.

Partly in response to this uncertainty, the first formal Copyright Act was passed in 1710 under Queen Anne. This gave protection to new books for fourteen years after first publication and the possibility of another fourteen years if the book were to be re-registered with the Stationers' Company. This sounded like good news for the book trade: for the first time rights to literary property had been confirmed in legislation. It also sounded like good news for authors: they would have something – clearly defined by law – to sell. Something to sell meant that more authors could live on their earnings; they could become 'professional' writers.

Many in the book trade assumed that the 1710 Act simply added further rights to the common-law right of perpetual ownership. But it proved not to be so. Through a series of legal test cases in the 1770s, it became apparent that 1710 *replaced* rather than *added to* common-law rights. In other words, the right to own literary property was time-limited: once the fourteen (or possibly twenty-eight) years had passed, the text went into the public domain and the copyright owner had no further rights over it.

From then on, the history of copyright was a history of trying to extend the time before a book went into the public domain. In 1814 another Act extended the copyright period to a full twenty-eight years from date of first publication, or the length of the author's life, whichever was the longer. This sounds a trivial alteration, but it was not. For the first time in copyright law, the author's life was mentioned as a determining factor. For the first time, albeit in a modest and quiet way, there was an attempt to link authors with the property they created. The 1710 Act was very definitely a pre-romantic piece of legislation that was concerned exclusively with property rights. By 1814 the romantic view of the author was sufficiently established to require legislation to link creator to the thing created.

The early Victorians went further. Encouraged by Thomas Noon Talfourd – lawyer, writer and friend of Charles Dickens – the 1842 Copyright Act extended the life of copyright to forty-two years from publication date or seven years after the author's death, whichever was the longer. Add to this an Act of 1838 (establishing a system by which a foreign country – if it granted copyright to British authors – would find its authors granted similar rights in this country), and we have the basis of copyright as most mid- to later nineteenth-century authors knew it. What did all this mean to the novelists of our period?

To an unpopular or unsuccessful novelist it would mean very little. If a novel did not sell well, the fact that it now had forty-two rather than twenty-eight years in which to sell very few copies meant nothing at all. But to a reasonably popular writer, and particularly to a very successful author, it could mean a great deal. An extra fourteen years of copyright meant a huge increase in possible income, and not just for authors but for their heirs as well. Dickens dedicated the first book edition of *Pickwick Papers* (1837) to Talfourd – and no wonder. Even to those novelists who sold their copyright immediately and completely for one lump sum, the longer time span meant that they could get a bigger lump sum from the publisher.

We ought to pause here and ask: how did writers in the nineteenth century convert these copyrights into cash when they published a book? There were four main ways of doing this:

**On commission:** this meant that the writer paid the publisher as an agent to organize production and publication; the writer also paid all the printing, binding and other costs. The advantage was that if the book was a success the author could take all the profits. The extreme form of this was when the author was charged for virtually everything and got nothing back – 'vanity' publishing was as common in the nineteenth century as it is now.

**Half profits:** under this system the author offered the manuscript as capital and the publisher invested money to pay the cost of production and distribution. The publisher would periodically deliver an account to the author in which the profit, if any, was calculated and divided equally. This would be fine with an honest and efficient publisher, but a less principled publisher could run up all sorts of fictitious costs so that the profit would vanish.

**Outright sale:** here the author was offered at the beginning a lump sum for the copyright of the book. In certain cases this would be a complete sale of rights, in others it might be for a fixed number of years, after which copyright reverted to the author. Given that many authors would be on the breadline, the temptation of ready cash might prove irresistible.

**Royalty:** this had originated in the USA but by the middle of the nineteenth century it was beginning to percolate through to the British Isles. A royalty deal usually consisted of an arrangement either for a number of editions or a number of years during which the author would allow publication in return for the publisher paying the author a certain percentage of the cover price (commonly 10 per cent) of each copy of the book sold.

Until the end of our period the two most common ways of turning a novel into cash were half-profits and outright sale of the copyright.

Many of those more successful novelists who did sell their copyright once and for all were almost certainly losing out in the long run. This was because a literary property, such as a novel, might have a number of rights attached to it. Many novels were serialized before they were published in book form, so there were the serial rights as well as book rights to sell. Then there were the rights to serialize outside Britain, and the book rights outside Britain – and the translation rights. Throughout the nineteenth century the number of subsidiary rights grew and grew, and thus so did their total value. The most extreme case of this is evident today, where film rights for a novel can be worth much more than all the other rights put together.

An endlessly expanding range of rights both here and abroad that an author could cash in on – it sounds ideal. There was, however, a problem for most of the nineteenth century, one that the 1838 International Copyright Act only partly answered. **What might this have been?**

The problem was that many countries did not offer copyright protection to British authors. There was no protection in France until 1851 and, much more significantly, no protection for British copyrights in the USA – the largest and potentially most profitable foreign market for British novels – until 1891.

With the industrial revolution in the British Isles came a growing population – an increasingly literate population with more disposable income and, among the middle classes at least, more leisure time in which to read. All these broad economic trends meant that there was a higher demand for novels, and higher demand meant higher prices. Add the 1842 Copyright Act to this and you have, for popular authors at least, the chance of realizing much higher incomes. The problem, however, with a rise in the value of literary property, is that there is an even greater incentive to steal it. For instance, during his earlier career, Dickens, along with many other British authors, suffered from a multitude of unauthorized editions published cheaply in America from which he derived little or no financial benefit. The exploitation, however, wasn't all one way: British publishers often copied American writers' work without authority or payment – Mark Twain was a frequent victim of this.

# Authors' rights and readers' interests

None of the three Copyright Acts that we have described (those of 1710, 1814, 1842) were passed easily. All met with objections from both inside and outside Parliament. Many of the objections came from individuals who were as socially responsible and as intellectually acute as those who were supporting copyright law. The problem of copyright is that by promoting authors' rights you are in immediate danger of threatening readers' interests. Imagine that you were a free-market liberal or a radical in Parliament in 1842. If you were a liberal you would believe in the need for free trade and the abolition of all monopolies. If you were a radical you would believe in the right of the people as a whole to be as well-informed and as well-educated as possible; you would certainly not believe in 'taxes on knowledge'. **If you were of either persuasion, why might you think that a Copyright Act would threaten your constituents and their interests?**

Because copyright is a double-edged sword: it not only allows the copyright owner to publish, it also allows the copyright owner not to publish, or only to publish at a high price, or in small quantities. Copyright could be viewed as a way of controlling, limiting or denying access to knowledge and opinion. And this was not an extreme position. Remember: copyright was an almost accidental by-product of the attempt of the Crown or the State to control the printing press. On such grounds, extension of copyright could be seen as a way of severely limiting a reader's access to knowledge.

As a way of measuring popular concern in the matter of copyright, consider the following: between 1838 and 1840 thirty-seven petitions (amounting to 341 signatures in all) were received by the House of Commons in favour of various copyright bills; in the same period the House received no fewer than 500 petitions (amounting to some 30,000 signatures in all) against the idea of extending copyright (Seville, 1999, chapter 5).

Throughout the eighteenth century, and for most of the nineteenth century as well, copyrights were not usually owned by authors: many professional authors tended to sell their copyrights immediately for ready cash. For this reason some of the most important copyrights were owned by the publishers. There was a dismal tradition in British publishing of maintaining high prices: publishers would, on the whole, rather sell small numbers of a book at a high price than large numbers of a book at a lower price. There is much evidence that most publishers would actually pulp, or sell for scrap, unsold copies of an edition rather than reduce its price and sell it off cheaply. This high-price culture should not surprise us, for parts of it survive even today: many people in the British Isles find it worthwhile to go over the Channel to buy all sorts of goods rather than paying higher British prices.

In the eighteenth and nineteenth centuries, to own the copyright of a book was frequently to keep its price high. Once a book was out of copyright, cheap reprinters would come in and its price would plummet. New books were copyright, so new books were expensive. To an extent that is still true today, but today we can expect a new novel, say, either to be discounted immediately (if it is very popular) or at least to appear as a much cheaper paperback within a year or so of first publication. In the late eighteenth and early nineteenth centuries you might expect a new novel or a new poem to sustain a high price for years or, perhaps, decades. Indeed, in the light of the Copyright Acts of 1710 and 1814, an exciting new book might, if the publisher chose, price itself out of the hands of most readers for nearly a generation (or twenty-eight years).

Let's turn this abstract idea into something more concrete and specific. We commonly imagine that when the great romantics were in full flood, everyone was reading them. This wasn't so. Only Scott and Byron were widely published and, even so, their work during their own lifetimes was usually very expensive. Hardly anyone read Wordsworth, Coleridge, Keats or Shelley. Readers in the great age of romanticism were overwhelmingly reading pre-romantic literature: the literature of the early and middle part of the eighteenth century which, by that time, was out of copyright and therefore subject to cheap reprinting by non-copyright-holding publishers. Even when the romantics were read, they were read by people who were reading much more Pope, Thomson, Gray, Cowper and Crabbe.

In the history of who read what when, one should never underestimate the impact of what we might call 'cultural inertia': that phenomenon in which high prices for current literature meant that most readers had easy access only to the literature, not of their own time, but of a generation before them. It was only by the middle of the nineteenth century, when cheap reprints were being produced more and more quickly after an expensive first edition, that this cultural inertia started to dissipate.

Given the relatively high cost of books until the mid-nineteenth century at least, they tended to be valued and therefore kept, frequently being passed on to the next generation. Dickens's taste in literature was formed by reading the works of the great eighteenth-century novelists, such as Fielding and Smollett, that he found in his father's small collection of books (clearly cheap late eighteenth-century editions). We know quite a lot about what seventeenth- and eighteenth-century middle-class readers valued in terms of books, because books were often listed in the inventory of property made after an individual's death. **Can you think of an incident in *Far from the Madding Crowd* that exemplifies this form of cultural inertia?**

In chapter 44 Bathsheba, not wishing to read 'new ones [books]', can call up from her uncle's collection seventeenth-century plays (by Beaumont and Fletcher) and eighteenth-century poetry and prose (*The Vanity of Human Wishes*, the *Spectator*), all of which, of course, allow her to dramatize and articulate her situation (Hardy, [1874] 2002, 44; p.300; all subsequent page references are to this edition).

Do notice, however, that having summoned up these books, she does very little reading: 'Bathsheba sat at the window till sunset, sometimes attempting to read, at other times watching every movement outside without much purpose' (ibid.).

Books in the past, as now, were used for many more things than reading. In Ptolemaic Egypt many affluent people were buried with papyrus scrolls of parts of Homer's *Iliad*, not because they had read them, or could read them, but because owning a scroll of Homer was an indication of status and culture. In the fifteenth century many affluent women would have owned 'Books of Hours' (beautifully illuminated, handwritten prayer books) despite being illiterate. Such books were often treated as jewellery (and would have cost as much) and might have hung from a jewelled belt. Since the seventeenth century, most gentlemen have collected libraries, though many of them used a library only as a place in which to have an afternoon nap. Who has not used a book to impress someone? Books are signs of intention or aspiration, and were indications of wealth and culture. Books may no longer indicate wealth, but they still function as expressions of worthy intention and intellectual endeavour: how many people have bought a copy of Stephen Hawking's *A Brief History of Time* – and how many have read it?

For those who cannot read, or who have difficulty in reading, books are mysterious objects – they are 'closed books' to them. Such objects can easily acquire a reputation for supernatural power – books as containers of spells. Notice that in chapter 13 of *Far from the Madding Crowd* Bathsheba and Liddy try the *sortes sanctorum*: the use of the Bible to find out what the future holds. The Bible was the most commonly used text for this (hence *sanctorum*), but *sortes* could employ Virgil's *Aeneid* and the poor were observed to use battered chapbooks for the same purpose. A book was not, and is not, just for reading.

# Marketing and packaging the copyright of *Middlemarch*

[H]er profile as well as her stature and bearing seemed to gain the more dignity from her plain garments, which by the side of provincial fashion gave her the impressiveness of a fine quotation from the Bible, – or from one of our elder poets, – in a paragraph of to-day's newspaper.

(Eliot, [1872] 1998, 1.1; p.7; all subsequent page references are to this edition)

'Fred's studies are not very deep,' said Rosamond, rising with her mamma, 'he is only reading a novel.' (1.11; p.95)

'She's got the newspaper to read out loud. That's enough for one day, I should think. I can't abide to see her reading to herself. You mind and not bring her any more books, do you hear?' (1.12; p.104)

For the publication of most of her major novels before *Middlemarch*, George Eliot had followed the conventional route: *Adam Bede* (1859), *The Mill on the Floss* (1860), *Romola* (1863) and *Felix Holt, the Radical* (1866) all came out initially as three-decker novels at 31s 6d. Less conventionally, they then appeared in a two-volume edition at 12s which in turn was followed a year or so later by a single-volume edition selling at 6s. In this way her publishers could satisfy the circulating libraries (Eliot's publishing life roughly spanned that period during which circulating libraries such as Mudie's were at the height of their powers) and, at the same time, explore what economists call 'price elasticity'. Price elasticity means, roughly speaking, that if you drop the price of an article by a significant amount, then that article suddenly becomes affordable by a whole new section of society, and this additional demand compensates the seller for a drop in profits on each individual item. Price elasticity was not something that appealed to copyright owners of the eighteenth century, but as literature moved into the era of mass production in the mid-nineteenth century, it was beginning to make sense to publishers. The 12s edition would appeal to one section of society and, in theory at least, the 6s edition would appeal to another. You obviously milked the higher payers before moving on to the less affluent: that way you maximized the number of copies bought at the higher prices, and thus maximized your income.

This scheme had worked well until *Felix Holt*. Blackwood, Eliot's main publisher, had printed 5,000 copies in June 1866 and had sold 4,615 of them (a huge number for a 31s 6d edition) by the end of the year. The 12s edition emerged in December 1866 and completely flopped: even ten years later only 726 of the 2,000 two-volume sets had been sold. Blackwood got the message: no single-volume 6s edition was produced. *Felix Holt* was the only Eliot novel published by Blackwood that made a loss for the publisher.

Despite this blip, Eliot's copyrights were a hot property, and not just in the British Isles. She had a market in the USA, and any novelist would know how important that market could be. However, as we have seen, there was no copyright arrangement between the British Isles and the USA during Eliot's lifetime, so getting money from America could be quite a challenge.

Quite apart from these international literary property issues, by 1871 the writing of *Middlemarch* itself was beginning to raise production and commercial problems. It was an ambitious novel in terms of size and structure: there were what appeared to be two separate plots (one concerning Dorothea Brooke, the other Lydgate) that could almost have been separate novels but which, by slow degrees, converged. This structure was technically difficult, of course, but also commercially awkward. The three-decker novel was a flexible and accommodating form, but even it had its limits. It soon became apparent to Eliot that *Middlemarch* would require four, not three, volumes. The book trade is, or at least was, a conservative trade. Publishers and librarians liked what they knew. Four-volume novels, reasonably common in the eighteenth century, were unusual in the nineteenth, and 'unusual' commonly spelled commercial trouble. However, Eliot was an uncompromising author. If she felt that her work required four volumes, she would write four volumes, whatever the commercial consequences.

Intractable author, worried publisher, potential problems with circulating libraries, US rights to be secured and a new novel form to be devised: how on earth were all these circles to be squared? **Nowadays, when distinguished (and less distinguished) authors have similar problems – or just want more money – what do they do?**

They hire a literary agent: someone who will negotiate with publishers and others, usually for a 10 per cent fee.

But in the 1870s there were no professional literary agents. Fortunately Eliot had the next best thing: her common-law husband, George Henry Lewes. On 7 May 1871 Lewes wrote the following proposal to Blackwood:

> you have more than once spoken of the desirability of inventing some mode of circumventing the Libraries and making the public *buy* instead of borrowing. I

have devised the following scheme ... to publish it in *half-volume parts* either at intervals of one, or as I think better, two months. The eight parts at 5/- could yield the £2 for the four volumes ...

If in a stiff paper cover - attractive but not bookstallish – (I have one in my eye) this part ought to seduce purchasers, especially if Mudies were scant in supplies.

It would be enough to furnish the town with talk for some time, and each part thus keep up and swell the general interest. *Tristram Shandy* you may remember was published at irregular intervals; and great was the desire for the continuation. Considering how slowly the public mind is brought into motion this spreading of the publication over 16 months would be a decided advantage to the sale – especially as each part would contain as much as one ought to read at a time.

Ponder this; or suggest a better plan!

(quoted in Sutherland, 1976, p.192)

Lewes followed this letter up with another one dated 21 August in which he detailed possible financial arrangements for the novel:

Assuming that the work will consist of 4 volumes to sell at 40/- if you propose to take the risk we should be willing to part with the *English* right only, for 4 years (which would bring it into your other terms of copyrights) for the sum of £6,000 – payable in the course of 1872–3 in any instalments you may think fit.

Or if we take the risk we should require a royalty of 2/- per copy sold, on each 5/- part, in the original form, and an equivalent royalty on copies in cheaper editions. Half yearly accounts.

(quoted in Sutherland, 1976, p.200)

This was not a wholly original plan. The popular novelist and friend of Dickens, Edward Bulwer Lytton, had proposed something similar to Blackwood in 1849 when discussing the publication of his work *My Novel*. It may not have been wholly new but it was designed to cope with a number of the pressures identified in the earlier discussion. It gave Eliot the scope she wanted: longer than the usual three-decker but not tied down to a monthly part-publication or a weekly serialization, both of which required a very tight writing schedule and imposed exacting word limits on what an author could or couldn't do within each part or within the span of the whole novel.

These restrictions could have a devastating effect on a novel. For instance, Mrs Gaskell's *North and South*, first serialized in Dickens's 2d weekly magazine *Household Words* in 1854, had to be crammed into just twenty-two weeks serialization. The consequence of this was that the conclusion was rushed and a number of characters had to die within very few pages of each other! Mrs Gaskell took the opportunity of the first book edition of the novel in 1855 to expand the ending and, later in the same year, issued a second revised edition which further enlarged and explained the development of the plot.

In Lewes's new scheme, a few pages more or less in a particular book would not signify. Despite avoiding the constraints of part or periodical publishing, it would keep the author in the public mind for a number of months, something that many novelists were used to and which was also invaluable in terms of pushing sales. Five shillings was a middle-class price, but it was an affordable price, so Lewes could legitimately expect quite a few buyers rather than borrowers, and as Eliot was emphatically an author who appealed to middle-class readers (she certainly did not reach as far down the social scale as Dickens, for instance), she would not lose many customers.

Blackwood had become more and more frustrated with the circulating libraries – particularly Mudie's (specifically on the subject of the huge discounts that Mudie's could demand and get from the publisher) – so anything that would allow him to reduce the significance of the libraries in distributing books would be welcomed.

There was another advantage – one that would have been invisible to Blackwood at the time. Lewes was also negotiating with American publishers. Although there was to be no Anglo-American copyright agreement until 1891, most self-respecting US publishers were keen to have some sort of working relationship with popular British authors. This desire led to an arrangement for rights to 'early sheets'. The sheets in question were printed sheets of the novel as they came off the press and before they were folded into gatherings and bound. These sheets would be transported across the Atlantic and delivered to the publisher who paid for them. That publisher would then have the novel set up in type, printed and bound in America and then distributed rapidly. This couldn't stop other American publishers then copying this first American edition but, with luck, by the time they did so the first publisher would have sold most of the edition and made a profit. This system just about worked, but it was very difficult to pull off if the novel in question was being serialized in a magazine or in monthly parts. In such circumstances there was hardly any gap between printing and publishing, so no chance to send off early sheets. Also, once out in the public domain, anyone could ship a copy of each part to the USA to any unscrupulous publisher they chose. By publishing in eight book-size chunks, with the usual delay between printing and distribution, Eliot made it possible for the 'early sheets' system to work and thus to earn an additional £120 from the US publisher Harpers.

Lewes was concerned to farm as intensively as he could Eliot's British copyright. **Take a look at his letter of 21 August again. He was offering two ways in which Blackwood might pay for the copyright. What were the two ways?**

One was the sale of the copyright for four years for £6,000; the other was a royalty of 2s per 5s copy (or 40 per cent of the cover price). Notice that in both cases the copyright sale was strictly limited. No complete sale for George Eliot! The lump sum payment was for only four years and only for English (i.e. British) rights. The royalty arrangement was also very tough: 10 per cent was the normal figure but here Lewes is asking for four times that rate.

Blackwood finally decided to pay Eliot the royalty. Why? Well, £6,000 was a lot of money. If the novel was successful it would be a bargain because within the space of four years Blackwood could have exploited price elasticity to the full: he could have published the eight volumes, the four books, an edition in two volumes and an edition in one volume. In those four years he could have milked *Middlemarch* – but only if it proved a success. A royalty meant you only paid on those volumes that sold: you would lose out, comparatively, if the novel were a success, because you would pay out an awful lot of 40 per cents, but if it was a sluggish seller you would only pay out on those sluggish sales. Who got it right: Blackwood or Lewes and Eliot?

Between November 1871 and December 1873 *Middlemarch* sold 5,650 sets in 5s numbers; between February and November 1873 it sold 3,249 sets of four volumes at 21s and between May 1874 and April 1876 it sold 18,406 copies of a single-volume 7s 6d edition. Roughly speaking, the 40 per cent royalty income on these sales would have been £8,645. April 1876 was a little beyond the four years offered for £6,000, so one might have to reduce that figure by a little. However, there is no doubt that *Middlemarch* was a financial success and that Blackwood lost out, to the tune of over £2,500, by not risking the straight purchase of the rights for four years.

This successful experiment in publishing left its mark on Eliot's novel as we read it today. Looking at most modern editions of novels by Dickens, Thackeray or Trollope, it is difficult without editorial help to work out where one serialized part ended and the next began. But *Middlemarch* retains the eight-book structure in which it originally appeared, and that continues to influence the way in which a modern reader responds to the novel.

# Thomas Hardy moulds himself

[N]ot much minding the kind of work he turned his hand to, he decided to offer himself in some other capacity than that of bailiff ... Now that Oak had turned himself into a shepherd it seemed that bailiffs were most in demand.

(Hardy, [1874] 2002, 6; pp.43–4; all subsequent page references are to this edition)

As we have seen, literary property, through the establishment of copyright and through the expansion of population and the growth of literacy (resulting in a larger reading market), was acquiring greater and greater financial value. This encouraged authors to work with informal, and later formal, literary agents, or obliged them to become, as we shall see with Émile Zola, their own literary agents and promoters. But these developments did not just affect authors. Publishers, too, had to develop new means of dealing with authors and potential authors.

As the nineteenth century progressed, many publishers – and particularly publishers of novels – started employing people who could sift and filter the huge number of submitted manuscripts and identify the sorts of book that would be worth publishing. Who these 'gatekeepers' were, and what sort of status they had within the firm, varied from publisher to publisher. John Forster (who was also a friend of, and informal literary agent for, Dickens) acted as a literary adviser to Chapman & Hall, as did the novelist and poet George Meredith. John Morely, scholar, critic and journalist, performed the same function for Macmillan. Somewhat further downmarket, there was Geraldine Jewsbury at the publishing firm of Bentley who was paid per novel for scrutinizing the creations of hundreds of would-be authors. She certainly earned her money. For every one publishable novel there were many that were not. Jewsbury sent her reports back to Bentley in the form of letters. Here are some of her judgements made between February and November 1868:

> *Lance Urquart's Lover* it wd. be perhaps worth yr. while to take if the lady were not likely to require a large sum for the MS.
>
> *Nelly Brooke* decline it altogether. It is dreadfully dull.
>
> *George Grey* It is great rubbish and I recommend you to have nothing whatever to do with it.
>
> *Between Life and Death* if published wd. make everybody laugh.
>
> *On the Brink* it is not altogether a bad novel – but it is not a good one ... I shd. say decline it.
>
> *Lord Nemmo* utter and entire rubbish
>
> *Guy Lovel Carrington* very dry and very dull.
>
> *The Two Rubies* a dull unwieldy story, ill put together.
>
> *On a Summer Evening* utter nonsense and rubbish.
>
> *Garibaldi's Novel* do not take it!
>
> *The Guards* you must please *refuse* it altogether and give no encouragement to the author.
>
> *Why did she leave him?* Imbecile.

> (quoted in Sutherland, 1976, pp.211–12)

One must always remember that, even at the very height of our period, there was a substantial group of mediocre but published writers who produced the ordinary literary fare that provided the context in which great writers were read. Below the mediocre writers were the hacks who survived by producing fiction and journalism on demand and almost by the line (George Gissing wrote movingly of these two classes in his novel *New Grub Street*; 1891). Below even these there was the huge, dismal underclass of the only-once-published and the never-published. Geraldine Jewsbury's comments give us a mercifully brief vision of this world.

Of course, even potentially good writers – unless they were very lucky or privileged – started from this world, though they hoped to leave it behind very quickly. In the very year Miss Jewsbury was enduring *Why did she leave him?*, Thomas Hardy submitted a novel, 'The Poor Man and the Lady', to Macmillan. Morley, as Macmillan's literary adviser, read it and was impressed by the description of country life but disliked what appeared to be a caustically satirical attack on the rich and their attitude to the poor. Alexander Macmillan, then head of the firm, wrote back to Hardy praising the novel but also pointing out that the novel was too dark, particularly when it dealt with London life:

> Your pictures of character among Londoners, and especially the upper classes, are sharp, clear, incisive, and in many respects true but they are wholly dark – not a ray of light visible to relieve the darkness, and therefore exaggerated and untrue in their result.

> (quoted in Sutherland, 1976, p.214)

In response to this, Hardy replied to Macmillan: 'Would you mind suggesting the sort of story you think I could do best, or any literary work I should do well to go on upon?' (quoted in Sutherland, 1976, p.215). Macmillan passed the novel on to Chapman & Hall who gave it Meredith to read. Though impressed as Morley had been, Meredith advised Hardy not to publish a book that, in his view, would be attacked by all critics as being 'socialistic, not to say revolutionary' (quoted in ibid., p.215).

Hardy's second novel, *Desperate Remedies*, was also taken to task by John Morley at Macmillan. After praising its treatment of dialogue and its general style, Morley raised a fatal objection:

> But the story is ruined by the disgusting and absurd outrage which is the key to its mystery. The violation of a young lady at an evening party, and the subsequent birth of a child, is too abominable to be tolerated as a central incident from which the action of the story is to move.

> (quoted in Sutherland, 1976, p.217)

Sex, politics and darkness: Hardy's first two novels were clearly using ingredients that were later, as we shall see, to be familiar to readers of Zola's novels. But Zola was to be presented to English readers not between the august covers of a Macmillan book or the respectable covers of Chapman & Hall, but first through cheap and dubious American translations and then through editions from a publisher on the margin, Henry Vizetelly. Hardy was making the mistake of going to the respectable, starched shirt front of the British publishing trade, not its more shabby and down-at-heel extremities.

William Tinsley ran a publishing house that offered mediocre – and worse than mediocre – writers an occasional home. He had even published one of the novels that Miss Jewsbury had slated in her report to Bentley (*The Two Rubies*), and was able to supply the circulating libraries with acres of three-decker novels at substantial discounts. Tinsley was the sort of publisher to whom new writers would go for a start before moving on to higher and better things. At one time or another the firm had published some of the most popular three-decker novelists, including Harrison Ainsworth, Mrs Henry Wood, Henry Kingsley and Wilkie Collins. Tinsley had made a great splash in 1862 by publishing Miss Braddon's *Lady Audley's Secret* – a sensational story of bigamy and murder. The Tinsley brothers had bought the copyright of Miss Braddon's novel for just £250 and had then proceeded to make a fortune from it. But then, hardly surprisingly, Miss Braddon moved on. For a mid-Victorian reader *Lady Audley's Secret* was a sensational and *risqué* book, and therefore it was not surprising that Hardy should try Tinsley as a publisher of *Desperate Remedies*.

Tinsley agreed to produce 500 sets of a three-decker version of the novel, but he wasn't taking any chances. He suggested a half-profits arrangement but in addition he required Hardy to pay a £75 'guarantee'. The author would get all this back if the novel made a profit of £150, and would then actually make some money if profits went above this sum. We have the rough costs of producing this edition: £194.29. **Given this information, do you think this was a good or bad deal for Hardy?**

You might argue that, as Hardy was desperate to get into print, any deal that got him published was a good deal. (Hardy might have agreed with you: much later, when he was an established author, he reported 'Never will I forget the thrill that ran through me from head to foot when I held my first copy of

*Figure 8.3 Cartoon of William Tinsley (d.1902), Hardy's first publisher. The titles on the spines of the books below the address indicate the range of authors Tinsley published at one time or another. Sadly for Tinsley, almost all of the most distinguished moved on to other publishers as they became more famous. Reproduced from Patricia J. Anderson and Jonathan Rose,* Dictionary of Literary Biography, *vol.106:* British Literary Publishing Houses 1820–1880, *London: Gale Group Publishers, 1991, p.299*

*Desperate Remedies* in my hand'; quoted in Gittings, 1978, p.213.) However, most half-profits deals assumed a burden of equal investment: that is, the publisher invested his skill and money and the author invested his text. To ask the author also to pay an indemnity is doubling the novelist's risk. As Tinsley's costs were £194.29, £150 represented roughly 77 per cent profit on investment – a very high expectation for an unknown novel. Tinsley actually made £313.50 which, when he had paid the costs of production, left roughly £119 of profit. This meant that Hardy got just under £60 back: he was £15 out of pocket but, one hopes, a wiser man.

Hardy's next novel, *Under the Greenwood Tree* (1872), was again published by Tinsley but this time Hardy received £30 plus £10 for the Continental rights; neither sum was generous but at least Tinsley was now paying Hardy rather than the other way around. This novel was a critical success, and it prompted Tinsley into a more generous offer: namely to pay £200 for the right to serialize Hardy's next novel and publish its first edition.

The serialization of *A Pair of Blue Eyes* in *Tinsley's Magazine* (between August 1872 and April 1873) and its publication in three-decker form in May 1873 was a great step forward. *Tinsley's Magazine* was not a distinguished publication; indeed, its printing of dubious stories concerning Queen Victoria and John Brown put it firmly with the other sensationalist publishing ventures of the firm. However, it did usher Hardy into the dignified and profitable world of prior serialization followed by a first, three-decker book edition. It also brought

Hardy to the notice of a distinguished man of letters, Leslie Stephen (later to become initiator of the *Dictionary of National Biography* and father of Virginia Woolf). Stephen was editing the *Cornhill Magazine*, a respectable and upmarket monthly magazine whose first editor had been William Makepeace Thackeray and whose publisher, George Smith, was keen to buy into new, rising literary talent. Smith doubled Hardy's income by giving him £400 for serial and first book-edition rights.

Hardy had arrived as a novelist. However, he was still not free from censure. Even the urbane and able Stephen objected to Fanny Robin's illegitimate baby. Hardy was always vulnerable to criticism, and perhaps more inclined to take guidance than he should have been. In chapter 43, for instance, when Liddy is suggesting that the coffin contains two bodies, Hardy's original text had Liddy telling Bathsheba: 'there's *two of 'em* in there' (43; p.285). The *Cornhill* text was much more prissy: 'Liddy came close to her mistress and whispered the remainder of the sentence slowly into her ear' (quoted in Gatrell, 1988, p.17).

Interestingly, Stephen suggested that Hardy might restore the original reading when he came to issuing it in book form. **Why do you think he did that?**

The *Cornhill Magazine* cost 1s, a three-decker novel 31s 6d: again we have an example of censorship related to price. A cheap publication could get to readers who might be corrupted; an expensive publication only to those affluent enough to buy or borrow it and they were, of course, much too well-educated and sophisticated to be corrupted. More cynically, one might say that as editor of the *Cornhill Magazine*, Stephen would have been tainted had it been published in his journal; once in book form he had no further responsibility for it.

Like Gabriel Oak at the Casterbridge hiring fair, Hardy as a novelist adapted himself to fit the market. He received advice from at least two publishers and three literary advisers as he made his way. Their advice was well meant and frequently to the point, but as a whole it was inconsistent and sometimes contradictory. Many critics have observed the peculiar heterogeneous nature of many of his novels, which seemed composed of bits of nature writing, pastoral idyll, rural naturalism, hints of almost Greek tragedy, melodrama and low comedy. Hardy's plots and style sometimes read like an author trying to please everyone simultaneously.

## *Reading and speaking in* Far from the Madding Crowd

Although it is still a contentious matter, many historians of the book now accept that at some time, probably in the mid- to late eighteenth century, a 'reading revolution' took place. This had a number of aspects, but the most important was the move from 'intensive' to 'extensive' reading. That is, a significant number of readers moved from reading a few texts again and again, to reading a lot of texts once. Before that time, most readers would own very few books. For instance, average, middling readers in 1700 might own the Bible, the Book of Common Prayer, a chapbook or two, *The Pilgrim's Progress*, and a few books relevant to their occupation. These texts would be read again and again, pored over, considered and re-considered. **What tends to happen when you read a text many times?**

One, you find yourself able to quote from it with ease; two, commonly you find that its style affects the way that you talk and write – the text becomes part of who you are and how you express yourself.

Extensive reading is the opposite. As the industrial revolution got underway all forms of printed matter became more widely available and, more slowly, cheaper. Libraries became much more common and cheaper to use. Readers could now read lots of material, but choose to read that material only once. The most characteristic forms of this new extensive reading system were the cheap, trashy novel and the newspaper, both clearly designed to be read just once by each reader.

Of course, like any cultural change, this reading 'revolution' was more of an evolutionary process than a truly revolutionary one. It affected different sorts of people at different rates at different times. Many of the well-educated, affluent, middle class were probably moving to extensive reading early in the eighteenth century. Many poor and educationally deprived but literate people were still intensive readers in the mid-nineteenth century. Those of a highly religious temperament would shun the frivolous and the temporary and would consciously restrict themselves to the Bible and a few pious works. Extensive reading would be more common in towns than in the countryside (towns would have more libraries, more bookshops, better distribution of newspapers, and so on).

There are two descriptions of book collections in *Far from the Madding Crowd*. One is clearly an intensive reader's collection, the other was collected by an extensive reader. **Can you identify these?**

We have already discussed Bathsheba's uncle's collection of books, described in chapter 44. This consisted of both new and old books and was very diverse in genre, style and content. Clearly an extensive reader's collection. But in chapter 8 Hardy describes Gabriel Oak's collection of books:

> *The Young Man's Best Companion, The Farrier's Sure Guide, The Veterinary Surgeon, Paradise Lost, The Pilgrim's Progress, Robinson Crusoe, Ash's Dictionary,* and *Walkingame's Arithmetic,* constituted his library; and though a limited series it was one from which he had acquired more sound information by diligent perusal than many a man of opportunities has done from a furlong of laden shelves. (8; p.72)

This was an intensive reader's collection; limited, but read and reread: 'diligent perusal' was exactly what intensive reading was all about.

The reading of *The Pilgrim's Progress* is mentioned again in the novel: ''Twas a bad leg allowed me to read the *Pilgrim's Progress*' (33; p.216), says Joseph Poorgrass, and we are reminded that illness or the results of an accident might provide one of the very few opportunities for the labouring classes to read at length.

However, text can be absorbed in ways other than by simple reading. **How else might religious texts be 'taken into the system'? Hardy illustrates at least two others in the novel.**

One, by hearing material again and again: on the very first page we are reminded that in the mid-nineteenth century, at least in the rural areas, many people still went to church on Sunday and there, week after week, they would hear readings from the Bible and, if they were Anglicans, the Nicene Creed. As Jan Coggan pointed out, non-Conformists 'can lift up beautiful prayers out of their own heads, all about their families and shipwracks [sic] in the newspaper' but Mark Clark confirms that Anglicans 'must have it all printed aforehand' (42; p.279).

Two, learning by rote. This was a central principle of much nineteenth-century education (and, indeed, of education prior to that century, for the 'art of memory' was much prized). To learn, however, is not to understand, and the schoolboy in chapter 44 whose repetitions of the Collect are paralleled by Hardy with the patterns of birdsong that Bathsheba has just heard, underscores the ritual aspects of printed and spoken language.

Bible language (specifically that from the King James Version of 1611), and more general religious prose, permeated nineteenth-century British culture. It seeped into the consciousness and into the vocabulary. **Can you think of examples in _Far from the Madding Crowd_ in which the most unlikely characters either quite naturally quote from religious texts or use language which is essentially biblical?**

In chapter 8, when Joseph Poorgrass is terrified he says:

> I kneeled down and said the Lord's Prayer, and then the Belief right through, and then the Ten Commandments, in earnest supplication. But no, the gate wouldn't open; and then I went on with Dearly Beloved Brethren, and thinks I, this makes four, and 'tis all I know out of book, and if this don't do it nothing will, and I'm a lost man. Well, when I got to Saying After Me I rose from my knees and found the gate would open. (8; p.62)

Notice that in this instance he is using religious text as a magical formula, just as Bathsheba and Liddy use the _sortes sanctorum._

Later in the same chapter Poorgrass adopts the biblical tone to justify Levi Everdene's way of keeping faithful to his wife; without this fantasy he might have 'given his eyes to unlawfulness entirely' (8; p.64). Poorgrass is particularly inclined to the biblical cadence: ''Tis the gospel of the body, without which we perish' (22; p.150). But others can also use the same style. Mark Clark, for instance, in order to justify a longer stay at the Buck's Head, says of the ability to enjoy a drink ''Tis a talent the Lord has mercifully bestowed upon us' (42; p.278).

But it was not just the religious language of the sixteenth and seventeenth centuries that had an influence on the language in which people talk and think in Hardy's novel. The world of ephemeral print could also have an impact. You should notice how frequently references to newspapers are made, even in this rural novel (chapters 4; p.34; 34; p. 211; 42; p.279; 48; p.320 and 50; p.336), but what I want to concentrate on here is something even more ephemeral: the advertising poster.

When discussing _Dombey and Son_ in chapter 1 we considered the fact that the nineteenth century was the first century of universal advertising, and then went on to discuss the way in which advertising invaded the physical form of the novel. Advertising did not stop there, of course. Today we complain bitterly of

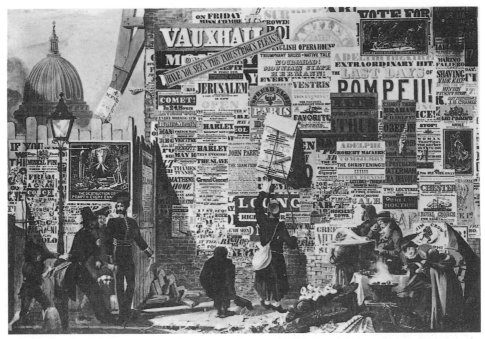

*Figure 8.4   John Parry, London Street Scene, 1835. Reproduced by courtesy of the Alfred Dunhill Museum & Archive, 48 Jermyn Street, St James's, London, SW1Y 6DL*

the way in which advertising seems to get everywhere, but at least now we have planning laws and legislation governing trade description. There are constraints on where you can advertise, what you can advertise and how you can advertise. Very few such constraints were in place in the nineteenth century. Unlike today, where we have radio, cinema, television and the internet on which to advertise, the nineteenth century had only print. Print was the only funnel through which all commercial communication had to flow. If you weren't in print you weren't selling.

Most blank walls were not blank in nineteenth-century towns and cities. They were posted, and fly posted, until the original brick or stone was wholly obscured by layer upon layer of printed paper.

There would be announcements of entertainments, of theatres, of fairs, of circuses, of lotteries; there would be advertisements for tobacco, for soap, for medicines, for false teeth and false hair; there would be promotions of sales: house clearances, bankruptcies and, in the country, of farms and of 'stock, plant, and implements' (5; p.42).

Nor was it just print. Goods for sale were not always contained neatly behind plate glass (remember how impressed Cainy Ball had been with Bath shops: 'Great glass winders to the shops' (33; p.218)) – frequently their contents burst into the street occupying the pavement and climbing the walls above and surrounding the shop.

*Figure 8.5 The excitement of the streets: the exotic animals and performers of the circus and, behind them, the garish and by now ubiquitous advertising posters. Photo of Barnum and Bailey's circus parading in Bristol, 1898. Reece Winstone Archive*

The street itself was full of walking advertisements: not merely the street sellers with their traditional cries, but hundreds of casual workers acting as sandwich-board men carrying mobile selling messages.

*Figure 8.6 Not all ephemera was static: script and print moved about in the form of sandwich boards and 'peripatetic placards'. This picture is a compilation; the artist has dated each example at the foot of the page. Reproduced from Peter Jackson, George Scharf's London, London: John Murray, 1987, pp. 34–5. By permission of John Murray, publishers, London*

This was not a new nor an exclusively industrial phenomenon. Hardy describes the hiring fair at Casterbridge where the labourers turn themselves into advertisements by wearing specific emblems:

> carters and waggoners were distinguished by having a piece of whip-cord twisted round their hats; thatchers wore a fragment of woven straw; shepherds held their sheep-crooks in their hands; and thus the situation required was known to the hirers at a glance. (6; p.43)

Just as our children now imitate the language and style of advertisements and pop videos, so *Far from the Madding Crowd* carries evidence that the trivial as well as the grand forms of print shaped the way in which people used language. Consider for a moment the scene in chapter 50 where the shepherds, with business over, turn their attention to the tent and ask the man working on it what was going on. His reply is distinctive: 'The Royal Hippodrome Performance of Turpin's Ride to York and the Death of Black Bess' (50; p.350).

This does not sound like a normal conversational response. **What does it sound like? And why are there so many words beginning with capital letters in the line?**

It sounds like an announcement on a poster or a handbill. This impression is confirmed by the use of capital letters to begin each significant word: this is how a title is usually presented. The man is speaking not in tongues but in headlines.

**There is another occasion slightly later in the chapter where again Hardy makes clear the impact of advertising on the contours of people's thoughts and speech. Can you find it?**

It occurs a few pages later:

> Bathsheba ... had, like every one else, read or heard the announcement that Mr Francis, the Great Cosmopolitan Equestrian and Roughrider would enact the part of Turpin. (50; p.352–3)

Here again the style of grandiloquence and the sprinkling of self-important capital letters indicates that the language comes from a public announcement.

In Hardy's novel, characters are not merely surrounded by printed texts; their language, indeed the way they see their world, is shaped and informed by those texts.

*Figure 8.7 Circus advertisement – the sort of advertisement that would be familiar to Hardy's agricultural labourers. Note the frequency of horse-based acts: Sergeant Troy would have had no difficulty finding employment in this circus. Reproduced from* The Victorian Scene, *London: Hamlyn Publishing Group, 1971, p.272*

# Zola: the author as his own promoter

Set the maiden fancies wallowing in the troughs of Zolaism,
Forward, forward, ay and backward, downward too into the abysm.

(Tennyson, *Locksley Hall Sixty Years After* (1886))

Despite the success of Lewes in marketing George Eliot's later novels, and Hardy's testing of the market, not all novelists felt the need for an informal agent to negotiate for them and promote their works. Some did it for themselves. Zola had a useful practical introduction into the world of book promotion before he began to publish novels. It provided an education that enabled him to push even his earliest books.

In February 1862 Zola started work in the packing department of one of the largest publishers in Paris, Hachette. The firm had originated in 1826 as a publisher of textbooks, classical texts and dictionaries but, by 1862, it was a mass publisher of guidebooks, novels and popular magazines. The guidebooks, particularly the 'Joanne' guides, rather like similar railway-based guides in Britain, were satisfying a new demand created by the growth of the French railway system.

Zola's first job was a menial one, but he was in an ideal position to make a map of French reading taste by simply observing what he had to pack a lot of (novels) and what he had to pack little of (poetry). He rose rapidly at Hachette, and by October 1863 was advertising manager and head of its small publicity department, writing copy for Hachette's monthly *Bulletin du libraire et de l'amateur de livres*, a free newsletter for booksellers and book lovers that was sent to all the publisher's regular clients. The *Bulletin* advertised Hachette's new publications by including exciting summaries, what we might now call 'blurbs'. Zola became adept at producing these and thus, when his own works began to appear, he knew exactly how to promote them.

During this period Zola had begun to publish short stories in various, mostly obscure, journals. As in the British Isles, the second half of the nineteenth century provided a remarkable range of newspapers and magazines, most of which were vehicles for, or at least published, both serialized and short-story fiction. Indeed, Zola's first published book, *Les Contes à Ninon* (1864; 'Stories for Ninon'), was a collection of his magazine fiction. (Similarly, Dickens's first book, *Sketches by Boz* (1836), was a collection of his magazine writings.) The deal Zola did with Hetzel, the book's publisher, was rather similar to a half-profits arrangement, but with an added burden of the novelist agreeing to 'place, in all newspapers, notices or advertisements worth at least as much as what it costs to print the work without ... you having to put yourselves to further expense' (quoted in Brown, 1996, p.119).

That this was not the burden it appeared to be was due to Zola's skill at what today we would call 'networking'. He had spent years making contacts in the world of journalism and publishing. If we add this to his skill at blurb-writing, we can see that he had become a natural and skilled self-promoter. He wrote off to editors of all sorts, requesting that they publish excerpts, or reviews, or comments on his book. If they did not wish to write their own material he would provide it for them: in one letter he enclosed the following shameless puff:

Émile Zola, belongs to the literary family of free spirits, of passionate and subtly mocking temperaments ... *Les Contes à Ninon* is sure to succeed with people of taste.

(quoted in Brown, 1996, p.119)

The exercise succeeded: the book was mentioned in nearly one hundred articles, many of which (for journalists were commonly lazy) were based on Zola's own puffs.

Zola's second book, *La Confession de Claude* ('Claude's Confessions'), was published in October 1865. It was a novel about the relationship between a young poet, Claude, and a prostitute. It was the sort of subject that in the British Isles would have guaranteed, had it been published at all, exclusion from the lucrative market of Mudie's circulating library. In France it ran greater risks, for it caught the attention of the police censor who reported on 2 December 1865: 'The author has exaggerated certain passages describing lustful passions ... a book which sets out to convey a moral should avoid anything suggesting pornography. Obeying tendancies of the realist school, the author has on certain pages delighted too much in analyzing shameful passions ... a book that purports to have a moral intention must avoid everything that might make it resemble a wicked book' (quoted in Brown, 1996, p.124).

The police themselves started investigating Zola, an investigation that included searching his room and asking Hachette's about him. Surprisingly, although mildly worried, Zola was also excited. There was a long tradition in France of great writers being persecuted by the authorities: only eight years earlier, in 1857, both Flaubert's *Madame Bovary* and Charles Baudelaire's collection of poems *Les Fleurs du mal* ('Flowers of Evil') had been prosecuted. If Zola had joined them, his reputation would have been made.

He had also been long enough in a publicity department to realize that any book that is prosecuted immediately becomes highly desirable and thus, commonly, a bestseller (books as diverse as *Lady Chatterley's Lover* and *Spycatcher* are but two twentieth-century examples of a similar process in this country). Disappointment followed as the police decided not to prosecute. Zola responded by using very similar techniques to those used to promote *Les Contes à Ninon*: he wrote to innumerable friends, colleagues and those who owed him a favour. The same self-puffery was used:

[A] tale of blood and tears that has Fall and Redemption as its lofty and pure moral. The frightful narrative relates a virgin heart's passion for one of those girls to whom poets have given the sweet names Mimi Pinson and Musette. The author bares himself therein with a strange talent that combines exquisite delicacy and mad audacity. Some will applaud and others will jeer, but this drama fraught with anguish and terror will leave no one indifferent.

(quoted in Brown, 1996, p.122)

**How effective a sales pitch do you think this was?**

A novel of 'Lofty and pure morals' but one that also describes prostitutes; 'delicacy' and 'audacity' combined in the same story; Zola had learnt his lesson well. As with a modern tabloid newspaper, the combination of sexual revelations and high moral tone always guarantees large sales.

On the principle that there is not such a thing as bad publicity, Zola was quite happy, if the police would not prosecute him, to create his own furore. These puffs were sent with the request that the editors review the novel, even if only to denounce it: 'It is understood that I prefer a sincere slating to routine compliments' (quoted in Brown, 1996, pp.122–3). By such means did Zola ensure that the first edition of 1,500 copies of *La Confession de Claude* sold out.

**Think for a moment about the differences between Hardy's and Zola's approach to marketing themselves**.

Hardy of course, had not had the useful and educational introduction to the marketplace that Zola had experienced at Hachette, so perhaps it is not surprising that Hardy invited the publisher to be his educator. The striking thing is that publishers and readers in Britain were advising Hardy not to make a stir, not to paint too darkly or attract critical condemnation. Zola, on the other hand, courted controversy as a means of drawing attention to his writings and therefore, he hoped, increasing his sales.

## *Obscenity and censorship*

In the culture of mid- to late nineteenth-century Western Europe, naturalism – at least as far as potential readers and buyers of books were concerned – drew on a much older tradition that cultural or political radicalism often associated with irreligion and sexual licence. This has deep roots, but in France the most obvious and immediate link was with the Enlightenment of the eighteenth century. Some of the most popular books with French readers in the Enlightenment were not critiques of politics or philosophy, but mildly pornographic works that were deeply anti-clerical and frequently quite radical, at least by implication. Novels such as *Thérèse philosophe* [1748?] was an example of what has been called 'Philosophical Pornography', and one that sold extremely well over decades.

Books that were not officially approved, 'clandestine' books, frequently printed outside France and then smuggled in, were a common feature among the bestseller lists in eighteenth-century France. Although it was not what the censors intended (it never is), books banned for political or sexual reasons almost always acquire a cachet that makes them highly desirable. Frequently, a notorious book is a godsend to both author and publisher, for people will pay high prices to get it.

In Britain censorship was much less well organized, particularly after 1695 and, probably as a consequence, the acquisition and reading of clandestine books was less a feature of its culture. It happened, of course, but on a smaller scale and in a less organized way.

The literary licensing that had existed from the first half of the sixteenth century had been designed mostly to suppress sedition and blasphemy rather than obscenity. The first modern case of a prosecution for what we might think of as a pornographic work was of James Read who, in 1708, was accused of publishing *The Fifteen Plagues of a Maidenhead*, it being alleged that this constituted an 'obscene libel'. Read was found guilty but the decision was

*Figure 8.8 Enlightenment philosophy, sex and anti-clericalism: an eighteenth-century bestseller in France. Frontispiece to* Thérèse philosophe. *Reproduced from Robert Darnton,* The Forbidden Best-Sellers of Pre-Revolutionary France, *London: HarperCollins, 1996, p.101. By permission of HarperCollins Publishers Ltd.*

reversed on appeal on three grounds: one, that it was not an offence known to common law; two, that because of this it was a matter for an ecclesiastical court rather than a temporal (secular) one; three, that it could not be a libel because the book was not directed at a specific person or persons.

Relatively little use was made of the offence of obscene libel in the eighteenth century. The more vigorous enforcement of the law had to wait for the major cultural shifts that occurred at the end of the eighteenth and the beginning of the nineteenth century. This change was best symbolized in Britain by the formation of the Society for the Suppression of Vice in 1802. Between 1802 and 1817 the Society conducted between thirty and forty successful prosecutions under the obscene libel law.

The major change, however, occurred in 1857 with the passing of the Obscene Publications Act, devised by the then Lord Chief Justice, Lord Campbell. This had the object of preventing 'the spread of those obscene prints and publications which had become of late most alarming'. The problem with the current law, Campbell explained, was that the prosecution was against the publisher who had most of the evidence in his control. Prosecutions were thus dependent on spies and informers acquiring the necessary proof. Campbell proposed a new procedure in which the police, armed with a Magistrate's warrant, could enter a publisher's premises and seize any obscene material found. It would then be up to the courts to decide whether the material was obscene, and if so, what was to be done with it. One of the problems with the Act was something that haunts all legislation designed to suppress obscene publications: the problem of definition. Campbell's Act made no attempt at definition, simply leaving it up to the courts to decide what constituted obscenity.

Case law, and the definitions associated with it, was therefore to be critical in the application of the 1857 Act. The crucial case occurred eleven years later in 1868 when, operating under the Act and with a warrant issued by a magistrate in Wolverhampton, the police seized a pamphlet from the premises of a member of the Protestant Electoral Union, Henry Scott. The pamphlet was entitled: *The Confessional Unmasked; shewing the depravity of the Romish priesthood, the iniquity of the Confessional and the questions put to females in confession.* **Judging by the title, how might this pamphlet, do you think, link with the sort of publication common in France in the eighteenth century?**

It was anti-clerical or, more specifically, anti-Roman Catholic, and employed the device of suggesting, in order to satirize Roman Catholicism, that the confessional was used by priests for their sexual gratification. Many obscene engravings, as well as books, on this very subject had been published in France in the eighteenth century

The pamphlet was brought before the justices and was found to be obscene. Scott appealed to Quarter Sessions where the Recorder (a barrister sitting as a part-time judge) found in his favour on the grounds that the pamphlet had not been produced for personal gain nor was the aim of the pamphlet to prejudice good morals. The case then went to the Queen's Bench Court in April 1868 which reversed the Recorder's decision on the grounds that an obscene publication could not be justified by a publisher having the 'right' motives. However, the case was famous not because of the final judgement, but because during the hearing at the Queen's Bench the then Lord Chief Justice, Sir Alexander Cockburn, articulated a definition of obscenity that has had a substantial influence on court proceedings and legislation ever since. Cockburn pronounced: 'the tendency of the matter charged as obscenity is to deprave and corrupt those whose minds are open to corruption and into whose hands a publication of this sort may fall' (quoted in Pearsall, 1971, p.470).

## Zola's novels in Britain

Given this context, how was Zola's work published in Britain, and how did his readers respond to him? In the early 1880s poor-quality, pirated translations of Zola produced by publishers in the USA were beginning to filter into Britain. They did not, of course, enter the respectable circulating library market. Instead they appeared on bookstalls and in backstreet shops.

Henry Vizetelly, originally a printer and engraver, established a publishing firm in London in 1880. At first he specialized in illustrated comical and satirical books, but then in 1884 he started branching out into continental fiction with such series (Victorians loved 'series') as 'Vizetelly's Popular French Novels', which were advertised as 'books that may be safely left lying about where the ladies of the family can pick them up and read them' (quoted in Anderson and Rose, 1991, p.317). **Why do you think Vizetelly was so keen to stress the inoffensiveness of his popular novels?**

The British have always tended to regard the French as suffering from lax sexual morals. Much, particularly visual, pornography was imported from France during the eighteenth and nineteenth centuries, 'dirty' French postcards were the subject of recurrent jokes, and writers such as Flaubert, Baudelaire and Zola confirmed the British prejudice. If you were going to use 'French' in a series title, you had to be very reassuring or the great British public would fear the worst.

Vizetelly also published another series, 'Russian Novels' (1884–8), which included major works by Tolstoy (*War and Peace, Anna Karenina*) and Dostoevesky (*Crime and Punishment*) in cheap editions. Vizetelly was a businessman who was looking for a decent profit, but he was also an adventurous publisher who was prepared to take risks in publishing 'difficult' foreign novels. However, this risk-taking increased dramatically with his next series, 'The Realistic Novels', in which he issued works by Flaubert (including *Madame Bovary*) and a novel by Alphonse Daudet whose subject was lesbianism (*Sappho*, 1886). These novels appeared in a cheapish format: one volume at 6s with illustrations, or at 5s without.

It was as part of this series that Vizetelly began to publish Zola in 1884. The translations that had been available before had been frequently poor and commonly heavily expurgated. Vizetelly's translations – many done by his son Ernest, who knew Zola personally – were much more accurate and all were described as being 'unabridged'. This was not strictly true, for some of Zola's most outspoken novels, such as *Nana* and *La Terre*, were toned down or, as Vizetelly himself put it, a sort of veil was put 'over those passages to which particular exception was likely to be taken' (quoted in Anderson and Rose, 1991, p.319).

*Figure 8.9   Henry Vizetelly, pioneer publisher who tried to combine profit with adventurous publishing and introduced many English readers to the great French and Russian authors of the period. The two prosecutions for obscene libel that he faced (1888, 1889) broke Vizetelly both financially and physically. Reproduced from Patricia J. Anderson and Jonathan Rose,* Dictionary of Literary Biography, *vol.106:* British Literary Publishing Houses 1820–1880, *London: Gale Group Publishers, 1991, p.315*

This did not save him. During a debate on 'Corrupt Literature' in the House of Commons in May 1888, Vizetelly was named and in June of that year a newly created 'National Vigilance Association' began a private prosecution of him under the 1857 Act. Soon after, the Conservative government of the time took over the prosecution and Vizetelly went to trial on 31 October 1888 at the Old Bailey. He pleaded not guilty. Although the prosecution had collected excerpts (twenty-one in all) from a number of Zola novels, the Solicitor General began with *La Terre* and had only got to the ninth extract when the following exchange took place:

FOREMAN OF THE JURY: I am requested to ask whether it is necessary to read all these passages? ...

SOLICITOR GENERAL: I can assure you, gentlemen, it is as unpleasant to me to read these passages as it is for you to have to listen to them. If you think the passages I have read are obscene of course I will stop.

SEVERAL JURYMEN: We think so.

(King, 1978, p.242)

After such an exchange it is not surprising that Vizetelly was advised to change his plea to 'guilty'. He was convicted and fined £100 and required to put up recognizances for good behaviour. This good behaviour was essentially an agreement not to circulate any works by Zola that included material of the sort objected to in court.

Vizetelly by this time was nearly seventy and a sick man. His business was near bankruptcy and yet he had many copies of no fewer than eighteen different novels by Zola in his warehouse waiting to be sold. Vizetelly assumed that if he sold novels that had not been mentioned in the original indictment, and expurgated those that had, he would be safe from prosecution and would be able to meet the additional demand from a reading public much less prissy than the Old Bailey jury. He was wrong. The National Vigilance Association prosecuted him again and, after a brief trial in May 1889 at which an incompetent defence counsel (an unhappily but aptly named 'Mr Cock Q.C.') told him to plead 'guilty', he was sentenced to three months in Holloway gaol. The prison sentence broke him physically and financially, and he died in poverty four years later, on 1 January 1894.

After Vizetelly's first trial, *The Times* commented that his crime was the worse because he had issued Zola's novels in cheap form. **Why would that have made it worse, as far as most contemporary readers of *The Times* were concerned?**

Because in publishing relatively cheaply, Vizetelly allowed such corrupting matter into the hands of the lower classes who could not have afforded more expensive books. In almost all trials based on the argument that something might corrupt someone, it is never those prosecuting who have been corrupted: they are always too sophisticated and/or mature to be vulnerable. Prosecutions are always conducted in the name of the weak (who are not represented); and weak tend to be women, children and the lower classes.

After Vizetelly's company collapsed, his copyrights in Zola translations were bought by the eminently respectable firm of Chatto & Windus. The three novels that had been specially named in the trial (*La Terre, Nana* and *Pot-Bouille*) could not be republished, but the other fifteen in Vizetelly's warehouse could be, as long as they were suitably expurgated. Chatto & Windus asked Ernest Vizetelly to do the job of expurgating the translations to make them publishable. The problem was that most of these novels had been stereotyped, and the cost of resetting them after all the cuts would have been prohibitive. What Ernest Vizetelly chose to do was simultaneously ingenious and disastrous. He cut significant chunks out and then wrote replacement passages that exactly fitted the space left by the excisions. In all, over the fifteen titles expurgated, he substantially changed 325 pages. Thus the demands of printing technology and publishers' economics ensured that the textual changes suffered by Zola's novels were much more radical than even the censors had required.

As you might expect, *Germinal* was not spared. **Can you think of passages that late Victorians of a prudish disposition might be inclined to remove?**

Maheu and La Maheude making love after the bath, La Maheude's discovery that Catherine has started to menstruate, the sexual mutilation of Maigrat after his death; all were modified so as to be either difficult to understand – or completely unintelligible.

*Germinal* sold about 110,000 copies in France between 1885 and 1903. Between 1886 and 1911 it sold 132,000 in English translations in Britain. Almost all those later copies would have been expurgated ones: the Zola the late Victorian and Edwardian English reader knew was a strange, diluted and sometimes mysteriously obscure writer.

There were a few readers who, though not reading French, would have access to text much closer to the novel that Zola wrote. In 1894 the Lutetian Society (a limited edition publisher) produced an unexpurgated edition translated by the sexologist Havelock Ellis. The critical detail here was that this was an expensive, private edition produced by a society whose members were select. There was no chance that people whose lives resembled those of the characters in *Germinal* would have any chance of reading the novel. This version would not be made available in a cheap format until Everyman's Library reprinted Ellis's translation in 1933, thirty years and more after Zola's death.

# Conclusion

In the nineteenth-century fiction market the pressures were intense. Novelists had to find new ways to market themselves in it, as Eliot did; or adapt and adjust to its expectations and demands, as Hardy in his early fiction struggled to do; or promote themselves by using it, as Zola did. Gabriel Oak at the Casterbridge hiring fair was not the only one capable of adapting to the twists and turns of a fickle market.

# Works cited

Anderson, Patricia J. and Rose, Jonathan. Eds. 1991. *Dictionary of Literary Biography,* vol.106: *British Literary Publishing Houses 1820–1880,* London: Gale Group Publishers, 1991.

Brown, Frederick. 1996. *Zola: A Life,* London: Macmillan.

Eliot, George. [1872] 1998. *Middlemarch,* ed. by David Carroll, with an introduction by Felicia Bonaparte, 3rd impression, Oxford World's Classics, Oxford: Oxford University Press.

Gatrell, Simon. 1988. *Hardy the Creator*, Oxford: Clarendon Press.

Gittings, Robert. 1978. *Young Thomas Hardy*, Harmondsworth: Penguin.

Hardy, Thomas. [1874] 2002. *Far from the Madding Crowd*, ed. by Suzanne B. Falck-Yi, with an introduction by Linda M. Shires, Oxford World's Classics, Oxford: Oxford University Press.

King, Graham. 1978. *Garden of Zola*, London: Barrie & Jenkins.

Pearsall, Ronald. 1971, *The Worm in the Bud*, Harmondsworth: Penguin.

Seville, Catherine. 1999. *Literary Copyright Reform in Early Victorian England*, Cambridge: Cambridge University Press.

Sutherland, John. 1976. *Victorian Novelists and Publishers*, London: Athlone Press.

Zola, Émile. [1884–5] 1993. *Germinal*, trans. by Peter Collier, with an introduction by Robert Lethbridge, Oxford World's Classics, Oxford: Oxford University Press.

# Further reading

Altick, Richard D. 1957. *The English Common Reader*, Chicago: University of Chicago Press. A broad introduction to the history of books and newspapers in the nineteenth century. Although written more than forty years ago, this is still a remarkably perceptive and useful book.

Altick, Richard D. 1991. *The Presence of the Present: Topics of the Day in the Victorian Novel*, Columbus, Ohio: Ohio State University Press. A big book to be dipped into rather read from cover to cover. If you want to know more about the links between the details of everyday life in the nineteenth century and the novels of the period, this is the book.

James, Louis. 1963. *Fiction for the Working Man*, Oxford: Oxford University Press. A marvellous study of the wealth of printed fiction in various forms available to the working-class reader in the period 1830–50.

Jordan, John O. and Patten, Robert L. Eds. 1995. *Literature in the Marketplace: Nineteenth-Century British Publishing and the Circulation of Books*, Cambridge: Cambridge University Press. A collection of essays dealing with the socioeconomic history of Victorian literature.

Neuburg, Victor E. 1977. *Popular Literature*, Harmondsworth: Penguin. A broad, short and very readable history of popular publishing with some interesting illustrations.

Patten, Robert L. 1978. *Charles Dickens and his Publishers*, Oxford: Oxford University Press. A comprehensive study of the stormy relationships Dickens had with his various publishers. Contains a wealth of information about print-runs and profits.

Sutherland, John. 1976. *Victorian Novelists and Publishers*, London: Athlone Press. Contains a useful set of three introductory chapters on novel publishing in general followed by seven chapters, each of which studies the publishing history of an author or a particular novel.

# CHAPTER 9

# *Middlemarch*: the social and historical context

*by Nora Tomlinson*

## Introduction

What kind of novel is *Middlemarch*? Perceptive readers at the time of its publication recognized the problems of trying to categorize a novel at once so long and so complex, and Henry James perhaps spoke for many of these Victorian readers when he wrote in an unsigned review in *Galaxy* in March 1873, that *Middlemarch* 'sets a limit ... to the development of the old-fashioned English novel' (James, 1987, p.81). While such an observation rather begs the question of what an 'old-fashioned English novel' might be, James seems tacitly to acknowledge both the extent to which *Middlemarch* was engaging with the familiar territory of moral, social and historical issues, and the extent to which it was breaking new ground in its references to and deployment of other literary forms, and in its awareness of its own fictional devices. The novel thus becomes both a kind of paradigm of Victorian realist fiction and at the same time a challenge to many of its conventions. Karen Chase summarizes this paradox clearly and effectively:

> It is impossible to consider the history of realism in the novel ... without quickly naming *Middlemarch* as a landmark ... To the impatient question, But what do you *mean* by realism? it is tempting just to lift the novel high and to say, I mean This. And yet if *Middlemarch* is a work which confirms and dignifies a central literary tradition, it is also a work which shows the unsteadiness, even the self-contradictions, of the realist project. George Eliot can usefully be seen as that English novelist who most forcefully expresses the claims of realism and who most vividly shows its instability.

> (1991, p.22)

The account of the novel which follows in chapters 9–11 aims to explore some of the issues involved in thinking about the question 'What kind of novel is *Middlemarch*?' Some of this discussion will be framed in terms of the more familiar notions of realism, such as some of the ways in which the novel engages with provinciality, with contemporary history and with ideas of vocation. Other sections will examine ways in which *Middlemarch* challenges our notions of realism. Does the very distinctive narrative voice, for example, heighten or subvert the novel's realist project? Does the complexity of the novel's organization reinforce or disguise the reader's awareness of the world of

*Middlemarch* as a fictional construct? Does the novel's engagement with contemporary scientific ideas extend or undermine our understanding of the operations of realist fiction?

You will notice I don't say that this account of the novel aims to provide an answer to the question 'What kind of novel is *Middlemarch*?', though I hope you will bear the question in mind as you read and reread the novel. I will be surprised if you reach any firm conclusions, except perhaps to acknowledge that the novel is so gloriously complex and rewarding as to defy simple answers.

*Figure 9.1   George Eliot (Mary Ann Cross), 1865; a drawing in chalks by Sir Frederick Burton. © National Portrait Gallery*

# *Middlemarch* as a provincial novel

Many novels convey a vivid sense of place – of a place, moreover, that was familiar to the novelist. *Northanger Abbey* draws on Jane Austen's knowledge of Bath, *Jane Eyre* on Charlotte Brontë's experience of Cowan Bridge and the moors around Howarth, *The Awakening* on Kate Chopin's life in New Orleans and *Heart of Darkness* on Joseph Conrad's own voyage up the Congo river. George Eliot is the novelist of an English region, the Midlands, which is where she locates all her novels except for *Romola* (1863) and *Daniel Deronda* (1876). Like Thomas Hardy, she writes about the kind of community and landscape in which she grew up, although, unlike Hardy, it is not the landscape in which she lived and worked for most of her adult life. Her father and her brother were land-agents in Warwickshire and experienced some of the changes wrought on rural communities, first by the building of canals to serve the new collieries of the district, and then by the construction of the railways and the gradual industrialization of towns such as Coventry and Birmingham. It is this world which provides the basis for most of her novels. *Middlemarch* is the last of several provincial novels Eliot wrote, and by the time of its composition she was writing not only about a world remembered from her youth, but also about a fictional reconstruction of this world with which she was now very familiar.

**Reread the first two paragraphs of book 1, chapter 12, of *Middlemarch*. What kind of landscape is evoked, and what is the narrator's relationship to it?**

The landscape is an attractive though undramatic one, and one that is long established and well used. The great oak has been there for centuries, and the stray hovel has been there long enough to acquire a veneer of charm. It is a working landscape, too, made up of meadows and pastures and small isolated communities, and containing reminders of former industrial activity in the form of the clay-pits that provide the bricks with which these communities were built. Crucially, as we shall see, it is also a midland landscape familiar to the narrator, who is one of the 'midland-bred souls' who remember 'Little details ... dear to the eyes that have looked on them from childhood' (Eliot, [1872] 1998, 1.12; p.96; all subsequent page references are to this edition). When she writes of 'the gamut of joy in landscape ... the things they toddled among, or perhaps learned by heart standing between their father's knees while he drove leisurely' (ibid.), the gap between author and narrator surely diminishes, as Eliot recalls the area of north Warwickshire in which she and her family grew up. Yet despite its biographical associations, this landscape is presented in visual, almost painterly language; there is an awareness of colour – the 'coral fruit', the 'red background for the burdock' – and an emphasis on 'wondrous modulations of light and shadow' (ibid.). It could be argued that this makes the landscape seem more vivid and 'realistic', but at another level the realism is perhaps undermined by the way the language emphasizes the artifice and construction of the description.

Although many novels have provincial settings, *Middlemarch* is unusual amongst English novels in having provinciality as an explicit subject: it is subtitled *A Study of Provincial Life*. So we need to ask ourselves what both we as readers, and Eliot as novelist, understand by the concept. 'Provincial' can be read as the reverse of 'metropolitan', with all that may be implied by this. If the metropolis is thought of as a centre of government and cultural life, as a place of intellectual excitement at the forefront of contemporary thought, then the provinces become some kind of 'other' – a place less exciting, less advanced, more conservative and altogether duller. 'Provincial' also suggests a geographical as well as an intellectual and cultural distance from the metropolis.

There are other ways of responding to the word, but thinking about the meaning of 'provincial' should provide a starting point for a discussion of Eliot's fictional representation of a provincial community. The word 'study' in the subtitle suggests, amongst other things, a careful and impartial analysis of a particular way of life; it does not necessarily have the critical and condescending overtones carried by the opposition of 'provincial' and 'metropolitan' outlined above. As you read this section, always bear in mind the question of how far the study of provinciality is genuinely impartial. This is an issue to which we will return in chapter 14, when discussing *Germinal*: Émile Zola's expressed views about the novel as a kind of sociological experiment become entangled with his anger at perceived social injustices and also with his actual artistic and imaginative practice.

First of all, then, let us consider some of the 'facts' about Middlemarch – where it is located in time and place, and who lives there. *Middlemarch* is a historical novel, published in 1872, but firmly located in pre-Victorian nineteenth-century English history between 1829 and 1832; Table 9.1 shows how the fictional events are precisely located in time, by the novel's references both to specific dates and times and to actual historical events that took place in the years covered by the narrative. Middlemarch is also, as the novel's title suggests, located in the middle of England. The town itself is generally thought to be based on Coventry, where Eliot started attending school in 1832, at the age of twelve, and where she lived with her father from 1841 to 1846; it could hardly be closer to the actual geographical centre of England. Whether 'middle' is meant to signify this central geographical location, or whether it signifies its middling, perhaps even mediocre, position on some kind of scale between the excitement of the metropolis and the relative inaction of a thinly populated region, is something you will have to decide for yourself. 'March' is a term for a political and defensive area between two countries, as in the Welsh and Scottish marches, and you may think that the 'march' part of the novel's title suggests something of the town's conservative defence against certain kinds of change. It is also clear that Middlemarch embraces more than simply the urban community of bankers, manufacturers, doctors, grocers, publicans, horse-traders and slum-dwellers: it also includes a considerable rural hinterland, which it serves and which in its turn serves the need of the town. This hinterland contains the rural parishes of Lowick, Freshitt and Frick; the estate of Tipton Grange, owned by Mr Brooke and including the run-down farm tenanted by Dagley; and the estates of Freshitt Hall, owned by Sir James Chettam, and of Stone Court, owned by Peter Featherstone.

The novel makes it quite clear that certain conventions exist which keep apart the urban world of trade and the rural world of the landed gentry. When Mr Brooke gives one of a series of dinner parties to celebrate Dorothea's forthcoming marriage to Mr Casaubon, he invites Mr Vincy as the newly elected mayor and a major Middlemarch manufacturer, Mr Bulstrode as a banker and a philanthropist, and various professional men from the town including lawyers and doctors; he does not, however, invite Mrs Vincy or Mrs Bulstrode or

*Figure 9.2    View of Coventry, watercolour, c.1847. By permission of Coventry City Libraries*

Rosamond, because, 'always objecting to go too far, [he] would not have chosen that his nieces should meet the daughter of a Middlemarch manufacturer, unless it were on a public occasion' (1.10; p.83). This separation of trade and gentry is what underpins the two meetings between Rosamond and Dorothea; although their husbands may meet socially and professionally, the two women's paths would not normally be expected to cross. It is, however, perfectly acceptable for Rosamond to visit Peter Featherstone at Stone Court, accompanied by Fred. This is partly, of course, because he is her uncle, but also because he, like her father, has made his money through industry and trade – in Featherstone's case through the extraction of manganese.

It is also clear that these social distinctions would have been perceived as old-fashioned by the novel's first readers. In a comment which links the old-fashionedness with provinciality, the narrator observes, 'For in that part of the country, before Reform had done its notable part in developing the political consciousness, there was a clearer distinction of ranks and a dimmer distinction of parties' (1.10; p.82). It is not, however, a static society, as the narrator's comments elsewhere make clear. **Reread book 1, chapter 11, from 'Certainly nothing at present ...' (p.88) to '... as we find in older Herodotus' (p.89). What kinds of movements are occurring in Middlemarch society?**

Change is an essential component of all societies, but Eliot is concerned with the very particular symptoms of change and the specific social dynamics of Middlemarch. There are changes in status both up and down, dramatic as well as

**Table 9.1 *Middlemarch* in history**

| Date | Historical events | References in the text |
|---|---|---|
| 1829 | The Duke of Wellington governs with Peel's support and the Tories remain in power until November 1830 | 'When George the Fourth was still reigning over the privacies of Windsor, when the Duke of Wellington was Prime Minister' (2.19; p.176) |
| April 1829 | Catholic Emancipation Bill passed | 'provincial families, still discussing Mr Peel's late conduct on the Catholic question' (1.1; p.9) |
| | | Casaubon has written 'a very seasonable pamphlet ... on the Catholic question', which may lead to a deanery, or even a bishopric (1.7; p.61) |
| 30 September | | Middlemarch action begins: 'It is the last day of September now' (1.1; p.11) |
| November 1829 – January 1830 | | Dorothea's marriage and honeymoon in Rome: 'Mr and Mrs Casaubon, returning from their wedding journey, arrived at Lowick Manor in the middle of January' (3.28; p.256) |
| 3 May 1830 | Robert Peel inherits a baronetcy | 'the celebrated Peel, now Sir Robert' (3.32; p.291) |
| 26 June 1830 | Death of George IV, Parliament dissolved, general election called | 'The doubt hinted by Mr Vincy whether it were only the general election or the end of the world that was coming on, now that George the Fourth was dead, Parliament dissolved, Wellington and Peel generally depreciated and the new King apologetic' (4.37; p.335) |
| July 1830 | Revolution in France | 'they're in the next century, you know, on the other side of the water. Going on faster than we are' (4.38; p.359) |
| 15 September 1830 | William Huskisson, former cabinet minister, killed at the opening of the Liverpool and Manchester Railway | 'he took the new-made railway, observing to his fellow-passengers that he considered it pretty well seasoned now it had done for Huskisson' (4.41; p.390) |
| Autumn 1830 | Disturbances among farm labourers, including the breaking of machines; Whigs in power under Grey | Possibly transposed in the novel to 1831, as 'the infant struggles of the railway system' (6.56; p.519) |

**Table 9.1 *Middlemarch* in history** *(continued)*

| Date | Historical events | References in the text |
|------|-------------------|------------------------|
| March 1831 | Bill for electoral reform passed by one vote | 'By the time that Lord John Russell's measure was being debated in the House of Commons, there was a new political animation in Middlemarch' (5.46; p.431) |
| | | Casaubon dies (5.48; pp.453) |
| 22 April 1831 | Parliament dissolved and another general election called | Mr Brooke stands for Parliament as an independent; he is forced to withdraw (5.51) |
| 22 September 1831 | Reform Bill passed by the House of Commons | |
| 8 October 1831 | Reform Bill thrown out by the House of Lords, and there are riots in Bristol, Derby and Nottingham | |
| 12 December 1831 | Reform Bill introduced to the House of Commons for the third time and carried | |
| *c.* March 1832 | | Lydgate and Bulstrode discuss 'the chances of the Reform Bill in the House of Lords' (7.70; p.669) |
| | | General discussion in Middlemarch of 'the question whether the Lords would throw out the Reform Bill' (7.71; p.676) |
| 13 April 1832 | Reform Bill is passed by the Lords but is blocked in committee; the king is asked to create new peers | 'It was just after the Lords had thrown out the Reform Bill' (8.84; p.763) |
| | | 'Mrs Cadwallader was strong on the intended creation of peers' (8.84; p.763) |
| May 1832 | Grey's government resigns, but Tories unable to form a government; the king sends for Grey again | Middlemarch ends |
| 7 June 1832 | Reform Bill receives the royal assent, and becomes law as the first Reform Act | |
| Unspecified date | | Will Ladislaw 'at last returned to Parliament by a constituency who paid his expenses' (8.finale; pp.782–3) |
| 1834 | English Municipal Corporations Act | Mr Brooke's 'pen had been remarkably fluent on the prospects of Municipal Reform' (8.finale; p.783) |

Source: Adapted from Purkis (1985). By permission of Pearson Education Ltd

gradual, occurring across the urban and rural divide: 'Municipal town and rural parish gradually made fresh threads of connexion.' The weaving image is important since it draws attention to the fundamental interconnectedness of individuals in society as well as serving for one of the ways in which the whole novel is structured. '[A]ny one', the narrator tells us – and by anyone she means her readers as well as herself – 'watching keenly the stealthy convergence of human lots, sees a slow preparation of effects from one life on another.' So we should expect the fictional society of provincial Middlemarch to change, and perhaps, since the novel takes place against the background of political reform, we might expect this change to be for the better. However, as in its representation of women's roles, *Middlemarch* explores the complexities of provincial society and is ambivalent about both the nature of the changes taking place within it, and whether these changes are a force for good.

One way of trying to get to grips with the way the novel handles the nature of provinciality is to consider a number of episodes, each involving a different aspect of that provinciality and a different fictional character. Each of these episodes will be explored with the aim of considering the extent to which provinciality is represented as a limiting restricting force, or as an innately conservative but essentially beneficent influence.

## *Dorothea's visit to Rome on her honeymoon*

**Reread book 2, chapter 20. How far is Dorothea's distress in Rome shown to be the result of her provincial background?**

You may be surprised that an examination of the ways in which *Middlemarch* deals with provinciality begins with an extract from one of the very few episodes in the novel not set in Middlemarch itself. However, the episode is valuable because it shows that the novel is not going to present simplistic notions of either metropolitan or provincial values.

Some of Dorothea's distress is caused by 'the dream-like strangeness of her bridal life' and by a dawning awareness that her life with Mr Casaubon would not be filled with 'the large vistas and wide fresh air which she had dreamed of finding in her husband's mind' but was likely to be 'replaced by anterooms and winding passages which seemed to lead nowhither' (2.20; pp.180, 183). But much of her distress is caused by the effect of Rome on 'the notions of a girl who had been brought up in English and Swiss Puritanism, fed on meagre Protestant histories and on art chiefly of the hand-screen sort' (2.20; p.181). Rome represents a kind of ultimate metropolis, lying at the centre both of a vast and ancient empire and of the Roman Catholic world; coping with it requires, the narrator seems to suggest, a degree of sophistication and knowledge in its visitors that Dorothea clearly lacks. George Eliot and her long-time companion, the critic and writer George Henry Lewes, had visited Rome in the spring of 1869, the year in which she started to write the novel. While the author is included in the visitors 'who have looked at Rome with the quickening power of a knowledge which breathes a growing soul into all historic shapes' (ibid.), she clearly understands its impact on an inexperienced young woman. Pagan Rome appears to Dorothea to be decadent, a 'vast wreck of ambitious ideals, sensuous and spiritual, mixed confusedly with the signs of breathing forgetfulness and degradation' (ibid.). Catholic Rome shocks her in a different way, and the visual impact of the vastness of St Peter's and its contents is described as being 'like a disease of the retina' (2.20; p.182) – an extraordinarily powerful image for the corrosive effects of Rome on Dorothea's happiness. Dorothea is inclined to blame her unhappiness on herself, with a 'self-accusing cry that her feeling of desolation was the fault of her own spiritual poverty' (2.20; p.180). The account of contemporary Rome, however, suggests that Dorothea's provincial instincts may be right. The vocabulary used to evoke her impressions suggests a Rome that needs to be rejected: 'Ruins and basilicas, palaces and colossi, set in the midst of a sordid present, where all that was living and warm-blooded seemed sunk in the deep degeneracy of a superstition divorced from reverence' (2.20; p.181).

The combination of these two causes of distress is exacerbated by the fact that there is no one to whom Dorothea can turn: the difference between her response to Rome and that of Mr Casaubon leads to the first marital misunderstanding, which is the immediate cause of her tears. 'What was fresh to her mind was worn out to his', and her husband's parroting of the received wisdom concerning the supposed glories of Rome 'did not help to justify the glories of the Eternal City, or to give her the hope that if she knew more about them the world would be joyously illuminated for her' (2.20; pp.184, 185). Significantly, at the moment in the novel when both Will Ladislaw and the reader see her illuminated in a shaft of sunlight, what Dorothea sees inwardly is Lowick. Yet the attractions of the English fields and elms and hedge-bordered highroads are subtly altered in her mind with her growing awareness of the many years she may have to pass there, and a feeling that the years may no longer be filled with 'joyful devotedness' (2.20; p.190).

Dorothea's response to Rome is presented not only as provincial but as limited, but Rome itself is not shown to be the embodiment of values that are somehow able to lift Dorothea out of her provincial ignorance. The end of chapter 20 hints that the provinciality of Lowick will not be a refuge for Dorothea. If we move forward in the novel to the Casaubons' return from their honeymoon, and to 'the stifling oppression of that gentle-woman's world', in which 'her blooming full-pulsed youth stood there in a moral imprisonment which made itself one with the chill, colourless, narrowed landscape' (3.28; pp.257, 258), we see that this suggestion is borne out. If Dorothea is to attain fulfilment, then this will have less to do with her place in a provincial world than with her own personal striving – 'the reaching forward of the whole consciousness towards the fullest truth, the least partial good' (2.20; p.190). The novel suggests that Dorothea's moral imprisonment is an aspect of the provincial life she leads with Mr Casaubon, and it takes the trip to Rome for her to discover her greatest gift – a sympathetic awareness of the needs of others. But the whole experience of Rome has been acutely painful to her, as her response to Lydgate's suggestion that foreign travel might help Mr Casaubon's illness shows; for Dorothea, Rome is an 'utterly hopeless' resource (3.30; p.271). The novel seems to suggest that her influence on the 'growing good of the world' (8.finale; p.785) transcends both her provincial and her metropolitan experiences, because she is able to learn from both.

## *Lydgate's dilemma over voting for the hospital chaplain*

**Reread book 2, chapter 18. To what extent is Lydgate's vote for Tyke presented as a triumph of provincial limitations over intellectual independence?**

The chapter repeats Lydgate's desire for intellectual independence, which has already been expressed in chapter 15. In the earlier chapter we learn that he has come to Middlemarch intending 'to do good small work for Middlemarch, and great work for the world' (2.15; p.139); the language in which these linked aims are expressed hints at Lydgate's own attitudes to the town's provinciality. Middlemarch will receive the benefit of 'good small work' – apparently all that it deserves – while the wider world will benefit from his real research. Lydgate's attitude to Middlemarch, in short, is condescending and patronizing. Chapter 18 also repeats the idea that Middlemarch is simply a means to an end for Lydgate – 'What he really cared for was a medium for his work, a vehicle for his ideas' (2.18; p.168) – and shows that he regards such matters as the choice of hospital chaplaincy to be beneath him: 'was he not bound to prefer the object of getting a good hospital, where he could demonstrate the specific distinctions of fever and test therapeutic results, before anything else connected with this chaplaincy?' (2.18; pp.168–9). What Lydgate is forced to acknowledge, as he inwardly debates his position on the chaplaincy, is that he is constrained by the very forces he despises: 'For the first time Lydgate was feeling the hampering threadlike pressure of small social conditions, and their frustrating complexity' (2.18; p.169). The interconnectedness of society is not, of course, found only in the provinces, but in Lydgate's mind it is always linked with the 'small social conditions' of provincial life. Long after the vote, 'The affair of the chaplaincy remained a sore point in his memory as a case in which this petty medium of Middlemarch had been too strong for him' (2.18; p.175). Forced to choose between his personal liking for Farebrother and his need to remain on good terms with Bulstrode for the sake of his professional research, between 'petty alternatives, each of which was repugnant to him' (2.18; p.169), Lydgate blames what he perceives to be the pettiness of Middlemarch not simply for the decision he makes, which turns out to have more far-reaching consequences than anyone could have foreseen, but for having to make such a decision at all.

But does Lydgate's desire to 'Confound their petty politics' (2.18; p.167) mean that his view of Middlemarch as merely provincial is the one that the novel endorses? Much of Lydgate's response to his dilemma is written in free indirect speech, which records his ideas and thoughts in the kind of vocabulary he might be expected to use, but places it in the third- instead of the first-person singular, so that the narrator can maintain a certain distance from him. The presentation of other persons involved in the dispute puts the affair in a slightly different light to the one that Lydgate sees by. Dr Sprague and Dr Minchin are gently mocked, the first having 'weight, and might be expected to grapple with a disease and throw it; while Dr Minchin might be better able to detect it lurking and circumvent it' (2.18; p.170). They are also clearly labelled as conservative in the practise of their professions, 'ready to combine against all innovators, and against non-professionals given to interference' (ibid.). The narrator also presents ironically the general distrust of Lydgate's unusual and advanced medical education, popular opinion being suspicious of 'a man who had not been to either of the English universities and enjoyed the absence of anatomical and bedside study there, but came with a libellous pretension to experience in Edinburgh and Paris, where observation might be abundant indeed, but hardly sound' (2.18; p.171).

Thus far, Lydgate's exasperation at what he sees as the limitations of provincial opinion appears to be supported by the amused ironical tone of the narrator. But the narrator, unlike Lydgate, does not condescend to these provincials. Dr Minchin 'liked to keep the mental windows open and objected to fixed limits', and was able to quote Pope's 'Essay on Man' in religious debate (2.18; p.170). This is no unthinking, unread doctor, however conservative his medical views may be. Other directors of the new hospital, assembling for the vote on the chaplaincy, are shown to be articulate and as aware as Lydgate of the issues involved in a choice between Farebrother and Tyke: Mr Hackbutt is a 'rich tanner of fluent speech', while Frank Hawley, lawyer and town clerk, is 'afraid of nobody' (2.18; pp.172, 174). Only Mr Brooke, here as elsewhere in the novel, is shown to have incoherent and confused views on the matter.

There are other chapters in *Middlemarch* where the weight of opinion against Lydgate is shown to be based on ignorance and prejudice, most notably chapter 45, which will be considered in chapter 10 below. The point to make about chapter 18 of the novel is that it is remarkably even-handed in its presentation of provincial debate. Provinciality has no monopoly on prejudice, and one of the reasons for Lydgate's failure in Middlemarch is his inability to recognize his own. Lydgate's failure as a doctor *is* presented as a failure, because of all the characters in *Middlemarch* his aspirations are the most clearly articulated and the most capable of being achieved. We have to ask ourselves, however, whether the greater failure is the town's assumption that it can swallow Lydgate and assimilate him very comfortably, or Lydgate's in not recognizing that in choosing to live and work in Middlemarch he inevitably becomes a part of the fabric of its provincial life.

## Mr Brooke's experiences as an election candidate

**Reread book 5, chapter 51. How is the provincial reaction to Mr Brooke's parliamentary candidacy presented?**

Mr Brooke is standing for Parliament as an independent reform candidate, and so, theoretically at least, the town's forceful rejection of him ought to suggest a dyed-in-the-wool provincial conservatism. In fact, this episode stands on its head the opposition between reform and conservatism, by exposing all the weaknesses of Mr Brooke's position and by highlighting the essential rightness of the opposition to him. The text does not reject reform in itself, but it does suggest that the ethical basis of reforming ideas needs to be both intellectually and morally sound. Mr Brooke's understanding of reform lacks both. He has the 'impression that waverers were likely to be allured by wavering statements' (5.51; p.469), and the chapter uses Will Ladislaw's exasperation with him ruthlessly to expose his intellectual shortcomings: 'he had begun to perceive that Mr Brooke's mind, if it had the burthen of remembering any train of thought, would let it drop, run away in search of it, and not easily come back again. To collect documents is one mode of serving your country, and to remember the contents of a document is another' (5.51; p.471). Additionally, the reader brings to this chapter an accumulation of memories of Mr Brooke's meanness and hypocrisy towards his own tenants, most notably in his encounter with the unfortunate Dagley in book 4, chapter 39. If this is what reform means, then Middlemarchers are absolutely right to reject him.

They reject him on self-interested but rational grounds. Mr Brooke's rambling account of the possible effects of reform is wonderfully refuted by Mr Mawmsey, the grocer, whose understanding of what the vote might mean is far clearer than Mr Brooke's: 'When I give a vote I must know what I'm doing; I must look to what will be the effects on my till and ledger' (5.51; p.470). This is self-interested, but it is at least articulate and honest. The actual election address made by a slightly intoxicated Mr Brooke is a comic exposure of political ineptness, so that when he rambles about 'freedom of opinion, freedom of the press, liberty – that kind of thing? The Bill, now – you shall have the Bill', the response from the invisible mocking Punch in the crowd seems entirely appropriate: 'You shall have the Bill, Mr Brooke, per electioneering contest, and a seat outside Parliament as delivered, five thousand pounds, seven shillings, and fourpence' (5.51; p.475). Despite the narrator's plea, 'Pray pity him', it is clear she wants her readers to do nothing of the sort: 'so many English gentlemen make themselves miserable by speechifying on entirely private grounds! whereas Mr Brooke wished to serve his country by standing for Parliament – which, indeed, may also be done on private grounds, but being once undertaken does absolutely demand some speechifying' (5.51; p.473).

Of course, the electioneering episode is not simply a rejection of the need for political reform: the references to Mr Brooke's agents – 'dirty-handed men in the world to do dirty business' (5.51; p.471) – shows how much this reform is needed. Eliot had explored this idea very thoroughly in *Felix Holt, the Radical* (1866), the novel she wrote before *Middlemarch*. What it does suggest is that reform needs something rather better than Mr Brooke's bumbling efforts, and that a vigorous rebuttal of such an approach to reform is a sign of a healthy, if conservative, community. It is also worth noting that Mr Brooke, man of the world though he likes to consider himself, is also provincial by birth, upbringing and occupation; actual political reform is left to the outsider Will Ladislaw, whose achievements as 'an ardent public man' (8.finale; p.782) take place outside the provincial environment of Middlemarch. Here, as in the other episodes we have discussed, the novel's representation of the nature of provinciality is complex.

# Caleb Garth's intervention in the protest against the railways

**Reread book 6, chapter 56, as far as '... and watched him in the gateway' (p.527). What light does Caleb Garth's encounter with the railway protesters shed on the kind of provinciality that the novel is projecting?**

Eliot sets the novel in the very early days of railway construction in England, before the railway mania of the 1840s. (In fact, this is one of the novel's few historical inaccuracies. Although England's first public railway, running from Stockton to Darlington, had been opened in 1825, railway construction in the Midlands had not actually started in 1830, when the events in Middlemarch are taking place: the London to Birmingham railway was not opened until 1838; see Table 9.2.) The coming of the railways is a topic of keen debate, and opinion in Middlemarch is divided between women, who think that railway travel will be intrinsically dangerous, and landowners, who, while disliking 'these pernicious agencies' (6.56; p.519), are determined to sell their land for as much profit as possible. In this there is nothing to distinguish the town's response to the coming of the railways from public opinion elsewhere. Charles Dickens, writing about railway construction in London in *Dombey and Son,* is torn between admiration at the railway's capacity for change and an appalled fascination at the disturbance it creates (see chapter 7 above). If Middlemarch responds cautiously to the coming of the railways, however, opinion amongst its rural neighbours is shown to be both unintelligent and reactionary. Peter Featherstone's brother and sister, already presented in a faintly ridiculous light during the account of Featherstone's death and funeral, are here pilloried for their provincial ignorance. Mrs Waule can only bleat about cows casting their calves, while Mr Solomon slowly organizes opposition to it. Although he is shown to be ultra-careful – 'The hour-hand of a clock was quick by comparison with Mr Solomon, who had an agreeable sense that he could afford to be slow' (6.56; p.521) – he has easy material on which to work:

> In the absence of any precise idea as to what railways were, public opinion ...
> was against them; for the human mind in that grassy corner had not the
> proverbial tendency to admire the unknown, holding rather that it was likely to
> be against the poor man, and that suspicion was the only wise attitude with
> regard to it. (6.56; p.520)

Thus he is able to recruit Hiram Ford, the waggoner, as a protester against the railway survey, Hiram believing that the railway agents are 'Lunnon chaps' and having 'a dim notion of London as a centre of hostility to the country' (6.56; p.521).

This is perhaps the most critical representation of provincial attitudes in the whole novel, but in this episode, as elsewhere, the novel is rather more even-handed than the preceding paragraph suggests, since Eliot chooses another rural inhabitant and worker, Caleb Garth, to put the case for the railways. His arguments are largely pragmatic, along the lines that the railroad 'will be made whether you like it or not' and 'It may do a bit of harm here and there, to this and to that; and so does the sun in heaven. But the railway's a good thing' (6.56;

p.525). The narrator acknowledges Garth's difficulties in 'attempting in dark times and unassisted by miracle to reason with rustics who are in possession of an undeniable truth which they know through a hard process of feeling' (6.56; p.526). Yet, although the protesters do not come to a willing acceptance of the railways, by his recognition of their hard lot in life and his avowed desire that they should not make things worse for themselves, Garth is able to win a grudging promise that they will not meddle further. His understanding of his fellow countrymen, and his belief that the railways are ultimately a force for good, contrasts sharply with Mr Brooke's meaningless platitudes about the benefits of political reform, and again confounds the notion that provincial opinion is necessarily opposed to progress.

# *Middlemarch* as a historical novel: the 'Woman Question'

All novels are located in history, but few as specifically and accurately as *Middlemarch*. Not only is the novel a study of provincial life, but it is a study of provincial life between the years 1829 and 1832. These are pre-Victorian years, and, as Table 9.1 shows, the time framework of the plot is closely associated with the debate about political reform and the eventual passing of the first Reform Act in 1832. Such a historical framework inevitably points to some of the major concerns of the novel, which include an exploration of the possibilities of change and improvement in certain areas of English life, and a debate on the question of how far any change is for the better. *Middlemarch* is a historical novel in the very specific sense that there is a gap of forty years between the final events of the narrative and the date of its publication (see Table 9.2); this enables readers to measure the events and opinions of the novel against what is known to have taken place in these forty years. Two Reform Acts had greatly extended the franchise to working men (though not to women of any class) in the years since Mr Brooke's speech, while the railways had transformed many aspects of English life since Caleb Garth encountered the railway protesters. More central to the concerns of the novel is what is known as the 'Woman Question'. The remainder of this section will explore how the novel handles the role of women, and, in the light of the historical changes that took place between 1829 and 1872, will try to reach conclusions about the kinds of changes the novel seems to endorse.

Contemporary reviewers of *Middlemarch* frequently saw the novel as dealing, at least in part, with the 'Woman Question'. R.H. Hutton, for example, in a review of the second book of *Middlemarch* in the *Spectator* on 3 February 1872, referred to 'the thesis of the "prelude" that these blundering lives are due to the inconvenient indefiniteness with which the Supreme Power has fashioned the natures of women'. Sidney Colvin said something rather similar in the *Fortnightly Review* on 19 January 1873: 'In her prelude and conclusion both, she seems to insist upon the design of illustrating the necessary disappointment of a woman's nobler aspirations in a society not made to second noble aspirations in a woman.' Although the novel was set in pre-Victorian times, it was written in full knowledge of developments in the Victorian women's movement, so that any reader with some awareness of what had happened in the intervening years could assess how much progress had been made towards giving women the rights to education, to financial independence, to divorce and to the vote.

George Eliot would seem exactly the novelist to urge women's rights. She was a highly intelligent, well-educated and extremely widely read woman, who had earned her own living as a translator, editor and writer since leaving Coventry in 1851. She was a close friend and correspondent of most of the women who were actively working to improve the lives of their fellow-women, and subscribed to the *English Woman's Review,* a feminist journal edited by her lifelong friend Barbara Bodichon. In 1855, she signed Bodichon's petition in support of the Married Women's Property Bill. She also gave money to the Elizabeth Garrett Anderson Hospital for women, and to the newly founded Girton College for women in Cambridge in 1869. Additionally, unable to marry Lewes, she had chosen to live with him without being married. (Although Lewes's wife, Agnes, was involved in a long-standing liaison with Leigh Hunt, because Lewes had already recognized Agnes's children by Hunt as his own, the law would not allow him to divorce her.) So on the face of it, Eliot looks as if she should have been at the forefront of any movement to improve the lot of her contemporary sisters.

In practice, she was extremely cautious, and in some cases, almost conservative in her views on women's rights, fearing perhaps that her irregular union with Lewes might damage the women's movement. In a letter to Mrs Nassau John Senior, dated 4 October 1869 – after she had started work on *Middlemarch,* but before she had begun to write about Dorothea – she wrote:

> I feel too deeply the difficult complications that beset every measure likely to affect the position of women and also I feel too imperfect a sympathy with many women who have put themselves forward in connexion with such measures, to give any practical adhesion to them. There is no question on which I am more inclined to hold my peace and learn, than on the 'Woman Question.' It seems to me to overhang abysses, of which prostitution is not the worst. Conclusions seem easy so long as we keep large blinkers on and look in the direction of our own private lives.

(in Eliot, 1954–78, vol.5, p.58)

This is not the first time she had voiced reservations about militancy in the women's movement. In an review in the *Leader* (13 October 1855) of Mary Wollstonecraft's *A Vindication of the Rights of Woman* and Margaret Fuller's *Woman in the Nineteenth Century,* which is radical in many respects, she also expressed the belief that it is necessary to proceed with caution to effect any change in the position of women: 'We must try and mend ... little by little – the only way in which human things can be mended. Unfortunately, many over zealous champions of women assert their actual equality with men, – nay even their moral superiority to men – as a ground for their release from oppressive laws and restrictions. They lose strength immensely by this false position'. Here Eliot is not so much claiming that women are inferior to men as expressing her reservations about the arguments employed by some feminists. She points out

**Table 9.2  Key events between the Reform Act and the publication of *Middlemarch***

| Date | Events in England | Events elsewhere |
|---|---|---|
| 1832 | Reform Act extends franchise to those occupying property rated at £10 or more a year | |
| 1833 | Factory Act limits hours of work for women and children | Abolition of slavery in the British Empire |
| 1834 | New Poor Law Commission establishes workhouses | |
| 1835 | Municipal Corporation Act gives votes for local government to men only | |
| 1836 | Founding of London University to award degrees to students at Kings College and University College | |
| 1837 | Victoria succeeds to the throne | |
| 1838 | Opening of London to Birmingham railway; first crossing of Atlantic by iron steamship, Brunel's *Great Western*; first Chartist demonstration | |
| 1839 | Daguerre patents early photographic technique | |
| 1840 | Introduction of penny post | |
| 1842 | Publication of Chadwick's *Sanitary Conditions of the Labouring Population in England* | |
| 1844 | Royal Commission on Health in Towns; start of railway mania | |
| 1845 | | Beginning of potato famine in Ireland |
| 1846 | Repeal of the Corn Laws | |
| 1847 | Chloroform first used as an anaesthetic | |
| 1848 | Public Health Act | Height of potato famine; revolution in several European states |
| 1849 | Bedford College for women established in London | |
| 1850 | Public Libraries Act; restoration of Roman Catholic hierarchy | |
| 1851 | The Great Exhibition | |
| 1854 | Founding of British Medical Association; establishment of Science and Art Department to support the teaching of art and science | Crimean War – to 1856 |
| 1857 | Matrimonial Causes Act makes divorce marginally easier for women | |

**Table 9.2  Key events between the Reform Act and the publication of *Middlemarch* (continued)**

| Date | Events in England | Events elsewhere |
|------|-------------------|------------------|
| 1858 | Founding of *English Woman's Journal*; Medical Act creates General Council of Medical Education and Registration; Newcastle Commission set up to enquire into state of popular education in England | |
| 1859 | Publication of Charles Darwin's *On the Origin of Species* and J.S. Mill's *On Liberty* | |
| 1863 | First underground railway opened in London | American Civil War – to 1865 |
| 1864 | Contagious Diseases Act | |
| 1865 | Antiseptic surgery developed by Lister; last severe cholera epidemic kills over 14,000 | |
| 1867 | Second Reform Act extends franchise to many working men, but not to women | |
| 1869 | Publication of J.S. Mill's *The Subjugation of Women*; opening of Girton College in Cambridge | |
| 1870 | Education Act establishes elementary schools for all; Married Women's Property Act | Franco-Prussian War |

that assertions as to the equality or superiority of women make dubious arguments for changes in their status, when, in her view, their current educational inferiority is the reason in favour of such improvements. If women were already superior to men, despite the disadvantages they faced, 'then there would be a case in which slavery and ignorance nourished virtue, and so far we should have an argument for the continuance of bondage' (ibid.).

The ambivalence between Eliot's sympathetic awareness of the movement to improve women's lives in the second half of the nineteenth century and the cautiousness of her actual response should perhaps prepare the reader for the complexity, and even the ambiguities, of her fictional representation of the position of women in *Middlemarch*. **Reread the prelude to *Middlemarch*. What differences are suggested here between the ideal and actual possibilities for women?**

The prelude allows that it is possible for a woman with a 'passionate, ideal nature' to demand 'an epic life' *and* also to achieve it, but – and it's a very big 'but' – not in England in the early years of the nineteenth century (prelude; p.3). What the prelude highlights is the gulf between women's aspirations and their achievements. Instead of a life which was a 'constant unfolding of far-resonant action' there was only 'a life of mistakes, the offspring of a certain spiritual grandeur ill-matched with the meanness of opportunity' (ibid.). The fault, the prelude makes clear, lies not in the women themselves but in the circumstances in which they find themselves and against which they have to struggle. The prelude prepares the ground for at least one aspect of Eliot's '*Study of Provincial Life*' in the limitations it imposes on the 'ardently willing soul' (ibid.) of the women who live provincial lives. They 'were helped by no coherent social faith and order' and are constrained by the conservatism of public opinion: 'Their ardour alternated between a vague ideal and the common yearning of womanhood; so that the one was disapproved as extravagance, and the other condemned as a lapse' (ibid.)

The third and final paragraph of the prelude acknowledges that there are those who think women are a naturally inferior species of humanity. 'Some have felt that these blundering lives are due to the inconvenient indefiniteness with which the Supreme Power has fashioned the natures of women' (prelude; p.3), though the parodying of the voice of these 'some' in the rest of the sentence makes it clear that this is not a view the narrator wishes to endorse. She goes on to point out that women's lives are far more varied than either women's appearance or literary representations of their lives would suggest, but ends, ominously, with the assertion that women can no longer achieve the kind of greatness gained by St Theresa: 'Here and there is born a Saint Theresa, foundress of nothing, whose loving heart-beats and sobs after an unattained goodness tremble off and are dispersed among hindrances, instead of centering in some long-recognizable deed' (prelude; p.4).

The phrase 'foundress of nothing' seems profoundly pessimistic and suggests that women's lives will inevitably be restricted by the 'hindrances' surrounding their everyday existence. The contemporary reader of *Middlemarch* could perhaps point to some of the improvements that had been achieved in women's legal and educational rights since the 1830s, and feel assured that the pessimism of the prelude had been confounded. The problem for a modern reader is to decide whether *Middlemarch* is a plea for greater opportunities for women as they try to escape the constraints of their limited education and upbringing, or whether the novel actually endorses the more traditional and domestic role of woman fulfilled as a wife and a mother. You should bear this dilemma in mind as you consider the representation of women in the novel.

## *A heroine*

Chapters 2–5 above, on *Northanger Abbey* and *Jane Eyre*, have discussed different ways in which the novels' heroines are constructed. In *Middlemarch* the prelude signals that a heroine and the nature of 'a heroine' are once again at issue. It seems entirely appropriate to use the word 'heroine' of Dorothea, since she, like the Theresa of the prelude, is 'enamoured of intensity and greatness' (1.1; p.8). Indeed, the opening chapters of the novel frequently use the same kind of vocabulary for Dorothea that is used of St Theresa. She is concerned for 'the higher inward life'; she has 'an exalted enthusiasm about the ends of life' and 'a nature altogether ardent, theoretic, and intellectually consequent'; and 'something she yearned for by which her life might be filled with action at once rational and ardent' (1.2; p.21; 1.3; p.26; 1.10; p.80).

At the same time as Dorothea's apparently unlimited potential for greatness is being outlined, the reader is also shown the constraints that are all too likely to limit this potential. Indeed, her very intensity of feeling is shown to be a handicap: 'with such a nature, struggling in the bonds of a narrow teaching, hemmed in by a social life which seemed nothing but a labyrinth of petty courses, a walled-in maze of small paths that led no whither, the outcome was sure to strike others as at once exaggeration and inconsistency' (1.3; pp.26–7). Dorothea has been an orphan since she was twelve and educated 'on plans at once narrow and promiscuous' (1.1; p.8), ensuring that she enters adult life ignorant and inexperienced in the ways of the world. Thus she has inappropriate expectations of marriage, which are doomed to be disappointed: 'The really delightful marriage must be that where your husband was a sort of father, and could teach you even Hebrew, if you wished it' (1.1; p.10).

She is also shown to be a misfit in the rural society in which she is placed, expected to marry because her beauty and wealth make her an excellent match, if only 'her love of extremes' (1.1; p.9) can be curbed. The narrator points sardonically to the extent to which Dorothea's aspirations towards spiritual greatness might embarrass a husband: 'Women were expected to have weak opinions; but the great safeguard of society and of domestic life was, that opinions were not acted on. Sane people did what their neighbours did, so that if any lunatics were at large, one might know and avoid them' (ibid.). The aphorism is amusing, and it could be argued that the ironic tone of much of the narrator's account of Dorothea in the opening chapters of the novel in fact deflates the reader's expectation of any heroic achievement, which might have been aroused by the prelude. Underlying the humour, however, is a frightening sense of the pressures that will be put on Dorothea to conform to the limited and limiting expectations of her family and friends.

Except for her desire to improve the living conditions of her uncle's tenants by designing cottages for them, Dorothea's aspirations, unlike those of Lydgate, are intangible and abstract, which is perhaps one of the reasons why it is so difficult to determine the novel's attitude to Dorothea. **What are Dorothea's achievements? Does the novel encourage us to think of these as successes or failures?**

Some of the achievements are rather personal and small in scale, such as acting as Casaubon's amanuensis and trying to persuade him to make financial provision for Will, believing in Lydgate after the death of Raffles and working to clear his name, and visiting Rosamond to help to save Lydgate's marriage. Other achievements might be described as philanthropic, such as persuading Sir James to build cottages for estate workers, employing Caleb Garth as a manager to improve her estate and encouraging her uncle to do the same, investing in the fever hospital and giving Mr Farebrother the Lowick living. Finally, she marries Will and becomes the wife of an 'ardent public man' (8.finale; p.782).

Outlining her achievements in this way makes it quite clear that Dorothea, unlike many of Eliot's contemporaries, does not attain fame and greatness for achievements in education, scholarship or social reform. Her role is a traditional supportive one, using her feminine influence where she can, supporting two husbands in their professional careers, and performing acts of charity and philanthropy; she has 'the ardent woman's need to rule beneficently by making the joy of another soul' (4.37; p.339). The question is really how far we should regard her life as a failure of unfulfilled potential and aspirations. If such questions are asked of Lydgate, the answer is clear, because his potential for achieving medical reform is so clearly articulated, and because 'he always regarded himself as a failure: he had not done what he once meant to do' (8.finale; p.781). Dorothea's aspirations are altogether more nebulous, and the prelude has already warned us not to expect her to become another St Theresa. And there is another powerful hint early in the novel that Dorothea's talents should best be applied in the traditional female role of wife and mother. As she waits for her uncle to give her Casaubon's letter of proposal, the narrator describes her hands: 'They were not thin hands, or small hands; but powerful, feminine, maternal hands' (1.4; p.36). Notice that the power is linked with femininity and motherhood, an idea repeated much later in the novel in the crucial meeting between Dorothea and Rosamond: 'Rosamond ... could not avoid putting her small hand into Dorothea's, which clasped it with gentle motherliness' (8.81; p.745). This is not to suggest that wifedom and motherhood are to be denigrated, but to query how far the novel presents them as a kind of second-best for a woman such as Dorothea.

Many readers have felt that Dorothea's ultimate fate as Will's wife is a tragedy of unfulfilled potential, though the finale makes it clear that this is not how Dorothea herself regards her life: 'Dorothea could have liked nothing better, since wrongs existed, than that her husband should be in the thick of a struggle against them, and that she should give him wifely help' (8.finale; p.783). The narrator even acknowledges that Dorothea's contemporaries feel she has not achieved what she might have done, thinking it 'a pity that so substantive and rare a creature should have been absorbed into the life of another, and be only known in a certain circle as a wife and mother' (ibid.). The argument the novel ultimately seems to endorse is that the time is no longer right for achievements on St Theresa's scale, and Dorothea's beneficence is best expressed through domesticity. It is not that Dorothea is less ardent for being a wife and mother, since 'Her finely-touched spirit had still its fine issues' (8.finale; p.785). Her influence cannot be assessed as St Theresa's can, but the influence is there none the less: 'The effect of her being on those around her was incalculably diffusive: for the growing good of the world is partly dependent on unhistoric acts; and that things are not so ill with you and me as they might have been, is half owing to the number who lived faithfully a hidden life, and rest in unvisited tombs' (ibid.).

In terms of the improvements that Eliot's contemporaries were seeking for opportunities for women, Dorothea's fate seems sadly limited. The novel is absolutely clear, however, that the world not only needs women like Dorothea but that it is a better place simply because she has lived in it. This may not be a feminist victory, but it is perhaps a victory for the possibilities of ordinary lives. And whether these ordinary lives become a 'far sadder sacrifice' than Dorothea's depends on our own sensitivity to them in our 'daily words and acts' (ibid.). The novel ends on an elegiac note, whilst reiterating the interdependence of human lives, and the need for a sympathetic understanding of them.

# *Alternative destinies*

Thus far Dorothea. But, as the narrator herself asks in a different context, 'why always Dorothea?' (3.29; p.261). We have seen that looking at the presentation of Dorothea's character in terms of the 'Woman Question' is more complicated than might have been supposed, and it is worth exploring the presentation of other female characters in the novel to see whether there is a common pattern. If we look at the representation of women such as Mrs Garth, Mrs Cadwallader and Mrs Bulstrode, it is possible to discern an endorsement of the notion that a woman's intelligence and energy are best deployed as supportive and even submissive wives.

All three are depicted as strong-minded and determined women, and the narrator appears to ask readers to admire these aspects of their womanhood. Mrs Garth has been educated to earn her own living as a teacher, and continues to take pupils after marriage and children. Mrs Cadwallader, 'a lady of immeasurably high birth', caustic wit and a 'feeling towards the vulgar rich [that] was a sort of religious hatred' (1.6; pp.48, 55–6), has defied her friends to marry a relatively impoverished clergyman. Mrs Bulstrode is not afraid to speak her mind to her niece, Rosamond, concerning what she sees as the impropriety of her behaviour with Lydgate. She is also deferred to by her husband: Mr Bulstrode, like Caleb Garth, 'in things worldly and indifferent was disposed to do what his wife bade him' (3.31; p.279).

Yet all of them are given a great loyalty and even submissiveness to the authority of their husbands, and these attitudes are held up for the reader's admiration. Mrs Garth accepts the hardships that fall on her and her children as a result of her husband's bankruptcy, renouncing 'all pride in teapots or children's frilling' because she adores 'her husband's virtues' and 'had that rare sense which discerns what is unalterable, and submits to it without murmuring' (3.24; pp.227–8). Additionally, she believes in a natural order of things in which women are subordinate to men; she was 'apt to be a little severe towards her own sex, which in her opinion was framed to be entirely subordinate' (3.24; p.228). Both Mrs Garth and her daughter are described affectionately by the narrator, but in terms which suggest that matrimony is the natural and inevitable role for women: 'Looking at the mother, you might hope that the daughter would become like her, which is a prospective advantage equal to a dowry' (3.24; p.229).

Mrs Cadwallader is hardly presented as a submissive female, since the narrator describes her as having a mind 'active as phosphorus, biting everything that came near into the form that suited it', but she accepts her relatively impoverished life with unfailing cheerfulness and a neat line in self-mockery: 'Young people should think of their families in marrying. I set a bad example – married a poor clergyman, and made myself a pitiable object among the De Bracys – obliged to get my coals by stratagem, and pray to heaven for my salad oil' (1.6; pp.56, 52). She, too, is affectionately presented, Mrs Fitchett's view that 'she would have found the country-side somewhat duller if the Rector's lady had been less free-spoken and less of a skinflint' (1.6; p.48) seeming to represent the narrator's own verdict on her. Mrs Bulstrode is presented as an altogether more earnest woman, and the narrator gently mocks her sense of her superiority to her friend Mrs Plymdale: 'more decided seriousness, more admiration for mind, and a house outside the town' (3.31; p.276). But her concern for Rosamond is shown to be genuine: she 'had a true sisterly feeling for her brother; always thinking that he might have married better, but wishing well to the children' (3.31; p.275). She admires and respects her husband, believing that he 'was one of those men whose memoirs should be written when they died' (4.36; p.326). What places Mrs Bulstrode on the side of the angels, however, is her response to her husband's downfall, and the account of this includes some of the most moving writing in the novel. The account is a complex one, acknowledging the difficulties she faces: 'Her honest ostentatious nature made the sharing of a merited dishonour as bitter as it could be to any mortal' (8.74; p.706). Yet, abandoning her rich garments for something altogether plainer, she goes to her husband, and because he 'seemed so withered and shrunken', 'a movement of new compassion and old tenderness went through her like a great wave' (8.74; p.707).

All these women are presented with warmth, understanding and compassion, and the qualities that are held up for the reader to admire are their loyalties and the sacrifices they make for the men in their lives. However, if these are the female virtues that the novel appears to endorse, there are also feminine characteristics that the novel criticizes. Specifically, the charity of the narrative voice is almost entirely withdrawn in the presentation of Rosamond, 'that combination of correct sentiments, music, dancing, drawing, elegant note-writing, private album for extracted verse, and perfect blond loveliness, which made the irresistible woman for the doomed man of that date' (3.27; p.252). In contrast to the 'epic life' of St Theresa, which the prelude offers as a possible model for women's lives, Rosamond is shown to be 'adorned with accomplishments for the refined amusement of man' (ibid.); she emerges, fully formed and beautifully groomed, from the pages of contemporary advice manuals for women.

One of the reasons for the harsh representation of Rosamond may be concern about the inadequacies of women's education. Although Eliot was writing *Middlemarch* forty years later than the events portrayed in it, opportunities for women to learn had not greatly increased. According to Maria Grey, writing in 1871, women

> are not educated to be wives, but to get husbands. They are not educated to be mothers; if they were they would require and obtain the highest education that could be given in order to fit them for the highest duties a human being can perform ... They would not give ... 5,520 hours of their school life to music against 640 to arithmetic.

(quoted in Beer, 1986, p.178)

This sounds remarkably like the education Rosamond received forty years earlier, and it could perhaps be argued that Rosamond, like Dorothea, should be seen as the victim of an inadequate education system. Dorothea, however, longs for learning not only for its own sake, but to enable her to assist others. Rosamond, 'the flower of Mrs Lemon's school', is perfectly happy with the notion that education enhances a woman's marriage prospects, rendering it easy for her to capture the 'lover and bridegroom who was not a Middlemarcher' (1.11; p.89; 1.12; p.109). For a writer as intellectual and as well educated as George Eliot, the creation of Rosamond provides the opportunity to fulminate not only at the inadequacies of educational opportunity for women, but also at the ways in which some women conspire to perpetuate these inadequacies.

*[handwritten margin note: Perhaps Eliot is contrasting contemporary values with old values of women's]*

Another reason for the hostile treatment of Rosamond may indeed lie in Eliot's own avowed contempt for frivolous women. This underpins her scathing article 'Silly novels by lady novelists', which appeared in the *Westminster Review* in October 1856, and in which she described such novelists as being 'entirely indifferent to publishers' accounts and inexperienced in every form of poverty except poverty of brain'. She also seems to have regarded women in society as essentially feather-brained, writing to her friend Sara Hennell in 1858:

> It is quite an exception to meet with a woman who seems to expect any sort of companionship from the men, and I shudder at the sight of a woman in society, for I know that I shall have to sit on the sofa with her all the evening listening to her stupidities, while the men on the other side of the table are discussing the subjects I care to hear about.
>
> (in Eliot, 1954–78, vol.2, p.454)

Her objection to stupidity will only carry us so far, however, since Rosamond 'was clever with that sort of cleverness which catches every tone except the humorous' (2.16; p.148). Neither can it be claimed that the ferocity with which she is presented is caused by her beauty alone, since the opening sentence of the novel draws attention to Dorothea's beauty. This differs from Rosamond's, however, in being entirely unselfconscious, and it is on her acute consciousness of self and a total lack of awareness of the needs of others that the critical representation of Rosamond is based.

For Rosamond's vision of the world is one that is entirely centred on self, and she more than any other character in the novel takes 'the world as an udder to feed [her] supreme [self]' (2.21; p.198). It is for Rosamond that the narrator reserves her greatest irony, with comments such as 'There was nothing financial, still less sordid, in her previsions: she cared about what were considered refinements, and not about the money that was to pay for them' (1.12; p.110). The narrator invites the reader's judgement of Rosamond, in much the same way as she invites our response to other characters in the novel, but always with that extra edge to her voice: 'Think no unfair evil of her, pray: she had no wicked plots, nothing sordid or mercenary; in fact, she never thought of money except as something necessary which other people would always provide' (3.27; p.252). Perhaps the detail to note here is not that we are urged to think no evil of her, but to think no *unfair* evil. The narrator is scathing about Rosamond's education, 'where the teaching included all that was demanded in an accomplished female – even to extras, such as the getting in and out of a carriage' (1.11; p.89). She is hostile to Rosamond's particular kind of beauty, and her 'controlled self-consciousness of manner which is the expensive substitute for simplicity' (5.43; p.407). And Rosamond's view of a wife's role is not that of loyal supporter of a husband's work; rather she sees marriage 'as a prospect of rising in rank and getting a little nearer to that celestial condition on earth in which she would have nothing to do with vulgar people, and perhaps at last associate with relatives quite equal to the county people who looked down on the Middlemarchers' (2.16; p.156).

Almost all of Rosamond's actions in the novel are shown to be self-centred and are presented critically. When she persuades Fred to accompany her to Stone Court to engineer a meeting with Lydgate, in pursuit of 'that middle-class heaven, rank' (1.12; p.110), the narrator's humour is at Rosamond's expense. When she refuses to give Lydgate a promise that she will not go riding with his cousin again, the narrator again highlights her self-centredness: 'she had been determined not to promise. Rosamond had that victorious obstinacy which never wastes its energy in impetuous resistance. What she liked to do was to her the right thing, and all her cleverness was directed to getting the means of doing it' (6.58; p.549). Confronted by Lydgate's anger at her countermanding his instructions to Trumbull, she shrinks ' in cold dislike ... in the conviction that she was not the person to misbehave, whatever others might do' (7.64; pp.619–20). When Lydgate berates her about writing to his uncle against his express wishes, the narrator highlights her inability to see any point of view but her own: 'there was but one person in Rosamond's world whom she did not regard as blameworthy, and that was the graceful creature with blond plaits and with little hands crossed before her, who had never expressed herself unbecomingly, and had always acted for the best – the best naturally being what she best liked' (7.65; pp.625– 6).

Rosamond's greatest sins are committed against Lydgate, both as a doctor and as a husband, though the novel attempts to be even-handed in showing the extent to which Lydgate and Rosamond 'Each lived in a world of which the other knew nothing' (2.16; p.155). This lack of understanding is explored by David Carroll (1992), in *George Eliot and the Conflict of Interpretations*. The book investigates ways in which Eliot's fictional characters reach a crisis in their lives in which decisions have to be made in order to make sense of their worlds – these moments are called by Carroll 'crises of interpretation'. At the end of the chapter on *Middlemarch*, Carroll explores Lydgate's crises of interpretation. Although his account appears to focus more on Lydgate than on Rosamond, it illuminates some of the differences, not simply in their characters, but in the ways in which they are represented. **Now read David Carroll, '*Middlemarch*: empiricist fables' (1992, pp.263–72; extract in Regan, 2001). What light does this passage shed on the relative charity with which Lydgate is presented and the harshness of Rosamond's representation?**

Part of the difference, Carroll suggests, lies in the greater complexity of the account of Lydgate, whose professional and domestic careers are shown to be in conflict and whose professional concerns with diagnostic medicine and anatomical research are of little use to him in his relationships with and understanding of women. Rosamond, on the other hand, experiences no such conflicts: 'There is no gap, no discrepancy possible between what she projects and the recognized image' (Carroll, 1992, p.268). She is a stereotype, with less capacity for experiencing crisis and responding to it and learning from it than her husband, and, the novel seems to suggest, should be judged accordingly. Rosamond's achievements are not held up as an example towards which any woman should aspire.

The novel seems to reject the concepts both of a dominant and of an ornamental woman, and to suggest that greatness on an epic scale is no longer possible. What kind of role for women does the novel then endorse? The answer may be a view of women that is both more conservative and more limited than we might have expected and hoped for. According to *Middlemarch,* a woman's greatest asset is her sympathy and her understanding, and the most satisfying fulfilment for these virtues is to be found as the supportive partner in marriage. And despite the model of St Theresa which broods over the whole novel, it is not clear whether its author sees such a marital fate as necessarily tragic.

# *Middlemarch* and reform

What emerges from the discussions of provinciality and the 'Woman Question' is that *Middlemarch* is conducting a debate about the kinds of transformations that are taking place in the fabric of English life across nearly half of the nineteenth century. These transformations are framed by the first political Reform Bill of 1832, which is part of the historical background of the novel, and by the second political Reform Bill of 1867, which was passed only two years before Eliot began to write *Middlemarch*; both the resulting Reform Acts extended the franchise to many working men but persisted in denying it to women. The novel also raises the possibilities of change in other spheres of life: through Dorothea, the novel explores the aspirations and education of women; through Lydgate it explores the possibility of significant changes in medical practice and scientific research; through Casaubon it explores the changes in research techniques; and through Sir James Chettam and Caleb Garth it explores the effect of changes in land-management and transport systems.

Eliot understood that the social changes through which she had lived were extremely complex and not necessarily a force for the good. Like the novelist herself, her first readers had seen a transformation in their world. (Some of these transformations are recorded in Table 9.2.) Between the two Reform Acts (the first in 1832, the second in 1867), the population of England and Wales had increased from almost 14 million to over 20 million – moreover, the population was now largely urban rather than rural. By the time *Middlemarch* was published, in 1872, a comprehensive railway network had extended into hitherto remote regions, enabling goods and people to be transported with great speed and efficiency. An increasingly interventionist state had passed legislation aimed at improving the working and living conditions of ordinary men and women, and at providing a wider range of education facilities. In 1872 Eliot's first readers were living at a time of relatively full employment, before the agricultural depression of the late 1870s had begun to take effect. So it could be assumed that they, as well as modern readers, who bring to the novel a wider historical perspective, might view the novel as a kind of celebration of the possibilities of reform. Whether the novel actually presents reform as an unambiguously good thing is open to debate.

Although by 1872 some progress had been made towards improved educational and employment opportunities for women and some enhancement of their status in law, there is no suggestion in the novel that any of its fictional female characters would have been in a position to take advantage of this. Only Dorothea is shown to have any aspirations towards the kind of greatness that will have a bearing on other lives, and much of this, in the early chapters of the novel, is clearly based on her misconception of what is possible. She, like Mary Garth, settles into domestic contentment, and their happiness is described in terms of their supporting roles as wives and mothers. Indeed the novel seems almost to discount the possibility of any other conclusion: 'A new Theresa will hardly have the opportunity of reforming a conventual life, any more than a new Antigone will spend her heroic piety in daring all for the sake of a brother's burial: the medium in which their ardent deeds took shape is for ever gone' (8.finale; p.785). There is a melancholy irony in Eliot's writing a celebration of women's hidden lives at precisely the historical moment when it seems possible for women to lead public lives. Whether you view this as a tragedy of missed opportunities may depend partly on the hopes and misgivings concerning the role of women that you bring to your reading of the novel. It will also be influenced by how you are affected by the language Eliot employs in the novel's finale. The final sentence of the novel can be regarded as an affirmation of the importance of the 'hidden life' yet the finale, whilst proposing on the one hand the validity of a 'home epic', also makes a reference to Antigone, which is a tragedy (8.finale; pp.785, 779). In the novel's prelude, the historical St Theresa is represented as aflame with religious vocation (prelude; p.3); at the end of the book we find Dorothea likened to a river that has 'spent itself in channels' (8.finale; p.785). If you turn back to the prelude after reading the end of the novel, you may be left with a stark sense of just how closely Eliot's choice of metaphor suggests that Dorothea's fate matches that of the mournful cygnet who 'never finds the living stream' (prelude; p.4). To have been 'born a Saint Theresa, foundress of nothing', could seem a powerful example of the 'tragedy' of everyday lives, which Eliot famously describes as lying on the 'other side of silence' (ibid.; 2.20; p.182). The narrator warns us at the outset that 'later-born Theresas' may achieve 'only a life of mistakes, the offspring of a certain spiritual grandeur ill-matched with the meanness of opportunity' (prelude; p.3). Of course, we come to the end of the novel after having read all that intervenes after the prelude. Specifically, we have just read the resolution of the novel's romance plots (Fred and Mary, Dorothea and Will). As readers we may feel torn between wishing to endorse the passionate romantic fulfilment that Eliot allows her heroine to attain, and dismay at the failure of Dorothea's more epic aspirations. This is illustrative of our sense of Eliot's deep ambivalence about female vocation and domestic roles.

If there is some ambiguity over Eliot's presentation of Dorothea's life as a tragedy of unfulfilled aspirations, there is none over the fate of Lydgate, which is presented as tragic in the extreme. What the novel leaves open is whether the provinces are places where medical and scientific advances can be made. Lydgate's scientific understanding and aspirations, as well as his intellectual capacity, are clearly articulated, and the novelist places him firmly in a historical context which shows the advances that were being made by his contemporaries. According to the finale, Lydgate dies aged fifty, which would have been in 1852

– that is, after major legislation had been passed to improve public health, but before cholera had been eliminated (see Table 9.2). Most of his working life is spent during a period of major advances in medicine and public health, yet his only publication is on gout, 'a disease which has a good deal of wealth on its side' (8.finale; p.781). In part Lydgate's failure is blamed on the provincial society which misjudges him, but the novel also makes it clear that it is Lydgate's own failure to understand the interconnectedness of this provincial life which brings about his own downfall. He may long 'to demonstrate the more intimate relations of living structure' (2.15; p.139), but, unlike his creator, he is unable to see that the scientific idea has its parallel in the fabric of provincial society of which he is part. Lydgate's failure is the greater because his understanding of current research methods is absolutely up to date; this is made clear by the contrast with Casaubon, whose own research is shown to take no account of new ideas and methodologies, and will lead nowhere. As Will Ladislaw forcibly puts it, 'it is no use now to be crawling a little way after men of the last century ... living in a lumber-room and furbishing up broken-legged theories' (2.22; pp.207–8).

The novel devotes less attention to changes in agricultural practices and transport systems than to the role of women and the possibilities of advances in medicine; where it does engage with them, though, it seems to suggest both that this kind of progress in itself is desirable and that the provinces have a robust and pragmatic attitude to them. Much of this has to do with the association of such changes with Caleb Garth, who is consistently presented in a sympathetic light, and, to a lesser extent, with Sir James Chettam, whose political conservatism is softened by his desire to improve the lot of the rural workers who are dependent on him, and with Fred, who finds his vocation in life as a 'theoretic and practical farmer' (8.finale; p.779).

Eliot's 'study of provincial life' does not reach firm and easily reducible conclusions; the opening paragraph of the finale of *Middlemarch* suggests that she knows herself to have been engaged on something much more complex than a straightforward investigation, something that requires her to interrogate the notions of both provinciality and the historical process. She accepts the limitations of fiction as a tool for such a study, acknowledging that 'the fragment of a life, however typical, is not the sample of an even web' (8.finale; p.779). The images, however, also seem to imply that the scope of fiction – 'the fragment of a life' – may ultimately be more valuable than any scientific or sociological enquiry, which produces only 'the sample of an even web'. In her assertion that the web is not even, that 'promises may not be kept', that 'an ardent outset may be followed by declension', that 'latent powers may find their long-waited opportunity' and that 'a past error may urge a grand retrieval' (ibid.), she also hints at the provisional nature of any conclusions about the nature of human progress. The novel is not a celebration of Victorian achievements, but a robust yet compassionate account of the human frailties lodged in an English provincial community on the cusp of change.

# Works cited

Beer, Gillian. 1986. *George Eliot*, Brighton: Harvester.

Carroll, David. 1992. '*Middlemarch*: empiricist fables', in *George Eliot and the Conflict of Interpretations*, Cambridge: Cambridge University Press. (Extract in Regan, 2001.)

Chase, Karen. 1991. *George Eliot: 'Middlemarch'*, Cambridge: Cambridge University Press.

Eliot, George. 1954–78. *The George Eliot Letters*, ed. by Gordon Haight, 9 vols, New Haven: Yale University Press.

Eliot, George. [1872] 1998. *Middlemarch*, ed. by David Carroll, with an introduction by Felicia Bonaparte, 3rd impression, Oxford World's Classics, Oxford: Oxford University Press.

James, Henry. 1987. '*Middlemarch*' (review), in *The Critical Muse: Selected Literary Criticism*, Harmondsworth: Penguin. (Extract in Regan, 2001.)

Purkis, John. 1985. *A Preface to George Eliot*, London: Longman.

Regan, Stephen. Ed. 2001. *The Nineteenth-Century Novel: A Critical Reader*, London: Routledge.

Suggestions for further reading can be found at the end of chapter 11.

# CHAPTER 10

# *Middlemarch* as a novel of vocation and experiment

*by Nora Tomlinson*

## *Middlemarch* as a novel of vocation

The prelude and the first book of *Middlemarch* set up two rather different sets of expectations for the novel. The seriousness of tone of the prelude and its outline of St Teresa's religious vocation seem to prepare the reader for a narration about vocation on a heroic, even an epic scale. The book's subtitle, and the first chapters of book 1, however, seem to suggest that the novel will deal with something rather more mundane. Yet there is a sense in which *Middlemarch* can be described as a novel about vocation. Not only does it explore how its two major protagonists, Lydgate and Dorothea, strive towards scientific, intellectual and emotional fulfilment, but, as with so many other strands of the novel, the idea of vocation is illustrated through a range of issues which confront some of the other inhabitants of the fictional provincial community.

How might we define 'vocation'? While it may be helpful to think of a vocation as a passionate desire for some kind of achievement, this achievement should not be seen simply in professional terms. The novel is clear, in its presentation of Lydgate, about the value it attaches to a professional vocation that is both intellectually fulfilling and socially useful, but it also recognizes the place of emotional and spiritual longings, such as those of Dorothea, which can have no professional outlet.

## Middlemarch *and the world of work*

While many nineteenth-century novels deal either directly or indirectly with the sources of wealth of their fictional characters, and some of them engage in a debate about the industrial working conditions that produced this wealth, fewer of them actually show work taking place. Émile Zola's *Germinal* is unusual in devoting so much space in the early chapters of the novel to an account of the actual extraction of coal, and the novel exposes the exploitative nature of hard physical labour. *Middlemarch*, in contrast, is concerned with the idea of work as vocation, explored largely, though not entirely, through the characters of Lydgate and Caleb Garth. The idea of mistaken vocation is explored too, through Fred's conviction that he should not be a clergyman, and Mr Farebrother's tacit admission to Lydgate that he 'felt himself not altogether in the right vocation' (Eliot, [1872] 1998, 2.17; p.162; all subsequent page references are to this edition). This vocational concept of work is highly selective, of course, and ignores the silk-weavers and dyers who work for Mr Vincy and Mr Plymdale, makes only the briefest of references to the cottage industry of straw-plaiting (1.9; p.71) and says nothing at all about the human effects of the building and working of the local canals and railways. Only in the account of Dagley's farm in book 4, chapter 39, are we given a glimpse of the misery of some agricultural living and working conditions:

> The mossy thatch of the cow-shed, the broken grey barn-doors, the pauper labourers in ragged breeches ... the scanty dairy of cows being tethered for milking and leaving one half of the shed in brown emptiness; the very pigs and white ducks seeming to wander about the uneven neglected yard as if in low spirits from feeding on a too meagre quality of rinsings. (4.39; pp.369–70)

This brief glimpse is included to show the hypocrisy of Mr Brooke's desire to stand for Parliament on a reform ticket, when his own tenants live in such a state of 'midnight darkness' (4.39; p.373).

This is not in any way to criticize the novel for omitting a full account of contemporary living and working conditions. *Middlemarch* has a different agenda from that of novels such as Elizabeth Gaskell's *Mary Barton* (1848) and *North and South* (1855), which explicitly set out to expose conditions in the Manchester cotton industry: Eliot's novel is concerned with exploring the possibilities of finding a vocation that is fulfilling. The work of individuals such as Caleb Garth and Lydgate, which will contribute to improvements in provincial life, is essentially work that satisfies their intellectual, spiritual and emotional needs. Both men are called to their work. The account of Lydgate discovering his vocation in book 2, chapter 15, shows that his work is 'an intellectual passion' and 'his scientific interest soon took the form of a professional enthusiasm' (2.15; pp.134, 135, 136). Garth, too, regards his work in vocational, almost religious terms. After reading the letter from Sir James Chettam offering him the management of the estates of Freshitt and Tipton, he says:

> it's a fine thing to come to a man when he's seen into the nature of business: to have the chance of getting a bit of the country into good fettle ... and putting men into the right way with their farming, and getting a bit of good contriving and solid building done – that those who are living and those who come after will be the better for ... I hold it the most honourable work that is ... It's a great gift of God. (4.40; pp.377–8)

The important thing about the vocations of both men is that they have as their aim the general and long-term improvement of human lives. Lydgate 'meant to be a unit who would make a certain amount of difference towards that spreading change which would one day tell appreciably upon the average, and in the mean time have the pleasure of *making an advantageous difference to the viscera of his own patients*' (2.15; p.137). His aim is twofold: to improve the health of those patients in his own personal care, and to be the means by which overall advances can be made in medical science to benefit future generations. In this he is like Garth, who knows himself capable of making improvements for 'those who are living and those who come after'. The novel is not *about* medical practice in 1830, nor about changes in land-management at the same date, but it does appear to present this kind of work in a favourable light; it does this partly through the attractiveness of the two characters with whom these callings are largely associated, but also by presenting both men as being concerned with immediate and long-term improvements in the lives of others.

Up to now we have considered the theory of work as explored in *Middlemarch*; however, the novel also provides the reader with opportunities to see the worker in action. **Reread book 5, chapter 45, of *Middlemarch*. How is Lydgate's performance as a doctor assessed by his patients and by other Middlemarch doctors? How does the narrator encourage the reader to assess him?**

The chapter amusingly illustrates the responses of a range of patients to the new doctor, from the downright hostility of Mrs Dollop, the landlady of the Tankard in Slaughter Lane, who is convinced that 'Dr Lydgate meant to let the people die in the Hospital, if not to poison them, for the sake of cutting them up without saying by your leave or with your leave', to Mr Trumbull, the auctioneer, who assures anyone who will listen to him that Lydgate 'knew a thing or two more than the rest of the doctors – was far better versed in the secrets of his profession than the majority of his compeers' (5.45; pp.415, 424). It is also clear that some of those patients who call him in, particularly in his early days in the town, do so with no special regard for his medical abilities, but because they think they can run up bills with a new doctor, or because, like Peter Featherstone, they are chronically ill and will try anything in desperation. Lydgate's status as outsider also means that 'there were particulars enough reported of him to breed much more specific expectations and to intensify differences into partisanship' (5.45; p.416).

This partisanship is exacerbated by some of the innovations Lydgate makes in his medical practice. Thus his refusal to dispense drugs, and his inability adequately to explain this policy to enquirers, leads to the hostility of the Mawmseys, who spread the mistaken rumour 'that Lydgate went about saying physic was of no use' (5.45; p.418). At the other end of the spectrum of public opinion, Mr Trumbull, whose pneumonia is 'left as much as possible to itself, so that the stages might be noted for future guidance', advertises Lydgate's skills as a doctor: 'he was not backward in awarding credit to the medical man who had discerned the quality of patient he had to deal with' (5.45; p.424). There are even patients such as Mr Powderell, who 'was inclined to esteem Lydgate the more for what seemed a conscientious pursuit of a better plan' (5.45; p.421), but who continues privately to persuade his wife to take Widgeon's Purifying Pills in parallel with Lydgate's treatment.

But if patient opinion is divided on Lydgate's ability as a doctor, medical opinion is united against him, culminating in the refusal of 'every medical man … to become a visitor at the Fever Hospital' (5.45; p.426) because Lydgate is given overall medical control. His decision not to dispense drugs is 'offensive both to the physicians whose exclusive distinction seemed infringed on, and to the surgeon-apothecaries with whom he ranged himself', and causes great irritation to Mr Wrench in particular: 'what I contend against is the way medical men are fouling their own nest, and setting up a cry about the country as if a general practitioner who dispenses drugs couldn't be a gentleman' (5.45; pp.417, 420). Neither does Lydgate endear himself to his fellow-doctors by providing the correct diagnosis of cramp for the medical condition of Mrs Larcher's charwoman, after Dr Minchin has diagnosed a tumour. Additionally there is the fear that Lydgate will poach patients, as he has already done in becoming the Vincys' family doctor instead of Mr Wrench: 'The new-comer already threatened to be a nuisance in the shape of rivalry, and was certainly a nuisance in the shape of practical criticism or reflections on his hard-driven elders, who had had something else to do than to busy themselves with untried notions' (5.45; pp.424–5).

The narrator is even-handed in the presentation of Lydgate's performance as a doctor. His innovations and diagnostic skills are noted, together with his concerns for the general welfare of his patients. For example, he sends a note to Mrs Larcher, saying that her charwoman 'was in need of good food', and explains both his diagnosis and his treatment to Mr Trumbull, because he 'was acute enough to indulge him with a little technical talk' (5.45; pp.422, 424). On the other hand, the narrator highlights his cavalier behaviour in his thoughtless explanation to Mr Mawmsey over his drugs policy, in his intervention in cases in the infirmary, and what is perceived as his arrogance, 'which nobody felt to be altogether deniable' (5.45; p.426).

By showing Lydgate at work, the narrator suggests that in some respects, he is indeed a skilful and innovative doctor, but also indicates the extent to which his reputation is outside his own control. She reveals the scale on which his innovations are misunderstood and misrepresented, and shows how his greatest medical successes are consistently misreported: 'Various patients got well while Lydgate was attending them, some even of dangerous illnesses; and it was remarked that the new doctor with his new ways had at least the merit of bringing people back from the brink of death' (5.45; p.422). Lydgate dismisses such talk as 'trash' but the narrator shows his powerlessness to correct popular opinion: 'his proud outspokenness was checked by the discernment that it was as useless to fight against the interpretations of ignorance as to whip the fog' (ibid.). The reader is reminded of the prophecy at the end of book 2, chapter 15, that Middlemarch will swallow and assimilate Lydgate very easily, and of Lydgate's difficulties in voting for the hospital chaplain; the chapter under discussion confirms a sense that Lydgate's professional as well as personal destiny is beyond his control.

Chapter 45 presents Lydgate at the turning point of his career, apparently successful, contented and fulfilled: 'There was something very fine in Lydgate's look just then, and any one might have been encouraged to bet on his achievement' (5.45; p.429). Yet the structure of the novel shows how his performance as a doctor is inextricably linked with major events of the narrative and thus with his own downfall. He first meets Rosamond by her design, when he attends Featherstone, and becomes closely acquainted with her when he is called in to attend her brother Fred. Marriage to Rosamond precipitates his financial downfall, while his association with Bulstrode brings about his medical downfall. His treatment of Raffles is impeccable, but while he suspects that 'somebody's ignorance or imprudence had killed him' he does not investigate further, because he fears to insult Bulstrode and also acknowledges that 'he himself might be wrong' (7.70; p.669). Lydgate's tragedy lies in the gap between his medical aspirations and his actual achievements; by showing the doctor at work the novel allows the reader to assess the extent of this tragedy.

The novel provides us with fewer glimpses of Caleb Garth actually at work; even the chapter on his involvement with the railways says little more than that he was taking measurements. There are, however, several references in the novel to the kind of work he undertakes. When he receives Sir James Chettam's offer of managing the Freshitt and Tipton estates, he immediately speaks of the improvements he will make: 'I shall make Brooke have new agreements with the tenants, and I shall draw up a rotation of crops. And I'll lay a wager we can get fine bricks out of the clay at Bott's corner. I must look into that: it would cheapen the repairs' (4.40; p.377). He is clearly interested in value for money, but also in achieving work of the highest quality. He admires Bulstrode because 'however [he] might ring if you tried him, he liked good solid carpentry and masonry, and had a notion both of drains and chimneys', and when Bulstrode purchases Stone Court from Joshua Rigg, Garth meets him 'to give an opinion on a question of stable drainage, and was now advising the bailiff in the rick-yard' (5.45; p.425; 5.53; p.490). Bulstrode in his turn wishes to employ Garth as 'the agent who was more anxious for his employer's interests than his own' (7.68; p.648). Most of all, he admires Dorothea, because, like the contemporary designer of the plan for a model cottage shown in Figure 10.1 (overleaf), she shares his views about the benefits of improvements to the living and working conditions of those who work on the land:

> 'She said a thing I often used to think myself when I was a lad: – "Mr Garth, I should like to feel, if I lived to be old, that I had improved a great piece of land and built a great many good cottages, because the work is of a healthy kind while it is being done, and after it is done, men are the better for it." '
> (6.56; p.518)

Garth is used by the narrator to celebrate certain kinds of work. Like Lydgate, he finds his vocation early, and the language used to describe this discovery is some of the most powerful anywhere in the novel. **Reread the last two paragraphs of book 3, chapter 24 (pp.235–6). How does the language operate to create a particular representation of labour?**

The language operates in a number of ways. First of all, there is a suggestion of grandeur conveyed by the scale of activities, by 'the great hammer', by the 'huge trunk' and by 'the piled-up produce', together with the lofty sounds produced by labour, the 'shouts of the workmen, the roar of the furnace, the thunder and plash of the engine', all of which appear to Garth as 'sublime music'. The repetition of the word 'sublime' towards the end of the first paragraph links the idea of labour to that of music. The passage also suggests the inspirational quality of labour, which for Garth acts as music, poetry, philosophy and religion. That labour is for him a kind of secular religion is reinforced in the second paragraph, where the nature of his 'virtual divinities' is spelled out: 'I think his virtual divinities were good practical schemes, accurate work, and the faithful completion of undertakings: his prince of darkness was a slack workman' (3.24; p.236).

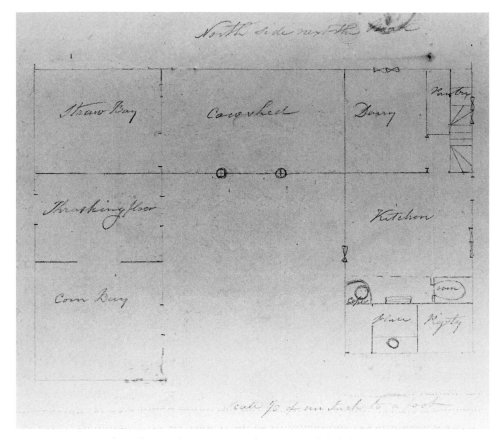

*Figure 10.1 Plan by Robert Evans for a model labourer's cottage, 1839. Warwickshire County Council Records Office CR 136/B3994B. By kind permission of the Newdegate Settlement*

What Garth represents in the novel is the honesty and integrity of work, and a belief in his ability to be a force for good. His aspirations are, perhaps, more practical and less theoretical than Lydgate's, but he shares with the doctor a desire to use his knowledge and experience for the good of others. He is shown to be, if anything, even less capable of managing finance than Lydgate. When he admires Dorothea's 'head for business' the narrator adds a rider that 'It must be remembered that by "business" Caleb never meant money transactions, but the skilful application of labour' (6.56; p.518). And unlike Lydgate, Garth is shown to be morally uncompromised by any financial misfortune or professional enterprise. When he is made bankrupt he lives narrowly, 'exerting himself to the utmost that he might after all pay twenty shillings in the pound' (3.23; p.217). More importantly, he is able to disentangle himself from Bulstrode's affairs: 'I can't be happy in working with you, or profiting by you. It hurts my mind' (7.69; p.653). The novel does not, of course, suggest any simplistic contrast between the moral probity of the two men. But it does show how two working lives are an integral part of both the social fabric of Middlemarch and the structural fabric of the novel.

One further aspect of the concept of work as vocation is worth a brief mention here. The preceding discussion has shown that the kind of work the novel holds out for our endorsement is work pursued for ends that are, for the most part, altruistic. This idea is supported by the novel's exploration of the implications of a mistaken or failed vocation. There are several examples, including Casaubon's pursuit of the Key to all Mythologies, Bulstrode's desire to be both eminent and Christian, and Will Ladislaw's search for a suitable occupation.

Casaubon's obsession with his research is presented as one of the reasons for Dorothea's unhappiness as his wife. As she lies awake agonizing over the unspecified promise her husband has tried to extract from her, she acknowledges the futility of his work, and her own part in it:

> had she not wished to marry him that she might help him in his life's labour? –
> But she had thought the work was to be something greater, which she could
> serve in devoutly for its own sake. Was it right, even to soothe his grief – would
> it be possible, even if she promised – to work as in a treadmill fruitlessly?
> (5.48; p.450)

Bulstrode's principle of gaining 'as much power as possible, that he might use it for the glory of God' (2.16; p.145) is exposed as both hypocritical and destructive, as the novel traces the damage this attitude causes to his family, to Lydgate and to Will Ladislaw.

As for Ladislaw, whom many readers, as well as many characters in the novel, regard as somehow lightweight, a dilettante and unworthy of Dorothea, it could be argued that his progress through the novel actually traces his search for a genuine vocation, though his aspirations are rather nebulous – he wants simply 'To love what is good and beautiful' (4.39; p.368). He is shown in the process of sampling several possibilities, but as eventually rejecting the careers of artist, journalist and political aide. It is not clear from the finale whether his career as 'an ardent public man' is solely the result of his marriage to Dorothea and her support for him, or whether we should regard him as always having had the potential for such a career. Perhaps the points to note are that Will is nearly always presented sympathetically, and that his ultimate career, which he pursues for the public good, suggests that he, too, like Lydgate and Garth, has found the kind of vocation the novel can endorse.

The prelude to Middlemarch makes a denigrating reference to 'favourite love-stories in prose and verse' (prelude; p.4). However, *Middlemarch* is, of course, a novel of romance as well as of vocation. Dorothea sees marriage in terms of vocation, and the ideal marriage would be one in which romantic love and vocational aspiration were in harmony. Often, however, the two are shown to be in conflict. Forewarning us of Lydgate's fate, Eliot points out that romance seems to kill vocation (2.15; pp.135–6). For Lydgate, and arguably also for Dorothea, marriage does spell the end of high vocational aspirations. This conflict has generic as well as thematic implications. The references to history, epic and tragedy at the beginning of *Middlemarch* suggest that it will explore the possibility of becoming a novel of heroic vocation, rather than a romance (prelude; p.3). In book 2, chapter 15, the narrator bemoans the assumption that romantic love is the proper subject of fiction, suggesting that Lydgate's 'moment of vocation' and 'growth of an intellectual passion' offer a more worthwhile theme (2.15; p.135). Nevertheless, *Middlemarch* does also develop romance plots. Is a novel of vocation feasible, or do we, as readers, require novels to be love stories? Perhaps what is most interesting from the point of view of the novel *form* is how the inclusion of epic and romance illustrates its capaciousness: the novel is able to contain and combine elements of numerous genres and resists restrictive definitions and categories. Moreover, even while the narrator is lamenting our unending appetite for love stories, rather than for the achievements which 'must be wooed with industrious thought and patient renunciation of small desires' (ibid.), the language employs the vocabulary of romantic love to describe vocational ardour – such as Lydgate's 'intellectual passion' – and thereby implies that vocation and romance are as much entangled as they are in conflict.

## *Representations of marriage*

Marriage, of course, is a fundamental element of both plot and theme in most nineteenth-century novels. It absolutely shapes novels as diverse as *Northanger Abbey, Madame Bovary, The Portrait of a Lady* and *The Awakening,* and is a key component in many others, including *Jane Eyre, Far from the Madding Crowd* and *The Woman in White.* Volume 1 of the autograph manuscript of *Middlemarch* bears this inscription: 'To my dear husband George Henry Lewes in this the nineteenth year of our blessed union.' The word 'union' seems to underline the fundamental importance to the novel of intellectual, emotional and sexual relationships in marriage – both as a means of shaping its plot and as a means by which ideas on the role of women and reform can be debated, and the novel's underpinning philosophies of the interconnectedness of human lives and the 'equivalent centre of self' (2.21; p.198) can be established. The inscription also suggests that for the novelist, as well as for her fictional heroine, marriage is every bit as much a vocation as work is.

*Middlemarch* explores and analyses thoroughly the failed marriages of Dorothea and Casaubon, and of Lydgate and Rosamond. One of the novelist's techniques is to provide the reader with a range of different and much more successful marital relationships against which they can be measured. These include the marriages of the Cadwalladers and of Celia and Sir James Chettam, the marriage of Mary Garth's parents and Mary's own marriage to Fred, and the marriages of the Vincys and the Bulstrodes. These pairings also serve to demonstrate the interconnectedness of provincial life; with the exception of the Cadwalladers, and Sir James Chettam, everyone listed in the preceding sentence has a family connection with someone else, as is confirmed by the family interconnections shown in Figure 11.1 in the next chapter of this volume. **What does the novel suggest that the successful marriages have in common?**

Some of the shared characteristics include: an awareness of the emotional needs of the other partner in the relationship; an understanding of and respect for the aspirations of the other partner; loyalty, especially in times of adversity; a sense of the value of the family unit, and a willingness to work together on its behalf. The marriage between Caleb and Susan Garth can perhaps be seen as the paradigm of these features. The narrator is at pains to draw the reader's attention to the virtues of both Garths, not just as individual characters, but in terms of their relationship to each other. Mrs Garth adored 'her husband's virtues, [and] she had very early made up her mind to his incapacity of minding his own interests, and had met the consequences cheerfully' (3.24; p.228). He in his turn

> would take no important step without consulting Susan ... With regard to a large number of matters about which other men are decided or obstinate, he was the most easily manageable man in the world. He never knew what meat he would choose, and if Susan had said that they ought to live in a four-roomed cottage, in order to save, he would have said, 'Let us go,' without inquiring into details.
> (6.56; p.529)

When we add to this those scenes in the novel that describe the Garth family at home, and the sense in which they are offered to us as an integrated, affectionate group, sharing in both the joys and the afflictions of their family life, we begin to see that the Garth family can be used as a measure for other marital and family relationships.

You may feel that this is to idealize and privilege the Garth family – and you would be right, but this is simply to reflect the way they are presented in the novel. With Mary and her parents, the narrator seems deliberately to blur the boundaries between fiction and reality and to suggest, if not that the Garths have an existence beyond the pages of the novel, then at least that they could and should. The reader is actually invited to find Mary Garth 'in the crowded street to-morrow, if [he or she is] there on the watch'. There is even a suggestion that we might speak to her, make her smile or make her angry, and 'if you did her a kindness, she would never forget it' (4.40; p.382). When Caleb is first introduced in the novel, the narrator provides a very careful account of how he puts his signature to Fred Vincy's bill, and adds in parenthesis, '(pardon these details for once – you would have learned to love them if you had known Caleb Garth)' (3.23; p.219). We can only guess at Eliot's motives for blurring the distinction between fictional and real lives. One reason is probably to enhance the realism of her representation by suggesting that the fictional characters have their counterparts in real life, but it is also likely that she is highlighting the special family virtues of the Garths. It is as if she is saying to her reader, 'This is the ideal. Do others measure up to it?' In almost all cases, the answer is 'Not quite'; the exception here is the marriage between Fred and Mary – though it isn't really appropriate to use this as a yardstick, since we see only their courtship, the marriage being summarized in the finale.

Thus, for example, the Vincys as a family, while financially and socially more successful than the Garths, are presented more critically. The Vincys are conscious 'of an inherent social superiority': Mrs Vincy frequently speaks of Mrs Garth 'as a woman who had had to work for her bread – meaning that Mrs Garth had been a teacher before her marriage; in which case an intimacy with Lindley Murray and Mangnall's "Questions" was something like a draper's discrimination of calico trade-marks ... no woman who was better off needed that sort of thing' (3.23; pp.217, 218). In comments such as this, the narrator's irony is directed towards an endorsement of the intelligence, integrity and independence of the Garths, whose married and professional lives are presented as a kind of template of the idea of service to and awareness of the needs of others; they, like Dorothea, have a deep awareness of these needs, which is one of the moral imperatives of this novel.

In marriage, more than in any other relationship the novel explores, it is the absence of this awareness of what the narrator calls the 'equivalent centre of self' (2.21; p.198) that is blamed for the tragedies of the unhappy marriages between Dorothea and Casaubon, and between Lydgate and Rosamond. Dorothea acquires an awareness of her husband's needs as separate from her own during their honeymoon in Rome, and Lydgate ultimately accepts his responsibility for Rosamond's happiness: 'He had chosen this fragile creature, and had taken the burthen of her life upon his arms. He must walk as he could, carrying that burthen pitifully' (8.81; p.752). The novel is clear-sighted in its presentation of the mistaken illusions that each character has of the married state. For Dorothea, 'the union which attracted her was one that would deliver her from her girlish subjection to her own ignorance, and give her the freedom of voluntary submission to a guide who would take her along the grandest path', while Mr Casaubon 'observed with pleasure that Miss Brooke showed an ardent submissive affection which promised to fulfil his most agreeable previsions of marriage' (1.3; p.27; 1.7; p.58). Rosamond's 'social romance ... had always turned on a lover and bridegroom who was not a Middlemarcher, and who had no connexions at all like her own: of late, indeed, the construction seemed to demand that he should somehow be related to a baronet', and Lydgate's illusion about Rosamond was that she possessed 'just the kind of intelligence one would desire in a woman – polished, refined, docile, lending itself to finish in all the delicacies of life' (1.12; p.109; 2.16; p.153). In each case, at an early stage in the presentation of each character, the reader is alerted to the knowledge that the expectations of marriage are both deluded and incompatible, and thus anticipates the doomed outcome of each relationship. This may mean that we read not so much to discover the outcome of each marriage, but more to trace the stages of its disintegration.

The two marriages invite comparison because of the careful way in which they are positioned in the novel. Each relationship is first presented separately, in books 1 and 2, and then gradually merged as the personal and professional lives of the four characters become linked. The relationship between Dorothea and Casaubon is explored first, with Casaubon's death occurring at the point in the novel where financial difficulties are beginning to threaten Lydgate's marital happiness (see the final paragraphs of book 5, chapters 46 and 49, respectively). We are therefore able to reflect on each relationship in the light of our response to the other. Thus, for example, Casaubon's useless research into the Key to all Mythologies, which has produced even in its author a 'despair which sometimes threatened him while toiling in the morass of authorship without seeming nearer to the goal', seems even more sterile when we read of Lydgate's confidence that 'the careful observation and inference which was his daily work, the use of the lens to further his judgment in special cases, would further his thought as an instrument of larger enquiry' (1.10; p.79; 2.15; p.137). The careful positioning also enables us to contrast the support given by the two wives to their husbands' work. Despite a growing awareness of the futility of her husband's research,

Dorothea begs Lydgate to advise her on how best she can help him: 'Advise me. Think what I can do. He has been labouring all his life and looking forward. He minds about nothing else. And I mind about nothing else –' (3.30; p.272). Rosamond, in contrast, is shown to have no understanding of Lydgate's vocation: 'Do you know, Tertius, I often wish you had not been a medical man.' Lydgate's reply pinpoints all that is wrong in their marriage: 'Nay, Rosy, don't say that ... That is like saying you wish you had married another man' (5.45; p.430).

Eliot also uses the character of Will Ladislaw as a structuring device to move the plot of the novel towards the resolution of relationships in the finale, as well as enabling the reader to use Will's perceptions as an additional tool to assess the nature of the two marriages being presented. Will is associated with all four major characters through the network of links that will be examined in more detail in chapter 11. He has family links with Casaubon, and social links with Lydgate and Rosamond – discussing politics with the one and singing and flirting with the other – and, of course, one of the major strands of the plot traces his emotional involvement with Dorothea. **How does the text of the novel draw attention to contrasts between Will and Casaubon, and to affinities between Will and Dorothea?**

Apart from the obvious difference between Will's youth and Casaubon's late middle age, the novel frequently associates Will with light and sunshine and Casaubon with dankness and gloom. As early as book 1, chapter 3, we are alerted to the 'ungauged reservoir of Mr Casaubon's mind', and as his wedding day approaches, the narrator comments on Casaubon's absence of delight in the prospects of his forthcoming marriage, finding such prospects less 'enchanting to him than the accustomed vaults where he walked taper in hand' (1.3; p.22; 1.10; p.78). The research he undertakes on his honeymoon confirms that he 'was lost among small closets and winding stairs ... With his taper stuck before him he forgot the absence of windows, and in bitter manuscript remarks on other men's notions about the solar deities, he had become indifferent to the sunlight' (2.20; p.185). Even his soul is associated with gloom: 'it went on fluttering in the swampy ground where it was hatched, thinking of its wings and never flying' (3.29; p.262). Will's 'sunshiny laughter' and 'sunny brightness' are explicitly contrasted with Casaubon's intellectual and emotional lack of light: 'When he turned his head quickly his hair seemed to shake out light ... Mr Casaubon, on the contrary, stood rayless' (2.19; p.179; 2.21; p.196). Will's presence is therefore used to remind the reader, as well as Dorothea herself, of the dark prison her marriage has become: 'the mere chance of seeing Will occasionally was like a lunette opened in the wall of her prison, giving her a glimpse of the sunny air' (4.37; p.339).

Dorothea and Will are associated through their youth and brightness. In contrast to the 'white vapour-walled landscape' of Lowick Manor, to which she returns after her honeymoon, she is described as 'glowing ... as only healthful youth can glow: there was gem-like brightness on her coiled hair and in her hazel eyes; there was warm red life in her lips' (3.28; pp.257, 256–7). Her aspirations, too, as expressed to Will, are voiced in terms of increasing light: 'That by desiring what is perfectly good, even when we don't quite know what it is and cannot do what we would, we are part of the divine power against evil –

widening the skirts of light and making the struggle with darkness narrower' (4.39; p.367). Small wonder, then, that the plot of the novel traces her progress from the darkness of her marriage with Casaubon to a life with Will 'filled ... with a beneficent activity' (8.finale; p.782).

Will's role in Lydgate and Rosamond's marriage is more problematic. Certainly, his association with Rosamond serves to highlight her selfishness and self-centredness. Indeed, the narrator observes that Will 'had more comprehension of Lydgate than Rosamond had ... easily imagining outdoor causes of annoyance' (6.58; p.555). You may feel, however, that his music-making and flirtation with Rosamond reflect as badly on him as they do on her, though the narrator confines herself to critical observation of Rosamond alone. Will's association with Lydgate serves to draw attention to the conflicts between independence and partisanship as they argue about their positions in relation to their respective sponsors. When Lydgate states that 'a man may work for a special end with others whose motives and general course are equivocal, if he is quite sure of his personal independence, and that he is not working for his private interest – either place or money' (5.46; p.438), the reader is reminded of the compromises made by both men: Lydgate has lost his independence by allying himself with Bulstrode to further his medical research, and Will has abandoned his high ideals to settle in Middlemarch and '[harness] himself with Mr Brooke' (5.47; p.440) so as to remain near to Dorothea. Will precipitates the crisis in Lydgate and Rosamond's marriage and in Dorothea and Casaubon's. That the outcomes in both cases are benign says a great deal about how we are encouraged to respond to him.

One aspect of marriage that English Victorian novels were unable to depict openly is sex – in marked contrast to later novels such as Zola's *Germinal*, where sexual acts, both within and outside marriage, are described in some detail. This is not to suggest that English novelists chose to ignore the nature of human sexuality, but rather that they chose more indirect methods of representing it in their fiction. Thomas Hardy's method of doing this in *Far from the Madding Crowd* is discussed in chapter 12. Many readers have felt that Eliot intended them to understand Mr Casaubon to be impotent, citing Dorothea's distress on her honeymoon in Rome as evidence. Part of this distress is linked to her 'deep impressions' of an 'unintelligible Rome' and its 'gigantic broken revelations' (2.20; p.181). Evidence of her husband's impotence is indirect, contained in the imagery of dank gloom referred to above, in the 'chill, colourless, narrowed landscape' (3.28; p.258) of her married home, and in the total lack of physical warmth between them. The only activity that appears to take place in their bedchamber is the annotation of his notebooks, and when she attempts to comfort him after Lydgate's visit he 'kept his hands behind him and allowed her pliant arm to cling with difficulty against his rigid arm' (4.42; p.398). Dorothea Barrett points out that the Dorothea in the novel is both sexually and vocationally passionate and that in marrying Casaubon,

> She is sacrificing the former passion for the latter. The pathos lies in the distance between the knowledge that narrator and reader share and Dorothea's lack of awareness ... she has no suspicion, as we have, that her sacrifice will be futile,

that neither her sexual nor her vocational needs will be satisfied by this marriage. (1989, p.128)

On the other hand, you may feel that the comment on Dorothea's pleasure in 'self-mortification' (1.2; p.17) when she speaks of giving up riding could refer also to the suppression of her sexuality in her marriage to Casaubon.

The narrator devotes considerable space to a discussion of Casaubon's jealousy of Will, and to his awareness of the age difference between himself and his young wife. One of the reasons he offers to himself for marriage is that 'he should receive family pleasures and leave behind him that copy of himself which seemed so urgently required of a man' (3.29; p.261), which seems to suggest that in theory, at least, Casaubon expects to consummate his marriage. But when the narrator goes on to express sorrow at his lack of powerful feeling, so that he is 'never to be fully possessed by the glory we behold, never to have our consciousness rapturously transformed into the vividness of a thought, the ardour of a passion' (3.29; p.263), she seems not only to be hinting at his impotence but also allowing that it is a tragedy for him as well as for Dorothea.

While Lydgate and Rosamond's marriage is marked by 'that total missing of each other's mental track', there is evidence of the physical warmth of the relationship. Lydgate's proposal of marriage is precipitated by his putting 'his arms round her, folding her gently and protectingly' (6.58; p.550; 3.31; p.283). Many pieces of dialogue between them include a phrase of narrative evoking this warmth of contact. Lydgate lets 'his hands fall on to his wife's shoulders', fastening her plaits and kissing 'the exquisite nape which was shown in all its delicate curves', putting his arm around her and asking for a kiss after their disagreement over their debts, and caressing her after another quarrel: 'Lydgate … pressed her delicate head against his cheek with his powerful tender hand' (5.43; p.411; 6.58; p.548; 6.58; p.561; 7.65; p.627). And when the bailiffs put a man in their house, he is shown joining Rosamond on their bed, letting 'his head fall beside hers' and weeping with her (7.69; p.659). In their last appearance in the novel before the finale, the image of the remainder of their married life together is expressed in physical terms as Lydgate takes 'the burthen of her life upon his arms' (8.81; p.752).

This is not to suggest that the novel is endorsing the idea that physical attraction and closeness are the most important aspects of marriage; the centrality of the concept of marriage as a relationship of mutual support is enough to rebut any such notion. But the emphasis on the physical warmth of one of the major marriage relations in the novel draws attention to its significant absence in the other, and also suggests that it is an aspect of marriage that the fiction cannot ignore. The fictional ideal that is presented in the novel consists of an awareness of the emotional, intellectual *and* physical needs of the other partner in the marriage.

Realism in fiction is complex and many-faceted. What the representations of work and marriage in *Middlemarch* show is something of the relationship between the fictional world and the world inhabited by readers of the novel. Such an overt narrative voice, constantly drawing attention to the complicity between narrator and reader, reminds us of the fictionality of what is portrayed, while the representation of the worlds of marriage and work, which have their parallels in the lives we actually lead, reminds us of the moral imperatives we can bring both to our reading of this novel and to our conduct and judgements in the world beyond the reading of fiction. These representations also serve to illuminate the nature of human aspirations and failings, and to suggest that these aspirations can reach their highest state in both professional and emotional experience. In this sense, *Middlemarch* is indeed a novel of vocation.

## *Middlemarch* and science: an experimental novel?

The years between the period in which *Middlemarch* was set and that in which it was written were marked by great changes in scientific and technological thinking (see Table 9.2 in chapter 9 of this volume), and both Eliot and her partner, Lewes, were familiar with the literature in which these new ideas were expounded. The novelist drew heavily on this new scientific knowledge when she wrote *Middlemarch* – so much so that Henry James, reviewing the novel in *Galaxy* in 1873, complained that it 'is too often an echo of Messrs Darwin and Huxley' (James, 1987, p.81). James's observation serves to show that the names of nineteenth-century scientists were sufficiently common currency for him to be sure that his readers would understand the point he was making, but it also shows the extent to which James failed to recognize the way scientific ideas, and indeed scientific language, are absolutely integral to the novel's workings. The problem for modern readers, most of whom will probably have 'science' and 'literature' in two separate mental compartments, is to grasp that for many Victorian writers and thinkers such categories were less distinct than they are now, and that science and literature had a shared language.

Although Eliot did not publicly expound a theory of the experimental novel, as Zola did, it is clear she felt there to be parallels between the writing of fiction and the work of the experimental scientist. In a letter written in 1876 to the positivist Frederic Harrison, she explained:

> My writing is simply a set of experiments in life – an endeavour to see what our thought and emotion may be capable of – what stores of motive, actual or hinted as possible, give promise of a better after which we may strive – what gains from past revelations and discipline we must strive to keep hold of as something more than shifting theory.

(in Eliot, 1954–78, vol.6, pp.216–17)

Her purpose in writing fiction, she seems to suggest here, is to investigate human behaviour to see whether she can discover a model or models that we can use to improve the ways in which we behave to our fellow human beings – to aim for 'the growing good of the world' (8.finale; p.785). Unlike the earlier novels of Jane Austen, Charlotte Brontë and Charles Dickens, which assume a shared set of religious and specifically Christian values, Eliot used aspects of scientific methodology based on secular humanist principles to see how any improvement might be achieved.

Although Eliot signalled her intention to explore 'the history of man, and how that mysterious mixture behaves under the varying experiments of Time' (prelude; p.3), it is only relatively recently, beginning in the 1970s, that critics have explored how the novelist deployed her knowledge of contemporary science. In his essay 'Optic and semiotic in *Middlemarch*', J. Hillis Miller concentrated on Eliot's striking use of optical imagery to show how constant shifts in perspective draw on her understanding of scientific method. He cites the image of microscope lenses of different strengths, which the narrator uses to explore Mrs Cadwallader's matchmaking (1.6; p.55; Miller, [1975] 1987, p.17). The stronger lens allows us to explore Mrs Cadwallader's behaviour in minute detail, and to gain a greater understanding of 'the play of minute causes' which produce it. Another crucial optical image in the novel is that of the pier-glass in the opening paragraph of book 3, chapter 27 (p.248). These images alert us to Eliot's method of suggesting that there are always alternative perspectives open to us. They are not simply about seeing, but are about interpretation.

Other studies of the novel have explored the use Eliot makes of nineteenth-century scientific ideas, particularly evolutionary theory. In her book *Darwin's Plots*, Gillian Beer (1983) shows how, in the nineteenth century, scientific texts could be – indeed often were – read as literature, while scientists drew on literary, historical and philosophical material as part of their argument. She argues that evolutionary theory had implications for narrative because of its preoccupation with time and change, and that it is 'a form of imaginative history'. It also gave authority to the ideas of cause and effect, and 'eschewed any notion of fore-ordained design' (ibid., p.8). The structure of *Middlemarch* will be discussed in detail in chapter 11, but you should be able to see in the broadest sense how Eliot's emphasis on the interconnectedness of human lives is essentially Darwinian in nature. Every action in her provincial society is both the cause and the effect of some other action: 'human lots ... were woven and interwoven' (2.15; p.132). The absence of preordained design, in the form of the Almighty, also shows itself in a series of chance encounters in the novel, all of which redirect the lives of characters into channels that were not what they had hoped or expected. Much of the early relationship between Lydgate and Rosamond can be seen in this way, though Rosamond is presented as the stronger species, who ultimately dominates her husband.

In the section of her book dealing with *Middlemarch*, Beer refers to the aspect of Darwin's argument that insists on variation being the key to evolutionary development. This idea is acknowledged in the prelude to the novel:

> if there were one level of feminine incompetence as strict as the ability to count three and no more, the social lot of women might be treated with scientific certitude. Meanwhile the indefiniteness remains, and the limits of variation are really much wider than any one would imagine from the sameness of women's coiffure and the favourite love-stories in prose and verse. (prelude; pp.3–4)

It is precisely because women cannot be analysed with 'scientific certitude' that the novelist is able to explore their diversity and to consider which species might evolve most effectively. In these terms, Rosamond is presented as coming from a long line of ornamental yet grasping women, who have been changed very little by social evolution and whose instincts for survival are highly developed.

Dorothea perhaps represents a different evolutionary strand, whose survival is less certain but whose long-term influence on 'the growing good of the world' is shown in the last paragraph of the novel to exist, though it is 'incalculably diffusive'. Scientific method, Eliot seems to be suggesting here, will carry us so far, but there comes a point where it simply will not provide a simple or a single explanation of human behaviour.

Beer's book provides many insights into *Middlemarch*, and there simply isn't the space to deal with all of them here. However, it is perhaps worth mentioning one further strand of Beer's argument here, since it is relevant to the secular morality on which the novel is based. She suggests that many writers of fiction in the second half of the nineteenth century were 'seeking sources of authoritative organization which could substitute for the god-like omnipotence and omniscience open to the theistic narrator' (Beer, 1983, p.160). Writers such as Eliot and Zola, she argues, sought to explore the natural laws that determined human behaviour. But both writers are also fascinated by the range of human diversity and by the workings of individual character. This makes, in Beer's words, 'for a painful display of energies between the scrupulous disclosures of law and the passionate unanswerable needs of human beings' (ibid., p.161). There is, in other words, a tension between the urge to find natural laws and the need to explore the nature of individuality. This tension is explored most completely in the novel in its representation of the character of Lydgate, himself a seeker after natural laws: 'he longed to demonstrate the more intimate relations of living structure, and help to define men's thought more accurately after the true order.' Lydgate's career exposes the limitations of scientific method, since he is an individual with 'both virtues and faults capable of shrinking or expanding'. Like so many of us, argues the narrator, he has 'better energies [which] are liable to lapse down the wrong channel under the influence of transient solicitations' (2.15; pp.139, 140).

Although she had been brought up as a devout evangelical Anglican, much of the reading Eliot did as a young woman, living with her father in Coventry, persuaded her that orthodox Christianity was no longer tenable; at the beginning of 1842, she refused to attend church with her father. Her reading began with works of biblical scholarship, such as John Pye Smith's *Relation between the Holy Scriptures and Some Parts of Geological Science* (1839) and Charles Hennell's *An Inquiry into the Origins of Christianity* (1841); this was followed, however, by a much wider course of scientific and philosophical reading and her own translation of Ludwig Feuerbach's *The Essence of Christianity*, which eventually appeared in 1854. Feuerbach's aim was 'to show that the antithesis of divine and human is altogether illusory, that it is nothing else than the antithesis between the human nature in general and the human individual' (Eliot's translation; quoted in Carroll, 1971, p.15). Her translation of Feuerbach was part of a lifelong enquiry – through her reading, her reviewing and her fictional writing – into an interpretative scheme that would explain the individual's place and role in the universe. If divinity and humanity are no longer meaningful distinctions, then divine rules no longer have relevance as control mechanisms for human behaviour. While the fictional world of Middlemarch predates most of the challenges that science and biblical scholarship were offering to Christian values, and although religious belief and churchgoing are presented as part of the fabric of provincial life, the novelist has to find an alternative set of values by which her characters can be judged. Caleb Garth's belief in his work as a virtual divinity, outlined in the preceding section, is an example of such values in operation.

There is no spiritual hereafter in *Middlemarch*; but ironically, although the novelist conducts her 'experiments in life' and makes great use of scientific analogies, her ultimate yardstick for judgement seems to derive more from St Paul's First Epistle to the Corinthians: 'Charity never faileth: but whether there be prophecies, they shall fail; whether there be tongues, they shall cease; whether there be knowledge, it shall vanish away' (13:8). The function of charity as a moral force in the novel will be discussed in greater detail in the next chapter. Here it will be enough to point out this duality in Eliot's realism, with its sympathetic and intuitive identification with the feelings of her characters, the narrator and the reader on the one hand, and the objectivity with which she tries to explain the forces that govern human behaviour on the other.

Another study of Eliot's relationship with and use of contemporary scientific ideas, Sally Shuttleworth's (1984) *George Eliot and Nineteenth-Century Science*, is concerned to explore Victorian ideas of organic social harmony. These ideas drew on nineteenth-century theories in biological science which stressed the interdependence of parts and whole in any organism, and transferred this to notions of society to explore the relationship between individuals and the society in which they lived. Eliot's partner, Lewes, wrote extensively on this topic, noting how, in contemporary social theory, 'The part exists only as part of the whole; the whole exists only as a whole of its parts' (Lewes, quoted in Shuttleworth, 1984, p.147). Lewes's observation shows how social science used a scientific analogy to explore the ways in which society was constructed, but, as Shuttleworth points out, Eliot used his ideas to write *Middlemarch* as if it were modelled on a scientific experiment. In *Middlemarch*, she explores the idea of organic union between the individual and society; it was the narrator's intention to watch 'keenly the stealthy convergence of human lots ... a slow preparation of effects from one life on another' (1.11; p.88).

Shuttleworth also points out that *Middlemarch*, largely through its presentation of Lydgate, is innovatory in having science itself as a theme. Lydgate, like his creator, is 'early bitten with an interest in structure' (2.17; p.161), but unlike her, he seems unable to understand that he himself is part of the social structure in which he has chosen to carry out his research. **Now reread the finale of the novel, and then read Sally Shuttleworth, '*Middlemarch*: an experiment in time' (1984, pp.143–55; extract in Regan, 2001). How far do you think the novel achieves 'the traditional realist demand for moral closure' (Shuttleworth, 1984, p.151)?**

Shuttleworth believes the result of Eliot's 'experiment' in the novel is to show that the interconnectedness between all parts of Middlemarch society is based on conflict and that therefore the familiar moral closure of many nineteenth-century novels cannot be achieved. Good does not always triumph, the wicked do not always receive their just deserts, and marriage does not always mean a life lived happily ever after. Eliot cannot entirely resist elements of the happy ending, and this is shown in her idealized account of the 'solid mutual happiness' of Fred and Mary, and the image of the two lovers at Stone Court 'in white-haired placidity' (8.finale; pp.779, 781). But Rosamond's domination of Lydgate is shown to be complete; she is always able to 'frustrate him by stratagem', while he compromises all his early scientific principles, dies early and angrily, seeing his wife as the basil plant 'which had flourished wonderfully on a murdered man's brains' (8.finale; pp.781–2, 782). (The reference is to John Keats's poem 'Isabella, or the Pot of Basil', in which the heroine's lover is murdered, his head cut off and buried in a pot, with a basil plant on top.) It is in her account of Dorothea that the novelist perhaps struggles most to achieve a moral and harmonious closure, and the honesty of the novelist as scientific experimenter contends with the writer of realist fiction as she refuses to make a clear and unambiguous statement about what Dorothea's life has achieved. The experimental scientist is still there in the penultimate paragraph: 'there is no creature whose inward being is so strong that it is not greatly determined by what lies outside it', and while she acknowledges that Dorothea's 'finely-touched spirit had still its fine issues', her actual achievement, however lyrically the novelist expresses it, is still seen in terms of organic theory – 'the effect of her being on those around her was incalculably diffusive' (8.finale; pp.784–5, 785). Only in the word 'incalculably' does the novelist seem to acknowledge that scientific experiment can never provide a complete answer.

*Middlemarch* can be described as an experimental novel in several ways. It engages with contemporary scientific ideas both as a theme and as a means of structuring its narrative, and these scientific ideas are embedded in the actual language of the novel in a way that may challenge conventional notions of realism; Eliot's use of the variable magnification of lenses, which has already been discussed, is a small example of this. The label 'experimental novel' is not, however, adequate on its own. *Middlemarch* is also a provincial and historical novel, as well as a novel about vocation in the widest sense. That it is also a superbly crafted text and a powerfully moral novel should emerge from the discussion in the next chapter.

# Works cited

Barrett, Dorothea. 1989. *Vocation and Desire: George Eliot's Heroines*, London: Routledge.

Beer, Gillian. 1983. *Darwin's Plots: Evolutionary Narrative in Darwin, George Eliot and Nineteenth-Century Fiction*, London: Routledge.

Carroll, David. Ed. 1971. *George Eliot: The Critical Heritage*, London: Routledge.

Eliot, George. 1954–78. *The George Eliot Letters*, ed. by Gordon Haight, 9 vols, New Haven: Yale University Press.

Eliot, George. [1872] 1998. *Middlemarch*, ed. by David Carroll, with an introduction by Felicia Bonaparte, 3rd impression, Oxford World's Classics, Oxford: Oxford University Press.

James, Henry. 1987. '*Middlemarch*' (review), in *The Critical Muse: Selected Literary Criticism*, Harmondsworth: Penguin. (Extract in Regan, 2001.)

Miller, J. Hillis. [1975] 1987. 'Optic and semiotic in *Middlemarch*', in *George Eliot's 'Middlemarch'*, ed. by Harold Bloom, Philadelphia: Chelsea House.

Regan, Stephen. Ed. 2001. *The Nineteenth-Century Novel: A Critical Reader*, London: Routledge.

Shuttleworth, Sally. 1984. '*Middlemarch*: an experiment in time', in *George Eliot and Nineteenth-Century Science: The Make-Believe of a Beginning*, Cambridge: Cambridge University Press. (Extract in Regan, 2001.)

Suggestions for further reading can be found at the end of chapter 11.

# Networks and narrative in *Middlemarch*

*by Nora Tomlinson*

## The writing and publishing of *Middlemarch*

*Middlemarch* began its life as two separate narratives. George Eliot's journal at the beginning of 1869 refers to the writing of a projected novel called 'Middlemarch' as one of her tasks for the year, and she began writing it in that July. By September she had written the first three chapters of what later becomes the Lydgate strand of the novel, but, distracted and depressed by the illness and death of her partner George Henry Lewes's son, affectionately known as 'Thornie', she made very slow progress. In November of the following year, she began 'Miss Brooke' as a separate story, and made much more rapid progress with this, reaching the middle of chapter 10 by the end of the year, and chapter 18 by March 1871. By this time, it was clear to her that the two stories could be intertwined, and by the end of June books 1 and 2 were finished, and the rest of the novel was clear in her mind. It was also clear to her that she needed something longer than the more usual three-volume novel to provide her with the space her new narrative required. This prompted Lewes – who for this novel, as for the rest of her fiction, acted as Eliot's literary agent – to write to her publisher Blackwood, with a proposal that *Middlemarch* be published in eight instalments (that is, in eight books, which he called 'half-volume parts') at two-monthly intervals, with final publication in four volumes, rather than the customary three:

> Mrs Lewes finds that she will require 4 volumes for her story, not 3. I winced at the idea at first, but the story must not be spoiled for want of space, and as you have more than once spoken of the desirability of inventing some mode of circumventing the Libraries and making the public *buy* instead of borrowing, I have devised the following scheme ... namely to publish in *half-volume parts* ... Each part would have a certain unity and completeness in itself with separate titles. Thus the work is called Middlemarch.
>
> (in Eliot, 1954–78, vol.5, pp.144–5)

What Lewes was proposing was in fact what John Sutherland calls 'an experiment in serialisation' (1976, p.198). It meant that, unlike Charles Dickens and Wilkie Collins, Eliot would not be required to write her story to a preset page-length for each projected part – 'ten or so pages either way would not matter' (ibid., p.196). Furthermore, the organization of the chapters into eight books – 'what had begun as a practical way of getting round problems of narrative lumpiness' – 'became, finally the way in which George Eliot "thought" about her work and its organisation' (ibid., p.205). Once the two stories had been merged into one novel, the writing seems to have proceeded smoothly and rapidly; the finale of the novel was posted to Blackwood on 2 October 1872, less than two years after she had begun the 'Miss Brooke' story. Although the writing process sounds fairly fraught – Eliot was still writing the later books of the novel after the earlier books had appeared in print – she never missed a deadline, though sometimes she came perilously close; book 8, for example, was sent to the publisher in four sections between 2 and 13 September, and was published in December. It is no surprise that she felt the need for the greater space that the eight books of the novel gave her; it is perhaps surprising, though, that she was willing to allow the novel to be published in parts, since her only other experience of this, with *Romola*, had proved very worrying and stressful. The writing of *Middlemarch* seems to have been an altogether easier experience for her. The experiment was also a commercial success; *Middlemarch* published in parts was a sell-out. (The publication of the novel is discussed in more detail in chapter 8 above.)

## How *Middlemarch* is organized

Henry James, reviewing *Middlemarch* in *Galaxy* in March 1873, described the novel as 'a treasure-house of detail but ... an indifferent whole' (James, 1987, p.75). The early struggles with the writing, the amalgamation of two distinct stories and the speed with which the novel was completed once these two stories were merged might well have led to the kind of writing James describes. However, the notebooks in which Eliot made notes towards the writing of the novel, with their outline of the contents of each chapter, suggest that she took great care to integrate all the elements of an extremely complicated narrative. Although book 5 is the first place in which all the narrative strands come together in one book, from book 2 onwards no one of the three main stories – Dorothea/Casaubon, Lydgate/Rosamond and Fred/Mary – is absent from an individual book.

## *Networks*

Eliot used a range of structuring devices to organize her material, and perhaps the most important of these arises almost organically from the subject matter of the novel itself. *Middlemarch* is subtitled *A Study of Provincial Life*: drawing on Darwinian ideas of evolutionary development and Lewes's discussion of organic theory (see the discussion on these ideas towards the end of chapter 10 above), Eliot underpins her novel with a network of professional, family and social links, which draw together all the elements of the fictional life of town and country. That this was deliberate can be seen clearly in some of the observations on narrative method she gives to her narrator. In chapter 11, which is really the first of the chapters describing Middlemarch society, she writes of 'the stealthy convergence of human lots' and the 'slow preparation of effects from one life on another' (Eliot, [1872] 1998, 1.11, p.08, all subsequent page references are to this edition), while in chapter 15, which offers a full account of Lydgate's history and aspirations, she describes her task as the 'unravelling [of] human lots, and seeing how they were woven and interwoven' into 'this particular web' (2.15; p.132). Both observations convey a powerful sense of the way in which every human life is inextricably bound up with the lives of others.

That this interconnectedness is more than simply a device for structuring her fiction is clear from an assertion made by the narrator as Dorothea watches Peter Featherstone's funeral: 'Scenes which make vital changes in our neighbours' lot are but the background of our own, yet, like a particular aspect of the fields and trees, they become associated for us with the epochs of our own history, and make a part of that unity which lies in the selection of our keenest consciousness' (4.34; p.306). This does not just prefigure the effects of Featherstone's death on Fred and Mary, but hints at the more indirect effects events may have on other fictional lives, by bringing to light the existence of Rigg and Raffles and the impact of their actions on Bulstrode and Lydgate. The narrator's comment also suggests that the model for this kind of interconnectedness is not merely an aesthetic device or an abstraction based on organic theory, but that it is a model drawn from her own experience, and one that will be familiar to her readers. It is worth considering in some detail how these networks of links – professional, family and social – actually operate.

## *Professional links*

Some of the leading characters in the novel have professions that bring them into contact with other characters. Listing some of these characters' professional contacts will show how strongly they bear on the events of the novel. Not surprisingly, such a list, although not intended to be exhaustive, consists entirely of men! It does, however, serve to illustrate some of the interconnectedness of these provincial fictional lives.

As a doctor, Lydgate has professional links with Mr Bulstrode, Peter Featherstone, Fred Vincy, Mr Casaubon and Sir James Chettam. He becomes associated in the minds of Middlemarchers with Mr Bulstrode from the moment he votes with him on the question of Tyke's chaplaincy, and thus his career and eventual downfall is inextricably linked with the banker's. Indeed the narrator reminds us, in case we had forgotten, that despite Lydgate's avowed desire for independence, he cannot help but feel 'the hampering threadlike pressure of small social conditions, and their frustrating complexity' (2.18; p.169). Rosamond first meets him when he pays a professional visit to Featherstone, and his emotional entanglement with her begins when he is called in to the house during Fred's illness. He is called in to see Mr Casaubon, and this begins his association with Dorothea, with all that this later entails for his marriage and Dorothea's marriage to Will Ladislaw. As a land-agent and surveyor, Caleb Garth works with or for Sir James Chettam, Mr Brooke, Mr Bulstrode, Dorothea and

Fred Vincy. It is Garth's refusal to continue to work for Bulstrode after he has listened to Raffles that gives substance to the rumours leading to Bulstrode's downfall. Because Fred works for Garth, he discovers his true vocation and thus is able to marry Mary. Ladislaw, as a newspaper editor and political reformer, works with Mr Brooke, and thus remains in touch with Dorothea, irritates Mr Casaubon and causes him to change his will. As a banker, Mr Bulstrode exerts a great deal of influence in the town. He persuades Lydgate to join him in planning the infirmary, and responds to appeals from Mr Vincy, who is his brother-in-law as well as his debtor, to refute rumours that Fred has been boasting about his expectations from Featherstone.

## Family links

**Try to establish clearly in your own mind some of the important family links in the novel. Probably the easiest way to do this is to draw a few diagrams of family connections, showing who was married to whom, and in what order. Again, consider the influence of some of these connections on the plot of the novel.**

This is quite a complicated activity, but one that is well worth doing because, as with the professional links, it uncovers some of the complexities of the plot and shows the force of unexpected family connections. Some of these links are highlighted in Figure 11.1. Notice particularly how Bulstrode's first and second marriages connect him both to Will Ladislaw and to the Vincys (see Figure 11.1a and 11.1c), and that although both of Peter Featherstone's marriages are childless, his one illegitimate child, Joshua Rigg, is both the means by which Fred Vincy is denied a large legacy from his uncle, and also the means by which his stepfather, Raffles, returns to persecute Bulstrode (see Figure 11.1b and 11.1c). The network of family relationships also provides the basis for some of Eliot's finest comic writing, in the form of her observations on the 'nice distinctions of rank in Middlemarch' (3.23; p.217), such as that existing between the Vincys and the Garths, and between the relatives assembled to wait for the death of Featherstone in book 3, chapter 32, and for the reading of his will in book 4, chapter 35.

## Social links

To these two networks of professional and family links can be added a third: social links. Thus, for example, Will Ladislaw mixes with visitors at Mr Brooke's house, with Miss Henrietta Noble on her missions of charity and with Rosamond and Lydgate. Rosamond keeps him in constant touch, not with Dorothea herself, but with a knowledge of her whereabouts, whilst Lydgate provides the final obstacle to the love that Dorothea and Will have for each other. Mr Farebrother is a friend both to Lydgate and to the Garth family. As the first he provides an ironic commentary on the difficulties of independence, and as the second he is the means of bringing Fred and Mary together. Finally, there are the networks of gossiping neighbours, which work so powerfully upon the reputations of Lydgate and Bulstrode.

In *George Eliot and Nineteenth-Century Science*, Sally Shuttleworth (1984) argues that gossip is another structuring device in Eliot's study of the interconnectedness of provincial life, and that this reflects the contemporary scientific theory of organic interdependence. 'Though the majority of characters in [chapter 71] scarcely know of each other's existence, they are all linked together by the connecting chain of opinion' (Shuttleworth, 1984, p.148). **Reread book 7, chapter 71, and identify each of the strands of Middlemarch society involved in this gossip and the impact each strand has on the lives of Bulstrode, Lydgate and Ladislaw.**

First, there is what might be termed the professional gossip of draper, horse-dealer and town clerk – men who socially have little to do with each other: this exposes Bulstrode's past and his role in Ladislaw's history, and points the finger of suspicion at Bulstrode and Lydgate over the death of Raffles. The gossip, as the narrator reminds her readers, 'was mainly what we know', but its impact is dramatic as it 'spread through Middlemarch like the smell of fire' (7.71; pp.674, 675). Further investigation by the town clerk, Frank Hawley, uncovers Caleb Garth's resignation as Bulstrode's agent, and the inference drawn from this is passed to one of the Middlemarch doctors, Mr Toller, who in turn passes it on, 'until it had quite lost the stamp of an inference' (7.71; p.675). Then there is the female domestic gossip of 'wives, widows, and single ladies [who] took their work and went out to tea oftener than usual' (7.71; p.676), which associates Bulstrode's loan to Lydgate with medical as well as financial scandal; this is reinforced by medical gossip as the town's doctors discuss Raffles's illness. There is the tavern gossip of the Tankard in Slaughter Lane, reported at length, which is blackly funny in its distortion of known facts. Finally there is the county gossip, which 'had been carried to Lowick Parsonage on one side and to Tipton Grange on the other' (7.71; p.680). The narrator makes the point that the gossip 'had been the common theme among all classes in the town' (ibid.), and the chapter links all aspects of Middlemarch society as well as most of its named major and minor characters in a way that seems genuinely organic. And, like a living organism, the gossip grows and feeds both on itself and on the community which disseminates it.

This is by no means an exhaustive account of the ways in which the fictional lives of Middlemarchers are inextricably linked; as you read and reread the novel, you will discover many other examples. But there should be enough here to convince you of how tightly and carefully Eliot structures the fabric of her 'provincial life' and how this fabric is an essential element in shaping and exposing the interdependence of Middlemarch lives. There is, as she wrote in *Felix Holt, the Radical*, the novel that preceded *Middlemarch*, 'no private life which has not been determined by a wider public life' (Eliot, [1866] 1988, 1.3; p.43), and the web of connections is both background to the novel and a tool by which its fictional lives are shaped. Into this web of connections come several outsiders who both influence and are influenced by the provincial life they join.

The role of outsider is a tool often used to challenge the status quo; the character of Étienne in Émile Zola's *Germinal* is used in this way, for example. It is worth looking at how Eliot uses those who come from outside the provincial life of Middlemarch, not only as instruments of plot to move the action forward,

## (a) WILL'S FAMILY

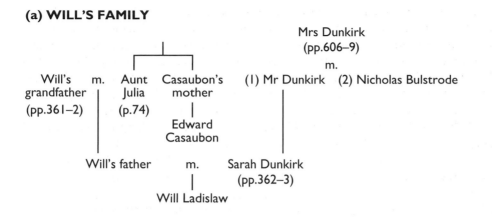

## (b) FEATHERSTONE'S WILL

Peter Featherstone  —  Rigg's mother  m.  Raffles

Joshua Rigg
(illegitimate son and heir to
Featherstone, pp.407–9)

## (c) THE GARTHS AND THE VINCYS

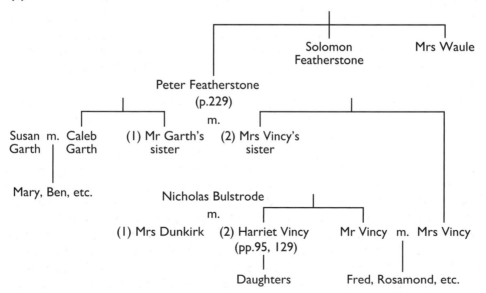

*Figure 11.1    A rough guide to some of the family links in* Middlemarch

but also to show how human lots are 'woven and interwoven'. **Which characters are explicitly recognized by the plot of the novel as outsiders to its fictional world, and what impact do they have on the plot?**

At the end of the opening paragraph of the first chapter of book 2, Eliot describes how Bulstrode is viewed by Middlemarchers:

> Mr Bulstrode's close attention was not agreeable to the publicans and sinners in Middlemarch; it was attributed by some to his being a Pharisee, and by others to his being Evangelical. Less superficial reasoners among them wished to know who his father and grandfather were, observing that five-and-twenty years ago nobody had ever heard of a Bulstrode in Middlemarch. (2.13; pp.115–16)

This observation, while it gently mocks the conservatism of the general view that Bulstrode is still an outsider after twenty-five years in Middlemarch, also highlights the general suspicion of him held by the town's 'Less superficial reasoners'. Even his second wife is aware 'that her husband's earlier connexions were not quite on a level with her own' (6.61; p.576). She 'liked to think that it was well in every sense for Mr Bulstrode to have won the hand of Harriet Vincy; whose family was undeniable in a Middlemarch light – a better light surely than any thrown in London thoroughfares or dissenting chapelyards' (ibid.). It is this tendency to distrust Bulstrode, together with a general ignorance of his life and actions before he came to Middlemarch, that causes the gossip about him to 'spread through Middlemarch like the smell of fire', in the process tarnishing not only his own reputation but also the reputations of Lydgate and Ladislaw, who are caught in its spread. Eliot's presentation of Bulstrode is far too subtle and complex to suggest a simple causal link between his position as an outsider and his inevitable downfall, and she credits her reader with the intelligence to recognize the complexities of his position. In a long analysis of Bulstrode's character and motives, in which the narrator discusses his past life and aspirations and his current difficulties with the attempts of Raffles to blackmail him, he is described as 'a man whose desires had been stronger than his theoretic beliefs, and who had gradually explained the gratification of his desires into satisfactory agreement with those beliefs' (6.61; p.581). While the narrator may be prepared to explain Bulstrode's behaviour, it is made absolutely clear that, because he is an outsider, Middlemarchers are not prepared to make any such allowances.

Whether Ladislaw should be considered as one of the outsiders to Middlemarch is debatable, since, as Figure 11.1a shows, he is directly related to Casaubon and has been educated at Casaubon's expense. He is not a Middlemarcher by birth or upbringing, but is shown to fit easily into a wide circle of Middlemarch society, including that of Mr Brooke, the Farebrothers and Lydgate and Rosamond. But as with Bulstrode, nobody knows who his father was, except that he was Polish and a musician, and consequently he is not uniformly welcomed. Sir James Chettam, who mentally refers to him as '*that* Ladislaw!' (6.54; p.513), views him as 'not a man we can take into the family. At least, I must speak for myself ... I suppose others will find his society too pleasant to care about the propriety of the thing' (8.84; p.767). Ladislaw is caught up in the swirl of rumour and gossip that accompanies Raffles's death. Even Mr Farebrother acknowledges Will's extraordinary 'queer genealogy', and in terms that sound almost anti-Semitic – 'A high-spirited young lady and a musical Polish patriot made a likely enough stock for him to spring from, but I should never have suspected a grafting of the Jew pawnbroker' – while Mr Hawley lumps him in with 'Any cursed alien blood, Jew, Corsican, or Gypsy' (7.71; p.676). Will's awareness that 'the Middlemarch tribes of Toller, Hackbutt, and the rest ... looked down on him as an adventurer' (6.60; p.567), and that Sir James never liked him, is in part responsible for the disappearance of Will and Dorothea from the Middlemarch scene at the end of the novel, he to become 'an ardent public man' and she to provide him with 'wifely help' (8.finale; pp.782, 783). Will is never assimilated into Middlemarch provincial life, and whatever his political achievements might be, they cannot be attained or sustained there.

Lydgate is the most visible outsider in the novel, visible because he was 'altogether foreign to Middlemarch, carrying a certain air of distinction congruous with good family, and possessing connexions which offered vistas of that middle-class heaven, rank' (1.12; p.110). There was also a 'general impression that Lydgate was something rather more uncommon than any general practitioner in Middlemarch' (2.15; p.133). He arrives in Middlemarch determined to retain his independence, both medically and emotionally, and 'to win celebrity ... by the independent value of his work' (2.15; p.136). A conflict is set up in which Lydgate's wholly admirable medical aspirations are placed in opposition to the forces of provincial life: and it is precisely the qualities that single him out as a newcomer to Middlemarch that bring about his downfall. Rosamond sees him as a means of achieving greater social status and escaping provincial life altogether; Bulstrode sees him as the means by which one of his philanthropic projects, the new hospital, can be advanced; and Lydgate's new approach to medical procedures ensures that he is misunderstood both by other doctors in the town and by many of his patients. Marriage to Rosamond embroils him in financial difficulties, while his association with Bulstrode proves extremely damaging to his reputation after the death of Raffles. The point here is that, as with Bulstrode, Eliot uses Lydgate's status as outsider as an essential element in the construction of this fictional world and the plotting of the novel.

Bulstrode, Ladislaw and Lydgate are all fully integrated into the social fabric of Eliot's fictional world; Rigg, too, might be said to have a place in it simply because he is Peter Featherstone's illegitimate son. However, both he and his stepfather, Raffles, seem much more a contrivance of plotting than do any of the major characters. Rigg first appears, in book 4, at his father's funeral and is immediately identified as an outsider by Mrs Cadwallader: 'there is a new face ... queerer than any of them: a little round head with bulging eyes – a sort of frog-face ... He must be of another blood' (4.34; p.308). His presence is also marked by other mourners as 'a new legatee; else why was he bidden as a mourner? Here were new possibilities, raising a new uncertainty' (4.35; p.312). And just in case her readers have not appreciated Rigg's importance, the narrator highlights the impact of an outsider on a hitherto familiar situation: 'We are all humiliated by the sudden discovery of a fact which has existed very comfortably and perhaps been staring at us in private while we have been making up our world entirely without it' (ibid.). This is almost heavy-handed, and it is no surprise that Featherstone's money is left to Rigg rather than to Fred. However, there is another glimpse of the plotting machinery at work at the end of the same chapter, when the narrator reminds the reader that 'Another stranger had been brought to settle in the neighbourhood of Middlemarch', but adding, somewhat portentously, 'No soul was prophetic enough to have any foreboding as to what might appear on the trail of Joshua Rigg' (4.35; p.320).

If Rigg's role in the novel appears at least partially to be no more than the mechanics of plot, then the role of his stepfather, Raffles, seems entirely mechanical and his appearances largely coincidental. However, it is clear that for Eliot coincidence was an acceptable and legitimate structural tool. Chapter 41 provides a brief history of the relationship between Rigg and Raffles. After referring to the exchange of letters between Rigg and Bulstrode about the sale of Stone Court, the reader is offered a paragraph on the nature of coincidence:

> Who shall tell what may be the effect of writing? ... it may end by letting us into the secrets of usurpations and other scandals gossiped about long empires ago: – this world being apparently a huge whispering-gallery ... a bit of ink and paper which has long been an innocent wrapping or stop-gap may at last be laid open under the one pair of eyes which have knowledge enough to turn it into the opening of a catastrophe. (4.41; p.386)

This is a clear enough signpost: when we are told at the end of the chapter that Raffles leaves Stone Court with a small flask wedged into its leather cover by a letter signed 'Nicholas Bulstrode', and that 'Raffles was not likely to disturb it from its present useful position' (4.41; p.390), we can feel the threat to Bulstrode poised like a sword of Damocles. That Raffles is Rigg's stepfather strains our credulity. That he is also the individual ordered to seek Mrs Dunkirk's daughter and then paid by Bulstrode 'for keeping silence and carrying himself away' (6.61; p.580) seems very unlikely indeed.

The point to note here is not that this mechanistic approach to structure in any way supports Henry James's criticism about the novel being an 'indifferent whole', but rather that Eliot combines two very different approaches to the structuring of her fiction. By using the natural networks of professional, family and social links she reinforces the reader's sense of entering a familiar world. In contrast, by drawing our attention to the devices of the outsider and of coincidence she draws aside this realist veil by foregrounding the actual mechanics and structure of her novel. It is a measure of her success that for the greater part of this very long novel, these two approaches work together extremely well. Only in some of the episodes concerning Raffles does the split appear obvious – and even here, Eliot's skilful handling of the circumstances of his death and the operations of gossip after it largely disguise any uneasiness over Raffles's role.

## *The image of the web*

By now, you have probably become fairly adroit at identifying ways in which Eliot organizes the complex structure of *Middlemarch* into a unifying whole, and for every technique that has been identified here, you should be able to supply your own examples from the text of the novel. Most of these techniques have been on a large scale, using networks of family and community. Another unifying device is the use of repeated images. As we have seen in chapter 10 above, Eliot was familiar with the writings of Charles Darwin. One of Darwin's ideas that she transfers to her own fiction is the idea of 'entanglement', which manifests itself in a web of complex relationships. In her book *Darwin's Plots*, Gillian Beer (1983) explores Eliot's use of Darwin's idea of the web both as a theme and as a structuring tool. In a study of provincial society, the image of the web ensures that theme and structure are inextricably linked and illuminate each other: 'The recurrent imagery of the web suggests simultaneously entanglement and creative order – and beyond them both, the web of human veins and tissues: human beings' (Beer, 1983, p.179). Eliot's use of the image demonstrates its flexibility and suggestiveness. It can be used on a grand scale to suggest the task of the novelist 'in unravelling human lots' and in concentrating 'on this particular web' (2.15; p.132). It can also be used on a rather smaller scale to illustrate the relationships between individuals, as well as their place in the larger scheme of things. **Now read Gillian Beer, '*Middlemarch*: the web of affinities' (1983, pp.167–80; extract in Regan, 2001), and then reread the paragraph in book 4, chapter 36, beginning 'The accepted lover ...' and ending '... of formal announcement' (p.325). How does the web image operate to inform the reader about Lydgate and Rosamond's courtship? What does it suggest about their future life together?**

The web is gossamer, which suggests both beauty and fragility, and its anchoring points are 'scarcely perceptible'. It is a web full of potential, 'made of spontaneous beliefs and indefinable joys, yearnings of one life towards another, visions of completeness, indefinite trust'. However, the web has two elements: Lydgate and Rosamond both spin their dreams, and these are both part of 'the mutual web' and yet incompatible. The narrator tells us, if we had not already guessed, that Lydgate has learned nothing from his experience with Laure, and confirms Rosamond's total self-centredness: 'she was in the water-lily's expanding wonderment at its own fuller life'. This web is surely a spider's web, rather than woven fabric, and while such webs are miracles of careful construction and transient beauty, they are also instruments of entrapment; the image, introduced with heavy irony by the narrator and reinforced by the exclamation mark, suggests that Lydgate and Rosamond are busy constructing their own doom. They are caught in the web of each other's imaginings, unaware of the greater web of the provincial society in which their courtship takes place. The individual web image reminds the reader of the wider web – both the fabric of Middlemarch society and the plot of the novel, which demonstrates the inescapable interconnectedness of human lives.

There is more that could be said about the possibilities the web image evokes here, and your own reading will have raised points other than the ones in the preceding paragraph. Beer points to a range of 'common contiguous metaphors (tree, family, web, labyrinth)' (1983, p.170), and as you reread the novel and encounter these images, think about how they operate, both thematically and structurally, to contribute to the reader's response. Think also about how such an image might contribute to the question of what kind of novel *Middlemarch* is. When the image reinforces our idea of the interconnectedness of Middlemarch life, it adds to our feeling that this is indeed a provincial novel. Because the web and its associated images, such as the labyrinth, are found in many myths, our sense of *Middlemarch* as a novel that is more epic than realist is enhanced. And because the web image figures so prominently in Darwin's scientific writing, our understanding of *Middlemarch* as an experimental novel may be increased. However we respond, it seems inevitable that our awareness of the novel's richness and complexity will be confirmed.

# The narrative voice in *Middlemarch*

Any discussion of the coherence of *Middlemarch* and the way in which the novel is organized would be incomplete without considering the operation of its narrator. The voice of the third-person narrator in *Middlemarch* is a striking one, perhaps one of the most striking voices in any fiction in English. **Now reread book 2, chapter 15. How you would describe the voice of the narrator?**

You may have been struck first of all by how much of the chapter consists of the narrator directly addressing the reader; there is relatively little dialogue here, which suggests that the reader is deliberately being placed in an active role in responding to the novel. The voice is also authoritative: this narrator knows exactly what they're doing. The familiarity with the work of Henry Fielding, the eighteenth-century novelist, together with the willingness to reject his 'remarks and digressions' (2.15; p.132) as a role model, suggests a wide-ranging familiarity with a whole range of English fiction, together with a confidence that allows for a new, distinctive narrative method and voice. Fielding's voice is not appropriate for the task Eliot has set herself because, instead of writing a piece of descriptive history, the narrator is involved in a much more active 'study' or experiment, which is not to be dispersed 'over that tempting range of relevancies called the universe' (ibid.). The task is to 'make the new settler Lydgate better known to anyone interested in him than he could possibly be even to those who had seen the most of him since his arrival in Middlemarch' (ibid.). The narrator's voice is also authoritative because it claims to know more about Lydgate than do any of the fictional characters with whom he interacts in the novel. This is not because Eliot pretends to be one of the Middlemarch citizens, but rather because the voice she crafts openly acknowledges its role as the creator of a fictional world. At the end of the chapter, Eliot reminds us both of her role as a storyteller and of our role as readers of her story. Lydgate's medical aspirations have been very clearly articulated and his chances of success laid before the reader as 'a fine subject for betting' (2.15; p.140), yet we can guess that these achievements will not come to fruition, since we have already been told more about Lydgate's 'spots of commonness' (ibid.) than the inhabitants of Middlemarch can possibly know, and can see that Middlemarch may very well 'swallow' him. The reader's response to the story, like the development of a fictional character, 'is a process and an unfolding' (ibid.).

The voice is confident and often amused, gently mocking the attitudes of Middlemarch inhabitants, particularly its women, towards its doctors: 'For everybody's family doctor was remarkably clever, and was understood to have immeasurable skill in the management and taming of the most skittish or vicious diseases' (2.15; p.133). The confidence is also demonstrated in the assured way in which Lydgate's strengths and weaknesses are outlined for us, showing that 'he meant to be a unit who would make a certain amount of difference towards that spreading change which would one day tell appreciably upon the average', but also showing, through his affair with the actress Laure, that he is prone to 'the sudden impulse of a madman' (2.15; pp.137, 143). Humour and confidence are both deployed in the penultimate paragraph of the chapter, where the narrator is ironic about Lydgate's mistaken belief that he has learned from his experience: 'henceforth he would take a strictly scientific view of woman, entertaining no expectations but such as were justified beforehand' (2.15; p.144). Alert readers will recognize an echo of Eliot's making reference in the prelude to *Middlemarch* to the notion that women's natures can be defined with 'scientific certitude' (prelude; p.4).

There are two further features of the narrator's presence in this chapter which it may perhaps be surprising to find deployed together: this narrator is formidably well-informed, yet also on intimate terms with the reader. Consider the range of knowledge that is brought to this chapter. There is an easy familiarity with the literary texts that the young Lydgate might have been expected to read. There is a sound knowledge of early nineteenth-century medical education and research, together with apparently casual use of quotations from King James I, a translation of the Latin inscription on the tombstone of the astronomer Herschel, a comparison of research in pathology with early voyages of discovery, and references to the contemporary fields of ideas and music encountered by Lydgate in Paris. So much learning might appear daunting were it not so easily integrated into the fabric of her account of Lydgate's upbringing, and all these details serve to add to the authenticity of the character the narrator is presenting.

Readers might be in danger of feeling overwhelmed by the sheer volume of learning that underpins not only this chapter but the whole novel, however lightly worn such learning might be. At times, such readers may be persuaded by the seductive and sympathetic voice of the narrator, who draws us gently into the discussion of character by insisting that fictional character and reader have many traits in common, and perhaps, more importantly, that the narrator too has experienced some of the same joys, doubts and sorrows. The 'we' of Eliot's narrator is not the royal 'we', but something more democratic. Shared between narrator and reader are not only intellectual assumptions about a breadth of culture and learning, but also assumptions about emotional delights and uncertainties. Thus, we are invited to share Lydgate's early delighted discovery of his vocation: 'Most of us who turn to any subject with love remember some morning or evening hour when we got on a high stool to reach down an untried volume, or sat with parted lips listening to a new talker, or for very lack of books began to listen to the voices within, as the first traceable beginning of our love' (2.15; p.134). Eliot suggests that we all play our part in cooling the early ardour of potential Lydgates: 'you and I may have sent some of our breath towards infecting them, when we uttered our conforming falsities or drew our silly conclusions' (2.15; pp.135–6). If this were simply described as the actions of ordinary mortals perceived by the narrator from some aloof and detached position, we should no doubt feel that we were being treated with condescension, but because the narrator admits also to not sufficiently understanding the nature of genius, we are more inclined to accept it. When the narrator asks us whether we find it incongruous that a Middlemarch surgeon should 'dream of himself as a discoverer', it suggests that perhaps we shouldn't, since 'Most of us', including the narrator, 'know little of the great originators until they have been lifted up among the constellations and already rule our fates' (2.15; p.137). And before revealing some of Lydgate's 'spots of commonness', the narrator makes a direct appeal for our continued attention: 'The faults will not, I hope, be a reason for the withdrawal of your interest in him' (2.15; pp.141, 140). Such an approach enhances the apparent realism with which Lydgate is depicted in that we are invited to acknowledge his existence. But it also serves to remind us that what we are involved in is a reading of and a response to fiction, and that the narrator expects us to perceive the extent to which the real and fictional worlds can shed moral illumination on each other.

Eliot seems always willing to subject both narratorial voice and the reader to any judgement made. These features are present throughout the novel. Even when the narrator is making a critical presentation of a character – and the tone can sometimes be very harsh indeed – there is nearly always the sense that both narrator and reader will share and recognize some of the weaknesses of character described. The characters who are given the most sympathetic as well as the most detailed analyses are Lydgate and Dorothea, who are linked in readers' minds by the grandeur of their aims and the failure both of their marriages and of the aspirations they have as the novel begins. The novel traces the process by which their ideals are modified or even destroyed by Middlemarch provincial life. But the narrator is almost always scrupulously fair in commenting on those characters whose aspirations and attitudes are less admirable than those of Lydgate and Dorothea. Mrs Cadwallader is not alone in regarding Mr Casaubon as 'A great bladder for dried peas to rattle in' (1.6; p.54); this is a view probably shared by most readers of the novel. Yet the narrator is prepared to give him the benefit of every possible doubt and, moreover, to encourage the reader to do the same – 'I protest against any absolute conclusion, any prejudice derived from Mrs Cadwallader's contempt for a neighbouring clergyman's alleged greatness of soul' – arguing that 'the chief reason that we think he asks too large a place in our consideration must be our want of room for him' (1.10; pp.77, 78).

Eliot famously demands the reader's sympathy for the less attractive characters in the novel. In the opening sentence of chapter 29, the narrator explicitly announces a changed point of view: 'One morning some weeks after her arrival at Lowick, Dorothea – but why always Dorothea? Was her point of view the only possible one with regard to this marriage?' Why, the narrator asks us, should youth and beauty be the only objects of interest? 'Mr Casaubon ... was spiritually a-hungered like the rest of us' (3.29; p.261). There follows a detailed analysis of Casaubon's reasons for marrying Dorothea, which carefully balances his 'self-preoccupation' with 'an egoistic scrupulosity' (3.29; p.262). The presentation is clear-sighted about Casaubon's lack of passion but also very perceptive in its recognition that uncharismatic characters have a call on our sympathies, and here the narrator makes a direct appeal to the reader's understanding: 'For my part I am very sorry for him. It is an uneasy lot at best, to be what we call highly taught and yet not to enjoy: to be present at this great spectacle of life and never to be liberated from a small hungry shivering self' (3.29; p.263).

This sympathetic presentation of unsympathetic characters, the charity that the narrator shows towards individuals whose actions seem morally or emotionally reprehensible, is perhaps the most distinctive feature of the narrative voice in *Middlemarch*. This charity is extended not only to Casaubon, but to Bulstrode, whose pawnbroking past and whose denial of Ladislaw's mother, his stepdaughter by his first wife, is exposed by his murder of Raffles and the subsequent gossip. Bulstrode aspires to that unachievable paradox of 'being an eminent Christian' (5.53; p.494); in the process of acquiring the eminence, he indulges in a great deal of self-deception, as he explains events in his past and present life to accord with his own understanding of Christian ethics. This, of course, is hypocrisy of the highest order, but we are warned against easy judgements of him: 'it was what he said to himself – it was as genuinely his mode of explaining events as any theory of yours may be, if you happen to disagree with him. For the egoism which enters into our theories does not affect their sincerity; rather, the more our egoism is satisfied, the more robust is our belief' (5.53; p.489). The first sentence above seems a little sharp, with the direct address to the reader, but it is effectively softened by the second sentence, which acknowledges the extent to which we all – Bulstrode, narrator and reader – rewrite our own autobiographies to fit an idealized perception of ourselves.

This idea is more fully explored in chapter 61, which provides us with the history of Bulstrode's life before he came to Middlemarch, and which reveals him to be not just corrupt but also capable of genuine suffering. In a remarkable paragraph, the narrator analyses this suffering, linking Bulstrode's fear 'of seeing disclosed to the judgment of his neighbours and the mournful perception of his wife certain facts of his past life which would render him an object of scorn and an opprobrium of the religion with which he had diligently associated himself' (6.61; p.577). Thus far these are Bulstrode's fears, but the narrator moves into a passage of more generalized comment about the 'terror of being judged' (ibid.), which applies to us all. 'With memory set smarting like a reopened wound, a man's past is not simply a dead history, an outworn preparation of the present: it is not a repented error shaken loose from the life: it is a still quivering part of himself, bringing shudders and bitter flavours and the tinglings of a merited shame' (6.61; pp.577–8). As with Casaubon's 'small hungry shivering self' (3.29; p.263), the narrator is able to present egoism as a human failing with which we can all identify. Bulstrode was not one of the 'coarse hypocrites ... He was simply a man whose desires had been stronger than his theoretic beliefs, and who had gradually explained the gratification of his desires into satisfactory agreement with those beliefs. If this be hypocrisy, it is a process which shows itself occasionally in us all' (6.61; p.581). As he struggles with his conscience when deciding whether to follow Lydgate's instruction for Raffles's medication, setting himself 'to keep his intention separate from his desire' (7.70; p.662), the narrator observes these struggles with enormous understanding and compassion:

Strange, piteous conflict in the soul of this unhappy man, who had longed for years to be better than he was – who had taken his selfish passions into discipline and clad them in severe robes, so that he had walked with them as a devout quire, till now that a terror had risen among them, and they could chant no longer, but threw out their common cries for safety. (7.70; p.663)

Not only does the narrator explicitly invite the reader into sharing this beneficent response to the fictional inhabitants of Middlemarch, but the evocation of this kind of response also lies at the moral heart of the novel. 'I know no speck so troublesome as self' (4.42; p.392), writes the narrator, not simply of Mr Casaubon but also of herself as omniscient observer of her fictional world, and she judges her characters according to their capacity to see beyond this troublesome 'self'. No character achieves this state easily or naturally, but those on whom the narrator bestows her highest approval acquire it sooner than others and use it, as Dorothea does, for 'the growing good of the world' (8.finale; p.785). For it is Dorothea, despite, or perhaps even because of her ardent impulses, who seems to grasp the concept of charity towards others most profoundly. 'We are all of us born in moral stupidity, taking the world as an udder to feed our supreme selves' (2.21; p.198), observes the narrator, adopting her familiar habit of including herself, as well as her characters and readers, in this judgement. Dorothea 'had early begun to emerge from that stupidity', yet even she had thought of her relationship with Mr Casaubon largely in terms of what it would mean to *her*, of 'how she would devote herself to Mr Casaubon, and become wise and strong in his strength and wisdom' (ibid.). What she learns instead, after a painful disagreement with her husband on her honeymoon, is that he, too, has his own needs, what the narrator calls 'an equivalent centre of self, whence the lights and shadows must always fall with a certain difference' (ibid.).

Although the narrator holds up other examples of disinterested behaviour for our admiration, such as Mrs Bulstrode's espousing her husband's sorrow, and Mr Farebrother's advocacy of Fred Vincy to Mary, the most obviously disinterested character in the whole novel is Dorothea. She is shown to emerge early from any preoccupation with self, and the account of her life is full of disinterested acts – though some of them, such as trying to persuade Mr Casaubon to provide for Will, have outcomes that are far from benign. It is Dorothea who takes up the cause of Lydgate's innocence: 'Let us find out the truth and clear him ... What do we live for, if it is not to make life less difficult to each other?' (7.71; p.687; 8.72; p.691). Dorothea's faith in him restores something of Lydgate's resolve, since, as the narrator points out, 'The presence of a noble nature, generous in its wishes, ardent in its charity, changes the lights for us: we begin to see things again in their larger, quieter masses, and to believe that we too can be seen and judged in the wholeness of our character' (8.76; p.717). This is perhaps the clearest statement in the novel of the beneficent moral effect of an awareness of 'an equivalent centre of self'; it does not simply express the narrator's approval of Dorothea, but also invites readers to recognize the value of such an awareness, and to endorse the way in which she uses it as a moral yardstick by which to judge both fictional Middlemarchers and actual inhabitants of the real world.

Perhaps the most powerful, as well as the most moving, illustration of the effect of this disinterested behaviour occurs in the encounter between Dorothea and Rosamond, in the final book of the novel. Dorothea's generosity of spirit comes as no surprise: 'How can we live and think that any one has trouble – piercing trouble – and we could help them, and never try?' (8.81; p.747). After her visit to Rosamond, the narrator describes Dorothea's generosity in terms of heroic self-sacrifice: 'it is given to us sometimes even in our everyday life to witness the saving influence of a noble nature, the divine efficacy of rescue that may lie in a self-subduing act of fellowship' (8.82; p.754). Such 'self-subduing ... fellowship' inspires Rosamond for the first and probably the only time in her life, to perform a disinterested action, delivering 'her soul under impulses which she had not known before' (8.81; p.750). In telling her that Will loves only Dorothea, Rosamond saves not only Dorothea's happiness, but also her own marriage. 'Poor Rosamond's vagrant fancy had come back terribly scourged – meek enough to nestle under the old despised shelter' (8.81; p.752).

An awareness of 'an equivalent centre of self' is not the only measure by which the narrator invites us to assess the moral probity of her characters. It is, however, arguably the most powerful tool, simply because it is also the most memorable and persuasive feature of the narrative voice itself. It is also the means by which the narrator constructs her readers in her own image. The constant and consistent inclusion of the reader in any judgements she makes, together with recurring suggestions that her readers should examine their own experiences and consciences before making any hasty assessment of the behaviour of the fictional characters, ensures that readers, too, are aware of 'an equivalent centre of self'. In Eliot's *Middlemarch*, readers as well as fictional characters are constructed by the tone and direction of its pervasive narrative voice.

We have established that the narrative voice of *Middlemarch* combines authority, confidence, ironical humour and sympathetic understanding. Who is this all-encompassing narrator? We cannot assume that the narrative voice is to be identified either with the historical Marian Evans, or with her pseudonym 'George Eliot'. We of course tend to say 'Eliot' and 'she' as a shorthand way of referring to 'the narrator' – yet the very incongruity here of using a male name with a female pronoun alerts us to the fact that this combination is merely a matter of convenience, and does not mean that author and narrator are one and the same. Indeed the sex of the narrator in *Middlemarch* seems doubtful or variable. Sometimes, as historian, or scientist, or when making a direct address to an apparently male reader, the voice seems distinctly masculine. This is J. Hillis Miller's view of the narrator, whom, for the purpose of his essay 'Optic and semiotic in *Middlemarch*', he finds it appropriate to describe as 'he' in order to distinguish the narrator of *Middlemarch* from its historically female author (Miller, [1975] 1987, p.13). Gillian Beer finds that the narrative of *Middlemarch*, which fuses intellect and emotion to work 'through passionate explanation', also fuses male and female voices: 'woman and priest are combined in the narrative discourse' (1986, p.192).

Such a pervasive narrator is often referred to in critical commentary as 'omniscient', and though this is something of a blanket term, it does seem particularly appropriate for the narrative voice in *Middlemarch*. Some of the complexities of this narrative voice are discussed by Beer (1986), who suggests that the reader is treated as if he or she has a role within as well as outside the novel. We are placed in what Beer calls the 'role of privileged newcomer, reading the social scene' (Beer, 1986, p.191). The reader's response to the narrative voice's 'passionate explanation[s]' becomes a 'contract between reader and writer' in which we appear to be equal partners (ibid., pp.191, 192). However, Eliot's use of networks and web imagery allows for a narrative focus which constantly shifts to different points of connection. This is discussed by Miller (1987) and by Beer (1983). Beer (1986) also looks at how the narrative voice encompasses numerous alternative viewpoints – not least through the proliferation of different metaphors, which draw the reader into an understanding of new connections and thus of multiple meaning. The result is that the contract between narrator and reader in fact limits our own capacity to function independently: 'Precisely because so many different kinds of explanation are afforded, it is hard for the reader to counter-interpret' (Beer, 1986, p.192).

The complexities of Eliot's narrative mean that not every commentator thinks that the narrative voice in *Middlemarch* should be described as omniscient. Like Beer, David Carroll believes that the voice invites the reader into the process of interpretation, but he also argues that the voice is not omniscient because it foregrounds the uncertain nature of character. Because the narrative voice itself points out that character is 'a process and an unfolding' (2.15; p.140), any attempt by the narrator (and thus by the reader) to encapsulate/summarize character will falsify it (Carroll, 1992, pp.7–8).

One critic who has attempted to convey the complex joys and frustrations of reading Eliot's narratives is Elizabeth Deeds Ermarth, whose 'George Eliot and the world as language' is a good way for you to round off your reading on *Middlemarch* for now. **Please read Elizabeth Deeds Ermarth, 'George Eliot and the world as language' (1997, pp.33–43; extract in Regan, 2001). How does Ermarth describe the characteristics of the narrative voice in Eliot's work, especially in *Middlemarch*? How is the idea of 'the world as language' relevant to these?**

Like Beer, Ermarth discusses how the reader is drawn into a sense of close relationship with the narrative voice in *Middlemarch*. She emphasizes the way in which the humour and wit of the narrative voice makes us assent readily to its propositions, and she suggests several examples from the novel (Ermarth, 1997, pp.33–4). Like Beer also, she discusses Eliot as a writer who constantly presents a multiplicity of interpretations and points of view, most conspicuously in *Middlemarch*, in the passage we discussed earlier, where the narrative voice interrupts itself: 'Dorothea – but why always Dorothea?' (3.29; p.261). Ermarth devises the concept of the ' "Nobody" narrator in order to distinguish it from anything so limited as a particular individual viewpoint' (1997, p.35). This concept is useful when discussing the plurality of perspective within much realist narrative, but is especially applicable to Eliot. Ermarth regards Eliot's ability to present a 'complex of awareness' as unequalled (ibid.). She suggests that one reason why webs and networks were so attractive a source to Eliot is that a web has a multitude of different centres; this is demonstrated amongst other things by the famous passage describing the scratched pier-glass as a metaphor for the novel's 'reflection' of reality, which she quotes in her essay (ibid., pp.37, 36). Like other critics, she points out that a consequence of the narrative perspective never being single is that explanation in Eliot is never final. There is, inspiringly and infuriatingly, always an '"on the other hand" that makes conclusions difficult' (ibid., p.35).

Ermarth develops an analogy with the way different languages relate to one another to convey the way in which Eliot's work encompasses multiple systems of interpretation. She suggests that Eliot's own 'deep knowledge' of the differences between the formidable number of languages that she herself knew was important to her awareness of the relative limitations of individual forms of explanation (Ermarth, 1997, p.38). In this respect she sees many of the issues central to recent literary theory as already examined in nineteenth-century fiction – particularly the post-structuralist interest in the extent to which '*everything* operates like language' (ibid., p.41). Post-structuralist theory is 'still working on this problem of plural systems, and the difficult problem of negotiating between them where there seem to be *no* common denominators, and no possibility of a common world' (ibid.). However, Ermarth stresses that Eliot is *not* a proto-post-modernist, not a deconstructive critic of her own work. Eliot's sophistication as a writer who confronts the inadequacy of all systems of explanation is always combined with her commitment above all to the real possibility of communication between the different viewpoints she examines: 'every language has its limit, but in her work crucially all limited languages coexist in a common world' (ibid., p.43). Ermarth concludes by stressing that 'The real beneficiaries of George Eliot's narrative style are of course not her characters but her readers. We are the ones ... who are continually forced to move from one private centre of interest to another, one place to another, one discourse or system of values to another' (ibid.). As readers, we can thus retain a sense equally of the intelligence and of the charity of the narrative voice of *Middlemarch*.

# Works cited

Beer, Gillian. 1983. '*Middlemarch*: the web of affinities', in *Darwin's Plots: Evolutionary Narrative in Darwin, George Eliot and Nineteenth-Century Fiction*, London: Routledge. (Extract in Regan, 2001.)

Beer, Gillian. 1986. *George Eliot*, Brighton: Harvester.

Carroll, David. 1992. *George Eliot and the Conflict of Interpretations*, Cambridge: Cambridge University Press.

Eliot, George. 1954–78. *The George Eliot Letters*, ed. by Gordon Haight, 9 vols, New Haven: Yale University Press.

Eliot, George. [1866] 1988. *Felix Holt, the Radical*, ed. by Fred C. Thomson, The World's Classics, Oxford: Oxford University Press.

Eliot, George. [1872] 1998. *Middlemarch*, ed. by David Carroll, with an introduction by Felicia Bonaparte, 3rd impression, Oxford World's Classics, Oxford: Oxford University Press.

Ermarth, Elizabeth Deeds. 1997. 'George Eliot and the world as language', in *George Eliot and Europe*, ed. by John Rignall, Aldershot: Scholar Press. (Extract in Regan, 2001.)

James, Henry. 1987. '*Middlemarch*' (review), in *The Critical Muse: Selected Literary Criticism*, Harmondsworth: Penguin. (Extract in Regan, 2001.)

Miller, J. Hillis. [1975] 1987. 'Optic and semiotic in *Middlemarch*', in *George Eliot's 'Middlemarch'*, ed. by Harold Bloom, Philadelphia: Chelsea House.

Regan, Stephen. Ed. 2001. *The Nineteenth-Century Novel: A Critical Reader*, London: Routledge.

Shuttleworth, Sally. 1984. *George Eliot and Nineteenth-Century Science: The Make-Believe of a Beginning*, Cambridge: Cambridge University Press.

Sutherland, J.A. 1976. *Victorian Novelists and Publishers*, London: The Athlone Press.

# Further reading

Ashton, Rosemary. 1983. *George Eliot*, Oxford: Oxford University Press. A brief, clear and helpful account of Eliot's work and its intellectual context.

Beer, Gillian. 1989. 'Circulatory systems: money, gossip and blood in *Middlemarch*', in *Arguing with the Past: Essays in Narrative from Woolf to Sidney*, London: Routledge.

Bloom, Harold. Ed. 1987. *George Eliot's 'Middlemarch'*, Modern Critical Interpretations, Philadelphia: Chelsea House. A collection of criticism on *Middlemarch* which includes J. Hillis Miller's 'Optic and semiotic' essay.

Buckley, Jerome H. Ed. 1975. *The Worlds of Victorian Fiction*, Cambridge, MA: Harvard University Press.

Carroll, David. Ed. 1971. *George Eliot: The Critical Heritage*, London: Routledge.

Chase, Karen. 1984. *Eros and Psyche: The Repression of Personality in Charlotte Brontë, Charles Dickens, George Eliot*, London: Methuen.

Creeger, George R. Ed. 1970. *George Eliot: A Collection of Critical Essays*, Twentieth-Century Views, Englewood Cliffs, NJ: Prentice-Hall.

Eliot, George. 1954–78. *The George Eliot Letters*, ed. by Gordon Haight, 9 vols, New Haven: Yale University Press.

Eliot, George. 1989. *George Eliot: Collected Poems*, ed. by Lucien Jenkins, London: Skoob.

Eliot, George. 1990. *George Eliot: Selected Essays, Poems and Other Writings*, ed. by A.S. Byatt and Nicholas Warren, Harmondsworth: Penguin.

Garrett, Peter K. 1980. *The Victorian Multiplot Novel: Studies in Dialogical Form*, New Haven: Yale University Press.

Haight, Gordon S. 1968. *George Eliot: A Biography*, Oxford: Oxford University Press.

Hardy, Barbara. 1997. 'The miserable marriages in *Middlemarch, Anna Karenina*, and *Effi Briest*', in *George Eliot and Europe*, ed. by John Rignall, Aldershot: Scholar Press.

Helsinger, Elizabeth K., Sheets, Robin Lauterbach and Veeder, William. Eds. 1983. *The Woman Question: Society and Literature in Britain and America, 1837–1883*, 3 vols, Manchester: Manchester University Press. Valuable context for the 'Woman Question' debate.

Kettle, Arnold. Ed. 1981. *The Nineteenth-Century Novel: Critical Essays and Documents*, rev. edn, London: Heinemann.

Levine, George. 1980. 'George Eliot's hypothesis of reality', *Nineteenth-Century Fiction*, vol.35, no.1, pp.1–28.

Mintz, Alan L. 1978. *George Eliot and the Novel of Vocation*, Cambridge, MA: Harvard University Press.

Neale, Catherine. 1989. *George Eliot: 'Middlemarch'*, Penguin Critical Studies, London: Penguin. A helpful and accessible guide to the novel and its context.

Newton, K.M. Ed. 1991. *George Eliot*, Longman Critical Reader, London: Longman, 1991. An extremely useful collection that includes essays on *Middlemarch* by David Lodge and D.A. Miller.

Pinney, Thomas. Ed. 1963. *The Essays of George Eliot*, New York: Columbia University Press.

Swinden, Patrick. Ed. 1972. *George Eliot, 'Middlemarch': A Casebook*, London: Macmillan.

Welsh, Alexander. 1985. *George Eliot and Blackmail*, Cambridge, MA: Harvard University Press.

Woolf, Virginia. 1925. 'George Eliot', in *The Common Reader*, First Series, London: Hogarth Press.

# CHAPTER 12

# *Far from the Madding Crowd:* vision and design

*by Stephen Regan*

## Introduction

*Far from the Madding Crowd*, Thomas Hardy's fourth published novel, first appeared as a magazine serial in 1874. It remains one of Hardy's most popular novels, widely regarded as his first major success in fiction-writing. The fascination and appeal of the novel have much to do with its subtle blend of popular literary forms and its striking array of powerful visual images. We might begin by asking 'What kind of novel is *Far from the Madding Crowd*?' Is it a realist novel or is it some other mode of writing? Is it a pastoral tale, a comic romance or a Victorian melodrama, perhaps? Hardy has often been portrayed as a rather naive and unsophisticated writer of rural fiction, but this chapter takes a very different line and argues that his way of constructing fictional situations and events is highly complex and unusual. What constitutes realism for Hardy is not always easy to establish, partly because his writing often seems to question the very notion of realism, by drawing attention to its own fictional devices, and by incorporating stylistic tendencies – Gothic, sensationalist, melodramatic – that seem at odds with realist aims and ambitions. Much of this chapter is preoccupied with 'ways of seeing' – including the framing of events as if they were scenes from paintings – mainly because the role of vision in the novel exemplifies Hardy's serious and persistent concern with how the world might be represented in art. **Reread chapter 1 of the novel (Hardy, [1874] 2002, pp.9–13; all subsequent page references are to this edition). How would you describe the narrative voice that we are introduced to here?**

The opening chapter of *Far from the Madding Crowd* brings into focus, in a vivid and concentrated way, the novel's abiding thematic and stylistic concerns. The account of Farmer Oak with which it begins is a set piece of character description that seems, in keeping with other late Victorian works of fiction, to be fairly conventional and unexceptional. The narrative voice quickly establishes a compact between a shrewdly observant author and a sophisticated readership. The voice is amiable and good-humoured, but also slightly ironic in its delineation of Gabriel Oak's religious and social appurtenances. 'On Sundays', we are told, Farmer Oak was 'a man of misty views, rather given to postponing ... he went to church, but yawned privately by the time the congregation reached the Nicene creed and thought of what there would be for dinner when he meant to be listening to the sermon' (1; p.9). What makes this opening description unusual, however, is its seeming refusal to pass any decisive judgement on the character it creates.

Identity, here and elsewhere in the novel, is held in abeyance as something provisional and unfixed, and readers are given a broad margin of interpretation. Gabriel is 'a man', but 'some relics of the boy' can be seen in his face (1; pp.9, 10). The more detail we have, the more elusive he seems to become: 'when his friends and critics were in tantrums he was considered rather a bad man; when they were pleased he was rather a good man' (1; p.9).

It is worth noting as well, even at this early stage in the novel, that much of the description is intensely visual. *Far from the Madding Crowd* is a highly pictorial novel, and it draws extensively on images and ideas from the visual arts. The opening paragraph reveals that the wrinkles in Gabriel's face extend 'like the rays in a rudimentary sketch of the rising sun', and a little later we learn that the dominant 'mental picture formed by his neighbours' was that of Gabriel in his working clothes (1; p.9). This pictorial idiom persists throughout the novel, illuminating its frequent passages of character and landscape description, but also serving to complicate our understanding of what constitutes 'realism' in Hardy's writing. If this strongly visual appeal seems to heighten the verisimilitude of particular incidents and scenes, it simultaneously draws attention to the patent fictiveness of Hardy's characteristic style. In other words, the framing devices of the novel – the very ways in which it seeks to represent the world – are brought self-consciously into the foreground.

As its title suggests, chapter 1 is a 'description of Farmer Oak', but the title also alludes to 'an incident' in which Bathsheba Everdene is brought dramatically into view. This twofold function is conspicuously evident when the narrative shifts from its casual description of Gabriel into an extended passage of action and dialogue. The shift is signalled by a sudden insistence on place and time: 'The field he was in this morning sloped to a ridge called Norcombe Hill' (1; p.11). Although we remain in the past tense, the effect of 'this morning' is to give the sentence a vivid present-tense immediacy. The passage that follows is remarkable for its highly organized visual design and its subtle articulation of shifting visual perspectives:

> Casually glancing over the hedge, Oak saw coming down the incline before him an ornamental spring waggon painted yellow and gaily marked, drawn by two horses, a waggoner walking alongside, bearing a whip perpendicularly. The waggon was laden with household goods and window plants, and on the apex of the whole sat a woman, young and attractive. Gabriel had not beheld the sight for more than half a minute when the vehicle was brought to a standstill just beneath his eyes. (ibid.)

The arrival of Bathsheba in the yellow waggon is framed by Gabriel's visual perceptions: by the initial casual glance with which he catches sight of the waggon on the incline, and then – as if in quick succession – by the close-up apprehension of the vehicle 'beneath his eyes'. It is almost as if the movement of the waggon has been filmed, but within that frame we have a geometrical vocabulary more suggestive of eighteenth- and nineteenth-century 'academic art' (i.e. paintings incorporating the formal precepts laid down by the official academies). The waggoner carries his whip 'perpendicularly', while the young woman (whose name is not revealed until chapter 4) is seated 'on the apex' of the waggon and its chattels. The fetching picture of the woman seated outdoors and yet surrounded by household objects owes much to the popular tradition of 'genre painting', in which figures from everyday life are depicted within a pleasing landscape or a recognizable domestic setting. Here, Hardy's narrative cleverly conflates the two possibilities. But apart from creating a pleasant 'picture', the incident plays ironically with ideas about the ways in which art might be said to mirror life. The incident contains reflections that prompt further reflections. The young woman blushes at seeing herself blush in the mirror; 'nobody knows' what provokes her smile, because this is a private indulgence, but of course 'nobody knows' anyway, because this is a work of fiction. Even so, the blush, we are told, ended in 'a real smile' (1; p.12).

# Ways of seeing

As several critics have pointed out (see especially Berger, 1990; Bullen, 1986), Hardy's interest in visual design extends beyond the influence of painterly techniques to a concern with the ways in which people perceive themselves and others. In a whimsical anticipation of this aspect of the novel, the narrative draws our attention to a cat in a willow basket, which 'gazed with half-closed eyes, and affectionately surveyed the small birds around' (1; p.11). As so often in *Far from the Madding Crowd*, the narrative proceeds according to the ways in which people perceive the world around them. The woman looks 'attentively downwards' at an oblong package and assures herself that the waggoner is 'not yet in sight'. Her eyes creep back to the package and what she reveals is the looking-glass in which she proceeds to 'survey herself attentively' (1; pp.11, 12). The passage in which Bathsheba blushes at her own reflection is full of brilliant visual effects. **Read the following passage and think about the ways in which it uses colour, light and contrast. Why is the passage so preoccupied with who sees whom?**

> It was a fine morning, and the sun lighted up to a scarlet glow the crimson jacket she wore, and painted a soft lustre upon her bright face and dark hair. The myrtles, geraniums and cactuses packed around her were fresh and green, and at such a leafless season they invested the whole concern of horses, waggon, furniture, and girl with a peculiar vernal charm. What possessed her to indulge in such a performance in the sight of the sparrows, blackbirds and unperceived farmer, who were alone its spectators – whether the smile began as a factitious one to test her capacity in that art – nobody knows: it ended certainly in a real smile; she blushed at herself, and seeing her reflection blush, blushed the more. (1; p.12)

The subtle gradations of scarlet and crimson in the morning sunshine are seen with a painter's eye, and so too is the vivid contrast between the woman's 'bright face' and 'dark hair'. The green of the plants adds further colour to the scene and also sets up a sharp contrast between the spring-like charm of the picture and the 'leafless season' in which the incident takes place. Entirely characteristic of Hardy's composition, both in this novel and in others, is the presentation of characters who, unknowingly, are watched by others. Bathsheba conducts her looking-glass 'performance' in the sight of the sparrows and blackbirds, but the 'unperceived farmer' is also one of the 'spectators'. We are later told that Gabriel 'withdrew from his point of espial' (1; ibid.).

Hardy's preoccupation with ways of seeing is clearly more than a novelty. The visual relationships established early in the novel have a profound structural importance and also carry a weight of social and cultural meaning. Although Gabriel pays twopence to the turnpike keeper to allow the waggon to pass (the first of several important economic transactions), his initial social distance from Bathsheba is immediately apparent: 'He looked up at her then; she heard his words, and looked down' (1; p.13). As if to reinforce the impression of condescension and belittlement, the narrator adds that 'The red jacketed and dark haired maiden ... carelessly glanced over him' when she 'might have looked her thanks to Gabriel' (ibid.). What Gabriel infers from the picture he has observed is 'Vanity' (ibid.), but this is only one perspective among many possibilities, and what Hardy's novel repeatedly suggests is the fallible, tentative nature of human perception. This abiding interest in multiple perspectives and different angles of vision has a powerful impact on Hardy's understanding of what constitutes 'realism'. Instead of an authoritative, single-minded account of what is 'true' or 'real', we are much more likely to encounter a conflicting and competing series of impressions.

# Vision and design

At one level, the narrative structure of *Far from the Madding Crowd* seems very bold and simple. Three suitors compete for the affections of Bathsheba Everdene: a shepherd, a gentleman farmer and a soldier. The narrative progresses according to the aspirations of each of these lovers, and much of the drama in the novel ensues from the overlapping and competing interests of the three, as well as from Bathsheba's fluctuating responses. This stark outline, however, is given a highly elaborate design by the repeated emphasis on visual codes of conduct and by the shifting degrees of visual attention and discrimination with which the principal characters regard each other. So Gabriel, in declaring his constancy to Bathsheba, remarks: 'whenever you look up there I shall be – and whenever I look up there will be you' (4; p.34). It is Gabriel who, in the end, sees Bathsheba most clearly, but before they reach the equilibrium he seeks, Bathsheba passes before the surveying gaze of both Farmer Boldwood and Sergeant Troy. In each case, the way in which Bathsheba is seen and appraised differs markedly from the way in which she is perceived by Gabriel. As J.B. Bullen argues, the action of the eye is 'a potent force in all the developing relationships of the book' (1986, p.72). Bullen points out that:

> Bathsheba's namesake is also looked upon and admired. The Second Book of Samuel reads: 'And it came to pass in an evening-tide that David arose from off his bed and walked upon the roof of the king's house: and from the roof he saw a woman washing herself; and the woman was very beautiful to look upon' (11:2).
>
> (1986, pp.73–4)

If the novel develops according to the ways in which Bathsheba is seen and admired, it is also the case that 'one interpretation of her history is a progression from vain self-contemplation to objective self-assessment' (Bullen, 1986, p.74). The way in which Bathsheba regards herself has been of paramount importance for critics interested in questions of gender, as we will see in chapter 13 below.

Before considering some of the more complex ways in which *Far from the Madding Crowd* is structured, it is useful to reflect for a moment on those occasions when Bathsheba encounters each of her three suitors for the first time. **Reread the first eight paragraphs of chapter 3, as far as '... the maid not at all' (pp.21–3), the point where Gabriel and Bathsheba speak to each other for the first time. What is the effect of Hardy's description of 'a girl on horseback' being conducted through a vocabulary of looking and seeing?**

The first dialogue between Gabriel and Bathsheba is carefully choreographed according to the subtle exchange of glances between the two. To begin with, we find Gabriel peeping from his hut as Bathsheba approaches on horseback. Believing herself to be unseen, she drops backwards, 'flat upon the pony's back' (3; p.21), allowing the animal to pass under the spreading boughs of trees in the plantation. Then, with even greater disregard for convention, and still believing herself to be unseen, she rides with her legs astride the pony: 'satisfying herself that nobody was in sight, she seated herself in the manner demanded by the saddle, though hardly expected of the woman' (3; p.22). Watching her, Gabriel is 'amused – perhaps a little astonished', while Bathsheba, having dismounted, sees 'with some surprise ... Gabriel's face rising like the moon, behind the hedge' (ibid.). When they meet, it is he who blushes first; however, when he casually reveals that he has witnessed her riding exploits, Bathsheba also blushes. The narrative records in minute detail how Gabriel first turns 'to meet his colloquist's eyes', and then turns away, wondering when he might face her again: 'He heard what seemed to be the flitting of a dead leaf upon the breeze, and looked. She had gone away' (3; p.24).

**Look briefly again at those chapters in which Bathsheba is first seen by Farmer Boldwood and Sergeant Troy (chapters 17 and 24). Each meeting is defined in terms of visual apprehension. How do these ways of seeing compare with Gabriel's earlier 'sightings' of Bathsheba?**

A good indication of Gabriel's feelings and perceptions as a lover can be found at the end of chapter 8, at the close of an evening's entertainment in Warren's Malthouse. Despite his closed eyelids, Gabriel is too full of emotional agitation to sleep: 'Night had always been the time at which he saw Bathsheba most vividly, and through the slow hours of shadow he tenderly regarded her image now' (8; p.72). Whatever the earlier instances of spying might imply, there is an indication here of a tender regard which becomes more pronounced as the action of the novel progresses. There is also a strong element of anticipation in the narrative, for 'the delight of merely seeing her effaced for the time his perception of the great difference between seeing and possessing' (ibid.).

Although Boldwood does not see Bathsheba until chapter 17, we have already been made aware of some aspects of his perception. His first meeting with her is delayed when he visits Weatherbury Upper Farm and she refuses to see him. Later, in the corn-market at Casterbridge, Bathsheba is conscious of being the focus of attention: 'Women seem to have eyes in their ribbons for such matters as these' (12; p.92). She is also conscious, however, of a certain 'recusant' (ibid.) who seems to withhold his gaze. The same man, who turns out to be Boldwood, passes her on the way home, 'with eyes fixed on the most advanced point along the road', and Bathsheba remarks to Liddy: 'I wonder why he is so wrapt up and indifferent, and seemingly so far away from all he sees around him' (12; p.93). As with Gabriel, Bathsheba's growing acquaintance with Boldwood is presented as an ocular drama. What seems to induce the fateful decision to send a valentine to Boldwood is Bathsheba's pique at being denied 'the official glance of admiration' (13; p.97). She finds it 'faintly depressing that the most dignified and valuable man in the parish should withhold his eyes' (ibid.).

Significantly, it is dusk when Boldwood is presented to us, contemplating the words 'MARRY ME' embossed on the seal of the valentine letter. So many crucial scenes, including decisive moments of judgement and confrontation, take place at night or in the half-light, when clear vision is difficult to obtain. We are told that 'the bachelor's gaze was continually fastening itself' on the letter, 'till the large red seal became as a blot of blood on the retina of his eye' (14; p.99). The obsessive, disturbed nature of Boldwood's vision is immediately apparent. He places the valentine in the corner of the looking-glass, as if registering its hold on his psyche, and is conscious of its presence even when his back is turned.

Boldwood's disturbed placidity is forcefully registered at the opening of chapter 17, which is once again set in the public sphere of Casterbridge market. The confrontation with 'the disturber of his dreams' is so powerful as to merit comparison with the most archetypal encounter between man and woman in Western civilization: 'Adam had awakened from his deep sleep, and behold! there was Eve. The farmer took courage, and for the first time really looked at her' (17; p.118). This very short chapter functions essentially as a mapping of emotional awakening, and it registers Boldwood's heightened sensibility pre-eminently through his gaze: 'Boldwood looked at her – not slily, critically or understandingly, but blankly at gaze, in the way a reaper looks up at a passing train – as something foreign to his element, and but dimly understood' (ibid.).

The double reference to a lack of understanding in Boldwood's perception does not bode well for his imagined engagement with Bathsheba. The physical beauty of the woman is vividly impressed upon him – he sees her black hair, her facial curves, her eyelids, eyes and lashes, the shape of her ear and even the soles of her shoes, all in erotic detail – but the ostensible reason for this acutely sensitive visual response is that Boldwood 'had never before inspected a woman with the very centre and force of his glance' (17; pp.118–19). More troubling still is the suggestion of Boldwood's 'blindness' in calculating the possible significance of the valentine. Bathsheba, meanwhile, is conscious of being watched – 'His eyes, she knew, were following her everywhere' – and though she regrets her teasing behaviour, she nevertheless regards the occasion as a 'triumph' (p.119).

Boldwood's hopeless courtship is conducted through a series of telling visual codes and allusions. When Bathsheba next sees the lovestruck farmer, he is standing by a gate (indicative, perhaps, of his uncertain future) and 'overhung by a willow tree in full bloom' (one of numerous allusions to melancholy in Boldwood's life) (18; p.124). In a scene entirely characteristic of Hardy's complex visual choreography, Gabriel watches Bathsheba watching Boldwood, and being 'ever regardful' of her facial changes he reads the signs of her behaviour and notes 'a keenly self-conscious reddening' (ibid.). In contrast, Boldwood is caught up in a confusing 'pantomime' of signs: 'Perhaps in her manner there were signs that she wished to see him: perhaps not: he could not read a woman' (ibid.). At the end of the following chapter, when his offer of marriage has been received with less than enthusiasm, Boldwood's dejection and disorientation are strongly registered through visual gesture: 'And then she turned away. Boldwood dropped his gaze to the ground and stood long like a man who did not know where he was' (19; p.129).

Bathsheba's first meeting with Sergeant Troy takes place at night in the gloom of the fir plantation. She finds herself 'hooked' to a soldier 'brilliant in brass and scarlet', and the contrast of this 'revelation' with her sombre expectations has upon her 'the effect of a fairy transformation' (24; p.162). Troy, in sharp contrast to Boldwood, is brazen in his way of seeing: 'He looked hard into her eyes when she raised them for a moment: Bathsheba looked down again, for his gaze was too strong to be received pointblank with her own' (ibid.). Troy's modes of perception and apprehension are sporadic and opportunistic: 'His outlook upon time was as a transient flash of the eye now and then' (25; p.166). In a sharp reversal of roles, it is Bathsheba who now comes to be dominated, and this is made emphatic in the novel's visual symmetry. At the end of chapter 25, it is Troy who emerges as 'a bright scarlet spot' (p.168) – the colour formerly associated with Bathsheba – and his attempted mastery is given a strongly visual manifestation:

> As soon as she had entered the field Troy saw her, and sticking his pitchfork into the ground and picking up his crop or cane, he came forward. Bathsheba blushed with half-angry embarrassment, and adjusted her eyes as well as her feet to the direct line of her path. (ibid.)

Chapter 24, in which Bathsheba encounters Troy in the fir plantation, opens with a reminder of Gabriel's constancy in love. Her nightly routine of 'looking round the homestead before going to bed' is preceded every evening by Gabriel 'watching her affairs as carefully as any specially appointed officer of surveillance could have done' (24; p.160). As in chapter 8, his watching is described neither as an obsession nor as a brazen affront, but as a 'tender devotion' (ibid.). One indication of Bathsheba's steady divergence from Boldwood and Troy towards the loyal and steadfast Gabriel Oak is her eventual appreciation not just of his patient forbearance but of his selfless vision. The 'simple lesson' Gabriel reveals 'by every turn and look' is that the interests most affecting his personal wellbeing are 'not the most absorbing and important in his eyes' (43; p.287). His way of seeing is tempered and serene, without any of the agitation that besets the other principal characters in the novel: 'Oak meditatively looked upon the horizon of circumstances without any special regard to his own standpoint in the midst' (ibid.).

# Structural principles

To the very end, the novel is propelled by this drama of visual attitudes and gestures, but its structure also depends on a skilfully orchestrated series of contrasts and parallels between people, situations and events, and on a highly elaborate arrangement of symbolic devices. The intricate design of Hardy's novel is such that certain episodes anticipate or prefigure later events and lead to an increasingly complex web of relationships. **Look again at the description of the shearing-supper in chapter 23 and consider the way in which certain events might be regarded as 'anticipatory'.**

At the shearing-supper, Gabriel's removal from the place of honour, at the opposite end of the table from Bathsheba, is emblematic of his displacement by Boldwood; but when Gabriel plays the flute to accompany Bathsheba's singing of 'The Banks of Allan Water', the words of the song anticipate the later action in a strongly dramatic and acutely ironic way: 'For his bride a soldier sought her / And a winning tongue had he: / On the banks of Allan Water / None was gay as she' (23; p.157). In the following chapter, Bathsheba encounters Troy in the fir plantation and finds the edge of her gown trapped in his spur. The incident is emblematic of her entanglement with Troy, in the same way that the lantern which Bathsheba holds creates distorted shadows prefiguring their destructive relationship: 'It radiated upwards into their faces and sent over half the plantation gigantic shadows of both man and woman, each dusky shape becoming distorted and mangled upon the tree-trunks till it wasted to nothing' (24; p.162).

A further example of the complex design and interplay of relationships occurs earlier in the novel, when a letter mistakenly delivered to Boldwood turns out to be a letter from Fanny Robin to Gabriel Oak, declaring her intended marriage to Troy (15; pp.111–12). Earlier still, Gabriel's arrival in Weatherbury coincides with Fanny's departure, and their fleeting encounter anticipates the desperate tragedy in Fanny's life. As Gabriel offers her money, their hands touch and he perceives the depth of her distress. The incident takes on a heightened emotional effect from its close association with Gabriel's work as a shepherd: 'Gabriel's fingers alighted on the young woman's wrist. It was beating with a throb of tragic intensity. He had frequently felt the same quick hard beat in the femoral artery of his lambs when overdriven' (7; p.54). It is in keeping with the novel's ironic perspective on the reading and misreading of signs that the narrator should pensively add that 'wisdom lies in moderating mere impressions, and Gabriel endeavoured to think little of this' (7; p.55). There is, however, a further significance to this event, since it recalls the newborn lamb that Gabriel delivers to Bathsheba on the occasion when he proposes marriage, and so obliquely sets up a contrast between Bathsheba's fortune and Fanny's distress.

Michael Millgate argues that 'Since Boldwood and of course Troy are also involved with the fate of Fanny, her relationship to Bathsheba becomes a strange shadow play of obvious contrasts and obscure rivalries' (1971, p.84). As Millgate points out, the sorrowful scene in which Fanny stands in the snow and the dark outside the barracks and calls to Troy is placed strategically between those chapters in which Bathsheba's fortunes are clearly ascending, first as mistress of the farm and then as an independent businesswoman at the Corn Exchange. Later, however, this pattern is reversed, so that Fanny in death wins back the affections of Troy, while Bathsheba is spurned and defeated.

# Hardy's style

Richard C. Carpenter draws attention to the 'tight-woven texture of symbolic and structural meaning' in *Far from the Madding Crowd*' (1964, p.345). **Now read Richard C. Carpenter, 'The mirror and the sword: imagery in *Far from the Madding Crowd*' (1964, pp.331–45; extract in Regan, 2001). What points does Carpenter make about the novel's 'imagistic design'?**

Carpenter's argument in this influential essay is that the 'imagistic design' of *Far from the Madding Crowd* is 'fundamentally musical. A motif, announced in an early scene, reappears time after time ... gaining in significance because of repetition in an expanding milieu, but more often transposed, inverted, taken up by a different character or situation' (1964, pp.332–3). He proceeds to show how particular images and colours, such as the yellow of the waggon and the red of Bathsheba's jacket, are repeatedly employed in the fire episode and in the meeting between Bathsheba and Sergeant Troy in the fir plantation, where the pervasive image pattern reappears in the scarlet and brass of the soldier's uniform. This time, however, the man is the tempter and the charmer.

Two significant aspects of *Far from the Madding Crowd* ought to be added to Carpenter's account of the novel's imagistic design. First, the quality of the writing in many of the scenes he describes is highly poetic, and this poetic charge involves more than the repeated use of familiar images; it extends to the rhythm and vocabulary of Hardy's prose. Second, it is worth noting that *Far from the Madding Crowd* is a highly episodic novel. This undoubtedly owes something to the exigencies of magazine publication, as we will see in the next chapter, but the result is a series of powerfully concentrated and memorable incidents such as the fire, the sheep-washing and sheep-shearing, the sword-exercise and the storm. While each of these episodes has its own narrative and dramatic interest, the cumulative effect gives the novel a tremendous sense of activity and momentum. Let us now look briefly at some of these episodes, in terms of both their poetic composition and their place in the larger narrative.

## *Norcombe Hill*

Hardy's interest in sense impressions and in the nature of human perception is vividly evident in those scenes in *Far from the Madding Crowd* that evoke a world of sound as well as sight. As we will discover in chapter 13 below, this strongly empiricist dimension in his writing – the preoccupation with what can be deduced from the evidence of the senses – is an aspect of his agnostic sensibility. It is almost as if, in the absence of any sustaining conventional belief, Hardy and his fictional creations are asking 'How can we now make sense of the world?' Much of the dramatic impulse in his fiction stems from the fact that people invest belief in sights and sounds, only to discover that their senses have been deceived. In many of his novels, including *Far from the Madding Crowd,* he is alert to the potentially tragic consequences of reading and misreading signs.

Hardy's principal characters are frequently presented in close relationship to the landscapes around them, because it is through the sights and sounds of the landscape that they struggle to invest the world with meaning. His landscapes have a vastness and a permanence that sometimes appear to diminish human strivings, casting a long shadow over the needs and concerns of the moment. **Reread chapter 2. How does Hardy describe Norcombe Hill, and what effect does the description of the landscape have on your reading of the novel?**

Norcombe Hill, where we encounter Gabriel Oak the second time, is described as 'a shape approaching the indestructible as nearly as any to be found on earth' (2; p.14). It is one of those 'smoothly outlined protuberances of the globe which may remain undisturbed on some great day of confusion when far grander heights and dizzy granite precipices topple down' (ibid.). The geographical contours and historical dimensions of Hardy's landscapes suggest solidity and permanence, though part of their function is to throw into relief the transient local, human activities and endeavours that happen in their vicinity. At the same time, these landscapes remain intriguing and puzzling, fundamentally impervious to human comprehension.

Hardy's view of nature is essentially post-romantic and post-Darwinian. In his writing there is little sense of the benign influences it affords to Wordsworth and his romantic contemporaries. Despite a common interest in rural life and labour, Hardy and Wordsworth are philosophically at odds. Written fourteen years after the publication of Charles Darwin's controversial study of evolution, *On the Origin of Species* (1859), *Far from the Madding Crowd* was strongly influenced by ideas of the natural environment as a place of struggle and survival. The highly metaphorical language of the Norcombe Hill chapter draws attention to the landscape as a site of fierce conflict, at times attributing human symptoms and responses to the environment. The events described in chapter 2 occur around midnight on the shortest day in the year, and Norcombe Hill seems curiously animated. Powerful gusts of wind 'smote the wood and floundered through it with a sound as of grumbling, or gushed over its crowning boughs in a weakened moan' (2; p.14).

The chapter is one of the early instances in the novel when sound, as much as sight, plays on the senses of an imagined observer:

> The instinctive act of human-kind was to stand, and listen, and learn how the trees on the right and the trees on the left wailed or chanted to each other in the regular antiphonies of a cathedral choir; how hedges and other shapes to leeward then caught the note, lowering it to the tenderest sob; and how the hurrying gust then plunged into the south to be heard no more. (2; pp.14–15)

What the novel is drawing attention to here is the function of what John Ruskin, the greatest art critic of the nineteenth century, termed 'the pathetic fallacy' (1903–12a, p.201). Ruskin, in *Modern Painters* (1843–60), illustrates the way in which poets as well as painters habitually colour the landscape with subjective moods and emotions. Hardy's fiction is powerfully imbued with the notion that we all imprint our human desires and longings on the world around us, and it plays a crucial role in his concern with the interpretation and misinterpretation of signs.

The Norcombe Hill chapter employs the device of pathetic fallacy very effectively, imprinting on the wind and the trees the sounds of groaning and crying. At the same time, the chapter also suggests the extent to which the world in all its magnitude can overwhelm human consciousness, creating unusual impressions and sensations: 'To persons standing alone on a hill during a clear midnight such as this, the roll of the world eastward is almost a palpable movement' (2; p.15). On these occasions, the narrator continues, 'the impression of riding along is vivid and abiding', and 'After such a nocturnal reconnoitre it is hard to get back to earth, and to believe that the consciousness of such majestic speeding is derived from a tiny human frame' (ibid.). *Far from the Madding Crowd* is a novel acutely interested in the psychology of sensation, especially those occurrences that render human consciousness vulnerable to illusion and deception.

Gabriel Oak is presented as a character who is firmly rooted in his landscape, who diligently responds to the sights and sounds of nature; this intimacy with the environment, however, does not insure him against catastrophe. The Norcombe Hill chapter, while effectively placing him in a meticulously detailed rural setting, also stresses the essential separateness of nature and humanity, and further highlights the deep division between human consciousness and the world it strives to know. Gabriel's presence in the chapter is revealed in a sudden and dramatic flourish:

> Suddenly an unexpected series of sounds began to be heard in this place up against the sky. They had a clearness which was to be found nowhere in the wind, and a sequence which was to be found nowhere in nature. They were the notes of Farmer Oak's flute. (2; p.15)

This unusual interlude is of a piece with the marvellous acoustic texture of the novel, but the sounds of Gabriel's flute are noticeably different from those of nature, and the tune he plays is 'altogether too curtailed in power to spread high or wide' (ibid.).

Later in the chapter, Gabriel carefully examines the sky 'to ascertain the time of night from the altitudes of the stars' (2; p.18). While in some respects he regards the sky as 'a useful instrument' and appreciates it as 'a work of art superlatively beautiful', he is also struck by the awe-inspiring immensity and indifference of the universe: 'For a moment he seemed impressed with the speaking loneliness of the scene, or rather with the complete abstraction from all its compass of the sights and sounds of man' (ibid.). For all his apparent stability, he is fallible in matters of perception and judgement. As if to reinforce this point, the narrator tells us that 'with eyes stretched afar, Oak gradually perceived that what he had taken to be a star low down behind the outskirts of the plantation was in reality no such thing. It was an artificial light, almost close at hand' (ibid.). Gabriel traces this light to a shed where Bathsheba and her aunt are attending a cow and its newborn calf. The manner in which he views the women is worth commenting upon, since it provides a further instance of Hardy's preoccupation with different angles of vision and also demonstrates the secretive and voyeuristic aspects of Gabriel's way of seeing.

In what becomes a characteristic mode of enquiry, Gabriel peeps through a crevice in the roof of the cowshed and spies on Bathsheba. With a scholarly flourish, the narrator explains that 'he saw her in a bird's eye view, as Milton's Satan first saw Paradise' (2; p.19). The elaborate simile here is typical of the learned allusions that appear in *Far from the Madding Crowd*, and we will return to their specific function later. The primary concern in chapter 2 is with sound and sight, so much so that even the animals that inhabit the shed provide an opportunity for the narrator to discourse on the unreliability of vision. Peering into the lamp-lit interior of the shed, Gabriel notices 'a little calf about a day old, looking idiotically at the two women, which showed that it had not long been accustomed to the phenomenon of eyesight, and often turning to the lantern, which it apparently mistook for the moon, inherited instinct having as yet had little time for correction by experience' (ibid.). The idiocy of the newborn calf has its corollary in the human sphere, and the closing paragraphs of chapter 2 are an explicit recognition of how seemingly impartial judgements are distorted by desire: 'In making even horizontal and clear inspections we colour and mould according to the wants within us whatever our eyes bring in' (2; p.20). In Gabriel's case, the 'void within him' gives scope for 'fancy' (ibid.), and even though he is denied access to Bathsheba's features, he creates them in his mind. With yet another explicit reference to the visual arts, we are told that Gabriel 'painted her a beauty' (ibid.).

## *A pastoral tragedy*

One of the most powerful episodes in the novel is Gabriel's devastating loss of his sheep over the precipice of a chalk-pit in chapter 5. Hardy's prose style in this chapter moves a long way from what might be regarded as conventional realist description and achieves the kind of poetic intensity associated with later modernist writers such as D.H. Lawrence, Virginia Woolf and Joseph Conrad. We have already seen how Hardy's prose draws overtly on techniques derived from painting. In the passage that follows, the stable, naturalistic description usually associated with realism dissolves and gives way to a style more reminiscent of impressionist and symbolist art. **What particular features of the passage might be regarded as pulling away from realist description?**

> By the outer margin of the pit was an oval pond, and over it hung the attenuated skeleton of a chrome-yellow moon, which had only a few days to last – the morning star dogging her on the left hand. The pool glittered like a dead man's eye, and as the world awoke a breeze blew, shaking and elongating the reflection of the moon without breaking it, and turning the image of the star to a phosphoric streak upon the water. (5; p.41)

It is not just the prominence of metaphor and simile that gives this passage its elevated quality; it is also the vivid, animated texture of the prose, derived in part from the rhythmic repetition of verbal participles – 'dogging', 'shaking', 'elongating', 'breaking', 'turning'. This rhythm is sustained by another repetition similar to the use of alliteration in poetry: the 'pit', 'pond' and 'pool' are followed in the passage by a breeze blowing over the water and turning the reflected star to a streak.

The structural importance of the passage is that it occurs immediately after Gabriel discovers the loss of a substantial part of his flock and therefore his livelihood. The unnatural skeletal and 'chrome-yellow' moon and the pool that glitters like 'a dead man's eye' obliquely register a momentary impulse towards suicide. Having seen his desire for stability established in relation to the stars in chapter 2, we are invited to interpret the image of a blurred star on the water as an indication of his sudden loss of control. As if to provide a window into his consciousness, the passage is preceded by an explicit instruction that this is what he witnessed as he 'surveyed the scene', and is followed by a similarly pointed remark: 'All of this Oak saw and remembered' (5; p.41). Here, and elsewhere, Hardy's interest in psychology can be seen to anticipate the insights that Sigmund Freud and Carl Jung were to bring to the mysterious and unexpected workings of the human mind.

# *The fire*

As Carpenter (1964) suggests, there are strong parallels and contrasts to be found between the opening episode describing Bathsheba's arrival and the episode involving the fire. One of the examples that Carpenter offers is the relationship between the 'incident' in chapter 1 (the arrival of Bathsheba on the yellow waggon) and the fire at the end of chapter 6. He notes that several images and other spatial relationships from the opening chapter are transposed and varied. As with the first encounter between Gabriel and Bathsheba, the meeting at the scene of the fire is one in which neither character is aware of the other's identity, though this is mainly because it is dark and Gabriel is on top of the rick fighting the fire. Ironically, though, he has now fallen below Bathsheba in social and economic terms. In the intervening space, he has lost his sheep, while she has acquired a thousand acres. The 'vernal' plants of the opening episode have been replaced by dry straw and grain; the yellow and scarlet colours are transposed into the 'rich orange glow' that lights up his face (1; p.12; 6; p.48); and the bright winter sunshine modulates into the darkness of the night. Once again, however, the poetic intensity of the episode calls for a more detailed analysis. The scene is presented through Gabriel's eyes, but this time he ceases to be 'a mere spectator' (6; p.48) and through his resourceful action succeeds in bringing the fire under control. **Read the following passage. What kind of imagery is used, and what does it contribute to Hardy's presentation of the fire?**

> This before Gabriel's eyes was a rick of straw, loosely put together, and the flames darted into it with lightning swiftness. It glowed on the windward side, rising and falling in intensity like the coal of a cigar. Then a superincumbent bundle rolled down, with a whisking noise, flames elongated and bent themselves about with a quiet roar, but no crackle. Banks of smoke went off horizontally at the back like passing clouds, and behind these burned hidden pyres, illuminating the semi-transparent sheet of smoke to a lustrous yellow

uniformity. Individual straws in the foreground were consumed in a creeping movement of ruddy heat, as if they were knots of red worms, and above shone imaginary fiery faces, tongues hanging from lips, glaring eyes, and other impish forms, from which at intervals sparks flew in clusters like birds from a nest. (6; p.48)

The passage contains a high density of figurative language, mainly in the form of similes: the fire glows 'like the coal of a cigar'; the smoke moves 'like passing clouds'; the straws burn 'as if they were knots of red worms'; and sparks fly 'like birds from a nest' (ibid.). The rhythm of the passage is dictated by its parallel syntactical structure: 'a superincumbent bundle rolled down ... Banks of smoke went off horizontally ... Individual straws in the foreground were consumed' (ibid.). The language of simile, in which one thing is likened to another, is lifted towards the end of the passage into a more overtly metaphorical and exuberantly creative set of images: 'imaginary fiery faces, tongues hanging from lips, glaring eyes, and other impish forms' (ibid.). Rather than purporting to offer a detailed verbal 'record' of events, the narrative aims at a more sensationalist effect. As we will see later, many of Hardy's narrative effects can be traced to the pervasive influence of Gothic art and literature in the nineteenth century. These fiery faces, reminiscent of medieval church gargoyles, owe something to Hardy's particular interest in Gothic architecture.

What is also worth noting is the way in which the fire episode plays deftly with light and shadow in a way that resembles the brilliant use of colour in works by Turner and late nineteenth-century British and French impressionist painters. What Hardy's prose shares with impressionist painting is a quality of perception that suggests a momentary apprehension of a particular object or event rather than a studied and settled account. Among the many fleeting impressions observed in the fire episode, our attention is drawn to the flashes of light on the tip of the shepherd's crook. As Gabriel approaches the fire, 'the metallic curve of his sheep-crook shone silver-bright in the same abounding rays', and later a woman passing by identifies the figure on top of the rick as a shepherd: 'See how his crook shines as he beats the rick with it' (6; pp.48, 50). The sheep-crook reappears at the end of the episode, 'charred six inches shorter': a potent image of his 'humility' (6; p.51). Although, as Carpenter (1964) argues, the positions of Gabriel and Bathsheba are briefly inverted, with Gabriel now occupying 'the apex' that Bathsheba formerly possessed, the closing line firmly restores the previous hierarchy: Gabriel, approaching 'the slight female form in the saddle', is seen 'stepping close to her hanging feet' (ibid.).

## *Sheep-washing and sheep-shearing*

The sheep-washing and sheep-shearing scenes in chapters 19 and 22 provide ample evidence of Hardy's intense preoccupation with questions of vision and design in *Far from the Madding Crowd*. **Read the following passage describing the 'sheepwashing pool'. How would you describe the angles of vision and what do you consider to be their purpose?**

The sheepwashing pool was a perfectly circular basin of brickwork in the meadows, full of the clearest water. To birds on the wing its glassy surface, reflecting the light sky, must have been visible for miles around as a glistening Cyclops' eye in a green face. The grass about the margin at this season was a sight to remember long – in a minor sort of way. Its activity in sucking the moisture from the rich damp sod was almost a process observable by the eye. The outskirts of this level water-meadow were diversified by rounded and hollow pastures where, just now, every flower that was not a buttercup was a daisy. The river slid along noiselessly as a shade – the swelling reeds and sedge forming a flexible palisade upon its moist brink. To the north of the mead were trees, the leaves of which were new, soft and moist, not yet having stiffened and darkened under summer sun and drought, their colour being yellow beside a green, green beside a yellow. From the recesses of this knot of foliage the loud notes of three cuckoos were resounding through the still air ... Boldwood went meditating down the slopes with his eyes on his boots, which the yellow pollen from the buttercups had bronzed in artistic gradations. (19; pp.125–6)

Perhaps the most distinctive feature of this passage is its subtle incorporation of several different viewpoints. In addition to a strong visual emphasis on shapes and surfaces, on light and colour, the description of the pool and the surrounding landscape involves a roving, shifting series of perspectives. We move unexpectedly from one perspective to the next, almost as if looking through one end of a telescope and then the other. As Bullen puts it, 'The bird's-eye view, unusual in itself, is made even more startling when the perspective is suddenly and radically changed. The panoramic is displaced by the microscopic, and from the aerial view of the pool and surrounding landscape, the narrator's eye moves rapidly to the pollen on farmer Boldwood's boots' (1986, p.62). This flexible, multiple series of impressions is characteristic of Hardy's narrative technique in *Far from the Madding Crowd*, and with it we find a familiar emphasis on the acoustic, as well as the visual, texture of the landscape: 'the river slid along noiselessly as a shade', while 'the loud notes of three cuckoos were resounding through the still air' (19; p.126). Hardy's landscape descriptions are infused with a sense of process, of things happening simultaneously. What we also find in this passage is Hardy's characteristic use of an idiom drawn explicitly from the visual arts: the reference to Boldwood's boots 'bronzed in artistic gradations' (ibid.) alludes to both sculpture and painting.

The visual diversity and complexity of Hardy's narrative technique is particularly evident in chapter 22. J. Hillis Miller (1970), in a highly detailed analysis of this chapter, has drawn attention to the constant shifts of temporal, as well as spatial, perspective. The way in which the narrator's distance from characters and events is continually modified has a significant bearing on questions of reader response. As Miller explains, at one point the reader might be sharing a close observation of events and identifying sympathetically with the characters involved, but then might suddenly be transported 'so far away in time and space that the events are seen from a godlike distance and with a godlike objectivity' (1970, p.393). Sometimes, the reader is explicitly put in both of these positions at once. In fact, the alternation is so constant that the effect of the narrator's language is to maintain the reader simultaneously both close and distant throughout. This combination of intimacy and separation is well illustrated by the narrative technique at work in the chapter. **Reread chapter 22 as far as 'So the barn was natural to the shearers ...' (p.144). In what ways do the shifting perspectives of the passage complicate its sense of narrative progression?**

The narrator's opening observations are heavily generalized and appear to deny the reader any secure position in relation to time and space. However, we gradually move into a close identification with Gabriel's consciousness and his awareness of time passing. The second paragraph offers us a more particular account of time and place: 'the first day of June' and a landscape 'all health and colour' (22; p.142). The 'vegetable world' of Weatherbury is detailed mainly in terms of its flowers, though the paragraph eventually closes in on the human inhabitants of the place and their occupations. The focus is adjusted further until we arrive at the place of work, the Great Barn or 'Shearing Barn', which prompts the narrator to deliver a eulogistic account of the building's harmonious blending of beauty and utility. As Miller explains, however, the point of view in these paragraphs upsets and complicates our understanding of what constitutes 'realism'. The narrator's account does not aim simply at a convincing representation of the physical appearance of the building; it also involves 'a temporal perspective on the barn which no physical vision, cinema, or stage set could provide' (Miller, 1970, p.394). What the narrative achieves is a double vision, which seems to wrap the present within the perspective of the past: 'Standing before this abraded pile the eye regarded its present usage, the mind dwelt upon its past history, with a satisfied sense of functional continuity throughout' (22; p.143).

The next paragraph suddenly alerts us to the here and now, and heralds its shift of focus with a flood of light: 'To-day the large side doors were thrown open towards the sun to admit a bountiful light to the immediate spot of the shearers' operations' (22; pp.143–4). The rest of the chapter describes the sheep-shearing going on in the barn, but the narrative perspective continues to fluctuate in terms of both spatial and temporal distance. Some of the most intimate moments in chapter 22 are those in which Gabriel works vigorously and contentedly under the approving gaze of Bathsheba. We are told that he 'flittered and hovered under her bright eyes like a moth' (22; pp.144–5). These are also some of the most erotic moments in the text. As with the description of the pond in chapter 5, both imagery and vocabulary imply a state of consciousness as well as affording a material description. This time, however, the prose carries us well away from the near despair of chapter 5 and shows Gabriel in blissful pleasure and desire. Carpenter casually understates the case when he comments that 'there seems to be a strong Freudian thread running through *Far from the Madding Crowd*' (1964, p.340). Gabriel appears to indulge in vicarious sexual pleasure as he sets about shearing a nervous ewe he has just flung upon its back: 'He lopped off the tresses about its head, and opened up the neck and collar, his mistress quietly looking on' (22; p.145). The narrator adds that he was 'fed with a luxury of content by having her over him, her eyes critically regarding his skilful shears, which apparently were going to gather up a piece of the flesh at every close and yet never did so' (ibid.). In a quiet state of bliss, he finishes the job with impressive precision:

> The clean sleek creature arose from its fleece – how perfectly like Aphrodite rising from the foam should have been seen to be realized – looking startled and shy at the loss of its garment which lay on the floor in one soft cloud, united throughout, the portion visible being the inner surface only, which, never before exposed, was white as snow and without flaw or blemish of the minutest kind. (22; pp.145–6)

The event is given such a highly charged erotic appeal that there appears to be an excess of signification: the language hints at depths of experience well beyond the mundane. As Carpenter suggests, 'This voluptuous picture, with all its sexual overtones, including the allusions to the goddess of erotic love and to Botticelli's painting, quite certainly means more than an exposition of a commonplace agrarian event should' (1964, p.341).

The depth of feeling aroused by Boldwood's arrival on the scene is powerfully registered within the context of shearing. Gabriel's belief that Bathsheba 'was going to stand pleasantly by and time him through another performance' is 'painfully interrupted' by Boldwood's presence in the barn (22; p.146). Bathsheba becomes 'red in the cheek', recalling the 'pink flush' of the ewe that Gabriel has just attended to (22; pp.147, 145). His sexual jealousy is rendered subliminally by the wound he inflicts on the next animal he shears. It is clearly significant, and entirely in keeping with the primacy Hardy attaches to clear-sightedness, that the injury should occur as Gabriel's eyes wander in the direction of Bathsheba and Boldwood: 'Oak's eyes could not forsake them' (22; p.147). He is stung by Bathsheba's 'severe remonstrance', but knows that 'she herself was the cause of the poor ewe's wound because she had wounded the ewe's shearer in a still more vital part' (ibid.). The 'vital part' is presumably the heart – the sentence echoes Sir Philip Sidney's sonnet 'The Bargain': 'His heart his wound receivèd from my sight' (1975, p.252) – but there are strong sexual overtones that hint at another vital part.

## *The sword-exercise*

Sergeant Troy's sword-exercise in chapter 28 lends itself remarkably well to the kind of Freudian psychoanalytical criticism practised in Carpenter's (1964) essay, but in fact the episode is so overtly erotic as to render Freud's insights superfluous. Although there is no direct reference to any physical contact beyond a kiss, Hardy's account of Troy's 'strange and glorious performance' (27; p.180) is one of the most sexually charged and sexually provocative scenes in nineteenth-century fiction. **Reread chapter 28. How is the impression of an erotic encounter created through language and imagery?**

'Yes, I should like to see it very much', Bathsheba confides to Troy (ibid.), and at the beginning of chapter 28, her anxiety is immediately apparent: 'She was now literally trembling and panting at this her temerity in such an errant undertaking: her breath came and went quickly and her eyes shone with an infrequent light' (28; p.181). Even before the sword-exercise commences, the landscape seems seductively inviting. The heath is dotted with 'tall thickets of brake fern, plump and diaphanous from recent rapid growth', while the pit is 'floored with a thick flossy carpet of moss and grass intermingled, so yielding that the foot was half buried within it' (ibid.). The sun is described as 'a bristling ball of gold' which sweeps 'the tips of the ferns with its long luxuriant rays', and Bathsheba appears in the midst of the ferns, 'their soft feathery arms caressing her up to her shoulders' (ibid.).

The close and daring cuts of Troy's sword-exercise are mimicked at the textual level by a commentary that is equally close and daring. When Troy produces his sword, it is 'raised ... into the sunlight ... like a living thing' (ibid.). In the act of impressing Bathsheba with his various 'thrusts', Troy darts the point and blade of the sword 'towards her left side just above her hip', and Bathsheba is conscious of the sword 'emerging as it were from between her ribs, having apparently passed through her body' (28; pp.182–3). 'Have you run me through?', she cries out in fright, to which Troy responds by telling her not to be afraid, 'Because if you are I can't perform' (28; p.183). Leaving aside the sexually symbolic aspects of the chapter's title, 'The hollow amid the ferns', the episode is remarkable not least because of its powerful crescendo of visual and aural sensations. The onomatopoeic effect of the sword-exercise is brought to a marvellously sibilant climax in the passage that follows:

> In an instant the atmosphere was transformed to Bathsheba's eyes. Beams of light caught from the low sun's rays, sparkled above, around, in front of her – all emitted by the skilful evolutions of Troy's reflecting blade, which seemed everywhere at once and yet nowhere specially. These circling gleams were accompanied by a keen rush that was almost a whistling – also springing from all sides of her at once. In short, she was enclosed in a firmament of light, and of sharp hisses, resembling a sky-full of meteors close at hand. (28; p.183)

It might be objected that chapter 28 simply does not bear the weight of a heavily symbolic interpretation, but, lest we emulate Bathsheba's temerity towards Troy, the narrator adds that 'She felt powerless to withstand or deny him. He was altogether too much for her', and towards the close of the chapter we are told that 'She felt like one who has sinned a great sin' (28; p.185).

## *The storm*

The storm episode extends across three chapters and occupies a central, strategic position within the structure of the novel. It marks a significant turning point in the relative fortunes of Gabriel Oak and Sergeant Troy, with one being recalled to Bathsheba's affections just as surely as the other is ousted. The storm scene, however, is important for a number of reasons: it contains some of the most vivid figurative writing in the novel; it exemplifies Hardy's abiding interest in the visual arts and their literary parallels; and it provides further evidence of the novel's preoccupation with ways of seeing and with the reading of signs. **Reread chapter 36 as far as the sentence beginning 'Gabriel looked in ...' (p.240). In what ways does the storm episode extend the novel's preoccupation with moments of perception and vision?**

Chapter 36 opens with the anonymous figure of 'a man ... motionless in the stackyard of Weatherbury Upper Farm, looking at the moon and sky' (36; p.236). As so often in Hardy's novels, the focus of attention narrows to the point where an identity is conferred upon the nameless spectator. It is, of course, Gabriel Oak, whose thoughtful, comprehending watch proves decisive in this particular episode: 'Oak gazed with misgiving at eight naked and unprotected ricks, massive and heavy with the rich produce of one half the farm for that year' (ibid.). Looking at the sky, he reads and interprets the signs of the impending storm: 'The night had a sinister aspect' and the moon 'a lurid metallic look' (ibid.). The contrast between Gabriel's resourceful ways and Troy's indulgent waste is vividly apparent when he strolls to the barn where Troy is celebrating his marriage to Bathsheba. As he peers through 'a knot hole in the folding doors' of the barn, his eye meets 'an unusual picture' (36; p.240). The description of the drunken revellers does, indeed, resemble a picture, and a little later, when Hardy describes the morning after, he recalls a drawing by John Flaxman (1775–1826) depicting Penelope's suitors (slaughtered by the returning Ulysses in Homer's *Odyssey*) being led into Hades. '[T]he whole procession', we are told, was 'not unlike Flaxman's group of the suitors tottering on towards the infernal regions under the conduct of Mercury' (38; p.251).

Another work of art is invoked in the novel's magnificent description of the storm, though here (as so often in Hardy's poetic evocations of landscape and environment) it is the combination of aural and visual impressions that lends force to the writing:

> Heaven opened then indeed. The flash was almost too novel for its
> inexpressibly dangerous nature to be at once realised, and they could only
> comprehend the magnificence of its beauty. It sprang from east, west, north,
> south, and was a perfect dance of death. The forms of skeletons appeared in the
> air, shaped with blue fire for bones – dancing, leaping, striding, racing around,
> and mingling altogether in unparalleled confusion. With these were intertwined
> undulating snakes of green, and behind these was a broad mass of lesser light.
> Simultaneously came from every part of the tumbling sky what may be called a
> shout, since, though no shout ever came near it, it was more of the nature of a
> shout than of anything else earthly. (37; p.246)

The reference is to a work by the German artist Hans Holbein, a series of woodcuts popularly known as *The Dance of Death*.

Hardy's impressionistic prose anticipates some of the more progressive, experimental techniques associated with the modernist fiction of James Joyce, Virginia Woolf and Joseph Conrad. In particular, the prose style assiduously avoids the neatly ordered linear description associated with a more conventional realist method, and aims instead at registering the simultaneity of events as they press upon the consciousness of the spectator or perceiver at any given moment. The red flash of Bathsheba's hat is a brilliant detail amidst the tumult of the storm: 'Oak had hardly time to gather up these impressions into a thought, and to see how strangely the red feather of her hat shone in this light when the tall tree on the hill before-mentioned seemed on fire to a white heat, and a new one among these terrible voices mingled with the last crash of those preceding' (37; p.246). Among the other radiant details in the storm episode is

*Figure 12.1  'The Ploughman', from Hans Holbein,* The Dance of Death *(originally entitled* Death*), 1526, woodcut. Cliché Bibliothèque nationale de France, Paris*

the memorable image (clearly drawn from Hardy's interest in sculpture) of the dying lightning illuminating Bathsheba's 'marble face high against the black sky' as she sits on the apex of the stack (37; p.248). A telling indication of the increasing rapprochement between Bathsheba and Gabriel, conducted in the novel's familiar ocular vocabulary, is that when Gabriel returns to peep through the chinks of the barn door, he senses someone breathing beside him and turns to find Bathsheba 'looking into the same chink' (ibid.).

# *Far from the Madding Crowd* and genre

The strong pictorial design of the novel, its intense concentration on visual impressions and its emphasis on the fallibility of perception, give it a distinctive place in nineteenth-century fiction. As we will see later, these aspects also, to some extent, question and challenge many of the assumptions that were commonly held about the nature of realism in the later nineteenth century. At a more fundamental level, we can begin to appreciate that *Far from the Madding Crowd* is not an easy novel to categorize. At the level of genre, it both complicates and extends our understanding of how literary realism functions. One of the hallmarks of Hardy's bold enterprise in writing *Far from the Madding Crowd* was the introduction of a bewildering variety of generic forms, many of which might be thought to sit oddly and awkwardly alongside each other: Victorian melodrama, classical tragedy, popular songs and ballads, hymns and sermons, travel writing, nature writing, art criticism, scientific discourse and political invective. In many ways the success of the novel might be said to be the achievement of a harmonious resolution of these various textual practices, within the subtle adaptation and modification of a prevailing realist model; in other ways, though, these multiple discursive forms refuse to coalesce, and reveal the actual diversity and multifariousness of what we commonly refer to as 'realism'. As we have seen in preceding chapters, the development of realism needs to be understood in relation to a diverse range of writing practices, including the use of Gothic and sensationalist devices. Hardy draws extensively on these devices and, in several novels, he also utilizes a well-established pastoral tradition in literature. **What kind of book, then, is *Far from the Madding Crowd*? What are its generic features?**

Some indication of what Hardy had in mind can be found in a letter he wrote in 1872 to Leslie Stephen, the editor of the *Cornhill Magazine*. In the letter he refers to 'a pastoral tale with the title of "Far from the Madding Crowd" – and that the chief characters would probably be a young woman-farmer, a shepherd, and a sergeant of cavalry' (quoted in Gatrell, 1998, p.xiii). At this point in his career, Hardy had already tried his hand at various popular modes of fiction. He had failed to find a publisher for an early work of social satire, 'The Poor Man and the Lady', the manuscript of which was lost and never printed. In 1871, he tried producing what came to be known as 'the novel of sensation' with *Desperate Remedies*, but failed to make an impact on the Victorian reading public. Aware that his own dissenting outlook was not likely to endear him to a broad readership, he later wrote in the 1889 preface to *Desperate Remedies* of 'feeling his way to a method', of seeking the appropriate form for his own 'idiosyncratic mode of regard' (Hardy, 1962, p.225).

Hardy had won praise for the rural scenes he introduced in *Under the Greenwood Tree* (1872), and was working on *A Pair of Blue Eyes* (1873) when Stephen wrote to him praising his 'descriptions of country life' in the earlier novel. Even though Hardy was undoubtedly persuaded by Stephen to develop the pastoral elements in his writing, it is clear that some of the generic forms he had already experimented with – satire, melodrama, sensationalism – found their way into *Far from the Madding Crowd*, along with a measure of the caustic irony and brooding tragic outlook he had begun to infuse into *A Pair of Blue Eyes*.

# *Pastoral*

In the late nineteenth century the term 'pastoral' had come to designate, in a loose and casual way, any work of art that dealt with rural life. *Far from the Madding Crowd*, however, owes much of its distinctive character and appeal to Hardy's subtle adaptation of allusions and conventions associated with a well-established pastoral tradition in classical and modern European literature. The word 'pastoral' (from the Latin *pastor*, meaning 'shepherd') is frequently associated with the idealization of the shepherd life, and with the artistic imagining of a peaceful and uncorrupted existence, though Hardy's particular use of the pastoral tradition does not necessarily endorse these associations.

Pastoral literature has its origins in the works of Theocritus (*c*.316–260 BCE), a Sicilian poet who wrote for the sophisticated Greeks of Alexandria. His *Idylls* (short mythological narratives and pastoral poems) establish a close relationship between pastoral writing and the theme of love, but they are also tinged with melancholy. The shepherd Thyrsis sings of the death of the lover Daphnis, providing a model for later pastoral elegies. The Latin poet Virgil (70–19 BCE) based his *Eclogues* on the works of Theocritus. In them he evokes a fabled 'golden age', in which primitive shepherds dwelt in blissful innocence. By the late Middle Ages, the classical tradition had been infused with the pastoral imagery of Christianity, with Christ as the good shepherd caring for his flock, and this merging of influences becomes apparent in the medieval mystery plays depicting the life of the Saviour. Among the earliest English pastorals are Edmund Spenser's *Shepheardes Calender* (1579), Sir Philip Sidney's pastoral romance *Arcadia* (1590) and Christopher Marlowe's poem 'The Passionate Shepherd to his Love' (1599). Pastoral drama was popular during the Renaissance, one of the notable plays being Shakespeare's comedy *As You Like It* (1600), but it was mainly in poetry that the pastoral tradition became established in English literature. John Milton's elegy 'Lycidas' (1637) provided the model for Percy Bysshe Shelley's 'Adonais' (1821), Matthew Arnold's 'Thyrsis' (1866) and numerous other examples.

As William Empson (1935) argues in *Some Versions of Pastoral*, the tradition has had a persistent and durable influence on European literature. The idealized world-view associated with it could not, however, be sustained, and decisive revisions and modifications of pastoral conventions proved inevitable. By the mid-eighteenth century, pastoral poetry was beginning to acknowledge conditions of disruption, hardship and misery in the countryside. The rise of the novel as a dominant literary form and the development of realism as a major literary technique profoundly affected the way in which pastoral themes were conceived and explored in imaginative writing. It might seem surprising that Hardy should seek to revitalize a literary tradition that predates (and in many ways runs counter to) the essentially realist mode of nineteenth-century fiction. Tales of rural life were undoubtedly popular in the nineteenth century, and some critics of his work are content to believe that *Far from the Madding Crowd* adopts a pastoral perspective largely as a way of invoking nostalgia for the past, and of asserting the virtues of the countryside over those of city life. However, there are good reasons for thinking that Hardy's use of pastoral conventions serves a much more complicated purpose than creating a world of antique simplicity. As we will see, he draws extensively on the close association of pastoral literature with rural occupations, but his version of the tradition is one that functions in dark and unsettling ways.

The title of the novel suggests that Hardy's vision is by no means simple or straightforward. It has its source in Thomas Gray's 'Elegy Written in a Country Churchyard':

> Far from the madding crowd's ignoble strife,
> Their sober wishes never learned to stray;
> Along the cool sequestered vale of life
> They kept the noiseless tenor of their way.
>
> ([1751] 1996, p.601)

While the novel certainly has its moments of quiet contemplation and serene composure, it is also riven with powerful and memorable images of destitution, misery and violence: Gabriel's loss of his flock, Fanny Robin's death in Casterbridge Union (the workhouse), Boldwood's murder of Troy and his subsequent imprisonment. In view of the novel's tendency to provoke and disturb its readers rather than gently lull them, the title's invocation of a pastoral idyll seems heavily ironic. Before looking in detail at some of the novel's pastoral allusions, it is useful to acknowledge how extensively and pervasively the notion of pastoralism informs Hardy's writing. **Leaving aside precise definitions, is there an obvious sense in which *Far from the Madding Crowd* might be described as a pastoral novel?**

Most obviously, perhaps, the novel invokes the pastoral tradition by taking as one of its central characters a shepherd who is also a lover. Like many of his literary predecessors, too, Gabriel sings and plays the flute. We are told that he 'could pipe with Arcadian sweetness' (6; p.45), a tribute that firmly links him with the classical origins of pastoral literature. Chapter 5, in which he loses his sheep, announces 'a pastoral tragedy', and later we see him at the hiring fair, having sunk 'from his modest elevation as pastoral king' (5; p.38; 6; p.43). His work as a shepherd provides the basis for much of the action in *Far from the Madding Crowd*. The novel scrupulously observes the seasonal activities going on at Weatherbury Upper Farm, but it gives particular emphasis to the importance of sheep-farming in the agricultural year. The very structure of the novel seems to be determined (like that of earlier pastoral works) according to the shepherd's calendar. There are three pastoral scenes in particular that carry a powerful symbolic resonance: the sheep-washing, the sheep-shearing and the shearing-supper.

As well as giving a prominent role to Gabriel Oak as the novel's most obvious pastoral figure, Hardy tightly integrates the shepherd's work within the overall time-scheme and structure of the novel so that pastoral episodes assume much more than a scenic significance. Gabriel and Bathsheba meet and part during early lambing in December; they meet again after the hiring fair in February and quarrel while Gabriel sharpens the shearing tools. The repercussions of Bathsheba's valentine greeting to Boldwood coincide with late lambing in February, while Boldwood's courtship of Bathsheba goes on throughout the washing and shearing of sheep and at the shearing-supper in late May and early June. Even when Gabriel is not immediately involved as a shepherd, his labour is closely associated with significant structural developments in the novel. It is while he is working on the oat harvest in August that he hears of Bathsheba's trip to Bath with Troy. In fire and in storm, he shows himself to be more than a shepherd to Bathsheba. The harvest supper and dance in late August mark a crucial turning point, both in terms of the agricultural cycle and in terms of the shifting loyalties and allegiances among the central characters in the novel.

In a broad sense, we can say that Hardy's knowledge and understanding of pastoral conventions inform both the setting and the structure of *Far from the Madding Crowd*. In addition, it is possible to identify specific allusions that link the novel to the pastoral tradition. At the shearing-supper, for instance, Jacob Smallbury volunteers a ballad 'as inclusive and interminable as that with which the worthy toper old Silenus amused on a similar occasion the swains Chromis and Mnasylus, and other jolly dogs of his day' (23; p.156). The amused reference here is to Virgil's sixth eclogue, in which two shepherds, Chromis and Mnasylus (usually spelled Mnasyllus), discover the satyr Silenus in a drunken sleep and persuade him to sing a song. Silenus complies with a lengthy account of Creation, drawing extensively on Greek mythology.

While explicitly invoking the pastoral tradition, however, *Far from the Madding Crowd* also departs significantly from some of its familiar conventions. The novel does not simply offer its readers an idealized world of bucolic innocence; nor does it suggest that the life of the country is necessarily preferable to that of the town. As we have seen, pastoral writing after the eighteenth century began to admit perceptions of the countryside that contradicted the older, idealized view; *Far from the Madding Crowd* goes much further, presenting a series of severe disturbances that threaten to demolish its pastoral affiliations completely. In generic terms we might say that the pastoral conventions of *Far from the Madding Crowd* are in perpetual tension with the conventions of realist fiction. The novel's generic instability is intensified by the existence of other literary conventions that complicate and occasionally undermine its realist credentials – so much so that Hardy's writing sometimes seems wilfully anti-realist. As well as employing pastoral devices, *Far from the Madding Crowd* also draws in strange and unexpected ways on Gothic fiction, the novel of sensation and popular melodrama.

## *The Gothic, the sensational and the melodramatic*

As we have seen in earlier chapters of this book, the Gothic novel usually involved a story of terror and mystery, often with ghosts and other supernatural occurrences, and tended to take as its setting a gloomy castle or monastery with dungeons, staircases and other claustrophobic places. The form was highly popular in the late 1790s and early 1800s. Among its many celebrated examples are Horace Walpole's *The Castle of Otranto: A Gothic Story* (1764), Ann Radcliffe's *The Mysteries of Udolpho* (1794) and Matthew Lewis's *The Monk* (1796). The term 'Gothic' originally referred to the medieval settings used by Walpole and others, but it was gradually extended to works such as Mary Shelley's *Frankenstein* (1818), which lacked such a specific setting but shared the atmosphere of terror. Elements of the Gothic persist in nineteenth-century novels such as *Jane Eyre* (1847), *Wuthering Heights* (1847), *Great Expectations* (1860–1) and *Dracula* (1897), and they can be found at work in more recent fiction, including the writings of Angela Carter.

Hardy, having trained as an architect, was thoroughly conversant with the principles of medieval Gothic architecture and its popular reproduction in Victorian Britain. Characteristic features included the pointed arch and vault, familiar in cathedrals and other church buildings throughout Europe between the eleventh and the sixteenth centuries. An elaborate and highly influential definition of such architecture was provided for Victorian readers by John Ruskin in his monumental work *The Stones of Venice* (1851–3). In the section 'On the nature of Gothic', Ruskin (1903–12b) develops a view of Gothic architecture that clearly coincides with some of the ideas informing Gothic literature. What Ruskin stresses are the characteristics of savagery and grotesquerie that are evident in the most imaginative work, such as the gargoyles that frequently adorn medieval churches and cathedrals.

Under the potent influence of Ruskin, Hardy began to explore the possibilities of a Gothic artistic revival at an early stage in his career. From 1856 to 1862 he worked as a trainee with John Hicks, an architect and church restorer based in Dorchester. Later, in London, he had the opportunity of assisting a well-established architect, Raphael Brandon, who (with his brother David) had in 1847 published a book entitled *The Analysis of Gothick Architecture* (the book was reprinted in 1874). Hardy read this and came to espouse a preference for English rather than French Gothic architecture.

Hardy's architectural interests shape his fiction, most notably in *A Pair of Blue Eyes*, and his descriptions of buildings tend to be elaborate and detailed. *Far from the Madding Crowd* is highly revealing in this respect. **Read the following passage describing Weatherbury Church. What characteristics of Gothic art does Hardy draw attention to here?**

> It has been sometimes argued that there is no truer criterion of the vitality of any given art-period than the power of the master-spirits of that time in grotesque; and certainly in the instance of Gothic art there is no disputing the proposition. Weatherbury tower was a somewhat early instance of the use of an ornamental parapet in parish as distinct from Cathedral churches, and the gurgoyles, which are the necessary correlatives of a parapet were exceptionally prominent – of the boldest cut that the hand could shape, and of the most original design that a human brain could conceive. There was, so to speak, that symmetry in their distortion which is less the characteristic of British than of continental grotesques of the period. (46; p.306)

The opening sentence is undoubtedly a reference to Ruskin, and much of what follows, including the observation on the boldness and originality of design and the hideousness of the gurgoyles (or gargoyles), owes much to Ruskin's research in *The Stones of Venice*. The contrast between British and continental forms of Gothic grotesquerie is also evident in this passage. Further references to Gothic architecture can be found in the novel. Bathsheba's house at Weatherbury Upper Farm appears to owe something of its design to Gothic influence: 'Fluted pilasters, worked from the solid stone, decorated its front, and above the roof the chimneys were panelled or columnar, some coped gables with finials and like features still retaining traces of their Gothic extraction' (9; p.73).

*Far from the Madding Crowd* reveals that Hardy's interest in Gothic architecture was complemented by a relish for Gothic romance. Think, for instance, of the lurid account of Troy's anticipatory delight at upsetting Boldwood's courtship of Bathsheba at his Christmas Eve party. **How would you describe the style of this short passage?**

> 'I expect I shall not be a very welcome guest if he has her there,' said the sergeant with a slight laugh. 'A sort of Alonzo the Brave; and when I go in the guests will sit in silence and fear, and all laughter and pleasure will be hushed, and the lights in the chamber burn blue, and the worms – Ugh, horrible! – Ring for some more brandy Pennyways, I felt an awful shudder just then.'
> (52.7; pp.356–7)

This is certainly a passage that shows a familiarity with Gothic fiction and its penchant for scenes of horror and fear. In fact, it explicitly acknowledges and borrows from 'Alonzo the Brave and Fair Imogine' (1795), in which the Gothic author Matthew 'Monk' Lewis imagines the ghost of the brave knight Alonzo appearing at the wedding feast of the faithless Imogine. In a bizarre moment of self-dramatization, Troy both imagines himself as a character in Gothic literature and simultaneously affects the shudder of an onlooker (or reader of Gothic tales).

In general it seems that, while Gabriel provides the impulse for scenes of pastoral meditation, the characters of Boldwood and Troy provide an opportunity for exploring the devices of Gothic and sensational fiction. As well as representing events that might be described as macabre or mysterious, Gothic fiction has a strong interest in aberrant or disturbed psychology. It is in this respect that Farmer Boldwood belongs to the realm of the Gothic novel: 'his was not an ordinary nature' we are told (18; p.122). At an early stage in the novel, we become aware of Boldwood's obsessive and vulnerable nature. At the beginning of chapter 14 we find that his gaze was 'continually fastening itself' on Bathsheba's valentine letter 'till the large red seal became as a blot of blood on the retina of his eye' (14; p.99). We have already seen how Hardy's visual perspectives provide an indication of personality and temperament. **Reread the descriptions of landscape in chapter 14, from 'the moon shone to-night ...' (p.100) to '... frozen to a short permanency' (p.101). What do they suggest about the 'disturbance' in Boldwood's life?**

Boldwood's fluctuations of mood are subtly evoked through details of landscape, especially through the interplay of light and shade. Words such as 'unnatural' and 'strange' (14; p.100) are given prominence in the chapter.

Boldwood's 'wan' expression and his 'nervous excitability' are captured and reflected in the image of a frozen landscape under the brilliant illumination of a winter sunset:

> In other directions the fields and sky were so much of one colour by the snow that it was difficult in a hasty glance to tell whereabouts the horizon occurred; and in general there was here too that before mentioned preternatural inversion of light and shade which attends the prospect when the garish brightness commonly in the sky is found on the earth and the shades of earth are in the sky. Over the west hung the wasting moon, now dull and greenish-yellow, like tarnished brass. (14; p.101)

In this instance, Hardy's elaborate observation of earth and sky serves as a symbolic exploration of Boldwood's increasing mental derangement. Elements of the Gothic blend with an intense and persuasive psychological realism.

Later, Boldwood is once again associated with Gothic fiction, this time through a host of references associated with monastic architecture and monkish solitariness. Chapter 18 is partly entitled 'Boldwood in meditation', and the stables where he walks are described as 'his almonry and cloister in one [where] after looking to the feeding of his four-footed dependents, the celibate would walk and meditate of an evening till the moon's rays streamed in through the cob-webbed windows or total darkness enveloped the scene' (18; p.121). The cobwebbed window is a familiar device in Gothic fiction, but the diagnosis of Boldwood's neurosis as sexual is distinctly modern and proleptically Freudian. Sexual excitement and its blockage are suggested in 'The restless and shadowy figure of a colt' that 'wandered about a loose-box at the end' (ibid.).

If *Far from the Madding Crowd* draws on the devices of Gothic fiction, it also shows the impact of the closely related 'sensation novel' that flourished in Britain in the 1860s. Wilkie Collins's *The Woman in White* (1859–60) was one of the most popular novels associated with this subgenre, and it spawned many imitations which exploited the evident taste for stories of crime and intrigue. Crimes of passion were especially popular. As Simon Eliot indicated in chapter 8 above, Hardy had already tried his hand at the form with *Desperate Remedies* and incurred the wrath of his publisher on account of his excessive zeal for sensation. *Far from the Madding Crowd* shows its affiliation with the sensation novel most pointedly in its narrative of Fanny Robin's brutal rejection by Sergeant Troy and the sordid circumstances of her death. Reports of Fanny's disappearance and repeated instances of her misery and distress serve to dispel any lingering suggestion of pastoral innocence in the novel. The most shocking revelation, and one that Leslie Stephen was at pains to tone down, occurs in chapter 43, entitled 'Fanny's revenge'. The Oxford World's Classics edition usefully reprints the manuscript version of this chapter rather than the version that appeared in the *Cornhill Magazine* and in subsequent editions of the novel. The fallen woman and the illegitimate child are 'sensational' in the mode of popular fiction of the 1860s and 1870s, but Hardy's original treatment of the corpses of Fanny Robin and her baby is unusually explicit, tending to what seems like a wilful indulgence in the grotesque. We need to keep in mind the possibility that Hardy not only utilizes popular subgeneric fictional elements, but also parodies them by pushing them to highly self-conscious, even ludicrous, extremes.

Hardy's original text has Liddy report to Bathsheba that 'a wicked story is got to Weatherbury within this last hour – that – there's *two of 'em* in there!' (43; p.285). Bathsheba's opening of the coffin and discovery of two bodies clearly emulates the sensation novel of the time, but the episode also contains stylistic flourishes which even now seem calculatedly perverse, as if challenging conventional moral and aesthetic ideals through a triumphant display of bad taste. In 'a miniature wrapping of white linen', Bathsheba perceives 'a face so delicately small in contour and substance that its cheeks and the plump backs of its little fists irresistibly reminded her, excited as she was, of the soft convexity of mushrooms on a dewy morning' (43; p.289). The same flouting of decorum and respectability is evident in the disturbingly incongruous comparison of the dead woman's hands with those in paintings by the Venetian artist Giovanni Bellini (*c*.1430–1516): 'Her hands had acquired a preternatural refinement, and a painter in looking upon them might have fancied that at last he had found the fellows of those marvellous hands and fingers which must have served as originals to Bellini' (ibid.).

Not surprisingly, passages such as this offended some of Hardy's readers, and some critics were apt to complain of his apparent naivety and crudity as a stylist. There is sufficient evidence, however, to suggest that Hardy was not only intent on manipulating a variety of styles and generic types to suit his purposes, but also strongly inclined towards the use of parody and satire as a way of provoking and engaging his readers. In this instance, the writing is extravagant and extreme to the point of dispelling any illusion of realism, calling attention instead to the nature of artifice. While apparently reinforcing its own descriptive accuracy by appealing to the veracity of another art form, the passage simultaneously undermines itself by a highly self-conscious rupturing of the narrative process.

A further example of this tendency can be found in Hardy's repeated use of theatrical devices from popular melodrama, a cultural form closely associated with the sensation novel and Gothic fiction, especially in terms of its elaborate plotting. As Rosemarie Morgan explains, melodrama is 'a heavily stylized form of sensational/romantic stagework relying on extravagance for its artistic effects' (1992, p.173). **Are there aspects of chapter 43 that might aptly be described as melodrama?**

The physical positioning, the gestures and the dialogue of Bathsheba and Troy in this chapter suggest that its composition was shaped to some extent by theatrical practice. Bathsheba 'knelt beside the coffin, covered her face with her hands, and for a time the room was silent as a tomb' (43; p.291). Troy arrives, as if on cue, and the narrative begins to resemble a set of stage directions: 'the front door opened and closed, steps crossed the hall, and her husband appeared at the entrance to the room, looking in upon her' (ibid.). The dialogue between them is highly stylized and theatrical:

'Well – what?' said Troy blankly.
  'I must go – I must go!' said Bathsheba ...
  'What's the matter in God's name – who's dead!' said Troy.
  'I cannot say – let me go out – I want air!' she continued. (ibid.)

*Figure 12.2    'Dick Turpin's Ride to York' (engraving), English School, nineteenth century. Private collection/Photo: Bridgeman Art Library, London*

Troy later sinks upon his knees and Bathsheba flings her arms around his neck, 'exclaiming wildly from the deepest deep of her heart' (43; p.292).

Troy's appearance as a masked highwayman at the sheep fair in chapter 50 is another instance of the novel's incorporation of popular theatrical forms. The persona of Dick Turpin is probably drawn from Harrison Ainsworth's melodramatic Gothic novel *Rookwood* (1834) – a work that might also have influenced Hardy's description of the storm in chapter 37 of *Far from the Madding Crowd*. The sudden appearance of someone assumed by other characters to be dead is a popular occurrence in theatrical melodrama, and Hardy exploits this to the full in the account of Troy's appearance at Boldwood's Christmas Eve party (chapters 52–4). There is, to begin with, something 'abnormal and incongruous' about the solemn and reserved Boldwood hosting a party (52.1; p.348). Once again, the positioning of characters, the use of gesture and the heightened dialogue are all highly theatrical. The description of Troy's arrival is particularly extravagant: 'Boldwood did not recognize that the impersonator of Heaven's persistent irony towards him, who had once before broken in upon his bliss, scourged him, and snatched his delight away, had come to do these things a second time' (53; p.366). Chapter 54, 'After the shock', announces that 'after Boldwood's exit, the scene was terrible', and proceeds to arrange the guests in a dramatic tableau: 'All the female guests were huddled aghast against the walls like sheep in a storm – and the men were bewildered as to what to do' (54; p.368). Bathsheba is presented 'sitting on the floor beside the body of Troy, his head pillowed in her lap where she had herself lifted it' (ibid.). The scene is strongly reminiscent of the staging of Victorian theatrical melodrama.

# Realism redefined

One of the commonplace critical notions about Thomas Hardy, and one that seems to have persisted since the late nineteenth century, is that his novels are flawed by crude and clumsy writing, and represent the unrefined products of an author largely self-taught and dwelling in the rural backwaters of a remote south-west corner of England. A frequent complaint is that they lack the quality of realism found in other nineteenth-century works of fiction, and that this is largely the result of their author's lack of an adequate theoretical and technical sophistication. That Hardy's novels might have been misjudged by an inappropriate set of critical standards is a view less frequently advanced. In this chapter I have concentrated on the narrative and generic complexity of *Far from the Madding Crowd*, before discussing its early critical reception. I have done so partly to encourage the unfashionable idea that Hardy's writing is informed by a remarkably subtle and discerning understanding of what constitutes literary realism – a view borne out by the various prefaces and essays on the nature of fiction that Hardy published in the later part of his career.

The earlier sections of this chapter considered the extent to which, in his writing style, Hardy both cultivated the powerful appeal of visual impressions and suggested that a full and comprehensive vision of the world is rendered problematic by partial perspectives and limited ways of seeing. What lies behind this preoccupation with visual impressions is an idea of novel-writing as an essentially explorative process, a tentative reaching after truths rather than an authoritative and confident declaration of 'what is really there'. The kind of fiction he writes requires a sympathetic and active response on the part of the reader. As Hardy puts it in his essay 'The profitable reading of fiction', an attentive reader will 'catch the vision the writer has in his eye, and is endeavoring to project upon the paper, even while it half eludes him' ([1888] 1997, p.247). This insistence on a tentative, exploratory mode of fiction-writing is found repeatedly in Hardy's work, especially in the 1890s, when his most controversial novels were being castigated for their social and moral ideas. In his preface to the fifth edition of *Tess of the d'Urbervilles*, he explains that a novel is an 'impression, not an argument' ([1891] 1983, p.5), and in his preface to the first edition of *Jude the Obscure*, he writes of 'a series of seemings, or personal impressions' ([1895] 1985, pp.xxxv–xxxvi).

Contrary to what his critical reputation has tended to suggest, Hardy certainly wasn't naive in his view of what constituted realism. In an essay entitled 'The science of fiction' (Hardy, [1891] 1997), he acknowledges that the nature of fiction must alter, so as to accommodate our 'widened knowledge of the universe and its forces' (ibid., p.262). **Now read Thomas Hardy, 'The science of fiction' ([1891] 1997; extract in Regan, 2001). How does Hardy view realism in fiction?**

'Narrative', Hardy insists, 'must adjust itself to the new alignment, as would also artistic works in form and colour' (1997, p.262). His mind is by no means closed to the idea of experiment in fiction; but even if it were possible to obtain in words the most 'accurate knowledge of realities', how would we begin to represent those realms of experience and perception that fall uncannily between the real and the unreal (ibid., p.261)? With marvellous felicity, Hardy concedes 'the impossibility of reproducing in its entirety the phantasmagoria of experience with infinite and atomic truth' (ibid., p.262). What is frequently overlooked in debates about realism, he asserts, is the importance of 'discriminative choice' (ibid.). In a move that surprisingly prefigures the instincts of James Joyce's artist-hero Stephen Dedalus, Hardy recognizes 'the need for the exercise of the Daedalian faculty for selection and cunning manipulation' (ibid., p.261). Against the idea of realism as mere 'copyism', he asserts the ideal of art.

'The science of fiction' is essentially a critique of the theories of 'scientific realism' or 'naturalism' that were associated with Émile Zola in nineteenth-century France (see chapter 14 below). Hardy employs a critical vocabulary that clearly demonstrates his familiarity with the writings of Zola and others: 'The most devoted apostle of realism, the sheerest naturalist, cannot escape … the exercise of art in his labour or pleasure of telling a tale' (Hardy, 1997, p.261). Once the principles of selection and omission have come into play, he continues, then art has been exercised, and the just aim of art is 'being more truthful than truth' (ibid.). The seeming paradox here succinctly conveys what Hardy sees as the futility of seeking to copy, rather than imaginatively transform or reorder, the world. If novel-writing is only about the accurate reproduction of things, then, to be frank, why bother? 'To advance realism as complete copyism', Hardy argues, 'is the hyperbolic flight of an admirable enthusiasm' (ibid., p.263), one that impetuously approaches the truth but fails to light upon it. Against the ideal of a scientific realism, Hardy proposes the intuitive power that enables a novelist 'to see in half and quarter views the whole picture, to catch from a few bars the whole tune' (ibid., p.264). What cannot be discerned by the senses alone must be apprehended by 'the mental tactility that comes from a sympathetic appreciativeness of life in all of its manifestations' (ibid.). Hardy closes the essay by illustrating how the most needy and illiterate people around him display what the true novelist upholds: 'a power of observation informed by a living heart' (ibid., p.264). This quality, as he observes, is probably innate rather than acquired. It nevertheless suggests that Hardy's view of fiction, for all its anti-realist tendencies, was one that was firmly based on moral instincts and social sympathies.

There is further evidence of what Hardy meant by distinguishing art from realism, and by suggesting that art is 'more truthful than truth'. In the putative *Life of Thomas Hardy* by Florence Emily Hardy, now generally believed to be Hardy's own work, there are several observations that stress the 'idiosyncrasy of the artist' and the role of art as 'a changing of the actual proportions and order of things'. In each case, he once again rejects the notion of mere 'copyism':

> Art is a changing of the actual proportions and orders of things, so as to bring out more forcibly than might otherwise be done that feature in them which appeals most strongly to the idiosyncrasy of the artist.

> (Hardy, 1962, p.228)

Just a few lines later, he is more explicit about the kind of aesthetic effects he aims for, and in his fascination with distortion he provides a plausible explanation of the outrage and hostility that his novels have sometimes elicited:

> Art is a disproportioning (– *i.e.* distorting, throwing out of proportion –) of realities, to show more clearly the features that matter in those realities, which, if merely copied or reported inventorially, might possibly be observed, but would more probably be overlooked. Hence 'realism' is not Art.

> (Hardy, 1962, p.229)

As Michael Wheeler suggests, this particular quotation constitutes 'a personal manifesto for the grotesque, which is broadly characterized by distortion or unnatural combination', and it helps to explain Hardy's characteristic way of 'viewing the world in varying lights or from unusual perspectives' ([1985] 1994, p.199). **Can you identify specific episodes or incidents in *Far from the Madding Crowd* that seem to answer Hardy's call for an 'art of disproportion'?**

There are numerous episodes in the novel that might be described as 'grotesque', but one of the most overt examples occurs in the fir plantation, where Bathsheba and Troy meet by the light of a lantern: 'It radiated upwards into their faces and sent over half the plantation gigantic shadows of both man and woman, each dusky shape becoming distorted and mangled upon the tree-trunks till it wasted to nothing' (24; p.162). This passage demonstrates very memorably what Hardy meant by an 'art of disproportion'.

What his fictional and non-fictional writings together reveal is that, while realism was immensely valued in the nineteenth century for its mimetic or representational powers, it was also a concept fraught with uncertainty and a subject of intense debate. 'Realism' remains for us, as for Hardy, 'an unfortunate, an ambiguous word' (Hardy, 1997, p.262). His invocation of the visual arts, his self-conscious parading of classical and artistic allusions, his strange mixing of pastoral, Gothic, sensational and melodramatic modes – all these threaten to sabotage what we commonly think of as realism, with its scrupulous and consistent observation of actuality. Hardy, by his own admission, sets art against realism. Yet there is a special sense in which his writing is supremely and enduringly realist: in that special sense of being 'more truthful than truth'. As Alison Byerly has argued, the Victorian novel's self-conscious preoccupation with 'art' and various art forms actually reinforces its claims to realism. Hardy's unnerving shifts of perspective and unabashed mixing of genres are not an evasion of 'the real' but part of a complex concern with various modes of description and representation. *Far from the Madding Crowd* confronts us with 'disjunctive artistic moments that shake our sense of what is real' (Byerly, 1997, p.12). Ironically, in contrast to those moments of heightened artistic expression, the rest of the narrative might be said to appear 'more real'.

This chapter has concentrated to a great extent on the nature of Hardy's realism, without saying very much about the social function he envisaged for his fiction or about its actual critical reception. It is often assumed that novels acquire a political power through their accurate depiction of 'the way things are'; one consequence of that idea is the emergence of the term 'social realism' as a way of describing a comprehensive vision and analysis of a particular society. But if Hardy's writing often tends towards an anti-realist stance, what kind of social and political charge might it possess? One possible answer might be found in the suggestion that Hardy's fiction has a capacity to 'shake our sense of what is real'. In other words, rather than seeking to confirm what is already there, Hardy's novels upset and disturb our familiar perceptions of the way things are: they challenge received opinion and refuse to conform to conventional social and moral values. The next chapter concentrates on the reception history of *Far from the Madding Crowd*; it explains why Hardy's readers frequently have been confounded by his idiosyncratic art; and it finds in the novel a radical politics concerned with overthrowing complacent and settled views about sexuality, social class, religious belief, community, work and environment.

# Works cited

Berger, Sheila. 1990. *Thomas Hardy and Visual Structures*, New York: New York University Press.

Bullen, J.B. 1986. *The Expressive Eye: Fiction and Perception in the Work of Thomas Hardy*, Oxford: Oxford University Press.

Byerly, Alison. 1997. *Realism, Representation and the Arts in Nineteenth-Century Literature*, Cambridge: Cambridge University Press.

Carpenter, Richard C. 1964. 'The mirror and the sword: imagery in *Far from the Madding Crowd*', *Nineteenth-Century Fiction*, vol.18, pp.331–45. (Extract in Regan, 2001).

Empson, William. 1935. *Some Versions of Pastoral*, London: Chatto & Windus.

Gatrell, Simon. 1998. 'Introduction' to *Far from the Madding Crowd*, ed. by Suzanne Falck-Yi, Oxford World's Classics, Oxford: Oxford University Press.

Gray, Thomas. [1751] 1996. 'Elegy Written in a Country Churchyard', in *The Norton Anthology of Poetry*, 4th edn, ed. by Margaret Ferguson, Mary Jo Salter and Jon Stallworthy, New York: W.W. Norton.

Hardy, Florence Emily. 1962. *The Life of Thomas Hardy 1840–1928*, London: Macmillan.

Hardy, Thomas. [1891] 1983. *Tess of the d'Urbervilles*, ed. by Juliet Grindle and Simon Gatrell, The World's Classics, Oxford: Oxford University Press.

Hardy, Thomas. [1895] 1985. *Jude the Obscure*, ed. by Patricia Ingham, The World's Classics, Oxford: Oxford University Press.

Hardy, Thomas. [1888] 1997. 'The profitable reading of fiction', in *Thomas Hardy: Selected Poetry and Non-Fictional Prose*, ed. by Peter Widdowson, Basingstoke: Macmillan.

Hardy, Thomas. [1891] 1997. 'The science of fiction', in *Thomas Hardy: Selected Poetry and Non-Fictional Prose*, ed. by Peter Widdowson, Basingstoke: Macmillan. (Extract in Regan, 2001.)

Hardy, Thomas. [1874] 2002. *Far from the Madding Crowd*, ed. by Suzanne Falck-Yi, with an introduction by Linda M. Shires, Oxford World's Classics, Oxford: Oxford University Press.

Miller, J. Hillis. 1970. *Thomas Hardy: Distance and Desire*, Cambridge, MA: Harvard University Press.

Millgate, Michael. 1971. *Thomas Hardy: His Career as a Novelist*, London: The Bodley Head.

Morgan, Rosemarie. 1992. *Cancelled Words: Rediscovering Thomas Hardy*, London: Routledge.

Regan, Stephen. Ed. 2001. *The Nineteenth-Century Novel: A Critical Reader*, London: Routledge.

Ruskin, John. 1903–12a. *The Works of John Ruskin*, ed. by E.T. Cook and Alexander Wedderburn, vol.5: *Modern Painters*, London: George Allen.

Ruskin, John. 1903–12b. *The Works of John Ruskin*, ed. by E.T. Cook and Alexander Wedderburn, vol.10: *The Stones of Venice*, London: George Allen.

Sidney, Philip. 1975. 'The Bargain', in *Silver Poets of the Sixteenth Century*, ed. by Gerald Bullett, London: Dent.

Wheeler, Michael. [1985] 1994. *English Fiction of the Victorian Period*, London: Longman.

Suggestions for further reading can be found at the end of chapter 13.

## CHAPTER 13

# *Far from the Madding Crowd:* the novel in history

*by Stephen Regan*

## Composition and serialization

In January 1873, Hardy went back to live and work in the cottage where he had been born, and where his parents were still residing, at Higher Bockhampton, Dorset. It was here that he composed the 'pastoral tale' that he had offered Leslie Stephen for serialization in the *Cornhill Magazine*. In his training for an architectural career, Hardy had shuttled between office work in London and church-restoration work in Cornwall and elsewhere. Returning to the familiar scenes of his childhood seems to have given him the confidence and composure he needed to plan and write a successful serial closely based on scenes of rural life and labour. In a letter to Stephen he explained that his home was 'within a walk of the district in which the incidents are supposed to occur', and that he found it 'a great advantage to be actually among the people described at the time of describing them' (quoted in Millgate, 1982, p.153).

*Figure 13.1 'Higher Bockhampton, T. Hardy's Birthplace', a pencil sketch of the cottage by Thomas Hardy in middle age. Trustees of the Thomas Hardy Trust, Dorset County Museum*

The writing of *Far from the Madding Crowd* was also coloured by less happy circumstances. In September 1873, Hardy's composure in writing the novel was severely shaken by the suicide of his friend and literary adviser, Horace Moule. Hardy's biographer Michael Millgate claims that 'Hardy was deeply shocked by the death of one who had, in many respects, been closer to him than anyone would ever be again' (1982, p.155). Moule had been a brilliant student at Cambridge University, but failed an exam in mathematics that hindered his academic ambitions and allegedly preyed on his mind. He took a job as an assistant Poor Law inspector, which involved frequent visits to workhouses, and this proved both demanding and depressing. Moule had been, for many years, an alcoholic, possibly an opium addict, and had previously shown suicidal tendencies. On 21 September 1873, he cut his throat in his rooms at Queens' College, Cambridge. Four days later, he was buried in Fordington churchyard, close to Dorchester, an area of Dorset Hardy knew well. Contrary to the Christian edict against suicide, a religious service was permitted after the inquest returned a verdict of 'temporary insanity'. Millgate suggests that 'it was perhaps fortunate for Hardy's state of mind that he was under pressure from Leslie Stephen to produce by the end of the month a completed first instalment of *Far from the Madding Crowd*' (1982, p.156). Even so, it seems likely that Hardy's conception of the novel was darkened by the tragic circumstances of Moule's death. It is perhaps significant that Hardy later gave considerable scope in the novel to the roles of Farmer Boldwood and Fanny Robin, and, by implication, to insanity and the workhouse.

Hardy and Stephen agreed with the publishers of the *Cornhill* that the first part of the serial would appear in January 1874, and it was eventually settled that the novel would be printed in twelve parts between January and December. Hardy continued to jot down ideas and snatches of conversation associated with the local community, and also recorded observations of weather and other natural occurrences, including a storm in November 1873. In *The Life of Thomas Hardy* he writes of having 'sketched in [his] note-book during the past summer a few correct outlines of smockfrocks, gaiters, sheep-crooks, rick-"staddles", a sheep-washing pool, one of the old fashioned malt-houses' (Hardy, 1962, p.97). Some of these sketches were sent to Helen Paterson, the illustrator of *Far from the Madding Crowd*.

All these details contributed to the fictional realization of 'Wessex', a place-name Hardy used for the first time in *Far from the Madding Crowd* and developed in later novels. The description of the great barn in chapter 22 contains a reference to 'these Wessex nooks' ([1874] 2002, 22; p.144; all subsequent page references are to this edition), and chapter 50 opens with the observation that 'Greenhill was the Nijnii Novgorod of South Wessex' (p.327; the reference is to the city of Gorky in Russia, the site of a large annual fair for many years). The unusual outdoor aspects of Hardy's process of composition are likely to have informed the novel's vivid physical realization of its regional locale, though we need to be cautious about seeking an exact correspondence between his fictional Wessex and historical actuality. One of the remarkable compositional features of *Far from the Madding Crowd*, and one that confirms the degree of planning and preparation that went into the novel, is that the temporal or seasonal setting of each instalment corresponds with the calendar month of its serial publication, as do the various occupations around the farm. Late lambing coincides with the April instalment; sheep-shearing with the May instalment; and summer storms with the August instalment.

Serialization of *Far from the Madding Crowd* required of Hardy a rigorous, disciplined method of writing, but proved immensely stimulating and inspiring. As well as writing to a tight set of deadlines, he was expected to keep the readers of the *Cornhill* engaged and entertained from one month to the next by providing a strong narrative outline, impressive dramatic incidents, sharply realized characters and a clear episodic structure. The powerfully visual, scenic dimension of his writing found an appropriate outlet in the monthly serial format, and this is evident in some of the revisions he made, both to the manuscript and to the proof pages of the *Cornhill*. In the passage announcing Bathsheba's arrival, in chapter 1, one sentence originally read: 'It was a fine morning, and the sun lighted up to a scarlet glow the crimson shawl she wore, and gave a soft lustre to her black hair.' The passage as published reads: 'It was a fine morning, and the sun lighted up to a scarlet glow the crimson jacket she wore, and painted a soft lustre upon her bright face and dark hair' (1; p.12).

**What are the effects of Hardy's revisions?**

Even this brief illustration suggests the extent to which his revisions were directed towards a heightening of visual impressions and a strong sense of contrast.

Not all the revisions were clear improvements, and some were made simply to appease Stephen's fears about offending the moral and religious principles of the magazine's readers. Stephen confessed to Hardy that he was 'ashamed' of his own 'excessive prudery', and that he was 'necessarily anxious to be on the safe side' (quoted in Millgate, 1982, p.160). Millgate claims that Stephen's close editorial scrutiny of Hardy's writing resulted in textual emendations of an important and positive kind, but other commentators have claimed that he often used aesthetic or stylistic requirements (such as the need for narrative pace) as an excuse for covert censorship (see Gatrell, 1988). Some of Stephen's recommended revisions are now likely to seem very minor and petty. All references to animals' 'buttocks', for instance, had to be altered to 'backs'.

Among the more extensive changes Hardy consented to were cuts to the description of the shearing-supper in chapter 23 (possibly because of the racy dialogue of the workers); cuts to the description of Fanny Robin and her baby in chapter 43 (very definitely to do with Fanny's status as a 'fallen woman' and the presence of an illegitimate child); and cuts to Troy's 'adventures by the shore' in chapter 47 (probably for genuine reasons to do with narrative pace). As Simon Eliot suggested in chapter 8 above, Hardy restored some of his original text at various times after serialization (a practice to which Stephen had no objection). The Oxford World's Classics edition of *Far from the Madding Crowd* is based very closely on the original manuscript of the novel and restores a number of excised passages.

Rosemarie Morgan has written a book-length study of Hardy's 'cancelled words', based on a searching analysis of the manuscript. Her assessment of his revisions is highly revealing, especially in showing how the novel's sharp focus on issues of social class and rural labour was cautiously modified for readers of the *Cornhill Magazine*:

> What the Victorian critic regarded as a tale of rural tranquillity refreshingly free from social conflict, class struggle and economic strife, and what has been regarded, more recently, as Hardy's avoidance of the actual conditions of the day, is not so clearly indicated to the reader of his manuscript.
>
> (Morgan, 1992, p.85)

In particular, the manuscript provides evidence of his careful registering of 'the codifications and demarcations of rank and status – of the class for whom he is writing' (Morgan, 1992, p.86). Accordingly, the novel's dialogue and characterization show a preoccupation with 'conventional codes, manners, modes of address, and so on, which denoted class difference and all the complicated little nuances of rank, status and social identity' (ibid., p.96).

It seems that Hardy seized the opportunity to expose the inequities of social class in a way that might appear to flatter rather than upset the prejudices of his largely middle-class readership. The way in which he both registers the cultural appurtenances of class society and simultaneously affords a subtle critique or exposure is very close to the technique of satire. This is an idea strongly endorsed by Peter Widdowson, who argues vigorously that the radical social satire of Hardy's unpublished first novel, 'The Poor Man and the Lady', persisted as 'a constant and crucial constituent of all his fiction' (1996, p.30). The meticulous attention paid to details of social class in the novel's descriptions of Sergeant Troy often border on satire. Liddy, impressed by stories of Troy's social status, tells Bathsheba, 'Ah – such a blessing it is to be high born: nobility of blood will shine out even in the ranks and files' (24; p.165). But the novel implies that Troy is, in fact, the illegitimate son of the Earl of Severn, with whom his Parisienne mother has had an affair. The French connection would, in itself, render Troy suspect for readers in the 1870s. (See Simon Eliot's comments in chapter 8 above.) Similarly, Boldwood's gentlemanly demeanour and air of social superiority are occasionally registered with both punctilious detail and a tone of wry amusement. In one telling revision to the manuscript, a reference to 'another gig' is carefully amended to: 'A low carriage, bowling along still more rapidly behind a horse of unimpeachable breed, overtook and passed them' (12; p.93). While clearly functioning, like the fine 'carriage', as an indicator of rank and status, the horse of 'unimpeachable breed' is a detail that seems to invite disdain for Boldwood's conspicuous display of wealth and cultivation.

An important aspect of Hardy's interest in social class is his depiction of the rural workforce, or 'workfolk', as the local labourers are called in *Far from the Madding Crowd* and in his essay 'The Dorsetshire labourer'. Cutting against a common critical opinion that Hardy's labourers are treated with condescension and mockery, Morgan argues that his initial design reveals a sustained and sympathetic awareness of economic insecurity and hardship in the rural community. She claims that the manuscript of *Far from the Madding Crowd* shows 'a greater distress and discontent in Weatherbury's labour force, a greater sense of their feelings of precariousness, than is apparent in the abridged version for the *Cornhill*' (Morgan, 1992, p.94).

Some critics have complained that Hardy was too willing to acquiesce in Stephen's recommended revisions to the manuscript of the novel. He, after all, obligingly told Stephen that he just wanted to be 'a good hand at a serial' (Hardy, 1962, p.100). Hardy, however, never simply conformed to literary propriety and decorum. While superficially appeasing Victorian moral guardians, *Far from the Madding Crowd* (even in its amended form) retained its capacity to trouble and disturb its readers, raising uncomfortable questions about love and labour, and about the kind of social organization under which both might flourish. Hardy's canny ability to play it both ways is amply evident in the strikingly diverse and conflicting critical opinions that his work continues to provoke.

# Hardy and his critics

The critical reception of any work of fiction is likely to involve a mixed and uneven response, and very few novelists are blessed with unanimous approval. Hardy's work, however, is unusual in frequently eliciting a fiercely divided and seemingly contradictory set of opinions within the same critical essay or review. Applauded for his painstaking fidelity to nature, he is then routinely castigated for the coarseness and vulgarity of his prose style. This tendency to find fault with his writing has been so strong and persistent, even in the twentieth century, that, as Terry Eagleton puts it, criticism 'has been able to do little more than inscribe a "Could do better" in the margins of Hardy's texts' (in Regan, 1998, p.46).

Hardy's iconoclastic views and his redoubtable anti-realist tendencies certainly confused and irritated some critics. While seeming in some ways to conform to critical expectations, he was apt to flout conventional standards of taste and literary decorum. The response of the literary establishment was to belittle him, by drawing attention to his social and regional origins and by denigrating his fiction as naive and unsophisticated. His talents were assumed to reside in the patient chronicling of the Wessex he knew, and any pretence at a deeper understanding of the world or attempts at stylistic and thematic diversity were treated with scorn.

When *Far from the Madding Crowd* was serialized in the *Cornhill*, some readers supposed that it might be a new novel by George Eliot. Early reviews of the book, then known to be by Hardy, refer to this early speculation, but in nearly every instance the comparison is refuted and Hardy's fiction found wanting. 'We cannot for our lives understand how any person of ordinary penetration, much more a skilled critic, could ever have supposed it to be written by George Eliot', the *Observer* declared in January 1875 (in Clarke, 1993, p.70). **Now read Henry James, 'Far from the Madding Crowd' ([1874] 1993, pp.80–3; extract in Regan, 2001, as 'Novels by Eliot, Hardy and Flaubert', subtitle 'Far from the Madding Crowd'). What is James's view of the novel?**

James sets the characteristic tone for much contemporary criticism in this condescending review, concluding that Hardy's 'superficial novel is a really curious imitation of something better' (1993, p.83). He is among those critics who praise Hardy's descriptions of nature, but the implied attitude is that of the cosmopolitan intellectual grudgingly acknowledging the humble efforts of some simple rustic scribe: 'Mr Hardy describes nature with a great deal of felicity, and is evidently very much at home among rural phenomena. The most genuine thing in his book, to our sense, is a certain aroma of the meadows and lanes – a natural relish for harvesting and sheep-washings' (James, 1993, p.82). Lest his readers mistakenly construe this verdict as unmitigated praise, James saves this memorable caveat for the end of his review: 'Everything human in the book strikes us as factitious and insubstantial; the only things we believe in are the sheep and the dogs' (ibid., p.83). The candid advice that Hardy should stick to farming appears repeatedly in reviews of *Far from the Madding Crowd* throughout 1874 and 1875.

The strong pictorial qualities in Hardy's writing are highlighted by some critics, though once again the focus is very much on Hardy's fidelity to rural life. R.H. Hutton, writing in the *Spectator* in December 1874, begins with lavish praise: 'The details of the farming and the sheep-keeping, of the labouring, the feasting, and the mourning, are painted with all the vividness of a powerful imagination, painting from the stores of a sharply outlined memory' (in Clarke, 1993, p.75). Hutton, however, cannot refrain from chastizing Hardy for what he perceives as stylistic flaws and lapses of concentration. The peculiar combination of praise and denigration in his review is entirely in keeping with the standards of Hardy criticism over the century that followed. Acknowledging the 'beauty' of Hardy's 'descriptive sketches' and 'watercolours in words', the review concludes that 'On the whole, the book is amusing and exceedingly clever even in its mistakes and faults' (in ibid., p.79).

The faults that Hardy's critics bemoan are frequently to do with violations of credibility, with coincidence and improbability. Can we really believe that Fanny Robin arrives at the wrong church for her wedding, or that Sergeant Troy would so callously reject her for this simple mistake? The *Observer* review concedes that 'Mr Hardy displays a fine imaginative disregard for probability', but nevertheless believes he goes too far: 'We confess we think it rather hard that a merely wilful young woman with a pretty face should be wooed by three different men, two of whom marry her, one of whom is killed for her, and the third of whom she drives crazy' (in Clarke, 1993, p.71). These criticisms of the improbability of events are frequently compounded with complaints about the implausibility of human behaviour in the novel. The *Observer* sees *Far from the Madding Crowd* as that kind of novel 'in which the characters and the march of events are more or less puppets, which remain to the last under the control of the narrator, who pulls the wires as he chooses' (in Clarke, 1993, p.71). James similarly complains that Hardy 'pulls the wires' (1993, p.81).

Those reviews that find Hardy's characterization credible and imposing turn out to be less than satisfied with the quality of his prose. An anonymous review in the *Athenaeum* praises his vigorous descriptive powers and then proceeds to castigate him for 'a sort of recklessness' and a 'coarseness' that 'disfigures his work and repels the reader' (in Clarke, 1993, p.73). Likewise, the *Saturday Review* reports that his 'sketches' show power in 'analysing the deeper shades of character', but then abruptly adds that 'Mr Hardy disfigures his pages by bad writing, by clumsy and inelegant metaphors, and by mannerism and affectation' (in Clarke, 1993, p.95). Hardy's writing obviously fails to conform to a particular set of aesthetic criteria. The extent to which it upsets conventional preferences for a smoother, more coherent realist narrative is evident in the puzzled response of the *Saturday Review* to the chapter entitled 'The hollow amid the ferns': 'we are led to question the truthfulness of such scenes as these. Are they a faithful rendering of real events taking place from time to time in the South-Western counties, or are they not imaginary creations with possibly some small groundwork of reality?' (in ibid., p.98). The same review provides an indication that negative criticism of Hardy's work was fuelled, to some extent, by presumptions about his social status and 'breeding'. We are asked 'how a man of good taste' could permit such 'a hideous' metaphor as that in which the element of folly in Bathsheba's character is described as 'lymph on the dart of Eros', which 'eventually permeated and coloured her whole constitution' (29; p.186). Such writing is thought to be crude and lacking in 'refinement' (in Clarke, 1993, p.96).

The most frequent observation regarding the agricultural workers in *Far from the Madding Crowd* is that Hardy has unconvincingly supplied them with a philosophical intelligence and habits of speech inappropriate to their station in life. The *Athenaeum* review, uncertain of where the novel is set, complains of his having given his 'Somersetshire rustics' a set of 'expressions which we simply cannot believe possible from the illiterate clods whom he describes' (in Clarke, 1993, p.73). The *Saturday Review* shares this observation, insisting that neither Shakespeare's clowns, nor George Eliot's rustics, nor Walter Scott's peasants, 'rise to anything like the flights of abstract reasoning with which Mr Hardy credits his cider-drinking boors' (in ibid., p.97). Andrew Lang, in a more measured review, complains with some justification that Hardy has idealized the material living conditions of rural labourers and that in 'telling clever people about unlettered people ... he adopts a sort of patronizing voice' (in ibid., p.92). The ferocity of some of these reviews, however, suggests that they were motivated in part by a concern that Hardy's estimation of the intelligence and ability of the rural workforce was, in fact, an accurate one.

Fears about the sexual behaviour and social independence of women inform a number of the early reviews and shape their apprehension of Bathsheba. The novel succeeds in confounding contemporary presuppositions about the proper behaviour of women; as the *Observer* review suggests: 'we can never make up our minds whether Bathsheba Everdene is intended to be a "lady" or the opposite; and it is quite certain that, on either supposition, she could not have done what she is represented as doing' (in Clarke, 1993, p.72). The *Westminster Review* offers its condolences to Gabriel Oak: 'We thoroughly sympathize with him and pity him, and we must say that he deserved a far better woman for a wife than such a vain and selfish creature as Bathsheba Everdene' (in ibid., p.89). James objects to Bathsheba's '*womanishness*': 'She is a young lady of the inconsequential, wilful, mettlesome type which has lately become so much the fashion for heroines' (1993, p.83).

On all counts, then, like the anonymous notice in the *Athenaeum,* the early reviews of *Far from the Madding Crowd* present Hardy as being 'at once an interesting and a disappointing writer' (in Clarke, 1993, p.73). What is difficult to comprehend, however, is that these sentiments should continue to provide the terms on which so much modern criticism of him turns. As Eagleton explains, the verdict very early on was that 'Hardy, regrettably, was really unable to *write*', and that 'since this is rather a major disadvantage for a novelist, it is not surprising that criticism has found such difficulties with his work' (in Regan, 1998, p.46). Time after time in twentieth-century criticism, the same back-handed compliments are meted out to Hardy.

One of the curiosities of later Hardy criticism is D.H. Lawrence's 'A study of Thomas Hardy'. This lengthy work was written in 1914, but not published until 1936; even so, it remains an influential and provocative response to his writing. Lawrence is moved by the passion and sensuality of Hardy's characters, and notes how 'all of them are struggling hard to come into being' (Lawrence, [1936] 1970, p.410). Not surprisingly, Lawrence sees a central concern in Hardy's fiction as 'the struggle into love and the struggle with love' (ibid.). Lawrence's critique is one of the first to take seriously the potential for tragedy in Hardy's work and to insist from the outset that the tragedy is prompted by social causes rather than by some mysterious 'fate'. Tragedy occurs when those who are struggling for self-realization and fulfilment transgress established social codes and conventions. Although Lawrence is principally interested in later novels, such as *The Return of the Native* (1878), *Tess of the d'Urbervilles* (1891) and *Jude the Obscure* (1895), his notion of 'the struggle into love' can be very clearly identified in *Far from the Madding Crowd*. Lawrence gives Hardy a decidedly modern appeal, in keeping with his own iconoclastic outlook and candid treatment of sex.

Virginia Woolf, on the other hand, writing an essay on the occasion of Hardy's death in 1928, seems inclined towards the equivocal Victorian attitudes we have already documented. She gives high praise to Hardy's vivid word-painting and to those 'moments of vision ... those passages of astonishing beauty and force which are to be found in every book that he wrote' (Woolf, [1928] 1994, p.509). *Far from the Madding Crowd* is singled out for its particular merits:

> We see, as if it existed alone and for all time, the wagon with Fanny's dead body inside travelling along the road under the dripping trees; we see the bloated sheep struggling among the clover; we see Troy flashing his sword round Bathsheba where she stands motionless, cutting the lock off her head and spitting the caterpillar on her breast.
>
> (Woolf, 1994, p.509)

'But', she continues with a heavy thud, 'the power goes as it comes' and 'the moment of vision is succeeded by long stretches of daylight' (Woolf, 1994, p.510). The novels are 'full of inequalities; they are hewn rather than polished ...' (ibid.). Perhaps because of the involvement of her father, Leslie Stephen, in Hardy's early career, she reserves her highest praise for *Far from the Madding Crowd* as 'a book which, however fashions may chop and change, must remain one of the great English novels' (ibid.).

T.S. Eliot likewise perpetuates the note of equivocation, implying that there is something almost involuntary or sporadic in Hardy's practice as a writer: 'He was indifferent even to the prescripts of good writing: he wrote sometimes overpoweringly well, but always very carelessly; at times his style touches

sublimity without ever having passed through the stage of being good'
(1934, pp.55–6). Eliot finds 'a note of falsity' in the novels that issues from a
refusal to 'leave nothing to nature' but always to be 'giving one last turn of the
screw himself' (ibid.). In this respect, Hardy is seen as wilfully morbid and
melodramatic, and Eliot cites the episode in which Bathsheba unscrews Fanny's
coffin as an instance of 'refined torture' (ibid., p.56).

F.R. Leavis, whose views on the novel were crucially influential throughout
the later twentieth century, simply omitted Hardy from his major critical study of
fiction, *The Great Tradition* ([1948] 1962), and since the criteria for inclusion
were moral seriousness and significant form, it can be assumed that he was felt
to be lacking in one or both. It fell to Lord David Cecil to construct a critical
appreciation that was to prove decisive in establishing the familiar terms on
which his work would be debated for at least the next three decades. *Hardy the
Novelist: An Essay in Criticism* was published in 1943, but reissued in a popular
reprint in 1969. Cecil is largely responsible for perpetuating two highly
questionable notions about Hardy's work. The first of these is the idea that the
novels are deeply nostalgic for a disappearing rural England; the second is that
Hardy sees humanity as eternally the victim of 'Fate' or 'Destiny'. Cecil also fuels
the myth of Hardy the flawed genius, attributing his lapses in taste and execution
to his simple country upbringing and his fundamental lack of worldly
sophistication. With fastidious class snobbery, he explains Hardy's awkward
learned allusions as 'the touching pedantry of the self-educated countryman,
naïvely pleased with his hardly acquired learning' (Cecil, 1969, p.146).
Interestingly, Cecil condemns as 'blemishes' precisely those aspects of the
novels that later critics would come to regard with fascination, including
'sensationalism', 'grotesqueness' and 'wild Gothic' tendencies (ibid., pp.113, 53,
119).

Those critics who reacted against Cecil's critical portrait tended to concentrate
on three main areas of interest: Hardy's claims as a realist, including his valid
depiction of rural Dorset; the validity of his philosophy or world-view; and the
narrative structure and language of the novels. Among the first group might be
counted those critics who were interested in exploring the social and political
significance of Hardy's work: critics such as Douglas Brown, Arnold Kettle and
Raymond Williams, to whom we will return. John Holloway, A.J. Guerard and
others were concerned to secure for Hardy a relevant place in the history of
ideas, while a more obviously 'formalist' line of enquiry was pursued by critics
such as David Lodge, Ian Gregor and J. Hillis Miller, all variously concerned with
patterns of imagery, narrative devices and recurring verbal and structural
features. The mid-1970s perhaps marked a critical turning point, with scholars
such as Michael Millgate (later his biographer and an editor of the letters)
insisting that Hardy be taken seriously both as a stylist and as a thinker. Since the
mid-1970s, however, the critical study of Hardy's work has undergone a radical
transformation, with some of the most engaging and original readings of the
novels coming from critics interested both in the imaginative representation of
gender and social class, and in the very question of representation itself,
including the meaning and function of realism. The best account of these shifts

in criticism can be found in Peter Widdowson's highly informative and illuminating essay 'Hardy and critical theory' (1999, pp.73–92).

# Sexual politics

Critics intent upon studying the role of women or ideas of gender in nineteenth-century fiction have frequently been puzzled by the seemingly contradictory views found in Hardy's novels. If there is a consensus of opinion, it tends towards an acknowledgement that the sexual politics of the novels are enigmatic and indeterminate. Katharine Rogers (1975) and Patricia Stubbs (1979) are both inclined to think that however enlightened and radical the novels may be in their ways of looking at the world, they retain some of the characteristically negative assumptions about women that were prevalent in the late nineteenth century. Novels such as *Far from the Madding Crowd, The Return of the Native* and *Tess of the d'Urbervilles* seem to show a deep and abiding sympathy for the plight of women oppressed by social convention, yet these novels also seem to reproduce some of the most obvious sexual stereotypes of their time. If Hardy succeeds in creating strong and attractive heroines, he also seems intent on exposing their limitations and depicting their ultimate downfall.

Discussions about sexual politics in *Far from the Madding Crowd* concentrate, not surprisingly, on the role of the independent woman farmer, Bathsheba Everdene; a more informed approach, perhaps, ought to consider the novel's attitude to manliness as well, since the struggle for love and fulfilment in the novel is defined primarily in terms of Bathsheba's relationships with three men. The character of Bathsheba certainly provoked surprise and hostility among early reviewers. We might recall Henry James's summary judgement of Bathsheba as 'a young lady of the inconsequential, wilful, mettlesome type' (1993, p.83), an opinion by no means confined to the pages of nineteenth-century reviews. A more moderate critical assessment regards the novel as being essentially concerned with the education or transformation of Bathsheba, though at least one twentieth-century critic sees Bathsheba as entirely beyond redemption (Casagrande, 1979). Does the novel endorse James's sentiments, or does it present a more positive and affirmative view of Bathsheba? **Look again at the moment in chapter 1 when Bathsheba blushes at herself in the mirror (p.12). How would you describe the presentation of Bathsheba here?**

What hinders any easy assessment of the novel's attitude to sexual matters is its complex array of visual perspectives and shifting narrative viewpoints. The narrative voice at first sounds censorious and slightly amused: 'Woman's prescriptive infirmity had stalked into the sunlight, which had clothed it in the freshness of an originality'. Frequently, in this way, an observation of a particular incident is made to serve a broad generalization about womanhood. Another perspective, however, becomes immediately available. We are told that 'A cynical inference was irresistible by Gabriel Oak as he regarded the scene', suggesting that the narrative voice does not necessarily share Gabriel's way of seeing. Similarly, at the end of the chapter, Gabriel's disapproval of Bathsheba's apparent 'vanity' is accompanied by the observation that Gabriel had been 'piqued' by her indifference (1; p.13). In other words, the novel allows a wide margin for interpretation on sexual politics, as on other matters. The narrative voice can jest about women's 'prescriptive infirmity', yet within the same space concede that 'nobody knows' the reason for Bathsheba's peering in the glass.

Recent feminist criticism has argued that *Far from the Madding Crowd* is not so much concerned with Bathsheba's growth to maturity as with the taming and subduing of her instinctive behaviour. Bathsheba herself seems to encourage such a response when she tells Gabriel, 'I want somebody to tame me' (4; p.36), but whereas some male critics, such as Richard C. Carpenter (1964), interpret this as rape fantasy, most female critics tend to read it less crudely as symptomatic of Bathsheba's repressed and thwarted desire. Penny Boumelha puts the case strongly:

> *Far from the Madding Crowd* is not only the story of the education of Bathsheba; her moral and emotional growth are paralleled by the breaking of her spirit. Images of taming pursue her. Her relationship with Troy is marked by instruments of violence, begun with the spurs, consummated by the sword, and ended by the gun. The scenes in which Oak jealously nips the ewe he is shearing in the groin, and in which Troy, after their marriage, walks beside her gig, holding reins and whip, lightly lashing the horse's ears as he walks, are a kind of surrogate for the physical punishment of Bathsheba herself. The stress on the humiliation to which she is subjected by Troy culminates in his repudiation of her before the dead bodies of Fanny Robin and her child.
>
> (1982, p.33)

Boumelha's purpose, however, is not to portray Hardy as the misogynistic author of the text, but rather to record the extent to which the novel candidly exposes 'the undercurrent of sexual antagonism' with which Bathsheba is confronted (Boumelha, 1982, p.32). She goes on to explore the complex structure of perceptions in Hardy's fiction, noting that contemporary ideologies of femininity are frequently thrown into question by conflicting and contradictory points of view.

A similar argument is proposed by Rosemarie Morgan (1988) in *Women and Sexuality in the Novels of Thomas Hardy*, one of the most enthusiastic feminist appraisals of his work. Morgan emphasizes the physicality of Hardy's women and his remarkably open-minded attitude to female sexuality; she draws attention, as well, to the depiction of women working outside the home in various occupations, and to that of women like Bathsheba, who travel unaccompanied outside their own neighbourhood, embark on projects of their own devising and take the initiative in relationships with the men they encounter. Although Morgan acknowledges the shifting narrative perspectives and conflicting points of view in Hardy's fiction, her analysis of *Far from the Madding Crowd* is apt to rely on a highly selective choice of quotations, which has the effect of elevating Bathsheba while sharply rebuking Gabriel. The overall result is to simplify the novel's narrative procedures and narrow its range of possibilities. The reading we are offered is one that concentrates relentlessly and over-insistently on Gabriel's 'vigilante method of shaming voluptuous womanhood', at the same time as exaggerating Hardy's 'refusal to censure the self-delighting, sexually responsive Bathsheba' (Morgan, 1988, p.48). **What other readings of the relationship between Bathsheba and Gabriel might be considered?**

It might be objected that any reading of *Far from the Madding Crowd* that consistently portrays Gabriel as a bullying censor or moral watchdog to an innocent, self-delighting Bathsheba fails to acknowledge the process of change in *both* characters. There is no allowance here for what Lawrence called 'the struggle into love and the struggle with love' (1970, p.410) – a struggle that arguably provides the central dramatic interest in the novel. Furthermore, the significance of Gabriel's changing perspectives can be fully apprehended only through the contrasting ideas of manliness afforded by Boldwood and Troy. Accordingly, Gabriel's 'watching over' Bathsheba might well be construed as relatively benign. Finally, a very different sense of the power relations in the novel begins to emerge when social class, and not just gender, is brought into play as a decisive factor. Not only does the focus on class relations draw attention to those moments in the novel where Gabriel is made subordinate, it also encourages a reading of the novel that recognizes the important socioeconomic distinction between the affluent status of Bathsheba and the desperate plight of Fanny Robin. With these points in mind, let us return to the novel and reconsider its depiction of sexual and marital relations. **Reread chapters 3 and 4, and look again at the earliest encounters between Bathsheba and Gabriel. Is the relationship simply that of a controlling male and a victimized female?**

There is no doubt that Gabriel watches Bathsheba in ways that are both disconcerting and offensive. The narrative endorses the suggestion that Bathsheba feels shame at having been spied upon: 'she appeared to feel that Gabriel's espial had made her an indecorous woman without her own connivance' (3; p.24). But the narrative also indicates some degree of misgiving on Gabriel's part – 'It was food for great regret with him' (ibid.) – and throughout the novel there are signs of him modifying his gaze and responding to desire in less overt and intrusive ways. Only a page later, we see him being roused from unconsciousness by Bathsheba after nearly suffocating to death in his shepherd's hut. The scene is a striking one, in which Bathsheba takes the initiative, almost as a lover, while Gabriel is prone beneath her: 'his head was upon her lap, his face and neck were disagreeably wet, and her fingers were unbuttoning his collar' (3; p.25). As Judith Bryant Wittenberg comments, the novel provides us with 'a tableau that intriguingly suggests both a *pietà* and a seduction scene with Bathsheba as the sexual aggressor' (1986, p.32). She adds that, ironically, Gabriel seems far more 'female' than Bathsheba in these early scenes. As well as effecting a striking reversal of conventional gender roles here and elsewhere, the novel also challenges conventional expectations about gender and power. **Reread chapter 3, from 'Whatever is the matter?' (p.25) to the chapter's end. What does the dialogue between Gabriel and Bathsheba reveal?**

This early conversation quickly establishes Bathsheba's intellectual command of an awkward situation. Her verbal exchanges with Gabriel are pointed and articulate. Physically, too, she takes control by inviting him to kiss her hand. The refusal to divulge her name is done 'teasingly', but, as John Lucas points out, it also involves 'the voice of class' (1977, p.138). Bathsheba tells Gabriel with cool reserve: 'you probably will never have much to do with me' (3; p.27). In chapter 4, she rejects his marriage-proposal with spirited independence, telling him: 'I *hate* to be thought men's property in that way', later elaborating on her reasons: 'You are better off than I ... I am better educated than you – and I don't love you a bit' (4; pp.33, 36). Class and economic considerations jostle for attention. Gabriel, unconvinced that Bathsheba has 'hardly a penny in the world', asserts the value of social class: 'You speak like a lady – all the parish notice it' (4; p.36). When Bathsheba inherits her uncle's farm, her economic position is vastly superior to that of the ruined Gabriel Oak. The role reversal at the end of chapter 6 is striking. So, too, is the angle of vision from which we perceive Gabriel and Bathsheba: Gabriel approaches with humility 'the slight female form in the saddle ... stepping close to her hanging feet' (6; p.51). His 'abashed and sad voice' registers his recent change of fortune, as well as the change in his immediate needs and desires: 'Do you want a shepherd, ma'am?' (ibid.).

**Now read Judith Bryant Wittenberg, 'Angles of vision and questions of gender in *Far from the Madding Crowd*' (1986, pp.25–40; extract in Regan, 2001). What are the main points she makes?**

Wittenberg makes the crucial point that there is not just one controlling male gaze but several different ways in which male characters respond to women visually, and that these are subject to fluctuation throughout the novel. She also argues that Bathsheba's own way of perceiving others and perceiving herself is vitally important, and that this, too, undergoes significant transformation. The social pressure to marry is seen by Wittenberg as part of Bathsheba's susceptibility to Boldwood and Troy, who are particular representatives of a patriarchal society with carefully delineated class affiliations: a gentleman farmer and a non-commissioned military officer of dubious noble lineage. Troy's mother, a Parisienne, married a doctor, but his 'natural' father is thought to be the last Earl of Severn, as Liddy confides to Bathsheba (24; p.165). Bathsheba's courtship with these men, as we have seen, is presented in powerfully visual terms, with the obsessive and self-destructive vision of Farmer Boldwood vying with Sergeant Troy's superficial delight in spectacle.

It is only through the competing claims of Boldwood and Troy that we finally come to know what kind of man Gabriel Oak is. If the novel is sensitive to different class affiliations and different ways of seeing, it is also acutely aware of different forms of masculinity and manliness. On several occasions, the novel throws the question of gender into disarray, unsettling distinctions between 'male' and 'female' behaviour and deliberately reversing conventional expectations. **Reread chapter 27, 'Hiving the bees'. Is this simply an amusing account of a familiar rural pastime or does it comment obliquely on questions of gender?**

Although this is a very short chapter, it neatly encapsulates the novel's abiding interest in disguise and the related question of identity. Troy clearly enjoys dressing up, and while this sometimes serves a narrative function – as with his concealment under the costume of Dick Turpin at the sheep fair – it also suggests that identity, far from being fixed and immutable, might well be fluid and provisional. A similar speculation about gender occurs in chapter 27, when Troy puts on the garments that Bathsheba has just been wearing:

> So a whimsical fate ordered that her hat should be taken off, veil and all attached, and placed upon his head, Troy tossing his own into a gooseberry bush. Then the veil had to be tied at its lower edge round his collar, and the gloves put on him. (27; p.179)

The superficial appearances distinguishing man from woman are momentarily erased. This time, it is Bathsheba who does the looking and Troy who is reduced to an object: 'He looked such an extraordinary object in this guise that, flurried as she was, she could not avoid laughing outright' (ibid.). Ironically, Troy's dressing up turns out to be a clever seductive ploy: 'It was the removal of yet another stake from the palisade of cold manners which had kept him off' (ibid.). Only minutes earlier, on Troy's arrival, Bathsheba had 'pulled the skirt of her gown tightly round her ankles in a tremendous flurry' (27; p.178). Displays of gender difference are countered with displays of gender blurring. Troy reasserts his soldierly identity by introducing the topic of sword-exercise, but his discomfiture in the hat and veil speaks eloquently of the limiting nature of traditional gender roles: 'Would you be good enough to untie me and let me out? I am nearly stifled inside this silk cage' (27; p.179). Here and elsewhere the novel challenges conventional constructions of both masculinity and femininity.

*Far from the Madding Crowd* asks if there is any natural or necessary relationship between gender and power. The fluctuating fortunes of Gabriel, seen in close relation to those of Bathsheba, dispel any easy conclusion on the matter. In various ways, Gabriel seems to be assigned those gender attributes that in other Victorian novels would traditionally be designated 'female': his tender care for animals, his patience in waiting, his constancy in love. Marjorie Garson argues that 'Gabriel is all the stronger for possessing both masculine and feminine qualities' (1991, p.28). As a shepherd, he is 'a nurturing figure, being both mother and midwife to his sheep', and he is also on intimate terms with Nature, the Great Mother: 'These female identifications give Gabriel's character stability and maturity; indeed, it is his solidarity with the Great Mother which is the basis of his own inner unity' (ibid., pp.28–9). At the end of the storm scene, a critical episode in terms of re-establishing warmth and camaraderie between mistress and shepherd, Gabriel speaks to Bathsheba as 'gently as a mother' (37; p.249).

Even though Gabriel's livelihood revives and prospers, he remains for the most part socially compliant and emotionally subdued. During the sheep-shearing, when he accidentally wounds a ewe, he tries with 'manly resolve' to conceal his love for Bathsheba, but continues to suffer 'the abiding sense of his inferiority to both herself and Boldwood' (22; p.147). The introduction of class-consciousness in this scene suggests that we ought to be wary of any easy distinction between male power and female victimization.

Bathsheba and Fanny Robin are both victims of the sexual predator, Sergeant Troy, but the cultural and economic contrasts between the two women are strongly marked. Bathsheba, we are told, 'had grounds for conjecturing a connection between her own history and the dimly suspected tragedy of

Fanny's end' (43; p.286). Only a few lines earlier, however, the narrator suggests that 'their fates might be supposed to stand in some respects as contrasts to each other' (ibid.). When Gabriel first meets Fanny, she is described as 'a slim girl, rather thinly clad', whose speech is hesitant and timorous (7; p.53). She tells him, 'I am rather poor and I don't want people to know anything about me' (7; p.54). Gabriel, noticing her shivering, offers her a shilling: 'Since you are not very well off perhaps you would accept this trifle from me' (ibid.). When Fanny is seen outside the barracks, she is repeatedly described in terms that emphasize her smallness and seeming insignificance: 'a form', a 'little shape', a 'figure', a 'blurred spot' (11; pp.86, 87). Wittenberg draws attention to the ways in which these visual references indicate a psychological condition and expose Fanny's vulnerability (1986, p.37). Garson similarly shows how Fanny is 'glimpsed only in culturally coded fragments (a lock of hair, a rapid pulse, a plaintive voice)' (1991, p.37).

In contrast to this 'slight and fragile creature' (7; p.55), Bathsheba appears opulent in a variety of silk and velvet gowns and dresses. In chapter 21, we see her in 'a rather dashing velvet dress, carefully put on before a glass', and during the sheep-shearing she appears in a 'new riding habit of myrtle green which fitted her to the waist as a rind fits its fruit' (21; p.137; 22; p.147). As Wittenberg points out, the contrasts between Fanny and Bathsheba are underscored by Hardy's technique of showing them in alternating scenes:

> Bathsheba's confident speech to her workers is followed by the chapter depicting Fanny in the snow outside the barracks, even as the chapter describing Fanny's agonizing trip into Casterbridge is bracketed by two scenes of Bathsheba with her husband, both times in emblems of prosperity, her gig and her house. The women may be 'sisters' in their susceptibility to sexual power, but Bathsheba has other qualities that make survival possible. Some of these could be called masculine.
>
> (Wittenberg, 1986, p.38)

Significantly, Fanny is identified very early in the novel as 'Miss Everdene's youngest servant' (8; p.70), a position that clearly establishes a hierarchical relationship and presents the contrast between the two women in obvious material and economic terms. While Bathsheba prospers and finally marries Gabriel, 'Fanny becomes the archetypal fallen woman of Victorian melodrama and visual art, a wandering outcast pictured most often in the dark and snow' (Wittenberg, 1986, p.37). Unlike some of the moralistic images of 'the fallen woman' in Victorian art, however, Hardy's picture of Fanny is compassionate and uncensorious. Chapter 40, 'On Casterbridge highway', shows us a woman who is literally 'fallen', desperately propping herself up with improvised crutches and struggling with the help of a dog until she finally collapses from exhaustion and dies.

Ironically, it is Fanny who acts as a powerful catalyst in transforming Bathsheba's thoughts and feelings, and in precipitating what she comes to recognize in her relationship with Gabriel as 'the genuine friendship of a sister' (41; p.269). **Reread chapter 43, as far as '... I should know all' (p.288). What kind of value does Bathsheba now recognize in Gabriel?**

It is in her worst moments of loneliness and doubt that Bathsheba turns to Gabriel as a teacher and a friend. Significantly, it is his way of looking at the world – his way of seeing things – that Bathsheba comes to value. The emphasis on perception suggests that his vision is not the possessive or threatening mode of apprehension often attributed to Boldwood and Troy. The following passage is crucially important in terms of how we might assess the adjustments in behaviour displayed by Bathsheba and Gabriel:

> What a way Oak had, she thought, of enduring things. Boldwood, who seemed so much deeper, and higher, and stronger in feeling than Gabriel, had not yet learnt any more than she herself the simple lesson which Oak showed a mastery of by every turn and look he gave – that among the multitude of interests by which he was surrounded, those which affected his personal well-being were not the most absorbing and important in his eyes. Oak meditatively looked upon the horizon of circumstances without any special regard to his own standpoint in the midst. That was how she would wish to be. (43; p.287)

In effect, both Gabriel and Bathsheba modify their ways of apprehending the world, and they learn to see each other differently. At the end of chapter 46, both have their eyes 'fixed' on Fanny's tomb. Gabriel's eyes momentarily alight on Bathsheba, but he gazes 'enquiringly' and feelingly (46; p.312).

The rapprochement between Gabriel and Bathsheba is presented in a way that draws attention to the complicated dynamics of desire rather than to the more obvious model of male power and female victimization. Chapter 37 is ostensibly concerned with the storm, but its subtitle is 'The two together': it shows Gabriel and Bathsheba working closely together, and it affords an opportunity for Bathsheba to explain her disastrous marriage to Troy. Gabriel admits that he now sees the matter 'in a new light' (37; p.248). Similarly, chapter 51 provides an occasion for Bathsheba to confide in Gabriel and confess her misgivings about Boldwood's proposal. The chapter is highly revealing in terms of the novel's sexual politics. While not explicitly condoning Bathsheba's 'rash' behaviour, it asserts a positive and enlightened view of gender and power imbalances. Bathsheba tells Boldwood, 'It is difficult for a woman to define her feelings in language, which is chiefly made by men to express theirs' (51; p.342). Equally striking is Bathsheba's memorable description of herself as 'a watched woman'. She tells Gabriel of her need for discretion in dealing with Boldwood: 'Some rash acts of my past life have taught me that a watched woman must have very much circumspection to retain only a very little credit' (51; p.345). Conceding that she has been 'a rake' in her treatment of Boldwood, she nevertheless rebels against the idea of marriage as a payment for damages: 'I *hate* the act of marriage under such circumstances, and the class of women I should seem to belong to by doing it!' (51; p.346).

Bathsheba's unconventionality and spirited independence at this point in the novel ought to mitigate against a simple account of the narrative as being primarily directed towards 'taming' her. **Now read John Lucas, 'Bathsheba's uncertainty of self' (1977, pp.137–47; extract in Regan, 2001). What does Lucas suggest the narrative is doing?**

Lucas suggests that the narrative exposes her 'radical uncertainties about herself', and that these are fundamentally connected with 'the nature of social movement' (1977, p.138). It is certainly the case, as we will see in the next section, that issues of social class, as well as gender, are crucially involved in the novel's constitution. Even as late as chapter 51, Bathsheba considers that Gabriel is 'far too poor a man to speak sentiment to her' (51; p.346). **How, then, are we to read the eventual marriage of Bathsheba and Gabriel, and in particular how should we respond to the narrative discourse on love and friendship in the final paragraph of chapter 56 (p.383)?**

Some critics regard the ending of the novel as the achievement of 'a harmonious equilibrium' worthy of celebration (Wittenberg, 1986, p.40). Others have tended to see it as problematical and subdued in tone. The dark and troubled events that precede the marriage of Bathsheba and Gabriel cast an unavoidable shadow over their eventual union. As Lucas suggests, Hardy seems to imply, 'through a narrative which elaborates on their separateness, how unlikely is their coming together' (1977, p.147). The passage in question is hedged about with doubts and uncertainties. The promising phrase 'substantial affection' is immediately followed by the parenthetical caution '(if any arises at all)', and good-fellowship, or camaraderie, which is 'unfortunately seldom superadded to love between the sexes', seems heavily dependent on 'happy circumstance'. As we will see in the next section, however, Hardy does recognize the value and importance of a love that is grounded in shared labour and shared endeavour.

# Social class

Hardy's first novel, probably written in 1867 and 1868, was entitled 'The Poor Man and the Lady – By the Poor Man'. The work was never published and no part of the manuscript has survived, but it is possible from letters, memoirs and other documents to detect what kind of novel it was. *The Life of Thomas Hardy* includes a revealing account of 'The Poor Man and the Lady' as 'a striking socialistic novel' (Hardy, 1962, p.56). It goes on to explain that the story was 'a sweeping dramatic satire of the squirearchy and nobility, London society, the vulgarity of the middle class, modern Christianity, church-restoration, and political and domestic morals in general' (ibid., p.61). More remarkable still is the disclosure in the *Life* that the author's views were 'obviously those of a young man with a passion for reforming the world ... the tendency of the writing being socialistic, not to say revolutionary' (ibid.).

*The Life of Thomas Hardy* also reveals that the publisher to whom Hardy had sent the manuscript, Alexander Macmillan, had praised the general conception of the novel, but expressed severe reservations about its pervasive class hostility. Macmillan had said it 'meant mischief' (quoted in Hardy, 1962, p.62). The *Life* also refers to a reader's report by John Morley, which remarks on the originality and promise of the novel, but also objects to a wild extravagance that makes it read 'like some clever lad's dream' (quoted in ibid., p.59). Another publisher's reader, the Victorian poet and novelist George Meredith, advised Hardy 'not to "nail his colours to the mast" so definitely in a first book', and warned him that 'if he printed so pronounced a thing he would be attacked on all sides by the conventional reviewers, and his future injured' (quoted in ibid., p.61). Hardy reworked parts of the manuscript for his novella *An Indiscretion in the Life of an Heiress* in 1878, and other sections appear to have been adopted by him in novels as late as *Jude the Obscure* (1895). As Millgate suggests, his failure to find a publisher was 'a severe setback, and Hardy, who always believed *The Poor Man and the Lady* to have been the most original work, for its time, that he had ever written, never forgot the bitterness of its several rejections and ultimate dismemberment' (1982, p.115).

Widdowson argues very persuasively that while Hardy endeavours to produce more 'acceptable' novels for the market, the subversive element in his writing persists in various guises. Most importantly, for a reading of *Far from the Madding Crowd*, the motivating idea behind 'The Poor Man and the Lady' 'points forward to all those other cross-class sexual relationships at the heart of Hardy's fiction', including that of Gabriel Oak and Bathsheba Everdene (Widdowson, 1996, p.29). These are relationships in which there is usually some 'significant economic disparity' (ibid., p.32). Also of importance is the persistence of satire – both on social aspirations and on fiction-writing itself. There are moments of explicit social satire in *Far from the Madding Crowd*, when the narrator turns abruptly from the course of events to address economic and social inequities. Shortly before the death of Fanny Robin, for instance, the narrative dwells on the irony that the inmates of Casterbridge workhouse should enjoy such a splendid view of the countryside: 'A neighbouring earl once said that he would give up a year's rental to have at his own door the view enjoyed by the inmates from theirs – and very probably the inmates would have given up the view for his year's rental' (40; p.263). The sardonic voice here is particularly pronounced, but the acute awareness of class distinctions is evident throughout the novel. As Widdowson points out, however, Hardy seems to turn on the pretensions of realist fiction with the same kind of fierce satirical energy. He appears to go 'underground', disturbing the very foundation of realist fiction by 'simultaneously creating illusion and deconstructing it' (Widdowson, 1996, p.30). As we have already seen, *Far from the Madding Crowd* is highly self-reflexive and self-conscious about its own fictive status. **What can be said, then, about the function of social class in *Far from the Madding Crowd*? Where might a political reading of the novel begin?**

One mode of criticism that was popular for many years has to do with the erosion of old rural England by the forces of modernity and change, usually represented by characters who are essentially 'outsiders'. Carpenter, for instance, writes about 'the dissolution of the old, stable, rural and provincial life under the pressure of urban encroachment and technological change' (1964, p.336). Arnold Kettle, writing on *Tess of the d'Urbervilles*, proposes that Hardy's fiction is fundamentally concerned with the destruction of the English peasantry ([1953] 1972, p.45). This kind of reading, however, involves a distorting view of what precipitates change in Hardy's novels, as well as a sentimental view of 'old' England. A great deal of historical evidence has been amassed, often to little avail, in trying to establish how 'accurately' the novels depict the changing rural society of their time. But, as Raymond Williams points out, the social disturbance portrayed in them is the consequence not of some outside pressure affecting a previously stable rural environment, but of social and economic conflicts already endemic in that environment (1970, pp.112–13). It is here that the question of social class becomes imperative. The architects of social change and disturbance in *Far from the Madding Crowd* – Bathsheba, Gabriel, Boldwood and Troy – are not characterized as 'outsiders' so much as social aspirants caught in complex patterns of cultural and economic change. **Now read Raymond Williams, 'Thomas Hardy' (1970, pp.97–118; extract in Regan, 2001), and note the points he makes about the rural social structure.**

As Williams makes clear, the rural society Hardy is writing about is not some timeless, settled order, but a shifting structure with a marked gradation of classes: landowners, tenant farmers, dealers, craftsmen and labourers. As the son of a builder, Hardy's own class position within this rural order might be described as an intermediate one. Though having direct relations with craftsmen and labourers, he was able to establish connections elsewhere in the social hierarchy. As an architect and then a writer, he moved to a different point in the social structure, mixing with a metropolitan as well as a rural society. Significantly, then, he comes to occupy an ambiguous class position and a curious vantage point as a writer. As Eagleton puts it, 'Hardy's situation as a literary producer was riven with contradictions. They are contradictions inseparable from his fraught productive relation to the metropolitan audience whose spokesmen rejected his first, abrasively radical work' ([1976] 1990, p.131). Widdowson endorses this view, suggesting that Hardy's principal characters are those who are 'displaced from their "true" class *locus*, being between classes, or being in the wrong place or community for their class type' (1996, p.32). Adopting a felicitous phrase from *The Hand of Ethelberta* (the novel that followed *Far from the Madding Crowd*), he draws attention to Hardy's acute and abiding interest in the 'metamorphic classes of society' (ibid., pp.32–3). **To what extent does *Far from the Madding Crowd* turn on ideas of social mobility and 'metamorphic' class relations? Where in the novel do we first see these ideas at work?**

It might be argued that, right from the outset, the novel evinces its interests in the class and cultural positioning of its protagonists. The picture of Bathsheba sitting aboard a waggon transporting her worldly goods is a striking one. So often, as with the opening of *The Mayor of Casterbridge* (1886), Hardy likes to depict the idea of social mobility through characters who are physically in transit. There are indications of social superiority in the suggestion that Bathsheba 'carelessly glanced over' Gabriel and 'told her man to drive on' (1; p.13). We are offered a replay of 'The Poor Man and the Lady', except that at this point in the novel Gabriel appears to be more financially secure than Bathsheba. **What is it, then, that signifies class distinction?**

Clearly, education has something to do with it, and this, in turn, is manifest in the way people speak. You might recall how Gabriel's marriage-proposal is rebuffed by Bathsheba's insistence that, although she has 'hardly a penny in the world' and is dependent on her aunt for sustenance, she is 'better educated' than he is (4; p.36). Gabriel, in deference, tells her 'You speak like a lady – all the parish notice it' (ibid.).

Social mobility, of course, has its downs as well as its ups, as Hardy demonstrates so powerfully in *The Mayor of Casterbridge*. Contrary to the popular wisdom that some malevolent Fate conspires against humanity in Hardy's novels, the tragic circumstances they depict are nearly always the consequence of a character's precarious position within the social and economic order. Gabriel is thrown into a subordinate class position when he loses his sheep. Lacking the capital to sustain his independent livelihood, he has not been able to provide insurance for his flock. Bathsheba, despite being the daughter of a 'celebrated bankrupt', inherits the property of her uncle, Farmer Everdene. Gabriel is then in the position of selling his labour to Bathsheba until such time as he can re-establish himself on the rung of ownership. *Far from the Madding Crowd*, then, meticulously establishes the specific class co-ordinates of its principal actors. **In what ways is this true of Troy and Boldwood?**

One of the earliest references to Troy is contained in the letter sent by Fanny Robin to Gabriel and intercepted by Boldwood. The letter states that although 'The sergeant grew up in Weatherbury', he is 'a man of great respectability and high honour – indeed, a nobleman by blood' (15; p.111). Boldwood reveals the scandal that Troy's mother was, in fact, married to 'a poor medical man', but formed 'a secret attachment' to 'the late Lord Severn', leaving Troy's parentage in some doubt (15; p.112). We later learn that Troy's watch, proffered as a gift to Bathsheba, carries the motto of the earls of Severn. Troy tells Bathsheba, 'It was all the fortune that ever I inherited', but he takes great pride in the spurious claims to nobility that it lends him: 'That watch has regulated imperial interests in its time – the stately ceremonial, the courtly assignation, pompous travels, and lordly sleeps' (26; p.175).

We learn that Troy was 'a fairly well educated man for one of middle class – exceptionally well educated for a common soldier', and that this explains why he 'spoke fluently and unceasingly' (25; p.167). Bathsheba later uses Troy's education and supposed nobility as justification for encouraging his interest in her. She tells Gabriel: 'Sergeant Troy is an educated man and quite worthy of any woman. He is well born' (29; p.189). Gabriel, however, has a different notion of what Troy's position implies: 'His being higher in learning and birth than the ruck o' soldiers is anything but a proof of his worth. It shows his course to be down'ard' (ibid.). In telling Bathsheba that Troy is not good enough for her, Gabriel clearly asserts an idea of value and worth at odds with the usual class preoccupation with rank and wealth. Ironically, Bathsheba has earlier told Liddy that she rejected the advances of a farmer (Gabriel himself) because 'He wasn't quite good enough for me' (9; p.77).

What *Far from the Madding Crowd* reveals is that love and marriage are not simply matters of the heart, but choices and decisions involving complicated economic and cultural factors. Within the chronic insecurity of the changing social order that Hardy depicts, these choices are particularly pressing and acute. Williams notes that 'One of the most immediate effects of mobility, within a structure itself changing, is the difficult nature of the marriage choice' (1970, p.115). This is everywhere apparent in *Far from the Madding Crowd*. It explains why Bathsheba, having little emotional 'want' of Farmer Boldwood, nevertheless feels compelled to consider his marriage-proposal: 'Bathsheba, not being the least in love with him, was eventually able to look calmly at his offer. It was one which many women of her own station in the neighbourhood, and not a few of higher rank, would have been wild to accept and proud to publish' (20; p.130). The class vocabulary of 'rank' and 'station' is particularly pronounced in this passage. Boldwood is perceived as a gentleman farmer, a 'well to do' and 'respected' man (ibid.). The same vocabulary of class distinction reappears in chapter 34, when Boldwood tries to persuade Troy to leave Weatherbury and Bathsheba behind, telling him, 'there's too much difference between Miss Everdene's station and your own for this flirtation with her ever to benefit you by ending in marriage' (34; p.225). Pondering whether to accept Boldwood's cash offer, Troy admits to liking Fanny 'best', but recognizes that 'she's only a servant' (ibid.). In a vivid realization of Hardy's 'metamorphic classes of society', Troy ceases to be a sergeant and becomes a gentleman farmer as soon as he has access to the resources of Upper Weatherbury Farm.

Marriage, education and work coalesce in *Far from the Madding Crowd* around the primary impulse of desire, and so often desire is thwarted and defeated. Hardy's later novels, *Tess of the d'Urbervilles* and *Jude the Obscure*, are the bleakest testimonies to this thwarted desire, but *Far from the Madding Crowd* also bears witness to the tragedy of unfulfilled aims, with the lives of Fanny Robin and Farmer Boldwood ending poignantly in terminal collapse and defeat. The social process in Hardy's novels tends towards isolation and separation within a community that might otherwise be nurtured and sustained: 'That all are frustrated is the essential action: frustrated by very complicated processes of division, separation and rejection. People choose wrongly but under terrible pressures: under the confusions of class, under its misunderstandings, under the calculated rejections of a divided separating world' (Williams, 1970, p.117). For Williams, the consolation and the hope can be found in the fact that, despite 'the tragically isolated catastrophe', Hardy 'created continually the strength and warmth of people living together: in work and in love; in the physical reality of a place' (ibid., p.116). Williams suggests that work is of critical importance for Hardy, because it represents 'a central kind of learning': 'Work enters his novels more decisively than in any English novelist of comparable importance' (ibid.). Williams also claims that 'Work and desire are very deeply connected in his whole imagination' (ibid., p.117). **Can you think of specific episodes in *Far from the Madding Crowd* where this perception is borne out?**

There are, in fact, many episodes in which love and labour are seen to be intricately related, with the sheep-shearing scene in chapter 22 being one of the most prominent and memorable. However, the preceding chapter very neatly suggests the extent to which Gabriel's work for Bathsheba is inseparable from his love for her. The chapter closes with the pertinent observation that 'When the love-led man had ceased from his labours, Bathsheba came and looked him in the face'. The question she asks is 'Gabriel, will you stay on with me?', but his reply is a curious anticipation of their eventual marriage-vows: ' "I will," said Gabriel' (21; p.141).

The hazardous nature of rural capitalism is such that Gabriel's desire for Bathsheba (dependent on rapid social advancement) cannot be abstracted from economic calculation, a realization clearly at work in chapter 36, entitled 'Wealth in jeopardy'. For the second time in his itinerant career, Gabriel risks his life for the woman he has 'loved so dearly' (36; p.240). That 'dear' love ('dear' in passion and in price) is measured against the value of five wheat ricks and three stacks of barley, which he mentally calculates as follows:

$$5 \times 30 = 150 \text{ quarters} = 500 \text{ £}$$
$$3 \times 40 = 120 \text{ quarters} = 250 \text{ £}$$
$$\text{Total } 750 \text{ £}$$

(ibid.)

Gabriel acknowledges that this is 'Seven hundred and fifty pounds in the divinest form that money can wear – that of necessary food for man and beast' (ibid.). His perception is an illuminating instance of what Karl Marx defined as 'commodification' (1977, p.435): the transformation of goods into money, to the point where the goods acquire a crude exchange value. As John Goode points out, there is a vital and necessary relationship between social class and work in the novel, because class and subordination are functions of the social relations of production: 'Society operates through work, and wealth – as Gabriel shows when he reckons wheat as the equivalent of gold after the storm – is expressed in terms of a developed, wage-based capitalist economy. The reality of class relations is in this novel, heavily disguised as idyll' (1990, p.28). Gabriel's resourceful labour accelerates his promotion, first as Bathsheba's bailiff, then as manager of Boldwood's farm. In chapter 49, appropriately entitled 'Oak's advancement', we see him on horseback, cheerfully surveying 'the length and breadth of about two thousand acres' (49; p.323), and we later learn that Boldwood has granted him shares in Lower Weatherbury Farm. So rapid is Gabriel's advancement that we might be tempted, as Goode suggests, to read the novel as 'a bourgeois fantasy' (1988, p.28) – except that his position is clearly exceptional, not easily attained, and always subject to the rise and fall he has already endured: 'Gabriel survives only by the pure luck of others' destruction' (ibid., p.32). Like Williams, Goode maintains that 'Work and love and their interdependence are the novel's central affirmation' (ibid.).

We might, in the end, question the adequacy of the novel's vision, investing as much as it does in the final, hard-won union of Gabriel and Bathsheba. The marriage is 'a case of eventual stability, after so much disturbance', but it carries with it, 'an air of inevitable resignation and lateness' (Williams, 1970, p.115). To the very end, romantic idealism seems compromised by strictly utilitarian considerations. In the immediate aftermath of his proposal, Gabriel walks up the hill with Bathsheba, 'explaining to her the details of his forthcoming tenure of the other farm' (56; p.383). We are told that 'They spoke very little of their mutual feelings' (ibid.). Nevertheless, the novel recognizes the possibility of a 'substantial affection' (ibid.), a sense of camaraderie, that might be found in mutually fulfilling work and a shared sense of purpose. If *Far from the Madding Crowd* is radically sceptical in its depiction of class and sexual politics, it is also poignantly affirmative.

*Figure 13.2    The wedding of Bathsheba (Julie Christie) and Gabriel (Alan Bates) in the film* Far from the Madding Crowd, *directed by John Schlesinger, 1967. Photo: The Ronald Grant Archive*

# Works cited

Boumelha, Penny. 1982. *Thomas Hardy and Women: Sexual Ideology and Narrative Form*, Brighton: Harvester.

Carpenter, Richard C. 1964. 'The mirror and the sword: imagery in *Far from the Madding Crowd*', *Nineteenth-Century Fiction*, vol.18, pp.331–45.

Casagrande, Peter. 1979. 'A new vision of Bathsheba Everdene', in *Critical Approaches to the Fiction of Thomas Hardy*, ed. by Dale Kramer, London: Macmillan.

Cecil, David. [1943] 1969. *Hardy the Novelist: An Essay in Criticism*, London: Constable.

Clarke, Graham. Ed. 1993. *Thomas Hardy: Critical Assessments*, vol.1, Robertsbridge: Helm.

Eagleton, Terry. [1976] 1990. *Criticism and Ideology*, London: Verso.

Eliot, T.S. 1934. *After Strange Gods*, London: Faber & Faber.

Garson, Marjorie. 1991. *Hardy's Fables of Integrity: Woman, Body, Text*, Oxford: Clarendon Press.

Gatrell, Simon. 1988. *Hardy the Creator: A Textual Biography*, Oxford: Clarendon Press.

Goode, John. 1988. *Thomas Hardy: The Offensive Truth*, Oxford: Blackwell.

Goode, John. 1990. 'Hardy and Marxism', in *Critical Essays on Thomas Hardy: The Novels*, ed. by Dale Kramer, New York: G.K. Hall.

Hardy, Florence Emily. 1962. *The Life of Thomas Hardy 1840–1928*, London: Macmillan.

Hardy, Thomas. [1874] 2002. *Far from the Madding Crowd*, ed. by Suzanne Falck-Yi, with an introduction by Linda M. Shires, Oxford World's Classics, Oxford: Oxford University Press.

James, Henry [1874] 1993. '*Far from the Madding Crowd*' (review), in *Thomas Hardy: Critical Assessments*, ed. by Graham Clarke, vol.1, Robertsbridge: Helm. (Extract in Regan, 2001.)

Kettle, Arnold. [1953] 1972. *An Introduction to the English Novel*, vol.2, London: Hutchinson.

Lawrence, D.H. [1936] 1970. 'A study of Thomas Hardy', in *Phoenix*, London: Heinemann.

Leavis, F.R. [1948] 1962. *The Great Tradition*, Harmondsworth: Penguin.

Lucas, John. 1977. 'Bathsheba's uncertainty of self', in *The Literature of Change: Studies in the Nineteenth-Century Provincial Novel*, Brighton: Harvester. (Extract in Regan, 2001.)

Marx, Karl. 1977. *Karl Marx: Selected Writings*, ed. by David McLellan, Oxford: Oxford University Press.

Millgate, Michael. 1982. *Thomas Hardy: A Biography*, New York: Random House.

Morgan, Rosemarie. 1988. *Women and Sexuality in the Novels of Thomas Hardy*, London: Routledge.

Morgan, Rosemarie. 1992. *Cancelled Words: Rediscovering Thomas Hardy*, London: Routledge.

Regan, Stephen. Ed. 1998. *The Eagleton Reader*, Oxford: Blackwell.

Regan, Stephen. Ed. 2001. *The Nineteenth-Century Novel: A Critical Reader*, London: Routledge.

Rogers, Katharine. 1975. 'Women in Thomas Hardy', *Centennial Review*, vol.19, pp.249–58.

Stubbs, Patricia. 1979. *Women and Fiction: Feminism and the Novel, 1880–1920*, London: Methuen.

Widdowson, Peter. 1996. *Thomas Hardy*, Plymouth: Northcote House.

Widdowson, Peter. 1999. 'Hardy and critical theory', in *The Cambridge Companion to Hardy*, ed. by Dale Kramer, Cambridge: Cambridge University Press.

Williams, Raymond. 1970. 'Thomas Hardy', in *The English Novel from Dickens to Lawrence*, London: Chatto & Windus. (Extract in Regan, 2001.)

Wittenberg, Judith Bryant. 1986. 'Angles of vision and questions of gender in *Far from the Madding Crowd*', *The Centennial Review*, vol.30, pp.25–40. (Extract in Regan, 2001.)

Woolf, Virginia. [1928] 1994. 'The novels of Thomas Hardy', in *The Essays of Virginia Woolf*, vol.4: *1925-1928*, ed. by Andrew McNeillie, London: Hogarth Press.

# Further reading

Brown, Douglas. [1954] 1968. *Thomas Hardy*, London: Longmans, Green & Co. Although Brown gives a simplified account of rural–urban relations in Hardy's fiction, his book contains some thoughtful and suggestive comments on the social and historical dimensions of the novels.

Chase, M.E. 1927. *Thomas Hardy: From Serial to Novel*, Minneapolis: Minnesota University Press. A valuable account of the publishing history of *Far from the Madding Crowd* and other Hardy novels.

Dalziel, Pamela. 1998. '"She matched his violence with her own wild passion": illustrating *Far from the Madding Crowd*', in *Reading Thomas Hardy*, ed. by Charles C. Pettit, Basingstoke: Macmillan. An informative and revealing account of the illustrations that accompanied the original *Cornhill Magazine* publication of the novel.

Fisher, Joe. 1992. *The Hidden Hardy*, Basingstoke: Macmillan. Fisher offers a theoretically astute and provocative approach to the novels, exploring Hardy's complex relations with his publishers and readers.

Gittings, Robert. 1975. *Young Thomas Hardy*, London: Heinemann.

Gittings, Robert. 1978. *The Older Hardy*, London: Heinemann. The two volumes by Gittings are worth reading alongside Michael Millgate's acclaimed biography of Hardy.

Gregor, Ian. 1974. *The Great Web: The Form of Hardy's Major Fiction*, London: Faber & Faber. A largely formalist reading of the novels, but one that significantly challenges the notion that Hardy was naive and clumsy in his composition and structuring of the novels.

Guerard, Albert J. [1949] 1964. *Thomas Hardy*, London: New Directions. Like Gregor, Guerard challenges narrow critical assessments of the novels, but does so by drawing attention to Hardy's progressive, proto-modernist ideas.

Hardy, Florence Emily. 1962. *The Life of Thomas Hardy 1840–1928*, London: Macmillan. A fascinating source of information. It was first published in two volumes after Hardy's death – *The Early Life of Thomas Hardy, 1840–1891* (1928) and *The Later Years of Thomas Hardy, 1892–1928* (1930) – purportedly written by Hardy's second wife, Florence Emily. However, it is now clear that both volumes were composed by Hardy himself in the 1920s. This single-volume edition, *The Life of Thomas Hardy, 1840–1928*, was published in 1962.

Holloway, John. 1953. *The Victorian Sage*, London: Macmillan. Holloway's book considers Hardy's work in the context of prevailing Victorian religious, philosophical and scientific ideas.

Jones, Lawrence. 1980. 'George Eliot and pastoral tragi-comedy in Hardy's *Far from the Madding Crowd*', *Studies in Philology*, vol.77, pp.402–25. Jones offers a stimulating account of the generic complexity of Hardy's writing, and draws attention to similarities and differences in the work of George Eliot.

Kramer, Dale. Ed. 1999. *The Cambridge Companion to Thomas Hardy*, Cambridge: Cambridge University Press. An excellent, up-to-date collection of new critical approaches to Hardy's work.

Lodge, David. 1981. *Working with Structuralism: Essays and Reviews on Nineteenth- and Twentieth-Century Literature*, London: Routledge & Kegan Paul. Lodge's book includes several essays on Hardy's fiction. His discussion of Darwinian ideas in *The Woodlanders* is particularly interesting.

Reid, Fred. 1986. 'Art and ideology in *Far from the Madding Crowd*', *Thomas Hardy Annual*, vol.4, pp.91–126. Reid's article explores the concealed politics of English pastoralism and makes excellent use of the writings of William Cobbett.

Shires, Linda M. 1993. 'Narrative, gender and power in *Far from the Madding Crowd*', in *The Sense of Sex*, ed. by Margaret R. Higonnet, Chicago: University of Illinois Press. An illuminating reading of the novel based on a potent blend of narratology and feminist theory.

Squires, Michael. 1970. '*Far from the Madding Crowd* as modified pastoral', *Nineteenth-Century Fiction*, vol.25, pp.299–326. A good introductory account of how Hardy adopts and transforms familiar pastoral conventions.

Thomas, Jane. 1999. *Thomas Hardy: Femininity and Dissent*, Basingstoke: Macmillan. A well-argued reappraisal of Hardy's work and one that challenges casual critical assumptions about the 'major' and 'minor' novels.

Widdowson, Peter. 1989. *Hardy in History: A Study in Literary Sociology*, London: Routledge. By far the most important and inventive work of criticism on Hardy in recent years; it briskly dispenses with the tired clichés of earlier criticism and establishes a new set of standards and methods for assessing the radical potential of Hardy's work.

Widdowson, Peter. 1997. *Thomas Hardy: Selected Poetry and Non-Fictional Prose*, Basingstoke: Macmillan. As well as arranging the poetry in a way that challenges commonplace critical assumptions about Hardy's achievements, this excellent book also includes a selection of essays such as 'The Dorsetshire labourer' and 'The science of fiction'. The accompanying notes are extremely helpful and informative.

Widdowson, Peter. 1998. *On Thomas Hardy: Late Essays and Earlier*, Basingstoke: Macmillan. A lively, stimulating collection of essays, providing a range of new critical perspectives on topics such as Hardy the satirist and cogent reviews of film versions of the novels.

Williams, Merryn. 1972. *Thomas Hardy and Rural England*, London: Macmillan. A comprehensive and detailed account of Hardy's work in relation to the rural society of its time.

Williams, Raymond. 1973. *The Country and the City*, London: Chatto & Windus. Williams's chapter on Hardy is a bold and inspiring appraisal. It has been crucially important in rescuing Hardy's critical reputation from the condescension of Henry James, F.R. Leavis and others.

Wotton, George. 1985. *Thomas Hardy: Towards a Materialist Criticism*, Dublin: Gill & Macmillan. A formidable Marxist reading of the novels, drawing impressively on theories of ideology and cultural production.

# CHAPTER 14

# *Germinal*: the naturalist novel

*by Nicolette David*

## What kind of a novel is *Germinal*?

Émile Zola's *Germinal* (1884–5) is a novel that portrays with unique power the revolutionary potential of the people and the urgent need for social change. The resonances of the title alone suggest as much: '"Germinal" was the name given to the month of April in the immediate aftermath of the French Revolution, and it was on "12 Germinal, year III" that starving Parisians staged a famous uprising against the government of the Convention' (Lethbridge, 1993, p.vii). These resonances pervade the events and imagery of the novel at many different levels, but critics remain divided as to their effect. Before we reach any final conclusion on that, however, it is important to try to define what kind of novel *Germinal* is.

All discussion of *Germinal* sooner or later has to come to terms with the literary movement known as 'naturalism', a movement which has become synonymous with Zola's name. One of the first novelists to attempt to theorize his work, Zola tried to persuade the public of the 'objective', disinterested nature of his literary project, starting in 1868 with his preface to the second edition of his first significant novel, *Thérèse Raquin* (1867), and continuing through to his lengthy essay 'Le roman expérimental' ('The experimental novel') in 1880. The matter-of-fact way in which Zola described working-class life and his (sometimes lurid) descriptions of sex repelled many readers. According to the critic David Baguley, Zola himself overstated the case for naturalism as a response to hostile critical reception:

> There has always been a strong tendency to take Zola's ideas literally and to interpret his novels as products of his stated principles. It would be more accurate to reverse the terms and to interpret the theory as an attempt to justify more forcibly than before his firmly established literary practice in the face of hostile criticism. Zola's ideas belong very much to the context of the reception of his works, to a situation in which he was led to harden his views and express them with an intensity that immediately discredited them in the eyes of his contemporaries.
>
> (Baguley, 1992, p.40)

Whether or not they should be taken literally, Zola's theoretical writings on the naturalist novel remain an important starting point for any critical discussion of *Germinal*. What, then, is meant by naturalism?

Naturalism is intimately related to and simultaneously distinct from realism. Broadly speaking, realism is a term applied to artistic texts which seek to imitate 'reality', texts which develop or bring to the fore certain techniques in order to represent all aspects of social or domestic life. In France between 1848 and 1870, realism became a key aesthetic movement, out of which a particular branch developed, known as naturalism. Of central importance to naturalism is a belief in scientific determinism, which pervades all aspects of life. It was the task of the naturalist novelist to emphasize the physiological and environmental conditions that determine individual character. Zola was also profoundly influenced by the scientist Dr Prosper Lucas, who wrote a *Traité de l'hérédité naturelle* (1850; 'Treatise on natural heredity'), and Zola's vast series of novels, the so-called Rougon-Macquart, which occupied most of his working life from 1868 onwards, was in part written to demonstrate the principle of heredity working through different characters from the same two families living within a wide spectrum of social environments at a certain period in French history, the Second Empire (1851–70).

At the same time, Zola was very interested in the ideas of the physiologist Claude Bernard, upon whose work he based 'Le roman expérimental'. 'The novel', Zola writes in that essay, 'is a real experiment that a novelist makes on man by the help of observation' ([1880] 1893, p.10); naturalistic novelists 'observe and experiment' (ibid., p.13). Science has entered 'the domain of us novelists, who are to-day the analysers of man, in his individual and social relations' (ibid., p.17). Naturalism is, therefore, 'the literature of our scientific age' (ibid., p.23). Physiology should not merely be confined to the domain of heredity, but should also be used to examine social relations:

> From this we shall see that we can act upon the social conditions, in acting upon the phenomena of which we have made ourselves master in man. And this is what constitutes the experimental novel: to possess a knowledge of the mechanism of the phenomena inherent in man, to show the machinery of his intellectual and sensory manifestations, under the influences of heredity and environment, such as physiology shall give them to us, and then finally to exhibit man living in social conditions produced by himself, which he modifies daily, and in the heart of which he himself experiences a continual transformation. Thus, then, we lean on physiology; we take man from the hands of the physiologists solely, in order to continue the solution of the problem, and to solve scientifically the question of how men behave when they are in society.
>
> (Zola, 1893, pp.21–2)

The novel is an experiment set up by the novelist, who starts with an idea, and watches it unfold:

> The experimental novelist is therefore the one who accepts proven facts, who points out in man and in society the mechanism of the phenomena over which science is mistress, and who does not interpose his personal sentiments, except in the phenomena whose determinism is not yet settled, and who tries to test, as much as he can, this personal sentiment ... by observation and experiment.
>
> (Zola, 1893, pp.23–4)

Zola claims that the novelist is a dispassionate observer, who does not control the experiment, and who does not 'interpose his personal sentiments'. Imagination plays a role only in the sense that it gives the writer the idea, and influences form and style, but the principal function of the writer is to observe the experiment and record. **Does this seem to be a view that we can take seriously?**

Critics have argued that the only way to conduct a real experiment would be to take a real character who possesses precisely the same genetic traits as one of Zola's characters, and place them in that social environment, and subsequently watch their character develop (or, more likely, decline). Fiction, on the other hand, functions on the basis of writers' (conscious or unconscious) manipulation of their medium. To us, the idea of the writer as a dispassionate observer may seem difficult to take seriously.

None the less, it is clear from his essay that Zola did take it seriously. Moreover, it is clear that he took the art of the novelist seriously.

In 'Le roman expérimental', Zola defends himself against the accusation that naturalists are fatalists. Naturalists are determinists, he says:

> All we do is to apply this method in our novels, and we are the determinists who experimentally try to determine the condition of the phenomena, without departing in our investigations from the laws of nature. As Claude Bernard very truly says, the moment that we can act, and that we do act, on the determining cause of phenomena – by modifying their surroundings, for example – we cease to be fatalists.
>
> (1893, p.30)

This may certainly be true in theory, but it remains the case that those characters from the Rougon-Macquart series in whom we are most interested have inherited genetic traits of madness or alcoholism: they are almost inevitably placed in social conditions that overwhelm them, and they become inextricably locked into patterns of events and interactions with other characters that herald their decline. A powerful strain of doom and gloom seems to pervade naturalist fiction. Baguley points out that there is a significant disparity between the optimistic belief in the value of scientific investigation held by many naturalist writers, including Zola, and this nihilistic tendency:

> Nature for the naturalists in general was a lethal force, heredity a fatal curse, humanity the prey to biological urges, to irrepressible drives, to primeval impulses, and ultimately to the natural processes of degeneration and decay. In naturalist works there is a constant drift towards disintegration and dissipation, towards a loss of purpose, order and form. Lives are constantly wasted and energies spent.
>
> (1992, pp.48–9)

In addition to 'Le roman expérimental', Zola wrote two other influential essays, 'Le Naturalisme au théâtre' (1881; 'Naturalism in the theatre') and 'Les romanciers Naturalistes' (1881; 'The naturalist novelists'). He clearly desired a theoretical framework through which naturalist novels could be read.

But while critics remain divided as to what kind of a writer Zola was, all agree that he did not stick to his doctrine. Baguley identifies a mixture of at least eight different genres operating in *Germinal*, which he arranges according to the letters in the title: **G**rotesque, **E**pic, **R**omantic, **M**ythic, **I**dyllic, **N**aturalist, **A**llegorical and **L**yric (1992, p.81). The Marxist critic Georg Lukács accused Zola of being flawed because he was essentially a romantic ([1940] 1950, pp.93–5);

others, like Irving Howe, argue that his work takes on a life of its own, bringing 'surprises' which 'could not have been foreseen' by studying the author's theories. For Howe, *Germinal* is great precisely because it exceeded in imagination the doctrine which conceived it (1970, p.54). The idea that the naturalist writer merely records with scientific objectivity is, and remains, paradoxical for the literary critic who engages with *Germinal* as a test. As Naomi Schor argues, 'Zola was nothing if not a superb craftsman, an ingenious and instinctive structuralist' (1978, p.35); and the leading French critic Henri Mitterand devotes several pages to an analysis of the structure of Zola's novels in *Zola et le naturalisme* (1986, pp.62–8). Other critics have written on how Zola's novels can be compared to music, and even to painting (see, for example, Keefe and Lethbridge, 1990, pp.7–8). **None the less, before we go on to consider how far Zola's novel exceeds the doctrine of naturalist fiction, ask yourself: what are the key features of naturalism?**

Naturalism in the novel means:

- the novel is an experiment (analogous to a scientific experiment)
- the role of the writer is that of a dispassionate observer who records the results of the experiment
- human nature and social relations can be analysed using the tools of science
- human nature is governed by the principle of heredity
- when the determining factors or social (and economic) relations impact upon a certain genetically determined temperament, the experiment unfolds
- the role of the writer's imagination is not foregrounded.

But how far does the novel bear out these aims? Let us think of the opening description of the mine:

> Now Le Voreux started to emerge from its shadowy dream world ... he worked out what everything was, and could even locate the pump letting off steam, with its long, raucous repetitive wheeze, like the hoarse snorting of some monster.
>
> (Zola, [1884–5] 1993, 1.1; pp.7–8; unless otherwise stated, all subsequent page references are to this edition)

From the very first moment we encounter Le Voreux there is a multitude of resonances, as Zola's prose sweeps us along in a tide of narrative fervour – a far cry from the dispassionate objectivity predicated of the naturalist writer. In the very fabric of his writing, Zola displays a great awareness of and sensitivity to the power that language possesses. Yet *Germinal*, like all the novels of the Rougon-Macquart series, privileges referential detail: it is extremely well researched and contains a wealth of very precise and accurate detail relating to each social milieu. The opening scenes of the novel, in which the Maheu family wake up, wash, and eat breakfast, are branded with an authenticity that draws us into their world. Yet if Zola's novel moves us, it is because it is also a superbly crafted narrative, full of symbolic meaning.

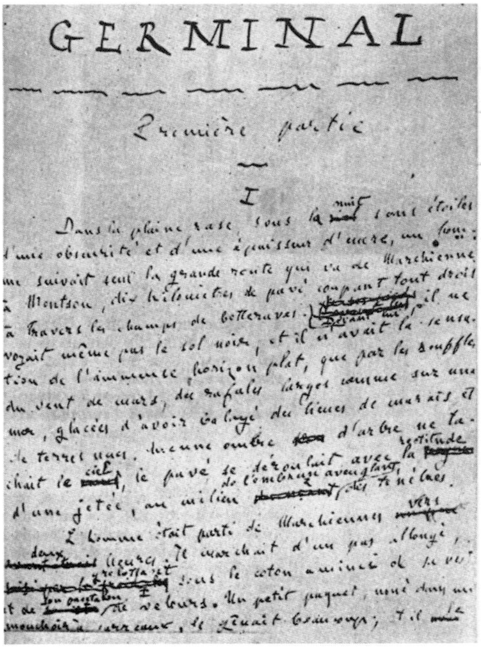

*Figure 14.1   First page of the manuscript of* Germinal. *Reproduced from Henri Mitterand and Jean Vidal,* Album Zola, *Paris: Éditions Gallimard, 1963, p.205. Bibliothèque nationale de France photographic plate*

In this chapter, we will explore the status of *Germinal* as a naturalist novel, through the examination of certain themes: the representation of social environment; characterization; the body and its appetites (violence, hunger and sexuality); and, finally, class conflict. The subtitle of the series to which *Germinal* belongs is 'Histoire naturelle et sociale d'une famille sous le Second Empire' ('A Natural and Social History of a Family under the Second Empire'), a description which emphasizes its historical nature. But Zola's characters, bearing the imprint of particular genetic traits, are enmeshed in the social fabric they are fated to inhabit as part of an 'experiment' spiced up by a powerful dose of heredity, insanity, alcoholism and violence. The common family ancestor is the neurotic Tante Dide, who originally marries Rougon, then, following his death, marries the drunken Macquart. The Rougon side of the family prospers fairly well, but it is the Macquart side of the family for which Zola is better known. Macquart's granddaughter, Gervaise, the heroine of *L'Assommoir* (1877; roughly translated as 'The Dram-Shop'), is the mother of Étienne, whom we encounter in *Germinal*. She is born with a stigma, a limp that symbolizes the violence her mother endured at the hands of her drunken husband. Gervaise herself slides into alcoholism and squalor in the slums of Paris. Étienne has two brothers, Claude and Jacques, and a half-sister, Nana. Claude is a talented painter who commits suicide in *L'Œuvre* (1886; 'The Masterpiece'), whilst Jacques goes on to become the homicidal train-driver of *La Bête humaine* (1890; 'The Human Beast'). The sensuous Nana, meanwhile, becomes a high-class prostitute who lives off the corruption of Paris under the Second Empire, before dying of syphilis, in the novel entitled *Nana* (1880).

# The representation of social environment

In *Germinal*, Zola shows very clearly how the environment of the characters conditions and deforms them. The development of Jeanlin into a physically and emotionally maimed human being is a good example. It is quite directly shown to be the outcome of years of suffering and poverty. For Zola, character creates destiny; yet character itself is forged by social environment, as it impacts upon inherited genes. The notions of character and environment are always difficult to separate; in the case of Zola, this is particularly extreme.

In *Germinal*, every aspect of the miners' existences – their bodies, their labour, their living arrangements, their poverty, their hunger, their sexuality – is powerfully shaped and marked by their relationship with the mine. The mine is the force that controls their lives and causes the terrible suffering portrayed. It represents the central core of their relationship to capitalism, and, consequently, to exploitation and suffering. It is most appropriately named 'Le Voreux', since in French this possesses connotations of the verb 'dévorer', meaning 'to devour', which is what it does. The representation of the mine is an important point for us to begin our investigation of Zola's portrayal of environment as a shaping force of human destiny, because it is here that the paradoxes inherent in the naturalist project are most vividly highlighted. Let us see, then, how Zola succeeds in describing the central environment for the miners.

There is no doubt that Zola was committed to feeding a wealth of referential detail into his narrative. His extensive research served him well, and every detail of the mine is described with attention to accuracy. But is that all? **Reread the opening pages of *Germinal*, especially part 1, chapters 1 and 3, and analyse the ways in which the mine appears in the eyes of the newcomer, Étienne.**

As the mysterious shape of the mine looms and takes shape in the dark night, the reader is introduced to the unfamiliar environment through the perspective of the newcomer, who is initiated through the old man, Bonnemort. The figure of the old man gives access to the community, in this case his own family. From the very beginning the mine is endowed with mythical qualities – it is portrayed as a beast:

> The pit, with its squat brick buildings crammed into the bottom of the valley, raised its chimney like a threatening horn, and seemed to take on a sinister air of a voracious beast, crouching ready to pounce and gobble you up. (1.1; p.7)

The regular motion of the pump is one of the first impressions made available to the senses: 'the pump letting off steam, with its long, raucous, repetitive wheezing, like the hoarse snorting of some monster' (1.1; p.8). The reader, like Étienne, is assailed by different sense impressions which we try to piece together in order to comprehend what we are witnessing: vision and sound, compounded by cold. The portrayal of the mine as a monster grows in intensity:

> There was no sign of dawn to relight the dead sky, only the blast-furnaces burning alongside the coke ovens, bloodying the shadows without illuminating their hidden depths. And Le Voreux lay lower and squatter, deep in its den, crouching like a vicious beast of prey, snorting louder and longer, as if choking on its painful digestion of human flesh. (1.1; p.15)

This is Zola's descriptive writing at its best – powerful, impressionistic, metaphorical, although occasionally lapsing into lurid melodrama. The beast is a predatory, devouring monster, who feeds on the human flesh of the miners and consumes them.

Later, when the miners enter the cages, it is as though to offer themselves up in a ritual sacrifice to the monster:

> It surged back up again, ready to swallow down another load of men. For half an hour the pit gulped down these meals, in more or less greedy mouthfuls, depending on the depth of the level they were bound for, but without ever stopping, always hungry, its giant bowels capable of digesting a nation. It filled and filled again, and the dark depths remained silent as the cage rose up from the void, silently opening its gaping jaws. (1.3; p.27)

The mine is no longer represented as merely a mine, a site of work, where labour is transformed into capital: Zola turns it into the body of a greedy, devouring creature. In the French original the syntax mirrors the devouring actions of the mine-monster, and the action of eating seems even smoother and more automatic. If you read a little French, you may find the quotation below from the original helpful. If not, that does not matter:

> Elle [la cage] replongea, puis jaillit de nouveau au bout de quatre minutes à peine, pour engloutir une autre charge d'hommes. Pendant une demi-heure, le puits en dévora de la sorte, d'une gueule plus ou moins gloutonne, selon la profondeur de l'accrochage où ils descendaient, mais sans un arrêt, toujours affamé, de boyaux géants capables de digérer un peuple. Cela s'emplissait, s'emplissait encore, et les ténèbres restaient mortes, la cage montait du vide dans le même silence vorace.

(Zola, [1884–5] 1978, 1.3; p.74)

The sense that the miners are being ineluctably devoured is even more powerful than in the English translation. The words used intensify the metaphor of the beast: only an animal can have a 'gueule' in French. Indeed, this beast is capable of devouring 'un peuple' (a population, a 'people'), a word in which only the first syllable is emphatically pronounced, and which carries tremendous force, placed as it is at the end of a sentence that conjures up inexorable repetition. The rhythm of devouring is created through the syntax in the French, by building up and suggesting the tireless repetition of the lifts, and through the repeated statement, 's'emplissait', 's'emplissait encore'. The mine is the Underworld, a place for the already dead: as the miners are swallowed, the 'shadows remain dead' ('les ténèbres restaient mortes'), a death the impact of which is emphasized by the alliterative use of 't' and 'r' consonants. Meanwhile, the cage rises up from 'the emptiness in the same voracious silence' ('du vide dans le même silence vorace'), the structure of the French original placing the emphasis upon the last word, 'vorace' (voracious). Thus the silence itself is an empty, magnetic void that is voracious, sucking everything living down into its dead depths.

The representation of the mine in *Germinal* is shot through with different myths, myths that intertwine continuously. **Which myths does Zola use to represent the mine, and what effect does this have?**

The mine is more than a devouring beast, it is a kind of Minotaur, as it devours human flesh. It is also portrayed as a labyrinth, whose arteries are mined by the miners. Étienne can be viewed as a modern Theseus, who is led into the mine by his Ariadne, Catherine. On another level, the mine is strongly associated with entombment and suffocation. It is a kind of Underworld, in which Étienne and

Catherine are eventually buried alive. Étienne can also be seen as Orpheus, who tries and fails to rescue his Eurydice. This idea can even be taken further by regarding Maheu as the king of this Underworld, a king who, by a kind of Oedipal prohibition, prevents the protagonist from possessing his daughter sexually, until his death removes him.

Henri Mitterand writes that humanity is part of a natural totality in Zola's novels, a totality in which the rhythms of nature hold sway. *Germinal* is dominated by the earth and rock, which possess mythical connotations, but this elemental nature, the earth and rocks of the mine, turns against the miners and destroys them: rocks crush them, earth blocks passages, fire burns them and water suffocates and drowns them. The earth is portrayed in a highly ambivalent manner: 'the earth ... in its ... depths, is dark, nocturnal, threatening, suffocating; it is underground and a tomb, a receptacle of death as well as a source of life, a site of origin and a site of forbidden return' (Mitterand, 1986, p.73; my translation). The earth is thus a location of death and a source of new life – for Étienne and his political vision at least. Yet the effect of seeing humanity as part of a natural totality highlights Zola's ambivalence towards his own political project. Maheu, working within the mine, is likened to a greenfly:

> He didn't want to stop cutting, and hacked away so furiously that he shook with the vibrations, wedged between his two levels of rock, like a greenfly caught between the pages of a book which threatened to slam suddenly shut. (1.4; p.39)

In using a simile that fuses Maheu with natural forces, Zola is not focusing on Maheu as the labourer whose work is turned into capital, and therefore exploited – in other words, he is not portraying him as a site of political conflict; rather he is taking his suffering and victimhood away from the specific stream of historical and political events.

Another mythical resonance, closely related to that of the Underworld, is that of Hell. The mine is quite explicitly represented as Hell, where the miners are subjected to unbearable torments: they are, in turn, burnt, suffocated, soaked, drowned and buried alive. Nowhere is the representation of the mine more hellish than in the seam close to Tartarus (Le Tartaret), appropriately named 'Désirée', where Catherine and Chaval work on the day they break the strike. Catherine looks at the miners working and the following mythical images fill her vision:

> She couldn't see them clearly in the reddish glow of their lamps; they were stark naked like beasts, but so black and caked with soot and coal that she wasn't disturbed by their nudity. All you could see of their obscure labours was their spines twisting and turning like monkeys and an infernal vision of reddened limbs, toiling away amid the dull thuds and subdued groaning. (5.2; p.307)

**What means does Zola use to achieve a hellish effect?**

The colours of Hell are traditionally thought of as black and red: the miners are blackened by the coal and reddened by the light of their lamps. Their labour not only causes them to twist and distort their bodies, but reduces them to animals. The sense of hellish torment is reinforced by the noise of the miners groaning with pain. To Zola's readers, who might well have been familiar with

Dante's *Divine Comedy*, the imagery of the toiling miners is strikingly similar to the depiction of the sinners in Dante's Hell. Indeed, Tartarus is an Inferno, a place of sulphurous legend, in which sexually promiscuous tram girls are eternally burning for their sins:

> the local miners told the tale of how a bolt from the heavens had fallen on this Sodom in the bowels of the earth, where the tram girls were guilty of the vilest abominations; it had happened so quickly that they had been unable to get back up to the surface, and still today they were roasting in their hell down below. The dark red, scorched rocks were covered in a leprous growth of alum. Sulphur grew like yellow flowers round the lips of the fissures in the rock. At night the foolhardy who risked their eyes to look through these cracks swore that they could see flames, and criminal souls crackling on the burning coals deep within. Wandering lights ran over the surface, and there was a constant stream of hot, poisonous vapours, rank with the faecal stench of this devil's kitchen. (5.1; pp.303–4)

Throughout *Germinal*, the mine is seen as a place where sexuality and violence burst out of control; we will discuss this in greater depth later on in this chapter when we explore the representation of sexuality. For the moment I am interested in showing how Zola uses myth in order to give the miners' experience a 'universal' dimension. Flagrant outbursts of sexuality on the part of the tram girls merit damnation, in which girls are burnt for eternity beneath the earth. In writing 'Sulphur grew like yellow flowers round the lips of the fissures in the rock', Zola transfigures the manifestation of sulphur into a signifier of sexual corruption and pleasure: the rock itself possesses lips, the flowers are like female genitalia. Similarly, the representation of the burning criminal souls and the explicit reference to the devil's kitchen reinforce the mythical layering.

Shortly afterwards we encounter Catherine, also a tram girl, struggling to work close by the Désirée seam (the parallel is deliberate). Subject to intolerable heat from both sides, she feels her throat burning:

> She felt so oppressed that she wanted to take her shirt off. The cloth was starting to torment her, as every fold cut into her and burnt her. She resisted the temptation, and tried to keep pushing, but she was forced to stop and stand up again. Then suddenly, telling herself that she'd cover up again when she got to the relay point, she took it all off, string and shirt together, feeling so feverish that she would have ripped her skin off if she had been able. And now, stark naked and reduced to the pitiful level of a scavenger scrabbling for a livelihood in the mud of the gutter, she struggled painfully along, her buttocks smeared with sweat and grim, wallowing belly-deep in the mire, pushing along on all fours like a horse hitched to a cab. (5.12; p.308)

This, then, is the ultimate consequence of the poverty and enslavement to the mine: the human being becomes an animal, naked and wallowing in mud. In the French original, the language used reinforces the bestial state to which Catherine is reduced. Her buttocks are 'la croupe', a word associated with a horse; she runs 'au trot', at a trot; and the final dramatic line of the paragraph, 'À quatre pattes, elle poussait' (Zola, 1978, p.366; 'On all fours, she pushed'), continues to work strongly with the animal vocabulary, because in French only an animal can possess a 'patte', a paw.

Mitterand and many other critics have made the vivid point that, in representing the working class as bestial, Zola was playing to the preconceptions of his bourgeois readers. Whilst Zola clearly shows that the miners are reduced to an animalistic state through unbearable working conditions and poverty, it is none the less difficult to escape the impression that they are *innately* bestial and violent. Zola's ambivalence, conscious or not, could be seen as undermining his naturalist, if not also his political, objective. When Catherine is portrayed as a squalid animal, wallowing in the mire, it seems as if, for those who have no choice but to work in the mine or starve, this is their inevitable and tragic fate.

Zola's novels can be viewed as tragic for we know from the very beginning that the central characters are doomed: they are pulled down by their fatal flaws, which are either inherited or have been absorbed from their environment. Placed within the social environment where they must live out their lives, enmeshed with the other characters fate chooses to throw in their path, they haven't got a chance. The modern gods of capitalism and industrialization are pitted against them. The social and historical context imbues and informs every fibre of their fictional lives. Catherine making the miners' breakfast, the Maheu family getting up in the morning, La Mouquette giving Étienne potatoes for the starving Maheu family, and the language used by the characters – all these serve to illustrate the enmeshment of the characters in their social environment.

**Can you think of an example of the kind of language used by the miners that reinforces this?**

Chaval's insults to Étienne represent one example among many of the miners' language:

> 'Ah, you bleeding swine, I'll have your nose, I will, I'll have your nose and stuff it! ... Let's have a look at your mug, let's see that little slut-fucking face, I'm going to mash it into pigswill, and then we'll see if the tarts still lift up their skirts for you.' (6.3; p.404)

We might read *Germinal* on one level as the story of how the working class acquire speech (Howe, 1970, p.55). It is only through speech that they can come to articulate their rights and arrive at a new stage of political consciousness. If this is so, then we might say that Zola does this at many different levels, one of which is that of their earthy language.

*L'Assommoir*, Zola's success of 1877, established him as a writer committed to portraying the suffering of characters enmeshed in a particular social milieu. In *L'Assommoir*, the central character's struggle to survive in working-class Paris is depicted at different levels, from the slang used by the characters to the description of the alcohol-generating machine that will precipitate their downfall. The environment of working-class Paris renders the central character's fate inevitable, just as, you could argue, Étienne will be forced to leave in the end. The tragic inevitability of the outcome is as powerful as the representation of the impact of their environment.

# Characterization

In a famous attack, launched in an essay entitled 'The Zola centenary', the influential Hungarian Marxist critic Georg Lukács accused Zola of being 'incapable of penetrating and convincing characterization' ([1940] 1950, p.95). Lukács developed what is known as 'the reflection model', according to which literature reflects 'reality' outside it. For Lukács, the form of the literary work reflects the form of the real world. According to Lukács, Zola, constrained by the self-imposed corset of naturalism, failed to reach the potential he was capable of as a writer; instead, he produced 'the monotonous commonplace of naturalism', which resulted from 'the direct, mechanical mirroring of the humdrum reality of capitalism' (ibid., p.93). In 'The Zola centenary', Lukács preserves Zola from the accusation that his characters are 'as puppet-like' as those of Victor Hugo (a romantic writer), but he argues that the doctrine of naturalism renders it impossible for Zola to produce fully fledged, complex characters in the 'realist' mode.

In an earlier essay, 'Narrate or describe?', Lukács ([1936] 1970) argued that before 1848 writers were inside the process of history, striving to narrate it. Later on, writers such as Zola were content to describe the world, to 'observe' the social reality they were portraying from outside, rather than 'experience' it from within. For Lukács, Zola condemns his characters to the role of mere spectators, whereas Leo Tolstoy or Honoré de Balzac depict the fabric of relations between their characters and the social reality that is being portrayed. According to Lukács's reflectionist model, a writer like Balzac is superior, because he shows the forces of history at work and is critical of the society he represents.

In Zola's defence we might point out that Lukács's model is based on judgements that privilege the novel of the early half of the nineteenth century – Walter Scott, Stendhal, Balzac. And even if we find a mixture of romanticism and realism in *Germinal*, this does not necessarily mean that Zola failed to reveal 'the human and social significance of the struggle for life' (Lukács, 1950, p.93), nor that his characters remain divorced from their environment. Lukács may, however, lead us to reflect upon what our expectations of a character in a realist novel might be. In Zola's 'experiment', he sought to trace genetic predispositions through the passions and vices of one family. **What implications do you think this has for characterization?**

It would be a mistake to expect the same kind of subtleties of characterization we find in George Eliot, for example. Zola's creative energies are simply not channelled into creating psychologically complex characters who are full of subtle contradictions and inner life. His interest lies predominantly in portraying a vast array of characters embedded in their social environment. In a sense, it is the people as a collective who most fully represent character in *Germinal*. What is of interest for us here is to address how Zola's method of characterization functions in the kind of novel *Germinal* actually is.

Let us begin with the protagonist, Étienne. Zola set out to prove through Étienne that disposition is inherited. So, when Catherine asks him why he hit his boss, we learn that it is because he had too much to drink: 'and when I drink, I lose control, I could kill myself or kill someone else ... Yes, I can't drink more than a glass or two without feeling the need to kill someone' (1.4; p.46). Zola continues:

> When he thought of those things, his black eyes swam and he went pale, for he was stricken with sudden anxiety at the thought of the hereditary flaw which festered unpredictably somewhere in the depths of his youthful vigour. (ibid.)

This hereditary flaw is represented as a festering cancer, corrupting from within. Coupled with Étienne's hatred of alcohol is an innate violence, which springs to life in the form of murderous rage towards Chaval: 'He clenched his fists, and his eyes lit up with homicidal fury, his intoxication brewing up within him an urge to kill' (5.4; p.338). This verges on the exaggeration of melodrama. Zola's belief in inherited traits intrudes into the fiction, rather than growing out of it. Although Étienne might have plenty of reason for wishing to kill Chaval, Zola does not present us with the inner workings of his mind to make this desire appear inevitable; instead he portrays the events which trigger Étienne's rage: drinking, sexual rivalry, mass hysteria, fury at Chaval's treachery. To a degree, we are excluded from identifying with the character. Compare the detailed and subtle way in which we are led to an understanding of Dorothea's reasons for marrying Casaubon in *Middlemarch* with the motivations offered in *Germinal* for Catherine's sexual involvement and subsequent loyalty to Chaval: Zola's approach is obviously different. None the less, surely it's a question of degree – and the kind of novel we are dealing with.

Zola's characters are revealed to us from the outside, through their external actions. Thus La Mouquette is generous: with her body, with her behind, with food, and even in death, trying to protect Catherine. Catherine is generous with her food to the newcomer, and submissive to Chaval, but she is never presented as a character who acts independently of her social environment. The mine has left its marks on her ravaged skin, as it has on the nature of women of her class: 'although her body wasn't ready, she let the male have his way with her, with the hereditary submissiveness that sent all the girls of her race rolling flat on their backs while they were little more than children' (2.5; p.130). Jeanlin – with his animalistic, almost mutant features and distorted, damaged body – is revealed to us through his whimsical cruelty to Lydie and Bébert, his creation of the hideaway in Réquillart, and the symbolic yet senseless murder of the little soldier; but the internal workings of his mind remain hidden.

Zola's characters are driven by their appetites; it is through these appetites and desires that they come to life for us. Étienne's rise to popularity as the organizer of the strike is motivated by the desire for popularity, the need to be important, to play a role, but also by the desire to impress Catherine.

The speech of the miners and the bourgeois families is important: it is a crucial indicator of class and, consequently, of character. Most English translations convey this to some extent, but it is difficult to be as vigorous or natural as the original:

> 'Philomène's coughing,' said Catherine, after listening quietly for a moment ...
>   'Oh yes, like hell!' Zacharie replied. 'Philomène doesn't give a damn, she's fast asleep ... What a slut, to think she can sleep until six o'clock!' (1.2; p.19)

In the French original, Philomène's desire to sleep is seen as the greed of a pig, which links it more directly to instinctive desires:

– Philomène tousse, reprit Catherine, après avoir tendu l'oreille ...
– Ah, ouiche! Philomène! répondit Zacharie, elle s'en moque, elle dort! ... C'est cochon de dormir jusqu'à six heures!

(Zola, 1978, p.64)

The characters in *Germinal* are all there to illustrate a particular point. Thus, Bonnemort, the old man who enables the newcomer to gain access to the community, brutalized and rendered insane through suffering, exacts a symbolic revenge by strangling Cécile Grégoire; Maheu comes to be the voice of the people, the working man who speaks to the bourgeoisie during the strike; and Catherine is not merely the woman Étienne loves, but in her he loves the oppressed, the suffering working-class woman. Rasseneur can be seen as the moderate, whilst Souvarine is the anarchist, the intellectual who has severed all emotional links with humanity. Étienne and Souvarine play out a dialectical relationship, out of which a new order is to be generated. Hennebeau is the tormented, sexually frustrated bourgeois, trapped between the economic realities of capitalism and the demands of the miners. Zola does not deprive his characters of a certain degree of complexity; he sees all too clearly that the leaders of the revolution are not heroes, but characters driven by ambition – in the position of the capitalist bosses, they might well behave exactly as they do.

# The body and its appetites

The body has emerged as an important area of investigation within recent feminist and psychoanalytic criticism. In Sigmund Freud's theoretical writings, the human body within civilization is never viewed as 'natural'. For Freud, the biological body is invested with psychical and social meaning. An individual's psychical and social history is thus 'written' on the body, just as in *Germinal* Catherine's skin and sexual development are marked by her labour in the mine. The miners' bodies in *Germinal* are visibly marked by their social history, but this psychical and social meaning can also be invisible or revealed through displacement. A body in a work of literature is never 'just' a body: it signifies all the things that being a body in a certain social context means (see Freud, [1905] 1991, pp.155–69). The body in *Germinal* can be characterized primarily as an appetitive body.

## *Violence*

When the drunk Étienne kills Chaval out of sexual rivalry, his heart beats faster 'with a kind of animal joy from a physical appetite satisfied' (7.5; p.502), 'la joie animale d'un appétit enfin satisfait' (Zola, 1978, p.570). The urge to kill is thus represented as an appetite that must be sated. At such moments, Zola's writing could be said to lapse into melodramatic rhetoric; but it is effective. In the act of killing Chaval,

He was seized with an irresistible urge to kill, a physical need, as if his tonsils
were swollen and choking his throat, forcing him to spew up or suffocate. It
rose and burst within him beyond the control of his will, under the impulse of
his hereditary flaw (7 5; p.502)

In Zola, 'la bête humaine', 'the human beast', is never far below the surface.
Étienne's 'hereditary flaw' overwhelms him, reducing him to an instinctual,
violent animal.

Hunger, sexuality and violence are fused in the horrific scene of Maigrat's
castration. **Reread part 5, chapter 6, from 'The mob had caught sight of
Maigrat on the roof of the shed' (p.366) to 'This dreadful mutilation had
been accompanied by a horrified silence' (p.368), and consider how the
themes of violence, hunger and sexuality are portrayed, and what effect
this scene has within the structure of the text.**

The castration of Maigrat comes at a moment of climax following a crescendo
of scenes in which the crowd have become increasingly vengeful and possessed
by blood-lust. A symbolic sacrifice is required: the scenes of the crowd running
in revolutionary fury have been built up so that in order to obtain a sense of
narrative release, an act of violence is required. Mitterand has pointed out that
the three symbolic murders in *Germinal* are indispensable to the destruction of
the old order and the possible foundation of a new society (1986, p.58). These
three murders thus constitute forms of revenge executed on the marginal
characters who come to represent, or are viewed as, attributes of bourgeois
oppression. Maigrat can be seen to represent revenge of this kind, because he
constitutes a link to capitalism. In this scene, the furious women exact their
revenge for starvation by stuffing earth into the dead man's mouth. The act of
castration, executed by the hideous fury, Ma Brûlé, is his punishment for having
demanded sexual favours of them.

# Hunger

Hunger is the primary appetite that drives the miners and the narrative of
*Germinal*. There is much to be learned from looking at the way in which hunger
and the body are portrayed in the novel.

Étienne's very first conversation with Bonnemort returns to the refrain: 'if only
there was enough bread' (1.1; p.8). As if to echo these words, the wind appears
to give a cry of hunger. Étienne surveys the surrounding countryside:

The shadows were still deep, but the old man's hand had somehow fleshed
them out with a breadth of suffering that the young man could now intuitively
feel living in the limitless space that surrounded him, as if the March wind were
wringing a cry of famine from the bare countryside. The squalls of wind
shrieked crazily, as if they were murdering work, bringing a famine which
would cause untold slaughter. (1.1; p.9)

The shriek of the wind gives voice to the miner's starvation. There are interesting
parallels between Charlotte Brontë's use of pathetic fallacy in *Jane Eyre* and
Zola's in *Germinal*. Here the desolation of the wind and the countryside both
mirrors and prefigures the suffering of the miners. The wind thus presents an

image of that suffering and an omen of catastrophe. The image used is one of famine, of hunger which causes death, and of the death of work – the inevitable consequence of the strike. Class and economics are reinscribed into the imagery of nature, while work follows the logic of the mortal body. **Try to identify some episodes in the novel that highlight the extreme hunger of the miners.**

In *Germinal*, only Le Voreux and the bourgeoisie eat: the miners constantly battle against starvation in their struggle to survive. This is nowhere more apparent than in the scene when La Maheude comes to beg the Grégoires for food (2.2; pp.92–6). This in turn follows the scene in which Cécile is presented with her delicious brioche, deliberately contrasted with the miners' meagre breakfast. Hunger is an ever-present, recurring torment: the savage demand of the body for food. On his first day in the mine, Étienne is shaking because of a cramp in his stomach; this prefigures Catherine's death by starvation when she and Étienne, trapped in the mine, are reduced to chewing his belt in order to give themselves the illusion of eating. The suckling Estelle constantly craves more breastfeeding (2.2; p.85), yet another symbol of the eternal demands of the body. Set against the vivid depiction of hunger, the desolation of starvation in the village is all the more devastating (4.5; pp.257–63). When La Maheude walks through the village, 'starvation seeped from every door', and 'you could hear the sleep of hunger coming' (4.5; p.262). The reiterated apocalyptic cry of the crowd, as they grow in revolutionary fury, is 'Bread, bread, we want bread!' (5.5; p.349).

Deprivation is therefore a central experience in this novel. Yet it is possible to talk about hunger both as a material and as an emotional experience. In *Germinal*, Zola is undoubtedly making a very strong point about exploitation. But there is a sense in which the experience of deprivation that lies at its core has resonances which go beyond the material reality depicted. We can add another dimension to our understanding of *Germinal* as a multilayered text if we examine the themes of hunger and maternity from a psychoanalytic perspective.

The child psychoanalyst Melanie Klein (1882–1960) founded her highly influential psychoanalytic theory upon the deprivation experienced by infants within the first few months of life. The first 'object' the child relates to is the figure of the mother, in particular the mother's breast. The infant splits this object into the 'good breast' and the 'bad breast', which do not literally mean that one is good and the other is bad, but which correspond to states of feeling, ways of relating. If the infant feels that it is being gratified by the breast, it imagines the breast as a good breast; if, on the other hand, it feels deprived, it imagines the breast as a bad breast, towards which it directs feelings of aggression. This in turn leads to an intensification of the sense of deprivation (Klein, [1929] 1975, pp.210–18). One of the principal sources of *Germinal*'s power derives from the fact that it is anchored in early childhood experience of hunger and a more general sense of emotional deprivation.

The themes of hunger, deprivation and gratification can be seen to crystallize in the figure of La Maheude, one of the most complex and interesting characters of the novel. She is constantly portrayed as the figure who fights the losing battle against starvation; it is her job to provide food for her hungry family, it is she whose body is a source of milk for the devouring Estelle: 'She said the cupboard was bare, the little ones kept asking for bread and butter ... And sure enough Estelle had started sucking ... the only sign of life she gave was a greedy little plumping of the lips' (1.2; p.21).

The oral fantasy of satisfaction at the breast is reflected in the references to eating, chewing and sucking which abound in *Germinal*, from scenes of the Maheu family at table to Catherine and Étienne chewing the belt when they are trapped in the mine. Oral satisfaction is therefore of primary importance. By the end of the novel, several conflicting strands of imagery can be seen to meet in the figure of La Maheude. She is both the suckling mother and the 'bad' mother who fails to protect her children from starvation; the mature, erotic woman, and a murderous wife and mother who incites Maheu to throw bricks at the soldiers: 'She lashed him with her tongue, dazing and numbing him with the murderous words that she spat out behind him, crushing her daughter in her arms against her breast' (6.5; p.430).

She becomes a figure of maternal suffering, the *Mater dolorosa*, who weeps at the death of her children and her man. In a seminal essay on the figure of the Virgin Mary in Western culture, the French psychoanalytic theorist Julia Kristeva identifies 'Milk and tears' as the 'privileged signs of the Mater Dolorosa' ([1977] 1986, p.173). For Kristeva, who is influenced by Klein, milk and tears signify 'the return of the repressed ... a semiotics that linguistic communication does not account for' (ibid., p.174), which surface through the figure of the Virgin Mary in Catholicism. In other words, the mother's milk and her tears communicate a primitive sense of loss and need in a way that lies beyond language. The infant satisfies its oral desires through sucking at the breast, while mother (and babe) weep at primordial loss. According to Kristeva, murderous aggression towards the mother (on the part of the child) is mitigated by the 'oral cathexis [relation]' and by her sorrowful tears (ibid., pp.180–1). Yet if we are to see La Maheude as a kind of *Mater dolorosa*, then she also becomes the character who emerges with the greatest burden of suffering: she has been the most punished.

The themes of hunger and sexuality come together in the representation of La Maheude as a mature, erotic woman. Zola is concerned to show sexuality in all its labyrinthine twists and turns, and one such moment occurs when Chaval bursts into the Maheu household while La Maheude is breastfeeding. Amidst the confusion, she forgets to replace her breast inside her blouse, and Étienne becomes transfixed by it:

> Despite his efforts to avoid it, Étienne's gaze kept returning to her breast, with its almost liquid expanse of white flesh, which he now found both voluptuous and embarrassing ... Slowly and unhurriedly she had taken her breast in both hands and put it back in place. A rebellious pink extremity resisted, which she thrust back in with her fingers, then she buttoned up her camisole, and slumped back into her chair, and became just a shapeless black body once more. (4.3; p.232)

Desire fixes upon the object of the breast, source of milk and erotic pleasure. It is as though it is Étienne who, gazing upon the breast, seeks to be fed and gratified, and in some way obtains satisfaction through a mesmerized voyeurism.

At the same time, this moment opens up another possibility: that Étienne may desire both the mother and the daughter. This is expanded in the final conversation between Étienne and La Maheude at the end of the novel, in which La Maheude states that she is glad they never entered into a sexual relationship (7.6; p.519). If Étienne is a kind of prodigal son, brought into the Maheu home, he could be said to feel an incestuous desire not only for his 'sister', Catherine, but also for her mother. This finds its bourgeois parallel in the relationship between Madame Hennebeau and her nephew Négrel, an incestuous sexual relationship which takes place within the home in part 4, chapter 1.

# *Sexuality*

The miners are constantly represented as driven by the appetite of sexuality. Much critical discussion has centred on Zola's ambivalent portrayal of the miners as animalistic and appetitive in their sexuality. This portrayal would have been shocking for his bourgeois readers at the time, especially if we consider the contrasting representation of the desiccated life of the bourgeoisie. Hennebeau is both aroused and repelled by the flagrant display of sexuality on the part of the miners and, indeed, his sexual frustration is one of the most interesting aspects of his character. Zola explicitly uses the theme of sexuality in order to bring his portrayal of both classes into sharper focus; yet his writing conveys an attraction for the sexual revelry and freedom of the proletariat that perhaps exceeds any political interest in supporting them. **Reread part 2, chapter 5, from 'A hundred paces further down the road ...' (p.124) to '... it was a force stronger than reason' (p.127), and part 5, chapter 5, from 'As he entered the room ...' (p.341) to 'But suddenly he heard Hippolyte coming back upstairs again, and he stopped, out of shame' (p.344), and compare the representations of working-class and bourgeois sexuality. You may wish to bring the earlier discussion of Tartarus into your comparison.**

In the description of Tartarus, female sexuality is figured ambivalently: it is simultaneously an alluring temptation and a leprous corruption, punished with eternal hellfire. The hill above Tartarus is both 'warmed by the fires from the lower regions' and so fertile that a 'miracle of eternal spring' takes place there. The mine is a place where sexual desire and violence burst out of control, but above ground the sexuality of the miners also renders them bestial. Indeed, Chaval's success in forcing himself upon the reluctant Catherine is a violation, once again driven by sexual appetite, alloyed with aggression. The name Chaval in French has echoes of the word 'cheval' (horse), which in itself suggests sexuality and virility. Old Mouque, stumbling over rutting couples in the fields, finds himself thinking 'How greedy were the young, oh, how they clutched and sucked at life!' (2.5; p.126). Here, too, sexuality is portrayed as the innate inheritance of generations of miners, who carry on producing babies 'fit only for toil and suffering' (2.5; p.127). It is a portrayal tinged with a voyeuristic desire. Hennebeau's torment at his wife's infidelity with Négrel may be seen as equally voyeuristic; yet here the atmosphere is distinctly different – oppressive, suffocating and poisonous. Hennebeau is as starved of sexuality as the miners are of food, and the parallel is clearly deliberate.

Within the mine, human beings (especially women) are reduced to animals. Women are constantly on all fours in the tunnels, followed by men. Étienne follows Catherine: 'He spent one whole trip following her, watching her run, with her behind up in the air and her hands placed so low down that she seemed to be trotting on all fours, like some small circus animal' (1.4; p.43). In the French original, the animal parallels are enhanced: he watches her 'filer, la croupe tendue, les poings si bas, qu'elle semblait trotter à quatre pattes' (Zola, 1978, p.90). Once again, she possesses a 'croupe' and trots on her 'pattes'. Yet at other moments the figure of Catherine appears almost alluring, when her pale body shines like ivory, or when she is clothed in coal dust: 'She had thick, pale pink lips, glittering with coal-dust, and he felt a painful surge of desire tug him towards them' (1.4; p.47).

The body, in particular the female body, is a sexual body. At the same time, it is also a politicized body. When the crowd is running and the quivering bourgeois women are hiding in the barn, La Mouquette shows them her behind: 'she suddenly lifted her skirts and thrust out her rear, displaying her enormous naked buttocks in the dying blaze of the setting sun. Her behind seemed savage rather than obscene, and there was nothing comic about it' (5.5; p.350).

Sexuality and class conflict fuse in this defiant exhibitionism. La Mouquette's behind is invested with sexual and political significance. She is constantly identified with her readily available proletarian body. In a sense, she *is* her body. Schor points out that 'this projection of repressed instincts and anxiety-producing phobias onto the people is hardly peculiar to Zola; rather it pervades nineteenth-century culture' (1978, p.127). She quotes the French critic Jean Borie, who, in a psychoanalytic study published in 1971, identified the way the body and the people represent one another in the work of nineteenth-century (bourgeois) writers and thinkers:

> The identification of the popular with the natural clearly shows us that the bourgeois is ready to use the puritan façade of his self-imposed repression as either the justification or the expiatory compensation of the social exploitation he benefits from: he has earned the right to dominate the people because he had succeeded in mastering Nature within himself, or else he constrains himself, sacrifices himself, castrates himself and thus demonstrates that his position as leader is not usurped but legitimate, for he occupies it not to derive any personal pleasure, but to serve the higher interests of social organization. In any case, the body and the people, those two repressed forces, will be very closely linked and will be able to function as metaphors for each other.
>
> (quoted in Schor, 1978, pp.128–9)

Sexual repression, like the repression of the miners in *Germinal*, is a constant struggle on the part of the bourgeoisie. Hennebeau's repression of sexual desire finds its political counterpart in the oppression of the miners by the mine bosses. At the same time, the identification of the body with the people can be seen to feed into the bourgeois discourse that seeks to keep the people in their place. This bourgeoisie, however, secretly longs to revel in their sexual freedom.

# Class conflict: the people and the bourgeoisie

According to the psychoanalytic critic Jean Borie, Zola created a double myth. Through unveiling the body, he unveiled the people, and vice versa. He thereby shocked respectable people who did not like to talk about either (Borie, 1971, p.26).

Throughout *Germinal*, Zola juxtaposes the proletariat and the bourgeoisie, in order to convey the sense of conflict between the two. The proletariat is often represented in a crowd, creating the effect of 'swarming' (Henry James, quoted in Howe, 1970, p.60), whilst the bourgeoisie are shown in families, in clans. Zola's crowd scenes are famous, and it is in these that his descriptive technique and his sense of how to structure a narrative are most vividly displayed. **Reread the description in part 3, chapter 2, of the crowd enjoying themselves at the fair, from 'They stayed there until ten o'clock' (p.160) to '... finishing off what was left of the morning's boiled beef' (p.161). How is the crowd portrayed?**

The scene bursts with sensuality and an earthy vitality: 'It was so hot that they felt they were roasting in an oven, and they let themselves go, not minding if their flesh spilled out of their clothes, glowing with a golden tint in the smoky light of the men's pipes; and the only problem was the nuisance of having to get up and pee; every now and then a girl got up, went down to the back of the hall near the pump, lifted her skirts, and then returned' (3.2; p.160). The people are portrayed as a collective, like a group of animals, their body parts and body fluids mingling and joining them together.

Zola makes use of different sense impressions to convey a sense of 'reality': the sounds of laughter, of music, the rhythm of the dancers, mixed with the colour of flesh, women's breasts, milk, streamers. A sense of smell is invoked too – we can almost smell the sweat, the beer and the urine – while the sense of touch is conveyed through the physicality of moving bodies. There is a great deal of movement: women arrive, leave with their men, children move after them, tram girls and pit boys fall over, girls go outside to relieve themselves. Everything combines to merge the crowd into one joyful, 'wallowing' mass. Interestingly, the tramping of dancing feet is likened to 'a landslide burying them alive', prefiguring the end.

Movement is a constant motif in *Germinal*. We encounter rhythm in the miners marching to the mine like herds of cattle, the breathing of Le Voreux, the movement of the cages, the movement of the miners' tools, the rhythmic feet of the revolutionary crowd. The repetition of rhythmical movement can be seen to effect what Peter Brooks terms 'the binding of textual energies':

> Repetition is one of the few factors of the text that allow the reader to see patterns of coherence, and thus at least the incipience of meaning, and to perceive how modification works, indeed how an entire narrative might be constructed on the minute variations within repetition.

(1984, p.316)

The sense of wallowing fleshiness, of people sticking together, is even more powerfully conveyed in the French; the clauses merge together like the crowd, an effect reinforced by the use of 'on' (the third-person singular, meaning 'one', 'we', or 'you'). The reader is drawn into the collective; it is as though we are all there together. 'Il faisait une chaleur de four, on cuisait, on se mettait à l'aise, la chair dehors' (Zola, 1978, p.213). The breasts of the women are 'mammelles', associated with the teats of animals, the girl relieving herself by the pump lifts her leg, 'se troussait', like a dog.

Zola's craft is evident in the representation of the growth of the starving people's fury. **Reread the crowd scenes in the forest in part 4, chapter 7, from 'The sound of applause echoed across to him …' (p.284) to the end of the chapter, and consider the narrative technique: what is its effect?**

Once again, the technique is impressionistic and gives the sense of a collective. Here the crowd is portrayed as 'a shapeless ocean of heads', 'a furious mass of faces', transfigured by suffering, transformed into a mass that is illuminated by mysticism. They loom out of the dark 'shadowy trunks' like the living dead, with disembodied eyes and open mouths. In chapter 4 on *Jane Eyre*, you will have become familiar with the term 'the uncanny'. Here, the crowd could be viewed as an 'uncanny' crowd; they are invested with the force of the political repressed, returning to exact their revenge, lit up by a dark ardour (see Freud, [1919] 1985, pp.339–40, 366, 372).

This revolutionary fury culminates in the scene where the bourgeoisie hide in the barn as the crowd run past. **Reread part 5, chapter 5, from 'But his witty remark was swept away in a hurricane of shouting …' (p.348) to 'Bread, bread, we want bread!' (p.349), and ask yourself: in what ways does Zola create a sense of movement and the collective power of the crowd? How do you think that the symbolic and hallucinatory details give a sense of grandeur?**

This passage is rich with references to the revolution of 1789, which eventually brought such bitter disappointment. The miners are singing 'La Marseillaise', and a raised axe 'took on the sharp profile of a guillotine blade against the light evening sky' (5.5; p.348). As we know, Zola's choice of title, *Germinal*, was also a deliberate reference to the month of April following the French Revolution. Furthermore, Zola almost certainly intended this revolutionary crowd, bathed in the red of sunset, to allude to the Paris Commune of 1871, the first working-class rule to be proclaimed in Europe, which ended in the bloody slaughter of its supporters.

Yet the way in which historical reference is used goes far beyond specific reference to the Revolution and the Paris Commune. The passage is invested with powerful symbolic and mythical associations, and the portrayal of the miners becomes a metaphor for revolution. Lucie and Jeanne, the bourgeois daughters, exclaim 'Oh, how exquisite' at the aesthetic beauty of the scene, in French 'cette belle horreur' ('that beautiful horror').

Zola employs a fabric of metaphors and similes to sweep us along. The proletariat are represented as a horde of barbarians, savages who will destroy the old order in a river of blood: 'It was a scarlet vision of the revolution that would inevitably carry them all away, on some blood-soaked *fin de siècle* evening' (5.5; p.349). Imagery of redness, blood and fire, pervades the scene. The masses are once again depicted as animals, this time savage beasts who will show no mercy: 'the men would look as gaunt as wolves, their fangs drooling and gnashing' (ibid.).

Once again, the whole passage loses that slightly melodramatic edge if read in the original. For example, in English the portrayal of the men as wolves is a simile. In Zola's original it is: 'les hommes auraient ces mâchoires de loups, ouvertes pour mordre' (1978, p.410), which literally translates as, 'the men would have [in the fantasized revolution] wolves' jaws, open to bite'. This is more powerful because it is leaner and identifies the men directly with the wolves' jaws. In the image of wolves' jaws, Zola fuses the idea of the miners' hunger and their vengeance. This is reinforced in the original, where the faces of the crowd are 'mâchoires de bêtes fauves', the jaws of wild animals, whereas in the translation they are portrayed as 'masks'. The effect in the French original is therefore more direct and economical. Zola's portrayal of the people as wild beasts and savage, revolutionary hordes takes the novel beyond naturalism into the realm of myth.

So, too, does the mythical layering of the writing. Indeed, the horde of emaciated women with unkempt hair, 'the dreadful old crones' (5.5; p.348), can be seen to invoke a crowd of avenging furies from Greek tragedy. They are inscribed into the rhythm of nature, 'like some natural disaster', 'buffeting their faces with its great hurricane wind' (5.5; p.349). Historic and social specificity are transcended, as the moment is raised up into the realm of the inevitable, the natural catastrophe.

As I suggested earlier, rhythm of movement is always very important in the novel. Here the rhythm of the stampeding crowd feeds the myth of the inevitability of revolution. Zola conveys the sense of the collective through movement: the crowd moves as one, powerful and inexorable. The men are a 'compact mass tumbling forwards like a single body' (5.5; p.348). The pace of the writing is conveyed through a chain of clauses following one another and an abundance of verbs referring to violent action. The use of the impersonal pronoun 'on' in the French once again suggests immediacy, drawing the reader into the crowd.

The figure of Maheu emerges as the representative of the working man: stoical in the face of suffering, showing solidarity to his comrades, ultimately destroyed. This is clearly revealed in the scene where he enters Hennebeau's home with the other delegates to speak for the people. Maheu silences the manager:

> Now that he had got going, the words came out unaided. At times he listened in surprise to the sound of his own voice, as if some stranger were speaking within him. Things which had been building up deep down inside him, things which he didn't even know he thought, came tumbling out as if his heart would burst. (4.2; p.218)

Here we see Irving Howe's notion that *Germinal* is the story of 'how the dumb acquire speech' (1970, p.55). Maheu has finally found his voice, which speaks like 'some stranger' from within him. Maheu's voice thus simultaneously becomes the symbol of the alienation of the proletariat within capitalism, and the vehicle through which that alienation is expressed. Within the text of

*Germinal* the characters cannot be said to overcome this alienation, to become whole, and to receive justice, despite Zola's redemptive vision of germinating revolution in the concluding pages. But can *Germinal* be said to sow the seed of revolutionary change?

# Conclusion

We have looked at the characteristics of the naturalistic novel outlined by Zola and then at Zola's craft as a writer of fiction. It is possible to trace in *Germinal* forms of writing usually associated with romanticism, realism, myth, tragedy and even poetry; these are the elements that render *Germinal* such a fine and memorable novel. So the question remains: **can *Germinal* be described as a naturalist novel?** I would argue that it cannot, because the naturalist novel, as Zola portrayed it, is a theoretical construct. The truly naturalist novel has not yet been written. Instead, we have a novel which contains powerful naturalist elements, but which far transcends the narrow mould that Zola made for it.

# Works cited

Baguley, David. 1992. *L'Assommoir*, Cambridge: Cambridge University Press.

Baguley, David. 1993. *Zola et les genres*, Glasgow: University of Glasgow French and German Publications.

Borie, Jean. 1971. *Zola et les mythes au salut*, Paris: Seuil.

Brooks, Peter. 1984. *Reading for the Plot: Design and Intention in Narrative*, Cambridge, MA: Harvard University Press.

Freud, Sigmund. [1919] 1985. 'The "uncanny"', in *Art and Literature: Jensen's Gradiva, Leonardo da Vinci and Other Works*, The Pelican Freud Library, vol.14, ed. by Albert Dickenson, Harmondsworth: Penguin.

Freud, Sigmund. [1905] 1991. 'Three essays on the theory of sexuality', in *On Sexuality*, The Pelican Freud Library, vol.7, ed. by Angela Richards, Harmondsworth: Penguin.

Howe, Irving. 1970. 'The genius of *Germinal*', *Encounter*, 34, pp.53–61. (Extract in Regan, 2001.)

Keefe, Terry and Lethbridge, Robert. Eds. 1990. *Zola and the Craft of Fiction*, Leicester: Leicester University Press.

Klein, Melanie. [1929] 1975. 'Infantile anxiety-situations reflected in a work of art and in the creative impulse', in *Love, Guilt and Reparation and Other Works, 1921–45, The Writings of Melanie Klein*, vol.1, London: The Hogarth Press and Institute of Psychoanalysis.

Kristeva, Julia. [1977] 1986. 'Stabat mater', trans. by Léon S. Roudiez, in *The Kristeva Reader*, ed. by Toril Moi, Oxford: Basil Blackwell.

Lethbridge, Robert. 1993. 'Introduction' to Émile Zola, *Germinal*, trans. by Peter Collier, Oxford World's Classics, Oxford: Oxford University Press.

Lukács, Georg. [1940] 1950. 'The Zola centenary', in *Studies in European Realism*, trans. by Edith Bone, London: Hillway. (Extract in Regan, 2001.)

Lukács, Georg. [1936] 1970. 'Narrate or describe?', in *Writer and Critic*, trans. by A. Khan, London: The Merlin Press. (Extract in Regan, 2001.)

Mitterand, Henri. 1986. *Zola et le naturalisme*, Paris: Presses Universitaires de France.

Regan, Stephen. Ed. 2001. *The Nineteenth-Century Novel: A Critical Reader*, London: Routledge.

Schor, Naomi. 1978. *Zola's Crowds*, Baltimore: Johns Hopkins University Press.

Zola, Émile. [1880] 1893. *The Experimental Novel and Other Essays*, trans. by Belle M. Sherman, New York: Cassell. (Extract in Regan, 2001.)

Zola, Émile. [1884–5] 1978. *Germinal*, Paris: Gallimard.

Zola, Émile. [1884–5] 1993. *Germinal*, trans. by Peter Collier, with an introduction by Robert Lethbridge, Oxford World's Classics, Oxford: Oxford University Press.

# Further reading

Baguley, David. Ed. 1986. *Critical Essays on Émile Zola*, Boston: G.K. Hall. A useful collection of essays including Irving Howe's 'The genius of *Germinal*' and Georg Lukács's 'The Zola centenary'.

Baguley, David. 1990. *Naturalist Fiction: The Entropic Vision*, Cambridge: Cambridge University Press. An illuminating study of naturalism.

Keefe, Terry and Lethbridge, Robert. Eds. 1990. *Zola and the Craft of Fiction*, Leicester: Leicester University Press. Contains essays that explore Zola's writing from the point of view of craft, thus highlighting the status of his novels as masterfully constructed fictions.

Nelson, Brian. 1983. *Zola and the Bourgeoisie: A Study of Themes and Techniques in 'Les Rougon-Macquart'*, London: Macmillan.

Schom, Alan. 1987. *Émile Zola: A Bourgeois Rebel*, London: Queen Anne Press.

Wright, Elizabeth. Ed. 1992. *Feminism and Psychoanalysis: A Critical Dictionary*, Oxford: Blackwell. A very useful introduction to the field of psychoanalysis and feminism.

# CHAPTER 15
# *Germinal*: Zola and the political novel

*by Dennis Walder*

## Introduction

Reviewing Charles Dickens's work in 1856, the leading French critic Hippolyte Taine (1828–93) wrote:

> Balzac, George Sand, Stendhal have also recorded human miseries; is it possible to write without recording them? But they do not seek them out, they hit upon them; they do not dream of displaying them to us; they were going elsewhere, and met them on their way. They love art better than men.

(quoted in Collins, 1971, p.339)

If it is true to say that Dickens's French contemporaries did not 'seek out' the human miseries that he depicted, then Émile Zola – their 'heir and follower' (Lukács, [1940] 1978, p.85) – was certainly breaking new ground when he consciously sought out the conditions of the mineworkers in northern France as the subject matter for *Germinal*. Does this mean Zola loved art less than men? Isn't it better to love men more than art? But is this a valid dichotomy anyway?

The answers to these questions touch on several issues, including the whole issue of politics in the novel. It is often argued that politics have no place in a novel, except indirectly. In *Le Rouge et le Noir* (1830; 'Scarlet and Black') Stendhal said that the effect of politics in the novel was like hearing a gunshot at a concert (1971, pp.384–5). But it all depends upon what one means by politics; and the kind of novel one is dealing with.

What I want to explore here are some of the ways in which Zola's novel may be thought of as political. It may be that in the end it is *Germinal*'s urge to represent 'the condition of the people' at the time that makes it most profoundly, and lastingly, a political novel – indeed, a kind of touchstone for politically inspired fiction, then and now. But it is important to keep in mind the literary-cultural environment in which Zola was writing, since this helps us to understand how far his work involved a different kind of intervention from that of the English novels of the time; and in particular, how far he extended the scope of fiction by his method and themes.

# The condition of the people

Despite the interest of George Eliot, Thomas Hardy and other nineteenth-century English novelists in offering to engage with contemporary society, their fiction was generally less concerned with commenting on, and stimulating debate about, the pressing issues associated with the new phase of industrialization developing in Britain during the 1840s and 1850s. It may be that, as the first industrial nation, Britain was likely to generate fiction concerned with what one might call the 'condition of the people' before other countries, since the discontent and degradation of the industrial working class was so obvious so quickly; but it soon became clear that, just as the suffering of working-class people became more apparent in Britain, more demanding of attention, so, too, did it become a topic for writers abroad, as the effects of industrialization spread. The so-called 'social problem novel' – a phrase used since the 1950s to identify a substantial number of novels published in Britain during the 1840s and 1850s – may be understood as a response to the contemporary plight of the newly industrialized working class, a plight that was significantly worse during the economic depression of the early 1840s. These novels, by writers such as Benjamin Disraeli (*Sybil; or the Two Nations*, 1845), Elizabeth Gaskell (*Mary Barton*, 1848; *North and South*, 1854–5), Charles Kingsley (*Alton Locke*, 1850) and Charles Dickens (*Hard Times*, 1854), revealed English writers attempting to alert their predominantly middle-class readers to the values and living conditions of the industrial working class, and to the political issues those conditions raised.

These English novelists dealt with such urgent political matters as the reforming Chartist movement (1838–48), strikes and master–worker relations; and they tended – understandably, perhaps, given the complexity of the issues, and their own backgrounds – on occasion towards simplistic or sentimental solutions. In *Mary Barton*, for example, reconciliation between employer and workman is finally effected by turning the latter into a murderer, who dies in his employer's arms. Dickens's representative workman in *Hard Times*, Stephen Blackpool, falls down a disused mineshaft and dies, offering the following as the novel's final comment on worker–master relations: 'It's aw a muddle' ([1854] 1989, 3.6; p.362).

With the exception of Dickens, all these writers adopted social-realist techniques as a way of engaging with the large questions facing society at the time, while attempting to inform their readers of the immediate and lasting effects of the industrial revolution. Dickens's unique blend of realism and fantasy enabled him to create an impression of a level of poverty, deprivation and anger of which many were totally ignorant, or about which they preferred not to know – Lord Macaulay notoriously criticized *Hard Times* for what he called its 'sullen socialism' (quoted in Collins, 1971, p.300).

But if many English novelists of the nineteenth century aimed to inform their more privileged readers about the conditions in which the mass of the population were living, they held back from suggesting that more than a change of heart on the part of the middle classes was the solution. *Middlemarch* offered some revealing reflections upon what was happening in the provinces during the 1830s, suggesting the need for an extension of the sympathies of the middle and landowning classes to the rural poor, while demonstrating the personal and local difficulties of achieving social justice. Hardy's work, including *Far from the Madding Crowd,* revealed a wider social range, and his interest in the changes overtaking rural communities suggests, I think, a political vision of greater depth than Eliot's. Moreover, nowadays, prompted particularly by the insights offered by feminist criticism, we can find in Hardy's work an engagement with questions of sexual morality and the position of women that is more illuminating than in Eliot's novel. **You may well disagree; and, after all, is it fair or appropriate to consider the politics of these novels in terms of our own current political or cultural preoccupations?**

Frankly, I don't think we can avoid doing so. Consider Irving Howe's classic work on the subject, *Politics and the Novel,* in which the author defined the political novel as 'a novel in which political ideas play a dominant role or in which the political milieu is the dominant setting' ([1957] 1987, p.17). Among nineteenth-century English novelists, this definition would bring in Disraeli or Trollope, but probably not Eliot, Hardy or Dickens. In fact, Howe's nineteenth-century exemplars were novels by Stendhal, Dostoevsky, Turgenev, Conrad and James. Predictably, perhaps, given Howe's rather limited emphasis upon 'political ideas' and a 'political milieu', no major (or even minor) English novelist features, although George Eliot is referred to occasionally, and *Middlemarch* finds itself in a footnote, where it is said to 'straddle' the categories of 'political novel' and 'social novel' (ibid., p.19).

Labelling novels always carries the danger of reductionism, especially when the novels are of the scope, variety and lasting power of *Middlemarch*; but Howe's remarks are useful in delineating two strands of fictional endeavour that may without distortion be called 'political': ideas and milieu. Moreover, his approach implies that what is called a political novel depends in the first place upon the sociopolitical environment at the time, as well as later. Underlying what Howe says is the assumption that life in mid-nineteenth-century Britain was more stable than abroad, that English novelists were simply not under the same pressures as those in France or Russia. There 'the novelist's attention had necessarily to shift from the gradations within society to the fate of society itself' – the point at which 'the kind of book I have called the political novel comes to be written' (Howe, 1987, p.19).

Howe was himself writing quite consciously at a time (the 1950s) when there was, he felt, a prevailing 'conservative mood', antagonistic to 'any sort of radicalism, even liberalism'. Hence his book was intended as, and came to be seen as, 'a dissident work' by the American intellectuals to whom it was addressed in the first instance (Howe, 1987, p.5). So his emphasis was upon identifying radical ideas in a wide range of novels from the nineteenth and twentieth centuries, which, according to him, confronted society as a whole. This meant inevitably widening the range of fiction he dealt with, beyond merely novels written in English – his twentieth-century exemplars included works by André Malraux and Ignazio Silone as well as George Orwell.

We might think that *Germinal* meets Howe's original criteria – in fact, two decades later, Howe went on to affirm the value of Zola's novel in a separate essay.

**Please read Irving Howe, 'The genius of "Germinal"' (1970, pp.53–61; extract in Regan, 2001). What was ultimately most important about *Germinal* according to this later essay?**

Howe proposed that what was ultimately most important about the novel was that it showed 'how the dumb acquire speech', and how those at the bottom transformed themselves into 'active subjects, determined to create their own history' (1970, p.55). This goes a long way beyond Howe's earlier emphasis on ideas and milieu. I am not sure how far *Germinal* succeeds in demonstrating so profound a transformation; but it is a viewpoint worth considering. And as a demonstration of how 'the dumb acquire speech', *Germinal* surely does represent a major achievement. As Howe suggests, when the mineworker Maheu begins to speak to the manager and 'the words came out unaided ... things which he didn't even know he thought, came tumbling out as if his heart would burst' (Zola, [1884–5] 1993, 4.2; p.218; all subsequent page references are to this edition), the transformation 'is at least as morally significant as that of the individual protagonist gaining access to self-knowledge in the earlier 19th-century novel' (Howe, 1970, p.56).

What I would suggest is that there are at least three broad senses in which novels may be considered political: (1) in terms of the depiction of politicians, political figures, institutions and/or contemporary ideas and debates; (2) in terms of their exposure of the condition of the people at a particular historical moment; and (3) in terms of what we, as readers today, would call political in the context of our contemporary debates, for example in relation to feminist issues.

These are, of course, fairly crude distinctions between what are overlapping and, in any really important novel, interweaving categories; and you will have your own sense of the politics of your own time as you read; but it may nevertheless be helpful to spell out some of what goes on in *Germinal* in these terms so as to begin to think through what we mean by talking about the politics of Zola's novel – and, indeed, other nineteenth-century novels as well.

# The wretched of the earth

According to F.W.J. Hemmings (1970, p.71), the novels by Zola preceding *L'Assommoir* and *Germinal* were obviously political, with 'the revolutions, wars, bomb-throwings and financial scandals that Zola recalled' appearing 'primarily in a political light' – indeed, the sixth of the Rougon-Macquart series, *Son Excellence Eugène Rougon* (1876; 'His Excellency') bore the subtitle *Scènes de la vie politique* ('Scenes of Political Life') when first published in instalments. If its subject matter was evidently political, that novel did not, however, reveal any great political insights: rather, it was a fairly obvious satire on power, and on the urge to dominate exhibited by its central figure. Zola did not know enough about the workings of government at that level to offer anything more complex or convincing.

None the less, as a journalist in Paris, Zola had informed himself about the Second Empire of Louis-Napoleon, which he attacked for corruption – criticizing, amongst other things, the military coup d'état of 2 December 1851

ich inaugurated Louis-Napoleon's imperial rule), French involvement in the
Crimean war (1854–6) and, most revealingly, the emperor's foolhardy
declaration of war on Prussia in July 1870 – a war which was to prove Louis-
Napoleon's downfall, the end of the Second Empire and, with its sequel, the
Paris Commune of 1871, a watershed in European history.

For a revealing example of Zola's politics while a practising journalist,
consider that a month after Louis-Napoleon's declaration of war on Prussia, and
the plebiscite the emperor hoped would support his latest move, it emerged that
a large portion of the army had voted 'non', prompting Zola to write an article
ironically entitled 'Vive la France' (1870; 'Long live France'), concluding: 'At this
very hour there are 50,000 soldiers along the Rhine who said "no" to the Empire.
They wanted no more war, no more permanent standing armies, no more of that
terrible power which puts the fortune of an entire nation in the hands of one
man' (quoted in Schom, 1987, p.48).

This sense of injustice, and sympathy with the common people, underlies
what one can detect of Zola's political opinions. The year after he wrote these
words, Zola left his journalistic career behind, and began 'Les Rougon-
Macquart', the great series of novels aimed at scrutinizing the natural and social
history of the Second Empire – including, in 1892, *La Débâcle* ('The Débâcle'),
the last but one of the series, in which he provided a near-factual account of the
Franco-Prussian war (which he spent in his native Provence, having been
declared unfit for military service), as well as the Commune (which he witnessed
for himself, back in Paris). The principal political figures, including Louis-
Napoleon (treated relatively sympathetically in this novel), were introduced, but
almost always as seen through the eyes of ordinary soldiers or civilians. This was
to prove the key to Zola's success as a political novelist, and it differentiated him
from other novelists of the time who attempted to deal with politics.
Nevertheless, it was only when he turned away from the direct depiction of
politics and politicians in *Son Excéllence*, and wrote his first novel about the lives
of the working class in *L'Assommoir* (1877; 'The Dram-Shop'), that he found the
approach that he sought – as well as the enormous critical attention which was
to attend his success thereafter.

That critical attention was far from entirely positive, however, especially in
terms of what was perceived as the novel's politics. Almost every prestigious
periodical in Paris attacked the so-called 'republican' Zola for what was
perceived as his disgusting and immoral depiction of urban working-people in
*L'Assommoir*, and his publisher was inundated with complaints (Schom, 1987,
pp.63–6). But, as with his succeeding novels (*Nana, Pot-bouille* ('Piping Hot')
and, above all, *Germinal*), what the critics attacked and the public claimed to
dislike, they nevertheless bought and read in increasing numbers.

Moreover, Zola had for some time thought that his plan of writing about the
people and their struggles had to include a second novel, an idea which
'crystallized in due course, when [he] became fully aware of the great socialist
movement that had been harrowing Europe to such redoubtable effect. A strike
naturally suggested itself as the most dramatic situation possible' (quoted in
Brown, 1996, p.520). In the political climate of the 1880s the broad workers'

movement had overtaken insurrectionary acts as a form of protest: the strike had replaced the barricade, so his decision made sense.

But which strike to write about? And where to set it? The novelist's friendship with a left-wing deputy and professor of natural science at Lille University, Alfred Giard, whose constituency included the Valenciennes area in northeastern France, provided an answer. Giard urged him to write about the mines, and when, towards the end of February 1884, strikes broke out at coalfields near Anzin, he met Giard at Valenciennes for a guided tour of *le pays noir* ('the black country', a phrase with similar overtones in French and English).

*Figure 15.1 Troops occupy the Renard mine at Anzin. From* L'Illustration, *19 April 1884*

Posing as the deputy's secretary, Zola spent eight days visiting miners' houses, attending meetings, discussing the strike and, most important of all, going down a mine himself to see what the workers' conditions were like. According to a recent biographer, he had been haunted since childhood by nightmares of being buried alive, and what he saw and experienced underground clearly had a profound impact upon him (Brown, 1996, p.528).

Zola thus consciously researched and documented his material before writing it up as a fiction. This was part of the method he propounded as 'experimental'. His extensive notes have been preserved, notes which prove how far he went to ensure the accuracy and authenticity of his depiction of the lives of the mineworkers. But Zola's preparation went further: returning to Paris, he attended political rallies, and read extensively on strikes, mines, mining accidents and diseases, and on socialist ideas.

According to the general plan of the Rougon-Macquart series, he had to locate the new novel during the Second Empire; but in any case, there had been several dramatic miners' strikes in the last years of Louis-Napoleon's regime (when strikes were still illegal); in particular a strike at La Ricamarie near Saint-Étienne in June 1869, put down by soldiers with the deaths of thirteen miners, and, in October of the same year, another at Aubin in the Aveyron, when fourteen more miners had been killed as a result of troops opening fire on stone-throwing strikers.

These events were the basis of the final action of *Germinal*, although as David Baguley has pointed out (1996, pp.xxvii–xxviii), Zola set the novel at a slightly earlier date, in the years 1866–7. This was a time of economic crisis and widespread unemployment in France, and not long after the formation in London in 1864 of the International Working Men's Movement under the aegis of Karl Marx (1818–83). Paradoxically, socialist ideas had become increasingly important in the industrializing nations of Europe with the success of liberal reforms from the 1840s onwards, since these reforms demonstrated that legal equality had failed to remove the massive inequalities of economic power created by industrialization. Increasingly, social revolutionaries like Marx, and the Frenchman Claude Saint-Simon (1760–1825) harnessed progressive and scientific ideas to an all-embracing theory of irresistible advance towards a socialist millennium and the triumph of justice for all. According to Marx, the capitalist system, while providing an unparalleled stimulus to the development of productive forces, systematically impoverished the masses. This in turn was creating a class of exploited industrial workers, the proletariat, who would eventually, by overthrowing capitalism, emancipate humanity. Although the title of *Germinal* harks back to the French Revolution, suggesting the continuity of radical hopes for fundamental change in society, there are many hints of more specific, historically located ideas in the novel. **Can you see how Zola's interest in engaging with socialist thought is quite specifically evident in the novel? For example, consider part 3, chapter 1.**

One of the most specific references is made in the scene in this chapter where for the first time we see Étienne discussing politics. We have already been informed that he had to leave his previous job as an engine-man for hitting his employer; but up to now the narrative has been preoccupied with giving us an impression of the mineworkers' lives, and with setting in motion the love-interest between Étienne and Catherine. Here, at his lodgings with Rasseneur, the looming possibility of a strike prompts debate, while simultaneously providing an opportunity for political allegiances and ideas to be articulated. Late one evening, when only the landlord, his wife and the two lodgers, Étienne and Souvarine, remain, Étienne reveals that he has had a letter from his former workmate, the activist Pluchart:

> For two months Étienne had been corresponding regularly with the mechanic from Lille, wanting to tell him all about his job at Montsou; but Pluchart was using the correspondence to indoctrinate him, now that he saw a chance of spreading his propaganda among the mining community.
>
> 'He's doing everything he can to make sure that his association is a great success. He's recruiting people on all fronts, so it seems.'

> 'And what do you think of their society?' Rasseneur asked Souvarine.
>
> The latter, who was gently stroking Poland's head, blew out a stream of smoke, and murmured dispassionately:
>
> 'Another load of rubbish!'
>
> But Étienne waxed lyrical. His whole rebellious temperament tempted him to embrace the struggle of labour against capital, in the first flush of his ignorant enthusiasm. It was the Workers' International Association, the famous 'International', that had just been founded in London. Wasn't it a superb achievement, to have launched this campaign through which justice would at last triumph? ... In another six months, they would have conquered the earth. (3.1; pp.141–2)

The anarchist Souvarine responds with another retort of 'rubbish' ('des bêtises' in the original), to what the narrator calls Étienne's 'ignorant enthusiasm'. But this does not undermine Étienne, whose thoughts are allowed to run on at some length in indirect reportage. The narrator's allusion to Étienne's 'rebellious temperament' reminds us of the importance Zola places on inherited tendencies, while the men's attempts to grapple with the new ideas of socialism in practice sway them this way and that. At this stage Étienne takes the Russian émigré Souvarine's destructive arguments ('To hell with you and your gradual evolution! Set fire to every town and city') to be a pose, and the landlord Rasseneur, 'who was even more down to earth than Étienne, and had that fund of good sense that comes with experience', 'didn't even bother to take offence' (3.1; p.142). Rasseneur asks if Étienne is going to try to set up a branch of the International in Montsou. This brings their arguments to bear on the immediate situation facing the miners. Pluchart says the Association will support them in a strike – 'And it just so happened that Étienne thought that a strike was imminent: the argument over timbering would turn sour, and it would only need one more demand from the Company to drive all the pits into revolt' (3.1; p.143). So a strike fund should be set up.

But a strike fund costs money, as Madame Rasseneur breaks in to say. Soon the men fall into rehearsing all the usual complaints, 'each adding his tale of misery', as they agree that the Revolution had only increased the working man's exploitation: 'Could anyone claim that the workers had had a fair share of the extraordinary growth of wealth and comfort that had taken place over the last hundred years? In declaring them free, the bourgeoisie had clearly taken them for a ride: yes, they were free to die of hunger, and they made liberal use of this right' (3.1; p.143).

Zola's strategy of showing us the sufferings of the mineworkers before introducing this argument contributes powerfully to its impact; so, too, does his interweaving of the individual, differing voices of these characters with the more general voice of radical protest. Souvarine, Rasseneur and Étienne represent different shades of left-wing opinion, all carefully articulated, even if here they are led to agree on the situation in which the miners find themselves. The observation that 'every evening there were similar conversations' (3.1; p.145) reminds us that Zola's method is to suggest the typical, rather than one particular event, as a way of dealing with large-scale social action and its political implications.

**How, then, would you define the different political views of the three men? Does the novel suggest any change or development in their views as the action of the strike progresses? Are they more than stereotypes?**

As the most extreme, Souvarine's position is perhaps the easiest to identify. It is hard, if not impossible, to conceive of any other nineteenth-century novel that would permit a character to walk away unharmed from wreaking deliberate destruction on such a scale. As the engineer Négrel observes in part 7, chapter 3, 'the thought of the man who had done the deed made his hair stand on end and filled him with the sort of religious awe that the presence of pure evil inspires, as if, mingled with the shadows, the man had loomed up again like some giant to commit his gargantuan crime once again' (7.3, p.470). But Souvarine is not presented to the reader as an evil giant. Zola avoids melodramatic stereotyping where the anarchist is concerned, thereby convincing us that characters such as Souvarine may be credible in times to come, even if they were not in the past.

Souvarine's background as an aristocratic assassin in St Petersburg is briefly sketched (3.1; p.140), as is the development of his nihilism when he resists the attempts of his fellow-radicals to get him involved in the strike, or even to agree on the ideals of socialist thought. Just before he goes down Le Voreux to hack away the lining where it holds back the underground sea, he is engaged in political discussion by the enthusiastic Étienne, who 'had now got up to Darwin' in his self-education. Charles Darwin's *On the Origin of Species* (1859) had been published in French by 1865: Étienne has read 'some fragments summarized and popularized in a five-sou volume' (7.2; p.450). Some socialists believed that the process of natural selection and the survival of the fittest would inevitably lead to socialism. The problem was that this could also lead to the view that the poor and the weak deserved their fate, as the more extreme Social Darwinists were to argue. But, in a rare show of passion, Souvarine attacks 'the stupidity of socialists who accepted Darwin, that apostle of scientific inequality' and, when Étienne persists, Souvarine finds himself saying that even if the whole world were swept away, the succeeding new world might develop the same injustices; and then, 'faced with this vision of eternal misery, the mechanic cried out in a ferocious voice that if justice was impossible in a world of men, then mankind would have to disappear' (7.2; pp.450–1).

Having got himself into this last, bleak position, Souvarine falls silent; then, in a final, confessional moment, he reveals to Étienne how his revolutionary group in Russia mistakenly blew up a passenger train instead of the Imperial train, and how he saw his mistress hanged: 'It's our punishment', he continues, 'We were guilty of loving each other' (7.2; pp.451–2). Now he has cleansed himself of such bourgeois weaknesses; and his puritanical dedication leads to the act of sabotage which, once again, causes the deaths of many innocents, including those whose sufferings were the rationale for action in the first place. But for Souvarine, remaining faithful to his beliefs is more important than personal feelings or ambitions. It was only in the 1880s that anarchist ideas were coming to the fore, and in this sense the character may have been an anachronism. Even so, the chilly conviction of Souvarine's behaviour provides a lasting image of a type of political extremist familiar to us in our own times.

Equally convincing, I would suggest, if less powerful as a character, must be Rasseneur, Étienne's other foil. He is portrayed as a moderate, a defender of what is 'possible'; his passivity and interest in compromise are fostered by his increasing jealousy of Étienne's power over the miners (3.4; p.175). But from the perspective of Monsieur Hennebeau, Rasseneur has been permanently sacked 'to protect our pits from his socialist filth' (4.1; p.220). Rasseneur is only too glad to let Étienne know that Pluchart's local association in Lille is on the verge of collapse, as a result of sectarian bickering: 'and already one could foresee the ultimate failure of this mass rising, which had threatened to blow away the old corrupt society with a single blast' (6.3; p.399). But Rasseneur's pessimism (or pragmatism, depending on your point of view) is, of course, a long way from that of Souvarine, who is prompted once again to utter his sense of the futility of it all and, in a telling phrase, to accuse his comrades of hating the bourgeoisie only because of their 'furious urge to become bourgeois in their place' (6.3; p.401).

Thus neither Rasseneur nor Souvarine seem to change their basic political standpoints. Étienne, however, is depicted as developing through the course of events. **Does this make him an 'active subject' in the sense suggested by Irving Howe (1970)? Where is his development most dramatically signalled, and how would you describe it?**

Étienne shifts from advocating violent revolution to an acceptance of a broadly Marxist position, according to which conflict is inevitable, and change will take place, though there is a severe limit upon what individuals can do to bring it about. His struggle to become a leader is presented as the product of mixed motives. On the private side, he works to show up Chaval, his competitor for Catherine's love, and to defeat Rasseneur, his competitor for the people. But his struggle is also presented as the result of a slow and confused journey towards political self-awareness. Apparently, it was at a fairly late stage in planning the novel that Zola decided to make Étienne the ringleader of the strike: his role was originally to have remained that of an observer, and a rank-and-file supporter, rather than the instigator (Hemmings, 1966, p.197). But Étienne finds it impossible from the start to accept the conditions the miners endure with what to him becomes a galling passivity:

> From the moment he had reached the bottom of this hell-hole, rebellion had been slowly simmering within him. He looked at Catherine, who had lowered her head submissively. How could they possibly drive themselves to death at such hard labour, in this mortal darkness, earning a pittance too small even to afford to buy their daily bread? (1.5; p.53)

The decision to strike is taken largely at his instigation, although Zola makes it clear that it is the cut in the miners' wages that drives them towards accepting Étienne's stand.

Initially, only the Maheu family provide an audience for his muddled ideas, but it is precisely their uncritical acceptance which propels him towards greater ambitions: both to educate himself and to gain power over his listeners.

Until then he had felt only an instinctive rebellion, amid the inarticulate discontent of his comrades ... he found himself seized with the uncritical taste for study that strikes the ignorant who are hungry for knowledge [but then] His shame at his ignorance diminished, and he grew in pride as he came to feel himself capable of thinking. (3.3; p.164)

Attended by this somewhat condescending authorial commentary, Étienne's development is clear, as is his impact upon the Maheus, signalled in terms of the overarching symbolism of the novel: 'Oh, things were moving, sure enough, there was a right little harvest of men growing up and ripening in the sunshine!' (3.3; p.167).

We have seen how the exchanges with Souvarine and Rasseneur, prompted by his correspondence with Pluchart, develop Étienne's understanding; but it is the responses of his uneducated audience that lend him increasing self-assurance until, in the forest meeting in part 4, he first tastes real power, defeats the moderate Rasseneur, and has a resolution passed to make the strike general.

The meeting is a great set piece in the novel, deserving close inspection for the brilliant way in which Zola links the personal with the public, individual feelings and ideas with the movements of the crowd, the whole highlighted by its dramatic moonlit setting. Étienne's rough rhetoric soon takes hold of his audience, as it does of himself. We have been prepared for what he says by the foregoing account of life down the mine, the timbering problem, the starvation of families, and so on:

'Do you want the strike to continue? And, if so, what do you propose to do in order to beat the Company?'
    A deep silence fell from the starry sky. The crowd was invisible in the darkness, and struck dumb by this speech which choked their spirits; and all that could be heard through the trees was a sigh of despair.
    But Étienne had already started up again in a different tone of voice. Already he no longer spoke as the secretary of the association, but as leader, or rather, as apostle entrusted with revealing the truth ... Wouldn't it be better to die straight away and at least make the attempt to overthrow the tyranny of capital which was starving the workers to death? ... No! The timbering tariff was not acceptable, it was only a crafty way of saving money by robbing each man of an hour's wages each day. This time they had gone too far, the time would come when the wretched of the earth would feel they had been pushed to the limit, and they would demand justice.
    He stood still, his arms outstretched.
    The crowd was shaken with a long tremor at the sound of the word 'justice', and they broke out in applause, which swept through the gathering with a sound like the wind rustling through autumn leaves. Voices cried out:
    'Justice! ... The time has come, justice!' (4.7; pp.281–2)

Étienne's audience becomes like the wind, like a natural force conveying a sense of the inevitability of what is about to happen, both within the pages of the novel and in the larger world. Phrases like 'the wretched of the earth' (borrowed by the translator from the first line of the 'Internationale', 1871, to represent the force of 'les misérables' in the original) will echo down the passages of time, to such classic calls for justice as Frantz Fanon's *The Wretched of the Earth* (1961; *Les Damnés de la terre*), written on behalf of the exploited around the world, whose miseries support those who have already won their rights and live in relative comfort.

But in Zola's novel the call for justice passes, and the crowd slips out of Étienne's control to become an undisciplined mob, carrying out acts of violence he had never envisaged or desired. As a result, the strike leader ends up hiding in a disused pit, like an animal. Étienne's sympathies with the proletariat disappear as he realizes not only that he has risen above them in knowledge, but in class terms – as Rasseneur predicted. He has himself become *déclassé*, alienated from the people he aimed to represent. His revolutionary fervour, derived from contemporary socialist thought, may have been intended to remain – an impression confirmed by the final novel of the Rougon-Macquart series, *Le Docteur Pascal* (1893; 'Doctor Pascal'), where Zola has Étienne arrested and condemned to death for taking part in the Paris Commune, before being pardoned and exiled to the French Pacific colony of New Caledonia.

In any case, unlike Souvarine and Rasseneur, Étienne *has* been shown to change, even (in Howe's terms) to transform himself to take an active part in history: 'Starting with the brotherly love of the novice, hoping to improve the condition of the wage-earner, he had finished with the intention of abolishing the system altogether' (4.7; p.283). This transformation in one of the workers sounded a warning to Zola's middle-class readers. And for others? It is worth considering some of the contemporary reaction to the novel, and the way in which it treats the middle classes, who may be said to represent the majority of his first readers. Any novelist who wishes to attack his or her own readers and their values will obviously need to proceed with caution – or avoid doing it too directly.

## *Germinal*, history and the bourgeoisie

The reaction to *Germinal* is a fascinating subject in its own right. Here I can do no more than sketch it in, as a way of indicating the extent to which the novel engaged with a particular historical – and indeed, political – moment. Many commentators were favourable, in some instances for fairly obvious reasons. Among the more interesting was the response of one fellow naturalist writer, Henry Céard, who remarked in a Buenos Aires newspaper, *Sud America* (17–18 April 1885), that the real subject of the novel is the crowd, 'the immense sob of humanity from which rises the echo, the clamour of universal suffering' (quoted in Baguley, 1996, p.440). Céard also suggested that Zola's art was an art of exaggeration, magnifying naturalistic detail way beyond the realism of mere verisimilitude so as to create a transcendent power. Indeed, he thought the author would have done better by dispensing with individual characterization altogether, and focusing upon the types he handled so well.

Zola's famous response to Céard was to assert that his main protagonists, like Étienne, did develop in the course of the novel, and that his subject was the reciprocal action and reaction of the individual and the crowd, one upon the other. As for exaggeration, he stated:

> I enlarge, that's undeniable, but I don't enlarge the way Balzac does, any more than Balzac enlarges the way Hugo does ... We all lie more or less, but what is the mechanism and mentality of our lie? Well – perhaps I delude myself here – I still believe that my lies serve to advance the truth. With a wingbeat, truth ascends and becomes symbol.
>
> (quoted in Brown, 1996, p.543)

Even those left-wing critics who had attacked *L'Assommoir* for its tendency to depict a working-class ruled by degenerate passions were generous in their praise for *Germinal*. Clovis Hugues, a militant left-wing deputy, exclaimed that he would defend the novel 'here, elsewhere, everywhere ... because, unlike Hugo, who in *Les Misérables* proposes charity as an answer to the social question, in *Germinal* Zola proposes justice' (quoted in Brown, 1996, p.544). 'Dear Citizen Zola', as he was addressed, was approached by a group of socialists in central France who wanted the novel for a local weekly because they knew of 'no comparable work of propaganda at once socialist and naturalist', and recognized 'how much it would help the workingman's organization of this region' to read the novel in their weekly (quoted in ibid.).

If, as seems to be the case, Zola's writing does reach towards the symbolic and mythical, its solid base in the historical realities of working life – depicted in terms of the interaction between individuals and the collective, between thought and action – ensured a positive reception not only from critics inspired by his method, but also from those inspired by his concern for justice.

This concern was evidently a profound part of his aim. The daily newspaper *Le Matin* quoted him as saying:

> My book is a work of pity, nothing else, and if readers experience this feeling, I shall be happy, I shall have achieved the goal I set for myself. When, indeed, one wishes to see and understand, it becomes quite clear that 1789 did not help the worker: peasants got land while the worker lost ground, and royalists are right in saying that the old guilds protected him better than the present regime. There is a great social movement afoot, a desire for justice that must be taken seriously, or bourgeois society will be swept away. I don't think that the movement will begin in France, however – our race is too flaccid. That's why, in my novel, a Russian embodies violent socialism.
>
> (quoted in Brown, 1996, pp.544–5)

### Who, then, does Zola suggest should take the blame for the condition of the people? The middle class, or the entire nation?

The quick answer is, both. But things are not quite so simple. Consider the role of the bourgeoisie in *Germinal*. According to Howe, Zola 'tries hard' to present his middle-class characters, the Hennebeaus and Grégoires, 'with some objectivity and even sympathy, but he usually fails'. Why? Because 'in this novel he is not interested in such people at all. They are there because his overall scheme demands it' (Howe, 1970, p.58). I have two problems with this view: firstly, because it seems to me to ignore the historical dimensions of the novel, which made the kind of treatment available later to, say, D.H. Lawrence unlikely if not impossible; secondly, I am not sure that it is borne out by closer analysis of the scenes in which the bourgeoisie appear.

We should remind ourselves that, although it was first published in 1884–5, *Germinal* is set in 1866–7, during the time of the Second Empire in France, which lasted from 1852 until 1870. As you know, the novel was part of a massive cycle, although not every reader nowadays may be in a position fully to appreciate the precision with which the twenty novels in it were located historically and politically. But contemporaries, even abroad in England, were clear: as the novelist George Moore put it in his 1885 preface to the English translation of Zola's *Pot-bouille* ('Piping Hot'), 'I am convinced that the living history of no age has been as well written as the last half of the nineteenth century is in the Rougon-Macquart series' (quoted in Nadel, 1986, p.vii). **Look back again to the opening pages of *Germinal*. How soon are we alerted to the historical dimension of the novel, in what way, and from whose point of view?**

The reader's awareness of the period in which the novel is set, and the larger sociopolitical climate of the time, is invited early on, within a few pages of the opening, when the driver Bonnemort makes the first speech of any length, in response to the new arrival Étienne's questioning: 'It's a crying shame round here, people laid off, workshops closing down, one after the other ... Maybe it's not the Emperor's own fault, but why does he need to go off and fight in America? Not to mention the cattle that's dying of cholera, like everyone else' (1.1; p.8).

The somewhat comic juxtapositions shouldn't blind us to the connection between character and history established here, when the question of blame is first raised. As readers today we are, of course, a lot further away from the mid-1860s than Zola's readers of the 1880s; but most editions of the novel provide notes which help bridge the gap, and Bonnemort's perspective helps us too, since what he does is express a familiar complaint, personalizing the difficulties of his class, while alerting us to the local and the broader context.

Foreign adventures have always been a way of trying to divert attention from problems at home, and the Emperor Louis-Napoleon's disastrous Mexican war (1861–7), amongst other things an attempt to establish Archduke Ferdinand Maximilian of Austria as ruler of that country, showed he was behaving no differently from rulers before him. Yet to begin with, Louis-Napoleon was a popular figure. Elected President of the Second Republic after the 1848 Revolution, Napoleon's nephew, Louis-Napoleon Bonaparte (1808–73), began as a liberal ruler who went on to assert his personal power by seizing control of the country in 1851. This was followed by a plebiscite in December 1852, after which he proclaimed himself emperor. We can presumably take it as typical that the miner's household should have a print (donated by the Company) of the emperor and his Spanish empress on the wall (1.11; p.22), just as mid-Victorian English working-class houses had Queen Victoria and Prince Albert on their walls, a sign of the allure of royalty to the poor, and a reaffirmation of the value of the family, alongside an unwillingness to blame royalty for their sufferings.

Rulers and government may be able to distance themselves from their political role, and remain invisible to the people whose lives they affect – people who show them the deference implied by Bonnemort's remarks. But in context we may discern an implicit questioning, which the events of the novel will pick up as part of the drive towards its terrible conclusion. Acceptance and resignation is going to become a thing of the past, even for someone as stuck in past structures as that living image of rigor mortis, old Bonnemort. In a peculiarly horrible, even melodramatic moment at the end of the novel, Bonnemort strangles Cécile Grégoire, the daughter of the mine-owner, as part of the violence unleashed by the strike and the reaction of the owners. Zola seems not to blame him for what he does.

If this seems at first an extraordinary, sensational outcome in terms of what we are used to as readers of English social novels of the time, we should perhaps remind ourselves of the fact that the French, unlike the English, had by the time *Germinal* was written witnessed horrific events. Britain had been involved in the distant Crimea during the 1850s without too much damage to national self-esteem, and during the years leading up to the passing of the Second Reform Bill in 1867 little more than the ripping up of the railings in Hyde Park by a few demonstrators had disturbed the mid-Victorian calm. The French, however, had faced famine and humiliation as a result of their disastrous defeat in the Franco-Prussian War. This was followed by the Paris Commune in 1871 – a fierce revolt crushed with exceptional viciousness (some 20,000 people were executed on the streets within a few days).

Less obvious to readers today, but of weight to contemporaries, were Bonnemort's allusions to industrial crisis and a cholera epidemic, both of which marked the year in which the events of the novel apparently take place. A severe economic depression, especially during a period otherwise noted for prosperity, may have impinged upon the minds of Zola's readers in the 1880s. Even if it hadn't, what we can recognize is a determination from the start of the novel to locate itself in terms of recent history, through the mouths of characters, rather than in terms of some long-winded scene-setting of the kind indulged in by Walter Scott or Honoré de Balzac. However, there are moments in *Germinal* where the novelist deploys rather more factual or documentary material, for example when the narrative appears to pause to give the precise details of the origins of the Grégoire family fortune ('around 40,000 francs a year in investment income ... derived entirely from their shares in the Montsou mines'; 2.1; p.78). It is a long account (two and a half pages). **The question is, can it be justified? Does this kind of narratorial digression or intervention distract the reader? If it does, you could argue that Howe is right to some extent when he suggests that Zola is concerned more about issues than 'art'. What do you think?**

In the first place, we cannot ignore the immediately preceding section of the narrative, the whole lengthy account of Étienne's descent underground, his first day at work in the mine, and the descriptions of the Maheu household. The novel's artful structure is designed to encourage the reader to endure with Étienne the conditions of mine and household before presenting, from the start of part 2, 'how the other half lives', initially at La Piolaine. The miners' desperate poverty has been grimly etched – for example, we might recall La Maheude 'dron[ing] on' about 'the little ones ... asking for bread and butter', complaining that 'there wasn't even any coffee left, the water gave you the runs, and day after day you kept your mind off the hunger by chewing boiled cabbage leaves' (1.2; p.21). The way the people of Village Two Hundred and Forty wake up and start the day, and in particular the Maheu family with their seven ragged children, is bound to come to mind as Madame Grégoire descends to the kitchen in her slippers and dressing-gown, to ask the cook to make a fresh brioche for her petted daughter Cécile as a nice little treat to accompany her usual morning chocolate.

The delicious aroma of this food permeates the house during the succeeding scene, which culminates in the arrival of La Maheude and two of her children, to ask for a hundred-sou piece to relieve their burden of debt. The request is in vain, of course, as the Grégoires pride themselves on being 'thinking Samaritans, constantly worried that they might make a mistake and encourage some immoral tendency' in the workers by their charity: 'they never gave money, never ever! Neither ten sous nor even two sous, for you know what the poor are like, as soon as they have two sous to rub together, they squander them on drink' (2.2; p.92).

Do 'they'? As we are made fully aware by the tumultuous scene at the Bon-Joyeux dance hall later, the workers *do* of course consume vast quantities of alcohol, given the chance (part 3, chapter 11); but the familiar, class-based assumption is that it is therefore better not to aid the poor, who are all the same – an assumption so neatly conveyed by the narrator sliding into the voice of the careful bourgeois. The bourgeois nature of the family is highlighted by the detailed, three-page account of the family history going back to their eighteenth-century investments, a history they 'enjoyed telling' (2.1; pp.78–80). It includes such details as the purchase of La Piolaine for a pittance 'after it had been confiscated by the State under the revolutionary regime' (2.1; p.79), a nice detail which calls to mind the revolutionary period and in particular at this point Marie Antoinette's legendary response to the demands of the starving poor, 'let them have cake', a response encapsulating the attitude which led to the revolution of 1789. (In part 5, chapter 4, the strikers march to the cry 'Bread! Bread! We want bread!' (5.4; p.328)). This historic resonance underlies and reinforces the effect of the totally inappropriate gift of brioche to the Maheu children, which they go away holding 'respectfully in their cold, numb little hands' (2.2; p.96).

We are invited to experience La Maheude's embarrassment and distress at asking for the money, a request which is refused. And yet Zola does not, it seems, ask us simply to condemn the affable and well-meaning Grégoires; any more than we are asked to condemn other representatives of the ruling class, such as Deneulin, a small mine-owner in difficulties the Hennebeaus, or their nephew, the engineer Negrel. The evidence of Zola's structural planning is clear from the fact that it is once again at the beginning of a part of the novel that we are invited to take the longer, historical view of characters whose behaviour we are about to witness under the stress of events. Thus, part 4 opens with the information that the long-expected strike has just broken out – an event anticipated by the timbering dispute in part 1, although it has taken several other factors, including Étienne's political development, to produce it. This might be the moment when we would expect to find the company manager and his wife depicted as blood-sucking capitalists, for whom we are invited to have little sympathy. **But how does the novel present the ruling group in chapter 1 of part 4? Are their political affiliations discernible, and credible?**

If the Grégoires are depicted as at best innocently ignorant of the human misery surrounding their comfortable lives, the Hennebeaus are revealed in a different, indeed more complex light, as we learn of their personal histories. Madame Hennebeau is shown as especially complicit, in her reaction to the whole area, 'its stupid fields stretching as far as the eye could see, and its endless black roads, with never a tree to be seen ... crawling with repulsive creatures who disgusted and frightened her' (4.1; p.202), and in her indifference to the misery of the workers, whose homes she and her Paris friends visit. Like another Emma Bovary in her frustrated sense of having failed to achieve 'the glamorous satisfaction she had dreamed of at boarding school' (4.1; p.201), she feels she has been locked away in the provinces with a boring husband, and takes her pleasure in an affair with Paul Négrel, 'her little playmate' (4.1; p.203), whom she decides it would be entertaining to marry off to some rich girl – Cécile Grégoire. Her husband, meanwhile, is presented as a mining-school graduate who carries out his professional functions as a salaried manager with a strict sense of duty, hiding his violent desire for his resistant wife beneath a cool and military bearing, and secretly envying the poor their promiscuous couplings.

While offering this sense of the private and individual shape of their lives, the novel does not forget to let us know the characters' politics, prompted by the sense of crisis. To the accompaniment of a 'restrained crunching' of crayfish shells, the conversation around the lunch-table at the Hennebeaus turns to politics: 'Monsieur Grégoire argued, with a tremulous voice, that he was a Liberal, in spite of all this; and that he regretted the overthrow of Louis-Philippe. As for Deneulin, he was in favour of strong government, and declared that the Emperor had gone too far down the road of dangerous concessions' (4.1; p.211). Louis-Philippe, who ruled France from 1830, had been deposed by the 1848 revolution, which inaugurated the short-lived Second Republic, followed in turn by Louis-Napoleon's coup d'état and the proclamation of the Second Empire in 1853. It is a neat irony to have Grégoire define himself as a 'Liberal' in such dated terms, and it reinforces our sense that the family as a whole live a life insulated from hardship by three generations of investment in the mines; while Deneulin, the new small capitalist, at least aware of the present dispensation, sets himself against such small moves towards liberalization as were introduced by Louis-Napoleon after 1860, when the Emperor came under intense pressure from reformers and republicans.

The novel's depiction of three representatives of the threatened middle class – Grégoire, Deneulin and Hennebeau – seems designed to balance the depiction of the three socialists – Rasseneur, Souvarine and Étienne. Yet that makes them sound more like mere types than they are. Self-indulgent, naive and even somewhat comical as the Grégoires may be, they are not presented unsympathetically. They are not indifferent to the misery around them, as Madame Hennebeau is, although they refuse to help the Maheu family. And Deneulin, when the strike ruins him, and he is forced to sell his mine to the faceless Company and become one of its servants (as Hennebeau anticipated;

4.1; p.212), is presented as a courageous and hard-working manager, who has lost out to forces larger than himself. Hennebeau is never merely a representative of his class. Unlike the Grégoires, with their inherited wealth, he has worked his way up from humble beginnings, made a rich but unfortunate marriage as part of his ambitious striving, and is always himself subject to inner and outer pressures: his frustrated sexuality on the one hand, his dependence upon the distant and anonymous Company directors on the other. None the less, of course, the responsibility for calling up troops to quell the rioters rests upon his shoulders; while the results of that action go beyond what he could have expected or imagined.

Perhaps it is only the lecherous shopkeeper Maigrat, among those depicted as exploiting the mineworkers, who is left without sympathy – although he does meet a bestial, violent end, reminiscent of the revolutionary Terror of the 1790s. This point leads me finally to consider the question of violence, especially political violence, in the novel.

# Violence

Despite the radical, if not revolutionary, implications of *Germinal*, and some of the more extreme events which take place in the course of the narrative, it was not until Zola adapted his novel for the stage that the authorities took any action against him. His collaborator on earlier dramatizations, William Busnach, anticipated the problems Zola was likely to face, in particular urging him to delete a scene in which policemen attack the strikers on stage. Characteristically, Zola refused the advice, and when, in October 1885 (only a year after the novel's first appearance), the Théâtre du Chatelet in Paris sent two copies of the play to the censor's office, as required by law, approval was denied. Zola seems to have been after a showdown over the whole question of censorship, but René Goblot, the minister concerned, was determined to prevent any public performance of Zola's dramatized novel. After consulting the radical Georges Clemenceau, Zola sent an account of the exchanges between himself and the minister to *Le Figaro*, and the paper printed it on 29 October 1885. Three years later the play was eventually staged. It proved a dismal failure. Nor did Zola's brief campaign against censorship succeed.

None the less, it is at least clear that the author wished to create the maximum impact with his novel, whatever the authorities might have felt about its politics. There is no question that the prospect of class war is anticipated in the novel, although it seems to have taken the simplifying immediacy of the stage to clarify this in a way which made the authorities feel action had to be taken. The strikers' rampage, followed by the stoning of soldiers and the subsequent shooting, is the central, most violent public incident in the novel, which is based, as we know, upon two actual events in 1869, the year before the fall of the Second Empire. But before that shooting, there is an event in the novel which may be said to anticipate it and, if you like, prepare us for it. This is the scene where the stunted little monkey-child Jeanlin, Catherine's younger brother, stabs the sentry. **Reread part 4, chapter 4, from 'But what caught Étienne's attention ...'**

**(p.412) to 'The blue eyes were wide open, looking at the sky, with the staring gaze that he had seen him turn towards the horizon, seeking his homeland' (p.413). What do you make of this scene? How far are we meant to condemn the killer, and how far sympathize with the victim? What are the political implications?**

The scene is unquestionably disturbing, even before we realize, through the skilful delaying of the information, that the sentry has a name and an identity: he is Jules, the shivering little soldier from Brittany with whom Étienne discoursed earlier, in an attempt to win him away from his soldierly duty (6.1; pp.382–4). That scene ensures that we feel sympathy for the victim, as we share Étienne's horror at what Jeanlin has done. But if Étienne is horrified 'by the grisly birth of this crime in the depths of the child's mind', kicking the boy away 'as if he were a dumb animal' (6.4; p.413), this comparison reminds us of the progressive dehumanization of Jeanlin from the start, as a result of the conditions of the mineworkers and their families. As in Dickens, attitudes towards children, and the treatment of them, provide an indicator of the level of humanity in societies subject to the overwhelming pressures of industrialization, and the inability of those in charge to do much about it. On one level, we might compare little Paul Dombey, effectively dying for lack of familial affection, on another, the two children, 'wretched, abject, frightful, hideous, miserable', presented to Scrooge in *A Christmas Carol*, 'this is Want, this is Ignorance ... Beware them both' (Dickens, [1843] 1971, p.108) or, even more forcefully, Jo, the crossing-sweeper boy in *Bleak House* (1852–3), who is compared with the dogs and cattle that pass him by on the streets of London, where tens of thousands of such children were known to run about neglected, lawless and violent.

When Jeanlin leaps onto the shoulders of the soldier 'like a wildcat' to plunge his knife into the man's throat, he has to press on the handle with both hands to get it through the soldier's thick collar. But: 'He had often cut the throats of chickens that he had caught behind some farm outbuilding.' As this reminds us, he and his 'faithful followers' (4.6; p.264), Bébert and Lydie, have been left to survive by their own devices from the start, which has meant theft, sex and general delinquency. Zola suggests that the boy is a mistake in evolution; but also that his upbringing – or rather, lack of it – has made him what he is. To Étienne, 'the boy, with his sharp features, green eyes, and big ears' has a 'degenerate frame' that harboured 'a kind of occult intelligence and primitive cunning, as if he was slowly reverting to his animal origins. The mine had shaped him, but then it had broken his legs' (4.6; p.273). On one level, Jeanlin shares the atavistic features emerging in such late nineteenth-century works as R.L Stevenson's *The Strange Case of Dr Jekyll and Mr Hyde* (1886) and Bram Stoker's *Dracula* (1897), expressions of the pessimistic side of Darwinism developed in the Austrian Max Nordau's influential treatise *Degeneration* (1892). But on another, in his attitude towards his little followers, and towards women, Jeanlin simply reflects the brutality of the adults around him.

When Étienne asks Jeanlin why he killed the soldier, the boy says he doesn't know, but the narrator's gloss expands on this, making explicit the connection between what he does and what has happened, as it shifts between free indirect reportage and narratorial comment:

Why should they worry, with these bloody soldiers who had come to push the colliers around in their own backyard? From the violent speeches in the forest, and the cries of death and devastation that tore through the pits, he had retained five or six words, which he kept repeating, like a child playing at revolution. And that was all he could say, no one had pushed him into doing it, it had come to him just like that, like the urge to steal onions he saw in a field. (4.4; p.413)

The boy knows about rape and murder, and has heard the justifications for confrontation and violence. It is not long before the confrontation between the mining community and the soldiers takes place, with the brick-throwing and then shooting that results. **Is this outcome presented as inevitable, the climax of antagonism between the classes?**

I do not think so: while having made the social and political issues clear, the novel does not insist that this is the way things have to go. The concluding comment on the awful scene of the shootings is not made by either Étienne or the narrator, but is cleverly left to the revolutionary priest Father Ranvier, from whom we are able therefore to distance ourselves to a greater or lesser extent, when he announces the arrival of 'the age of justice, and the imminent extermination of the bourgeoisie' who had 'brought their crimes to a climax', by having 'the workers and the poor of the earth massacred' (6.5; p.433; 'en faisant massacrer les travailleurs et les déshérités de ce monde').

None the less, the image of Maheu baring his chest, 'tattooed' as it is with coal (6.5; p.425), to the soldiers' bayonets, partakes of the heroic. It is no surprise that this should have become a lasting image of the novel (see Figure 15.2). And yet it is the murder of the women and children that is most affecting, I think, including that brief image (the whole scene is highly cinematic) of Bébert and Lydie hit by the first few shots, lying clasped together in their final convulsions: 'Then Jeanlin, who had arrived from Réquillart at that very moment, still drowsy with sleep, came hopping through the smoke, and saw him embrace his little wife, and die' (6.5; p.431). Is this sentimental? Or a moment of pathos justly felt, for the victims of the larger social movements we have been made aware of throughout the novel – movements which have led to the violence? Zola's ambivalence towards violence, which is also represented in symbolic terms towards the end as the shedding of blood from 'this incurable wound' (7.6; p.522), is part of that ambivalence which helps create the conditions for the novel's lasting qualities, its unwillingness finally to endorse revolution, while insisting that readers understand what may, and probably will, bring it about: ignorance and oppression.

In broad terms, then, I would agree with Irving Howe's observation, that in *Germinal*, Zola 'shows as no other European novelist before him, the emergence of a new historical force, and he reveals the conflict that must follow; but its outcome remains uncertain, shadowy, ambiguous' (1970, p.57). This might make it sound as if only by remaining uncertain or ambiguous is it possible to tread the difficult path between what writers owe to art, and what they owe to the people. Perhaps, on the other hand, what makes a novel more lasting than a work of propaganda is that willingness to engage with the issues of one's time with a depth that precludes simple answers, or clear-cut resolutions.

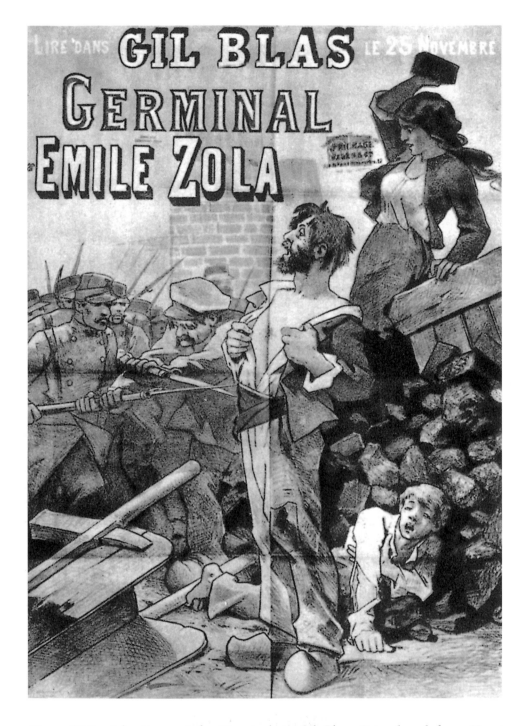

*Figure 15.2 Advertisement for* Germinal *in* Gil Blas. *Reproduced from Henri Mitterand and Jean Vidal,* Album Zola, *Paris: Éditions Gallimard, 1963, p.221. By permission of the Musée Carnavalet, Paris*

For Henry James, Zola's courage as a writer and a man, and the greatness of his work, nevertheless left him 'never but once obliged to quit, to our vision, the magnificent treadmill of the pigeonholed and documented' ([1903] 1987, p.417) – as if it were a flaw that the French novelist should have maintained his close link to the research that enabled him to write books such as *Germinal.* James praised this novel in high terms, however, arguing that the miners' strike was one of those episodes 'for which our author established a new measure and standard of handling, a new energy and veracity' (ibid., p.419) – high praise indeed, from a writer who, as he freely admits, worked within a quite different field of vision.

The one occasion on which, according to James, Zola 'quit' his 'treadmill', was that when his moral courage testified to his ability to live 'for himself and out of the order of his volumes' (1987, p.417): the Dreyfus affair. Zola himself evidently knew the difference between what role a novel might play in effecting political change – very little, immediately – and the role of journalism. This much is evident from what was to become one of the most famous pieces of journalism ever written, Zola's open letter to Félix Fauré, President of the French Republic, 'J'accuse …!' ('I accuse!'). The letter appeared on the front page of the new daily paper *L'Aurore* for 13 January 1898, and by writing it, the novelist not only ensured himself a place in history, but probably also ensured the manner of his unnecessarily early death. Writers and intellectuals in Britain and America certainly were prepared to stand up for political ideas – witness Eliot and Dickens declaring themselves on opposite sides over whether or not Governor Eyre of Jamaica should stand trial for putting down a rebellion there with extraordinary ferocity in 1864 (Eliot was in favour); but Zola's willingness to engage in public polemic for a cause he believed in was unparalleled. He was not particularly a supporter of the Jewish Captain Alfred Dreyfus himself, the man whose wrongful conviction for espionage in 1894 set the case rolling; but it was because of his growing awareness of the monstrous fabrications and dishonesty involved that Zola became determined to speak out for justice, with the result that he was prosecuted for slander, convicted on the basis of more false evidence, and forced to flee to England to avoid imprisonment. He returned after a year, but he did not live to see the full rehabilitation of Dreyfus (by then a pathetic prisoner on Devil's Island), dying of carbon monoxide poisoning produced by a faulty flue – an 'accident', it now seems, brought about by anti-Dreyfusards (Brown, 1996, p.793). Some 50,000 people attended Zola's funeral, including a mob shrieking their hatred of the author; Dreyfus was also present. But so, too, were groups of miners, who chanted 'Germinal! Germinal!' through the streets.

# Works cited

Baguley, David. 1996. 'Introduction' and 'Zola and his critics', in Émile Zola, *Germinal*, Everyman Library edition, London: J.M. Dent.

Brown, Frederick. 1996. *Zola: A Life*, London: Macmillan.

Collins, Philip. 1971. '*Hard Times*', in *Dickens: The Critical Heritage*, ed. by Philip Collins, London: Routledge & Kegan Paul.

Dickens, Charles. [1854] 1989. *Hard Times*, ed. by Paul Schlicke, Oxford World's Classics, Oxford: Oxford University Press.

Hemmings, F.W.J. 1970. *Émile Zola*, 2nd edn, Oxford: Clarendon Press.

Howe, Irving. 1970. 'The genius of 'Germinal', *Encounter*, 34, pp.53–61. (Extract in Regan, 2001.)

Howe, Irving. [1957] 1987. *Politics and the Novel*, New York: Columbia University Press.

James, Henry. [1903] 1987. 'Émile Zola', in *The Critical Muse: Selected Literary Criticism*, ed. by Roger Gard, Harmondsworth: Penguin.

Lukács, Georg. [1940] 1978. 'The Zola centenary', in *Studies in European Realism*, trans. by Edith Bone, London: Hillway.

Nadel, Ira Bruce. Ed. 1986. *Victorian Fiction: A Collection of Essays from the Period*, New York: Garland.

Schom, Alan. 1987. *Émile Zola: A Bourgeois Rebel*, London: Macdonald.

Stendhal. [1830] 1971. *Scarlet and Black*, trans. by Margaret Shaw, Harmondsworth: Penguin.

Taine, Hippolyte. [1856] 1971. 'Charles Dickens: son talent et ses œuvres', in *Dickens: The Critical Heritage*, ed. by Philip Collins, London: Routledge & Kegan Paul.

Zola, Émile. [1884–5] 1993. *Germinal*, trans. by Peter Collier, with an introduction by Robert Lethbridge, Oxford World's Classics, Oxford: Oxford University Press.

# Further reading

Guy, Josephine M. 1996. *The Victorian Social-Problem Novel*, Basingstoke: Macmillan. An excellent introduction to the subgenre, its critical history and recent approaches to it.

Joll, James. 1983. *Europe since 1870: An International History*, 3rd edn, Harmondsworth: Penguin. A good broad survey of the period.

Pagès, Alain. Ed. 1998. *Émile Zola: The Dreyfus Affair: 'J'accuse' and Other Writings*, trans. by Eleanor Levieux, New Haven and London: Yale University Press. Anthology of Zola's writings about Dreyfus.

Wilson, Angus. 1965. *Émile Zola: An Introductory Study of his Novels*, London: Mercury Books. A short, lively and sympathetic introduction.

Zola, Émile. [1892] 1972. *The Débâcle*, trans. by Leonard Tancock, Harmondsworth: Penguin.

Zola, Émile. [1877] 1995. *L'Assommoir*, trans. by Margaret Mauldon, with an introduction by Robert Lethbridge, Oxford World's Classics, Oxford: Oxford University Press.

# Index